Dimensions of World Politics

GLENN P. HASTEDT
KAY M. KNICKREHM
James Madison University

 HarperCollinsPublishers

For our families
Cathy, Sarah, and Matthew
Steve, Dylan, and Mark

Sponsoring Editor: Lauren Silverman
Project Editor: David Nickol
Art Direction/Cover Coordinator: Heather A. Ziegler
Cover Design: Circa 86
Production: Willie Lane/Sunaina Sehwani

DIMENSIONS OF WORLD POLITICS

Copyright © 1991 by HarperCollins Publishers, Inc.

Library of Congress Cataloging-in-Publication Data

Hastedt, Glenn P.
    Dimensions of world politics / Glenn P. Hastedt, Kay M. Knickrehm.
        p.   cm.
    Includes bibliographical references and index.
    ISBN 0-06-042674-8
    1. International relations. 2. World politics—20th century.
    I. Knickrehm, Kay M. II. Title.
    JX1391.H37 1990   90-38910
                                                      CIP

90 91 92 93 9 8 7 6 5 4 3 2 1

Contents

Preface

Students often find introductory courses among the most difficult they encounter. Not only is the language of a field or discipline unfamiliar, but it often seems to them that as soon as they master one set of ideas, new material is taken up that demands familiarity with still more concepts. Compounding the problem is the likelihood that students do not have a sense of perspective on either the development of the field or the major events that are studied in it. In addition to overcoming these obstacles, instructors face the tasks of condensing a vast amount of material into a semester or quarter format and presenting it in such a fashion that students get a sense of the sweep and logic of the subject matter. In writing *Dimensions of World Politics*, we have sought to meet the needs of both students and instructors.

Students require two things of a text. First, it needs to be written in a straightforward fashion. New to the subject, they need to be able to identify clearly the central points of the discussion. Second, they need case-study and background information that helps place the ideas being presented to them in context. We have sought to provide both of these things in *Dimensions of World Politics*. Where a choice had to be made between elegance of language and the direct identification of major themes or elements to a theme, the latter was chosen. Virtually every chapter contains case-study material. There is also a chapter devoted to a review of post–World War II international relations, with an emphasis on the U.S.-Soviet cold war rivalry, and chapters that examine the evolution of the international economic system. In addition, we have provided a series of maps to help students orient themselves to the cases and events being discussed.

Instructors require that a text be of manageable length and not so long as to preclude the use of supplemental readings. We believe that this goal has been realized, although it forced us to limit our discussion at certain points. Second, there is a need for a text to address both the current concerns of the discipline as well as the enduring issues. Too often the table of contents of a text, especially in later editions, captures only the state of the field at the time it was first written and not more recent developments. We have sought to deal with both sets of concerns by dividing *Dimensions of World Politics* into three parts. The text begins by introducing students to the enduring concepts used to analyze world politics. The next two sections deal with the most important forms of military and economic interaction found in the contemporary international system. Third, a text must provide students with an exposure to the way in which theorists in the field organize their thoughts without forcing instructors into using a particular paradigm or organizing scheme. To this end we begin by discussing the development of the field and highlight three competing approaches to its study: realism, globalism, and dependency theory. We do not argue that one approach is correct, nor do we discuss every topic through each one of these filters. Instead, we return to them selectively and at various points throughout the text as the subject matter warrants.

We owe thanks to many people at HarperCollins for their help in our preparation of *Dimensions of World Politics*. Foremost among them are Marianne Russell, Lauren Silverman, and David Nickol. We would also like to thank the following reviewers for their thoughtful comments on the early drafts of the text: Carroll R. McKibbin, California Polytechnic & State University; Andrei Markovits, Boston University; Ronald Meltzer, SUNY, Buffalo; Peter Merani, Towson State College; Patrick Morgan, Washington State University; Barbara Yarnold, Saginaw Valley College. Their ideas were of great value in clarifying our thinking about what we wanted to accomplish in writing *Dimensions of World Politics*. Three colleagues at James Madison University, Steven Bowers, Anthony Eksterowicz, and Richard Flaskamp, also provided us with help at various stages of the project. As always, the invaluable assistance of our secretary, Diane Sellers, is greatly appreciated. Of course, we are solely responsible for any errors of fact or interpretation in the text.

Those to whom we owe the greatest thanks are our families, and we dedicate this book to them.

Glenn P. Hastedt
Kay M. Knickrehm

MAPS

THE WORLD

GREENLAND

ICELAND

NORWA

GREAT BRITAIN

NETHERLANDS

DENMARK

IRELAND

BELG.

GE

SWITZ

FRANCE

PORTUGAL   SPAIN

MOROCCO   ALGERIA

CANADA

UNITED STATES

MEXICO

CUBA

HAITI

DOMINICAN REPUBLIC

JAMAICA

GUATEMALA

EL SALVADOR

HONDURAS

NICARAGUA

COSTA RICA

PANAMA

VENEZUELA

GUYANA

SURINAM

FRENCH GUIANA

COLOMBIA

ECUADOR

PERU

BRAZIL

BOLIVIA

PARAGUAY

URUGUAY

ARGENTINA

CHILE

MAURITANIA

SENEGAL

MALI

BURKINA FASO

THE GAMBIA

GUINEA-BISSAU

GUINEA

SIERRA LEONE

LIBERIA

IVORY COAST

GHANA

TOGO

BENIN

EQUATORIAL GUINEA

CAM

NI

FINLAND

THE SOVIET UNION

POLAND
CZECHOSLOVAKIA
HUNGARY
ROMANIA
YUG.
BULGARIA
ALB.
GREECE
TURKEY
LEBANON
ISRAEL
SYRIA
JORDAN
IRAQ
IRAN
KUWAIT
QATAR
LIBYA
EGYPT
UNITED ARAB
EMIRATES
OMAN
SAUDI ARABIA
CHAD
NORTH YEMEN
SUDAN
SOUTH YEMEN
DJIBOUTI
CENTRAL
AFRICAN
REP
ETHIOPIA
UGANDA
SOMALIA
ZAIRE
KENYA
RWANDA
BURUNDI
TANZANIA
ANGOLA
MALAWI
ZAMBIA
MOZAMBIQUE
ZIMBABWE
MADAGASCAR
BOTSWANA
SWAZILAND
LESOTHO
SOUTH AFRICA

AFGHANISTAN
PAKISTAN
NEPAL
BHUTAN
INDIA
BANGLADESH
MYANMAR
SRI LANKA

MONGOLIA

CHINA

NORTH
KOREA
SOUTH

JAPAN

TAIWAN

LAOS
VIETNAM
CAMBODIA
THAILAND
MALAYSIA

PHILIPPINES

INDONESIA

PAPUA NEW GUINEA

AUSTRALIA

NEW ZEALAND

EUROPE

SOUTHEAST ASIA

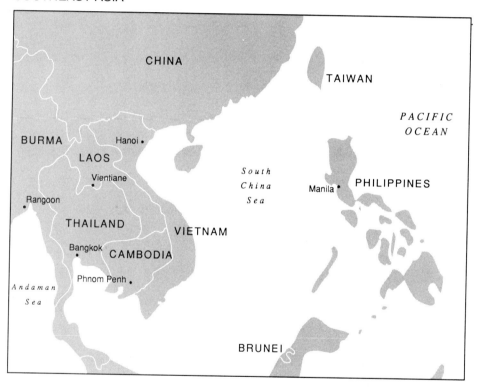

THE KOREAN PENINSULA

CHINA

U.S.S.R.

NORTH KOREA

• P'yongyang

Sea of
Japan

JAPAN

• Seoul

Tokyo •

Yellow
Sea

SOUTH KOREA

Pacific
Ocean

East
China
Sea

THE MIDDLE EAST

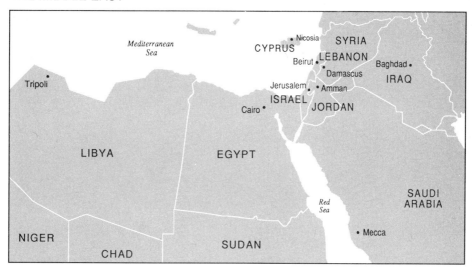

THE PERSIAN GULF

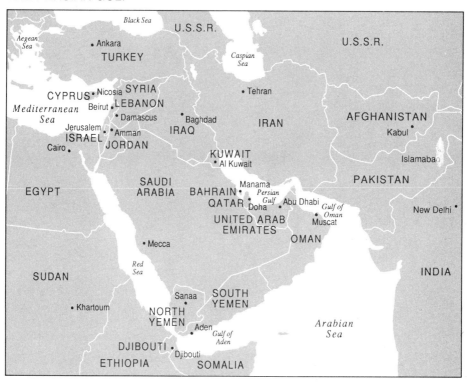

CENTRAL AMERICA

SOUTHERN AFRICA

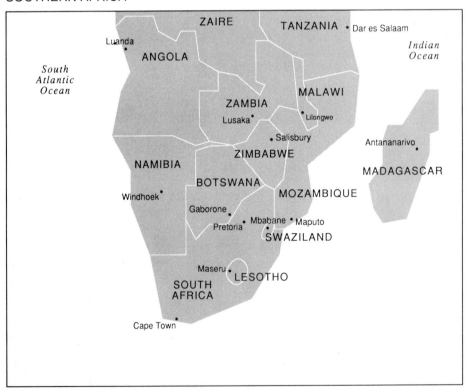

ONE

The Conceptual Dimension

Chapter
1

Issues and Approaches to the Study of World Politics

WORLD POLITICS IN THE NEWS

Rarely does a week go by that some aspect of world politics does not make news headlines. What follows is a recent sampling.

GERMAN REUNIFICATION

On March 18, 1990, the Christian Democratic Party won nearly half the vote in East Germany's first post-cold war election. An important factor in its victory was a promise by West German Chancellor Helmut Kohl, leader of the West German Christian Democratic Party, to carry out currency unification at a 1:1 exchange rate at a time when the black market exchange rate between the two currencies was about six East German marks for one West German mark. Within one month of the election the Kohl government began to backtrack from its promise. East German savings were estimated to be valued at approximately 160 billion East German marks. Printing this much money was seen as creating the real risk of higher inflation and interest rates that would threaten West German economic stability. East German leaders reacted angrily to rumors that something less than a 1:1 exchange would occur, with the leader of the East German Christian Democrats noting that East Germans earned about one-third what West Germans earned and that with a 2:1 exchange rate the disparity between the two populations would double. Strikes, demonstrations, and marches were threatened as was an even greater exodus of East Germans to West Germany.

Twice before in German history monetary unification has played a major role in political unification. Germany did not exist until 1871 when Otto von Bismarck brought many of the independent German-speaking principalities together under Prussian control. Along with increased trade and the presence of a common external threat, one of the measures he used to bring this about was the creation of a single currency to be used by all German states. The second time that currency unification played a key role in political unification was in 1946. Dissatisfied with the pace of talks designed to bring about economic and political reform in occupied Germany, and leery of Soviet intentions towards its occupation zone, the United States and Great Britain announced that they were merging the two occupation zones into one ("Bizonia"). Fearing that control over its occupation zone would be threatened by the planned introduction of a new German currency by the Western powers, the Soviet Union cut off all Western access to Berlin in June 1948. The Soviet Union lifted the blockade in May 1949. That same month the Federal Republic of Germany (West Germany) came into existence as France gave up control over its occupation zone. In October the Soviet Union announced the establishment of the German Democratic Republic (East Germany).

More than any other city, Berlin has served as a symbol of the cold war and a barometer by which to measure its intensity. The end of World War II found it a city divided into U.S., Soviet, British and French occupation zones deep within the Soviet occupation zone of Germany. The 1948 Berlin blockade was only the first of many times that Berlin dominated cold war headlines. Soviet troops were used to put down a 1953 spontaneous general uprising against communist rule that began in East Berlin and spread through the rest of the country. In 1958, 1959, and again in 1960 the Soviet Union threatened the West with unilateral action in the form of a peace treaty with East Germany designed to alter the status of Berlin. The Berlin Wall was constructed in 1962 as the Soviet Union and East Germany sought to stem a massive exodus to the West. Some 10 years later Berlin again made headlines, but this time it was in connection with *detente*, the name given to the period of relaxed tension between the U.S. and Soviet Union that characterized much of the 1970s. In June 1972 the four World War II occupying powers signed an agreement in which the Soviet Union guaranteed Western access to Berlin and eased travel restrictions between the two Berlins. Thus, it was not surprising that many proclaimed an end to the cold war when, in November 1989, East Germany's borders and the Berlin Wall were opened after more than 80,000 East Germans had already fled to the West since September.

The International Drug Trade

In January 1987, Colombia's ambassador to Hungary was assassinated. He was a former minister of justice who was responsible for extraditing to the United States

Colombians accused of drug trafficking. He had been assigned to Budapest because it was thought he would be safe there from the drug cartel that had threatened his life. His predecessor had been slain in 1984. These are only two of scores of public officials, including several judges and an attorney general, who were casualties in Colombia's effort to stop the flow of drugs to the United States. Two dozen judges were killed between 1979 and 1989.

In 1986 more than 125 tons of cocaine entered the United States. In spite of the war on drugs declared by this country, there has been little success in stopping this influx. Most of the cocaine that finds its way to the United States is grown in Peru and Bolivia, and much of it is refined and shipped from Colombia. The enormous profits generated by the international drug trade make it virtually impossible to stop. It is estimated that the cocaine trade generates $500 billion a year in revenue. A Peruvian peasant can make four times as much money by growing coca than by growing any other crop. The refiners and shippers make considerably more money. Drug money corrupts government and law enforcement officials and pays for the assassinations of those who cannot be bought. The situation is further complicated by the importance of coca to Indian culture and religion, by the increasing involvement of revolutionary groups in the drug trade, and by the importance of cocaine production to the regional economy. It is estimated that in 1986 all of Bolivia's legal exports brought $543 million into the country, whereas the cocaine trade brought in more than $600 million. Noriega in Panama, senior military officers in Honduras, officials in Cuba, and several Contra leaders in Nicaragua are just a few of those who recently have been accused of involvement in this lucrative business. In July 1989, General Arnaldo Ochoa Sanchez and 13 other officers were tried in Cuba for drug smuggling. Ochoa and three others were convicted of treason and executed. The remaining defendants were sentenced to prison.

The Medellin cartel is the world's largest association of cocaine traffickers, and it is wealthier and more powerful than many governments. It is estimated that this cartel controls 80 percent of the 165,000 pounds of cocaine reaching the United States from South America. Bribery, intimidation, and murder are only a few of the tactics that it uses to influence policy in Colombia and abroad. The cartel has bought protection from Panamanian officials and has taken over businesses in Haiti. In some areas, the cartel has bought the allegiance of the local poor by providing welfare systems that are more generous than those provided by the government. It has entered into an alliance with M-19, a leftist guerilla movement attempting to overthrow the Colombian government. It supplies weapons and money to the guerrillas, who then guard the cartel's airstrips and carry out assassinations. M-19 was responsible for the 1985 murders of 11 Colombian Supreme Court justices whom the cartel wanted eliminated. In 1984 the cartel offered to pay off the Colombian national debt—which at that time was more than $9 billion—in exchange for Colombia dropping charges against them and abandoning its extradition treaty with the United States. In July 1988, the cartel offered to negotiate a deal with the U.S. government. In return for amnesty from prosecution, it offered to work for U.S. intelligence by informing on leftist guerrillas and Cuban personnel in Colombia and by supplying information about Libyan arms shipments. The United States declined the offer, noting: "We don't do business with international outlaws."

Colombia and the United States signed an extradition treaty in 1979 that allowed drug traffickers to be extradited to the United States even if they had never actually entered the United States to do business. In December 1986, the Colombian Supreme Court, terrorized by assassinations and threats from drug lords, declared the treaty unconstitutional. In the summer of 1989, in response to renewed killings, President Barco of Colombia decreed measures that allowed for extradition and for seizure of drug traffickers' assets. In response, the Medellin cartel declared "total war." The Bush administration proposed a $65 million package, including helicopters, aircraft, boats, small arms and other equipment. Raids against drug lords' estates resulted in 11,000 arrests and the seizure of $125 million worth of property in a single weekend, but most of the leaders of the cartel remained at large. Meanwhile, Colombia pressed for U.S. funds to protect judges and other officials as bombings and assassination attempts continued. By February 1990, when President Bush flew to Cartagena, Colombia, for a summit with Latin American leaders, the Colombian Government had earned international praise for its commitment to the drug war.

Famine in Africa

In early 1984, the United Nations (UN) and private relief organizations began urgently to request help in fighting a growing famine in East Africa. Drought, deforestation, and war had combined to create a disaster. Over 7 million Ethiopians had suffered from food shortages in 1983, and relief agencies were estimating that 4.6 million would suffer in 1984. In spite of repeated warnings from the relief agencies, however, it was not until graphic television coverage of the famine was aired in the fall of 1984 that world interest was aroused. By this time, the famine had reached epidemic proportions in 12 of the 14 Ethiopian provinces, and an estimated 43 percent of the Ethiopian people were malnourished. Once the extent of the tragedy became known, there was a tremendous response from the public and from governments. Relief organizations received thousands of contributions, rock stars donated profits from recordings and concerts, and the players in the NBA All-Star Game donated their salaries. By the end of November, 325,000 tons of food had been pledged by Western nations. Some relief organizations charged that Western nations had been slow to respond in the hope that the famine would bring about the collapse of the communist government in Ethiopia. Western officials blamed poor coordination and planning by the UN relief organizations. The United States blamed the Ethiopian government, which had spent $100 million on a celebration of its tenth anniversary in the midst of the famine and practiced a policy of concentrating resources in the urban areas that were most friendly to the regime to the detriment of agricultural production. Relief efforts were complicated by the ongoing civil war. Separatists in Eritrea and Tigre were battling the Ethiopian government, and the famine hit hardest in these regions. Both sides were accused by relief workers of impeding the flow of food to the hungry. Additional problems were created by the inaccessibility of many of the refugee camps. These problems continue, and by Spring, 1990, Ethiopia was once again facing widespread famine.

The 1984 famine was not confined to Ethiopia. The UN Disaster Relief Organization has called the drought the worst human disaster to strike the African continent in recent history. Additionally, badly designed foreign-aid programs and development strategies that neglect agriculture have been blamed for exacerbating the drought and for food problems in other areas of the continent. In all, 36 countries have suffered serious food shortages, and 35 million people have been placed in danger of starvation. Worldwatch Institute blames the drought on rapid population growth, which has outstripped food production and contributed to the drought through deforestation. Nevertheless, few Third World governments have adopted policies to encourage food production and soil conservation, and hunger is expected to become more prevalent in the future.

Acquired Immune Deficiency Syndrome

The London Summit in January 1988, attracted high-level officials from nearly 150 countries. By the end of the conference, in a spirit of cooperation rarely found when so many diverse cultures come together, all had agreed to develop a multinational strategy to deal with a major international threat to humanity. They agreed that no one is to blame for the problem and that all are at risk. In addition, they unanimously pledged to work against discrimination and for tolerance. The subject of this harmonious summit was Acquired Immune Deficiency Syndrome (AIDS), and the participants were health ministers and other high-level officials. Although the London Summit was not the first international conference on AIDS, it was the first to deal with AIDS as a political rather than a scientific issue. The Fifth International AIDS Conference met in Montreal in June of 1989. Eighty-seven countries were represented.

Since reporting on AIDS began in 1979, 73,670 cases of AIDS have been reported to the World Health Organization (WHO). It is expected that for every case that is reported there are between 50 and 100 unreported cases; thus, by 1986 WHO estimated that there were between 5 and 10 million cases worldwide. By 2000 there are expected to be between 50 and 100 million carriers of the AIDS virus. If only 30 percent of those infected actually develop the disease within five years, then by 1995 there will be 15 to 30 million people dying from AIDS.

Presently, WHO distinguishes among three distinct epidemiological patterns of AIDS infection. Pattern I countries, which are found in Western Europe, North America, parts of South America, Australia, and New Zealand, account for most of the reported cases. Here the groups that are most affected are homosexual and bisexual men and intravenous drug users. It is expected that the virus will increasingly be spread through heterosexual contact as bisexual men pass on the virus to more and more female partners. Pattern II countries are located in parts of Africa and the Caribbean. In these areas, AIDS is prevalent among heterosexuals and is spread primarily through heterosexual contact, with 25 percent of the 20- to 40-year-olds in some urban areas affected. In these countries, it is estimated that 75 to 90 percent of prostitutes carry the AIDS virus. Another important method of transmission is from mother to child during pregnancy. Cases are underreported in these countries because of poor record keeping and communication. It is unknown why so many more heterosexuals are affected in these countries than in Pattern I countries, but it is theorized that the prevalence of other sexually transmitted diseases, such as syphilis and gonorrhea, is a factor. The lesions resulting from these diseases make it easier for the AIDS virus to enter the bloodstream during ordinary heterosexual contact. Pattern III countries have the lowest incidence of infection, and, although the virus has been found to be present here, it has not reached the general population. These are the countries of Asia, the Pacific, the Middle East and Eastern Europe. Most AIDS cases here are transmitted through sexual contact or blood transfusions.

One of the world's hardest hit areas is Africa. Poor hygiene practices, parasitic and infectious diseases that weaken the immune system, the greater need for transfusions coupled with a lack of resources necessary to insure a safe blood supply, and the fact that 40 percent of the population is in its sexually active years have come together to produce an epidemic. It is estimated that 2 million Africans are infected—an infectious rate that is 100 times higher than that of the United States. In Africa and throughout the Third World, AIDS undermines health gains by diverting already inadequate funds from other health programs, by increasing infant mortality rates, and by damaging immunization programs. These programs are affected as mothers, fearing AIDS contamination through dirty needles, refuse to have their children vaccinated against other illnesses such as smallpox and measles.

In addition to its impact on health and human suffering, AIDS also has substantial economic consequences. A major impact is on lost productivity. The AIDS virus attacks those age groups that are most economically productive and also those who are most likely to leave behind children requiring care by surviving relatives or by the state. Since AIDS strikes urban areas more heavily, those who die are often the better educated and more skilled. In the copper-rich regions of Zambia, 68 percent of the men testing positive for AIDS were skilled workers on whom the mining industry depends. One study projects that in the 1990s AIDS will have cost Eastern Africa $980 million dollars because of economic slowing alone. Other threats to the economy that are attributable to AIDS come from the loss of tourist dollars and the costs of medical care for the victims.

Although Africa is hardest hit, AIDS has been found in every region of the world. Unlike malaria, smallpox, and various parasitic diseases, AIDS cannot be labeled a Third World disease and dismissed as unimportant in the developed world. Unlike other diseases, it is always fatal. At this time, scientists can talk of reducing risks but cannot promise either a vaccine or a cure.

Although in many ways AIDS appears to be a problem that unites rather than divides humanity, it has also contributed to international tensions. There have already been some problems concerning persons with AIDS crossing international boundaries. In 1987 the U.S. Senate voted 96 to 0 for an amendment adding AIDS to the list of diseases that bar infected immigrants and aliens from entering the country. In April 1989, a Dutch official with AIDS was jailed briefly when he entered the United States to attend a conference on health. Many members of Congress objected, noting that the intent of the legislation was to bar those seeking residence and that the policy as enforced endangered scientific and cultural exchanges. A judge subsequently granted the visitor a waiver from the exclusion, and he was allowed to attend the conference. One month after the incident, the Immigration and Naturalization Service established new regulations allowing persons who are infected with AIDS to enter the country for conferences and treatment. Presently, only Iraq routinely screens visitors for AIDS. Cuba requires testing for visitors who plan to remain in the country three months or longer, and the Soviet Union provides for testing if there is a reason to suspect that a visitor is infected. In September 1989 an American bridge player with AIDS was denied a visa to travel to Australia for a bridge championship.

The *Vincennes* Incident

The $1.2 billion *Vincennes* was called by its captain, "the most sophisticated ship in the world." Its Combat Information Center contained four huge computer screens that served as the crew's window on the world. In modern warfare, the speed and accuracy of weaponry does not always permit the visual identification of targets. Once an incoming aircraft is in sight on radar equipment, its target is already within range. When the sophisticated radar of the *Vincennes* reported an approaching aircraft during a battle with Iranian gunboats, the captain attempted radio contact with the plane. When the plane failed to respond to warnings, the *Vincennes* fired two missiles. The plane, an Iranian Commercial Airbus carrying 290 people, was destroyed. In the initial aftermath of the incident, suspicion fell first on the equipment itself. The *Vincennes'* radar, despite being the latest in technology, is incapable of distinguishing between a 177-foot-long Airbus and a 62-foot F-14 fighter plane. Originally the *Vincennes* reported that its Aegis system showed that the plane was descending and picking up speed—a maneuver suggesting that the plane was an F-14 preparing to attack. Other ships in the area disputed the claim that the plane had been descending. Their radar showed that the plane was ascending or leveling off and that it was at a much higher altitude. A military inquiry that reviewed data from the *Vincennes* later determined that the Aegis air defense system had functioned correctly. Human error at several critical points had sealed the fate of the Iranian victims. The crew had been alerted to the possibility of an air attack and were mindful of an earlier incident in which another ship, the USS *Stark*, had been seriously damaged and had several crewmen killed when it failed to intercept an Iraqi fighter plane. Under stress, the data supplied by the Aegis system was misinterpreted so that the ascending plane was identified by the crew as descending. Its altitude, although correctly identified by the computer, was misidentified by the crew so that it appeared much lower than it actually was. Although the crew had a list of commercial flights operating in the Persian Gulf, they failed to notice the Iranian flight when they scanned the list. The conclusion reached by the investigators was that "human error arising from the psychological stress of being in combat for the first time" caused the tragedy.

The Aegis system is just one example of the increasing sophistication of military hardware. Some critics have argued that the complexity of this equipment may be beyond the ability of some operators. The crew of the *Vincennes* had undergone a year's training with the Aegis equipment. Yet, when the crew was required to interpret a large amount of data very rapidly in a stressful situation, the result was a tragic decision that cost 290 innocent lives. Other sophisticated equipment is planned. The air force is trying to develop a computerized helmet for combat pilots that would result in their being able to "fly blind." Pilots would watch radar and infrared signals projected on the inside of their helmets and would no longer visually identify targets.

This type of advance is made necessary by the speed of modern weaponry. If the system fails, however, the pilots would be crippled. The reliability of some of these highly technical defense and weapons systems has presented problems in the past. When sophisticated equipment breaks down, it is costly and often difficult to repair. The M-16 rifle used in the Vietnam War was criticized for its design flaws, which gave it a tendency to jam and made it acutely vulnerable to dirt. Soldiers in Vietnam complained that it was unreliable, and some preferred less sophisticated weapons that required less maintenance. Equipment failure can doom a mission, as in the U.S. attempt in 1981 to rescue the American hostages held captive in the American Embassy in Iran. Problems with the helicopters, in combination with other factors—dust storms and a lack of replacements—caused the United States to abandon its attempt. That failure made any subsequent rescue attempt impossible, since the element of surprise had been lost. Perhaps the most sophisticated of all defense systems is the Strategic Defense Initiative (SDI), popularly known as "Star Wars." Scientists cannot agree on whether such a system is possible, and even those who believe that the system is feasible are troubled by the fact that the system could never be fully tested. If we assumed the system would work and it failed, we would be annihilated.

Chernobyl

The world's worst nuclear accident occurred on April 26, 1986, when an explosion occurred at the Chernobyl nuclear power plant in the Soviet Union. Only two persons died in the initial explosion, but within a few weeks 29 of those who received high doses of radiation were dead, and many others had been exposed to radiation. Although some design flaws were reported as contributing to the accident, most of the blame was attributed to errors on the part of the operators. The emergency cooling systems, designed to protect the reactor if it should become unstable, had been shut down by operators to facilitate a test that they were running. Heat caused the two explosions that destroyed the plant. The explosions and fire propelled radioactive fragments and gases more than 3,600 feet into the air. Immediately after the accident, Soviet officials downplayed the severity of it, noting that radioactive fallout would present no danger beyond a 60-mile radius of the plant. Subsequently, however, the Soviets released an extensive report, which was praised by Western experts for its openness. The report indicated that 192,000 people who had been evacuated from the area of the accident would not be able to return for at least four years. Extensive cleanup plans included burying the topsoil from the 18-mile evacuation zone, washing all buildings, and possibly burning the forests in the area. From April 27 to May 10, helicopters dropped 5,000 tons of sand, clay, limestone, lead, and boron onto the reactor in an attempt to stop the leakage of radiation. Nevertheless, people in the area of the plant received exposures up to 400 rem. Blood changes begin at a dose of 25 rem and one-half of those exposed to 400 rem would be expected to die soon after exposure. It is estimated that in the area around the plant there will be approximately 280 additional deaths from cancer over the next 70 years. Throughout the remainder of the Soviet Union, 4,750 deaths are expected to occur from atmospheric radiation exposure and 1,500 deaths from cancer in people who consumed contaminated milk and food. Nearly three years after the accident, *Pravda* reported that contamination was worse than previously reported. It noted that about 4,000 square miles of territory had contamination levels exceeding the maximum set by the government for the accident zone. Nearly one-quarter of a million people are living in the affected area.

Increased levels of radiation were not restricted to the Soviet Union. An estimated 3.5 percent of the radiation escaped into the upper atmosphere. This is more radiation than resulted from the bombs dropped on Hiroshima and Nagasaki in World War II. Air currents caused this radiation to travel around the world. Higher levels of radiation were detected over the next few months in many different areas of the globe.

Cooperation to help the Chernobyl victims was immediately forthcoming. Dr. Robert Gale, a specialist in bone marrow transplants, contacted Armand Hammer, chairman of Occidental Petroleum, who has business ties with the Soviets. Hammer called the Soviet embassy and arranged with the Soviets for American and European assistance. Ultimately, 15 countries sent doctors and other assistance to help in the treatment of victims.

In the aftermath of the accident, the Soviet Union called for international cooperation to prevent future nuclear incidents. Its report stated: "The accident at the Chernobyl nuclear power plant has again demonstrated the danger of uncontrolled nuclear power and highlighted the destructive consequences to which its military use or damage to peaceful nuclear facilities during military operation could lead."

The Falkland Islands

On Friday morning, April 2, 1982, the sound of gunfire from Argentine commandos was heard in Port Stanley, the capital of the Falkland Islands. These soldiers were part of a 2,500-man invasion force, backed by a naval task force, which included an aircraft carrier (the British-built *Veinticinco de Mayo*), and three missile-carrying destroyers. The next day a second Argentine invasion force landed on South Georgia Island. The approximately 1,800 people living on the Falkland Islands were protected by a British garrison numbering 84 Royal Marines. Within days these British defenders were removed from the Falkland Islands, and Argentina set about to reinforce its position on the renamed Malvinas Islands. This was not the first time that a dispute had broken out between Argentina and Great Britain over who controlled these islands. Earlier challenges took place in the 1880s, 1927, 1933, 1966, and 1976.

Great Britain countered by dispatching a task force to the South Atlantic. Ultimately comprised of 60 ships, it was the largest armada that the British had put together since World War II. The British navy was not prepared for a war in the South Atlantic. The primary contingency for which it had prepared itself centered on the defense of Europe and the North Atlantic sea lanes, and this task did not require the capability to transport troops long distances. When war broke out, the Royal Navy consisted of two light aircraft carriers, 14 destroyers, 46 frigates, 12 nuclear-powered submarines, 16 conventional-powered submarines, and 4 Polaris armed submarines. The British government was forced to requisition four British Petroleum (BP) tankers and use them as fuel transporters, an educational cruise ship was turned into a hospital, and the 1,600 passenger cruise ship *Canberra* became a troop and supply ship.

It took three weeks for the British fleet to reach the Falkland Islands. In that time the United Nations Security Council called for a cease-fire and peace talks, the European Economic Community imposed economic sanctions against Argentina, and U.S. Secretary of State Alexander Haig sought to mediate between these two American allies. All of these efforts were futile. In early May a major sea and air battle erupted with important losses on both sides. A British submarine sank the Argentine cruiser *Belgrano*, while Argentine jet fighters disabled the British destroyer *Sheffield*. At this point, the United States officially gave its support to Great Britain, accused Argentina of armed aggression, and placed sanctions against it. The United States also provided Great Britain with political and military intelligence. In late May British forces established a firm beachhead on the main island, and on June 14, the 13,000 Argentine forces on the Falkland Islands surrendered. British losses were estimated at 255 dead, while an estimated 577 Argentine soldiers died in the fighting.

Other World Events

To this list could be added the conflicts in Nicaragua and Afghanistan, the hostages in Lebanon, the bombings in Northern Ireland, apartheid, the exodus of refugees from East Germany, acid rain, an INF treaty, the U.S.-Japanese trade controversy, human rights violations, the 1988 summer Olympics, and many others.

STUDYING WORLD POLITICS

Why do these stories make headlines? No doubt it is partly because news editors expect that we will find them interesting. They also make news headlines because of their presumed importance to our lives. The time is long past when Americans can go about their daily lives free from any concern about what is happening beyond U.S. borders. Initially, the realization that the United States could not isolate itself from the World led to an attempt to control it—"to make the world safe for democracy." More recently, many Americans have come to believe that the United States no longer possesses the ability to control or to manage the international challenges and opportunities that present themselves. The combination of a sensitivity to events beyond U.S. borders and a vulnerability to them lies at the heart of the growing interdependence of states in the international system and the heightened need to study world politics.

Observers of international relations disagree—often quite strongly—about how to make sense out of these and other events in world politics. For example, do all of these news stories touch upon equally important aspects of world politics? Are some of them interesting and important and others just interesting? Do some deal with issues that lie at the heart of world politics and others deal primarily with domestic political issues that only occasionally spill over into the international arena? What part of the news stories are most important: Is it the events leading up to the event, the event itself, or the international reaction to the event?

Three different theoretical viewpoints compete for prominence today, each claiming to provide the correct method for answering these types of questions. They are the *realist*, the *globalist*, and the *dependency* approaches.[1] Before comparing them, we want to talk about the two prerequisites for studying world politics and review the development of the field of international relations.

The Need for Facts and Theory

The intuitive starting point for coming to grips with a problem is to acquire the basic facts. However, given the complexity of world politics, getting "all of the facts" about such widely differing phenomena as arms control and military strategy, international economics, terrorism, environmental pollution, and human rights before making a judgment about them is all but impossible. The task is made even more difficult because most students and policymakers new to the field of world politics are far more knowledgeable about domestic American politics than about events happening outside U.S. borders. The temptation arises to look for shortcuts: to assume that others hold the same values that we do; to assume that history will repeat itself; to assume that the future can be predicted as if it were a straight-line extension of the past and present with no unexpected curves or zig-zags; and to assume that the proper interpretation of an event is self-evident.

The problem is that all of these shortcuts are brimming with danger. Not all peoples or countries have the same set of values, and often international conflicts are not over facts but over ideologies and symbols. History does not repeat itself. The war in Afghanistan may be very similar to the Vietnam War, but it is not Vietnam II. If nothing else, the proximity of Afghanistan to the Soviet Union and the U.S. provision of modern antiaircraft missiles to the Mujahadin make it different. The future will often differ from the present in unexpected ways. Low oil prices had been the norm in international politics for decades, but events following the 1973 Arab-Israeli War changed that forever. Finally, facts are not self-interpreting. Just what are we to make of *glasnost* or *perestroika*, the Soviet pullout from Afghanistan, and Gorbachev's arms control proposals? Are they to be taken as genuine signs of a new era in Soviet foreign policy? Are they only tactical retreats in a continuing Soviet drive for world domination? Are they signs of domestic political strength or the acts of a desperate leader?

Acquiring an understanding of world politics requires more than just presenting a chronological ordering of facts or a review of who did what to whom. It demands answering such questions as the following: How significant are these events? Do events in one part of the world have any bearing on what happens in other parts of the world? Should they be judged as good or bad, desirable or unwanted? Can they tell us something about the future? If getting the facts is not enough, and getting all of the facts is probably impossible, where do we turn for help in deciding what facts we should try to get and what we should do with them once we have them?

Students of world politics have turned to theory to guide them through this process of simplification and analysis. While theories can take many different forms, the purpose of a theory is to place a set of interrelated concepts into a logical frame-work in order to describe, explain, and predict phenomena. By emphasizing certain concepts (for example, power, the rule of law, economic exploitation) over others and by specifying how they are related to one another (the balance of power prevents war; revolutions occur when the level of poverty in a society falls below a certain level), theoretical frameworks organize our thinking about events. They lead us to emphasize certain facts over others (and even help to define for us what a fact is) and guide us in making judgments about the significance of what we find. Disagreement over which theoretical perspectives to use is not new to the study of world politics. The current debate over the relative advantages of the realist, globalist, and dependency perspectives is only the latest in a series of controversies that has marked the development of the field of international relations.

DEVELOPMENT OF THE FIELD

Idealism versus Realism

Prior to World War I the study of world politics existed at the fringes of several academic disciplines—most notably history, philosophy, and law. A unifying theme running through these writings was the conviction that the structure of the international society was unchangeable. The peace, prosperity, and stability of the period between the late 1880s and the onset of World War I reinforced this bias and created a sense of complacency that led observers to be content with describing events rather than analyzing them and with exploring the writings of philosophers such as Machiavelli, Thucydides, Hobbes, and others for what they said about the nature of world politics.

World War I changed that. It created a need to explain why the war happened as well as to account for other developments in the changed international order. Building upon their liberal intellectual tradition, American scholars sought answers within the context of an essentially legalistic and moralistic framework. War was not inevitable; it occurred because of the way the system was structured and as a result of bad leadership. The cure for the first problem was to do away with the prewar emphasis on power politics and its primary method of keeping the peace—the balance-of-power system. In its place, international laws, agreements, and institutions would be established that would allow the inherent reasonableness of individuals to flourish and would make collaborative peace efforts possible. The solution to the problem of bad leadership was democracy. Wars occurred when people either did not know what was happening or when they were misled by bad leaders. The more democratic the process by which foreign policy was conducted and the greater the control of the people over their leaders, the less able were leaders to lead their countries into war.

This scholarship was also optimistic in tone. The League of Nations, international disarmament conferences such as the Washington Naval Conference, and a greater attention to the development and articulation of international law all made progress possible. The international system could be changed in such a way as to ensure true peace and prosperity. The optimism of the early 1920s faded in the 1930s. In Europe, Hitler came to power in Germany and set it on the road to rearmament, expansionism, and war. In Asia, Japan had pulled out of arms control agreements, built up its military establishment, and invaded Manchuria. In Africa, Mussolini's Italy annexed Ethiopia as part of its plan to establish an Italian empire. By 1939 the world was once again at war.

There were two very different responses to the growing gap between the principles of international relations, as put forward by scholars, and the reality of world politics.[2] One group of writers insisted that the principles were correct and could ensure peace if they were applied correctly. The problem was that European leaders had not done so. A second group concluded that the principles were at fault. World politics was not an exercise in writing laws and treaties or in creating international organizations; it was a struggle for power carried out under conditions that bordered on anarchy. Adherents to this new school of thought referred to themselves as *realists* and labeled the others *idealists*.

Realists argued that the focus of research in international relations must be on discovering the fundamental forces that drive world politics. A focus on these forces would reveal that leaders have far less freedom to maneuver when they are engineering solutions to problems than idealists have believed to be the case. Realists maintained that laws and morality have played little part in the workings of world politics and that a state's primary obligation is to itself, not the international community, other states, or humanity. Self-preservation under such conditions demands that a state be able to protect itself, because it cannot count upon help coming from any other quarter. Policymakers, concluded realists, therefore must always engage in a pursuit of power. To do otherwise (to put one's faith in the defensive ability of laws, organizations, or international public opinion) invites war and defeat, as other states position themselves to take advantage of this mistake in judgment by acquiring more power. Peace is possible only when all states follow their own narrowly defined national interests. Creating institutions that ignore these fundamental realities or trying to change them are utopian and bound to fail.

Realism emerged from World War II as the preeminent theoretical perspective for defining world politics.[3] The next great controversy in the field of international relations was over how to study world politics.[4]

Traditionalism Versus Behavioralism

Realists inherited the methodology of the idealists but changed its focus from laws, diplomacy, and international organizations to the study of power. At the core of this methodology was the study of history. We acquire knowledge of a problem or an issue by first-hand observation and by devoting a lifetime to its study. The task of the scholar is to recreate what and why soldiers, statesmen, and diplomats did and to present their interpretation of it. A significant portion of that recreative effort is directed at providing the context for action. As employed by historians, this "traditionalist" methodology worked from the assumption that events were largely unique and could only be understood if all of the basic forces relevant to the event were presented and accounted for. Realists deemphasized the inherent uniqueness and complexity of specific events and stressed instead the elements of continuity that were shared by them. For realists, world politics was marked by recurring patterns and was governed by the influence of geography, nationalism, ideology, climate, the drive for power, or some other basic force. It was these concepts that realist scholars relied upon to interpret the events that they observed firsthand or had studied for a lifetime.

During the 1950s, some realists, as well as those who rejected realism, began to apply an alternative methodology to the study of world politics. Referred to by some as the *scientific approach* and to others as *behavioralism*, this new methodology took as its point of departure the belief that events in world politics could be understood if they were taken "out of context" and examined with other events of the same kind in a "controlled" fashion. In doing so, behavioralists turned to the natural sciences in search of methodologies for carrying out these comparisons and to disciplines such as sociology, economics, anthropology, and psychology in search of concepts to guide their study.

Highly detailed case studies that concluded with personalistic interpretations of the phenomena were rejected in favor of cross-national comparisons in which dependent and independent variables were identified, the nature of causation was specified, and terms were operationally defined. In concrete terms, they did not study revolutions by presenting a series of in-depth case studies and conclude by giving their interpretations. Instead, they identified what it was that they were trying to explain (the dependent variable—revolutions); what it was that caused revolutions (the independent variables—the level of poverty in a society and rioting); and how the two were related (the pattern of causation—high levels of poverty lead to rioting, which leads to revolution). They also operationalized their terms: A high level of poverty exists when x percentage of the population has an income below y. This is important, because a critical goal of behavioral research is to present enough information about how the research has been conducted to allow another scholar to replicate it and come up with the same findings, just as chemists can duplicate each other's results in the laboratory by following the same procedures.

The controversy between the two methodological approaches became quite intense. Behavioralists argued that generating explanations and predictions in world politics was possible only if researchers became more exact in their methodology and tested the theoretical propositions that they put forward. Traditionalists countered with two arguments. First, they argued that, by importing the value-free approach of the natural sciences and by applying it to world politics, behavioralists had become obsessed with quantifying things and had lost sight of the larger normative questions that were at the heart of international relations. Second, they argued that all too often behavioralist research produced inconclusive or contradictory results because of its inability to measure accurately key concepts or even to agree upon which data sets to use. From the point of view of traditionalists, the net result was a tendency to measure what was easily observed rather than what was important in world politics.

For example, traditionalists charged that behavioralists did not ask why nations go to war, but rather whether the number of borders that a state has influence the likelihood of going to war. Nevertheless, is the relationship between borders and warfare so obvious that it can be taken for granted? This is what Harvey Starr and

Benjamin Most found when they began to look at the role that borders play in world politics.[5] They found that, while it was generally recognized that international borders "shape" world politics, little attention had been paid to how borders were defined, operationalized, or measured. They were able to identify six different types of borders, and they found that not all types of borders were related to war in the same way. For example, when they reviewed the period 1946–1965, they found that the more colonial borders a major power possessed, the more likely it was to become involved in a new war. The reverse relationship held for noncolonial borders. The more noncolonial borders a major power possessed, the less likely it was to become involved in a new war.

The traditionalist-behavioralist debate did not end with a clear-cut winner, as was the case with realism's triumph over idealism. Instead, traditionalism and behavioralism now coexist. They have also been joined by a third methodological approach, postbehavioralism, which tries to combine the positive features of both into one approach. It acknowledges that the study of world politics must be carried out in a more exacting fashion than was the case with traditionalist research, while at the same time insisting that attention must be paid to the larger, normative issues in the study of world politics: security, welfare, justice, power, peace, freedom, and war. In the eyes of many, these issues had become lost in the debate over methodology. The behavioral approach, with its emphasis on scientific inquiry, largely ignored these issues, while realists tended to treat the debate over which ones to emphasize as closed and as having been decided in favor of power and security-oriented values.

REALISM, GLOBALISM, AND DEPENDENCY THEORY

Today methodological pluralism—the coexistence of competing approaches to the study of world politics—has been joined by a type of conceptual pluralism. While it has never been without challengers, realism now coexists with two other major theoretical perspectives: *globalism* and *dependency-based approaches*. Together these three approaches dominate American writings on world politics. We will compare them along four dimensions: (1) who they identify as the primary actor(s) in world politics; (2) the nature of the relationship between these actors; (3) the potential for changing the nature of the international system; and (4) their basic philosophical orientations. Table 1.1 presents a summary of these points.

Realists continue to hold that the state is the only international actor of significance. It is involved in a competitive struggle with other states in an international system in which laws, organizations, and morality have little influence over how states define their interests or conduct their foreign policy. Because they operate in an environment that is best characterized as anarchic, states must consistently place power considerations at the center of their foreign policy and define their national interest in narrow terms, with the survival of the state as the core goal. States owe little, if anything, to other states or to the international community. Finally, realists are pessimists about the possibility of changing the fundamental nature of world politics. Thus, from a normative perspective, realism is a conservative philosophy that stresses acceptance of the status quo and cautions against undertaking utopian

Table 1.1   REALISM, GLOBALISM, AND DEPENDENCY THEORY

	Realism	Globalism	Dependency
Primary actor(s)	States	States and nonstate actors	Economic interests
Relationship between actors	Competitive pursuit of national interest	Cooperative interdependence	Exploitation
Potential for changing the international system	Limited	Optimistic	Improbable
Philosophical orientation	Conservative	Reformist	Radical

Source: Adapted from the discussion in Michael Smith, Richard Little, and Michael Shackleton, eds., "Introduction," in *Perspectives on World Politics* (Chatham, N.J.: Chatham House Publishers, 1981), pp. 13–21.

schemes to bring about peace. Not only will they fail, but also these plans run the risk of endangering the most fundamental value of all: the survival of the state.

Globalists argue that the realist view of world politics is time bound and outmoded.[6] They contend that realists have developed a set of concepts based on nineteenth-century European diplomatic history and applied them to twentieth-century international politics. Until recently, the fit between the two has been relatively close, but, as the twentieth century comes to an end, the gap between reality and the realists' vision of it has become so great that the model has become increasingly irrelevant to the study of world politics.

Globalists concede that states are still the major players in the game of world politics, but they disagree that they are the only actors of importance. The foreign policies of a host of nonstate actors, ranging from international organizations and multinational corporations to terrorist groups, must also be studied if world politics is to be understood. Moreover, globalists argue that the state is not the unitary actor that realists have made it out to be. In discussing U.S. foreign policy, for example, we spend so much time talking about the foreign-policy positions of Congress, the Central Intelligence Agency (CIA), and lobbying groups that the terms "U.S. foreign policy" or "U.S. national interest" lose some of their conceptual clarity and importance.

The emphasis given to studying power is also questioned by globalists. First, they maintain that military power, in particular, has become increasingly ineffective as a means of wielding international influence and furthering a state's national interest. This is true, both for the pursuit of the traditional state objectives stressed by the realists and the much longer list of welfare-related goals that now compete with them for the attention of policymakers. Second, they argue that the attention given by the realists to competitive power politics has blinded researchers to the amount of cooperation that exists between actors in world politics. Models of international relations rooted in calculations of power politics are unable to explain why many of these cooperative ventures grow and prosper.

As seen by the globalists, the central changes in world politics revolve around the growing interdependence of actors and the global nature of the problems that they face. Together they create a situation in which states will not be able to accomplish their objectives by acting alone. Success demands that joint efforts be undertaken to put global management systems into place. As a philosophy, globalism is reformist in nature. Globalists are optimistic about the potential for changing the international system by creating a new set of rules and norms that will curb international behavior.

The third theoretical framework frequently employed today to study international relations is *dependency theory*.[7] In the forefront of those who adopted the dependency perspective were Latin American scholars, who were responding as much to what they perceived as the failings of the comparative politics literature on political development as they were to the realist approach to studying world politics. In their view, writings on Third World political development (which was dominated by American scholars) had two major blind spots. First, they emphasized political variables to the virtual exclusion of economic factors when they explained the fate of Third World states. Second, they treated Third World development from a domestic political perspective with little regard for the international context within which these states were trying to develop.

Shifting one's attention to economic and international system variables placed the plight of Third World states in an entirely different light. For example, the end of colonialism no longer marked the end of the exploitation of Third World states by industrialized states; it only changed the form of that exploitation from military to economic. Third World states remained in an inferior, dependent position when they were interacting with the financial and commercial power centers of the rich states of the world. These states used their position of economic dominance in order to structure the international economy to serve their interests. Their position of dependency left Third World states unable to define effectively their own development goals or to advance the welfare concerns of their population because their economies were set up and organized to serve the interests of the industrialized states. Goods were manufactured for export to these states, while the production of basic goods for domestic consumption was neglected.

Dependency theory draws heavily upon Marxist-Leninist theory in the formulation of its arguments. Marxist-Leninist theory argues that the structure of a society is determined by the dominant mode of production (the way goods and services are produced). As explained more fully in Chapter 5, Marxism uses the dialectical method to explain history and to critique capitalism. Capitalism is an inherently exploitative system, because, while it is the workers who produce a profit through their labor, it is the capitalists who prosper. Under capitalism, the long-term tendency is for profits to fall, which leads to a series of ever-worsening crises that culminate in revolution. The workers seize the capitalists' property and institute a socialist system, in which profits are shared by all. In order to postpone this inevitable revolution, the capitalist countries embarked on a course of imperialism and established colonies. They exploited these colonies by taking raw materials, by using the inhabitants as cheap or slave labor, and by creating new markets for their goods. In many ways, the relationship between the mother country and the colony is analogous to that between capitalist and the worker: The colony produces something of value that is taken by the mother country.

For dependency theorists, then, the dominant actors in world politics are economic classes whose relations are best characterized in terms of exploitation and dependency. Because the struggle between economic classes is rooted in the structure of the international system, dependency theorists hold out little prospect for changing the exploitation inherent in this relationship unless a fundamental transformation of the system takes place. Thus, from a normative viewpoint, dependency theory takes exception with the reformist thrust of globalism and instead advocates an agenda of "radical political action to exacerbate the contradictions of a system which systematically oppresses some of its members."[8]

PLAN OF THE BOOK

The realist, globalist, and dependency approaches present us with three quite different pictures of what world politics is all about. It is not our intention to argue that one theoretical approach or methodology is better than the others. Each has strengths and weaknesses. Their usefulness depends upon the questions that we are asking about world politics. As such, we do not try to force our discussion of topics to fit the language of these three perspectives, but rather we come back to them selectively in order to clarify points or highlight areas of disagreement. What we want to do in this book is to put forward a historical record of events and to present questions and concepts that will encourage students to decide for themselves which approach is most useful for studying world politics.

We take the concept of world politics to be a broad one, encompassing both the interaction between actors (states, multinational corporations, international organizations) and the forces that give rise to their actions. Consistent with our earlier observation about the growing interdependence of states, our view of world politics deemphasizes the traditional distinction between domestic and foreign policy in favor of an emphasis on those events—regardless of where they happen—that hold significant consequences for the global condition.

This book is divided into three parts. Part One covers the conceptual dimension. It combines case studies, heavily drawn from the post-World War II experience of the United States, and basic concepts from the field of international relations, in order to create a foundation from which we can analyze world politics. Part Two examines the military dimension of world politics. It presents an overview of the cold war, examines military strategy and principles at both the nuclear and conventional levels, and addresses the question of why nations go to war. Part Three examines the economic dimension of world politics. It begins by reviewing the development of the post-World War II international economic system and then addresses problems associated with development, regional integration, and the activities of multinational corporations.

NOTES

1. For reviews of the development of the field of international relations, see Paul Viotti and Mark Kauppo, *International Relations Theory* (New York: Macmillan, 1987); K. J. Holsti, *International Politics: A Framework for Analysis*, 5th ed. (Englewood Cliffs, N.J.: Prentice-Hall, 1987), pp. 1–22; Theodore Couloumbis and James Wolfe, *Introduction to International Relations*, 3d ed. (Englewood Cliffs, N.J.: Prentice-Hall, 1986), pp. 2–39; and Michael Smith, Richard Little, and Michael Shackleton, eds., "Introduction," in *Perspectives on World Politics* (Chatham, N.J.: Chatham House Publishers, 1981), pp. 11–22.
2. See E. H. Carr, *The Twenty Years Crisis* (London: Macmillan, 1951).
3. The classic early post-World War II realist text is Hans Morgenthau, *Politics Among Nations* (New York: Alfred Knopf, 1948).
4. This debate is reviewed in Ray Maghroori, "Introduction: Major Debates in International Relations," in Ray Maghroori and Bennett Ramberg, eds., *Globalism vs. Realism* (Boulder, Colo.: Westview Press, 1982), pp. 9–22.
5. Harvey Starr and Benjamin Most, "The Substance and Study of Borders in International Relations Research," *International Studies Quarterly* 20 (1976), 581–620.
6. See Robert Keohane and Joseph Nye, *Power and Interdependence* (Boston: Little, Brown, 1977) for an elaboration of what here is referred to as the *globalist position*.
7. For an example of dependency theory, see Fernando Cordoso and Enzo Faletto, *Dependency and Development in Latin America* (Berkeley Calif.: University of California Press, 1979). The literature on dependency theory is reviewed in James Caporaso, ed., *International Organization* 32 (1978), which is a special issue.
8. Smith, Little, and Shackleton (eds.), *Perspectives on World Politics*, p. 21.

Chapter
2

Power

In 1979, a group of militant citizens in a relatively small developing nation (Iran) stormed the embassy of a superpower (the United States) and took the workers there hostage. Over the next year, the government of Iran, in defiance of international law, refused to release the hostages. By any standard, the United States was the more powerful of these two states. It possessed a huge nuclear arsenal, as well as approximately 2 million soldiers. It had an annual military budget that was almost three times the size of Iran's, yet its efforts to free its own citizens were spectacularly unsuccessful. In its efforts to gain the release of the hostages, the United States tried everything, from engaging in quiet diplomacy directly with Iran and through other states, to freezing the assets of Iran that were held in U.S. banks, to mounting a military rescue attempt.

U.S.-IRANIAN RELATIONS: A CASE STUDY OF POWER[1]

U.S. relations with Iran in the years prior to the fall of the Shah in 1979 and at the onset of the hostage crisis could not have been more different. During the Shah's rule, the United States had little difficulty in realizing its foreign-policy objectives. Then, as today, three objectives were paramount: (1) maintaining the flow of oil, (2) containing Soviet influence, and (3) establishing and maintaining regional stability. The Shah also had a consistent set of goals. Under the heading of the "White Revolution," he sought to transform Iran into an industrialized state and a major international power. Through single-mindedness of purpose, repression, and terror, he attempted to overcome centuries of backwardness in one generation. The key to achieving this dream was manipulating Iran's oil resources in order to acquire military power and an industrial base.

During the Nixon-Ford administrations, a number of trends came together that catapulted Iran from the position of a peripheral state in U.S. foreign-policy priorities to that of a central pillar. Great Britain informed the United States that it was going to withdraw its military forces and political authority from the Persian Gulf. The United States was already financially burdened and socially divided by Vietnam. The withdrawal of British military forces from the Persian Gulf would create a power vacuum that would have to be filled in order to forestall communist expansion. The United States, however, would not step in directly. Under the 1969 Nixon Doctrine, the United States stopped playing policeman of the world and began to function as an arsenal that would help regional powers maintain order and security. Iran and Saudi Arabia were among the states selected to play a surrogate role in the Persian Gulf and receive U.S. arms and support. For Iran this meant not only the realization of the Shah's long-standing goal of creating a large military but also U.S. acceptance of the Shah's definition of Iran's role in world affairs. During the last decade of the Shah's rule, the single most important link between the United States and Iran was arms sales. The Shah's philosophy became "buy the best at the greatest quantity and at the fastest rate." The volume of activity was staggering. One-third of all U.S. arms sales were to Iran, and 27 percent of Iran's government spending was directed at arms purchases. This massive spending spree also brought with it a rapid and visible influx of Americans to sell, service, and train Iranians in the use of their newly purchased equipment. By July 1976, 24,000 Americans were working in Iran. Throughout this period, the Shah did stand by the United States. For example, when the Arab states joined together in refusing to sell oil to the United States and Israel in the aftermath of the 1973 Arab-Israeli war, he continued to sell oil to both countries. He provided the United States with listening posts against the Soviet Union and fuel for U.S. naval vessels. Yet, the Shah had not abandoned his ultimate goal of creating a powerful and independent Iran. The purpose of acquiring U.S. weapons was to free Iran from dependence on the United States for protection.

There also occurred during the last decade of the Shah's rule a progressive breakdown of Iran's socioeconomic system and an increase in his reliance on the secret police (SAVAK) to maintain order. A charismatic challenger to the Shah emerged in the person of the Ayatollah Khomeini, who had been in exile since 1964. His opposition to the Shah and the Shah's White Revolution reflected the thinking of the Moslem Shiite clergy. They believed that the Shah had sold Iran's resources to the West in return for personal wealth and glory. The White Revolution and its goals were held to be sinful. They felt that Iran needed to cut its ties to the United States and return to tradition and the teachings of the Koran.

The Carter administration's emphasis on human rights altered the relationship between Iran and the United States. Carter criticized the Shah for his human rights violations, pressed him for reform, and tried to put a cap on the arms sales policies of the Nixon-Ford administrations. Reluctantly, the Shah began to ease restrictions and institute reforms. Neither the United States nor the Shah were ready for what followed. Rioting began in January 1978, within days followed by an appearance by Carter in Iran in which he publicly praised the Shah and spoke of the Iranian peoples' love for him. Throughout the rest of the year, both the Shah and the Carter administration temporized in the face of mounting Iranian discontent. The Shah gave no evidence of being able to deal with this challenge in a meaningful manner. At first he shuffled ministers around; next he established an all-military government and finally he turned to Shapour Bakhtiar, an old opposition leader, to form a government. By the time the Shah was ready to compromise, it was no longer possible to do so. The opposition National Front had become radicalized and intransigent in its demands. On January 16, 1979, the Shah went into exile. Throughout 1978 the Carter administration had been unwilling or unable to act decisively. The United States was now left with the worst possible situation. It had neither saved the Shah nor aligned itself with his victims, who now competed for power.

In February 1979, Khomeini returned from exile. The age-old rule of Iranian politics to never allow oneself to be outflanked in militancy took on a very real meaning for the United States. From the American perspective, the Shah had been removed and would not return. The goal became one of cutting losses to a minimum. Khomeini and his followers saw matters differently. They believed that the United States was a satanic force—the real power behind the Shah's throne. They remembered the events of 1953, when, with U.S. aid, another nationalist reformer, Mossadegh, was ousted in a coup and the Shah's powers were drastically increased. Iranian militancy reached an unprecedented level on November 4, 1979. With the Shah terminally ill in New York, Iranian students seized the U.S. embassy, took hostages, and demanded the return of the Shah and his wealth to Iran. The Shah's death in July 1980 did not resolve the crisis. The hostage issue had become embroiled in Iranian internal political maneuvering. No resolution appeared likely unless the power struggle ended and the hostages were no longer valuable pawns for the contending parties to manipulate. Ultimately, with the help of Algeria, an agreement was reached in which Iran received the money that was owed it by U.S. banks in exchange for the release of the hostages. They were set free on January 21, 1981 as Ronald Reagan was inaugurated as president.

The Iranian hostage situation illustrates the complexity that is involved when we analyze power. No concept is more central to the study and the practice of world politics, yet, regardless of its importance, power remains an ill-defined concept. Great extremes exist in the precision and the detail used to define *power*. For Hans Morgenthau, power borders on being an all-encompassing concept. It is anything "that establishes and maintains the control of man over man. Thus power covers all social relationships which serve that end, from physical violence to the most subtle psychological ties."[2] Others are quite precise in specifying what power is. Ted Gurr defines *power* as the capacity to organize and deploy more human and material resources in the service of state policies than other states can organize and deploy.[3] We will employ a middle-range approach and adopt a definition of *power* that is concise and allows for a more detailed discussion of its fundamental qualities. Following John Spanier, we will define *power* as "the capacity to influence the behavior of others in accordance with one's own objectives."[4] Embedded in this definition are three distinct notions of power: (1) It is a resource that one possesses; (2) it can be used as a means to an end; and (3) it establishes a relationship. The remainder of this chapter is devoted to exploring these three aspects of power.

POWER AS A RESOURCE: CONSTRUCTING A POWER PROFILE

Elements of Power

The first step in constructing a state's power profile is to inventory the factors that go into making states powerful (or weak). Only a moment's reflection is needed to recognize that such a listing could be endless, especially if Morgenthau's definition were to be used as a starting point. With that caveat in mind, we will identify seven factors that commonly form the core of a state's power base.

Geography   First and foremost, geography refers to size and location. Geography is crucial to a state's power base in two ways. First, indirectly it is all but a prerequisite for possessing significant amounts of the other elements considered crucial to a state's power base: a large population, natural resources, and a large economic capacity. Second, size and location play a key role in defining when national security threats exist and the proper way to meet those threats. Consider the case of the Soviet Union and Israel. With an area of 8.6 million square miles, the Soviet Union is the world's largest state, and, throughout its history, it has been able to repel invaders from Napoleon to Hitler by trading territory for time. Israel, with an area of only 7,992 square miles cannot afford such a strategy. In 1967, convinced that war was inevitable, it struck first and captured the Golan Heights, the Gaza Strip, the West Bank, and the Sinai Peninsula. With this added territory, Israeli leaders reacted differently in 1973 to information that war was again imminent. Rather than attack first, they chose to accept the first blow and then counterattack.

Large size in itself is not necessarily an asset for a state. Other geographic features, in particular location and terrain, can negate its potential benefits. In many respects, the history of the Soviet Union can be read as an attempt to overcome the geographic obstacles that have been placed in the way of exploiting its size. The Soviet Union does not possess a natural frontier with Europe, and, while its vastness has ultimately contributed to the downfall of invaders, the absence of a stark geographic barrier on its border has made it an inviting target for would-be conquerors. Although it is richly endowed with natural resources, many of these lie in remote areas where climate, the expense of transportation, and the absence of workers conspire to make resource extraction an expensive undertaking. Official Soviet estimates have placed the cost of extracting oil from its Siberian fields at two or three times above the average cost of extracting Soviet oil. Agricultural productivity is similarly handicapped, for only 10–20 percent of the total area of the Soviet Union is suitable for cultivation.

These factors come together quite differently for the United States. The Atlantic and Pacific Oceans have long provided the United States with a degree of protection from external threats. Although, like the Soviet Union, it possesses long borders, the identity of its neighbors (Canada and Mexico for the United States, versus China, Germany, and the old Austrian-Hungarian Empire for the Soviet Union) has made the task of border defense far less expensive. In fact, the United States is particularly blessed in terms of its geography. Most of its land mass lies within the temperate zone, where conditions are most favorable to large-scale agriculture—so much so that the United States pursues a policy of deliberately removing land from crop production. Similarly, the climate is favorable to human productivity, with very few areas of the country being inhospitable to human habitation. The large amount of inhabitable land and the abundance of natural resources have made it possible to support a large and productive population. The absence of significant natural barriers have made the early development of extensive transportation and communication systems possible. Overall, size and location have contributed to U.S. power without imposing large costs.

The importance of location to a state's capacity for power is aptly illustrated by the experiences of less developed countries. Most of the Third World is located within a 30° latitude of the equator. High temperatures create soil and weather conditions that are not conducive to development. The type of agricultural production needed to sustain industrial development requires large areas of cleared land and dependable rainfall. In the tropics, the rain forest canopy protects the soil from the effects of excessive heat and erosion. Once the rain forest is cleared, the condition of the soil deteriorates rapidly. The prevailing weather patterns produce alternating periods of too much and too little rain. Drought and erosion destroy the thin topsoil. In the Sahel region of Africa alone, 250,000 acres of arable land become desert each year. High temperatures also create a favorable environment for the proliferation of insect pests. Agricultural production is costly and uncertain under these conditions. In addition to creating agricultural problems, heat diminishes human productivity and fosters conditions under which debilitating diseases such as malaria flourish.

Climate is not the only geographic problem that Third-World nations face. This portion of the globe is particularly prone to natural disasters. Droughts, floods, earthquakes, volcanos, hurricanes, and tornados are more common here than elsewhere. These disasters cause major setbacks to development in poor countries. It is no accident that development occurred first in the more temperate regions. Geographic location is an important factor contributing to delayed development and diminished power in the Third World. As a result, these countries have been vulnerable historically to domination by those states that are located in the more temperate regions.

Population   Although no element of power automatically confers great power status upon a state, the absence of a large population historically has made attaining that rank all but impossible. Large populations have been valued because they provide the foundations for large armies and large work forces. However, the structure and the rate of growth of a population, as well as its size, are of importance. Not all members of a society contribute equally to defense or the production of goods and services. The elderly and young consume more resources than they contribute to current strength. Growth rate is also a crucial factor that influences a state's power. A state with large numbers of young citizens can expect to have a large work force in the future, even if there is a low rate of population growth, whereas a state with an aging population faces the need to make difficult decisions about what types of economic and military activity it can support in the future. Figure 2.1 illustrates the relative size of the world's countries based on population figures.

Today a large population is more often a handicap than an asset, for the bulk of the world's peoples are concentrated in the less developed countries. Here, rapid population growth means enormous yearly increases in the number of citizens who must be provided for. Having large numbers of people entering the work force is not beneficial when there are not a sufficient number of jobs for them. Even in a relatively wealthy country, rapid growth strains resources. Schools, housing, and waste disposal systems are just a few of the services that must be provided. In developing countries, population growth can overwhelm and weaken the state. The higher the growth rate, the more pressing the problems become. Nigeria provides an excellent illustration of this phenomenon.[5]

In 1984 Nigeria, with approximately 88 million people, was the tenth largest nation in terms of population size. The United States, with over 236 million people, was fourth, yet Nigeria in that year had nearly twice as many births as the United States. At its present growth rate, there will be 532 million people in Nigeria by the year 2050. At that point, Nigeria would have almost as many people within its 572,880 square miles of territory as presently exist in all of Africa (17,978,140 square miles). Long before this point could be reached, however, the strain on political and economic resources would become so great that Nigeria's social and political systems would collapse. Although it is one of the more serious cases, the population problem in Nigeria is in no way unique. In 1985 more than three-fourths of the world's population resided in the Third World. Unless population growth can be significantly slowed, these states will fall further and further behind the developed world.

One final aspect of population that bears special mention is its ethnic composition. As we shall discuss in greater detail elsewhere, ethnic tensions are a major contributing factor to international and domestic conflict. Few states possess homogeneous populations, and the greater the ethnic tensions, the less a large population contributes to a state's power base. In 1972 only 12 of 132 states could be classified as ethnically homogeneous; in 39 states the largest ethnic group made up less than 50 percent of the population; and in 53, the population contained at least 5 major ethnic groups.[6] Because of the way in which the colonial powers drew boundaries, Third-World states have been hit particularly hard by ethnic conflict. Nowhere is this more evident than in Africa, where boundaries were established on the basis of administrative convenience or as a result of negotiations among the European powers with no regard for preexisting African nations and ethnic divisions. Uganda presents one of the most serious cases of ethnic conflict resulting from colonial rule. During Idi Amin's tenure in office, an estimated 1 million Ugandans died. Most of these victims belonged to particular ethnic groups. Under Amin's successor, Milton Obote, the killings continued, although they were targeted at a different ethnic group. Although the extent of ethnic violence is more severe there than elsewhere

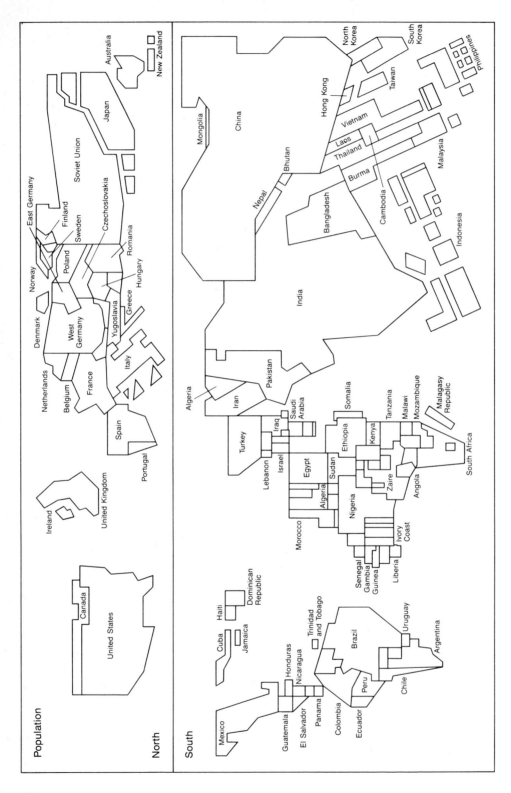

Figure 2.1 World map based on population (*Source: Newsweek*, October 26, 1981, p. 38. Copyright 1981, by Newsweek, Inc. All rights reserved, reprinted by permission.).

the Ugandan situation is, in a number of ways, representative of the effects of arbitrary boundaries. Ethnic conflict is not the only cause of the problems that Uganda now faces. The effects of Idi Amin's personality, as well economic pressures, cannot be ignored. However, without ethnic divisions, Amin's rule might well have taken a different course.

The problems associated with ethnic tension are not restricted to Third World states. During the 1970s, Canada had to contend with a strong separatist movement in Quebec; and the British and Spanish have long had to deal with violent regional separatist movements organized among the Catholics in Northern Ireland and the Basques in Spain, respectively.

As we enter the 1990s, the Soviet Union faces acute ethnic problems. Ethnic Russians account for about 50 percent of the population, and some 150 different ethnic groups can be found within its borders. Moreover, the Asiatic Russian population is growing at a far more rapid rate than its European counterpart. Built-up tensions over longstanding attempts to "Russify" these peoples and resentment over the great disparities in wealth, status, and political power between the European and Asiatic Russians (the European Russians hold the better jobs and positions of authority within the government and military) along with traditional conflicts among regional ethnic groups are major factors contributing to the violence in Georgia, Armenia, and the Soviet Central Asian Republics of Uzbekistan, Tajikistan, and Azerbijian. Ethnic tensions are also present in European Russia. All of the Baltic republics have demanded independence and the Ukrainian Popular Movement has called for the transformation of the Soviet Union into a confederation of fully independent republics. Ethnic tensions have also reappeared in East Europe. A region long known for conflicts among, these disputes have resurfaced with the replacement of Soviet-dependent leaders with nationalistic ones. Some observers expect the Baltic Republics to achieve independence by the mid 1990s. Ironically, *glasnost* has actually contributed to ethnic tensions by publicizing for the first time the disparities in standards of living between regions.

Natural Resources   The OPEC-led oil embargo of the early 1970s sent the price of oil skyrocketing in the industrialized world, touched off a wave of inflationary pressures, and brought great wealth to the oil-producing states. The embargo illustrates the important role that natural resources play in establishing a power base. The quite different situation of the mid-1980s drove home the point that the importance of any given natural resource to a state's power base changes over time. In 1971, prior to the first oil crisis, the posted price of oil was $1.80 per barrel. In 1973 it rose to $11.67 per barrel. In 1980 it skyrocketed to over $30 per barrel, only to fall back to $16 per barrel in 1986. One consequence of this rapid fall in the price of oil was that in 1985 Saudi Arabia's balance-of-payments deficit of $20 billion was exceeded only by the United States. Its oil revenues fell from $113 billion in 1980 to $43 billion in 1985.

Of critical importance to the value of a given natural resource is the nature of the technology used to extract that resource and the distribution of that resource among states. The United States, Germany, and Great Britain all became industrialized and achieved great power in part by exploiting their vast coal reserves. It was only after World War II that oil replaced coal as the dominant energy source in the industrialized world, and it was the concentration of oil in a relatively small number of Third World states that laid the foundation for the West's vulnerability to oil embargoes.

States that are not able to become self-sufficient with regard to oil (as few are) must acquire this needed resource from other states or forego the military and economic structures for which it is a prerequisite. In earlier periods, great powers either traded or established colonies to guarantee access to key raw materials. Today more complex forms of exchange and domination exist. The term *neocolonialism* has been used by some economists to refer to the economic relations between the developed and the less developed countries. *Neocolonialism* refers to a situation in which the subservient state is legally independent but in reality dependent on the developed nations. Instead of direct control, the stronger power uses indirect means to influence the weaker power. Sometimes this relationship is described by the term *dependency*. Economic and even social and political decisions on the periphery (the less developed countries) are made to meet the needs of the center (the developed market economies). Periphery nations continue to supply cheap labor and raw materials to the center nations and to import manufactured goods and technology.

Oil is not the only critical resource. The developed nations are dependent on the less developed nations for a number of raw materials. According to figures released in 1989 by the CIA, the United States imports 100 percent of the sheet mica, strontium, manganese, and chromium that it uses and over 90 percent of its bauxite, cobalt, and platinum group metals. Mineral resources tend to be concentrated in a few places. South Africa is particularly well endowed. It possesses 95 percent of the platinum, 75 percent of the chromium, 60 percent of the diamonds, 70 percent of the gold, and 73 percent of the manganese that are now produced in the world. South Africa's possession of these and other important minerals is one reason that the developed nations have been cautious in exerting pressure on the South African government to change its apartheid policies. Other nations also possess significant mineral wealth. Much of the world's copper comes from just four countries (Chile, Peru, Zambia, and Zaire). Over 70 percent of the world's tin is supplied by Bolivia, Malaysia, and Thailand. Jamaica and Guinea supply more than half of the bauxite that is now traded.

Economic Wealth   A state's wealth always has been an important contributor to its power base. Traditionally, wealth was valued more for its ability to contribute to military power than as a measure of status in its own right. The greater a state's wealth, the more readily it can produce both "guns and butter." States at all power levels face the potentially constraining effects of inadequate resources. During the mid-1980s, a major force behind interest in arms control in the Soviet Union and the United States was the heavy burden that arms spending placed on the two economies. More than anything else, it was limited economic resources that forced Great Britain to abandon its empire and to accept the status of a second-rate nuclear power heavily dependent on U.S. technology. France, in contrast, made a conscious decision to ignore the costs involved and established an independent nuclear capability. The poorer nations of the world find these decisions to be even more significant.

Whereas military spending in the Soviet Union involves foregoing the production of consumer goods, in a poor nation it can mean going without basic necessities. For example, in Ethiopia in 1980, the government spent almost 11 percent of its gross national product (GNP) on the military and only 1.4 percent of its GNP on health. During that same period, life expectancy in Ethiopia was 40 years, and the country ranked 127th out of 142 countries on infant mortality.[7] During the course of the cold war between the United States and the Soviet Union, economic well-being became an important measure of power status separate from its contribution to military strength. One measure of a state's wealth is GNP: the total monetary value of the goods and services produced by a state. Figure 2.2 presents the relative size of the world's countries based on GNP. Although the GNP gives an overall indication of the total amount of wealth that is being produced in a society, it is of limited use when we are comparing states, since it does not take into account the state's size. The standard measure employed for comparative purposes is the per capita GNP, which is simply the overall GNP divided by the nation's population.

Although per capita GNP is the most common indicator of wealth used, it is often criticized. It probably overstates the distance between rich and poor countries, and it underestimates the well-being of persons in socialist countries. In addition, per capita GNP does not address the question of income distribution. There may be a relatively small number of very wealthy citizens and a very large number of very poor citizens. What matters in the long run in terms of power is how much wealth a state possesses and what a state chooses to do with its economic resources. While economic wealth does not guarantee power, it is a prerequisite to it.

Political Capacity The existence of the factors that we have just listed can enhance a state's power, but what is ultimately important is the extent to which these factors can be manipulated by policymakers to realize foreign-policy objectives. A strong state is one in which policymakers have the capacity to shape society into new forms and to adapt it to the demands of change. The problems associated with building a strong state have long been identified with the Third World. In terms of formal structure, many less developed countries (LDCs) appear to have very strong states. The executive branch is not constrained by a strong legislature, competing parties, and the other institutions of democracy. Many observers have argued, however, that in spite of the existence of a dominant executive structure in many LDCs, the state actually has too little power rather than too much. The absence of the power resources that we discussed earlier and the presence of high population growth rates and ethnic divisions constrain policymakers. Additionally, as government policymakers become strong, so do leaders of other groups, resulting in fragmented societies that are prone to stalemate.[8]

Recently, the concepts of weak and strong states also have been applied to advanced industrial market economy states in order to explain why these states have adopted different international economic policies.[9] Under this scheme, the United States can be classified as a weak state—one in which the government is heavily influenced by pressure group activity, in which power is decentralized, and in which policymakers have few policy instruments to choose from as they pursue policy goals. At the other extreme lies the Japanese state, with its close ties between the long-

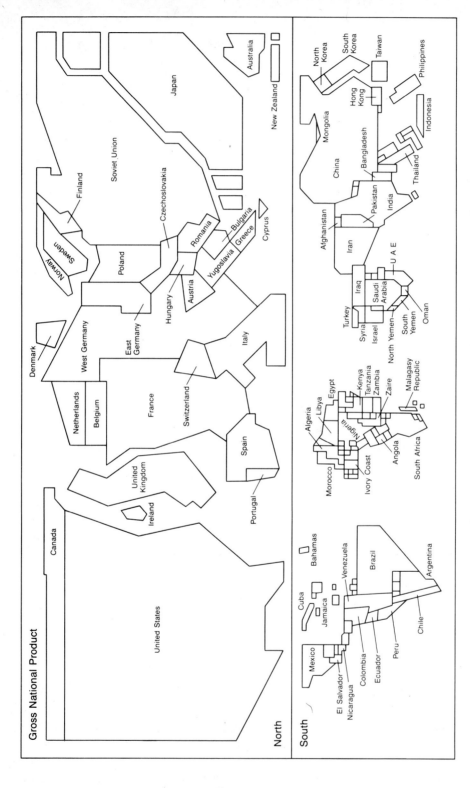

Figure 2.2 World map based on gross national product (GNP) (*Source: Newsweek,* October 26, 1981, p. 38).

ruling Liberal Democratic party and the bureaucracy, the close working relationship that exists between the bureaucracy and the large businesses and trading firms, and the resulting ability to intervene in the economy at the level of a specific economic sector or firm. In between lie the European states, with Great Britain falling closest to the United States and France falling closest to Japan. Lacking significant numbers of policy tools to realize their economic foreign-policy objectives, weak states such as the United States and Great Britain are forced to rely upon appeals to ideology (the inherent value of an open international economic system) and vague statements of foreign-policy objectives when they try to deal with problems related to interdependence, such as trade deficits, high inflation, and the flood of comparatively cheap foreign-made goods in their markets. Strong states are able to call upon administrative regulations, nationalized industries, and the judicious use of monetary policies to pursue more finely tuned policies of restricting foreign investments or pursuing a strategy of export-led growth.

Military Power   Military capability is an indispensable component of power. The capacity of a state to defend itself and its potential to inflict losses on another state are important considerations in international negotiations. Although there is not a one-to-one relationship between military and political power, they are certainly related, and military capabilities remain an important measure of power. At first glance, assessing a state's military power seems a straightforward exercise, but the reality is quite different. It is true that the two primary measures of military power (expenditures, and work force and equipment) are readily available. *World Military Expenditures and Arms Transfers* (1986) lists U.S. military spending in 1983 at $217,154 million and that of the Soviet Union at $258,000 million. The Soviet armed forces are calculated at 4,400,000 soldiers, while the U.S. armed forces are calculated at 2,222,000 soldiers.[10] *The Military Balance*, an annual volume that has been produced for over 20 years, puts together detailed accounts of the armed forces of virtually every state. Table 2.1 presents selected expenditure, and work force, and equipment figures for several states. Table 2.2 presents a comparison of conventional force levels between NATO (North Atlantic Treaty Organization) and the Warsaw Pact. Notice that, in absolute terms, the developed nations spend much more money on the military than do the less developed nations. Relative to their resources, however, the Third World nations spend heavily. Many of the poorest nations spend between 5 and 10 percent of their GNP on the military. Among the developed nations, the average expenditure is between 5 and 6 percent. Military spending can be beneficial to the economy. For example, the armed forces and weapons manufacturing provide training and employment. However, the trend in Third World countries is for greater proportions of money to be spent on sophisticated weaponry that must be imported. This type of spending hurts rather than helps the domestic economy. On average, the less developed countries spend more money on military expenditures than on health or education. In the long run, these countries may be sacrificing one type of power (economic) for another (military).

We encounter significant problems as soon as we try to determine what the figures in Tables 2.1 and 2.2 mean. Consider the problem of establishing the Soviet Union's level of military expenditures.[11] Until recently the Soviet Union did not

Table 2.1 SELECTED COMPARISON OF WORK FORCE AND SPENDING LEVELS

State	Military Expenditures (millions)	Armed Forces (thous.)	Military Expenditures as a Percentage of GNP	Armed Forces per 1000 Population
Argentina	$ 1,523	175	2.7	5.9
Canada	6,439	81	2.2	3.3
China (PRC)	34,500[e]	4,100	8.6	4.0
Egypt	2,679[eb]	447	8.3	9.8
East Germany	9,806[e]	240	6.4	14.4
West Germany	23,565	496	3.4	8.1
Israel	6,229[e]	180	24.2	45.0
Japan	11,500	241	1.0	2.0
Mexico	872	131	0.6	1.7
Nigeria	1,723	222	2.5	2.6
Saudia Arabia	27,192	55	24.3	5.3
South Africa	3,132[e]	77	4.3	2.5
Soviet Union	258,000	4,400	14.0	16.1
United States	217,154	2,222	6.6	9.5

[e] = estimate

[eb] = estimate with arms import data added to military expenditures

Source: United States Arms Control and Disarmament Agency, *World Military Expenditures and Arms Transfers* (Washington, D.C.: Government Printing Office, 1985).

publish a detailed military budget but instead announced a single figure. This amount changed little from year to year, and, for the period 1970–1984, the announced level of Soviet military expenditures actually dropped by 4 percent. The Soviet Union now publishes a much larger figure for defense spending than it did in the past, but even this figure leaves out a good deal that the West would consider to be military spending. Unwilling to work with this figure, analysts in the West have developed two approaches (called the *add-on* and the *building-block* approaches) for putting together an estimate of Soviet military expenditures. Using the *add-on approach*, analysts take the official Soviet figure as a starting point and add on the presumed cost of items that are not mentioned at all or that are hidden in the spending figures of other departments. With the *building-block approach* analysts divide the Soviet military establishment into separate categories (training, construction, weapons, work force, research and development, etc.) and set a cost for each. All of the numbers are then added together to produce an estimate of Soviet military spending. The building-block approach is used by the Central Intelligence Agency (CIA), and its calculations of Soviet military expenditures traditionally have been among the most controversial of its estimates. At issue have been both the types of items listed (for example, should some civil defense, health, and education costs, pensions, and the cost of premilitary training be included) and their costs. The government of the Soviet Union has promised to provide a more complete and detailed budget in the future.

Table 2.2 A COMPARISON OF WARSAW PACT AND
NATO DATA ON MILITARY FORCES IN
EUROPE

	Warsaw Pact Count	NATO Count[1]
Tanks		
Warsaw Pact	59,470	51,500
NATO	30,690	16,424
Armored Troop Carriers		
Warsaw Pact	70,330	55,100[2]
NATO	46,900	23,340[2]
Artillery		
Warsaw Pact	71,560	43,400
NATO	57,060	14,458
Combat Aircraft		
Warsaw Pact	7,876	8,250[3]
NATO	7,130	3,977[3]
Helicopters		
Warsaw Pact	2,785	3,700[3]
NATO	5,270	2,419[3]
Ground Forces		
Warsaw Pact	3,573,100	3,090,000
NATO	3,660,200	2,213,593

[1]NATO count includes only equipment in fully or partially manned units. NATO has the following equipment levels in storage: tanks—5,800; ATCs—5,260; artillery—2,870; combat aircraft—530; and combat helicopters—180. NATO estimates that Warsaw Pact stored equipment levels are in excess of NATO stored equipment levels in all categories.

[2]Figures were released by NATO in May 1989.

[3]Figures do not include trainer combat aircraft and are not based on the same definitions used in determining the ceilings on combat aircraft and combat helicopters that NATO proposed in CFE negotiations in July 1989.

Source: Soviet Military Power, Prospects for Change, 1989 (Washington, D.C.: Department of Defense, 1989), p. 99.

A comparison of the level of defense spending among states is difficult for several reasons. How does the cost of a Soviet tank (in rubles) compare to the cost of a U.S. tank (in dollars)? Some type of common measure is needed to make this comparison. The most commonly used standard measure is the U.S. dollar, but both the add-on and the building-block approaches calculate Soviet military spending in rubles. This means that their ruble figures must be converted into our dollars. Again, two basic choices exist.

The simplest method is to take the total figure and just convert it into dollars by using the existing exchange rate. The problem with this method is that the price of the ruble is fixed by the Soviet government. It does not reflect balance of payments, the level of inflation, or international supply and demand. While the official exchange rate in the summer of 1989 was 1 ruble = $1.60, the black-market exchange rate was 1 ruble = $.10.

The CIA uses the *pricing-elements approach.* In it each element of the Soviet military budget is valued at the price that it would cost to purchase that item in the United States. The large number of unknowns that must be guessed at in such a calculation can produce widely differing conclusions. For 1983 CIA calculations of Soviet military spending were $236 billion dollars greater than the official figure of $22 billion. Using the same methodology, *World Military and Social Expenditures* came up with a figure that differed from the CIA's by $46 billion.

An even more fundamental problem in making comparisons occurs because of the "index number effect," which happens whenever we compare states at different levels of economic development. Labor is extremely expensive in the United States, while technology is relatively cheap. As a result, industry and the military establishment rely as much as possible on technology to hold down costs. The opposite is the case in the Soviet Union. Labor is more abundant than in the United States and less expensive. It is technology that is expensive and whose use must be minimized. Pricing the cost of the Soviet labor that goes into building a tank or the cost of maintaining the large Soviet army in U.S. dollars distorts the true level of spending by the Soviet Union, just as pricing the large amounts of technology used in the U.S. production process and by the military in rubles would overstate its cost. Adjustments can be made to try to offset these distortions, but they do increase the amount of subjectivity in the estimate and the potential for error.

Comparative calculations of military expenditures are not easier, even if we restrict ourselves to those Western states whose currencies are traded on the international market. Repeatedly, powerful political leaders in the United States have complained that the NATO allies are not paying their fair share for the defense of Europe and that, if a greater percentage of the burden is not borne by these allies, the United States should pack up and go home and leave the defense of Europe to the Europeans. Selected military spending levels for some NATO states can be found in Table 2.3. European states claim that a straight comparison of military expenditures does not provide an answer to the defense burden of each state because more is involved than just a disagreement over dollars.

West Germany has put forward a particularly vigorous defense of its contribution to the common defense of Europe.[12] Among the points they raise are the following. West Germany, a country whose territory equals only about the combined size of New York and Pennsylvania, notes that within its territory are stationed more than 400,000 allied troops, and over 40,000 military installations and training areas are provided on a no-cost basis. The value of the real estate involved amounts to over $18 billion. Each year three or four major military exercises take place that involve about 40,000 soldiers and 10,000 vehicles, which criss-cross German public and private lands and often block off major public transportation systems. The total number of yearly military exercises approaches 5,000, and the cost of damages resulting from military maneuvers amounted to $40 million in 1984. Each year over 580,000 military flights are conducted in German air space. Over 11,000 of these are conducted at low altitudes (between 250 and 500 feet). The country's transportation system has

Table 2.3 SELECTED MILITARY SPENDING LEVELS FOR SOME NATO
STATES, 1987

State	Total (in millions of dollars)	Per capita	Percent government spending	Percent GNP
Canada	$ 8,773	$ 342	9.3	2.2
France	$ 34,530	$ 620	19.8	3.9
FRG	$ 34,244	$ 560	22.9	3.1
Italy	$ 16,817	$ 293	4.9	2.2
Norway	$ 2,632	$ 630	6.7	3.1
Portugal	$ 1,135	$ 109	8.7	3.2
Turkey	$ 2,890	$ 55	22.4	4.8
United Kingdom	$ 31,774	$ 667	11.3	4.9
United States	$288,433	$1,185	28.7	6.7

Note: The figure for military spending as a percent of GNP is for 1986.

Source: The Military Balance, 1988–1989 (London: International Institute for Strategic Studies, 1988), p. 224.

been designed with military requirements in mind (for example, major highways are intended to double as alternative landing strips for combat planes). Finally, major political costs result from the fact that a majority of NATO's nuclear and chemical forces are stationed in West Germany.

Notice that we have not yet even raised the question of quality. How good is the Soviet tank compared to the American tank? Does it matter that in the area stretching from the Atlantic Ocean to the Ural Mountains (the geographic boundary of European conventional arms control talks) the Warsaw Pact has 52,200 main battle tanks compared to NATO's 22,200, if they are unequal in quality? Do we judge the antisubmarine warfare capabilities of NATO by comparing them to the antisubmarine warfare capabilities of the Warsaw Pact or by deciding how many submarines the Warsaw Pact has? After 20 years of presenting force and equipment levels for the two sides, the editors of *The Military Balance* in 1987 decided not to present a single overall assessment of the military balance in Europe. In fact, the editors concluded that it was ". . . a misnomer to speak of a single, overall military 'balance.' "[13] Judgments about the comparative capabilities of the two alliances could only be made in the context of a series of assumptions about the war to be fought. Which military forces would be included: What role would Spanish and French troops play; would the Poles and the Czechs fight with the Russians? What percentage of Soviet forces would have to be used to prevent possible uprisings in Eastern Europe? How would the conflict begin? Was either side surprised? What was the state of readiness of the two alliances? Are there other conflicts elsewhere in the world, such as the Persian Gulf?

Leadership James MacGregor Burns defines leadership as the "reciprocal process of mobilizing . . . resources, in a context of competition and conflict, in order to realize goals independently or mutually held by both leaders and followers."[14] Leadership is an important element of a state's power base because of its ability to promote social cohesion, to foster the efficient use of resources, and to define common objectives. Without quality leadership, the objective elements of power that we have concentrated upon to this point do not easily contribute to a state's overall strength. Although there is often general agreement as to which policymakers have been strong leaders and which have not, it is difficult to identify exactly which individual characteristics provide the basis for leadership. A few, that are often cited are charisma (which is, in itself, a quality that is difficult to define), organizational ability, powers of persuasion, decisiveness, courage, and dedication to purpose. The qualities of leadership that are most useful depend largely on the context in which they are used. The potential leader must have the peculiar combination of skills that are necessary to succeed in a particular time and place. This is not to say that leadership depends entirely on being in the right place at the right time (and thus that Hitler could not have risen to power in a different country or in Germany during another era). Leaders are themselves products of their cultures and so naturally reflect them. In addition, part of being a successful leader lies in recognizing opportunities available in a particular context and in taking advantage of them. Many leaders have shown remarkable skill at adapting their ideologies and leadership styles to changing circumstances. Nevertheless, not every skill is useful in all situations, as the example of Churchill's failure to lead in peacetime illustrates. Because the qualities necessary for leadership vary depending on the situation, it is difficult to predict when, where, and if a strong leader will arise. Leaders are not easily found. No school produces them. Burns goes so far as to argue that the crisis in leadership today lies in the mediocrity or irresponsibility of so many people in leadership positions. Graduation from West Point, winning elections, working one's way up the party bureaucracy to a seat in the Soviet politburo, or leading a successful coup or independence movement is no guarantee that the individual will possess the ability to lead once in power. For every Eisenhower, Churchill, Stalin, Lenin, Nasser, Castro, or Gandhi there are far more policymakers who have failed to provide effective leadership when needed. Many of these individuals are now forgotten save for brief references in historical texts. For example, the leaders of Weimar Germany after World War I cannot be named now by any but the most serious scholars of that period. Other leaders may be remembered as much for their later failures as for their early successes. Many initially strong leaders prove unable to sustain power. Sukarno rose to prominence in the Indonesian independence movement. When Indonesia became independent in 1949, Sukarno became its first president. During the 1950s, Sukarno consolidated his rule and built a centralized government with a strong executive. He possessed many of the characteristics necessary for leadership, including considerable charisma, and during the independence movement he exercised his skills to his and Indonesia's advantage. Yet, conditions in Indonesia deteriorated under his rule. His desire to become an international leader led him to ignore Indonesia's domestic problems. While the economic condition of the country drastically worsened, he emphasized with pride his unorthodox approach to economic development. In truth this approach consisted of indifference and mismanagement. He failed to control the Communist party (PKI) with the result that there was increasing unrest among military leaders. In 1965 General Suharto seized effective power following an abortive military coup. Although Sukarno retained a formal position for a brief period of time, his rule had in fact come to an end. In other instances, a strong leader has been disastrous to the long-range strength of the country. Pol Pot's rule in Kampuchea (Cambodia) led directly to the disintegration of the economy and infrastructure and to the invasion and occupation of his country by Vietnam. Idi Amin had a similar effect on Uganda.

National Will   National will is an even more elusive component to a state's power base than is leadership. Alternatively referred to as morale, social unity, or national pride, national will refers to the existence of a socially accepted sense of purpose and morality behind a state's action. The Vietnam War, the Arab-Israeli wars, and colonial wars for independence are vivid examples of the ability of less powerful states to defeat more powerful states or alliances because they possessed a strong sense of purpose and their opponents did not. In the case of Algeria, it is estimated that it took 450,000 French troops to combat 8,500 active Algerian revolutionaries. Soviet policy toward Afghanistan and U.S. policy toward Nicaragua are recent conflict situations in which similar discrepancies in national will may influence the outcome.

Power Equations

Doing no more than identifying the ingredients of a state's power base leaves us with a vague definition of power. We know where to look for it, and we know it when we see it, but how do we measure it? How do the ingredients that we have listed come together to make a state strong? Measuring power is important. It is the basis on which states compare themselves to one another. Furthermore, if one current research project is correct, a state's calculation that it is more powerful than its enemy is a necessary condition for going to war.[15] Measuring power requires a movement away from simply talking about power in general terms toward developing indicators of power that both accurately and reliably capture its essence. The objective is to operationalize ingredients of a state's power base such that all who employ these indicators reach the same conclusions. Doing this is not easy. Recall the qualifications that we placed on large populations as an element of power and the different measures that we suggested could be used to measure economic and military strength. In this section we will review four efforts to construct power equations that claim to grasp accurately the nature of power and allow for cross-national comparisons.

Working with data collected by the Correlates of War project, which has collected data on wars occurring between 1816–1980, James Ray states that power is made up of three dimensions: demography, industrial strength, and military strength.[16] Demography is operationalized as the total population of the state *(tpop)*. Industrial capacity is measured by three indicators: total urban population *(upop)*, steel production *(sp)*, and fuel (coal) consumption *(fc)*. Military strength is measured by two indicators: the size of the military budget *(mb)* and the size of its armed forces *(saf)*. In calculating these figures, Ray is concerned, not with the absolute amount of that resource (fuel, urban population, military budget), but with the state's great power percentage of it. All six of these indicators are given equal weight, and his power equation takes the following form:

$$\text{power} = \frac{tpop + upop + sp + fc + mb + saf}{6} \tag{2.1}$$

The United States in 1900 had a power score of 22. It possessed 16 percent of the population identified as living in great power states, 21 percent of the urban population, 39 percent of the total steel production, and 38 percent of the coal consumption. Its military budget represented 12 percent of all military spending by great power states, and its armed forces had 4 percent of all military personnel. When we place these percentages into the equation, the result is as follows:

$$\text{U.S. power} = \frac{16 + 21 + 39 + 38 + 12 + 4}{6} = 22$$

Table 2.4 presents the power scores of major powers in selected years from 1938 to 1975.

Several objections to using this type of power equation can be raised. One problem is that the equation does not accurately measure power for all states. A.F.K. Organski and Jacek Krugler argue that equations such as this do not accurately predict the outcome of conflicts in the Third World because they omit the political capacity of the government to extract resources from society.[17] This is particularly true in the area of taxation. In 1986 industrialized states' taxes on income, profit, and capital gains averaged 40 percent of their GNP, while in the poorer states this revenue accounted for only 16.8 percent of their GNP. To be truly a part of a state's power base, weapons, large populations, natural resources, and economic wealth must be available for use by policymakers. They operationalize political capacity by dividing a state's actual extractions from society (i.e., taxes, profits from government monopolies, and funds obtained by borrowing) by its expected level of extraction (a figure arrived at by applying a model to the predicted socioeconomic conditions of the state). They argue that the greater the ratio arrived at by this method, the more capable is the state. It will possess a greater ability and more flexibility to undertake foreign and domestic policies.

A second objection that can be raised about the equation concerns how the elements are related to one another. All six elements are treated as equally important. There is no reason that this must be the case. Some elements might be capable of dramatically increasing or decreasing a state's power. This could be indicated in a power equation through the use of multiplication, as is done in Equation 2.2, which was constructed by Ray Cline, a former intelligence analyst with the CIA and the State Department.[18] Note that his equation not only includes the idea of power multipliers but also pays explicit attention to one other dimension of power excluded from Equation 2.1 the intangible aspects of power. Efforts to measure power often shy away from including leadership, strategy, or national will because of the difficulty of operationalizing them. Calculating a state's national will, for example, involves far more subjectivity and room for disagreement than does measuring its coal consumption. In Equation 2.2 Cline treats strategy and national will as power multipliers. His equation is made up of five elements: critical mass (*C*), which refers to territory and population, economic strength (*E*), military strength (*M*), strategy (*S*), and national will (*W*) and looks like this:

Table 2.4   STATE POWER COMPARISONS (1938–1975)*

1938			1946	
State	Index score		State	Index score
Soviet Union	25		United States	45
United States	24		Soviet Union	34
Germany	20		Great Britain	14
Great Britain	10		France	7
Japan	10			
France	6			
Italy	5			

1950			1955	
State	Index score		State	Index score
United States	38		United States	39
Soviet Union	30		Soviet Union	30
China	17		China	17
Great Britain	9		Great Britain	9
France	5		France	5

1960			1965	
State	Index score		State	Index score
United States	35		United States	33
Soviet Union	29		Soviet Union	32
China	24		China	24
Great Britain	7		Great Britain	6
France	6		France	5

1970			1975	
State	Index score		State	Index score
United States	33		Soviet Union	34
Soviet Union	32		United States	30
China	25		China	26
Great Britain	5		Great Britain	5
France	5		France	5

*The data for this table were supplied by the Correlates of War Project at the University of Michigan. (Sums for years that deviate from 100 are accounted for by rounding error. The figure for urban population in China in 1975 is based on extrapolation.)

Source: James Ray, Global Politics (Boston: Houghton Mifflin, 1987), p. 194.

$$\text{power} = C + E + M \times (S + W) \qquad [2.2]$$

In Cline's analysis, the "normal" situation is for strategy and will to leave the other elements of the power equation unchanged by totaling 1 (0.5 + 0.5). The states that Cline credits with having greater than normal amounts of strategy or national will, or both, include the Soviet Union, West Germany, Israel, Japan, Cuba, North Korea, South Korea, Sweden, and Brazil. The states that he considers to be lacking in strategy or national will, or both, include the United States, Canada, the People's Republic of China, India, the Philippines, Nigeria, and Argentina.

A third problem with Equation 2.1 is that it may be time bound. Did coal consumption accurately reflect industrial strength in the 1980s? Most would argue that oil or nuclear power, or both, must also be considered. However, doing so seriously complicates the calculation of power over time. At what point should additional measures of energy consumption be added to an equation? When they are added, how much weight should they be given? How often should the elements of a power equation be changed? Peter Beckman has incorporated the idea that the elements of a power equation will change over time into his effort to construct a power equation.[19] His equation starts with 1900 and is made up of three elements: the state's percentage of world steel production (steel), its percentage of world population (pop), and a political stability score (pol. stab.). His equation is as follows:

$$\text{power} = \frac{\text{steel} + (\text{pop} \times \text{pol. stab.})}{2} \qquad [2.3]$$

The total is divided by 2 in order for the scores to fit on a scale of 0–100 percent. Beckman feels that advances in technology and transportation systems require that this equation be changed for the period 1920–1929. He adds to it the state's percentage of world energy production. For the decade beginning in 1940, Beckman modifies his equation again by adding the state's percent of deliverable nuclear weapons and changing his political stability indicator in recognition of the unrest that followed in the immediate postwar period. Table 2.5 presents the size of the U.S., Soviet, Chinese, British, and Indian power base during the mid-1970s as calculated by all three power equations. Does it make a difference which equation we use? In terms of overall rankings the only disagreement is with the placing of India and Great Britain. All agree that the Soviet Union, the United States, and China are first, second, and third, respectively. However, if we convert the power scores to a standard scale by taking the highest score (in each case that of the Soviet Union) and making it 100 percent, then calculating the other scores as a percentage of it, considerable disagreement emerges. According to Equation 2.3, the United States has 91.7 percent as much power as the Soviet Union. In Equation 2.2, it has only 80.5 percent, and in Equation 2.1 it has only 81.8 percent. China's power varies even more dramatically. According to Equations 2.2 and 2.3, it has either only 22.9 percent or 29.2 percent as much power as the Soviet Union. Nevertheless, Equation 2.1 credits China with having 69.7 percent as much power as the Soviet Union.

Many observers argue that power equations (regardless of how they are constructed) leave us with only a partial and misleading definition of power. For example, each of the equations we have given assigns the predominant amount of power

Table 2.5   POWER CALCULATED BY ALL THREE
               EQUATIONS, MID-1970s

	Raw score	Standardized score

Equation 2.1:

$$\text{power} = \frac{\text{tpop} + \text{upop} + \text{sp} + \text{fc} + \text{mb} + \text{saf}}{6}$$

	Raw score	Standardized score
Soviet Union	33	100.0
United States	27	81.8
China	23	69.7
India	12	36.4
Great Britain	5	15.0

Equation 2.2:
$$\text{power} = C + E + M \times (S + W)$$

	Raw score	Standardized score
Soviet Union	523	100.0
United States	421	80.5
China	120	22.9
Great Britain	99	18.9
India	58	11.1

Equation 2.3.: updated to the 1970s

$$\text{power} = \frac{\% \text{ steel} + (\% \text{ pop} + \text{pol. stab.}) + \% \text{ world energy} + \% \text{ nuc. power}}{4}$$

	Raw score	Standardized score
Soviet Union	24	100.0
United States	22	91.7
China	7	29.2
India	4	16.7
Great Britain	2	8.3

Sources: Equation 2.1: James Ray, *Global Politics* (Boston: Houghton Mifflin, 1987), p. 194. Ray does not include India in his calculations. We have recalculated the scores by substituting India for France and by using data from the UN, the CIA, and U.S. Arms Control and Disarmament Agency. Equation 2.2: Ray Cline, *World Power Assessment* (Washington, D.C.: Georgetown University Center for Strategic and International Studies, 1977. Equation 2.3: Peter Beckman, *World Politics in the Twentieth Century* (Englewood Cliffs, N.J.: Prentice-Hall, 1984), p. 326.

to the Soviet Union. However, many analysts would argue that Gorbachev's reforms are partially motivated by a sense that the power of the Soviet Union is actually lower than these calculations would suggest. The primary problem is the absence of any type of contextual analysis. Power equations implicitly treat power as money— a type of international currency that can be used with equal ease to accomplish (purchase) any goal or objective. Conflict situations such as rescuing hostages, promoting human rights, deterring terrorism, dealing with international debt and trade imbalances, combating guerrilla forces in Afghanistan or supporting them in Nicaragua, and countless others suggest that there is a vast difference between a state's power base, its potential power, and its actual power or ability to realize foreign-policy objectives under a given situation. The next two sections of this chapter will illustrate two general ways in which we can establish the context within which power as a resource can be used.

POWER AS A MEANS TO AN END

There is no automatic way of exercising power. A state's power base can be transformed from potential power to actual power in a number of ways. The challenge facing policymakers is to manage this transformation by selecting among the various options available, so that goals are realized and costs are kept to a minimum. A convenient way that policymakers can conceptualize the range of choices available to them is to visualize a continuum, with persuasion and force as the two opposite end points on that continuum[20] In between these 2 points lie a series of possibilities. Persuasion involves attempts to convince another state to adopt one's position on an issue through the use of reason, propaganda, or appeals to loyalty, or some other emotive force. Next comes the offering of rewards. In some cases, offering rewards may be insufficient, and policymakers may actually have to grant the rewards before the other state complies. Failing that, states may threaten punishment, such as increasing tariffs or denying most-favored-nation status. Threats alone may prove insufficient, so the next option is to inflict nonviolent punishment, such as breaking diplomatic relations or carrying out a boycott of a state's products. Finally, there is force. Unlike the other policy options, which leave the ultimate decision to comply or to resist with policymakers in the other state, force involves imposing a position on them. By invading Czechoslovakia in 1968, the Soviet Union imposed its will by force. For all practical purposes, once Soviet troops arrived on Czech soil, the Dubcek government no longer had the option of complying with or resisting Soviet demands. In contrast, during the Polish crisis of 1980, while the specter of a Soviet invasion constantly loomed in the background, Polish authorities retained their decision-making powers. The consequences of resisting Soviet demands were no doubt clear, but the decision remained formally theirs. The actual choice of options on this continuum rests upon a number of factors. Before examining them, we need to stress that not all states are able to select from the same menu of options. The size of a state's power base typically places severe restraints on that state's range of options. For example, in responding to incidents of terrorism, the United States has far more options to choose from than do its European allies, largely because of its greater military capabilities. (The bombing of Libya in retaliation for its support of terrorist activities was an option available to the United States but certainly not available to all states.) Terrorism itself is highly valued by small states and revolutionary groups because it is inexpensive, requiring only a few people and relatively small amounts of explosives or other weapons. Acts of terrorism allow smaller states and groups within states to have a major impact on events and attract global attention to their causes, even though they lack the power bases of large states.

Expense is the major consideration for a state when it is selecting a point along this continuum through which to exercise its power. There are inevitable translation costs involved in moving from power as a resource to power as a means to an end.[21] These costs can take various forms, such as the bureaucratic expense of mobilizing resources, domestic opposition to a course of action, the embarrassment of a prematurely leaked or failed strategy, and problems surrounding the actual implementation of a course of action. Given the time-consuming nature and expense involved in accumulating power resources, prudent policymakers seek to minimize these translation costs by operating as much as possible at the persuasion end of the continuum. The costs of persuasion are small compared to the costs of making (or implementing) rewards and punishments. Translation costs are greatest when force is employed. Many observers argue that the repeated use of force is a sign of weakness rather than strength, because it suggests that a state cannot realize its objectives through any means other than directly imposing its will. The Soviet invasions of Czechoslovakia (1968) and Afghanistan (1979), the presence of U.S. forces in Vietnam (1961–1973), and the repeated Israeli incursions into Lebanese territory in the early 1980s can all be seen in this light. In each case, these states were unable to use the powers of persuasion, promises, rewards, threats, or punishments to induce a smaller state to act as they wished. Translation costs are likely to run particularly high when force is used, because, as countless observers have noted, even the simplest activity becomes difficult in war. Israeli Prime Minister Begin felt the full consequences of higher-than-expected translation costs that stemmed from the 1982 Israeli invasion of Lebanon. Designed to drive Palestinian guerrillas out of southern Lebanon and to counter Syria's growing influence, the invasion resulted in tragedy when Israeli forces allowed Lebanese Christian forces to enter Palestinian refugee camps now under its control. Hundreds of men, women, and children were massacred. The resulting outcry in Israel forced Begin, who categorically disclaimed responsibility for the tragedy, to establish an investigatory commission. It called for the dismissal or censure of several top officials, including Defense Minister Sharon. Several months later, Begin also resigned, unable to recover politically or emotionally from the furor over the massacre.

A second set of considerations that a state uses when it selects a means of moving from power as a resource to power as a means to an end involves the specific circumstances of the situation. How important is the objective—are the means proportionate to the ends? What other issues are being contested at the time, and are there links among them? What is the underlying pattern of relations with the other state: Is the state an ally or one with which one is constantly at odds? Where is the conflict taking place? Research findings suggest that a state's ability to project its power declines as the distance that must be covered increases. Distance worked to the United States' advantage during the Cuban missile crisis in 1962 but created problems during the early cold war confrontations over Berlin and the Persian Gulf crises of the 1980s.

We need to make one final observation regarding power as a means to an end. In a very real sense, a state's power is what others believe it to be. Victory on the battlefield, putting a human on the moon, and high standards of living project the image of power and give a state the reputation for being powerful, so much so that a state's reputation for power may outstrip its actual ability to exercise its power. The lag between a state's reputation for power and its actual power may go unchallenged for a long period of time, allowing the state to remain a force in world politics for longer than any power equation would suggest. Great Britain was such a state during the late nineteenth and early twentieth centuries. France represents the opposite case. Its reputation for power also exceeded its actual power, but the gap was closed with crushing speed in 1940 as Hitler's armies raced across the French countryside to Paris. In defeat, the state's reputation for power was tarnished. It can be quite difficult and expensive for a state to reverse popular perceptions and to reestablish its reputation for power. A case in point is President Reagan's effort to restore the image of the United States as a powerful state and to escape the shadow of the Vietnam War through such actions as invading Grenada, sending troops to Lebanon, retaliating against terrorists, and giving support for the pro-U.S. forces in Nicaragua and Afghanistan.

POWER AS A RELATIONSHIP

A second way that we can build context into the concept of power is to stress that any exercise of power involves a relationship. Power is either exercised over something or someone.[22] The former is referred to as *the scope of power*, while the later is referred to as *its domain*. The scope of a state's power can be quite broad, covering a wide variety of issues and behaviors, or rather narrow, giving the state very little capacity to shape events beyond its borders. *Scope of power* can also be seen as comprising behavioral and structural dimensions. *Behavioral power* allows a state to determine the outcome of a specific issue: a vote against the membership of a country in the UN; establishing a specific tariff level on imported cars; or joining in an economic boycott against a country because it has invaded another country. *Structural power* gives a state power over the rules of the game: establishing that admitting a new country to the UN is an important issue that must be decided by a two-thirds vote instead of a simple majority; organizing an international organization (GATT) whose purpose is to work toward low tariff levels and a free-trade international economic system; or getting other states to agree that Soviet expansion must be contained and punished. These two types of power are not mutually exclusive: A state may possess both or may have neither one. Structural power is of special interest to states for several reasons. First, it is extremely difficult to foresee all of the specific decisions that might have to be controlled in resolving an issue. Second, to control the specific decisions made by a large number of states on issues such as tariffs, UN votes, nonproliferation, or economic sanctions involves a great deal of expense and can quickly exhaust a state's power base. Third, and most important, the rules of the game are not neutral in their impact and may go far in determining who will win and who will lose. For example, long-term U.S. foreign-policy goals may be better served by having a framework for a Middle East settlement accepted by all parties that excludes participation by the Soviet Union than by the acceptance of a specific peace plan. Many observers saw in President Reagan's military buildup, harsh anti-Soviet rhetoric, Strategic Defense Initiative, and willingness to send U.S. troops abroad an attempt to change the rules of the superpower game and to make it less favorable toward Soviet involvement in Third World states.

Terms that capture the domain of a state's power (or the lack of it) are a standard part of the language of world politics. *Colonialism, imperialism, exploitation, client states*, and *buffer states* all speak of the existence of a specific power relationship among states. Once again, a continuum can be employed to illustrate the variety of possibilities involved when we characterize the relations among states. Each end of the continuum is marked by a condition of dependence, in which one state relies heavily upon another for the provision of goods or services and is therefore greatly affected by that state's decisions. The reverse situation holds for the providing state: It is relatively unaffected by the actions of the dependent state. Midway on the continuum lies a point of interdependence, in which both states are equally vulnerable to the actions of the other. It needs to be stressed that relations of conflict and cooperation are not confined to specific points along this continuum. Conflict occurs under conditions of interdependence as much as it occurs under those of dependence, because often the cause of the conflict grows out of factors outside of the power relationship existing among states, such as differing cultures and ideologies, incompatible policy priorities, and historical traditions. Because of the differing power relationships involved at different points, what does vary is the process of managing conflict and cooperation. At the two extremes, unilateral directives and the use of force are likely to dominate, while a reliance on mutual accommodation and bargaining are most likely to be found when interdependence exists. For us to capture accurately the power relationship that exists among states may require the construction of more than one continuum. It may also require that we be sensitive to changes taking place over time. While dependence once characterized the full scope of the relations that existed between an imperial power and its colonies, the picture became more varied in the post-World War II era, as the colonial state moved toward independence and the power of the imperial state declined. Significant changes can also be seen in U.S.-Japanese relations. Since the end of World War II, U.S.-Japanese military relations have been characterized by Japanese dependence on the United States. Of late the United States has begun to pressure Japan to increase its defense spending. If it is coupled with cutbacks in U.S. defense expenditures, this pressure, if successful, could bring about an altered relationship between the two states—one that is positioned further toward the center of the continuum. The evolution of U.S.-Japanese economic relations shows just how dramatic this change can be. In the early postwar era, Japan was heavily dependent on the United States for its economic recovery and growth. By the mid-1980s, this economic relationship was characterized as one of a growing U.S. dependence on Japan. Japan was able to achieve this growth in economic power in part because of its dependence on U.S. military might, since Japan did not have to divert its own resources to defense spending. In 1984, Japan spent $12.7 billion on defense, or 1 percent of its GNP, while the United States spent $237.1 billion, or 6.3 percent of its GNP. Over the period 1965–1986, the average annual growth rate of the Japanese economy was 4.3 percent, compared to 1.6 percent for the United States.

CONCLUSION

To summarize our discussion of power, let us look at U.S.-Iranian relations by using the three meanings of *power*. First, *power* is a resource that a state possesses. By using any of the three power equations we introduced, we would show that the United States had an overwhelming advantage over Iran. Equation 2.2 [power $= C + E + M \times (S + W)$] would put the U.S. power base in 1975 at 421 and Iran's at

128. Several factors negated this superiority during the hostage crisis. In particular, geography worked against the United States. Not only was Iran far away from the United States, thus creating logistical problems for any type of military operation, but also Teheran was located deep inside Iran, and the embassy compound often was surrounded by thousands of demonstrators. Iran's power was also dramatically multiplied by the national unity and the sense of rage that were created by the Shah's fall and the Ayatollah's coming to power.

By viewing power as a means to an end, we can categorize and evaluate the policy options that are open to the United States. In its efforts to secure the release of the hostages, the United States used power located at all points along the continuum, from persuasion and secret negotiations to the use of force (the failed military rescue effort). Two considerations were introduced as important in the selection of an option: (1) translation costs and (2) the appropriateness of the option to the circumstances. The high translation costs associated with power at the *force* end of the continuum were fully evident in the political fallout that followed the rescue effort, President Carter's steadily plummeting popularity in the polls, and his defeat in the 1980 presidential election. The difficulty of using economic sanctions against Iran illustrates how circumstances can limit the effectiveness of a policy tool.[23] It takes a long time for economic sanctions to have an impact, and they are most effective when they are applied quietly and out of view. This was not how the United States applied its economic sanctions against Iran. The highly visible nature of these sanctions, although important to reassure the American people that the United States was doing something, made their success unlikely. In fact, U.S. economic sanctions only began to have an effect after the Iran-Iraq war broke out in 1980 and Iran needed hard currency in order to obtain military spare parts.

Finally, power can be viewed as a relationship. U.S.-Iranian relations can be placed at several points along our continuum. In 1953, when the United States and the British engineered the coup that overthrew Mossadegh and brought the Shah back from exile, Iran was almost completely dependent on the United States. During the early 1970s, a relationship of near equality and interdependence existed. Iran needed weapons from the United States to realize its goal of being a regional power; the Nixon Doctrine made Iran an important surrogate power for the United States. The oil crisis also helped to bring an element of equality to the U.S.-Iranian relationship because Iran could now buy the weapons it wanted from the United States (or anyone else) and did not have to accept obsolete weapons as foreign aid.

At the end of the Shah's rule, a curious situation of mutual dependency existed. The Shah could not survive in power without the support of the United States, while the United States was dependent upon the Shah because it had no pro-U.S. Iranian leader with whom to replace him.

NOTES

1. For reviews of the U.S.-Iranian relations, see Gary Sick, *All Fall Down* (New York: Penguin, 1986); and Barry Rubin, *Paved with Good Intentions* (New York: Penguin, 1981).
2. Hans Morgenthau, *Politics Among Nations*, 5th ed., rev. (New York: Alfred Knopf, 1978), p. 9.

3. Ted Gurr, "War, Revolution, and the Coercive State," *Comparative Politics*, 21, no. 1 (April 1988): 45–65.

4. John Spanier, *Games Nations Play*, 6th ed. (Washington, D.C: Congressional Quarterly Press, 1987), pp. 161–200.

5. Michael Todaro, *Economic Development in the Third World* (New York: Longman, 1985), p. 184; and Lester Brown, ed., *The State of the World 1985* (New York: Worldwatch Institute, 1985), p. 23.

6. Walker Conner, "The Politics of Ethnonationalism," *Journal of International Affairs*, 27 (1973): 1–21.

7. Ruth Sivard, *World Military and Social Expenditures, 1983* (Washington, D.C.: World Priorities, 1983).

8. Joel Migdal, "Strong States, Weak States: Power and Accommodation," in Myron Weiner and Samuel Huntington, eds., *Understanding Political Development* (Boston: Little, Brown, 1987), p. 393.

9. See Peter Katzenstein, ed., *Between Power and Plenty* (Madison, Wis.: University of Wisconsin Press, 1978); and Stephen Krasner, *Defending the National Interest* (Princeton N.J.: Princeton University Press, 1978).

10. United States Arms Control and Disarmament Agency, *World Military Expenditures and Arms Transfers, 1986* (Washington, D.C.: Government Printing Office, 1987).

11. See Sivard, *World Military and Social Expenditures*, pp. 44–45 for a discussion of the methodology involved.

12. Embassy of the Federal Republic of Germany, *The German Contribution to the Common Defense, 1986*.

13. International Institute for Strategic Studies, *The Military Balance, 1987–1988* (London, International Institute for Strategic Studies, 1987), p. 226.

14. James MacGregor Burns, *Leadership* (New York: Harper & Row, 1978), p. 425.

15. Bruce Bueno de Mesquita, *The War Trap* (New Haven, Conn.: Yale University Press, 1981).

16. James Ray, *Global Politics*, 3d ed. (Boston: Houghton Mifflin, 1987), p. 190.

17. A. F. K. Organski and Jacek Krugler, "Davids and Goliaths: Predicting the Outcomes of International Wars," *Comparative Political Studies* 11 (1978): 141–180.

18. Ray Cline, *World Power Assessment* (Washington, D.C.: Georgetown University Center for Strategic and International Studies, 1975).

19. Peter Beckman, *World Politics in the Twentieth Century* (Englewood Cliffs, N.J.: Prentice-Hall, 1984).

20. K. J. Holsti, *International Politics: A Framework for Analysis*, 5th ed. (Englewood Cliffs, N.J.: Prentice-Hall, 1987), Chapter Six.

21. Robert Keohane and Joseph Nye, *Power and Interdependence* (Boston: Little, Brown, 1977), p. 18.

22. Karl Deutsch, *The Analysis of International Relations*, 3d ed. (Englewood Cliffs, N.J.: Prentice-Hall, 1988), pp. 20–45.

23. For an analysis of economic power and economics as an instrument of foreign policy, see David Baldwin, *Economic Statecraft* (Princeton, N.J.: Princeton University Press, 1985).

Chapter
3

Foreign Policy and the National Interest

ACTORS IN WORLD POLITICS: WHO ARE THEY AND WHAT DO THEY WANT?

The modern state is defined by its possession of (1) a fixed and clearly identifiable border, (2) a permanent population (as opposed to a nomadic one), and 3) a government that exercises ultimate power over its territory and population. A state that possesses these characteristics is considered to be sovereign. Its decisions are not subject to the approval of any higher authority, such as a pope, emperor, or international organization, and it is free to define its foreign-policy goals and to protect its interests in any manner it chooses. Sovereignty has always been more of a legal concept than a statement of political reality; few of the more than 160 independent states that exist in the 1990s could be said to be truly sovereign. As Robert Tucker argues, states are "born unequal." They possess different combinations of population, geography, resources, and other ingredients that make states powerful enough to define their own national interests.[1] Grenada, Lebanon, and Afghanistan are contemporary examples of states that are formally sovereign but lack the capacity to define their own national interest or to choose a foreign policy. It is in recognition of this reality that the term *state* is often prefaced by such qualifiers as *imperial*, *buffer*, *micro*, *client*, or *war-torn*.

In spite of its current prominence, the state is a relative newcomer to the arena of world politics. The Treaty of Westphalia (1648) ended the Thirty Years War in Germany and served as a dividing line between two eras.[2] Prior to it, European politics were dominated by the overarching authority of the Holy Roman Empire and the pope, and the political landscape was dotted with fortified castles and cities, duchies, and feudal holdings. At the conclusion of the Thirty Years War, the church had lost its power over the political affairs of Europe, and the state had emerged as the central political unit in European (and, therefore, world) politics. The change-over from small to large political units did not come about overnight, just as in earlier ages the Greek city-states and the Chinese empire did not suddenly disappear.[3] Political units possessing the core characteristics of states as we know them today had begun to appear before the Thirty Years War, and units lacking them continued to exist after the Treaty of Westphalia was signed.

The number of states in world politics has increased dramatically. The deliberations of the Congress of Vienna (1814–1815), which restructured the political landscape of Europe in the aftermath of the Napoleonic Wars, were dominated by 8 states. In 1899, 26 states attended the Hague Peace Conference. Forty-two states were charter members of the League of Nations, and 51 states came together to form the United Nations (UN). By 1955, the UN's membership had grown to 76, and in 1965 it stood at 107. In 1987, 159 states were members.

States are not the only actors of importance in world politics today. Even more dramatic growth has taken place in the number of intergovernmental organizations (IGOs) and international nongovernmental organizations (NGOs). In addition to the UN, examples of the former include the North Atlantic Treaty Organization (NATO), the Organization of Petroleum Exporting Countries (OPEC), and the International Monetary Fund (IMF). Examples of NGOs include General Motors, the Catholic church, Amnesty International, and the Palestine Liberation Organization (PLO). In 1850 there were only five IGOs. At the turn of the century, there were less than 40 IGOs, and in the mid-1950s there were less than 120, yet by 1985 there were 3,897 IGOs in existence. The growth rate for NGOs is even more startling. In 1909, less than 180 NGOs existed, and by 1954 there were just under 1,000. In 1985 the number had grown to 23,248.[4]

The fundamental problem facing states (and nonstate actors) in world politics is how to balance their power resources and commitments while leaving a comfortable surplus of power in reserve. Walter Lippmann, an American journalist who wrote of this problem in 1943, argued that, when such a balance exists, there will be widespread domestic support for a state's foreign policy. Should commitments exceed power, the result will be a foreign policy that is characterized by "insolvency," "bankruptcy," and deep domestic dissension.[5] Avoiding this so-called Lippmann Gap is a perpetual problem that policymakers encounter as they put together a foreign policy and define their state's national interest. The Lippmann Gap also is not unique to the Unites States or to the twentieth century. In *The Rise and Fall of the Great Powers*, Paul Kennedy argues that the fundamental problem facing every great power is balancing its short-term security needs with its long-term needs to preserve a healthy and productive economy that is based on the most modern technology, because it is rapid and sustained economic growth that generates the resources that allow states to pay for the instruments of military power.[6] Kennedy's survey of great powers from 1500 to the present leads him to conclude that, over the long run, none have succeeded in maintaining such a balance. Inevitably, "imperial overreach" sets in, with military commitments and spending exceeding the economy's ability to pay for them. The result is economic slowdown, which, when coupled with rapid economic growth in other states, leads to the loss of great-power status.

Perhaps nowhere in the post-World War II era has the dilemma of balancing power and commitments been more evident and the consequences of failure been so clear as in the Vietnam War. In the following sections, we will examine the history of that conflict and use it to examine the concepts of foreign policy and national interest. A policy is a course of action that is designed to realize some goal or objective. A state's foreign policy is made up of those actions that policymakers take to influence the behavior of actors and the outcomes of events beyond their borders. A state's national interest consists of those fundamental and enduring goals and objectives that justify and give direction to its foreign policy.

VIETNAM

America's involvement in Vietnam spanned the terms of six presidents. The cost of the war and its levels of destruction were enormous: 55,000 Americans lost their lives; at its height, 541,000 Americans were fighting there; $150 billion were spent on the war effort; hundreds of thousands of Vietnamese died and were wounded; 7 million tons of bombs were dropped; and 20 million craters were left behind.[7]

To understand the war in Vietnam, we need to go back to the closing stages of World War II and the efforts of three forces to fill the vacuum that was left when Japanese forces were withdrawn. The Vietminh was a guerilla force under the leadership of Ho Chi Minh. It was organized in 1941 as a national front organization, bringing together Vietnamese Communists and others opposed to French and Japanese domination. Ho Chi Minh had helped to found the French Communist party in 1920, and in 1930 he oversaw the creation of the Vietnam Communist party. In 1945, the Vietminh proclaimed Vietnam, formerly a French colony, an independent country. However, at the Potsdam Conference of July 1945, the last of the wartime conferences of the Allied powers, it was agreed that Vietnam would be divided at the sixteenth parallel, with Chiang Kai Shek's Chinese forces controlling the northern half of Vietnam and British forces controlling the southern half. The British, short of troops, rearmed the French forces, which had been interned at Saigon, and on September 23, 1945, permitted them to seize control of the Saigon government from the Vietminh.

In February 1946, Chiang Kai Shek withdrew his forces in return for French concessions in China, leaving France and the Vietminh as the two opposing powers in Vietnam. Attempts to negotiate an acceptable distribution of power between these two sides failed. In the fighting that ensued, French military forces were unable to assert their control over the Vietnamese countryside and settled on a strategy of holding cities and towns. In 1948, the French made one last political effort to block Ho Chi Minh's growing popularity. They named Bao Dai as head of the state of

Vietnam. Under the terms of the agreement drafted by the French, France would retain control over Vietnamese foreign affairs and its army, and Vietnam could not interfere in any way with French property there. Not only the terms of the agreement but also Bao Dai, who had been made Emperor of Annam (a region of Vietnam) by the Japanese just before their defeat, were unacceptable to the Vietminh.

The United States began to take an active interest in Indochina in mid-1949, as the strategy of containing communist expansion took on an Asian dimension. Mao Zedong had won the civil war in China, and tensions on the Korean peninsula were rising. In February 1950, the United States recognized Bao Dai's government one week after the French formally granted "independence." Weeks before, seeing the French decision as imminent, Ho Chi Minh sought and received diplomatic recognition for his government from China and the Soviet Union. Matters came to a head with the entry of Chinese troops into the Korean War in 1950. At the same time that Truman sent troops to Korea, he increased arms shipments to the French in Indochina. By 1952, the United States was providing France with $30 million in aid to defeat Ho Chi Minh, and in 1953 the United States was paying one-third of the cost of the French war effort.

Ho Chi Minh had, at one point, held out hope for U.S. support in his bid to create an independent Vietnam, but none was forthcoming, although at that time the United States was resisting calls for help by France. He based this hope on the Atlantic Charter, which was signed in 1941 and spoke of the importance of national self-determination, and on Roosevelt's general opposition to the reestablishment of colonial empires by the British and the French. However, in the United States, decisions on Indochina came to be viewed in a larger context. France was reluctant to participate in a European defense system, which the United States saw as vital if Europe was to contain communist expansionism there. In a virtual quid pro quo, the United States agreed to underwrite the French war effort in Indochina in return for French participation in plans for the defense of Europe. In the process, Ho Chi Minh was also redefined from a nationalist to a communist threat to U.S. security interests.

The Eisenhower administration reaffirmed Truman's financial commitment to France and enlarged upon it. By the end of 1953, U.S. aid rose to $500 million and covered approximately one-half of the cost of the French war effort. For Eisenhower and Secretary of State John Foster Dulles, expenditures of this magnitude were considered necessary to prevent a Chinese intervention that both felt was otherwise likely to occur. Unfortunately for the French and its strategy of backing Bao Dai, U.S. aid had not lessened Ho Chi Minh's popularity enough to secure military victory. The end came for the French at Dienbienphu. In mid-1953, France was encouraged by the United States to attempt one final military campaign against the Vietminh. The offensive was a disaster. As originally envisioned, the Vietminh would be lured into attacking French strongholds, where superior French firepower would destroy the massed Vietminh forces. Instead, it was the attacking Vietminh forces that were able to overwhelm the French defenders. With its forces under siege at Dienbienphu, France informed the United States that, unless it intervened, Indochina would fall to the communists. The Eisenhower administration was divided on how to proceed. Some, including Vice President Richard Nixon and the Chairman of the Joint Chiefs of Staff Admiral Radford, favored prompt military action, while others, including Army Chief of Staff General Matthew Ridgway and many in the State Department and Congress, urged restraint. In the end, no aid was forthcoming, and the process of withdrawal began.

France's involvement in Indochina officially came to an end with the signing of the 1954 Geneva Peace Accords. According to this agreement, a "provisional demarcation line" would be established at the seventeenth parallel. Vietminh troops loyal to Ho Chi Minh would regroup north of it, and pro-French Vietnamese forces would regroup south of it. Elections were scheduled for 1956 to determine who would rule over the single country of Vietnam. The Geneva Accords provided the French with the necessary face-saving way out of Indochina. Ho Chi Minh's troops controlled three-quarters of Vietnam and were poised to extend their area of control. All parties to the agreement expected Ho Chi Minh to win the 1956 election easily.

The United States did not sign the Geneva Accords but pledged to "refrain from the threat or use of force to disturb" the settlement. However, only six weeks after the Geneva Peace Accords were signed, the South East Asia Treaty Organization (SEATO) was established as part of an effort to halt the spread of communism in the wake of the French defeat. Signatory states to this collective security pact were: Great Britain, France, New Zealand, Pakistan, the Philippines, Thailand, Australia, and the United States. A protocol extended coverage to Laos, Cambodia, and "the free people under the jurisdiction of Vietnam." The Vietminh saw the protocol as a violation of the Geneva Accords, because it treated the seventeenth parallel as a political boundary and not a civil war truce line.

Political developments below the seventeenth parallel supported the Vietminh interpretation. In 1955, the United States backed Ngo Dinh Diem, who had declared himself President of the Republic of Vietnam. He had been appointed to the post of prime minister by Bao Dai during the Geneva Conference and quickly moved to establish himself as the dominant political force in the South.

The United States provided Diem with considerable amounts of military-related aid. Approximately three-quarters of the South Vietnamese military budget was paid for by the United States, and 30 percent of all nonmilitary U.S. aid went for transportation projects. Only minor amounts went to health, sanitary, education, or housing projects. The primary recipients of these benefits were the urban middle class and not the rural peasant population. By the time Eisenhower left office, U.S. military aid reached the point where 1,000 U.S. military advisors were stationed in South Vietnam.

Diem's grip on power in the South was not secure enough for him to win an election, and with U.S. support he argued that, since South Vietnam had not signed the Geneva Accords, it did not have to abide by it and hold elections. The year 1956 came and went with no elections. In moving to solidify his position, Diem began to turn on his opposition. In January 1956, he issued Presidential Ordinance Number 6, which stated that "individuals considered dangerous to national defense and common security" could be confined in "concentration camps." His first targets were Vietminh supporters who had remained in the South, but gradually all those who had opposed continued French rule were suppressed. The years 1958 and 1959 saw even more stringent and oppressive measures put into place. In 1960, there was a failed military coup. Opposition to Diem reached its most dramatic level in 1963, when a number of Buddhist monks set themselves on fire to protest his continued rule. Nevertheless, when Kennedy came into office, his administration also supported Diem. Gradually, however, the Kennedy administration came to the conclusion that Diem had to be removed from power, and in October 1963 he was overthrown by army officers who had been assured by U.S. officials that the United States would not act to save Diem.

North Vietnam had not immediately tried to bring down the Diem regime. Facing an immediate and severe food shortage, the North concentrated its efforts on economic reconstruction. It sought economic aid from China and the Soviet Union, and tried to reestablish trading ties with the South, on which it was dependent for rice. This ranking of priorities by the North led many Vietminh in the South to feel abandoned as Diem moved against them. On December 20, 1960, southern dissidents took matters into their own hands and announced the formation of the National Liberation Front of South Vietnam (NLF). Six weeks later Hanoi endorsed it.

When the Kennedy administration first looked at Southeast Asia, its primary concern was Laos and its goal was to create a neutral state. For many, Laos was also seen as a potential test case of the Soviet Union's ability to work constructively with the United States. The Vietminh had long supported the communist Pathet Lao forces, but the Soviet Union only had begun to do so openly just before Kennedy's inauguration. If the Vietminh triumphed in Vietnam the fear was that the Soviet Union would be unable to restrain its support for other communist parties in Indochina. Under such conditions, the value of Laos as a test case of U.S.-Soviet cooperation would be greatly lessened, and the establishment of a communist government in Laos would become a real possibility.

The landmark decision on Vietnam during the Kennedy administration came in October 1961 with the Taylor-Rostow Report. Because he had received contradictory information and advice on how to proceed, Kennedy sent General Maxwell Taylor and Walt Rostow to Vietnam on a fact-finding mission. They reported that South Vietnam could be saved only by the introduction of 8,000 U.S. combat troops. Kennedy rejected this conclusion, but, although he was skeptical of the argument, he authorized an additional 15,000 military advisors. Kennedy's handling of the Taylor-Rostow Report is significant for two reasons. First, his decision was typical of those that he made on Vietnam. He never gave the advocates of escalation all that they wanted, but neither did he ever say no. Some increase in the level of the American military commitment was always forthcoming. Second, in acting on the Taylor-Rostow Report, Kennedy helped to shift the definition of the Vietnam conflict from a political problem to a military one. Up until this point, Vietnam was seen by the Kennedy administration as a guerilla war, in which control of the population was key. From now on control of the battlefield was to assume priority.

Under President Johnson, U.S. involvement in the war steadily escalated. Pressures began building in January 1964 when the Joint Chiefs of Staff (JCS) urged him to put aside U.S. self-imposed restraints so that the war might be won more quickly. They especially urged for aerial bombing of North Vietnam. In August 1964, this bombing began in retaliation for an incident in the Gulf of Tonkin. The United States stated that two North Vietnamese PT boats fired upon the C. *Turner Joy* and *Maddox* in neutral waters. President Johnson also went to Congress for a resolution support-ing his use of force against North Vietnam. The Gulf of Tonkin Resolution passed by a unanimous vote in the House of Representatives and by an 88-2 vote in the Senate. It gave the president the authority to "take all necessary measures to repel any armed attack against the forces of the United States and to prevent further aggression." The incident itself is clouded in controversy. Later studies suggest that the incident was staged or that it never occurred. These views hold that President Johnson was merely looking for an excuse to begin the bombing. In the eyes of many, the Gulf of Tonkin Resolution became the functional equivalent of a declaration of war.

From that point forward, the war became increasingly Americanized. Operation Rolling Thunder, a sustained and massive bombing campaign, was launched against North Vietnam in retaliation for the February 1965 Viet Cong attack on Pleiku. In March 1965, General William Westmoreland requested that two marine corps divi-sions be sent to Vietnam. By April, the JCS recommended that 50,000 U.S. combat troops be sent. In May, this figure was revised upward to 80,000. In June, General Westmoreland sought 200,000 ground forces and projected a need for 600,000 troops by 1967. The goals of the United States were also changing. A *Pentagon Papers* memorandum put forward the following priorities: 70 percent to avoid a humiliating defeat; 20 percent to keep South Vietnam from China; and 10 percent to permit the people of South Vietnam to enjoy a better, freer way of life.[8]

The Tet offensive in January 1968 brought yet another challenge to the Johnson administration, and in many ways it was the final challenge. The Tet offensive was a countrywide conventional assault by communist forces on South Vietnam. It pene-trated Saigon, all of the provincial capitals, and even the U.S. embassy compound. The U.S. response was massive and expanded bombings of North Vietnam. In the end, the communist offensive was defeated. As a final thrust to take control of South Vietnam, it had been premature, but it did demonstrate the bankruptcy of U.S. policy. Massive bombings and hundreds of thousands of U.S. combat troops had not brought the U.S. any closer to a final victory. In March 1968, President Johnson announced that he would halt the bombings against North Vietnam and that he would not be a candidate for reelection.

Vietnam was for President Nixon, as it had been for President Kennedy, a sec-ondary issue. Establishing détente was Nixon's primary concern, and this policy of détente could be threatened by any weakness or vacillation in U.S. policy on Viet-nam. American commitments to Vietnam had to be met if the Soviet Union and China were to respect the United States in the post-Vietnam era. The strategy se-lected for accomplishing this was *Vietnamization:* Gradually the United States would reduce its combat presence such that, by 1972, the South Vietnamese army would be able to hold its own when supported by U.S. air and naval power, and economic aid.

The inherent weakness of Vietnamization was that the strategy could succeed only if the North Vietnamese did not attack during the transition period before the South Vietnamese army was capable of fighting on its own. President Nixon and his national security advisor Henry Kissinger designed a two-pronged approach to lessen the likelihood that an attack would occur. Cambodia was invaded with the hope of cleaning out North Vietnamese sanctuaries, and the bombing of North Vietnam was increased. Nevertheless, the potential danger became a reality when in the spring of 1972 North Vietnam attacked across the demilitarized zone (DMZ). At this point, President Nixon was forced to re-Americanize the war in order to prevent the defeat of South Vietnam. Bombing of North Vietnam reached unprecedented levels, and North Vietnamese ports were mined.

Against the backdrop of this fighting were the Paris peace talks. They had begun in earnest in 1969, but little progress had been made. With the escalation of the war, President Nixon offered a new peace plan that included a promise to withdraw all U.S. forces after an Indochina-wide cease-fire and exchange of prisoners of war. Progress was now forthcoming. Hanoi was finding itself increasingly isolated from the Soviet Union and China, both of whom had become more interested in establishing a working relationship with the United States than in defeating it in Vietnam. It was now South Vietnam that began to object to the peace terms and stalled the negotiating process. In early December, the final talks broke off without an agreement. On December 18, 1972, the United States ordered the all-out bombing of Hanoi and Haiphong to demonstrate U.S. resolve to both North and South Vietnamese leaders. On December 30, talks resumed and the bombing was ended. A peace treaty was signed on January 23, 1973.

President Ford was in office when South Vietnam fell in 1975. What had begun as a normal military engagement ended in a rout. On March 12, 1975, the North Vietnamese attacked across the DMZ. On March 25, Hue fell. Five days later, Danang fell. The United States evacuated on April 29, 1975, and on April 30, 1975 South Vietnam surrendered unconditionally.

CHARACTERIZING A STATE'S FOREIGN POLICY

Events Data Analysis

Some questions arise regarding U.S. foreign policy in Vietnam:

Can we place U.S. foreign policy during its long involvement in Vietnam in a larger context?

Is it typical of how the United States deals with guerilla movements?

Does the United States respond differently to challenges in Asia than it does to challenges in Latin America?

Is its response pattern consistent over time?

Is U.S. foreign policy toward North Vietnam typical of how a great power deals with a troublesome small power?

One approach for us to take in answering these types of questions is known as *events data analysis* and involves grouping individual foreign-policy acts into categories in order to determine if a sequence or a pattern exists. Of particular concern to observers of world politics is the amount of conflict and cooperation between a pair of states or in the international system as a whole.

Table 3.1 WORLD EVENT INTERACTION SURVEY EVENTS CATEGORIES

1. **Yield**
   011 Surrender, yield to order, submit to arrest, etc.
   012 Yield position; retreat; evacuate
   013 Admit wrongdoing; retract statement

2. **Comment**
   021 Explicit decline to comment
   022 Comment on situation—pessimistic
   023 Comment on situation—neutral
   024 Comment on situation—optimistic
   025 Explain policy or future position

3. **Consult**
   031 Meet with at neutral site; or send note
   032 Visit; go to
   033 Receive visit; host

4. **Approve**
   041 Praise, hail, applaud, condolences
   042 Endorse others' policy or position; give verbal support

5. **Promise**
   051 Promise own policy support
   052 Promise material support
   053 Promise other future support action
   054 Assure; reassure

6. **Grant**
   061 Express regret; apologize
   062 Give state invitation
   063 Grant asylum
   064 Grant privilege, diplomatic recognition; de facto relations, etc.
   065 Suspend negative sanctions; truce
   066 Release and/or return persons or property

7. **Reward**
   071 Extend economic aid (for gift and/or loan)
   072 Extend military assistance
   073 Give other assistance

8. **Agree**
   081 Make substantive agreement
   082 Agree to future action or procedure; agree to meet, to negotiate

9. **Request**
   091 Ask for information
   092 Ask for policy assistance
   093 Ask for material assistance
   094 Request action; call for
   095 Entreat; plead; appeal to; help me

10. **Propose**
   101 Offer proposal
   102 Urge or suggest action or policy

11. **Reject**
   111 Turn down proposal; reject protest demand, threat, etc.
   112 Refuse; oppose; refuse to allow

12. **Accuse**
   121 Charge; criticize; blame; disapprove
   122 Denounce; denigrate; abuse

13. **Protest**
   131 Make complaint (not formal)
   132 Make formal complaint or protest

14. **Deny**
   141 Deny an accusation
   142 Deny an attributed policy, action, role, or position

15. **Demand**
   150 Issue order or command, insist; demand compliance, etc.

16. **Warn**
   160 Give warning

17. **Threaten**
   171 Threat without specific negative sanctions
   172 Threat with specific nonmilitary negative sanctions
   173 Threat with force specified
   174 Ultimatum; threat with negative sanctions and time limit specified

Table 3.1   Continued

18. **Demonstrate**	20. **Expel**
181 Nonmilitary demonstration; walk out on	201 Order personnel out of country
182 Armed force mobilization, exercise, and/or display	202 Expel organization or group
19. **Reduce relationship (as negative sanction)**	21. **Seize**
191 Cancel or postpone planned event	211 Seize position or possessions
192 Reduce routine international activity; recall officials, etc.	212 Detain or arrest person(s)
194 Halt negotiations	22. **Force**
195 Break diplomatic relations	221 Noninjury destructive act
	222 Nonmilitary injury-destruction
	223 Military engagement

Source: Philip Burgess and Raymond Lawton, *Indicators of International Behavior* (Beverly Hills, Calif.: Sage, 1972), p. 6.

Two of the most influential coding schemes are the World Events Interaction Survey (WEIS) and the Conflict and Peace Data Bank (COPAD). Based on an analysis of WEIS data for 1966, two researchers found that accusations were the most prominent single type of event in world politics. Ultimatums were the type of behavior least employed.[9] Almost two-thirds of all international activity was verbal. They also found that 20 of the most active states accounted for just short of 70 percent of all events, and that 5 states accounted for 40 percent of all events, with the United States and the Soviet Union accounting for 18 and 9 percent, respectively, of all events. Finally, contrary to the general image that we have of world politics as being an arena of conflict, they found that conflictual, cooperative, and participatory (talking, meeting, explaining one's foreign policy) events occurred with about the same frequency.

The coding scheme used in the WEIS study is reprinted in Table 3.1. Table 3.2 places selected examples, drawn from our case study of U.S. foreign policy in Vietnam, into the WEIS classification scheme. Doing so points out quite clearly the wide range of strategies and tactics that were employed by the United States. The examples of actions range from comments, consultations, and promises to agreements, rejections, demonstrations, and the use of force. Constructing a similar table for the actions of the other participants would allow us to map out the conflict and to explore the ways in which it compares to other international conflicts.[10]

National Roles

A second approach to characterizing state behavior operates at a higher level of generalizations. It is not concerned with specific foreign-policy acts but with a state's general orientation toward world politics. K. J. Holsti defines this to be "general attitudes and commitments toward the external environment and its fundamental

Table 3.2 SELECTED EXAMPLES OF U.S. FOREIGN POLICY IN VIETNAM ACCORDING TO THE WEIS CLASSIFICATION SCHEME

WEIS category	Example of U.S. foreign policy in Vietnam
1. Yield 011 Surrender, yield to order, submit to arrest, etc.	U.S. evacuation of Vietnam—April 29, 1989
2. Comment 022 Comment on situation—pessimistic 025 Explain policy or future position	Taylor-Rostow Report Gulf of Tonkin Resolution
3. Consult 031 Meet with at neutral site; or send note	Paris peace talks
4. Approve 042 Endorse others' policy or position; give verbal support	Advance approval of 1963 South Vietnamese military coup against Diem
5. Promise 053 Promise other future support action	SEATO pledge to come to the defense of South Vietnam, Laos, and Cambodia
6. Grant 064 Grant privilege, diplomatic recognition; de facto relations, etc. 065 Suspend negative sanctions; truce	Recognition of Emperor Bao Dai's government President Johnson's announcement of halt in bombing
7. Reward 072 Extend military assistance	U.S. military aid to France and the various South Vietnamese governments President Kennedy's sending military advisors to South Vietnam
8. Agree 081 Make substantive agreement	Establishment of SEATO; signing of Paris Peace Accords
10. Propose 101 Offer proposal	President Nixon's 1969 peace proposal
11. Reject 111 Turn down proposal; reject protest demand, threat, etc.	Turning down of French request for U.S. intervention in 1953
18. Demonstrate 182 Armed force mobilization, exercise, and/or display	December bombings in 1972 following failure of Paris peace talks
22. Force 223 Military engagement	Rolling Thunder bombing campaign in retaliation for bombing of Pleiku

strategy for accomplishing domestic and external objectives and for coping with persistent threats."[11] A state's orientation is not revealed in any one foreign-policy act but is a way of characterizing the cumulative impact of large numbers of foreign-policy actions taken over long periods of time.

We can characterize a state's general orientation toward world politics in any number of ways. On a most general level, *isolationism, nonalignment, multilateralism,* and *imperialism* are terms frequently employed for this purpose. Holsti suggests that we can think in more specific terms and identify national role orientations for states. National roles incorporate the basic fears and aspirations of policymakers, as well as economic, geographic, domestic, and systemic constraints on a state's actions. On the basis of content analysis of speeches by high-level policymakers in 71 states, he identifies 16 national roles. They are listed in Table 3.3. The most activist role orientations are at the top of the table, whereas those associated with passive foreign policies are at the bottom. States are not restricted to holding one national role orientation at a time, nor is it impossible for states to adopt new national roles or shed old ones. The important point is that national roles have a greater staying power than does the impact of an individual policymaker's personality. This allows analysts to make predictions about how a state will act under given circumstances. For illustrative purposes, we will discuss four national roles.

Some states see themselves as *bastions of revolution.* They believe that they have a duty to organize or lead revolutionary movements around the world. Such leadership requires that they give some combination of moral, monetary, economic, or military aid to revolutionaries who share their vision of world politics. Holsti concluded that both the United States and the Soviet Union tend to hold this role orientation. The United States sees itself as having a duty to promote democracy abroad, while the Soviet Union has repeatedly pledged its support to anticapitalist national liberation movements in the Third World. States also may see themselves as *regional leaders.* In this national role orientation, states believe that they should be in the forefront of all regional diplomatic, military, or economic initiatives. Egypt has long adopted this role orientation in the Middle East, while China sees itself as occupying a similar position in Asian politics. Again, both superpowers have adopted this role orientation. The United States sees itself as a leader in the Western Hemisphere, and the Soviet Union sees itself as a leader in Eastern Europe. A *faithful ally* national role orientation stresses the identity of interests between itself and another state. The similarity may be rooted in historical or ideological bounds, or in the perception of a common threat, and it produces a tendency to support its ally almost in reflex-type fashion in international disputes. British foreign policy has shown such a tendency in the postwar era in its support for U.S. diplomatic and military initiatives. Our last example is that of *mediator–integrator.* In this role orientation, the state sees itself as a regional or global "fixer." Frequent participation in UN and multinational peacekeeping efforts and international conferences characterize the behavior of states adopting this role orientation. Canada, France, Hungary, Yugoslavia, and the Scandinavian countries are prime examples of states that have adopted this national role. In terms of the typology presented in Table 3.3, during its involvement in Vietnam the United States can be seen as having adopted three national role orientations: regional leader, regional protector, and defender of the faith.

Table 3.3 A SAMPLING OF NATIONAL ROLES

Role conception	Sources
Bastion of revolution	Ideological principles; anticolonialism; desire for ethnic unity
Regional leader	Superior capabilities; traditional national role
Regional protector	Perception of threat; geographic location; traditional policies; needs of threatened state
Active independent	Antibloc attitudes; economic needs; geographic location
Liberator–Supporter	Anticolonial attitudes; ideological principles
Antiimperialist agent	Ideological principles; perception of threat; anticolonial attitudes
Defender of the faith	Perception of threat; ideological principles; traditional national role
Mediator–Integrator	Cultural-ethnic composition; traditional noninvolvement in conflicts; geographic location
Regional subsystem collaborator	Economic needs; sense of belonging; common political-ideological traditions; geographic location
Developer	Humanitarian concern; superior economic capabilities; anticipated consequences of underdevelopment
Bridge	Geographic location; multiethnic composition of the state
Faithful ally	Perception of threat; insufficient capabilities; traditional policies; ideological compatibility
Independent	Antibloc sentiment; economic needs; threat perception
Internal development	Socioeconomic needs; perception of threat through foreign involvement
Isolate	Perception of threat; insufficient capabilities
Protectee	Perception of threat; insufficient capabilities

Source: K. J. Holsti, "National Role Conceptions in the Study of Foreign Policy," *International Studies Quarterly* 14 (1970): 206–207.

THE NATIONAL INTEREST

Foreign policies are justified because they further the "national interest." Yet, as we saw in our case study on Vietnam, invoking the "national interest" seldom ends disagreement over the wisdom of a course of action. Should we be surprised by this inability to agree on a definition of the U.S. national interest? Is this problem unique to the United States? The answer to both questions is no. Arnold Wolfers in his classic treatment of the subject argued that, in order to provide a meaningful guide to policy, the concept of *national security* (and the related idea of national interest) must specify how much protection is to be given to a value and the means to be used for that purpose.[12] National interest does neither. Instead of providing policymakers with objective guidance in constructing a foreign policy, definitions of national inter-est are put forward in a normative fashion in order to direct foreign policy down a preferred path—one that gives emphasis to a set of goals or values which the individ-ual feels are being ignored or underprotected. Farmers demand increased govern-ment price supports and greater access to foreign markets in the name of the national interest. Industrialists argue for quotas on foreign-made goods, increased govern-ment support for scientific and technological research, and increased trade with com-munist states in the name of national interest. The military argues for less trade with communist states and increased expenditures on weapons systems in the name of national interest.

Competition to define the national interest is often intense because, while the goals and values that a state may pursue are virtually endless, the same is not true for the resources needed to realize them. Decisions must constantly be made about which goals to emphasize and which to neglect. The definition given to the national interest is a major factor affecting which values will be favored. This is because not all foreign policies (and, therefore, the values that they protect) are compatible with a given definition of national interest. Human rights cannot easily be the centerpiece of U.S. foreign policy toward Latin America if the primary national interest in that area is defined as stopping the spread of communism.

Because of its limiting quality, the debate over defining the national interest is closely watched. By studying how it is defined and the challenges to that definition, we can learn much about which groups are wielding influence over the formation and the execution of a state's foreign policy.[13] Because of the lack of extensive and detailed information about the dynamics of Soviet decision making in the pre-Gorba-chev era, debates over the definition of Soviet foreign-policy goals have been watched with special interest by American Kremlinologists. Changes in nuance and emphasis, omissions of frequently invoked themes, and the introduction of new slo-gans are used to gauge what is going on inside the Kremlin and where Soviet foreign policy is going.

The National Interest and Societal Interests

While the national interest is an ambiguous symbol and therefore limited in its ability to guide policy, it is not altogether lacking in meaning. It directs the attention of policymakers to a category of goals that a state's foreign policy should value most: national or societal goals. Those goals that advance only the interests of certain indi-viduals or groups are by definition not eligible for placement at the center of a state's foreign policy. To be in the national interest, quotas on Japanese cars entering the United States must benefit more than the automobile industry; they must also pro-mote the welfare of the United States as a whole. The same holds true for the stepped-up agricultural exports or the advancement of human rights. We can identify three possible ways by which particularistic societal interests can come to define the national interest.

First, it is possible that one segment of society can come to dominate and control the policy process to the point where its views, and only its views, shape the content of foreign policy. Whatever disagreements exist within this elite class are over tactics and not the fundamental direction of policy. A concern for particularistic interests masquerading as the national interest in this fashion lies at the heart of the long-standing fascination with the influence of the *military-industrial complex.* The term was coined by C. Wright Mills in 1956 and was given high visibility by President Eisenhower in his farewell address when he warned against its unwarranted influence and the dangers of misplaced power.[14]

Many different formulations of the military-industrial complex argument exist, and efforts to prove its significant influence over policy have produced mixed results. All start from the assertion that, although society as a whole does not benefit from military spending or the adoption of a definition of the national interest that takes as a given the existence of a hostile, threatening, and anarchic international system, certain segments of society do prosper because of them. At a minimum, these segments include the professional military, industries heavily dependent on defense contracts, labor unions whose members work in these industries, and members of Congress, whose districts are home to military installations or production facilities. Numerous linkages exist among these groups that help to forge them into a powerful political force able to impose its agenda on the political system as a whole. Generals and admirals upon retirement find employment with leading defense contractors. Congresspeople who formally oversee the military tend to come from districts in which exceedingly high levels of military spending take place. The military-industrial complex is not unique to capitalist societies. A similar phenomenon has been found to exist in socialist states. Composed of members of the professional military and intelligence services, managers of heavy industries, and the party and state ministries with responsibility in these areas, this constellation of forces has consistently been able to set Soviet priorities at the expense of forces engaged in the production of consumer goods, agricultural products, and public services.[15]

Second, interest groups can gain control of a state's foreign policy through a process of building coalitions. Under this theory, no permanent elite group dominates the policy agenda. Instead, policy reflects the relative power of various groups within a society and their ability to translate that power into control over parts of the policy process. In essence, the government acts as an impartial umpire by judging who the winner is in the struggle to control policy and registering that victory by altering a policy to reflect the values of the dominant group or coalition of groups. Because power resources change over time, no group or sector of society is permanently able to control policy. Foreign policy and definitions of the national interest will change as new groups come to dominate the political landscape.

According to this pluralist view of policymaking, arms control policy within the United States, France, the Soviet Union, and elsewhere reflects the balance of political power between those groups in society that oppose arms control and those that support it rather than the interests of the military-industrial complex. The same holds true for foreign economic policy, human rights, and military interventions abroad. Many foreign-policy professionals and scholars take a dim view of pluralism's impact on foreign policy. They see foreign policy and defining the national interest as too important to be left to a power struggle among societal groups who tend to be uninformed about world affairs and who often base their decisions on narrow definitions of self-interest or emotionalism. What is needed is the ability to recognize and to respond to the dynamics of world politics in a consistent and objective fashion. The pressures of competing interest groups trying to control policy work against this. Politics must stop "at the water's edge" if policymakers are to pursue effectively the national interest.

Third, the process of defining the national interest may be overly influenced by bureaucratic politics. In this view, competition to control foreign policy is not carried out among groups within a society but between rival bureaucratic interests whose concern is not so much to solve a problem as it is to maintain (or gain) control over the formulation and implementation of policy. The foreign-policy bureaucracy is not a machine responding to the orders of the heads of government, but a series of competing fiefdoms each of which has its own view of what should be done. Selecting a foreign policy or a definition of the national interest is not so much a matter of finding a policy that will work as it is one of finding a policy around which a bureaucratic consensus can form. This is no easy task. Over time, governmental bureaucracies develop vested interests in policy areas, organizational routines on how to deal with problems, and memories of past policy battles. These combine to cause organizations to see problems differently. What to the military is a problem of placing added troops on the border to provide for greater defense may appear to the treasury to be an unacceptable increase in government spending and to diplomats to be a provocative act that will produce war rather than ensure peace. Reaching a consensus becomes a time-consuming game in which the various preferences of the players are bargained into a single position. Consequently, there is a tendency to hold to a consensus position as long as possible and to make only incremental or minimal changes in the direction of policy when forced to by events abroad.

The National Interest and the Global Interest

Conflict of a different sort surrounds the debate over the relationship between the national interest and the global interest. Many realists view the two as incompatible and caution against giving primacy to global interests over national ones. The primary obligation of policymakers is to provide for the security of the state in a competitive, hostile, and anarchic international system. Concepts like *global interest* and *global community* are illusions in a system in which there are no permanent rules or bonds uniting states. Self-help and self-interest are the keys to survival. Peace is not a condition that can be engineered into existence through the creation of institutions, signing treaties, or appeals to common interests. Peace is a condition that comes about when states pursue their own (limited) definitions of national interest.

Not all realists share this assessment. Arnold Wolfers found it to be shortsighted. He argued that states have two classes of goals: *possession goals* and *milieu goals.* Included in the former category would be efforts to acquire territory, to gain a seat on the UN Security Council, to get most-favored-nation status as a trading partner, or to gain access to oil. Possession goals tend to be treated as zero sum in nature; that is, to the extent that one state "possesses" the goal, that goal is seen as being denied to another. In contrast, milieu goals are not so much possessed by a state as they are forming a common or shared environment within which states act. All states are able to partake of global prosperity, peace, stability, and respect for environmental pollution standards. Wolfers acknowledges that milieu goals are often no more than a means to realizing a possession goal, but he believes that this need not be the case. He cautions against downplaying the value of milieu goals simply because they can also be in the interests of other states. He argues that "it is wise for governments and peoples to be aware of—and in fact to stress—the element of national self-interest, however farsighted, that leads nations to improve the milieu by rendering services to others."[16]

Globalists take strong exception to the primacy given to the national interests of states by realists. They raise two points. First, the state is no longer the central unit in world politics whose interests must receive attention ahead of all others. The interests of regions, nonstate actors, substate actors, international organizations, and the world as a whole must now also be given their due attention. As we have already seen, it is only recently that world politics has centered around the state. There is no reason to expect that it will always be so. John Herz argues that the history of world politics has been marked by the emergence of political units of ever-increasing size as rulers sought to establish defensible boundaries.[17] Following this logic, the state can remain the central unit of world politics only so long as its borders constitute a "hard shell" behind which a population is secure from attack. Globalists argue that this is no longer the case. Advancing military technology has made it impossible for the state to protect its citizens, and economic interdependence has had a similar effect on the state's ability to provide unilaterally for the socioeconomic needs of its population.

Second, globalists assert that the problems confronting policymakers today cannot be solved within the context of a logical decision that places state interests at the center. Successfully addressing the problems of overpopulation, environmental decay, nuclear proliferation, hunger, and poverty that face our endangered planet requires that we give precedence to the goals of the whole rather than to any of its individual parts.[18] Globalists recognize that moving the global interest from a marginal concern to one that is at the center of world politics will not be easily realized. The state's freedom to pursue its national interest will have to be restricted in favor of the global interest, and foreign policies will have to be framed in terms of state responsibility for the global condition and not narrowly defined possession goals.

The National Interest: Long-, Middle-, and Short-Term Goals

So far we have discussed what the national interest is not: It is not a clearly stated guide for action, and it is different from subnational interests and the global interest. However, what is the national interest? How do we know when a goal or an objective is in the state's national interest? Many argue that the dynamics of world politics establishes a universal ranking system into which all foreign-policy goals can be placed. As we can see in Figure 3.1, three levels of goals (long-, middle-, and core) can be identified, which come together to form a triangle in which core goals form the base of the pyramid and take precedence over the pursuit of middle and long term goals.[19] They are distinguished from each other by their importance to the survival of the state, the time element involved in realizing them, and the kinds of demands that pursuing these goals places on other states.

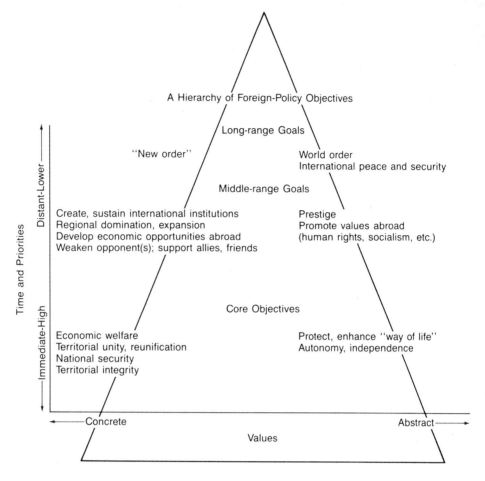

Figure 3.1 A hierarchy of national goals [*Source:* Adapted from chart on p. 124, K. J. Holsti, *International Politics*, 5th ed. (Englewood Cliffs: Prentice-Hall, 1988)].

Core goals are those values and interests for which the state is willing to demand the ultimate sacrifices from its own people and to place the greatest demands upon others. The defense of its borders, the perpetuation of its political, economic, and social system, the control of strategically vital areas, and the realization of ethnic or religious unity are the most frequently pursued core goals. These are short-term goals whose realization is a prerequisite for the pursuit of all other foreign-policy objectives.

Middle-term goals are of three types. The first of these are efforts to improve domestic social and economic conditions through such international activities as entering into trade agreements, acquiring foreign aid, and gaining assured access to raw materials that are controlled by other states. The second of these are policies designed to enhance the state's international prestige. This is often done through diplomatic activity, participation in international cultural or technological exchange programs, or displays of one's military capabilities through highly visible troop exercises or naval maneuvers that are designed to "show the flag." The third of these are efforts at self-extension or imperialism. These need not mean physically taking control of other states or extending one's boundaries. They may take the form of establishing spheres of influence, promoting the state's ideology abroad, or dominating foreign markets.

Long-term goals are "plans, dreams, and visions concerning the ultimate political or ideological organization of the international system."[20] Whereas middle-term goals make specific demands against specific states, long-term goals make universalistic demands against all states in the international system. Hitler's Thousand Year Reich, Japan's Greater East Asia Co-Prosperity Sphere, the Soviet vision of worldwide communist revolution, and U.S. efforts to make the world safe for democracy are some examples of long-term goals that are held by major powers.

Approached in this fashion, the concept of national interest appears to take on an objective meaning. Policymakers cannot simply state that they are acting in the national interest. Groups and individuals within a society cannot merely assert that their preferred goals are identical to the national interest. The correctness of these claims can be judged against the standards for placing goals in each of the three categories. On closer examination, however, this objectivity turns out to be largely illusory, and the concept of national interest still remains basically normative in nature. For, while this approach does allow us to make distinctions between goals, the actual placement of a goal in one of the three categories is still a matter of judgment.

Consider the case of Israel. Should Israel treat control over the West Bank and Gaza strip as core goals or as medium- or long-term goals accepting a trade of land for peace? The latter was proposed during President Reagan's 1982 peace initiative and again in 1988 when widespread rioting broke out in these predominantly Arab-populated areas. Israel came into possession of these occupied territories as a result of the 1967 war and began a policy of encouraging Jewish settlement in them. The practical result of this policy would have been to enlarge the Israeli state—something that, given its small size and its hostile neighbors, could provide Israel with an additional measure of security should it have to fight another war. However, as events in 1988 clearly showed, incorporation into Israel in this fashion remains unacceptable to the Palestinians who live there and who see Israeli control as provocative and exploitative. So long as these territories remain under Israeli control and no Palestinian state exists, periodic violence seems inevitable. We could argue that, rather than providing for increased security for Israel, control over these territories is an example of self-extension—a middle-term goal that ought to be sacrificed if doing so would provide for the protection of Israeli core values through a meaningful peace treaty. The unanswered question is whether or not a peace treaty would do so. It is because of this question that we come back to the inherently normative nature of the concept of national interest.

Vietnam and the National Interest

How would the various approaches to defining the national interest, which we introduced earlier, evaluate the U.S. involvement in Vietnam? Realists are divided on its wisdom. For some, the U.S. involvement was necessary to protect core security interests and was rooted in the need to halt the outward thrust of aggressive states and the logic of a bipolar system. Drawing analogies with Nazi aggression and the failure of appeasement at Munich (1938), the Korean War (1950), and the fall of China (1949), these realists saw the Vietnam War not as a civil war, but as a case of aggression that had to be stopped in order to (1) protect other states from wars of national liberation and (2) maintain the integrity of the international order. The problem with the Vietnam War was not U.S. involvement but the nature of that involvement. For these realists, "no more Vietnams" means not fighting a war in which U.S. forces are added incrementally; in which restrictions are placed on what can be done, where it can be done, and against whom; and in which the American public is not willing to make the sacrifices to realize core security goals.

Other realists question whether the threat posed by a communist victory in Vietnam ever constituted a core threat to U.S. security interests. Writing in the 1960s, Hans Morgenthau, one of the founders of the realist school, argued that the evidence did not support any of the stated reasons for the growing U.S. involvement in Vietnam: resistance to aggression, the containment of China, the containment of communism, and the prestige of the United States.[21] Of these goals, Morgenthau felt that the last was the most plausible, but it was not a core security goal and therefore not worth the cost that the war in Vietnam placed on the United States. The previously cited study by the Defense Department on the U.S. involvement in Vietnam (*The Pentagon Papers*) agreed with Morgenthau that prestige had become the driving force behind the U.S. presence in Vietnam.

Globalists are negative in their assessment of the U.S. involvement in Vietnam and view it as the product of thinking that occurs when policymakers are trapped within a "national security straightjacket."[22] This conceptual straightjacket defines the national interest in terms of power, views world politics as a zero sum game played under conditions of anarchy, and places the survival of the state at the center of its value hierarchy. By deemphasizing the importance of individuals and by being predisposed to the use of force to solve problems, the national security straightjacket prevents policymakers from dealing with such emerging problems of the global order as hunger, poverty, discrimination, and a clean environment. Instead of promoting these values in its foreign policy, the U.S. ended up supporting a series of tyrannical South Vietnamese regimes.

Elite theorists are also critical of the U.S. involvement in Vietnam, although their reasons vary. One school of thought sees Vietnam as evidence of the influence of the military-industrial complex on U.S. foreign policy. The United States fought in Vietnam, not because it was in the national interest, but because it was in the interest of U.S. business interests. It was not so much the size of the U.S. economic stake in Vietnam that made it important as it was what a communist triumph in Vietnam would symbolize. Big business could not allow a Third World government to adopt with impunity policies that threatened U.S. access to raw materials or that limited the size of the global capitalist market. Success in Vietnam would only invite further challenges in more profitable settings. The existence of a communist threat was used as a pretext to protect U.S. dominance of the global economy.

A second school of thought among elite theorists rejects the neo-Marxist explanation just offered and suggests that the U.S. involvement in Vietnam was the result of a different type of perceptual blinder that colors policymakers' thinking about the nature of the U.S. national interest. J. William Fulbright, Chairman of the Senate Foreign Relations Committee during much of the Vietnam War and a leading critic of it, refers to this set of beliefs as an "arrogance of power."[23] The United States, unprepared with historical experience for the role of superpower, during the post-World War II era became corrupted by power and lost its spirit and sense of values. It succumbed to the temptation to use power and dominate others simply because it was possible to do so. In the process, policymakers came to assume U.S. omnipotence and the universality of American values. They did not take the time to acquaint themselves with local conditions or to adapt their policies to the preferences of others.

In the pluralist view, the U.S. presence in Vietnam could be considered to be in the national interest, because a societal consensus equated the initial U.S. involvement as being in the national interest. Pluralists would also argue that Vietnam ceased being in the national interest when a majority of the groups in society no longer supported the war effort. According to some observers, this is exactly what happened. Leslie Gelb and Richard Betts argue that, although many things went wrong in Vietnam, one of the ironies of the Vietnam War was that the U.S. political system "worked": It allowed five presidents to continue the war until a consensus was reached that it was either time to leave or time to achieve victory on the battlefield.[24]

Lastly, one can evaluate the U.S. involvement in Vietnam through a bureaucratic perspective. Here again, two lines of thought exist. One stresses the bureaucratic culture of the national security apparatus that formulated the plans for the war, while the other stresses the negative consequences of bureaucratic bargaining that dominated the decision-making process. According to the first view, personal survival in the upper circles of decision making in Washington required that an image of toughness be created. The source of this lesson for elected officials was the "loss" of China. The Republicans had successfully leveled this charge against the Democrats. Kennedy applied the same strategy against Nixon in 1960, accusing the Eisenhower administration of losing Cuba. Politically, President Kennedy saw Vietnam as his China. President Johnson saw the same lessons in the Vietnam War as did Kennedy. As President Johnson stated many times, he would not be the first president to lose a war. The national security managers also drew upon the fall of China for lessons. To this they could add lessons from decision making in the Korean War. In each case, a reputation for toughness was the most highly prized virtue that one could possess.[25] The bureaucratic casualties in the decision-making process on China were those who, even though they were correct, were identified with the dove side of a policy debate. Those who had been hawkish—but wrong—emerged relatively unscathed from the anticommunist witch hunts of the 1950s. According to the bureaucratic politics perspective, this need for toughness existed apart from personality traits or the balance of domestic political forces. It was rooted in the organizational culture of the national security bureaucracies. Anyone who hoped to get ahead in them had to adopt these values in much the same way as those who work for General Motors or Xerox must also adhere to the "company line" if they wish to move up the organizational ladder. To a lesser extent, Korea produced a similar pattern. Dean Rusk, who had failed to predict Chinese entry into Korea but was staunchly anticommunist, did not pay a price for being wrong. In 1961, he became Kennedy's secretary of state.

The second school argues that policymaking in Vietnam was becoming stuck in a quagmire as a result of the incessant infighting among the national security bureaucracies.[26] In contrast to the first bureaucratic perspective, less emphasis is placed on the values that unite bureaucrats, and greater attention is paid to the forces that separate them. The State Department, CIA, and Defense Department each had their views on how to fight the Vietnam War and who should "control the action." These views were reconciled through a process of bureaucratic bargaining that produced inconsistent policies and caused the United States to stay in Vietnam longer than it should have, if one accepts the pluralist argument.

CONCLUSION

According to American political folklore, "politics stops at the water's edge." By this is meant that the wide-ranging, highly public debates, the political name-calling, and the back-room bargaining that often typifies the process by which domestic policies are made are inappropriate for deciding questions regarding foreign affairs. Foreign policies should be selected on the basis of U.S. national interests, and the debate should be conducted in a bipartisan fashion. As we have attempted to show in this chapter, politics cannot and should not stop at the water's edge. A great deal of legitimate disagreement exists over how to define both the national interest and foreign policy. Neither term is self-defining.

The definitions selected do make a difference. John Lovell observes that the idiom of national security (the language that is used to characterize foreign policies and definitions of the national interest) tells us a great deal about the behind-the-scenes politics that occurs when national security decisions are made.[27] Participants in the policy debate over what to do in Vietnam, Nicaragua, the Middle East, or elsewhere try to manipulate the symbols and images associated with different definitions of the national interest and characterizations of foreign policies in order to frame the policy problem in such a way that it is compatible with their ideological outlook of world politics. The work of William Ascher also points to the significance of the central images associated with different ways of portraying the national interest and characterizing foreign policies.[28] In his study of forecasting in such areas as population growth, technological innovation, transportation, and economic activity, he notes the importance of *core assumptions* to the accuracy of the forecast. Core assumptions embody the forecaster's basic outlook on the nature of the context within which the forecast is being made. In the arena of world politics, no assumptions anchor policymakers' thinking so firmly as do definitions of national interest and the labels attached to foreign policies. They provide policymakers with a point of departure from which they can raise and answer such questions as what the Soviet Union is doing in Afghanistan; what difference it makes who rules South Africa; whether the United States should recognize the Palestine Liberation Organization; and how Great Britain should respond to calls for further arms control initiatives in Europe.

NOTES

1. Robert Tucker, *The Inequality of Nations* (New York: Basic Books, 1977), p. 3.
2. For a discussion of the historical origins of the modern state, see James Ray, *Global Politics*, 3d ed. (Boston: Houghton Mifflin, 1987), pp. 157–163.
3. For a discussion of the Chinese empire, Greek city-state, and Renaissance Italy, see K. J. Holsti, *International Politics: A Framework for Analysis*, 5th ed. (Englewood Cliffs, N.J.: Prentice-Hall, 1988), pp. 20–45.
4. Data on the growth of IGOs and NGOs can be found in Union of International Association, *Yearbook of International Organizations*, (Munich: K. G. Saur, 1987).
5. For a discussion of the Lippmann Gap as it relates to contemporary U.S. foreign policy, see Samuel Huntington, "Coping with the Lippmann Gap," *Foreign Affairs* 66 (1988), 453–477.
6. Paul Kennedy, *The Rise and Fall of the Great Powers* (New York: Random House, 1987).
7. For histories and commentaries on the U.S. involvement in Vietnam, see Daniel Ellsberg, *Papers on the War* (New York: Simon & Schuster, 1972); Robert Gallucci, *Neither Peace Nor Honor* (Baltimore, Md.: Johns Hopkins University Press, 1975); George Kahn and John Lewis, *The United States in Vietnam* (New York: Dell, 1967); and Stanley Karnow, *Vietnam* (New York: Viking, 1983).
8. *The Pentagon Papers as Published by the New York Times* (New York: Quadrangle Books, 1971), p. 271.
9. For additional details, see Charles McClelland and Gary Hoggard, "Conflict Patterns Among Nations," in James Rosenau, ed., *International Politics and Foreign Policy: A Reader in Research and Theory*, rev. ed. (New York: Free Press, 1969), pp. 711–724. See also the discussion in Patrick Morgan, *Theories and Approaches to International Politics: What Are We to Think*, 3d ed. (New Brunswick, N.J.: Transaction, 1981).
10. For such a comparison of international events, see Charles McClelland, "Action Structures and Communication in Two International Crises: Quemoy and Berlin," in Rosenau, *International Politics and Foreign Policy*, pp. 473–482.
11. Holsti, *International Politics*, p. 93.
12. Arnold Wolfers, "National Security as an Ambiguous Symbol," in *Discord and Collaboration: Essays on International Politics* (Baltimore, Md.: Johns Hopkins University Press, 1962), pp. 147–166.
13. On this point, see John Lovell, "The Idiom of National Security," *Journal of Political and Military Sociology* 11 (1983), 35–51.
14. C. Wright Mills, *The Power Elite* (New York: Oxford University Press, 1956). Also see Steven Rosen, ed., *Testing the Theory of the Military-Industrial Complex* (Lexington, Mass.: D.C. Heath, 1973).
15. Morton Schwartz, *The Domestic Policy of the USSR: Domestic Factors* (Encino, Calif.: Dickenson, 1975); and Vernon Aspaturian, "Vulnerabilities and Strengths of the Soviet Union in a Changing International Environment: The Internal Dimension," in Erik Hoffmann and Frederick Fleron, Jr., eds., *The Conduct of Soviet Foreign Policy* (New York: Aldine, 1980), pp. 694–718.
16. Wolfers, "The Goals of Foreign Policy," in *Discord and Collaboration*, p. 77.
17. John Herz, *International Politics in the Atomic Age* (New York: Columbia University Press, 1959).
18. Richard Falk, *This Endangered Planet: Prospects and Proposals for Human Survival* (New York: Vintage, 1972).
19. Holsti, *International Politics*, pp. 124–134.
20. Holsti, *International Politics*, p. 129.
21. Hans Morgenthau, *A New Foreign Policy for the United States* (New York: Praeger, 1969).

22. Gerald Mische and Patricia Mische, *Toward a Human World Order: Beyond the National Security Straightjacket* (New York: Paulist Press, 1977).
23. J. William Fulbright, *The Arrogance of Power* (New York: Random House, 1966).
24. Leslie Gelb with Richard Betts, *The Irony of Vietnam: The System Worked* (Washington, D.C.: Brookings, 1979).
25. See Richard Barnett, *The Roots of War* (New York: Penguin, 1973), pp. 76–136.
26. See Arthur Schlesinger, Jr., *The Bitter Heritage: Vietnam and American Democracy, 1941–1966* (Boston: Houghton Mifflin, 1976).
27. Lovell, "The Idiom of National Security," *JPMS:* 35–51.
28. William Ascher, *Forecasting* (Baltimore, Md.: Johns Hopkins University Press, 1978).

Chapter
4

Contemporary International Perceptions

"Americans tend to think that they invented world politics and that world politics did not exist before 1945." This observation is typical of foreign commentaries on the conduct of U.S. foreign policy, and it contains more than a kernel of truth. Americans often fail to appreciate the perceptual "baggage" that states bring to bear on foreign-policy problems. The purpose of this chapter is (1) to highlight the historical and ideological influences that shape state perceptions of world politics and (2) to identify competing visions of current superpower foreign-policy orientations. Ideology and national interest are generally held to be the two most important contributors to a state's national style. Often they are pictured as competing with one another in influencing foreign-policy decisions. This is not necessarily the case. Much of the time they are mutually reinforcing.

Finally, it needs to be stressed that, while no state can escape its past in formulating its foreign policy, contemporary Chinese or Soviet foreign policy should not be expected to be a carbon copy of Tsarist, Stalinist, or Maoist foreign policy any more than U.S. foreign policy should be explained completely by references to Washington's Farewell Address or by invoking images of Manifest Destiny. Past expressions of ideology and national interest are important because perceptual systems are resistant to change and they set limits on the types of foreign policies that can be undertaken. Also, they serve as a yardstick against which we can measure current foreign policies by allowing us to identify better which are truly revolutionary break-throughs and which should be seen as changes in tactics designed to realize long-standing objectives.

THE AMERICAN WORLD VIEW

Ideological Influences

No formal ideology exists in the United States that is comparable to that of Marxism-Leninism; instead, the primary ideological influence on the U.S. national style comes from the writings of such eighteenth-century liberals as Thomas Jefferson and John Locke. Liberalism is no less influential than Marxism-Leninism in spite of the fact that it is not formally sanctioned. In fact, Louis Hartz argues that one of the fascinating aspects about liberalism in the United States is that its influence is everywhere, yet it is not recognized as an ideology.[1]

Classical liberalism holds that people are inherently rational and fully capable of making their own decisions concerning their interests. Individuals identify goals and then choose the courses of action that are most likely to achieve those goals that are most important. They need no interference from government for this purpose. All individuals have an inherent right to life, liberty, and the unfettered pursuit of prop-erty. The purpose of government is to guarantee individuals their freedom by pro-tecting them from arbitrary power and to regulate conflicts that may arise as they pursue their own self-interests. Because people are basically rational, they recognize that it is in everyone's self-interest to cooperate with a state that protects their ability to pursue wealth and security. The concept of the free market is an important compo-nent of liberalism. In it, individuals compete freely. Sellers are free to set their own price, and buyers are free to decide whether or not to buy. The mechanisms of supply and demand result in a rational price structure when there is no government interference. Ultimately, as individuals pursue their self-interests, the system as a whole benefits. No conflict of interest is seen between individuals pursuing profit and gain and society as a whole advancing and developing. Both move forward to-gether.

These beliefs have a number of implications for the conduct of U.S. foreign pol-icy when they are applied to the arena of world politics. First, there is the rejection of power politics. Seeing world politics as a struggle for survival in an anarchic setting, European powers advocated power politics as the proper foundation for an effective foreign policy. Operating under a different set of assumptions, the United States is inclined to see power politics as a cause of conflict and not a method of conflict resolution. Rational people recognize that war is a costly and wasteful method of solving problems. Preserving peace is in each state's best interest. Common inter-ests, rather than conflict, are emphasized. Evidence of the continuing faith that Americans have in the noninevitability of war and the search for common interests can be seen in the importance given to international summit conferences and in the optimism with which they have greeted Gorbachev's ascension to power in the So-viet Union.

The rejection of power politics also leads to a clearly perceived distinction between war and peace. The difficulties of conducting a foreign policy based on such a dichotomy have plagued U.S. policy-makers repeatedly during the post-World War II era, as the domestic debates over Korea, Vietnam, and Nicaragua readily attest. It is also a distinction not recognized by European powers who adhere to the view put forward by von Clausewitz that "war is a continuation of politics by other means." War and diplomacy cannot be totally divorced from one another. Both are legitimate instruments for pursuing foreign-policy goals, and the line separating them is unclear. Rejecting this view, Americans tend to consider themselves to be either at war or at peace. Different rules apply to each situation. During war, the professional soldiers are in charge, and their task is to achieve victory on the battlefield as quickly as possible with the least loss of life and without regard for political considerations. During times of peace, the professional soldier is expected to remain silent and on the sidelines as the United States pursues its security through nonviolent means.

Second, the United States has traditionally been a forceful advocate of international commercial transactions between states. Just as the marketplace brings together individuals in a mutually profitable way within a society, international trade is the best mechanism for bringing states together and helping them to realize their shared interests. Further, just as governments should not interfere with the operation of the domestic market, states should not place arbitrary restrictions such as tariffs, quotas, embargoes, or domestic content regulations on international trade. U.S. trade policy has not always lived up to these injunctions, largely due to the pressures of domestic politics. In the interwar years it was very protectionist, and today there are calls for an international trade policy of "fair trade" rather than "free trade."

Third, foreign-policy problems are approached from a legalistic perspective.[2] Just as rational individuals recognize that their freedom is best protected through the rule of law, so states can also agree on rules. Instead of starting from the assumption that states have conflicting interests and searching for the solution that is least destabilizing for the international system, Americans assume a harmony of interests and seek to establish formal legalistic criteria against which they can measure the appropriateness of state behavior. This legalistic perspective makes it difficult for Americans to appreciate the deeper sources of many contemporary problems in world politics and to sympathize with the aspirations of those who feel they need to resort to violence in order to bring about change in their societies or the international system. It also leads to a tendency to think in terms of permanent solutions to problems rather than to treat problems as constantly evolving, with each "solution" being a part of a larger process and not a final step. Arms control agreements are supposed to end the arms race; the Camp David accord which brought together Egyptian President Anwar al-Sadat and Israeli Prime Minister Menachem Begin to sign the Egyptian-Israeli Peace Treaty of 1979 is supposed to bring peace to the Middle East; and a negotiated withdrawal of foreign troops is supposed to bring peace to Angola. When the problem continues, the inevitable result is disillusionment, which, in turn, is often followed by a period of withdrawal.

Expressions of Historical National Interest[3]

The best known formulation of the U.S. national interest is George Washington's injunction to "avoid entangling alliances." At the time of independence, the only viable alliance partners of the United States were the great powers of Europe. In his farewell address, President George Washington laid out the reason that the United States had not entered into any form of association with them: "Europe has a set of primary interests which to us have none or very remote relation."[4] Behind these words of caution was the belief that the United States and Europe were different (the United States was young, strong, and liberal in outlook, while Europe was old, decadent, and conservative in its ideology) and that involvement in European affairs could only sap U.S. strength and dilute its uniqueness.

In rejecting participation in a balance-of-power system, the United States did not embrace isolationism or completely turn its back on Europe. It embarked upon a course of unilateralism. Contact with Europe was largely limited to trade and was conducted largely on its own terms. The Monroe Doctrine, for example, was a unilateral statement that told European powers to stay out of Latin America and was issued after a British proposal for a joint declaration was turned down. A similar pattern of behavior surrounded the issuing of the Open Door notes in China at the turn of the century. This outlook carried over into the twentieth century. The United States participated in World War I as an Associated Power and not as an Allied Power. In the post-World War II era, U.S. participation in international organizations, although multilateral in appearance, remains fundamentally unilateral in nature. Within the United Nations, the freedom of the United States to conduct foreign policy on its own terms is protected by the veto power, and the system of weighted voting in international financial organizations similarly protects U.S. interests.

The principal geographic focus of U.S. foreign policy was on westward expansion. While treated by Americans as domestic policy, settling the West was very much an exercise in foreign policy. The continent was not empty or free for the taking: The Louisiana Territory was purchased in 1803; Texas was annexed in 1845; the Mexican-American War was fought in 1846; the Oregon territory was acquired by a treaty with Great Britain in 1846; Alaska was purchased in 1867; and the U.S. army fought over 943 battles with Indians between 1865 and 1898. This westward expansion took place in the context of secure borders and hemispheric preeminence, the reasons for which were not fully appreciated by most Americans. Not only did the oceans provide a large measure of security, but preoccupied with other concerns, the European powers showed little interest or ability to intrude into the Western Hemisphere. Spain and Portugal were in a period of decline, the entire European continent was embroiled in the French Revolution, and Great Britain with its powerful navy was as much a buffer between Europe and the United States as it was a competitor for influence in the Americas.

By virtually any standard, the United States' first ventures into foreign policy-making were highly successful. Americans read into these successes proof of the superiority of liberal values and a problem-solving approach that stressed self-reliance and pragmatism over ideological formulations. Talk of Manifest Destiny became commonplace as foreign-policy successes and economic growth reinforced one another to produce a sense of mission among many in the United States.

Competing Visions of U.S. Foreign Policy

As we noted earlier in the chapter, disagreement exists within every society over the direction and conduct of its foreign policy. The United States is no exception. Washington's advice to steer clear of involvement with European powers was not immediately endorsed by all Americans. Alexander Hamilton favored keeping close ties with Great Britain, while others advocated an alliance with France. In its first 200 years, three wars served as focal points in the debate over how best to orient U.S. foreign policy. The first of these was the Spanish-American War (1898). The rapid industrialization and population growth that was experienced in the decades after the Civil War convinced many that the United States had outgrown its role as a hemispheric power and that it was now positioned to assume the part of a great power. Victory in that war transformed the United States into a colonial power through the acquisition of Puerto Rico, Guam, and the Philippines. The United States also annexed Hawaii and became a key participant in international peace conferences that were organized to mediate conflicts in Asia and Africa. While endorsed by some, this burst of global activism worried others, who demanded that the United States return to its foreign-policy traditions and not follow the European states down the road of imperialism.

The breakdown in the elite consensus, brought about by the United States' increased involvement in world politics, continued until World War II. Its failure to join the League of Nations and the popularity of the neutrality legislation of the 1930s served as proof of the extent to which participation in World War I had brought only a temporary respite to the ongoing debate between the "internationalists" and the "isolationists."

A consensus did form in the wake of World War II with the onset of the cold war. It was solidly internationalist in makeup and organized around eight points:

1. The United States had the responsibility and capability to be actively involved in undertakings that would create a just and stable world order.
2. Peace and security were indivisible.
3. Soviet and Soviet-sponsored efforts to alter the status quo by force were the primary threats to a stable world order.
4. Containment represented the most effective means of meeting the Soviet expansionist challenge.
5. The United States should both join and take the lead in organizing alliances during peacetime.
6. The United States should be actively involved in a broad range of international organizations.
7. A free-trade policy was essential for contributing to political stability and for avoiding destructive trade wars.

8. Military and economic foreign aid was both an obligation and in the U.S. national interest.[5]

This consensus endured until the Vietnam War. Since then, public opinion polls and surveys of elite attitudes show Americans to be deeply divided.[6] The Iranian hostage crisis and the Soviet invasion of Afghanistan of 1979, and the conflict in Nicaragua in the 1980s have done little to affect the pattern of thinking that came out of the experience of the Vietnam War. The current debate over the proper direction of U.S. foreign policy is not simply a rehashing of the old struggle between isolationists and internationalists. A far more complex pattern exists—one that some characterize in terms of a "three-headed eagle."[7]

Cold-war internationalists continue to approach world politics largely in terms of the assumptions that guided pre-Vietnam foreign policymaking. The Soviet Union remains the primary threat to the United States, so cold-war internationalists favor an active internationalist foreign policy centered around the possession of a strong military capability and geared to stopping Soviet expansionism. *Post-cold war internationalists* also advocate an activist foreign policy for the United States but one that is focused on North-South issues. The Soviet threat is seen as manageable. Far more serious are the largely ignored and mounting problems for the international system stemming from the large gap between rich and poor states in such areas as the environment, population, trade, natural resources, and human rights. Lastly, there are the *Semiisolationists*, who hold that the major threat to U.S. security lies in its excessive involvement in world politics. They reject the role of "policeman of the world" and "do-gooder" for the United States. Table 4.1 presents a more detailed comparison of these competing outlooks.

THE SOVIET WORLD VIEW

Gorbachev's New Thinking

A great deal of uncertainty exists today over what Soviet foreign policy is all about and where it is headed. The focal point of this uncertainty is Mikhail Gorbachev. He is the fourth head of the Communist Party Soviet Union (CPSU) since 1982. Where his three predecessors (Brezhnev, Andropov, and Chernenko) could be characterized as typical products of the Soviet system, Gorbachev strikes many in the West as being new and different. In an astonishingly short period of time, he has changed the language and underlying premises of Soviet foreign policy.

The impact of Gorbachev's "New Thinking" is evident throughout Soviet foreign policy.[8] No longer is the defense of Soviet security interests viewed as attainable solely by military means. Political measures such as arms control and diplomatic settlements of regional conflicts are also seen as playing a vital role. Moreover, Soviet security is no longer seen as something in competition with or distinct from the security interests of other states or the global community as a whole. In making this change, Gorbachev has replaced the class struggle with interdependence and the common fate of humanity as the central imperative of world politics today. Funda-

Table 4.1 COMPETING VIEWS ON U.S. FOREIGN POLICY

Nature of the international system	Cold-war internationalism	Post-cold-war internationalism	Semiisolationism
Structure	Bipolar (and likely to remain so) Tight links between issues and conflicts	Complex and interdependent (and becoming more so) Moderate links between issues and conflicts	Multipolar (and becoming more so) Weak links between issues and conflicts
World order priorities	A world safe from aggression and terrorism is a necessary precondition for dealing with other issues	International regimes for coping with a broad range of issues, with high priority on North-South ones	It is utopian to think in such terms; top priority should be to reduce linkages, dependencies, and interdependencies
Primary threats to the United States	Soviet and Soviet-sponsored aggression and terrorism Military imbalance favoring the USSR Soviet ability to engage in political coercion based on nuclear blackmail	North-South issues (e.g., rich-poor gap), which threaten any prospects for world order International environmental problems Danger of nuclear war	Danger of war by miscalculation Domestic problems (inflation, unemployment, energy, crime, drugs, illiteracy, racial conflict, etc.) Arms trade

Soviet-American relations (Nature of the conflict)	Conflicts of interest are genuine Largely zero-sum	Some real conflicts of interest, but these are exaggerated by hard-liners on both sides Largely non-zero-sum	Few if any genuine conflicts of interest [mostly arise from failure to see that real threats are unresolved domestic issues] Largely non-zero-sum
Primary dangers of war	Military imbalance will lead Soviets to threaten vital U.S. and Western interests Recent successes will make Soviets more aggressive, perhaps recklessly so	Uncontrolled arms race Both sides equally likely to misperceive other's actions, leading to unwanted war	Misperception, miscalculation of true national interests and threats to them U.S. and Soviet meddling in volatile Third World areas Uncontrolled arms race
The Third World role in present international system	Primary target of Soviet and Soviet-inspired subversion and aggression	Primary source of unresolved social/economic problems that must be resolved to create a viable world order	With a few exceptions, largely peripheral and irrelevant, especially to U.S. interests
Primary U.S. obligations	Help provide security from aggression and terrorism but on a selective basis (to strategically important ones, oil producers, etc.)	Economic and other forms of nonmilitary assistance Play a leading role in structural systemic changes (N.I.E.O., etc.)	Few, if any, obligations for either security or economic development

Source: Adapted from Table 4.4, pp. 130–132 in Ole Holsti and James Rosenau, *American Leadership in World Affairs* (Boston: Allen & Unwin, 1984).

mental changes have also taken place in how the Soviet Union views the Third World and Eastern Europe. The Third World is now seen as a drain on limited Soviet resources and as a catalyst to international tensions rather than as an arena for competition with capitalism. Gorbachev's rhetoric and reform agenda sent shock waves throughout Eastern Europe. He has renounced the Brezhnev Doctrine, which made the Soviet Union the ultimate judge of what was permissible behavior by other Communist parties, and in its place stressed the "absolute independence of all fraternal countries." Stability appears to have replaced absolute loyalty as the primary Soviet interest in the region. Beyond that, Eastern Europe is "on its own."[9] The fundamental pressures that are pushing Gorbachev's foreign policy forward are relatively clear. First, Brezhnev's foreign policy failed. The Soviet military buildup of the late 1960s and 1970s produced neither a lasting détente with the West nor any substantial increase in Soviet security. Instead, the Soviet Union's large inventory of weapons, its rhetorical emphasis on needing to be prepared to fight and win a nuclear war, and its involvement in Third World regional conflicts only served to refuel Western fears about Soviet intentions and provoked the United States to undertake a major military buildup of its own, the net result of which was to impose new military requirements on the Soviet Union.

Second, and more fundamentally, the Soviet economy and social structure were badly in need of repair. Throughout its history, the Soviet Union—and Tsarist Russia before it—had been a one-dimensional power. There had never been an economic counterpart to its immense military strength. The problem faced by Gorbachev was that in combination with chronic alcoholism and corruption, the constant emphasis on military spending over consumer goods and investment had actually served to undermine and erode what economic strength it possessed. Gorbachev's answer to this domestic crisis has been economic reform centered on the concepts of *glasnost* (candor) and *perestroika* (restructuring). Among the concrete measures he has undertaken are an emphasis on economic efficiency, even at the cost of unemployment, greater worker discipline, the establishment of free-trade areas, and the importation of Western technology. Addressing these problems has been made difficult because the Communist party has become so discredited in the eyes of many that Gorbachev felt compelled to try and establish a new power center, The Council of People's Deputies, from which to rule the Soviet Union.

There is a close linkage between *glasnost* and *perestroika* and Gorbachev's foreign policy. If they are to succeed, his domestic initiatives require a stable and predictable international system. On the other hand, foreign-policy successes (in terms of access to Western technology and the ability to reduce military spending) are vital to the success of his domestic reforms. Yet, such an environment cannot guarantee their success. In its first years, Gorbachev's reform agenda has produced more opposition than positive economic results. Opponents across the political spectrum spoke out against him, and ethnic rioting and protests for greater independence took place in the Baltic Republics, the Ukraine, Georgia, and Armenia.

All of this has left Western analysts unsure of how to evaluate his actions and Western policymakers divided on how to respond to his initiatives. Some analysts foresee an inevitable return to more traditional Soviet foreign-policy actions and attitudes as the more conservative elements of the Communist party leadership reassert themselves. The linkage between Gorbachev's foreign policy and Soviet economic problems leads others to conclude that the change in Soviet foreign policy will be an enduring one. In this view, the need for economic reform is so great that whoever rules the Soviet Union will be compelled to travel down a similar foreign-policy path. In order to understand more fully the range of views existing in the United States on a response to Gorbachev's new Soviet foreign policy, we must examine the traditional frameworks used for presenting the Soviet view of world politics.

Ideological Influences

Doctrine   The distinction between ideology as a set of principles formally endorsed by the regime (doctrine) and as a set of beliefs that guide action has been central to attempts to assess the role of Marxism-Leninism in Soviet foreign policy, because each appears to have a different type of influence. Doctrine is seen as providing Soviet policymakers with the language that they must use in presenting Soviet foreign policy. The symbols and phrases of this language are rooted in the writings of Marx and Lenin. Marxist theory argues that the structure of relationships in a society is determined by the economic system. Marx's basic tool of analysis is the dialectic applied to history. In any society, there exists a dominant mode of production that determines property relations (thesis). Because changes in the mode of production occur more quickly than changes in the property relations, contradictions arise (antithesis). As these contradictions are resolved, a new mode of production comes to dominate (synthesis). In capitalism, the owners of the means of production, the bourgeoisie, seek to maximize profits or "surplus value." Surplus value is produced by extracting from labor more value than it is given. Thus labor, the proletariat, is exploited. Labor creates value but does not receive in wages as much value as it creates; rather, wages tend toward subsistence—the amount required to keep workers alive and working. Capitalists seek to increase profits by decreasing labor costs. As workers are paid less money, they cannot purchase goods produced by the capitalists, and overproduction occurs. As profits fall, weaker capitalists are forced out of business and capital becomes more concentrated. Under capitalism, the state exists as a tool of the capitalists and is used to oppress the proletariat. As the gap between the classes widens and the class struggle becomes more pronounced, the proletariat becomes aware of its role in history and seizes the means of production from the capitalist class. Socialism becomes the new mode of production. Gradually, as classes (and thus class antagonism) disappear, the state ceases to serve any useful purpose and withers away. For Marx, history is progress. The world is gradually moving to a better state. Marx expected the revolution to occur first in the societies where technology was most advanced and where the contradictions in capitalism would logically develop. He viewed his analysis as objective and scientific and thus believed that the eventual establishment of communism was inevitable.

Marx believed that national boundaries were artificial lines created by capitalists to keep people apart. People of the same social class from different countries have more in common than people from different classes living in the same country. Consequently, workers of the world would support each other in revolting from capitalist oppression. The socialist revolution would spread naturally from one country to another.

Early Russian Marxists argued that the revolution would begin in the states on the edge of capitalism. The more advanced systems had learned to export their crises through imperialism. Colonialism provided access to cheaper resources, cheaper labor, and wider markets. By exploiting the colonies, capitalists could keep wages higher and workers docile at home and yet still increase profits. Thus, the revolution had been postponed in these countries. Nevertheless, the revolution, once it had begun in the periphery, would become worldwide. Lenin did not believe that class consciousness would develop spontaneously among the workers, and so he envisioned an important role for the party as the leader (vanguard) of the proletariat. The party would be composed of dedicated revolutionaries and organized on the principle of democratic centralism. Before a decision was made there would be freedom of discussion, but once the party reached a decision, everyone had to accept it and abide by it. Until such time as the state could wither away—this is not possible as long as capitalism continues to exist anywhere—government was to be organized on the principle of democratic centralism, with decisions made by those who were ideologically pure.

According to traditional doctrinal formulations, Soviet foreign policy was held to be peaceful due to its class character. The opposition of capitalist states to socialism was also taken as a given. Given the international nature of the class struggle, victory was only possible on a worldwide scale. The concepts of world revolution and Soviet security were thus one and the same. The "correlation of forces" was a central concept in the process of selecting the correct policy against this type of enemy.[10] Unlike its Western counterpart's concept of the balance of power, the correlation of forces is concerned with more than measuring military capabilities. It is fundamentally a net assessment of class forces and is broken down into such headings as economics, military affairs, politics, and international movements. One of the key doctrinal assertions of the Brezhnev era was that the global correlation of forces had begun to shift in favor of socialism.

Soviet leaders must use this language, because the legitimacy of Communist party rule depends upon its ability to fulfill the promise of Marxism-Leninism and to construct policies that benefit Soviet society as a whole. As a consequence, the language of Soviet foreign policy tends to be quite rigid at any one point in time. Simply put, there is an ideologically correct way to interpret events and trends that cannot be challenged, because to do so would be to cast doubt on the Communist party's ability to interpret Marx and Lenin. Over time, however, movement and reinterpretation does take place as new leaders assume power and conditions inside and outside the Soviet Union change. Robert Legvold argues that Gorbachev's reformulation of the logic behind Soviet foreign policy is the third time the concept of revolution has been dramatically altered by Soviet leaders. The first time came when the concept of *socialism* in one country was substituted for that of *global revolution*. The second came when Khrushchev adjusted Soviet thinking to the nuclear era. According to Legvold, Gorbachev's New Thinking marks the end of revolutionary faith on the part of Soviet leaders.[11]

Joseph Stalin first put forward the idea of "socialism in one country" in 1924.

He disagreed with Leon Trotsky, his defeated rival to succeed Lenin as head of the Communist party, who argued that the Soviet Union could not build socialism on its own and that victory over the bourgeoisie could only be achieved in the context of a "permanent revolution." Stalin maintained that, by drawing upon its immense resources, the Soviet Union could establish a socialist system, in spite of the hostility of capitalist states, without being part of a simultaneously occurring world revolution.

In putting forward "peaceful coexistence" in 1956, Nikita Khrushchev sought to bring Soviet foreign-policy doctrine into line with the realities of the nuclear age. Doing so required abandoning three elements of communist doctrine as it existed under Stalin: (1) the inevitability of war and capitalist encirclement of the Soviet Union, (2) the impossibility of establishing socialism through peaceful means, and (3) the presence of "permanently operating factors" that governed the outcomes of wars. This last point led Stalin to downplay the significance of nuclear weapons by arguing that victory in war was determined by leadership, morale, good weapons, and trained soldiers. Khrushchev held that war was no longer possible, because, while capitalist hostility toward socialism was still present, the power of socialist states made war unthinkable. Peaceful coexistence did not, however, mean an end to class conflict. It only meant that the struggle could not take the form of direct confrontations between the United States and the Soviet Union. The class struggle would continue, with "wars of national liberation" in the Third World emerging as a particularly important battleground during the 1950s and 1960s.

Ideology as a Practical Guide to Action: An Operational Code A technique used by Western analysts for capturing the way in which they believe Marxism-Leninism serves as a practical guide to action is to frame it in the context of an *operational code.*[12] An operational code consists of the beliefs that shape, and thus constrain, how a policymaker looks at events. It can be broken down into two parts: philosophical and instrumental. The former is composed of beliefs about the fundamental nature of world politics: Is it purely conflictual? Is there a role for cooperative ventures? Do accidents happen? The instrumental side of the operational code is made up of beliefs concerning what type of actions and strategies are appropriate for conducting foreign policy: Can one lie or conduct covert operations? Must one honor agreements?

Marxism-Leninism has traditionally been seen as making four contributions to the philosophical side of the Soviet operational code. First, it identifies capitalism as the primary national security threat to the Soviet Union. Capitalist hostility is portrayed as shrewd, determined, and thorough. While pinpointing capitalism as the enemy may seem to be stating the obvious, it does provide a focus for Soviet foreign policy that many see as missing in U.S. foreign policy, where no consensus exists as to who or what the enemy is. Second, Marxism-Leninism teaches that all politics, domestic and foreign, involve conflict and struggle and that little importance can be given to moderating influences. This contrasts with liberalism, which stresses that peace is the normal condition of world politics.

Third, working from the perspective of the dialectical process, Soviet leaders tend to adopt an all-or-nothing perspective on events. Any position between the extremes of total victory and total defeat is held to be unstable. Here again, a contrast exists with liberalism. Compromise and accommodation are the keys to conflict resolution for the liberal. For a Marxist, conflict can only be resolved by the final defeat of one party. Rather than seek compromise, the psychological tendency is to adopt an aggressive, defiant posture. Closely linked to this attitude is the final component to the philosophical side of the operational code—the belief that change is inevitable. Permanent rules are impossible, because conditions change. Strategies and tactics thus must constantly be reevaluated. Action appropriate for one setting or phase of a conflict may be unsuitable for another. The contrast between Soviet and U.S. thinking on this point is quite evident in how the two sides approach arms control talks. Freeman Dyson notes that the United States "treats nuclear war as a mathematical exercise," from which will emerge a formula capable of permanently guaranteeing U.S. security. The Soviet Union thinks in terms of "goals to be striven for, not conditions to be guaranteed."[13]

The Marxist-Leninist contribution to the instrumental portion of the Soviet operational code can be summarized as follows:

1. Pursue an optimizing strategy, in which a series of escalating goals are pursued simultaneously, so that, even if the utmost goal is not realized, some lesser objectives will be reached.
2. Push the opponent to the limit.
3. Engage in pursuit.
4. Know when to stop.
5. Avoid adventures.

Note that these guidelines do not provide a perfect blueprint for action that can be applied mechanically in all situations. Room for disagreement and misinterpretation exists. The dividing line between engaging in pursuit and knowing when to stop is a fine one, with the final choice reflecting the influence of nonideological factors.

Expressions of Historical National Interest

Two different types of historical experience are important in shaping the Soviet world view. First, there are the lessons learned from the successes and failures of Soviet foreign policy. Second, there are the traditional foreign-policy concerns of the Russian state. The relative importance attached to these two forces depends upon whether Soviet foreign policy is seen as a modern day extension of Tsarist foreign policy or as if history begins with the 1917 revolution.

Long-term historical influences on Soviet foreign policy can be grouped under two headings. First, there is the traditional Russian sense of mission. For centuries, Moscow has been considered by Russians to be the "Third Rome," the center of true Christianity. The previous centers of Christianity (Rome and Constantinople) had become corrupt and were conquered. Writing in 1510, a Russian monk told Tsar Vasily III, "Thou alone, in all that is under heaven, art a Christian Tsar . . . all Christian kingdoms are merged into thine alone . . . [the] two Romes have fallen, but the third stands, and there will be no fourth."[14] Just as Manifest Destiny allowed American leaders to justify territorial expansion as something other than imperialism, so too the self-image of Moscow as the Third Rome provided the basis for viewing Russian expansion in positive and benevolent terms.

Second, there is the Soviet fear of invasion. Ken Booth writes that

> the invaders of Russia in the last 800 years read like a *Who's Who* of military aggression: the Mongols between 1240–1380; the Poles 1607–1612; the Swedes 1611–1614 and again in 1709; Napoleon in 1812; Germany and Austria in 1914–1918; Britain, the United States, Japan, France, and Italy, 1918–1919; Poland in 1920; and Germany between 1941 and 1944. . . . Within living memory the Russians lost 45,000 military dead in the Russo-Japanese War, nearly two million military and an uncounted number of civilian casualties in the First World War, 30,000 in clashes with Japan in the late 1930s, approximately 50,000 in the Soviet-Finnish War, . . . and between fifteen and twenty million in overcoming the gratuitously brutal invasion by Hitler's Germany.[15]

Russia's vulnerability to invasion has left an enduring mark on Russian foreign policy. It has produced what can be called "a defensive expansionist impulse." Russian leaders have tried to substitute territory for secure borders. The more territory under Russian control, the further back becomes the starting point for the next attack, and the greater is the likelihood that the war will not have to be fought entirely on Russian soil. The permanent sense of insecurity brought on by the constant fear of invasion has also given Russian diplomacy a quasi-military character. George Kennan asserts that Russia has never experienced truly friendly relations with neighboring states, but only periods of armistice with hostile enemies. As a result, its diplomacy has not been concerned with producing compromise positions acceptable to all parties, but with impressing the adversary with the "terrifying strength of Russian power, while keeping him uncertain and confused as to the exact channels and means of its application."[16]

Lessons concerning the Soviet national interest are also drawn from the successes and failures of Soviet foreign policy. Too often there is a tendency in the United States to present Soviet foreign policy as a string of unending victories. A more balanced presentation would characterize it in terms of victories and setbacks. Moreover, the victories have often come with a high price tag. For example, the Soviet Union has incurred great economic and military costs in propping up the Cuban and East European governments. The reform movement that spread through Eastern Europe in 1989 and brought noncommunists into positions of power also casts doubt upon the long-standing belief that communist victories are irreversible.

Competing Visions of Soviet Foreign Policy

Three alternative visions of Soviet foreign policy exist within which we can try to understand Gorbachev's initiatives: the *essentialist*, the *mechanist*, and the *interactive*.[17] None holds a monopoly on U.S. thinking, and recent U.S. administrations have embraced all three. Each presents a different interpretation of such issues as the driving force behind Soviet foreign-policy behavior, the nature of the Soviet threat, and the possibility of reaching a meaningful accommodation with it. These contrasts are summarized in Table 4.2.

In the *essentialist* view, Soviet foreign policy is highly deterministic in nature,

Table 4.2 COMPETING VISIONS OF SOVIET FOREIGN POLICY

	Essentialist	Mechanist	Interactive
Source of behavior	Highly deterministic Origins lie in very nature of system: communism or totalitarianism	Expansion seen as natural behavior for USSR Geopolitics and historical national interests are stressed	External events and policy disagreements among elite seen as driving force Learning seen as possible
Nature of threat	Alarmist Blueprint for world hegemony and revolution exists Little emphasis given to constraints Domestic problems seen as promoting foreign-policy adventurism	"Preponderance" seen as ultimate goal Influence and status seen as short-term goals Opportunism and not a master plan seen in Soviet actions	Reactive Domestic problems seen as placing constraints on foreign policy Threats can be met with policy of linkage
Possibility of accommodation	Likelihood of war seen as high USSR not seen as interested in global stability Little reason seen to enter into negotiations	Negotiations seen as a supplement to military power Arms control seen as a tool to manage global competition	Interdependence stressed Negotiations seen as a substitute for military power USSR seen as a potential partner in managing world affairs

Source: Derived from Lawrence Caldwell and Alexander Dallin, "U.S. Policy Toward the Soviet Union," in Kenneth Oye, Donald Rothchild, and Robert Lieber, eds., *Eagle Entangled* (New York: Longman, 1979), pp. 199–227.

and the source of that behavior can be found in the principles of Marxism-Leninism. This view discounts the possibility that there can be any real change in the nature of Soviet foreign policy and sees no basis for accommodation with it. The likelihood of war with the Soviet Union is held to be rather high, and the Soviets are seen as having little interest in stabilizing the world order or in entering into meaningful negotiations. For the essentialist, Gorbachev's New Thinking is either an aberration that will eventually be corrected or a planned deception.

The *mechanist* perspective sees Soviet foreign policy as largely a product of geo-politics. In place of the blueprint for world revolution or hegemony alluded to by the essentialists, the mechanists see the Soviets as opportunists who act to exploit favorable situations and who seek greater status and prestige in the international system but who also have real security concerns and face major constraints on what they can hope to accomplish. Limits can be placed on the degree and intensity of competition and conflict with such an enemy if they are rooted in a policy of meeting power with power. The mechanist is likely to credit Gorbachev with sincerity but, at the same time, is unsure of how many concessions to make because the mechanist believes that the ultimate aim of the New Thinking is not to create a more peaceful Soviet Union, but to create a Soviet Union that is better able to play the game of power politics against the United States.

The third approach, the *interactive* vision, sees Soviet foreign policy as a product of elite choice, and it holds that learning is possible. Much of Soviet foreign policy is held to be reactive in nature. The interactivist believes that if the United States can structure its foreign policy so that "bad" Soviet behavior is punished and the "good" rewarded, over time Soviet foreign policy will adjust. The strategy of détente has rested heavily upon such assumptions. Through a policy of linkages, it sought to engineer the transformation of the Soviet Union from a competitor to a partner. Alone among the three perspectives, the interactive perspective favors a positive response to Gorbachev's foreign-policy initiatives. Interactivists note that, unlike the détente of the 1970s, it is now the Soviet Union that needs the United States' help in engineering a stable international system and that it is U.S. and not Soviet military power that is on the rise. These altered conditions, plus the presence of a leader such as Gorbachev, are seen as presenting the West with a rare opportunity fundamentally to alter the nature of U.S.-Soviet relations.

THE CHINESE WORLD VIEW

The radicalism and defiant rhetoric of Chinese domestic and foreign policy found in the Maoist era is no longer present. It has been replaced by an emphasis on the development of a decentralized quasi-market economic system within China and the creation of special economic zones designed to attract foreign technology and invest-ment. Significant though they are, these policy changes are fully consistent with the underlying thrust of both Chinese ideology and the Chinese national interest. Their purpose is to make China strong and capable of resisting foreign influences and to fashion a distinctively Chinese approach to world politics.[18]

The transition has not been painless. Just as in the Soviet Union, economic re-form in China has led to expressions of political unrest. Matters came to a head in the summer of 1989 when hundreds and possibly thousands of student protesters and their supporters were killed by Chinese forces in Beijing's Tiananmen Square. The United States and many of its allies, as well as international economic organizations, responded to this display of brute force with economic sanctions. Unlike economic sanctions against Cuba, the Soviet Union, Nicaragua, or Chile, these sanctions were not motivated by any desire to punish China or to bring down a government. They were expressions of moral outrage. Both China and the rest of the world seemed anxious to put the events of the summer of 1989 behind them, and by the fall of 1989 steps toward normalizing relations were well under way. However, not everyone was willing to forget as was clear with the negative reaction in the United States to the secret diplomatic mission that President Bush sent to China.

Ideological Influences

Three elements come together to form Chinese ideology.[19] All are revolutionary in nature and were advocated by individuals intent on regaining for China its past greatness and power. The first component is the May Fourth Movement (1919). It symbolized the awakening of Chinese intellectuals to the need for revolutionary change within China as a prerequisite for regaining full sovereignty. The igniting spark was a decision made by the Allied Powers at the Paris Peace Conference (1919) to transfer German rights in Shantung Province to Japan. These rights had been acquired by Germany as part of the spheres-of-influence system that had been imposed upon China by Western powers. Many of the ideas put forth by the May Fourth Movement, such as education and language reform, the introduction of scientific methods, and an emphasis on the values and goodness of the common people, would become central elements of the political agenda when the communists took power in 1949. The May Fourth Movement also advocated the exploration of non-Chinese political ideologies. One of these was Marxism-Leninism, which is the second component to Chinese communist ideology.

Prior to the 1917 Bolshevik Revolution, Marxism-Leninism was almost unknown to Chinese intellectuals. However, the success of that revolution, plus the intellectual fervent unleashed by the May Fourth Movement, led many to explore it. What they found was a body of thought that provided an emotional link between their antiimperialist feelings and a growing sense of nationalism. It not only accounted for China's ongoing exploitation at the hands of the West but also laid out a plan for revolutionary action.

The third component to Chinese communist ideology is Maoism. Just as Lenin did before him, Mao Zedong did not leave Marxism unchanged. For Marx, revolution would come when objective economic conditions deteriorated to the breaking point. Lenin modified this by adding that political consciousness must also be molded in order for revolution to occur. Mao took Marxism-Leninism one step further away from economic determinism by stressing the importance of human willpower in directing the course of history. The dialectical process became less a contest of class interests and more a struggle between the spirit of revolutionary progress and the tendency for capitalism to reassert itself.

Maoist thought stresses the superiority of the human spirit over machines and technology. Diligence, hard work, self-sacrifice, self-reliance, and correct thinking are capable of overcoming even the greatest objective roadblocks to making a revolution. In China, this meant substituting a peasant-based movement for a large working-class movement, establishing a modern economy through the organized efforts of the masses (the Great Leap Forward), and building a powerful military strength that rested on the participation of the whole population (the concept of a People's War). Mao also believed that conflict and tension are an inherent feature of life. There is a constant need to be on guard against backsliding and allowing reactionary elements in society to reestablish their influence. Lucian Pye argues that, in doing so, Mao "transformed Communist ideology into a morality play between the forces of good and evil . . . [he] gave to socialist morality a sense of omnipresent, if not original, sin.[20]

Fewer doctrinal statements exist in Chinese ideology as compared to its Soviet counterpart. This is a result of the greater flexibility of Maoist thought and the less activist nature of Chinese foreign policy. Three doctrinal statements from the Maoist era (1949–1977), however, do merit special mention, because they capture the revolutionary and nationalistic character of Chinese communist ideology and serve as a yardstick against which we can measure contemporary Chinese foreign-policy initiatives.[21] As Allen Whiting notes, contemporary Chinese leaders, while they no longer embrace all of what Mao said, have not yet put forward a coherent alternative theoretical framework for Chinese foreign policy.[22]

The first doctrinal statement from the Maoist era is the Theory of Three Worlds. Originally put forward by Zhou Enlai at the first conference of nonaligned countries at Bandung in 1955, it was reaffirmed by Mao in 1974. The United States and Soviet Union comprise the first world; Japan, Canada, and Europe form the second; all other states, including China, comprise the third world. This formulation is significant because of where it places China in relation to other states. It is also quite different from the three-worlds imagery that is used in the United States, which has the United States and other advanced capitalist states in the first world, the Soviet Union and other communist states in the second world, and the less developed states in the third world.

The second doctrinal statement of enduring importance is closely related to the first: Anti-Superpower Hegemony. This concept was included in the Shanghai Communique that was signed by President Nixon and Premier Zhou Enlai at the end of Nixon's historic trip to China in 1972. It states that no country should be allowed to exercise preponderant influence over another. Both the United States and Soviet Union are regarded as potential national security threats in this formulation. A major cause of war in the international system is believed to lie with efforts by the first world to dominate and exploit the other two. A natural harmony of interests exists between the second and third worlds. Success demands that no compromises or acts of appeasement be entered into with these hegemonic powers. Third world states are also encouraged to enter into an economic struggle with the two hegemonic powers and exploit their need for raw materials and natural resources.

The third doctrinal statement can be summed up as a pronuclear posture. Chinese leaders have long been suspicious of U.S. and Soviet advocacy of nonproliferation agreements and efforts to get other nuclear powers to enter into test ban pacts. China exploded its first nuclear device in 1964, and between 1964 and 1978 it conducted at least 36 tests. Chinese leaders have come to regard the possession of (defensive) nuclear weapons by third world states as legitimate and even necessary to prevent superpower exploitation. They were also suspicious of détente in the 1970s because they saw it as a smoke screen behind which the United States and the Soviet Union could intensify the arms race while at the same time giving a false sense of security to other states in the international system.

Expressions of Historical National Interest

The Chinese historical legacy is imposing both in its length and its extremes. Frederick Hartmann observes that "three hundred years ago China was at the height of its power and glory while the United States consisted of only a few struggling colonies and Russia was equally weak and preoccupied with matters of survival."[23] Standing in sharp contrast is the period 1840–1945, known as the Century of Humiliation. The establishment of communist rule in China marks the beginning of a third era, which is characterized by China's reemergence as a major power. Each of these periods has left its mark on Chinese foreign policy.

Distant though it may be, the pull of China's past greatness on the leading figures of the twentieth century should not be underestimated. Whatever their political differences, Mao Zedong, Chiang Kai-Shek, and Sun Yat-sen all believed in China's inherent superiority and uniqueness. International relations in this period of greatness was carried out according to a very different set of principles from that which emerged in the European dominated part of the world. Most notably absent was the concept of sovereign equality. China saw itself as the Middle Kingdom, the only power in a world of lesser states. Robert North writes that "for the better part of two millennia, at least, China perceived itself as the only great empire on earth, the only civilization, the only culture that really mattered."[24] The Chinese also rejected the European idea that peace was best ensured through a balance-of-power system. Confucian thought held that a natural order existed and that stability was attained when this order was recognized. Problems arose when individuals were confused about their proper roles.

The tribute system symbolized this sense of inequality and natural order. Periodically, barbarian states were expected to send a mission to the emperor, at which time they would bring gifts and demonstrate their submissiveness. In return for this tribute, China was expected to protect the barbarian state. The relationship fell short of that associated with Western colonialism, remaining more as a set of rituals than as an administrative system. The net effect was to bolster trade between the two. Tribute missions to China continued well into the Century of Humiliation. Between 1840–1894 there were at least 46 missions from Korea. Missions arrived from Burma until 1875, from Vietnam until 1883, and one from Nepal arrived in 1908.

The early Western presence in China was innocent enough. Commerce and Christianity were its primary forms, and neither elicited an enthusiastic response. Western merchants were restricted to operating in certain cities and were allowed to deal only with specified Chinese merchants. If European and American merchants were to succeed in unlocking the riches of China, a product had to be found that the Chinese wanted, and the Westerners had to break free from the restrictions placed on them by Chinese authorities. The product was opium. Although at one time trade with the West was heavily skewed in China's favor, by 1830 Chinese exports were no longer earning enough to pay for the imported opium, and China began to experience an outflow of bullion. The imperial Chinese government made numerous efforts to stop the trade in opium, but, until 1839, these largely amounted to issuing decrees and were ineffective. In that year, a Chinese official in Canton seized $11 million in opium and tried to drive the opium dealers from the city. The British, charging that it was a violation of international free trade, took military steps to counter this action.

The Opium War lasted until 1842, when the Treaty of Nanking was signed. By its terms, Hong Kong was ceded to Great Britain, and five cities became treaty ports in which British merchants would be governed by British authorities. British merchants were free to trade with any Chinese merchant, and British and Chinese officials were designated as equal in standing. Finally, China was forced to compensate Great Britain for the opium seized in 1839 and for the cost of the British war effort. It was not long before other Western powers demanded and received similar trade agreements: the United States (1844), Belgium (1845), Sweden and Norway (1847), and Russia (1851).

Chinese fortunes continued to decline for the remainder of the century. During the 1850s, 10 more treaty ports were created, foreign embassies were established, and the Chinese interior was opened up to trade. The power of the Chinese government was dealt a major blow by the Taiping Rebellion (1861). A peasant-based movement led by Christian converts, the Taipings put forward a puritanical communal reform agenda that opposed materialism and promoted equality of the sexes. At first, the West was neutral in the conflict, but in the end it came to the aid of the Manchu Dynasty. Concern grew that the value of the series of unequal treaties might be jeopardized should the Taipings gain power or the imperial government become too weakened. The rebellion was not easily put down. Estimates place the loss of life at between 20–40 million. In comparison, the Civil War in the United States, which was taking place at the same time, resulted in approximately 400,000 deaths. From this point forward, the Manchu Dynasty existed only because of Western support and became a government that did not rule.

Yet another major setback in the Century of Humiliation came with the Boxer Rebellion (1900). A conservative reaction to the moderate reform efforts of the Chinese government, the Boxer Rebellion bore no trace of Western ideas. The Boxers grew out of local militia and were manipulated by the Chinese government. They directed their attacks at foreigners and those Chinese who worked for them. The rebellion was put down by a multinational army drawn from the forces of the Western powers that had interests in China after the Boxers laid siege to foreign embassies in Peking. For Chinese nationalists, success would not come until 1911, when Sun Yat-sen's followers overthrew the Manchu Dynasty. Even that victory was less than complete. True governing power did not go immediately to the Nationalist revolutionaries but passed first to warlords, whose grip on China was not broken until the 1930s, when they were defeated by Chiang Kai-shek. Even then, the Chinese civil war and Japanese occupation forces stood in the way of China laying full claim to its sovereignty.

While dating only from 1949, Chinese communist foreign policy has traveled down several paths.[25] From 1950 to 1953 the primary concern was border security. China sent its forces into the Korean peninsula when U.S. forces approached the

Chinese border with Korea and into Tibet over the protests of neighboring India. The years 1954–1965 were a period of great activism but little consistency for Chinese foreign policy. The first few years saw China participate in two major international conferences: Geneva (1954), which marked the end of French colonialism in Indochina, and Bandung (1955), which was the first meeting of nonaligned states. By the late 1950s, Chinese foreign policy had become highly militaristic as the Great Leap Forward radicalized Chinese society. The Great Leap Forward was an attempt by Mao to speed up greatly the process of economic development in China by stressing the role of human willpower and peasant-based industry over large-scale industrialization projects. China provoked an international crisis in 1958 when it began shelling Quemoy and Matsu, two Taiwanese-held islands. China backed down when President Eisenhower responded by sending the Seventh Fleet to escort shipping and when Premier Khrushchev failed to support its actions. The Soviet Union's unwillingness to use its nuclear forces as a protective umbrella became a primary ingredient (along with ideology, personality conflicts, and historical conflicts centering on Russian exploitation of China and its early manipulation of the Chinese Communist Party) in the Sino-Soviet dispute that came to light in 1963. Next came a period of isolationism and paralysis, as China went through the Cultural Revolution (1966–1969). The Cultural Revolution was an attempt by Mao and his political allies to rekindle the revolutionary spirit within China, but it resulted in anarchy and chaos.

Since then, Chinese foreign policy has begun to resemble that of the other great powers. Today it has a crowded foreign-policy agenda. Economic modernization heads the list. To this end, Chinese leaders have actively sought out foreign capital. By 1988, the World Bank had approved approximately $5.5 billion in loans for China and had provided it with feasibility studies for agriculture, health, transportation, science, and energy projects. China has also borrowed over $3.5 billion in low-interest loans from Japan since 1979. Economic modernization is sought after not only as an end in itself but also for its ability to help China realize two long-standing objectives. The first is national security. The second is the reincorporation of such outlying territories as Taiwan, Hong Kong, Macao, and a number of disputed islands in the South and East China Seas.

Three states are central to China's ability to realize its foreign-policy goals. One is the United States. The nature of U.S.-Chinese relations changed dramatically when President Nixon announced in 1971 that he was going to visit China. Since then, there have been several ups and downs in U.S.-Chinese relations, but no formal break has occurred. In particular, China objects to the idea, frequently voiced in Washington, that it is a pawn (the "China Card") to be used by the United States in its struggle with the Soviet Union. U.S.-Chinese relations also became noticeably chilly during the early years of the Reagan presidency because of its support for Taiwan. Also of great concern to Chinese leaders are its relations with the Soviet Union. As evidenced by the 1989 Sino-Soviet summit conference that was held in Beijing, relations with the Soviet Union, while still less than "normal," have also improved greatly since 1969, when Chinese and Soviet forces fought over a disputed island on their border. Gorbachev has gone far in meeting the three conditions that Chinese leaders established as preconditions for normalizing Sino-Soviet relations.

He has withdrawn Soviet forces from the Chinese border, pulled Soviet troops out of Afghanistan, and placed pressure on Vietnam to end its occupation of Cambodia. Finally, there is the question of Sino-Japanese relations. Chinese leaders are of two minds regarding Japan. On the one hand, Japan is a natural trading partner and source of high-technology imports. On the other hand, historically Japan has been an enemy, and concerns with contemporary Japanese militarism are very much in evidence.

Competing Visions of Chinese Foreign Policy

Given its history of foreign policy reversals, its resentment of foreign influence, and its past willingness to isolate itself from the international system, the key questions for the future become: (1) How long will Chinese foreign policy run on its current course, and (2) If it changes direction, what will that path look like? Michel Oksenberg suggests that answers can be found if we recognize that an underlying theme in Chinese communist foreign policy is nationalism.[26] Oksenberg identifies four types of Chinese nationalism: *emotional*, *xenophobic*, *assertive*, and *confident*. He argues that they are rooted in different assessments of Chinese weaknesses and that each suggests a different foreign policy. The key to the future thus lies in understanding how the Chinese leadership evaluates China's position in the international system.

Emotional nationalism is self-pitying, self-righteous, and hypersensitive to perceived insults. It is ambivalent in its feelings about the outside world, seeing China as having been wronged by others, feeling that the world owes China a debt, yet looking at the world with a certain amount of admiration. Emotional nationalism thus has much in common with the type of nationalism in many Third World states. *Xenophobic nationalism* is isolationist in spirit. It believes that China's problems are due to the presence of Western ideas and values and that the solution is to cleanse China of them. China can regain its greatness only when its ideological purity and cultural uniqueness are restored. The Boxer Rebellion and Cultural Revolution are expressions of this type of nationalism. *Assertive nationalism* also sees China's weaknesses as a result of foreign economic exploitation and cultural penetration. Its proposed solution is a limited involvement in the international system, which would allow China to modernize through its contacts with the outside world without becoming more dependent upon it. The perceived need to protect China from further humiliation makes it militant and rigid. China's unyielding stance on Taiwan, its relations with Vietnam, and Mao's provocative rhetoric toward the Soviet Union are examples of assertive nationalism. Lastly there is *confident nationalism*. It flourished in the mid-1980s, but its roots date back to the nineteenth century. According to it, China's weaknesses are due to such factors as an inadequate industrial base, poor communication facilities, underdeveloped transportation systems, a poorly trained work force, and inefficient political and economic institutions. Nothing is wrong with Chinese culture. It is strong and resilient. Confident nationalism recommends a calculated policy of economic and political development based on importing foreign ideas and technology. Extensive contacts with the outside world are welcomed, and China is seen as playing a significant role in maintaining stability in the region. Oksenberg cautions that confident nationalists have never been able to control the political stage for long periods of time and that the other forms of nationalism are always lurking in the background and could quickly reassert themselves.

THE THIRD WORLD PERSPECTIVE

The Third World includes the more than 125 less developed countries of Latin America, Africa, the Middle East, and Asia. The derivation of the term is generally attributed to Alfred Sauvy, a French demographer. Mohammed Ayoob has suggested that Third World states approach the international system from a dual perspective. On the one hand, they are individual states that have interests to protect and advance. On the other hand, they are "intruders" into the world arena who are seeking to change the rules of the system.[27] Joan Spero notes that Third World states are least successful in achieving significant change in the international system when the industrialized nations perceive their demands as indicative of a desire to change the international decision-making structure. The wealthy states have proved to be more willing to agree to concessions in areas in which proposals are designed to aid development without threatening the existing structure. Because the Third World is made up of very diverse states, it is difficult to generalize about Third World foreign policy, and we will not attempt to frame our discussion here in the same terms as we did with the individual states discussed earlier. To the extent that Third World states can be said to share a dominant perspective on world politics, they are guided by (1) nationalism, (2) the philosophy of nonalignment, and (3) perceptions of weakness.

Nationalism

The nationalism of Third World states is influenced by their history of domination by more powerful states and, particularly, by colonialism. The leaders of the early independence movements in the colonies were usually Western-educated elites. The education received by these individuals emphasized the larger entities of states over kinship and locality and provided them with a concept that could be used to unite their people against colonial rule. By focusing on the idea that their people constituted a nation, these leaders could argue for the right of self-determination. Nationalism was also used to overcome the sense of inferiority engendered by foreign domination. Today the foreign policies of the Third World states continue to revolve around attempts to end economic dependence and to improve their status in the international pecking order.

Once independence was achieved, nationalism provided a mechanism for state building. Particularly in Africa, colonial boundaries were determined by administrative needs and as a result of treaties and negotiations among the colonial powers. They paid no attention to existing political entities or ethnic configurations. Consequently, the citizens of states such as Nigeria shared no past history as a united people prior to colonialism. Nationalism was used to unite people behind the concept of the new nation, to overcome their attachments to ethnic or kinship groups, and to instill national pride.

That nationalist sentiments in many cases developed out of the struggle for independence has meant that Third World nationalism is often tinged with anti-Western rhetoric and feeling. This hostility toward the West, combined with the inherent appeal of Marxism for the powerless, gave the Soviet Union an early political advantage in its relations with the Third World. However, economic concerns have intervened. The Soviet Union has not been generous with economic aid, and few Third World countries have been willing to alienate Western donors by placing themselves completely in the Soviet camp. Between 1954 and 1983, Soviet aid to sub-Saharan Africa totaled $836 million, whereas, in 1983 alone, Western aid totaled $8 billion. In fact, today most Third World states have either political or economic ties with the West—even those with a socialist orientation.[28]

Charismatic leaders can use nationalist sentiments to their advantage by representing themselves as the embodiment of the nation and as a rallying point in the struggle to achieve international security. Under such leaders, foreign policy becomes very personalistic: The characteristics of the leader are the major determinants of policy. For many of these leaders, emotional nationalism remains the only identifiable ideological focus. They argue that they were wronged by past injustices (imperialism) and by a current world order in which they are merely pawns of the superpowers. They view their own position as self-righteous and unassailable. Further, they can use external enemies as a diversion from domestic problems and to unify their citizens in a common cause. Gaddafi in Libya and Khomeini in Iran are examples of leaders who believe that virtually anything that they direct at their perceived enemies is justified. Ideology takes precedence over practicality. For example, Khomeini's international death sentence on Salman Rushdie (because Rushdie wrote *The Satanic Verses*, a book termed heretical by Khomeini) pushed back the normalization of relations between Iran and Western states.

While it provides a basis for unity, Third World nationalism also places roadblocks in its way. This can be seen most clearly in the failure of various attempts at regional unity. Intent upon protecting the often fragile basis of national unity within their states, beset with a wide range of domestic problems, and suspicious of foreign encroachments on their newly won sovereignty, Third World leaders have been reluctant to enter into the type of long-term sovereignty-limiting agreements that are necessary to make international cooperative efforts work. Still, there exists the realization that, because of their individual weaknesses, collective action must be pursued. African and Middle Eastern states have been most active in pursuing regional cooperation.

The thrust toward African unity is epitomized by the Organization of African Unity (OAU), which was founded in 1963. The OAU has been united in its attempts to end colonialism and the interference of the superpowers, and, more recently, in its opposition to the white minority government of South Africa. Article III of its charter emphasizes noninterference, sovereignty, and the inviolability of the borders inherited from colonial rule. The OAU is restricted from interfering in the domestic affairs of any member country, which seriously curtails its authority. Conflicting interests have kept the African nations from achieving any real political unity. The

OAU has attempted to mediate disputes between African states. The OAU asked states not to choose sides in the Angolan conflict, and initially its members complied. However, over time, as the South African and U.S. CIA support for the National Union for the Total Independence of Angola (UNITA) was exposed, more and more states came out in support of their opponents, the Popular Movement for the Liberation of Angola (MPLA). From May to June of 1989, 18 presidents and prime ministers under the leadership of President Houphouet-Boigny of the Ivory Coast negotiated a cease-fire agreement between the government of Angola and the UNITA rebels. This was the largest meeting of African heads of state, other than the conferences held by the OAU. This effort illustrates the continuing consensus among African states over the question of Southern Africa.

The Arab states of the Middle East have shared a number of foreign-policy goals. These states are united by a common religion, history, and culture; and, in spite of significant differences in their regimes, they have each supported—albeit to different degrees—the concept of Arab nationalism. This philosophy has resulted in support for independence movements in the region (such as Egypt's support for the Algerian revolt against French rule), support for the liberation of Palestine (and its reverse image, opposition to Israel), attempts at political unity, and economic cooperation. The Ottoman Empire (1517–1918), which united the Arab world, was at one time the largest empire that has ever existed. It was founded through "holy wars," which sought to bring Islam to the world's infidels, and was administered according to the dictates of the Koran, the Muslim bible. Muslim leaders use this glorious history to evoke nationalist spirit. In spite of this heritage, however, the Arab states have had little success with attempts at political unification. The Arab League, which has persisted since its establishment in 1945, has had very limited success in settling conflicts among member states. It does not have the authority to make binding decisions regarding its members. The United Arab Republic was formed by the political unification of Egypt and Syria in 1961, and it lasted for three years, before dissension between the states led to its demise. It was more effective in limited, functional areas such as health and education programs. Other attempts at unification have failed in earlier stages of the unification process, with the notable exception of the United Arab Emirates, a federation of small oil-rich states in the Persian Gulf area.

The politics of oil is one area in which Arab cooperation has been forthcoming. During the 1970s, the Middle Eastern oil-producing countries banded together to wrest control of oil production and exporting from Western hands. The Organization of Arab Petroleum Exporting Countries (OAPEC) was formed in 1968 and has been used to further the interests of Arab nationalism. Its Arab members have used oil to pressure other states in their treatment of Isreal. During the Yom Kippur war, in response to the U.S. decision to airlift weapons to Israel, OAPEC agreed to cut production by at least 5 percent as part of its strategy of placing pressure on European governments to withdraw their support for Israel.

Nonalignment

The second major element of Third World foreign policy is nonalignment. The concept of nonalignment—remaining independent of both the United States and the

Soviet Union—was advanced at the Afro-Asian conference at Bandung, Indonesia in 1955. The United States, which opposed the conference, attempted to sabotage it, and that it occurred at all is an indication of Third World determination to escape superpower domination. The 29 states that attended the meeting affirmed the idea of Third World unity and made clear their refusal to bow to U.S. pressure. The conference marked a new era in Third World self-esteem and independence. As one delegate noted: "We are the two greatest continents on earth. We have the greatest pool of manpower, the greatest of all materials. We have the greatest pool of fuel. We have every strategic military base and area. If we are determined, all of us, with our collective will, no strategic war will take place—if we do not participate in any sense."[29] In 1961, the Nonaligned Movement (NAM) was founded by Sukarno of Indonesia, Nehru of India, Nasser of Egypt, and Tito of Yugoslavia. It grew from an original membership of 25 to over 100 members. NAM schedules periodic meetings and elects a three-year chair. Additionally, there is a coordinating bureau that performs some managerial functions, such as administering membership. Countries that are thought to be too closely aligned to a major power are denied membership. This criterion is inconsistently applied, however. South Korea and the Philippines were rejected on the basis of being too closely aligned with the United States, but Cuba, North Korea, and North Vietnam were admitted. In theory, all states except members of NATO, the Warsaw Pact, the Central Treaty Organization (CENTO), and the South East Asia Treaty Organization (SEATO) are eligible for membership. The NAM addresses political, as well as economic, issues. Between 1979 and 1983, the NAM was chaired by Cuba, which took a radical position—approving the Soviet invasion of Afghanistan, for example. Not all members shared this orientation, and disagreements were frequent along both ideological and geographic lines.

The major purposes of NAM are to protect the independence of Third World countries in a world that is dominated by the superpowers, to increase Third World power by aggregating it, and to provide a forum for Third World interests. An earlier purpose, to provide a neutral, nuclear-free zone as a buffer between the superpowers, is generally regarded today as less important. Since the 1970s, economic issues have become increasingly important to NAM.

One state that continues to identify itself with the philosophy of nonalignment is India. Its official policy of nonalignment is rooted in two traditions. The first is inherited from British India and espouses a concern for the territorial integrity of South Asia. The second is that of the Indian National Congress, which focuses on world peace, anticolonialism and antiracism. Its nonalignment position is not one of isolation (India has been active in regional and world politics) but, rather, emphasizes pragmatism and independence.[30]

New states are characterized by the need to build both internal and external security. Ayoob notes that NAM membership remains valuable to Third World states, in part, because it provides them with some freedom to maneuver in their relationships with the major powers. By using the argument that they are committed to a nonaligned foreign policy, states can resist superpower pressure to adopt particular stands.[31] Both nationalism and nonalignment are related to the quest for security and autonomy. Many Third World governments are faced with significant internal and regional challenges to their authority. The insecurity that these governments face leads them to make alliances, particularly with the superpowers, but also with other states in the region. Consequently, a tension develops between the desire for autonomy and the desire for security. This ambivalence can be seen in the current controversy in the Philippines concerning the future of American bases there.

The Weakness of Third World States

Stephen Krasner notes that political weakness and vulnerability are fundamental sources of Third World behavior.[32] Severe economic problems, the enormous disparity between the rich and poor states, and the history of foreign domination create perceptions of the world order that differ from those of the East and West. After they achieved independence, many Third World states continued to have their resources controlled by firms operating out of the developed states. The extractive policies of multinational corporations led to a period of economic nationalism on the part of some Third World governments during the 1960s. This was especially prevalent in Latin America. Bolivia, Peru, and Mexico nationalized foreign-owned oil companies during the 1960s, and Chile nationalized the copper companies in 1971.

The tendency for weaker states to look outside the country for both the solutions to their problems and the sources of their weakness makes dependency theory an attractive explanation to many Third World leaders. Rather than focusing on internal problems as the primary source of backwardness and poverty, dependency theory blames the international order and offers solutions that depend more on changes in that order than on sacrifices at home. As Third World countries have embraced dependency theory, they have rejected liberalism. They argue that the market system works to reward those who are already better endowed. They want to restructure fundamentally the international economic system to give Third World states more influence over policymaking in international organizations, to provide for more development assistance, to make technology the common property of humanity, to give each state exclusive control over its own resources and over multinational firms operating on its soil, to establish trade policies that will encourage agricultural production and increase their export earnings, and to stabilize prices for raw materials. The less developed countries have worked together to pass the Declaration of the Establishment of a New International Economic Order in the UN General Assembly, as well as producing other documents at various conferences. These economic concerns provide the basis for the one area in which there is considerable Third World unity.

The call for a New International Economic Order (NIEO) was formally endorsed by a Special Session of the General Assembly in 1974 and stated as its purpose:

> to work urgently for the establishment of a new international economic order based on equity, sovereign equality, common interest and cooperation among all states, irrespective of their economic and social systems, *which shall correct inequalities and redress existing injustices, make it possible to eliminate the widening gap between the developed and the developing countries* and ensure steadily accelerating economic and social development and peace and justice for present and future generations [author's emphasis].[33]

The NIEO touched on a number of issues. Important proposals included a call to renegotiate Third World debt, to reform the IMF, particularly in its decision-making process, and to stabilize the value of primary-product exports by tying commodity prices to those of manufactured goods and by creating a common fund to be used to establish buffer stockpiles. Other proposals were aimed at opening markets in the developed countries to Third World products, lowering tariffs on Third World exports, and increasing technical assistance in agriculture. Further, the less developed countries asked that the more developed countries increase development assistance to a minimum of 0.7 percent of their respective GNPs. By 1981, only five developed countries had increased development assistance to this level.

Although the NIEO has provided a sense of solidarity to less developed states, its goals (which are vague and open to differing interpretations) have not been realized. When changes occur, they are often limited and uneven in effect. For example, one area of major interest concerns opening markets in the industrialized countries to Third World products. There has been some limited progress in this area. In 1965, the United Nations Conference on Trade and Development (UNCTAD) asked states to refrain from increasing barriers and to give priority to reducing barriers on those products that comprise the principal exports of the less developed countries. Additionally, exceptions to free-trade rules were asked for less developed states. UNCTAD II in 1968 instituted what was to become the Generalized System of Preferences (GSP), passed in 1976 and extended in 1980. The original idea behind the GSP was to exempt the exports of developing states from trade barriers.

There is also a growing appreciation that Third World states must change their domestic policies, as well as the international system. At the Lusaka Conference of Non-Aligned Nations in 1970, the delegates agreed that, in order to achieve greater autonomy and more power in the international system, they must place a greater reliance on themselves and on economic cooperation among themselves. One important organization formed to address economic issues is the Group of 77, which has more than 120 members—virtually all the Third World states. At its 1967 meeting in Algiers, it formulated a charter that still governs the negotiating position of these states in regard to trade, finance, development assistance, and the international economic structure.[34]

CONCLUSION

In this chapter, we have argued that understanding the perceptions that policymakers bring to foreign-policy decision making requires more than just an understanding of textbook ideology. Looking solely at ideology would not help us to predict the foreign-policy positions adopted by the Contadora states (Mexico, Venezuela, Colombia, and Panama) with regard to U.S.-Nicaraguan relations. In essence, these four capitalist states have come out in favor of seeing a communist government safely installed in power in Nicaragua rather than join with the United States in supporting the Contras. What they fear most is not communism in Central America, but the destabilizing effect that a large-scale U.S. military presence would have on their own fragile political systems. Their position also reflects the problems posed by a close geographical proximity to the United States and the legacy left by past U.S. interventions into the region.

Views of policymakers are also colored by such diverse factors as geography, interpretations of their country's historical experience, and the need to address problems in a pragmatic fashion. These forces do not come together in a single package. There is no single U.S. or Soviet perspective on international relations, any more than there is a single Third World perspective. Within every society, competing views exist. Care must thus be taken that, in our dealing with the current Chinese approach to world politics, we do not lose sight of the existence of competing approaches that may one day come to guide Chinese foreign policy.

NOTES

1. Louis Hartz, *The Liberal Tradition in America* (New York: Harcourt Brace Jovanovich, 1955).
2. George F. Kennan, *American Diplomacy, 1900–1950* (New York: Mentor, 1951).
3. See John Lovell, *The Challenge of American Foreign Policy* (New York: Macmillan, 1985), pp. 51–82.
4. Quoted in Howard Bliss and Glen Johnson, *Beyond the Water's Edge* (Philadelphia: Lippincott, 1975), pp. 52–53.
5. Ole R. Holsti and James N. Rosenau, *American Leadership in World Affairs: Vietnam and the Breakdown of Consensus* (Boston: Allen & Unwin, 1984), pp. 218–220.
6. See Holsti and Rosenau, *American Leadership in World Affairs*; Michael Maggiotto and Eugene Wittkopf, "American Attitudes Towards Foreign Policy," *International Studies Quarterly* 25 (1981): 601–631; and the symposium on beliefs, opinions, and American foreign policy in *International Studies Quarterly* 30 (1986): 373–484.
7. See the analysis in Holsti and Rosenau, *American Leadership in World Affairs*.
8. Robert Legvold, "The Revolution in Soviet Foreign Policy," *Foreign Affairs* 68 (1989): 82–98.
9. Charles Gati, "Eastern Europe on Its Own," *Foreign Affairs* 68 (1989): 99–119.
10. This account is based on Stephen Gilbert, *Soviet Images of America* (New York: Crane, Russak, 1977).
11. David Holloway, "Gorbachev's New Thinking," *Foreign Affairs* 68 (1989): 66–82.
12. For treatments of Marxism-Leninism that employ the operational-code approach, see Nathan Leites, *A Study of Bolshevism* (Glencoe, Ill.: Free Press, 1953); Alexander George, "The 'Operational Code': A Neglected Approach to the Study of Political Leaders and Decision Making." *International Studies Quarterly* 13 (1969): 190–222; and Joseph Nogee and Robert Donaldson, *Soviet Foreign Policy Since WW II*, 3rd ed. (New York: Pergamon, 1988).
13. Freeman Dyson, "On Russians and Their Views on Nuclear Strategy," in Charles W. Kegley and Eugene R. Wittkopf, eds., *The Nuclear Reader: Strategies, Weapons, War* (New York: St. Martin's, 1985), pp. 97–99.
14. Quoted in Gordon Smith, *Soviet Politics: Continuity and Contradiction* (New York: St. Martin's, 1988), p. 7.
15. Ken Booth, "Soviet Defense Policy," In John Baylis, et al., eds., *Contemporary Strategy: Theories and Policies* (New York: Holmes & Meier, 1975), p. 219.
16. George F. Kennan, *Memoirs* (New York: Bantam, 1967), p. 599.

17. These views are outlined in Lawrence Caldwell and Alexander Dallin, "U.S. Policy Toward the Soviet Union," in Kenneth Oye, et al., eds., *Eagle Entangled: U.S. Foreign Policy in a Complex World* (New York: Longman, 1979), pp. 199–227. The terminology used there is somewhat different.

18. Allen Whiting, "Foreign Policy of China," in Roy Macridis, ed., *Foreign Policy in World Politics*, 7th ed. (Englewood Cliffs, N.J.: Prentice-Hall, 1989), pp. 251–297.

19. James C. Wang, *Contemporary Chinese Politics: An Introduction* (Englewood Cliffs, N.J.: Prentice-Hall, 1980), pp. 43–64.

20. For a discussion of Maoist thought and its relationship to Marxism-Leninism, see Lucian Pye, *China, an Introduction*, 2d ed. (Boston: Little, Brown, 1978), pp. 189–213.

21. Wang, *Contemporary Chinese Politics*, pp. 242–248.

22. Allen Whiting, "Foreign Policy of China," p. 268.

23. Frederick Hartmann, *The Relations of Nations*, 6th ed. (New York: Macmillan, 1983), pp. 584–585.

24. Robert North, *The Foreign Relations of China*, 2d ed. (Encino, Calif.: Dickenson, 1974), p. 51.

25. Wang, *Contemporary Chinese Politics*, pp. 236–242.

26. Michel Oksenberg, "China's Confident Nationalism," *Foreign Affairs* 65 (1987): 501–523.

27. Mohammed Ayoob, "The Third World in the System of States: Acute Schizophrenia or Growing Pains?" *International Studies Quarterly* 33, no. 1 (March 1989), 67–80.

28. Paul Cammack, David Pool, and William Tordoff, *Third World Politics* (Baltimore: Johns Hopkins University Press), 1988.

29. Bahgat Korany, "Coming of Age Against Global Odds," in Bahgat Korany, ed., *How Foreign Policy Decisions Are Made in the Third World: A Comparative Analysis* (Boulder, Colo.: Westview Press, 1984), p. 11.

30. Robert Hardgrave, *India: Government and Politics in a Developing Nation* (New York: Harcourt Brace Jovanovich, 1980), p. 238.

31. Ayoob, "The Third World in the System of States," pp. 72–73.

32. Stephen Krasner, *Defending the National Interest* (Princeton, N.J.: Princeton University Press).

33. Krasner, *Defending the National Interest*, p. 560.

34. Krasner, *Defending the National Interest*, pp. 20–30.

Chapter
5

The International System

Analysts do not agree on what factors are most important for explaining a state's behavior. For some, key foreign-policy decisions are best explained in terms of the personality or perceptions of individual policymakers. Others stress the influence of interest groups, types of governments, or economic considerations. Still others argue that state actions can best be understood in terms of the constraints and imperatives created by conditions beyond state borders. A shorthand term for these forces is *the international system*. The idea of a system is borrowed from the natural sciences, in which it is used to indicate that the fates of certain objects are linked together. The ecological chain of life is an example of a system that brings order and meaning to what otherwise would appear to be a series of unrelated events and objects.

So it is with world politics. At first glance, the global environment in which states act appears to be made up of a bewildering array of nonconnected events and forces: a coup d'etat in Nigeria; the destruction of the Amazon rain forest; a global grain shortage; East Germans fleeing to West Germany with the help of Hungary; government attacks on student protesters in China; and Palestinian rioting in the West Bank. However, upon closer examination, a different picture begins to emerge. Events are not totally random. World politics is not a game or a struggle conducted under conditions of absolute anarchy. Patterns and regularities do exist. While not all events and happenings in the global environment are linked together by some grand logic—accidents do happen, and chance does play a role in world politics—it is possible for us to establish in advance the impact that certain types of events will have on other parts of the international system. Let us consider the Korean War.

THE KOREAN WAR

At dawn, June 25, 1950, over 100,000 North Korean troops crossed the thirty-eighth parallel and invaded South Korea. Caught by surprise, South Korean troops and their American advisors offered only ineffective resistance. By 9:00 A.M., the ancient Korean capital of Kaesong had fallen and the South Korean capital of Seoul was being bombed by North Korean planes. So great was the level of unpreparedness on the part of the South Koreans that a real danger existed that they would run out of ammunition as they tried to halt the North Korean attack. Nevertheless, the attack was not "a bolt from out of the blue." Tensions had been rising on both the regional and the global level since mid-1948. In the first six months of 1949, some 400 North Korean border violations were reported, along with several hundred guerrilla skirmishes inside South Korea. Already in 1950 the Soviet Union had begun to boycott United Nations Security Council meetings over the continued membership of Taiwan and the failure to seat Communist China. Reports were also circulating that the Chinese had begun to send aid to the Vietminh, who were fighting the French in Indochina.

The reasons for the attack are still debated. Possible explanations run from a probing action by Stalin against the West (generally held as the most likely explanation) to a decision made independently by North Korea (judged as the least likely explanation).[1] Regardless of why it occurred, the North Korean attack produced a quick two-pronged response by the United States. The first line of action involved mobilizing the United Nations. At the request of the United States, an emergency meeting of the Security Council was convened the morning of the attack (New York time). The Soviet Union continued its boycott of these meetings, and by evening a Security Council resolution was passed calling for North Korea to remove its forces from the South and for the immediate establishment of a cease-fire. A two-day adjournment was also agreed to, in order to allow delegates to receive instructions from their governments over exactly what the UN's response should be. On Tuesday, June 27, 1950, the Security Council reconvened and passed a resolution calling upon member states to furnish "such assistance to the Republic of Korea as may be necessary to repel the armed attack and to restore international peace and security in the area." On July 7, the Security Council voted to establish a Unified Command under the leadership of the United States. This arrangement accurately reflected the pattern of military aid made available by UN members. The United States contributed 50 percent of the ground forces, 86 percent of the naval forces, and 93 percent of the air forces. South Korea contributed 40 percent of the ground forces, 7 percent of the naval forces, and 6 percent of the air forces.

The second line of action involved sending unilateral U.S. military aid to South Korea. On the evening of the attack, President Truman met with his advisors and agreed to send arms and supplies to South Korea, to evacuate U.S. dependents, and to place the Seventh Fleet in the Formosa Straits in order to seal off Taiwan from China. The following day, General Douglas MacArthur, Commander of United States forces in the Far East, was authorized to provide South Korea with limited military assistance. On June 30, MacArthur's instructions were broadened to the point at which he could give South Korea as much help as he felt necessary, provided that he left enough forces in reserve to protect Japan from an attack.

The North Korean attack was not easily stopped. It was not until September that UN forces were able to go on the offensive, and then it was possible only because MacArthur gambled and landed a portion of his forces behind enemy lines at Inchon, thus catching North Korean forces in a pincer movement. So successful was MacArthur's strategy that, by early October, U.S. troops were crossing the thirty-eighth parallel and entering North Korea. With the acquiescence of the United Nations, U.S. goals were now redefined as the unification of Korea. For that purpose, President Truman authorized MacArthur to send his forces into North Korea, provided that neither China nor the Soviet Union entered the war. Optimism ran high among U.S. officials, because they believed that victory was near. In November, the final offensive began. Instead of a quick victory, there occurred the longest retreat in American military history. On November 27, over 200,000 Chinese forces counterattacked and drove the UN troops out of North Korea and all the way down to the tip of the Korean peninsula. While the Chinese counterattack had been unanticipated, it had not come without warning. The Chinese had signaled both by words and deeds that they felt threatened by the advancing UN forces and would not permit the challenge to go unmet. On October 10, the Chinese Foreign Ministry warned that "now that American forces are attempting to cross the 38th parallel on a large scale, the Chinese people cannot stand idly by." On October 26, Chinese forces launched a surprise attack against UN forces, and they followed with an even larger attack on November 1. As the year ended, MacArthur's staff was making plans for the evacuation of Korea. MacArthur called for drastic action. He recommended using Chinese Nationalist forces in Korea, allowing the Chinese Nationalists to launch a diversionary attack on China, an air and naval bombardment of China, and a blockade off the Chinese coast. Truman rejected these proposals, because he wanted to keep the Korean War limited in scope. Conflict between Truman and MacArthur was temporarily averted, since the UN forces were able to hold their positions and mount a counterattack. By March 1951, they had once again reached the thirty-eighth parallel. Truman and MacArthur held opposing views on how to proceed from that point of advantage. Truman favored pursuing a negotiated settlement, while MacArthur favored a strategy based on dictating surrender terms coupled with slightly veiled threats of further military action. Eventually, Truman came to regard MacArthur's public questioning of his preferred line of action as "open defiance of the president," and, on April 5, 1951, relieved MacArthur of his command. In June 1951, truce talks began at Kaesong. In July 1953, an armistice was finally signed.

For our purposes in this chapter, what is important here is the logic that seems to have driven the responses of both American and Chinese officials to the pending military gains of their adversaries. Both sides, although cautious and limited in their initial moves, felt that they had no choice but to deny the other a military victory.

Prior to the North Korean attack, neither the words nor the actions of U.S. officials suggested that South Korea was a place in which the United States would fight a war. In a major foreign-policy address in January 1950, Secretary of State Dean Acheson defined the U.S. defense perimeter in the Far East as including "the Aleutians, Japan, the Ryukus, and the Philippines." Acheson went on to say that other areas were expected to defend themselves, pending the arrival of United Nations support.[2] General MacArthur made similar comments in 1949. U.S. military support for South Korea was also minimal. By June 1950, only $1,000 of an appropriated $10 million for fiscal year 1950 (due to end June 30) had arrived in South Korea. Yet, once the North Korean attack began, U.S. policymakers were united in their belief that an American response was necessary. The United States moved quickly to involve the United Nations, and President Truman stated that he was not going to let the attack succeed and that the United States was going to "hit them hard."

Less information is available concerning China's decision to counterattack in November 1951, but here too, it appears that Chinese leaders changed their minds about the need to use military force. From the outset, the Chinese recognized the importance of the Korean peninsula to China's security. When the war began, they expected a quick North Korean victory that would not require their military involvement. As stalemate set in, Chinese public pronouncements still did not give any indication that it was considering intervening. It was only when UN forces began preparing to cross the thirty-eighth parallel that China began issuing warnings. The failure of Soviet diplomacy at the UN to arrange for a diplomatic solution to the war and the inability of the North Korean army to stop the northward movement of UN forces appeared to have convinced the Chinese leaders that "it was absolutely necessary to prove the willingness of the bloc to risk general war in order to preserve established Communist regimes."[3] The alternative of U.S. dominance over all of Korea and a Washington-Tokyo-Seoul military alliance pointing at China's industrial area of Manchuria was considered to be unacceptable.

International Systems and World Politics

During the Korean War, U.S. and Chinese policymakers were responding to what they perceived to be demands placed upon them by the structure of the international system. In a very real sense, they felt that they had no choice but to go to war. Clearly, this was incorrect. Policymakers always have a choice regarding what course of action to take or whether to do anything at all. Yet, the logic of international-system analysis suggests that their fears were not totally without merit and that the failure to act on them would have jeopardized their state's national security. Not going to war might have allowed the enemy to gain a significant and perhaps permanent advantage over them. The net result would have been to transform radically the national security problem currently facing the United States or China and to change the terms under which future foreign-policy decisions would have to be made. For China, it would have meant having a hostile pro-U.S. ally as a neighbor. Not only would this have denied it a defensive buffer zone along one of its borders, but also it would have called into question any future hopes of establishing China as a regional superpower. The danger for the United States was that a Chinese success might invite further "limited attacks" on its allies in Asia or Europe. Were this to happen, the United States' reputation as a superpower capable of protecting its allies' would be seriously damaged. Additionally, should too many of its allies fall, the United States might also have to fight a major war in order to protect its security interests and to reestablish itself as a dominant world power.

The challenge that policymakers face is to identify correctly the aspects of the international system that place the greatest constraints on the state's behavior. The most frequently cited system characteristics are the distribution of power and the pattern of interaction among the major actors. Based on these features, "rules" for survival can be formulated to guide their actions. System rules may take the shape of formally spelled out declarations of international law or treaty obligations, or informally agreed upon ways of conducting foreign relations. Rules are established in one of two ways. First, rules may be formulated by examining earlier international systems (such as those in existence during the period of the Chou Dynasty, Renaissance Italy, and the Greek city-states) to see how system members who operated under like conditions behaved, and then a judgment can be made as to whether those actions contributed to the prosperity and survival of that actor.[4] Second, rules may be arrived at by looking at the logical implications that a particular distribution of power holds for system members and then translating those findings into rules. As our discussion will show, regardless of how it is done, a certain inconsistency results. Sometimes the rules read like descriptive statements (states *do* this), and at other times they read like prescriptive statements (states *should* do this).

Note that the rules of an international system are dependent in large part upon the distribution of power in the system. If the distribution of power in the international system changes, the rules for survival change as well. Actions that will protect the national security interests of a state in one type of international system may not do so under another. Lawrence Eagleberger, a retired career foreign-service officer who has held a series of important Defense and State Department positions since the late 1960s, was alluding to this when he argued in a 1989 article that "the beginning of wisdom for Americans, and for America's friends and allies, is to recognize that we are leaving the atypical period of a bipolar world . . . and returning to a more traditional and complicated time of multipolarity." He goes on to note that "the transitional period through which we are now passing is itself the author of substantial problems and makes a creative Western response to a host of other challenges more difficult" and that the United States "will of necessity play a lesser role" in the decades ahead.[5]

Left unanswered by these observations but addressed by Eagleberger in his article are the questions of what type(s) of power and power relationships are changing and why. Realist writers emphasize the distribution of military power, while dependency theorists and globalists stress the central role of nonmilitary factors in world politics. We will provide examples of how each approach has been used to organize thinking about the nature of the international system and the type of constraints that each places on state behavior.

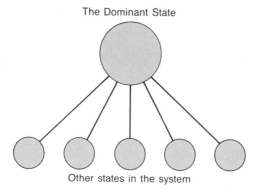
The Dominant State

Other states in the system

Figure 5.1 A unipolar system (Solid lines indicate primary interactive links in the system.).

TYPES OF INTERNATIONAL SYSTEMS BASED UPON THE DISTRIBUTION OF MILITARY POWER

Unipolarity

In a unipolar system, all power is concentrated in one place. The principal forms of interaction and communication run vertically from the dominant state downward to the weaker states and are controlled by it. Significant autonomous contacts between the weaker states are relatively few in number. A graphic depiction of a unipolar system is found in Figure 5.1. By definition, true defensive alliances are not present in a unipolar system. The dominant state has no need for an alliance, because it can impose its will upon all others in the system. For the same reason, alliances do not offer the weaker states any added degree of protection from the dominant state. Individually and collectively, their governments run the risk of ruin if they adopt policies that displease the dominant state.

There are very few examples of unipolar systems, which suggests that it is extremely difficult to bring such a system into existence. While the great disparity of power in a unipolar system makes it very stable, the system is not impervious to the forces of change. The dominant state thus needs to take great care in exercising its power, so that it does not inadvertently set in motion forces that will undermine its position of strength. Just because it is capable of destroying the weaker members of the system does not mean it is in the interest of the dominant state to do so. Based on the historical analysis of previous unipolar systems and the logic of its structure, observers have identified "rules" to help the dominant state select the "correct" policy option:

1. Seek to maintain or increase one's power.
2. Insist on the status quo regarding the distribution of power in the system.
3. Respond to probes or challenges to one's power with restraint.[6]

The Holy Roman Empire and China in the Western Chou period (1122–771 B.C.) are examples of two international systems that generally are acknowledged as being unipolar. One observer suggests that Europe during 1871–1890 can also be seen as unipolar, and some consider the period immediately following World War II to be unipolar because of the American monopoly of the atomic bomb and the ruinous state of the European, Soviet, and Japanese economies.[7] More typically, however, the early post-World War II international system is considered to be bipolar.

The closest post-World War II approximations to unipolar systems have occurred in two regional systems: Latin America and Eastern Europe. As we noted earlier, the fit between the real world and a model of it is never perfect, but, especially from the late 1940s through the early 1970s, the international politics of both regions conformed closely to the rules of unipolarity. The United States and Soviet Union, the two dominant states, were able to impose their will upon the weaker states in each regional system. The Soviet Union sent troops into East Germany (1963), Hungary (1956), and Czechoslovakia (1968) to bring wayward governments back into line or to put down domestic unrest. The United States helped to engineer the overthrow of the Arbenz government in Guatemala (1956) and that of Salvador Allende in Chile (1973), and sent troops to the Dominican Republic (1965). Alliances can be found in each region: the Rio Pact and the Organization of American States in Latin America, and the Warsaw Treaty Organization and the Council For Mutual Economic Assistance (COMECON) in Eastern Europe. These are symbolic alliances designed to legitimize the preeminent position of the dominant state and to make it easier for that state to exercise its control over the system. They have neither provided any meaningful consultation among the members of the system nor controlled the actions of the superpower. In each case, the major deviation from true unipolarity is the presence of a state that openly and successfully challenges the dominant position of the superpower. In Latin America, this state has been Cuba, and, in Eastern Europe, it has been Yugoslavia. Until recently, however, the United States and the Soviet Union have been successful in isolating these states within their regions and preventing others from following their example.

Bipolarity

In a bipolar system, power is evenly concentrated at two opposing poles. Around each pole exists a tightly knit and hierarchically organized alliance system. Members of the two alliance systems have virtually no meaningful contacts with each other that are not controlled or directed by the bloc leaders. Figure 5.2 presents a graphic description of a bipolar system. Because of this distribution of power, each of the two dominant states regards the other as an adversary that must be kept in check at all times. In failing to do so, by allowing the other superpower to gain a power advantage, a state runs the risk of placing itself in a position of permanent inferiority—and hence, domination—because there are no other states in the system that are powerful enough to help it preserve its independence. Counteraction thus becomes inevitable. Every potential gain on the part of one's opponent must be rebuffed or compensated through gains of one's own. The conflicting logic inherent in a bipolar system makes neutrality of any significance impossible for states. Neither superpower can be sure that a neutral state will remain neutral should conflict break

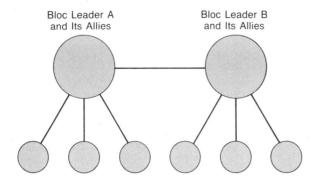

Figure 5.2 A bipolar system (Solid lines indicate primary interactive links in the system.).

out. The prudent course of action is to bring that state into one's own bloc before the enemy tries to do so. The essential rules for a bipolar system can be summarized as follows:

1. A bloc must increase its capabilities compared to those of the opposing bloc.
2. A bloc must engage in a major war rather than permit the rival bloc to achieve a position of preponderance.
3. A bloc must seek to eliminate the rival bloc.
4. A bloc must negotiate rather than fight, fight a minor war rather than a major war, and fight a major war rather than fail to eliminate the rival bloc.[8]

Examples of bipolar systems can be found in ancient China, in the Greek city-state system, with Athens and Sparta being the two poles, as well as in nineteenth-century Europe. Most observers classify the early post-World War II era as bipolar. The cold-war competition between the United States and the Soviet Union of drawing lines around the world through the creation of alliance systems is very much in accordance with the rules of bipolarity. So, too, is the absence of neutrality. It was only at the 1955 Bandung Conference that the idea of neutrality in the East-West struggle was raised as a viable course of action for the emerging Third World states. The actions of the United States and China in the Korean War were also in accord with the rules of bipolarity. No matter how unimportant U.S. policymakers felt South Korea was to U.S. security interests, once it was attacked, the logic of bipolarity demanded a response. Similarly, as long as the U.S. goal was only to reestablish the status quo, the communist bloc could stand on the sidelines, but, once the stated goal became unification, the rules of bipolarity demanded that the communists take counteraction.

Loose Bipolarity

In a loose bipolar system, power remains concentrated in two opposing and competing poles around which alliance systems form. The fundamental dynamics of the system also remain unchanged as each superpower continues to view the other with

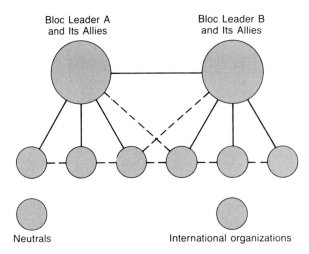

Bloc Leader A
and Its Allies

Bloc Leader B
and Its Allies

Neutrals

International organizations

Figure 5.3 A loose bipolar system (Solid lines indicate primary interactive links in the system. Dashed lines indicate emergence of new paths of interaction in a loose bipolar system.).

suspicion and counters any move that it might take. Loose bipolarity differs from tight bipolarity in the lessened ability of the two superpowers to control their allies and, as a consequence, in the reduced desirability of competing for additional allies. Hierarchically organized blocs have given way to alliances in which the secondary powers can successfully challenge the position of the bloc leader and seek out contacts on their own with members of the other alliance system.

Neutrality is a real policy option for states in a loose bipolar system. Forced by the logic of bipolarity to continue to oppose each other but faced with the increased costs and reduced benefits of leadership, the two superpowers do not automatically view claims of neutrality with the same suspicion as they did in a tight bipolar system. True neutrality on the part of a state can serve both their interests by removing it as an area of competition. For similar reasons, universal-member international organizations now become prominent actors. Given the constraints of loose bipolarity, these organizations present the bloc leaders with a potentially low-cost way of exercising their influence on the fringes of the system. Figure 5.3 presents a graphic depiction of a loose bipolar system.

The rules for a loose bipolar system are far more complex than those for bipolarity. Not only must the two superpowers deal with two additional types of actors (neutrals and universal-member international organizations), but variation in the structure of the alliance systems is also possible. Complicating matters further, rules are needed to guide the actions of neutrals and the universal-member international organizations. Only by obeying these rules can neutral states and international organizations hope to play active and independent roles in the international politics of a loose bipolar system. Here we will only present the essential rules for the superpowers in a loose bipolar system. These rules are in addition to the ones specified for the superpowers in the bipolar system:

1. A bloc must attempt to increase its membership but tolerate the actions of nonmembers if nontolerance might drive that state into the enemy's bloc.
2. A bloc must keep the objectives of the universal-member international organization secondary to its own objectives, while trying to subordinate the goals of the rival bloc to those of the international organization.[9]

Most observers hold that the post-World War II international system during the 1960s and 1970s had become loose bipolar. With increasing frequency, large numbers of Third World states were now declaring themselves to be neutral in the East-West struggle between the United States and the Soviet Union. Following the Sino-Soviet split in 1956, China could no longer be considered to be a subservient ally of the Soviet Union. Strains also became plentiful within NATO, centering largely around the issue of burden sharing. Because the United States was becoming even more deeply involved in Vietnam, the United States wanted its European allies to pay a larger percentage of the cost of defending the alliance. The European allies were reluctant to do so. Many of them doubted the wisdom of the Vietnam War effort. There also existed a feeling that the United States was excluding them from key decisions within NATO and that it did not appreciate the political costs the European states were incurring by allowing large numbers of U.S. forces and missiles to be based on their territory. The high-water mark in this European reluctance to support U.S. defense initiatives came when France withdrew from the military structure of NATO. European states, led by France and West Germany, also began pursuing cooperative commercial and cultural contacts with East European states at a time when neither the United States nor the Soviet Union was officially endorsing such moves.

Multipolarity

Mobility and flexibility replace confrontation and counteraction as the key words in a multipolar system. In a multipolar system, there are at least five major poles, all of which are relatively equal in power. The large number of poles and the even distribution of power between them means that the identity of friends and foes is not determined in advance by the structure of the system. Any pole is as much a potential friend as it is a potential enemy. The particular alignment of forces in existence at any time will depend upon the specific issue being contested. Alliances are formed to deal with issues as they arise and are dissolved when the security threat has passed. Moreover, with the ideological differences between poles held to be of secondary importance to the need to maintain flexibility in selecting alliance partners, challenges in the system and imbalances of power are not seen as irreversible. They are treated more as problems to be managed to a successful conclusion, a process facilitated by the trust built up by the past cooperative ventures that all poles have engaged in at one time or another. Neither neutral states nor universal-member international organizations play significant roles in a multipolar system. The absence

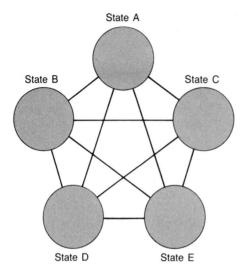

Figure 5.4 A multipolar system (Solid lines indicate primary interactive links in the system.).

of intense ideological conflict between two warring blocs leaves states little to be neutral toward, and the ability of the major actors to form alliances to solve particular problems robs permanent international organizations of much of their purpose in the international system. Figure 5.4 presents a graphic depiction of the structure of a multipolar system. The rules that the five major powers should follow in conducting their foreign policy in such a system are as follows:

1. They should increase their capabilities but negotiate rather than fight.
2. They should fight rather than pass up an opportunity to increase their capabilities.
3. They should stop fighting before they eliminate one of the other major states.
4. They should permit a defeated major state to reenter the system as an acceptable alliance partner or elevate a secondary state to major state status to take its place.
5. They should act to oppose any state or coalition of states that tries to assume a position of predominance within the system.
6. They should act to constrain actors whose foreign policy is based on the realization of some unlimited or utopian vision of world order instead of the pursuit of narrowly defined national goals. [10]

The most famous multipolar system was the balance-of-power system that existed in Europe from the end of the Napoleonic Wars in 1815 until the outbreak of World War I in 1914. The five major powers were Great Britain, Austria-Hungary, Prussia, Russia, and France. The unique characteristic of this system was the manner in which Great Britain worked to create a balance by shifting its power from alliance to alliance so that no side gained a dominant position on the continent. World War I destroyed the balance-of-power system, and it was not until the 1930s that a new and global multipolar system began to take shape. Its major actors were Great Britain, France, Russia, Germany (the successor to Prussia), the United States, and Japan. This system proved to be short-lived. Its swift decline occurred because the major states failed to follow the rules of multipolarity. At a minimum, the unwillingness or inability of the other major states to take early steps to stop Hitler violated rules 5 and 6.

THE PRESENT AND FUTURE INTERNATIONAL SYSTEM

Systems do matter. The conflicts in Korea and Vietnam, the invasion of Czechoslovakia, and aid for the Contras in Nicaragua all make sense in the context of a bipolar system, in which there is no such thing as a small, isolated war. Any potential gain of the opposing power must be countered or negated. Failure to do so raises the prospect of setting off a series of falling dominos as ally after ally is defeated. These same undertakings do not make sense if the system is multipolar. Because no setback is irreversible, the superpower does not need to involve itself in every conflict. Over time, the loss of Vietnam would have been compensated for by either the defection of a communist ally (Afghanistan?) or by subsequent actions taken by the Vietnamese to assert their independence from Moscow or Beijing.

The problem today facing policymakers who want to follow "the rules" is that the current international system does not fit into any of the categories that we have identified so far. Elements of bipolarity and multipolarity are present, yet neither model alone can be said to capture the essence of the current situation. On the one hand, this is not surprising, since our system models are "ideal types" and will never perfectly match up with reality. On the other hand, the combined presence of vast numbers of nuclear and conventional weapons and national economies under stress heightens our sensitivity to the consequences of following the wrong set of rules. These concerns lay behind the feeling of unease that many had over superpower maneuvering in the Persian Gulf region in the late 1980s. Should the rules of bipolarity be followed because United States and Soviet geopolitical interests are directly at stake, or should multipolar rules be adhered to because the conflict so directly touches on the price and supply of oil? The fact that the current international system does not fit into any one of our previously discussed categories leads to the important question of where it is going. One possibility is that one of the four traditional types of international systems will surface. A second possibility is that an entirely new type of international system will emerge. An additional concern is how we will get to wherever it is that we are going. We will conclude our discussion of international systems organized in terms of the distribution of military power by addressing these questions.

Tripolarity

A tripolar system has three relatively equal poles. Such a system might come into existence if the power of the United States and the Soviet Union should decline relative to other states and if the power of China were to increase significantly. Respect for spheres of influence and limited foreign-policy goals should characterize the foreign policies of the three major powers. There also would be no need to counter each gain made by one of the other poles, because the third pole is always available as an ally. The primary danger to be avoided in a tripolar system is diplomatic isolation.[11] The best way that the powers can ensure that this does not happen is to avoid foreign-policy undertakings that would force the other two poles into a counteralliance. The Soviet invasion of Afghanistan is an example of what should not be done. It served as a stumbling block to improved Sino-Soviet relations and pushed China into closer relations with the United States. One observer has suggested the following as rules for a tripolar system:

1. The existence of an "adversary number one" leads to "objective collusion" with number two.
2. Each of the three players should aim to reduce collusion between the others to a minimum.
3. At the same time, it is in the interests of each to bluff or blackmail its chief adversary by threatening collusion with the other.
4. The surest way for any one of the three to provoke the other two into collusion is to display undue aggressiveness.[12]

A Unit Veto System

A unit veto system takes as its point of departure the universal, or near universal, spread of nuclear weapons among all major political actors in the international system to the point at which each can threaten the destruction of any attacker, even though it cannot guarantee its own survival. To survive as a "pole," actors must be prepared to resist all threats made against them and to retaliate when attacked. As a consequence, a unit veto system is a standoff system in which virtually no changes in the status quo are possible. Universal-member international organizations are nonexistent. There are few peaceful international transactions for such a body to facilitate, and actors see little use for it in advancing their own security interests. Actors rely on their own nuclear arsenal to "veto" developments that they find to be threatening. The rules for a unit veto system might look as follows:

1. All nuclear powers must resist threats and retaliate if they are attacked.
2. All nuclear powers must engage in military action rather than refuse to use force.[13]

HOW SYSTEMS CHANGE

We can follow two different strategies when we are dealing with the occurrence of changing systems. Both will be used here. The more conservative approach develops a checklist of questions that need to be asked in addressing the topic. The second, and more ambitious, approach develops a theory that explains systems change.

Systems Change: A Checklist Approach

A systems change checklist contains at least five questions. The first of these is, "Where is the source of the change located?" Does it arise from within the boundaries of the system, or is its origin external to it? Many believe that a truly global international system is a relatively recent phenomenon, brought about by advances in communication, transportation, and economic and military technologies. In this view, regional systems (Europe, Latin America, the Far East, etc.) have been far more common throughout history. Others, who view international systems change from the perspective of recurring long cycles, see that there is a global layering to world politics, whose roots go back to the fifteenth and sixteenth centuries. For example, George Modelski argues that five "long cycles" of international politics can be identified beginning in 1494, each of which lasted approximately 100 years:[14]

Time period	Leading power
1. 1494–1580	Portugal
2. 1580–1688	the Netherlands
3. 1688–1792	Great Britain
4. 1792–1914	Great Britain
5. 1914–2000	the United States

The second is, "What is the rate of change?" Is change slow and gradual, or does it come about in a sudden episodic burst? The Russian and French Revolutions are examples of sudden and unexpected events that led to systems change. The dismantling of the French and British colonial empires after World War II are examples of a slower process of change.

The third question is, "What is the underlying cause of the change?" Economic problems, a lack of societal agreement on the goals of a state's foreign policy, and government instability are among the many factors that may prevent an actor from obeying the rules of the system and thereby set in motion the process of systems change. A particularly important underlying cause of change in the contemporary international system is the unprecedented pace of technological innovation that has created a lag between the consequences of technological change and the ability of governments and international organizations to manage those effects.[15]

The fourth question is, "What is the immediate catalyst for the change?" While the underlying causes of systems change are many and are often present in combination, the most frequent immediate catalyst of systems change is war. The central role that war plays in our thinking about how international systems operate is evident in the fact that we tend to designate historical epochs by the wars that were taking place. It also creates an interesting potential problem for those seeking to prevent wars. If wars play a key role in the process of systems change, and if wars do not occur, how will systems change? Can a functional equivalent for war be found—something that will allow systems to change without war's negative consequences?[16]

The fifth question is, "What direction is the change taking?" Is it leading to the creation of a new system, or is it leaving chaos in its wake? There is nothing automatic about systems change. The decay of a bipolar system does not have to lead to the establishment of a loose bipolar one. Systems also do not move in an orderly progression from one type to another. Not only is it possible for systems to be in a state of transition, as appears to be the case today, but also it is possible that the fall of a system may be followed by anarchy, as when the Holy Roman Empire fell and Europe lapsed into a period that was known as the Dark Ages.

Systems Change: A Theoretical Explanation

One of the most prominent lines of investigation into the phenomenon of systems change centers on the rise and fall of hegemonic, or dominant, powers. The reasons for the decline of the hegemonic position of the world powers are many. Robert Gilpin suggests that they center on the changing distribution of costs and benefits experienced by the dominant state as its rule over the international system advances.[17] In order to bring more resources under its control, powerful states seek to expand their control over territory and their influence over the international economy. The problem is that over time the costs of controlling territory and organizing and running the international economy grow more rapidly than does the capacity of the dominant state to allocate funds for supporting the status quo.

On the domestic scene, the tendency is for less and less of society's wealth to be reinvested in the economy. As a society ages, more and more of its national income is spent on the consumption of goods and services. The result is an aging and growing obsolescence of its economic infrastructure. Compounding matters further is the tendency for the cost of the most advanced military technology to rise rapidly, thus making the exercise of military power a doubly expensive undertaking. It demands a large investment of funds for research and development at a time when comparatively little is available for such purposes, and it is costly to replace equipment lost in battle.

On the international scene, the costs of leadership are heightened by two factors. One of these factors is the free-rider problem. Having assumed responsibility for military security, the dominant state benefits most from the distribution of prestige, power, and rules. Other states realize this and are in a position to shirk their responsibilities for system or alliance maintenance since they know that, because the dominant state benefits so much from the status quo, it will have to act on its own to preserve the existing order. Thus, France, knowing that the United States will still have to protect it, can withdraw from NATO, or Japan, certain that the United States will provide military security, can invest its resources in its economy. The second factor is a result of the rapidly growing power of the secondary states, which is brought on by the inevitable diffusion of technology to its military opponents and economic competitors.

Gilpin argues that a state or a group of states will only contest the international status quo when they believe the benefits of doing so exceed the costs. An increasing difficulty of the dominant state in meeting its obligations creates such an occasion for the secondary states. The hegemonic state is left with two options in meeting this challenge. The preferred course of action is to allocate more resources to its foreign policy. This means either increasing taxes or improving the efficiency of its economy, both of which are difficult to accomplish. The second option is to reduce its foreign-policy commitments without undermining the structure of the system. The Nixon Doctrine, détente with the Soviet Union, and the establishment of relations with China can all be seen as examples of attempts by the United States to reduce the cost of its world leadership by cutting down the number of threats against which it must defend itself. The danger of this second strategy is that what the dominant state intends as a prudent consolidation of power is seen by others as appeasement and a loss of will. Rather than preserving its leadership, this strategy may only invite additional challenges, thus setting the stage for a global war.

INTERDEPENDENCE

As we have noted previously, not all observers of world politics accept the realist emphasis on conflict and the primacy of military power. Constraints also come from the interdependence of states. A perspective on the interdependence of states takes as its starting point the fact that, by definition, all the parts (members) of a system are interconnected. The actions of any state, whether it is imposing a tariff, signing a peace treaty, giving foreign aid, or building a new weapons system, create potential opportunities and challenges for the other members of the system. The fundamental foreign-policy problem for any policymaker is to construct a foreign policy that allows the state to gain the maximum benefit from its international exchanges while minimizing the negative costs. If states were able to retreat into isolationism or self-sufficiency whenever the costs of dealing with others became too great, then there would be no reason to study the effect that interaction patterns have on world politics and state behavior, but they cannot. Furthermore, while some members of the system will experience far greater difficulty than others in either exploiting or coping with this interconnectedness, all will experience some sense of "not being in control" of their own destiny. It is this combination of interconnectedness, plus loss of control, that is the hallmark of interdependence.

Cost and benefits are not necessarily distributed equally, and it is the existence of asymmetries in cost and benefits that allows some members to exercise power over others in an interdependent world. The costs of interdependence can be grouped under two headings: sensitivity and vulnerability costs. Sensitivity costs refer to how quickly changes in one country bring about costly changes in another and how costly those changes are. Vulnerability costs refer to the disadvantages suffered by a state, even after it has changed its policies to try and cope with the actions of another state.

Much as earlier writers on world politics used the phrase "balance of power" without giving it concrete or consistent meaning, contemporary commentators have used the term "interdependence" in a variety of ways. A balance of power has been used to refer to the structure of the international system (a balance-of-power system); a situation in which power is distributed evenly (a balance of power exists); a situation in which one side has an advantage over the other (the balance of power favors state

A over state B); and a situation in which the distribution of power is in flux (the balance of power is shifting in favor of state A).[18] In the case of interdependence, some treat it as an inescapable feature of contemporary world politics, while others see it as the joint product of trends in world politics and foreign-policy decisions. A second point of dispute is whether, by definition, interdependence involves only instances in which harmony and mutual gain prevail or whether it is possible for conflict to be present as well.

To cut through this conceptual confusion, Robert Keohane and Joseph Nye have put forward an ideal model of "complex interdependence."[19] In doing so, they stress that they are not attempting to describe interdependence as it exists, but to conduct a thought experiment about what an interdependent world would look like if it existed. In their view, complex interdependence has three main characteristics.

1. Multiple channels connect societies. Not only are state-to-state relations (interstate relations) present, but also important transgovernmental and transnational relations exist. Transgovernmental relations refers to situations in which parts of a government (such as Congress or the CIA) become important independent international actors in their own right and interact with other societies. Transnational relations refers to situations in which one of the actors is not a state. It might be an international organization, a multinational corporation, or a nonstate actor, such as a terrorist group.

2. There is no clear or consistent hierarchy of issues on the policy agenda, and the distinction between domestic and foreign policy becomes blurred. Most importantly, military issues do not consistently dominate over all others.

3. Military force is not used by governments against other governments within the region or on issues in which complex interdependence prevails. It still may be used outside of this context.

These three defining features of complex interdependence establish the underlying framework within which states interact. That framework finds concrete expression in a network of formal and informal procedures, rules, and institutions that regulate and control international interactions. Collectively, these governing arrangements are referred to as *international regimes.*[20]

International Regimes

Analysis of international regimes is a relatively recent addition to the ways in which international systems are studied, and its use holds several implications for our perceptions about how the international system shapes the behavior of its members.[21] One of the most important of these is that we need to develop a more differentiated picture of how the international system operates.

There is no single international regime in the sense that we speak of global bipolarity. Nor is there a Middle Eastern or a Latin American regime. Regimes are organized around issue areas (trade, monetary policy, oil, food) and generally have some form of institutional or legal structure to them. A state that is participating in multiple regimes will find that it must play by several different sets of rules. Complicating matters further, there are some areas of international cooperation in which no regimes exist. In some cases, this is because states do not interact with each other frequently enough to perceive a need for rules to govern their interactions. This was the case 50 years ago with regard to using oceans. The absence of a regime can also be explained when the link between cooperative behavior and self-interest is immediate and direct. Regimes come into existence when states share common interests but when their decisions, independently arrived at, fail to produce the most desirable results for the group as a whole.[22] U.S.-Soviet restraint is a form of cooperation, but it is seen as falling short of being a true regime for this reason.[23]

The International Food Regime: An Example

The international food regime began to take shape in the first years after World War II, but it has only been since the 1970s that food issues have become an integral part of world politics. As recently as the 1950s and 1960s, domestic agricultural production was still not considered a matter capable of affecting the shape of world politics. In order to understand the contemporary global food system, we need (1) to identify the key foods that are exchanged internationally and (2) to look at those foods in terms of three categories: production, distribution, and consumption. A familiarity with each of these parts is necessary, because it is the way in which they interact that determines the movement and availability of food worldwide.[24]

The centerpiece of the international food regime is grain. Not only is far more arable land devoted to its production than for any other crop, but also grains are an essential food in many countries. Wheat and rice are staples in many diets, and coarse grains such as corn are both consumed directly and used to feed livestock, dairy animals, and poultry. A much higher percentage of wheat production is involved in international transactions than is the case for any of the other grains. About 20 percent of all wheat that is produced crosses international borders, as compared to only 3 or 4 percent of the world's rice production and about 15 percent of the coarse grain crop.[25] Put another way, between 1978 and 1980, about 1 in every 6 tons of wheat grown was traded internationally, as compared to approximately 1 in every 9 tons of other grains and 1 in 25 tons of rice.[26]

Production The primary factors affecting overall food production are area and yield. Because virtually all of the land suited for agriculture is already being used for this purpose, increasing global food production is very much a question of increasing yield through the application of modern technology. Few states, however, possess either the large amounts of arable land or the advanced scientific capabilities, or both, that are needed to produce large quantities of grain. Even fewer are able to provide for their own population's needs and have enough left over for the international arena. International transactions in grain are thus dominated by a few producers.

While wheat is produced around the globe, only seven states account for approximately 75 percent of the world's total wheat production. They are, in order: China, the Soviet Union, the European Community (EC), the United States, India, Canada, and Australia. World trade in wheat is even more tightly centered, with five states accounting for over 80 percent of the total: the United States, France (part of the EC), Canada, Australia, and Argentina. (The United States is by far the biggest exporter of wheat, although its dominance eroded steadily during the 1980s. In 1980–1981, 45 percent of the world wheat trade was controlled by the United States. In 1985–1986, this figure had fallen to 26 percent.) These same states also dominate the coarse-grain export field. Here too the United States saw its commanding position in the export market deteriorate. In the late 1970s, the United States accounted for nearly 60 percent of the world's coarse grain exports. In 1985–1986, this number had fallen to a low of 38 percent.

China, India, Indonesia, Bangladesh, Thailand, and Japan are the world's leading rice producers. In 1985–1986, they accounted for approximately 77 percent of the world's total rice production of 320 million metric tons. Only two of these states, Thailand (which controlled 34 percent of the rice export market in 1985–1986) and China, are long-term exporters of significant quantities of rice. After Thailand, the United States controls the next largest share of the rice export market (19 percent in 1986). As was the case with wheat and coarse grains, the United States saw its market share decline during the 1980s. Nevertheless, the United States still occupies a unique place on the production side of the international food regime. When the overall figures are adjusted for the small size of the rice export trade, the United States produces about 30 percent of all grain and is responsible for almost 50 percent of total world sales.

Not only are there relatively few producers of food for the international marketplace, but also, given dependence on favorable weather conditions, the supply of food tends to be unpredictable. During the 1970s, this led to erratic fluctuations in food prices and undependable trade flows. The link between fluctuating supplies and erratic prices and international trade problems was new. During the 1950s and 1960s, variations in crop size produced only relatively minor price changes in the international marketplace. Canada and the United States were able to draw upon large food reserves to buffer the effect on prices of food scarcity. Several factors came together to change this situation. First, the size of these buffer stocks fell. Canada, the United States, and Australia all undertook a series of programs designed to reduce the number of acres in production. Then, unexpectedly, the international demand for food intensified. The amount of grain traded in the world marketplace increased by 25 percent in the years 1971–1972 and 1972–1973, and the price of rice, corn, and wheat doubled. In some countries, such as the Soviet Union, a series of bad harvests had made international grain purchases a virtual necessity, while in other countries, such as China, changes in governmental agricultural policies brought new states into the international marketplace. Producers had great difficulty adapting to this new situation. In much of the world, the problem remained one of low productivity. In the developed states, where agricultural productivity is high, the problem was the high cost of energy brought on by the OPEC-led oil price hikes. No longer able to rely upon cheap energy to produce their crops, farmers throughout the United States, Canada, and Australia found that, in spite of the higher prices for which grain sold, it was hard to make a profit. As a result, they were forced to grow less or to concentrate on selected high-yield crops.

Two of the three constants of agricultural production and trade policy since the early 1950s have been overreaction and overproduction.[27] The 1970s were no exception to this rule. In time, producers did adjust, and during the 1980s, the problem once again was overproduction. Now, however, the United States, Canada, and Australia face stiff competition in their efforts to dispose of excess food production abroad. States such as Argentina and Thailand have seen their agricultural export earnings plunge. By the mid-1980s, Great Britain, Pakistan, and Saudi Arabia had all gone from being major importers to exporters of wheat; China had become a corn-exporting state; and Pakistan, Taiwan, Indonesia, and China had become rice exporters. The combination of overcapacity and increased competition has shaken the foundations of the international food regime in a way that the scarcity crisis of the 1970s did not. In order to understand why, it is necessary to examine the next phase in the food trade cycle: distribution.

Distribution   It is only relatively recently that food has become a major point of interaction between states in the arena of world politics.[28] Up until the industrial revolution, most of the world's food was consumed where it was produced and by those who produced it. The process of specialization, mechanization, and urbanization, set in motion by the industrial revolution, created national rather than local food systems. In time these national food systems became international and were linked to one another as a result of the transportation revolution that was brought on by the development of railroads and the steam engine. By the 1870s, grain grown in the Unites States was being imported by European states. Still, as we have already seen, as late as the 1960s, international food transactions were not a major component of world politics.

International food transactions can be grouped into four categories: trade, aid, investment, and information and technology exchanges. First, there is international trade in food. International food sales are heavily affected by the actions of government agencies. Frequently, at least one of the participants in these transactions is a government agency such as the Canadian Wheat Board, which sells grain on the international market, or Exportkhleb, the Soviet grain-purchasing agency. Governments also affect the international selling price of food and its availability through their price support programs, management of food reserves, and pricing policies. Seldom are these decisions made with an eye for their international consequences.

While not as well known as their oil-producing counterparts, a select few international grain-trading firms exercise the same type of mastery over international grain transactions. Six firms (Cargill, Continental, Louis Dreyfus, Bunge, Garnac, and ADM) manage about 85 percent of all U.S. grain exports. Because these firms are privately owned, even less is known about their inner workings, net worth, and policy preferences than is the case with the multinational oil companies. They have proven themselves to be highly independent actors capable of taking positions and carrying out policies that contradict and challenge the U.S. positions on issues. A case in point is the 1980 U.S. grain embargo against the Soviet Union. While these firms technically complied with the U.S. edict, their European subsidiaries continued to export food to the Soviet Union. A decade earlier, these firms were selling grain to the Soviet Union without the knowledge of the U.S. government.

The second type of international food transaction takes the form of food aid. Here too, states are the dominant actors, with most international food aid being given by one government to another. Up until the early 1970s, when the size of international food surpluses began to shrink, the United States was the principal source of international food aid. Between 1965 and 1972, it provided 80 percent of all food aid. Much of this aid was channeled through the Food for Peace Program. Also known as PL 480, the program distributed $30 billion worth of food aid between 1965 and 1980. The purposes of the Food for Peace Program are to dispose of the U.S. agricultural surplus, to create new markets for U.S. products, and to support regimes favorable to the United States. Most of the food distributed under this program is sold to foreign governments, which pay for it in local currency (some of the major recipients have been South Vietnam, South Korea, Taiwan, Pakistan, and Egypt) and then sell the food on the open market. Low-interest loans are provided to these governments to enable them to purchase the food from the United States. Critics of the program have argued that the availability of the aid gives governments little incentive to improve agricultural production or to institute land reform. Since the food is usually sold for less than local farmers can produce it, the existence of food aid helps to drive them out of business. Additionally, the food is sometimes sold on a ration basis to those groups that the government deems important. These are the police, members of the military, and the urban middle class. Thus, the food becomes a dole for the relatively wealthy rather than for the most needy. The Food For Peace Program also makes some food available under Title II (Direct Assistance). This aid goes to private voluntary organizations such as CARE.

Since the early 1970s, efforts have been made to encourage other food-producing states to increase their food aid contributions. An important tool in this process has been the Food Aid Convention. Established by the 1967 International Grain Agreement, its members in 1980 committed themselves to doubling the amount of food aid dispensed between 1967 and 1979.

With the onset of international food scarcity, international organizations began to play a more visible role in the international food regime. The most important of these is the United Nations' World Food Program. Set up in 1962, it has over 100 members. Unfortunately, its efforts have been handicapped by a lack of resources and the tendency for the amounts of aid pledged by member governments to fall short of its needs. The United States has been the primary contributor to the World Food Program, accounting for almost one-half of its resources since its founding.

The third and fourth forms of international food transactions do not involve food per se. Instead, they involve information and resources that move across international borders. As recently as the 1940s, yields per acre in rich and poor countries were not very different. Today the situation has changed. In part, the widening gap between agricultural productivity in rich states and agricultural productivity in poor states is due to the availability of modern agricultural techniques that have revolutionized the process of food production. This knowledge is not yet widely available in the Third World, and introducing it is not an easy matter. A number of complex issues are involved. What type of technology should be transferred to the Third World? Should it be the agricultural technology developed in the rich states to meet the problems faced by rich states (i.e., expensive labor and abundant land), or should it be modern agricultural technology especially suited to the needs of Third World states? To whom should the technology be provided? Women do much of the agricultural work in Third World states in Africa and Southern Asia, but the social structure is such that aid officials cannot come into an area and talk to the women without alienating the entire community. The decision making is often left entirely to the men, who in many cases understand less of what is needed because they are not actively involved in farm labor. Who should control the transfer of this technology? Information is not as easily controlled by governments as is trade, aid, or resources. Yet, many question whether multinational corporations can be trusted to give primary attention to the needs of the Third World states if they are placed in control of the international transfer of information.

One of the worst examples of a multinational corporation mismanaging information for its own gain occurred with infant formulas. Nestlé Corporation began an aggressive marketing campaign during the 1970s that was designed to convince Third World mothers of the benefits of infant formula. Nestlé was accused of using questionable practices, such as having off-duty nurses in uniform visit new mothers to talk of the advantages of formula over breast-feeding. The decline in breast feeding that followed had disastrous consequences for infant health. Breast-feeding has particular advantages in Third World countries. First, the mother's immunity to many life-threatening diseases that flourish there is passed on to the infant through the milk. Second, when formula is used instead of breast milk, the unavailability of clean water means that the powdered formula is contaminated when mixed with water and the infant will die from bacterial infections transmitted through the liquid. Finally, many Third World mothers are not well enough educated to recognize the importance of following directions carefully. In the case of the infant formula, many tried to save money by mixing the formula at half its strength, and their babies became malnourished. The Nestlé case is considered to be just one example of how a firm can take a potentially beneficial technology and use it in such a way that it causes considerable damage in states where few restrictions on marketing and advertising are enforced.

A final consideration is whether unrealistic expectations will be created in the Third World. A number of agricultural projects, including the famous Green Revolution, have promised results that have never materialized. The Green Revolution is a term that encompasses many different scientific and technological advances which have been introduced into Third World countries. In particular, it refers to new, high-yield strains of wheat and rice. When used properly, these technologies have produced results. From 1961 to 1976, India's food production rose at an annual rate of 2.6 percent. However, these strains require the use of an integrated technology of irrigation, fertilization, and pesticides that is often beyond the ability of Third World farmers to provide, so in many countries food production has not kept pace with population growth.

By itself, information will not produce dramatic increases in agricultural productivity. Additional resources in the form of equipment, fertilizers, and money for things such as land and water development projects are also necessary. The need is great. In 1974, the UN's Food and Agricultural Organization estimated that food production in the Third World would have to double by 1980 in order to meet the growing demand for food in that part of the world. Because of their lack of wealth, Third World states do not have the wherewithal to meet these needs themselves. Most of the needed resources must be transferred internationally. As was the case with food aid, food-producing states often have failed to provide the required resources. The Food and Agricultural Organization found that the money given by the rich states to help the agricultural sector in poor states fell about 45 percent below what was needed.

Consumption   Food consumption can be viewed from two different perspectives—either in terms of need or demand.[29] In the first case, food consumption issues are approached from the perspective of meeting minimum nutritional needs. The average number of calories consumed daily varies greatly around the world. On average, humans need a minimum of 2,200 calories per day. In the United States, the average consumed in 1985 was 3,682 calories per day, while in India it was 2,126 and in Ethiopia it was 1,704.[30] One further comment on the relationship between food and nutrition must be made. As James Harf and Thomas Trout note, the question is not always whether there is something to eat, but whether there is enough to eat based on the adequacies or inadequacies of the individual diet. Healthy people can be hungry. People with enough to eat can be unhealthy because of the nature of their diet."[31]

In the second case, demand, food is treated as a commodity that will be produced for a profit and sold to the highest bidder. As we have already seen, the major exporters of food are developed states. Measured by volume, so are the major importing states. In 1985–1986, the Soviet Union accounted for 18.5 percent of all wheat and 16.2 percent of all coarse-grain imports; Japan accounted for 6.5 percent of global wheat and 25.8 percent of global coarse-grain imports; and the European Community imported 3.4 percent of the world's wheat and 6.6 percent of the world's coarse-grain sales from non-European Community member countries. China (7.8 percent) and Egypt (7.4 percent) are the two major Third World importers of wheat, while Saudi Arabia (8.9 percent), Taiwan (4.9 percent), and South Korea (4.8 percent) are the major Third World importers of coarse grains.[32] The predominance of developed states and newly industrializing states among the major food importers holds two major consequences for the large number of poor Third World states that depend upon external sources of food to meet their consumption needs. First, the price structure within which they must compete to purchase food is determined by the buying habits and domestic agricultural policies of the wealthier states. Second, in times of food scarcity, it is they who are least able to compete for import market shares.

International Food Regime Rules

The three aspects of the international food regime—production, distribution, and consumption—are held together by a set of informal rules that guide the decisions made by the "international food managers." Based on their study of the international food regime as it existed during the period 1946–1980, Donald Puchala and Raymond Hopkins identified eight norms that were central to its operation:

1. There should be respect for international free trade in food. Any actions that violated the principles of free trade of which there were many must be characterized by such terms as "temporary" or "politically imperative."

2. Policymakers should undertake corrective action within their states to compensate for price fluctuations brought on by international surpluses or deficits.

3. International food aid is acceptable so long as it does not take precedence over the international free trade in food.

4. Famines are extraordinary conditions that demand extraordinary responses on the part of the international food regime. They are not to be treated as a standard problem or normal occurrence for which the regime should develop regular procedures.

5. There should be a free flow of scientific and crop information throughout the regime.

6. National food self-reliance should be given a low priority. Members of the international food regime were not encouraged to become self-sufficient with regard to food supplies. States were urged to see food dependence as legitimate and responsible international behavior.

7. There should exist respect for the sovereignty of states. The international food regime did not concern itself with activities occurring within the borders of states. Most important, this meant that consumption patterns and agriculture price and support policies were not matters of international negotiation.

8. Little concern is given to the problem of chronic hunger. As with food aid, an attention to the problems associated with chronic hunger were of secondary importance to the international food regime. The primary objective was to maintain the international free trade in food.[33]

As can readily be seen, these rules were not neutral. They favored the interests of the exporting states and did little to advance the interests of the poor importing states. Stockpiles of food were designed to ensure price stability and not to ensure that those who needed food would be able to get access to it in times of need. While the international food regime did mobilize in the face of a major famine, efforts by Third World states to become more self-sufficient in the production of food were not actively supported.

The norms of the regime also encouraged the growth of interdependence. Initially, this worked to the clear advantage of the food-producing states, because it guaranteed them foreign markets for their food exports. However, over time, interdependence increased the vulnerability of the exporting states to the ripple effects of actions occurring in any corner of the regime. For example, large quantities of U.S. grain were sold to the Soviet Union in 1972, and shortly thereafter grain prices in the United States rose to their highest levels since 1917. Higher grain prices, in turn, meant higher food prices, and in 1972–1975 almost $54 billion was added to the U.S. food bill.

The problem of reforming the rules of international food trade has become a recurring issue in world politics. In 1974, a World Food Conference was held in Rome. The main topic of debate was the unequal nature of the regime's rules. Since then, a new set of norms has emerged that challenges the priority given to protecting the international free market in food, but, overall, the current international food regime's norms differ only marginally from those just outlined. During the 1980s, a continuing dissatisfaction with the rules governing international agriculture on the part of Third World states led them to demand that agricultural programs affecting trade in agriculture or access to markets be included in GATT (the General Agreement on Tariffs and Trade) negotiations. Since the end of World War II, GATT has been the primary forum for negotiating reductions in international trade barriers. Trade in agricultural products has largely been excluded from its deliberations, which are known as negotiating "rounds." The latest negotiations, agreed to in 1986, are referred to as the Uruguay Round. The developed states wanted to keep agriculture off the agenda but were forced to accept its presence as the price for getting the Third World to enter into negotiations on barriers inhibiting international free trade in services.

CONCLUSION

International systems are artificial creations. We, as observers, have a great deal of choice as to whether we will define an international system in military or economic terms; where its boundaries will begin and end; whether they will be cultural, geographic, economic, or political in nature; how the rules will be defined; and who the members of the system will be. International systems are used to help us better understand what is happening in world politics. It is a way of cutting through the clutter of all that is going on so that we can focus on those forces that govern state behavior. In the process of simplifying reality, we end up leaving out some details and features in order to emphasize others. As a result, the real world never perfectly matches the systems that we create to explain it. These discrepancies place limits on the predictive and explanatory power of international systems theory. However, they do not rob it of its ability to provide insight into the forces that shape state behavior but, rather, serve as a way of distinguishing between different historical periods or generate insights into the nature of world politics.[34]

NOTES

1. John Stoessinger, *Why Nations Go to War*, 4th ed. (New York: St. Martin's, 1985), pp. 55–56.
2. Quoted in Allen Whiting, *China Crosses the Yalu: The Decision to Enter the Korean War* (Santa Monica Calif.: The Rand Corporation, 1960), p. 39.
3. Whiting, *China Crosses the Yalu*, p. ix.
4. K. J. Holsti, *International Politics: A Framework for Analysis*, 5th ed. (Englewood Cliffs, N.J.: Prentice-Hall, 1988).
5. Lawrence Eagleberger, "The 21st Century: American Foreign Policy Challenges," in Edward Hamilton, ed., *America's Global Interests* (New York: Norton, 1989), pp. 242–260.
6. Adapted from Peter R. Beckman, *World Politics in the Twentieth Century* (Englewood Cliffs, N.J.: Prentice-Hall, 1984), pp. 238–239. Beckman also puts forward rules for other states in the system.
7. On China, see Holsti, *International Politics*; on Europe, see Richard Rosecrance, *Action and Reaction in World Politics* (Boston: Little, Brown, 1963); and on the immediate post-

World War II era, see Ernst B. Haas, "Collective Security and the Future International System" in *Monograph Series in World Affairs*, Vol. 5 (Denver: University of Denver, 1967–1968).

8. Adapted from Morton A. Kaplan, *System and Process in International Politics* (New York: John Wiley & Sons, 1957), pp. 38–45.

9. Adapted from Kaplan, *System and Process in International Politics*, p. 38. Kaplan also presents rules for neutrals and universal-member international organizations.

10. Adapted from Kaplan, *System and Process in International Politics*, p. 23.

11. John Spanier, *Games Nations Play*, 6th ed., (Washington, D.C.: Congressional Quarterly Press, 1987), pp. 148–149

12. Michael Tatu, quoted in Spanier, *Games Nations Play*, p. 148.

13. Adapted from Kaplan, *System and Process in International Politics*, pp. 50–52.

14. George Modelski, *Long Cycles in World Politics* (Seattle: University of Washington Press, 1985). For a review of different approaches to the existence of long cycles, see Richard Rosecrance, "Long Cycles and International Relations," *International Organization* 41 (1987): 283–301. We will take up the question of long cycles in more detail in our discussion of why states go to war.

15. Michael Blumenthal, "The World Economy and Technological Change," *Foreign Affairs* 66 (1988): 529–550.

16. See Patrick Morgan, *Deterrence* (Beverly Hills, Calif.: Sage, 1977).

17. Robert Gilpin, *War and Change in World Politics* (Cambridge, Mass.: Cambridge University Press, 1981).

18. For a discussion of the various meanings of the balance of power, see Inis Claude, Jr., *Power and International Relations* (New York: Random House, 1962).

19. Robert Keohane and Joseph Nye, *Power and Interdependence*, 2d ed. (Glenview, Il.: Scott, Foresman, 1989), pp. 24–38.

20. Stephen Krasner, "Structural Causes and Regime Consequences: Regimes as Intervening Variables," in Stephen Krasner, ed., *International Regimes* (Ithaca, N.Y.: Cornell University Press, 1983), p. 1. In addition to the other essays in this volume, see Robert Keohane, *After Hegemony, Cooperation and Discord in the World Political Economy* (Princeton, N.J.: Princeton University Press, 1984).

21. For a dissenting view on the importance of regimes to the study of world politics, see Susan Strange, "Cave! Hic Dragones: A Critique of Regime Analysis," in Stephen Krasner, *International Regimes*, pp. 337–354.

22. Arthur Stein, "Coordination and Collaboration: Regimes in an Anarchic World," in Stephen Krasner, *International Regimes*, pp. 115–140.

23. Robert Jervis, "Security Regimes," in Stephen Krasner, *International Regimes*, 173–194.

24. This account of the international food system is largely derived from James Harf and B. Thomas Trout, *The Politics of Global Resources* (Durham N.C.: Duke University Press, 1986); and Raymond Hopkins, Robert Paarlberg, and Mitchel Wallerstein, *Food in the Global Arena* (New York: Holt, Rinehart, & Winston, 1982).

25. Dennis Pirages, *Global Technopolitics* (Pacific Grove, Ca.: Brooks/Cole Publishing Company, 1989), pp. 93–94.

26. Raymond Hopkins, Robert Paarlberg, and Mitchel Wallerstein, *Food in the Global Arena* (New York: Holt, Rinehart & Winston, 1982), pp. 11–14.

27. Dale Hathaway, *Agriculture and the GATT*, Vol. 20 (Washington, D.C.: Institute for International Economics, 1987), p. 17.

28. Hopkins, Paarlberg, and Wallerstein, *Food in the Global Arena*, p. 15.

29. Harf and Trout, *The Politics of Global Resources*, p. 44.

30. World Bank, *World Development Report, 1988* (London: Oxford University Press), 1988.

31. Harf and Trout, *The Politics of Global Resources*, p. 35.

28. Hopkins, Paarlberg, and Wallerstein, *Food in the Global Arena*, p. 15.

29. Harf and Trout, *The Politics of Global Resources*, p. 44.

30. World Bank, *World Development Report, 1988* (London: Oxford University Press), 1988.

31. Harf and Trout, *The Politics of Global Resources*, p. 35.

32. Calculated from tables presented in Hathaway, *Agriculture and the GATT,* pp. 45, 47.

33. This case study is based on the account presented in Donald J. Puchala and Raymond F. Hopkins, "International Regimes: Lessons from Inductive Analysis," in Stephen Krasner, *International Regimes,* pp. 61–92.

34. Robert J. Lieber, *Theory and World Politics* (Cambridge, Mass.: Winthrop, 1972).

Chapter 6

International Law and International Organization

None of us question the need for cooperation among states in world politics. The dilemma is how the conditions in which cooperation is possible can best be created. The two most frequently advocated mechanisms for creating those conditions in which cooperation is possible are international law and international organization. In this chapter, we will examine the various issues surrounding their operation and effectiveness. By way of introduction to the topic, we will review the role played by international law and international organization in response to the Soviet Union's 1983 attack on commercial flight KAL 007. This was not the first time that a civilian airliner had been shot down in peacetime for violating a country's airspace. In 1952 the Soviet Union shot down an Air France flight over East Germany; in 1954 China shot down a Cathay Pacific airliner; in 1955 Bulgaria attacked an El Al plane; in 1973 Isreal attacked a Libyan airliner; and in 1978 the Soviet Union shot down a South Korean airliner. It was also not the last attack. As we noted in Chapter 1, in 1988 the U.S. Navy shot down an Iranian airliner over the Persian Gulf.

KAL 007

At 3:46 A.M. on September 1, 1983, KAL 007, a Boeing 747 with 240 passengers and a crew of 29, en route from New York City to Seoul, South Korea via Anchorage, Alaska, was hit by a Soviet air-to-air missile and crashed into the Sea of Japan.[1] There were no survivors. KAL 007 was assigned route "Red 20," the westernmost of five internationally established air lanes used for trans-Pacific travel. Red 20 would bring KAL 007 within 50 miles of the Soviet Union. Because the flight and voice recorders were never found, it is unclear exactly what happened after the flight left Anchorage. What is certain is that at some point KAL 007 left Red 20 and flew over the Soviet Union. First, it crossed over the southern Kamchatka peninsula without incident and returned to international airspace over the Sea of Okotsk. It then reentered Soviet airspace on a course that took it over Sheklin Island, the site of a major Soviet naval facility. KAL 007 was within minutes of once again exiting Soviet territory when it was hit by one or two air-to air missiles launched from Soviet fighters.

Little agreement exists on the particulars of KAL 007 beyond this bare outline of events. In spite of its designation as a civil aircraft, the Soviet Union argued that KAL 007 gave the appearance of being on a military reconnaissance mission and that, in fact, Soviet military personnel had mistaken it for a military reconnaissance plane, the RC-135. It argued that not only were the profiles of the two planes similar, but also KAL 007 and an RC-135 approached the Soviet Union at identical altitudes—thereby merging their radar images—before the RC-135 turned off and flew to the Aleutian Islands and the KAL flight proceeded to fly over an area often frequented by U.S. reconnaissance aircraft. International navigation maps clearly identified this area as militarily sensitive and restricted. The Soviet Union also contended that KAL 007 had failed to respond to a series of warnings and instructions to land. These signals included flashing lights, rolling wings, and firing 120 rounds of tracer fire. Furthermore, it contended that KAL 007 had acted as if it were on a military reconnaissance mission by engaging in evasive maneuvers, flying without its navigation lights on, and emitting signals similar to those emitted by short-code radar transmissions. As a final indictment of KAL 007, the Soviet Union stated that the crew was heard informing Tokyo that it had safely passed over southern Kamchatka and was proceeding normally.

The United States took the lead in condemning the Soviet Union. It acknowledged that KAL 007 had violated Soviet airspace but rejected the assertion that the Soviet action was justifiable. The United States argued that (1) KAL 007 was not spying on the Soviet Union; (2) even if it had been, the Soviet Union had not made enough of an effort to resolve the incident without using force; and (3) even at night, the profiles of a Boeing 747 and an RC-135 were clearly distinguishable. In challenging the Soviet interpretation of events, the United States made public Japanese intelligence intercepts of radio conversations between the Soviet fighter pilots and ground control stations. These transcripts of the radio conversations effectively refuted the Soviet allegations that KAL 007 had acted in a suspicious manner; they showed that Soviet pilots had KAL 007 clearly in sight for 20 minutes before they shot it down and that no concerted effort had been made to make contact with the airliner. Soviet authorities did not challenge the authenticity of the transcripts but chose to argue that they demonstrated that Japanese authorities knew that KAL 007 was in danger and took no steps to alert them. For its part, the United States had no explanation for why KAL 007 was so far off course other than to insist that pilot error could not be ruled out.

Both the United States and the Soviet Union, the two states most involved in the post-incident political maneuvering, justified their positions as permissible under international law. The Soviet Union offered no apologies, admitted no fault, and did not compensate the families of the victims. In large measure, it based its arguments on the internationally recognized principle that a state has the right to protect its territory from the hostile military actions of other states. The United States countered that the Soviet action was illegal under international law because this principle did not extend to attacks on civil airliners in peacetime. Each side also cited the 1944 Chicago Convention on International Civil Aviation to support its position. In defense of the Soviet position, it can be argued that the Convention declares that every state possesses exclusive sovereignty to the airspace over its territory and that it may designate areas as militarily sensitive and ban civil flights above them. In support of the U.S. position, it is noted that there is nothing in the Convention that justifies the use of force against intruding aircraft. In fact, the Convention requires states to "have due regard for the safety of navigation of civil aircraft." The only use of force that is specifically sanctioned by the Convention is forcing the intruding aircraft to land. Omitted in the Convention are instructions as to how a state is supposed to respond if an intruding aircraft ignores signals that it must land.

The exact nature of state responses to the incident varied considerably. Unilateralist measures were taken by several states. For example, Canada denied Aeroflot, the Soviet airline, the use of Montreal's airport for 60 days, and the United States notified the Soviet Union that it would not renew a bilateral agreement for cooperation on transportation issues. Other states, notably Mexico, China, Romania, Albania, and India, adopted a wait-and-see attitude. They refused to condemn or endorse the Soviet action because of their uncertainty over the specifics of KAL 007's flight and its downing.

Most of the activity after the incident took place within international organizations. False starts were made on a number of fronts. On September 12, 1983, the UN Security Council voted on a resolution that had been submitted by the United States that condemned the Soviet Union for using force in ways "incompatible with the norms governing international behavior and elementary considerations of humanity." The resolution passed by a vote of 9-2, with four states abstaining, but because the Soviet Union cast one of the two negative votes (Poland also voted no), the resolution was defeated. The European Community also considered adopting a strongly worded statement condemning the Soviet action but failed to act on it because of Greece's opposition. Members of the North Atlantic Treaty Organization (NATO) were said to be unanimously in favor of condemning the Soviet action but did not do so because they felt NATO was not an appropriate international organization to call for sanctions.

While collective international action was blocked or muted on these fronts, more specialized international organizations did act. Three days after KAL 007 was shot down, the International Federation of Airline Pilots' Associations voted to classify the Soviet Union as an offending state and called for a 60-day ban on flights to Moscow. More than 12 states participated in this boycott before it was called off, pending an investigation by the International Civil Aviation Organization (ICAO). The ICAO study was highly technical in nature and concluded that (1) KAL 007 was not on a reconnaissance mission; (2) KAL 007 drifted off course due to a combination of errors and oversight; (3) the air traffic controllers did not know that the plane was off course; and (4) the Soviet Union had simply assumed that KAL 007 was an intelligence aircraft and based its actions on this assumption. In addition to conducting this investigation, the ICAO also voted to condemn the Soviet Union for action "incompatible with the norms governing international behavior," and agreed to call an Extraordinary Assembly meeting to consider an amendment to the 1944 Chicago Convention that would address the use of force against civil aircraft.

One hundred seven member states, eleven international organizations, and one observer state attended this meeting, which began in April 1984. Six different versions of a possible amendment were introduced, and efforts to forge a consensus position took place in meetings of a Plenary Group, an Executive Committee, and a Working Group. Participants also worked together in informal regional groupings such as the French-speaking African states, the English-speaking African states, members of the European Civil Aviation Conference, and members of the Latin American Civil Aviation Conference. The initial presentations made in the Plenary Group meetings indicated that less than 40 states favored an amendment. Most members felt that there already existed an international consensus opposing the use of force against a civil aircraft and that any amendment should do no more than reaffirm this understanding. East European states opposed the idea, and Third World states were largely silent. Those Third World states that did speak out came down on both sides of the issue. According to ICAO rules, two-thirds of those in attendance must vote yes for the amendment to be adopted. The amendment would only take force after two-thirds of the total membership ratified it.

The six versions of an amendment were then introduced and debated in the Executive Committee. Two fell outside of this area of agreement. A South Korean proposal called for sanctions against the offending state, and a Soviet proposal stressed "the rights of a contracting state to protect its sovereignty or safeguard its security." Ecuador did not push its proposal, and it received little attention. The remaining three proposals, by the United States, France and Austria, and the Latin American Civil Aviation Conference, all fell within the general area of consensus. The major difference was that the proposal by the Latin American Civil Aviation Convention did not place the ban on using weapons against civil aircraft within the context of the UN Charter, which recognizes the right of self-defense, while the other two proposed amendments did.

At approximately the midpoint of the Executive Committee's deliberations, the Communist states mounted an attack on the emerging consensus that states should not use force against civil aircraft. Their efforts were blocked when Venezuela, supported by Colombia, succeeded in ending this debate through a vote of cloture. At a subsequent meeting, the Executive Committee appointed a 23-state Working Committee to draft an amendment for consideration by the Executive Committee. It did so and used the French-Austrian proposal as the basis for its discussions. The primary point of controversy within the Working Committee centered on a proposal put forward by Poland that, in addition to banning the use of weapons against civil aircraft, the amendment should also contain a clause that justified the use of force by alleging that the state of registry or the state of the operator had not prevented the intrusion into the offended state's airspace.

The Polish proposal was not included in the draft amendment that was sent back to the Executive Committee. It was then that compromise language was agreed upon that allowed the Polish proposal to be included in the amendment in such a way that it would not take away from the force of the prohibition on using weapons against civil aircraft. This was done in two ways. First, Ghana sponsored a motion that substituted "prohibit" for "prevent" in characterizing the responsibilities of states regarding the deliberate misuse of civil aircraft. Second, the amendment specifically stated that this requirement did not affect the responsibility of a state to refrain from using force laid out in an earlier paragraph. Significantly, the amendment is silent on two important points: When does a civil aircraft become a state (military) aircraft, and what constitutes evidence of hostile intent? As of April 1987, only 36 states had ratified the amendment. Of the key actors in the KAL 007 incident, only South Korea has done so to date. The United States, Soviet Union, and Japan have not yet ratified it.

As our case study shows, international cooperation, imperfect as it may be, is carried out primarily through two mechanisms: international law and international organization. We now turn to an in-depth examination of each.

INTERNATIONAL LAW

Many are quick to dismiss international law as largely irrelevant to world politics. This judgment is often based on comparisons of international law with its domestic counterpart. A structural feature-for-feature comparison with domestic law finds international law wanting in virtually every respect. In national political systems, laws are made in designated political institutions (most frequently, legislatures), a set of institutions exist for dealing with controversies over the application of law to a problem (the judiciary), and a central enforcement mechanism exists (a police force). International law possesses none of these qualities. Laws come from multiple sources, there is no enforcement mechanism, and the International Court of Justice lacks the authority to make binding interpretations of international law. Others reach a similarly negative conclusion based on the inability of international law to bring an end to war and violence. Again, the comparison is made to domestic political systems: Whereas violence is not sanctioned as an acceptable way to solve disputes in domestic law, rules have been formulated to govern how violence is conducted in international law.

Defenders of international law argue that these comparisons and the negative conclusions that follow from them are unfair. First, domestic legal systems are presented in overly idealistic terms. All of us can think of numerous instances in which domestic laws failed to prevent illegal behavior or in which domestic laws were all but totally ignored. It is simply not the case that international law always fails and domestic law always succeeds. Second, it is not at all clear why the standard for comparison should be domestic law in advanced industrial societies. One researcher,

Roger Masters, has argued that a more logical point of comparison for international law would be to primitive stateless societies.[2] He notes that violence and law play different roles in primitive societies than they do in civilized ones. Self-help, deterrence, and retaliation are characteristically primitive approaches to law and organization.

International law deserves to be analyzed on its own terms. Two questions are especially relevant for an understanding of its potential and limitations as an instrument of cooperation among states: Where do we look for international law, and when and why does it get obeyed?

Where Does International Law Come From?

Multiple Sources[3]   Article 38 of the statute of the International Court of Justice recognizes four sources of international law. They are:

1. International conventions, whether general or particular, establishing rules expressly recognized by the contesting states;
2. International custom, as evidence of a general practice accepted as law;
3. The general principles of law recognized by civilized nations;
4. . . . Judicial decisions and the teachings of the most highly qualified publicists of various nations.

International conventions more commonly are called *treaties*. They are formal written documents that lay out permissible and impermissible behavior. The number of treaties in existence has grown dramatically in the course of the twentieth century. In 1892, the official listing of treaties entered into by Great Britain filled 190 pages. The listing published in 1960 ran to 2,500 pages. It needs to be stressed that treaties are a source of law only for those states that have signed and ratified the agreement. Violations of the SALT II Treaty, for example, are not violations of international law, because the treaty was never ratified by the United States. Similarly, since France has never signed the Nuclear Non-Proliferation Agreement, legally it is not bound by the restrictions that this agreement places on the transfer of nuclear technology from nuclear states to nonnuclear ones. The treaty most relevant to the Soviet attack on KAL 007 was the 1944 Chicago Convention on Civil Aircraft. As we have already noted, both the United States and Soviet Union were able to use portions of this treaty on which they could base their positions. The United States pointed out that the treaty did not justify the use of force against civil aircraft, while the Soviet Union cited those provisions that recognized a state's right to sovereignty over its airspace.

Unlike treaties, customary international law is not written. Traditionally, international jurists have sought to identify the content of customary law by examining the well-established and normal ways in which states interact with one another. Not all routine behavior qualifies as international law. For it to do so, two conditions must be met. First, the behavior must be consistent with general international practice. Second, it must be accepted as law by the international community. Diplomatic immunity and the notion that a state's jurisdiction extends into the ocean three miles beyond its coastline are prominent examples of customary international law. Both the United States and the Soviet Union also were able to cite long-standing international customs in support of their positions on the KAL 007 incident. The United States argued that, in shooting down KAL 007, the Soviet Union had violated international norms that prohibited the deliberate destruction of civil aircraft. The Soviet Union did not reject this norm but argued that it did not apply. Instead, it cited as a defense of its action the internationally recognized norm that a state has a right to take military action against an intruding spy plane.

As we mentioned, general principles are a third source of international law. They exist at a more fundamental level than do customs, and they have proven to be most useful in new areas of international law where treaties and customs do not specify what type of behavior is permissible. For example, individuals and multinational corporations enter into a wide range of contractual relationships with states and international organizations. Because international law is primarily concerned with how states interact with one another, few treaties have been signed or customs developed to deal with problems growing out of relationships concerning such matters as terms of employment and oil concessions. General principles from domestic and international law can be used as starting points for reaching decisions. In the case of KAL 007, the general principle that each side clothed its position in was sovereignty. The Soviet Union argued that the logic inherent in the principle of sovereignty gave every state an absolute right to protect its airspace from unwanted intrusions. The United States argued that the national security concerns inherent in the concept of sovereignty are limited by human values.

Notice that it is only at the level of principle that the United States and Soviet Union truly disagreed with each other over the meaning of international law. When the question was framed in terms of treaties or customs, they only disagreed over the relevance of a particular law to the incident. At the level of general principles, they disagreed over the very meaning of *sovereignty:* Did it give states absolute or only relative rights?

Which Sources Are Most Important?   It is too much for us to expect that treaties, customs, general principles, court decisions, and the writings of international jurists will always be in agreement. Even if they were, there would be no reason to treat them with equal deference. Some sources of international law might quite legitimately be considered more important than others. The International Court of Justice, for example, holds that judicial decisions and the teachings of jurists are "subsidiary means for the determination of the rules of law." Two long-standing schools of thought exist on which of the remaining sources of international law should be considered most important. The older of the two is the natural-law approach. According to this approach, international law grows out of universal and unchanging principles that possess eternal validity. The task facing policymakers is not to make international law but to find it. This search has led natural law promoters in two directions. Originally, they searched the writings of the Roman Catholic Church for general principles that could be used to establish rules of conduct for international actors. Hugo Grotius (1583–1645) shifted the focus from theology to secular principles. He argued that laws were an automatic consequence of people living together and thus would exist even if there were no God. Rules were necessary for the survival of a society and could be uncovered by a process of logical and reasoned inquiry. In the eighteenth century, the natural-law interpretation of international law was challenged by the positivist approach. The positivist view of international law held that laws were not derived from general principles, nor did they exist above or apart from states. International law was made by states and was restricted in scope and time to whatever states agreed upon. Accordingly, treaties and customs were seen as the central source of international law. Today, the debate between the natural-law and positivist approaches to international law continues, but it is overshadowed by a larger controversy. Operating outside of Western culture and tradition, Third World and Communist states question the validity of international laws that stem from either of these philosophical positions.

Richard Sterling summarizes the Third World position this way: "for non-Westerners, all the main sources of today's international law—court opinions, and treaty law as well as customs and the commentators—bear the stamp of white parochialism."[4] The historical reality is that contemporary international law originally was European international law, which became global in scope through the expansion of trading relations and the establishment of colonies. It thus came into existence prior to the emergence of Third World states as sovereign actors. Western states simply took it as a given that, upon becoming independent, Third World states would embrace the existing body of international laws. The situation improved little after those states gained their independence. Western powers either used their influence over the postcolonial elite to force unequal treaties upon Third World states or acted in concert to formulate treaties whose terms Third World states were expected to endorse without question. Until international law becomes the product of equal participation of all states, Third World states do not see any chance that international law will be relevant to world politics.

Immense practical and philosophical problems stand in the way of realizing this goal. Consider the task facing a global conference that is called to establish rules of warfare for the twenty-first century. For those raised in the Western cultural tradition, the intuitive starting point for such an effort is the concept of a *just war*. For those raised in the Islamic cultural tradition, the intuitive central ordering concept is that of a *holy war*, or *jihad*. The phrases *just war* and *holy war* are not perfectly synonymous, but they sound very much alike. The problem is that, when used within their proper cultural contexts, they convey very different sets of symbols and images.

Plato, Cicero, Augustine, and Thomas Aquinas are among the host of philosophers and theologians whose ideas have contributed to the development of the concept *just war*. The modern just-war doctrine has two parts. The first part deals with the proper justification for going to war and has four elements. These are: (1) There must be proper authority behind the decision to engage in violence, (2) there must be a just cause, (3) there must be a rightful intent of the action, and (4) the war must be consistent with and supportive of peace. The second part of the just-war doctrine defines what acts are justifiable in warfare. It has two major elements. The principle of proportionality requires that the amount of violence used be proportional to the gravity of the issue being contested. The principle of discrimination requires that a distinction be made between combatants and noncombatants. Only combatants may be the targets of proportional violence.

Also, strongly embedded in the Western tradition is the notion that a penalty must be paid by the state which has acted unjustly and forced others to go to war (although it is clear that in practice this principle has long since been transformed into "the loser must pay"). This notion can be found in the writings of the early Dutch international jurist, Hugo Grotius; references to it can be found in the documents that came out of the 1907 Hague Conference; it is present in the Treaty of Versailles, which ended World War I and required that Germany pay reparations; and it is present in the Potsdam Agreement, which allowed the Soviet Union to exact reparations from German territory under its control. The Nuremberg war trials added yet another dimension to the concept of war crimes by punishing individuals for violations of the just-war doctrine and by rejecting as a legitimate defense the argument that the accused were following orders. Table 6.1 presents a listing of some of the more prominent examples of war crimes.

Muslims believe that God meant for them to struggle to establish Islam as the universal religion. Accordingly, they divide the world into two parts: Dar al-Islam ("the House of Islam") and Dar al-Harb ("the House of War"). The latter refers to that part of the world that has yet to be brought into the House of Islam. Islamic teachings stress that the "believers" are obliged to wage a *jihad* (holy war) until such time as the entire world is united in the House of Islam. Those holy warriors who do so are sometimes known as *mujahedin*. Where the entire thrust of the just-war doctrine is on placing restraints on the use of force, the concept of a jihad points in the opposite direction. Its emphasis is on justifying the use of whatever violence is necessary in order to vanquish or convert the nonbeliever. Although in premodern times the concept of a jihad gave Islam an expansionist and aggressive character, commentators note that it also can be interpreted in a defensive or protectionist light: The House of Islam must be kept pure and protected from outside encroachments. This desire to cleanse Muslim society from foreign and corrupting influences, whether it be Western values or Soviet-backed domination, is seen by many as the central thrust to the fundamentalist Islamic revival now taking place in the Middle East.

Communist states have traditionally objected to international law because of its capitalist roots and exploitative nature. According to Marxist theory, law is part of the superstructure of a society and does not exist independently of the underlying system of class-based economic relations. The purpose of law is to help the representatives of the dominant class in a society to retain their hold on power. In the process, other classes in the society are oppressed and exploited. International law will become just only when it sheds its capitalist roots and is based upon the principles of socialism. Prior to Gorbachev, Soviet writings long argued that, given the existence of different economic systems in world politics, there can be no single set of international laws. Instead, three different bodies of international law exist. First, there is the international law that governs relations between capitalist states. Second, there is the international law that applies to the relations between socialist states. By definition, the former are exploitative, whereas the latter are progressive and just. A

Table 6.1 INTERNATIONAL LAW: WAR CRIMES
_____

1. Making use of poisoned or otherwise forbidden arms or munitions;
2. Treachery in asking for quarter or simulating sickness or wounds;
3. Maltreatment of corpses;
4. Firing on localities which are undefended and without military significance;
5. Abuse of or firing on a flag of truce;
6. Misuse of the Red Cross or similar emblems;
7. Wearing of civilian clothes by troops to conceal their identity during the commission of combat acts;
8. Improper utilization of privileged (exempt, immune) buildings for military purposes;
9. Poisoning of streams or wells;
10 Pillage;
11. Purposeless destruction;
12. Compelling prisoners of war to engage in prohibited types of labor;
13. Forcing civilians to perform prohibited labor;
14. Violation of surrender terms;
15. Killing or wounding military personnel who have laid down arms, surrendered, or are disabled by wounds or sickness;
16. Assassination, and the hiring of assassins;
17. Ill-treatment of prisoners of war, or of the wounded and sick—including despoiling them of possessions not classifiable as public property;
18. Killing or attacking harmless civilians;
19. Compelling the inhabitants of occupied enemy territory to furnish information about the armed forces of the enemy or his means of defense;
20. Appropriation or destruction of the contents of privileged buildings;
21. Bombardment from the air for the exclusive purpose of terrorizing or attacking civilian populations;
22. Attack on enemy vessels which have indicated their surrender by lowering their flag;
23. Attack or seizure of hospitals and all other violations of the Hague Convention for the Adaptation to Maritime Warfare of the Principles of the Geneva Convention;
24. Unjustified destruction of enemy prizes;
25. Use of enemy uniforms during combat and use of the enemy flag during attack by a belligerent vessel;
26. Attack on individuals supplied with safe-conducts, and other violations of special safeguards provided;
27. Breach of parole;
28. Grave breaches of Article 50 of the Geneva Convention for the Amelioration of the Condition of the Wounded and Sick in Armed Forces in the Field, of 1949 and Article 51 of the Geneva Convention of 1949 Applicable to Armed Forces at Sea: "wilful killing, torture or inhuman treatment, including biological experiments, wilfully causing great suffering or serious injury to body or health, and extensive destruction and appropriation of property not justified by military necessity and carried out unlawfully and wantonly".
_____

Source: Gerhard von Glahn, *Law Among Nations,* 2d ed. (New York: Macmillan, 1970).

third body of law, known as the Law of Peaceful Coexistence, governs the relations between capitalist and socialist states. The content of the Law of Peaceful Coexistence has emerged over time and is a product of treaties and agreements entered into by the two alliance systems; thus, it is viewed as neither inherently just nor unjust. Rather, peaceful coexistence is a special form of class struggle that is conducted between states based on a "practical and realistic approach to the relations between countries." It is based on the "mutual renunciation of the use of armed force as a means of settling disputes between countries." Soviet commentators are quick to point out that this statement should not be interpreted as pointing to a reconciliation between East and West. "Peaceful coexistence is one of the principal forms of the struggle against imperialism. . . . The easing of tensions and the successes of the policy of peaceful coexistence paralyze the most bellicose elements of imperialism and hinder the export of counterrevolution."[5]

When and Why Does International Law Get Obeyed?

Because states are sovereign, compliance with international law is voluntary. The question naturally arises as to why states should obey international law. The answer tends to be quite simple and straightforward. States obey international law out of self-interest. When it is followed, international law brings an element of predictability and certainty to world politics, which helps mute the struggle for power and the anarchic tendencies that are always present. Customs are followed because states see more benefits than costs in adhering to them. Treaties are agreements voluntarily entered into, and it stands to reason that states will not sign a treaty that is not in their best interest or that they will be tempted to break. If they expect other states to honor commitments and to observe the practices and customs of international law in their dealings with them, they must do likewise.

In a more generalized sense, states also fear the chaotic consequences that would follow from widespread disregard for international law. Twice in recent years the focus of international concern in this regard has been on Iran. In 1979, Iran's seizure of the U.S. embassy produced widespread condemnation. If duplicated by other states, this act would undermine the entire system of diplomatic representation on which diplomacy and the peaceful settlement of disputes rest. The second wave of intense international criticism came in 1989, following Iranian Parliament Speaker Ali Rafsanjani's call to Palestinians to kill five Americans or other Westerners in retaliation for each Palestinian who had died as a result of Israel's occupation policies on the West Bank and the Gaza Strip. His cry for revenge came only months after the Ayatollah Khomeini issued a public death sentence against British author Salman Rushdie because of his novel *The Satanic Verses.* Less than one week after making these remarks Rafsanjani retracted his comments.

Quite clearly, compliance does not always happen. When it does not, it is because the influence of international legal prohibitions against a pattern of behavior has been overridden by other concerns. Although violations of international law are a sign of its weaknesses, it should also be noted that they are not random. The fact that they tend to be clustered around certain types of incidents or situations can be taken as a sign of the importance of international law as a constraint on behavior under certain circumstances.

The key question thus involves the circumstances under which international law is most likely to serve as an instrument of cooperation among states. Legal commentator Charles de Visscher suggested that the answer can be found in the attitudes of states and not in the existence or perfection of legal doctrines and standards.[6] No matter how precisely it is written, no statement of international law will be likely to overcome the presence of incompatible objectives and conflicts of interest. Borrowing from the work of K. J. Holsti, the following scheme might be used as a working hypothesis regarding state attitudes toward international law:[7]

1. In "routine matters" involving states that normally maintain friendly relations with one another, legal norms will be of considerable importance.
2. When the issue involves a real conflict of interest and core values and the states involved normally maintain friendly relations with one another, international law will tend to be interpreted in an arbitrary manner so as to put each nation's actions in the best possible light.
3. When the issue involves a real conflict of interest and core values and the states involved consider themselves to be enemies, international legal obligations will be ignored in the interests of fashioning an effective response.

Holsti notes that there are two important conclusions to be drawn from this scheme. First, most transactions between states fall into the first category, thus reaffirming the importance of international law. Second, in crisis situations, such as the Soviet attack on KAL 007, international law does not constrain state behavior but serves a different function. It is primarily used to mobilize support both at home and abroad for one's policy.

Should a state feel that it is a victim of a violation of international law, it has two basic options at its disposal. One option is to take the case to the International Court of Justice (ICJ) for adjudication. This strategy has not been pursued very often. The principle of sovereignty and the unwillingness of states to trust a third party to settle their disputes are factors limiting the Court's effectiveness. Since its creation in 1946, only about 60 cases have been brought before the ICJ, and virtually one-half of them were heard before 1960. They are listed in Table 6.2. Approximately one-third of the time the ICJ was unable to reach a decision.

No state is required to take an issue to the ICJ or to accept its verdict. A state acknowledges the Court's automatic jurisdiction over disputes involving it by signing the Optional Clause of the International Court of Justice Statute, its founding document. Only about one-third of all UN members have signed it, and most of them have attached qualifications. In the case of the United States, the Connally Reservation stated that U.S. recognition of compulsory ICJ jurisdiction was limited to matters that did not involve disputes falling within the domestic jurisdiction of the United States as determined by the United States. In 1986, the United States withdrew its acceptance of the Optional Clause when the ICJ agreed to hear Nicaragua's claim that the United States had violated international law by mining its harbors. The United States boycotted the hearing, which resulted in a guilty verdict against the United States for committing acts of war against Nicaragua.

The U.S. refusal to recognize the ICJ's jurisdiction was not unprecedented. In 1972, Iceland refused to accept the ICJ's right to hear a dispute with Germany and Great Britain over its unilateral establishment of a 50-mile exclusive fishing zone. In the following year, France rejected ICJ jurisdiction when New Zealand and Australia sought to block its nuclear testing program in the Pacific. Instances such as these, in which one state brings a case before the ICJ while knowing that the other party will reject any claim to compulsory jurisdiction, point to still another way in which the ICJ makes international law. It can play a consciousness-raising role, thereby speeding up the development of an international consensus on such matters as nuclear testing, covert action, or seizing embassies. A very real danger of this strategy is that, instead of serving as the basis for an international consensus, the ICJ action will polarize the international community or alienate key states.

The second option that a state has at its disposal if it feels that is has been a victim of a violation of international law is to pursue the matter unilaterally. Traditionally, the ultimate unilateral sanction has been war. Today, a consensus exists that, except in the case of self-defense against an armed attack, war is no longer a legitimate means by which a state can ensure that its legal rights are respected. More commonly, states resort to retorsions and reprisals. A retorsion is a legal action that is taken by the injured state that is designed to punish or harm the state that violated international law. Cutting off economic or military aid to a state is an example of a retorsion. The United States' decision to boycott the 1980 summer Olympic games in Moscow as a protest over the Soviet invasion of Afghanistan is another example. Reprisals are retaliatory actions taken by the injured state that in normal circumstances would be considered illegal. Expropriating the property of citizens or multinational corporations headquartered in the law-violating state is an example of a reprisal. So, too, was the seizure of Iranian assets in U.S. banks following the takeover of the U.S. embassy. In the case of the Soviet attack on KAL 007, the primary response involved retorsions. Soviet airliners were denied access to several Western airports, and several states boycotted flights into the Soviet Union.

Ethical and practical considerations enter into the decision of whether or not to retaliate against a state in the name of justice. Practical considerations enter into the decision of policymakers because no act of retaliation is without its costs. Allies may be offended by the action, or domestic political groups may oppose it, or both may occur. There is also the possibility that retaliation may bring counterretaliation, which will inflict even greater harm upon the state. Steve Chan has identified three conditions that must be met before a state can legitimately resort to force in order to right a wrong.[8] He applies them to the use of retaliatory military force, but they can also be seen as guidelines for the use of economic, political, or diplomatic force. First, the state must make every effort to settle the dispute peacefully. Second, the retaliation must be directed against those who were directly responsible for the illegal act. Third, the damage caused by the retaliation must not exceed the damages suffered or the scope of the other side's initial provocation. These criteria are not always easily met. Consider the problem of retaliating against acts of terrorism. How does one go about trying to settle the issue peacefully? Both the United States and Israel—two states that have used military force in retaliation against terrorists—have a stated policy of not negotiating with terrorists for fear of giving a certain amount of legitimacy to the actions of these groups, thereby encouraging additional terrorist acts. Who does one retaliate against—states supporting terrorism (i.e., Libya) or the terrorists themselves? Regardless of who the target is, military retaliation against

Table 6.2 INTERNATIONAL COURT OF JUSTICE CASES

I. Cases in which judgments were rendered

Title	Parties	Dates
1. Corfu Channel	United Kingdom v. Albania	1947–1949
2. Fisheries	United Kingdom v. Norway	1949–1951
3. (a) Asylum	Colombia/Peru	1949–1950
(b) Request for Interpretation of Judgment in Asylum Case	Colombia v. Peru	1950
(c) Haya de la Torre	Colombia v. Peru	1950–1951
4. Rights of Nationals of the United States in Morocco	France v. United States	1950–1952
5. Ambatielos	Greece v. United Kingdom	1951–1953
6. Anglo-Iranian Oil Co.	United Kingdom v. Iran	1951–1952
7. Minquiers and Ecrehos	France/United Kingdom	1951–1953
8. Nottebohm	Liechtenstein v. Guatemala	1951–1955
9. Monetary Gold Removed from Rome in 1943	Italy v. France, United Kingdom, and United States	1953–1954
10. Certain Norwegian Loans	France v. Norway	1955–1957
11. Right of Passage over Indian Territory	Portugal v. India	1955–1960
12. Application of Convention of 1902 Governing the Guardianship of Infants	Netherlands v. Sweden	1957–1958
13. Interhandel	Switzerland v. United States	1957–1959
14. Aerial Incident of 27 July 1955	Israel v. Bulgaria	1957–1959
15. Sovereignty over Certain Frontier Land	Belgium/Netherlands	1957–1959
16. Arbitral Award Made by the King of Spain on December, 23 1906	Honduras v. Nicaragua	1958–1960
17. (a) Barcelona Traction, Light and Power Co., Ltd.	Belgium v. Spain	1958–1961
(b) Barcelona Traction, Light and Power Co., Ltd. (New Application)	Belgium v. Spain	1962–1970
18. Temple of Preah Vihear	Cambodia v. Thailand	1959–1962
19. South-West Africa	Ethiopia v. South Africa; Liberia v. South Africa	1960–1966
20. North Cameroons	Cameroon v. United Kingdom	1961–1963
21. North Sea Continental Shelf	Federal Republic of Germany/Denmark; Federal Republic of Germany/Netherlands	1967–1969
22. Appeal Relating to the Jurisdiction of the ICAO Council	India v. Pakistan	1971–1972
23. Fisheries Jurisdiction	United Kingdom v. Iceland	1972–1974
24. Fisheries Jurisdiction	Federal Republic of Germany v. Iceland	1972–1974
25. Nuclear Tests	Australia v. France	1973–1974
26. Nuclear Tests	New Zealand v. France	1973–1974
27. Continental Shelf	Tunisia v. Libyan Arab Jamahiriya	1978–
28. Continental Shelf	Libyan Arab Jamahiriya/Malta	1982–1985

Table 6.2 Continued

I. Cases in which judgments were rendered		
Title	Parties	Dates
29. Military and Paramilitary Activities in and against Nicaragua	Nicaragua v. United States	1984–1986
30. Application for revision and interpretation of Judgment of February 24, 1982 concerning the Continental Shelf	Tunisia/Libyan Arab Jamahiriya	1984–1985

II. Case in which special order was rendered		
Title	Parties	Dates
1. United States Diplomatic and Consular Staff in Teheran	United States v. Iran	1979–1981

III. Contentious cases before a chamber		
Title	Parties	Dates
1. Delimitation of Maritime Boundary in Gulf of Maine Area	Canada/United States	1981–1984
2. Frontier Dispute	Burkina Faso/Mali	1983–

IV. Cases removed without judgment		
Title	Parties	Dates
1. Protection of French Nationals and Protected Persons in Egypt	France v. Egypt	1949–1950
2. Electricite de Beyrouth Co.	France v. Lebanon	1953–1954
3. (a) Treatment in Hungary of Aircraft and Crew of United States	United States v. Hungary	1954
(b) Treatment in Hungary of Aircraft and Crew of United States	United States v. USSR	1954
4. Aerial Incident of March 10, 1953	United States v. Czechoslovakia	1955–1956
5. (a) Antarctica	United Kingdom v. Argentina	1955–1956
(b) Antarctica	United Kingdom v. Chile	1955–1956
6. Aerial Incident of October 7, 1952	United States v. USSR	1955–1956
7. Aerial Incident of July 27, 1955	United States v. Bulgaria	1957–1960
8. Aerial Incident of July 27, 1955	United Kingdom v. Bulgaria	1957–1959
9. Aerial Incident of September 4, 1954	United States v. USSR	1958
10. Compagnie du Port, des Quais et des Entrepots de Beyrouth and Société Radio-Orient	France v. Lebanon	1959–1960
11. Aerial Incident of November 7, 1954	United States v. USSR	1959
12. Trial of Pakistani Prisoners of War	Pakistan v. India	1973
13. Aegean Sea Continental Shelf	Greece v. Turkey	1976–1978

Source: A Leroy Bennett, *International Organizations: Principles and Issues,* 4e, copyright, 1988, p. 185, Adapted by permission of Prentice Hall, Inc., Englewood Cliffs, NJ.

terrorists always runs the risk of injuring innocent civilians. What can be considered proportional retaliatory damage for the hijacking of an airliner, the assassination of a government official, or an attack on an embassy?

INTERNATIONAL ORGANIZATION

The second basic mechanism for fostering international cooperation is through international organization.[9] International organizations can be classified as either international governmental organizations (IGOs) or international nongovernmental organizations (NGOs). The difference between the two is that IGOs are created by the agreement of sovereign states and have states as their members and NGOs are created by private groups and do not have states as members. In our case study of the Soviet attack on KAL 007, both IGOs (the UN and the International Civil Aviation Organization) and NGOs (the International Federation of Airline Pilots' Associations) became involved in the effort to formulate an international consensus on the use of force against civil airliners in peacetime. In 1987, there were 1,649 IGOs and 16,592 NGOs. Our focus will be on IGOs rather than NGOs. Despite their larger numbers, NGOs do not play as important a role in the game of world politics as do IGOs. States are the central actors in world politics, and because IGOs are composed of states and NGOs are not, it stands to reason that IGOs should be the more prominent of the two in our discussions. As a measure of relative importance, we can compare the typical organizational infrastructure of NGOs and IGOs. The average NGO has a staff of 10 professionals and a budget of less than $1 million. The average IGO has a staff of 200 professionals and a budget approaching $10 million.[10]

The Growth and Development of International Organizations

International organizations are so prevalent today that it is easy to take them for granted. For all their numbers, they are relatively new actors in the game' of world politics, and this newness must be kept in mind when we are judging their effectiveness as instruments of international cooperation. We can gain a better appreciation for the novel nature of international organizations by charting their growth. This can be done two ways. The first approach involves a graphic depiction of how their numbers have increased. As Figure 6.1 indicates, international organizations are creatures of the twentieth century and the post-World War II era. By the end of 1865, there were only five IGOs. On the eve of World War I, there were only 29 in existence. In 1980 there were 337 "conventional" IGOs and 702 "other" IGOs in existence, for a grand total of 1,039. By 1987, this grand total had jumped to 1,649. The growth rate for NGOs is even more startling. In 1909, less than 180 existed, and by 1954 there were just under 1,000. In 1987 the total number of IGOs in existence had swelled to 16,592.

The second approach to understanding the novel nature of international organizations is to focus on the factors that gave rise to their growth and development. For this we turn to the nineteenth century. Inis Claude cites four prerequisites—two objective and two subjective—for the development of international organizations.[11]

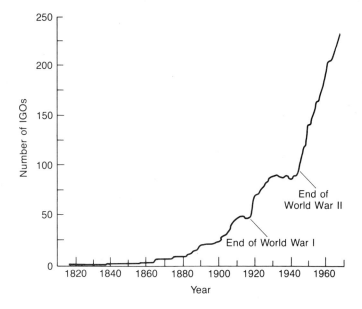

Figure 6.1 The growth of international governmental organizations in the global political system, 1815–1970 [*Source:* Harold Jacobson, *Networks of Interdependence* (New York: Alfred Knopf, 1979), p. 41].

Objectively, the world must be divided into sovereign states, and a substantial measure of contact must exist between them. Subjectively, policymakers must perceive that their interactions create problems and that the possibility exists for regulating their relations in a manner that will be beneficial to all. If states were not sovereign but subject to the authority of a higher political unit, as was the case when the pope and the Roman Catholic church stood above states before the Treaty of Westphalia, then cooperative measures could be imposed upon them. If states seldom came into contact with one another, there would be little reason to expend a great deal of time and effort to establish regularized procedures governing their interactions. Furthermore, if those interactions only occasionally led to conflict, then the isolated problems that did arise could be dealt with on a case-by-case basis. Movement toward creating international organizations reflected the belief that states could no longer do just as they please and that a method existed for bringing a measure of order and predictability into world politics without challenging the underlying principle of state sovereignty.

Nineteenth-century policymakers struck out in three directions in search of an appropriate institutional model. Each was based on a different sense of what the fundamental ordering principle should be. The first effort at building an institution stressed the principle of compromise and took the form of a system of multilateral, high-level political conferences known as the Concert of Europe. The Concert of Europe was a self-appointed group of "great powers" who took it upon themselves to organize the political landscape of Europe. As such, its meetings went beyond mere peace conferences, which officially registered the end of a war and at which terms of peace were agreed upon. The Concert of Europe concerned itself with such matters as regulating the use of European rivers, redividing the Balkans, maintaining peace on the continent, and establishing agreement on the rules of imperialism. Claude credits the Concert of Europe with creating the psychological prerequisites for successful multilateral negotiations by establishing the principle of consultation and the expectation of collective diplomatic attention to the major issues of world politics.

The second effort at building an institution rested upon the principles of regulation and universality. It took the shape of the Hague System of international conferences. In 1899, and again in 1907, small and large European and non-European states met together to address the problem of war. Significantly, the focus of their deliberations was not so much on a particular war as on the problem of war in the abstract sense. The solutions arrived at were highly legalistic in nature. The conferees succeeded in cataloging and getting agreement on the rules of war on land and on sea, and on the rights and responsibilities of neutrals. What is important about the Hague System for the growth and development of international organizations is the support shown for regularly occurring international conferences (the third Hague Conference was set for 1915 but did not take place because of World War I) and the experience gained in the techniques of conference diplomacy.

The third effort at building an institution emphasized the principle of cooperation and led to the creation of public international unions. Prominent early examples included the Central Commission for the Navigation of the Rhine, the International Telegraphic Union (1865), and the Universal Postal Union (1874). As can be seen by the names of these international organizations, the central force behind activity in this area was the increasingly complex nature of economic, cultural, social, and technical international transactions. They served as forums in which policymakers could discuss common problems, gather and exchange information, and coordinate national policies. Public international unions contributed to the growth and development of international organizations in at least two ways. First, they expanded the definition of what was a problem in world politics and thus a fitting subject for international collaboration. Second, the combined presence of the three basic organizational units (a secretariat, an assembly, and a council) found in most contemporary international organizations can be traced to the operation of public international unions. Finally, experimentation took place with various voting schemes, resulting in those commonly used by international organizations today.

These three streams of institution building came together in the aftermath of World War I to provide the organizational foundation for the League of Nations. The League's Council drew upon the Council of Europe for its model; its Assembly was rooted in the principles that governed the operation of the Hague System; and its Secretariat traced its lineage back to the International Telegraphic Union, which established the first permanent international bureaucracy. While the great organization-building experiments of the nineteenth century provided the intellectual model for the League of Nations, the immediate event that gave force to its creation was World War I. The League's blueprint was put together at the Paris Peace Conference. It was essentially drafted by the United States and Britain. Although the leaders gathered at Paris looked back with horror at the ruin left by the war that their armies had just fought and won, they saw no need to change the basic nature of world politics. The League of Nations was not intended to lead to the creation of a fundamentally new type of world politics. Its goals were far more limited and reformist in nature. The League of Nations was designed to prevent the kind of system-wide breakdown that took place in 1914 and to legitimize the international distribution of power that was in place at the end of the war.

The rise to power in Germany of Adolph Hitler and the inability of the "victors" to meet his challenge in a timely fashion stand as testament to the failure of the League of Nations to accomplish either of these goals. While many factors contributed to the outbreak of World War II, the failure of the League of Nations can be traced to two specific structural faults in its design. The first problem lay in the area of membership. Inis Claude dubs it, "the problem of the empty chair."[12] The League of Nations was unable to get appropriate states in and to keep them in. The United States never joined. The Soviet Union did not join until 1934 and was expelled in 1939. Germany's effective dates of membership ran from 1926 to 1933. Japan and Italy withdrew from the League in 1933 and 1937, respectively.

The second problem lay with the principle of collective security, which seeks to deter threats to peace by making the response of a larger group of states automatic. The principle of collective security was written into the League's Covenant, its founding document, but, in practice, it failed to materialize when Italy invaded Ethiopia in 1935. For a collective security system to work, two requirements must be met: (1) the identity of the aggressor must be quickly and unambiguously established, and (2) states must respond in the agreed-upon manner, regardless of who the aggressor is. Neither requirement is easily met, either today or in the past. The most common forms of international warfare (guerilla wars, terrorism, low-intensity conflicts) all cloud the identity of the aggressor. The second requirement fails to take into account the fact that states are unlikely to want to go to war or to impose sanctions against an ally and that policymakers will naturally be hesitant to commit themselves to an automatic response of any kind. Prudence dictates that they always leave themselves a way out.

The United Nations System

Types of International Organizations International Governmental Organizations can be grouped into one of four categories, depending upon their membership and function. Membership is either universal, in which case all states are free to join, or limited. There is no single standard for limiting membership. In most cases, geography is the primary limiting factor, such as in the Organization of American States, the Organization of African Unity, or the Arab League. Economics may also be a limiting factor. Membership in the European Community is limited both by geography and economics; member states have capitalist economies. Ideology or political affiliation tends to serve as the limiting factor in military organizations, such as the North Atlantic Treaty Organization (NATO) and the Warsaw Pact, which are designed to protect members from external attack. Finally, history may provide the

Table 6.3 TYPOLOGY OF INTERNATIONAL ORGANIZATIONS

	Purpose	
	Special purpose	Multifunctional
Membership		
Limited	North Atlantic Treaty Organization Organization of Petroleum Exporting Countries International Cocoa Association	Organization of African Unity Organization of American States Arab League Council of Europe
Universal	UN High Commission on Refugees World Health Organization UNICEF International Civil Aviation Organization	United Nations League of Nations

unifying and limiting criteria. The members of the British Commonwealth were all once British colonies.

With regard to function, IGOs can be classified either as multifunctional or special purpose. In the former case, the organization will deal with a wide variety of issues, whereas, in the latter case, it is set up to deal with a specific problem. Table 6.3 combines these two dimensions and presents several examples of each type of IGO. Our case study of the downing of KAL 007 made reference to three of the four types of IGOs. The UN is a universal member, multipurpose IGO; the International Civil Aviation Organization is a universal member, specialized IGO, and the Latin American Civil Aviation Convention is a limited membership, specialized organization.

The principal international organization today is the United Nations.[13] The planning of it began during World War II, even before the United States entered the war. The first time the phrase "United Nations" appeared on an official document was in 1942, when 26 states met in Washington and used the phrase to sign a declaration of principles. In 1943, representatives of the United States, Great Britain, China, and the Soviet Union met in Moscow and committed themselves to the creation of a universal international organization. Preliminary plans were worked out in 1944 at Dumbarton Oaks and in 1945 at Yalta. The UN Charter was signed in San Francisco on June 25, 1945 and was scheduled to come into effect as soon as the governments of all five permanent members of the Security Council and one-half of the other members ratified it. This happened by the end of October 1945, and the UN General Assembly convened for the first time on January 10, 1946 in London.

Structure of the United Nations The founders of the UN purposefully gave the impression that the UN was a new international organization and not a resurrected League of Nations. While creating a sense of distance between the UN and the

League of Nations was necessary from both a psychological and a political perspective, it obscured the fact that, structurally, the UN really could be seen as a revised version of the League of Nations. Its main structural features could be found there, and, just as the League of Nations did, the UN system drew upon all three of the nineteenth-century experiments in organization building for its inspiration. There is one important respect in which the structure of these two international organizations differed. According to Inis Claude, the League of Nations took as its point of departure the concept of accidental war and the need to prevent another war from starting in the same fashion.[14] No such conceptual unity was present at the creation of the UN system. Instead, it was recognized that multiple paths to war existed. One way of understanding how the different parts of the UN system relate to one another is to see each as directed at preventing states from traveling down as many of these paths as possible.[15]

The Security Council has representatives from 15 states, 5 of whom (the United States, the Soviet Union, Great Britain, France, and China) are designated as permanent members and are given veto power over its substantive deliberations. Other states are elected as nonpermanent members by a vote of the General Assembly for a two-year term, with the general understanding that no state is eligible for immediate reelection. Nonpermanent seats are allocated on the basis of a regional-quota formula in the following manner: five for Asia and Africa, two for Latin America, one for Eastern Europe, and two for Western Europe and other states. An unwritten rule allows members from each of these regions to choose which state will occupy its seats, with the full General Assembly then giving automatic approval to these choices.

According to the UN Charter, the Security Council alone is empowered to adopt economic and military sanctions. In giving it this power, the founders of the UN were not seeking to reestablish a collective security system. The veto power held by the five permanent members guaranteed that the UN could never be used against one of them. Disputes between any of permanent members would be settled outside the scope of the UN system. The true parent of the Security Council is the Council of Europe, and the logic behind its incorporation into the UN system is the belief that, unless provisions are made for the cooperation of the great powers, war is inevitable. The Security Council thus was seen as providing a standing instrument for the great powers to use when they were in agreement on what should be done about a problem.

The General Assembly was seen as a body that could prevent war by providing states with a place to talk and to clarify misperceptions about each other's intentions. As did the Assembly of the League of Nations, the UN General Assembly draws upon the Hague System and its principle of universality for its inspiration. The General Assembly expresses its opinion on the matters that come before it in one of three ways. First, it can pass a resolution that would call upon members to act in a specified way, or it can condemn or applaud an action already taken. Second, it can pass a declaration, which is a statement of principle. Among the most significant declarations issued by the General Assembly have been the Universal Declaration of Human Rights (1948), and the Declaration on the Establishment of a New International

Economic Order (1975). Third, it can pass a convention, which is a multilateral treaty. United Nations treaties only come into force and bind the behavior of members after states have ratified them.

Regardless of how the General Assembly chooses to express its views, the UN Charter places limitations on what it can say. The General Assembly is not allowed to make any decisions that are binding on its members, it is prohibited from making any recommendations concerning a dispute under consideration by the Security Council, and it may not intervene into matters that are essentially within the domestic jurisdiction of any state. This last restriction applies not only to the General Assembly but also to the UN as a whole.

A third key organization in the UN system is the International Court of Justice. It was hoped by some that states would be less likely to go to war if there existed clearly established rules and procedures for settling disputes and for conducting interstate relations. The International Court of Justice is a reincarnation of the Permanent Court of International Justice that was set up by the League of Nations and formally came into existence in 1921. The International Court of Justice plays two different roles in world politics. First, it is a court where states can take disputes to be settled. Second, it is the constitutional court of the UN, where questions concerning the meaning of the UN Charter or the constitutionality of acts are resolved. Unlike the U.S. court system, the International Court of Justice can be asked to give advisory opinions on questions as well as to settle disputes. Fifteen justices sit on the International Court of Justice. They are elected by concurrent votes of the General Assembly and the Security Council, and it is expected that the composition of the Court will cover all major legal systems. Should a state that does not have representative on the Court be involved in a dispute that comes before it, that state is allowed to appoint a jurist of its choosing to the bench to hear the case.

In the belief that some wars are rooted in the misery and poverty experienced by many of the world's people, a fourth principal organization of the UN system, the Economic and Social Council, was designed to raise global living standards and to improve economic conditions. It attempts to do so in three ways: (1) by discussing global problems in such areas as food, health, housing, labor, transportation, and trade and then recommending solutions, (2) by sponsoring research and issuing reports, and (3) by coordinating the activities of the many agencies involved in international economic and social work.

The complexity of the problem facing the Economic and Social Council in coordinating UN efforts to eradicate poverty and misery can best be appreciated by examining the diversity of organizations involved in these tasks. Most directly under the control of the Economic and Social Council are a series of regional and functional commissions and committees. Numbered among them are the Commission on Human Rights, the Commission on the Status of Women, and the Economic and Social Commission for Asia and the Pacific. One step further removed from the direct control and supervision of the Economic and Social Council are such UN agencies as the United Nations Children's Fund (UNICEF), the United Nations High Commission for Refugees (UNHCR), the World Food Council, and the United Nations Conference on Trade and Development (UNCTAD). The primary services that the Economic and Social Council provides to these agencies lie in the area of coordination.

Even further removed from the control of the Economic and Social Council are a group of specialized and more or less autonomous UN agencies. Each was created by a treaty produced at an international conference, and membership in each organization is separate from membership in the UN. In its dealings with them, the Social and Economic Council is limited to making recommendations for the coordination of policies and activities. Listed among these agencies are the World Health Organization (WHO), the United Nations Educational, Scientific and Cultural Organizations (UNESCO), and the International Monetary Fund (IMF).

A fifth organization in the UN system, the Trusteeship Council, was created to redefine the way in which colonial powers view their colonies. The goal was to have them seen less as pieces of property to be exploited and more as pieces of property whose possession confers a great and expensive responsibility on the owner. Without this change in thinking, it was feared that states would continue to go to war in order to acquire colonies and that states would not prepare their colonies for independence. An inevitable by-product of this latter possibility would be bloody colonial wars for independence. Beyond this normative task, the Trusteeship Council is also charged with the operational responsibility of supervising the administration of regions designated by the UN as trust territories. In each case, a state is assigned to administer the territory and to prepare it for independence. All but one of the 11 trusteeship territories that came into existence by 1950 occupied a similar position in the League of Nations mandate system.

Most problematic for the UN has been the case of Namibia. Under the League of Nations mandate system, Namibia, then referred to as South West Africa, was administered by South Africa. When the UN was created, South Africa refused to place Namibia under a trusteeship arrangement and instead unilaterally annexed it. This decision was never accepted fully by the UN, which lists itself as the administering authority in official UN documents. A permanent resolution to the Namibian problem only began to take shape in the late 1980s and then only after the issue became embroiled in the Angolan civil war, in which South Africa and the United States opposed forces supported by the Soviet Union and Cuba. A peace agreement that was signed on December 22, 1988 essentially traded Namibian independence for the withdrawal of 50,000 Cuban troops from neighboring Angola. As part of the agreement, the UN sent a Transition Assistance Group to supervise Namibia's independence elections and the evacuation of South West African People's Organization (SWAPO) guerrillas from Namibia back into Angola.

The sixth and final structure created by the founders of the UN is the Secretariat. A full-time, professional, international civil service was seen as essential if peace was to have a chance. Without bureaucrats and diplomats who are loyal to the international community, only narrowly defined and competitively cast national interests are likely to be put forward and to receive careful consideration at international conferences. At the head of the Secretariat sits the secretary-general. Secretary-generals serve a five-year term and are elected by a two-thirds vote of the General Assembly upon the recommendation of the Security Council. There have been five secretary-generals: Trygve Lie of Norway (1946–1953), Dag Hammarskjold of Sweden (1953–1961), U Thant of Burma (1961–1972), Kurt Waldheim of Austria (1972–1982), and Perez de Cuellar of Peru (1982–present). For reasons that we shall discuss shortly, the Soviet Union has frequently been displeased by the actions and decisions of the secretary-general. After the death of Dag Hammarskjold from an airplane crash as he was returning from an inspection trip to the UN Peacekeeping Force in the Congo, the Soviet Union unsuccessfully proposed that the office of the secretary-general be made a collective position. One secretary-general would be selected by the West, one by the Soviet bloc, and one by the UN as a whole. Then, only when all three members of this *troika* were in agreement could the office of the secretary-general issue instructions. If this effort had been successful, the Soviet Union would have succeeded in acquiring a de facto veto power over the actions of the Secretariat.

Figure 6.2 presents an overview of the key features that we have just identified in the UN system.

The Five Different United Nations   The description of the UN that we have given so far focuses on the nuts and bolts of the UN system. It does not give a sense of how the UN has changed and evolved over time. We will divide the history of the UN into five phases.[16] The exact point in time at which we can separate one UN from the next is not easily determined and can be debated at great length. For our purposes, identifying these precise points in time is not as important as is the process of thinking about the UN as a dynamic organization rather than one that was created in 1945 and has become frozen in place ever since. There is nothing really surprising about the fact that the nature of the UN has been transformed over time. The UN is an international organization, and, by definition, ultimate power in international organizations resides with the member states. As the power relationships of these member states change, so too does the nature of international organizations. The changes that international organizations experience do not, however, fully mirror the changes taking place in the power relationships among states. This is because, once in place, the norms, institutions, and informal networks that form the essence of an international organization are difficult to abolish or drastically rearrange.

The first UN came to an end almost upon creation in 1945. It was to be a way of keeping together the World War II Great Power alliance that had defeated Germany and Japan. This conception of the UN became outmoded as the cold war heated up and the international system moved into a bipolar configuration. The actual date of its demise might be set as early as August 6, 1945, when the United States dropped the atomic bomb on Hiroshima. Questioning the military need to use the atomic bomb, some see the true target of this attack as the Soviet Union. In destroying Hiroshima, the United States sent a strong political signal to the Soviet Union regarding where real power would lie, and, therefore, who would set the rules in the postwar international system.

It was the United States that pushed hardest at World War II summit conferences. International law and international organization are central elements in the liberal approach to world politics, which lies at the heart of the American perspective on international relations. Soviet participation in the UN was secured at the price of concessions in other areas (one concession within the UN system was to allow two Soviet Republics—the Ukraine and Byelorussia—to join as full members). The Soviet Union approached the role of the UN as a peacekeeper from a realist perspective. Power, not laws and organization, would determine the nature of the interna-

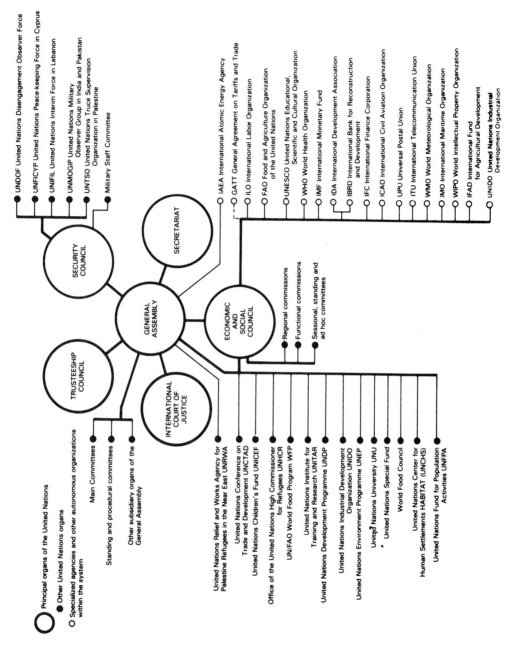

Figure 6.2 The United Nations system [*Source: Basic Facts About the United Nations* (New York: United Nations, 1987)].

tional order. No international organization could make the United States and Soviet Union get along and cooperate. Soviet membership in the UN was vital, because the United States would be a member and might try to use the UN against it should they become enemies.

The Soviet fear was not groundless, and the second UN can be seen as an instrument of American foreign policy. It did not last very long, ending around the mid-1950s. The United States was successful in using the UN for its own purposes for three reasons. The first came about as the result of a tactical error made by the Soviet Union. Upset over an earlier UN decision not to recognize the People's Republic of China as the legitimate occupant of China's seat, the Soviet Union was boycotting UN meetings when the Security Council took up the question of how the UN ought to respond to the North Korean invasion of South Korea. As a result, it was not present to veto resolutions labeling North Korea as the aggressor, calling upon member states to help South Korea repel the attack, and requesting the United States to designate a commander and help organize a unified UN command in South Korea.

It was clear to all that the Soviet Union would not repeat this mistake, and the search began for a way to get around future Soviet vetoes of Security Council Resolutions that called for the use of military force to stop aggression. The instrument chosen was the Uniting for Peace Resolution. Passed in November 1950, it stated that an Emergency Special Session of the General Assembly could be called whenever the Security Council was deadlocked and "fail[ed] to exercise" its responsibilities in the face of threats to international peace and security. Such a session may be called (and must meet within 24 hours) either at the request of nine members of the Security Council or by a majority of the UN's membership. As is clear from reading Table 6.4, the distribution of states within the UN left no doubt that the United States could muster the necessary votes whenever necessary. This is the second reason for the United States' success in using the UN to further its foreign-policy goals. Of the 55 states that were members of the UN in 1945, 34 could be classified as U.S. allies, whereas only 5 could be classified as Soviet allies. In 1950, when 60 states belonged to the UN, 37 were U.S. allies and there were still only 5 Communist bloc states.

A third and more limited reason for the United States' success in using the UN to form its own purposes was that Third World states had grounds of their own for wanting to find a way of circumventing Soviet vetoes. The UN was valued by them as a potential modifier of the actions of the Great Powers. They feared that if the UN did not respond to the North Korean attack, it would be permanently discredited as a peacekeeper in the same way that the League of Nations was discredited following Italy's attack on Ethiopia in 1935. If that were to happen, then Third World states might well become the prime victims of Great Power aggression. Third World states also saw the Uniting for Peace Resolution as a way of increasing their influence in the UN, because it took power away from the Security Council and gave it to the General Assembly, where they were better represented.

Further evidence that the second UN tended to function as an instrument of American foreign policy comes from the frequency of Soviet vetoes. As Table 6.5 illustrates, this is the period when most Soviet vetoes took place. Between 1945 and 1955, the Soviet Union cast 77 of the 117 vetoes it had cast by 1985. During that same period, only three other vetoes were recorded, one by China and two by

Table 6.4   GROWTH OF UN MEMBERSHIP, 1945–1986

Year	Number	New member states
1945	51	Argentina, Australia, Belgium, Bolivia, Brazil, Byelorussian SSR, Canada, Chile, China, Colombia, Costa Rica, Cuba, Czechoslovakia, Denmark, Dominican Republic, Ecuador, Egypt, El Salvador, Ethiopia, France, Greece, Guatemala, Haiti, Honduras, India, Iran, Iraq, Lebanon, Liberia, Luxembourg, Mexico, Netherlands, New Zealand, Nicaragua, Norway, Panama, Paraguay, Peru, Philippines, Poland, Saudi Arabia, South Africa, Syria, Turkey, Ukrainian SSR, USSR, United Kingdom, United States, Uruguay, Venezuela, Yugoslavia
1946	55	Afghanistan, Iceland, Sweden, Thailand
1947	57	Pakistan, Yemen
1948	58	Burma
1949	59	Israel
1950	60	Indonesia
1955	76	Albania, Austria, Bulgaria, Democratic Kampuchea, Finland, Hungary, Ireland, Italy, Jordan, Lao People's Democratic Republic, Libyan Arab Jamahiriya, Nepal, Portugal, Romania, Spain, Sri Lanka
1956	80	Japan, Morocco, Sudan, Tunisia
1957	82	Ghana, Malaysia
1958	83	Guinea
1960	100	Benin, Burkina Faso, Central African Republic, Chad, Congo, Côte d'Ivoire, Cyprus, Gabon, Madagascar, Mali, Niger, Nigeria, Senegal, Somalia, Togo, United Republic of Cameroon, Zaire
1961	104	Mauritania, Mongolia, Sierra Leone, United Republic of Tanzania
1962	110	Algeria, Burundi, Jamaica, Rwanda, Trinidad and Tobago, Uganda
1963	112	Kenya, Kuwait
1964	115	Malawi, Malta, Zambia
1965	118	Gambia, Maldives, Singapore
1966	122	Barbados, Botswana, Guyana, Lesotho
1967	123	Democratic Yemen
1968	126	Equatorial Guinea, Mauritius, Swaziland
1970	127	Fiji
1971	132	Bahrain, Bhutan, Oman, Qatar, United Arab Emirates
1973	135	Bahamas, Federal Republic of Germany, German Democratic Republic
1974	138	Bangladesh, Grenada, Guinea-Bissau
1975	144	Cape Verde, Comoros, Mozambique, Papua New Guinea, São Tomé and Principe, Suriname
1976	147	Angola, Samoa, Seychelles
1977	149	Djibouti, Vietnam
1978	151	Dominica, Solomon Islands
1979	152	Saint Lucia
1980	154	Saint Vincent and the Grenadines, Zimbabwe
1981	157	Antigua and Barbuda, Belize, Vanuatu
1983	158	Saint Christopher and Nevis
1984	159	Brunei Darussalam

Source: UN Chronicle 23, no. 2 (1986), inside front cover.

Table 6.5 VETOES IN THE SECURITY COUNCIL, 1946–1985

Time period	Number of vetoes				
	China	France	United Kingdom	United States	Soviet Union
1945–1950	0	2	0	0	47
1951–1955	1	0	0	0	30
1956–1960	0	2	2	0	15
1961–1965	0	0	1	0	11
1966–1970	0	0	2	1	2
1971–1975	2	2	8	11	5
1976–1980	0	5	4	10	5
1981–1985	16*	4	7	28[†]	2
1986	0	1	2	8	0
Total	19	16	26	58	117

Source: Robert Riggs and Jack Plano, *The United Nations* (Chicago: Dorsey, 1988), p. 77. Reprinted by permission of Brooks/Cole Publishing Company, Pacific Grove, CA.

*All 16 vetoes by China were cast in closed session to block the reelection of Kurt Waldheim as Secretary-General in 1981. The vetoes are not recorded in the official records but appear in press accounts.

[†]Five of the 28 U.S. vetoes were cast in closed session to block the election of Tanzanian candidate Salim Ahmed Salim as Secretary-General in 1981.

France. Many of these Soviet vetoes were cast to prevent additional pro-Western states from joining the UN. It vetoed Italy's bid to join the UN five times. The United States was able to realize a great deal of public relations out of this "obstructionist" Soviet behavior, because the United States was able to argue that it had never vetoed any membership application. The truth is that the United States was never forced to veto the application of a pro-Soviet ally, because the state could never get enough "yes" votes from Western states to qualify for membership. All that the Soviet Union could say in its own defense was that the West was exercising a silent collective veto.

By the final years of the second UN, the stalemate over admitting new members had reached crisis proportions. Only nine states had been added to the UN's membership roll between 1946 and 1950, and none were added between 1950 and 1955, although more than 20 had applied for admission. The deadlock was finally broken in December 1955 when 16 states were admitted as a package. The expansion in membership that began then brought a third UN into existence. It was dominated by the newly independent Third World states who were now joining the UN in large numbers. Although initially they were quite hostile to the interests of the West and supportive of Soviet concerns because of the positions that each side had taken on the question of decolonization—the United States had sided with its European colonial allies in urging that a slow approach be taken toward Third World independence, while the Soviet Union had positioned itself as a champion of rapid decolonization—Third World states soon sought to distance themselves from both superpowers.

The Third World states came to the conclusion that their security interests would best be served by keeping United States and the Soviet Union out of their internal and regional problems. The central instrument of the third UN that would be used to make this goal a reality was the United Nations Peacekeeping Force, and the key concept behind it was *preventive diplomacy.* Preventive diplomacy sought to identify a positive role for the UN in a bipolar world. Secretary-General Dag Hammarskjold envisioned preventive diplomacy as a means of preventing power vacuums and marginal conflicts from becoming the object of superpower competition.[17] Hammarskjold cited the early United Nations peacekeeping operations as evidence of the potential for success inherent in the concept of preventive diplomacy. Although he did not treat preventive diplomacy and peacekeeping in the same way, over time the two ideas became merged into one and less and less attention was given to the possibility of having the UN engage in quiet diplomacy that was designed to prevent a crisis situation from developing.

There have been 15 UN peacekeeping operations. Twelve of them came before 1970, beginning in 1956 when a United Nations Emergency Force (UNEF) was sent to Egypt to serve as a buffer between the Egyptian and the Israeli forces. A full listing of UN peacekeeping operations is presented in Table 6.6. Their duties have varied considerably. In some cases they have acted as observers; in others they have served as buffers between hostile forces; and in still others they have gone into countries to restore the peace. Given these varied roles, the size of UN peacekeeping forces has also shown great variation. Observer units have been as small as 20, while forces engaged in military activities have ranged in size from 5,000–7,000 in the Middle East and Cyprus to 20,000 in the Congo (Zaire). Regardless of their size or purpose, the presence of UN peacekeeping forces cannot be imposed upon a state, for to do so would violate the principle of sovereignty. They must be invited into a country, and they must leave when they are told to. Egypt expelled the UNEF in 1967, and war broke out before they had been fully evacuated. United Nations Peacekeeping Forces are also not allowed to interfere in the domestic politics of the host state, although this has happened, most notably in 1960 when the United Nations Congo Operations (UNCO) force became involved in the ongoing civil war.

The UN has had mixed success in its role of peacekeeper. One researcher has calculated that, of 282 disputes in the international system between 1945 and 1981, 123 were referred to the UN and the UN succeeded, at least partially, in resolving 51 percent of those cases. Twenty-eight cases were settled with assistance of the UN, and in another 35 cases the situation improved because of the UN's efforts.[18] Another study found that, of the 160 international crises that occurred between 1945 and 1975, the UN became involved in 95 cases and successfully resolved 28 of them.[19] Whether our final judgment about this record is positive or negative largely depends upon the standards of judgment and expectations that we bring to the question, "Can the UN keep the peace?" Ernst Haas, the author of the first study that we cited, argues that *failure* is an inappropriate term to use in assessing the UN's peacekeeping record, but he does feel that its ability to play peacekeeper has gradually lessened or decayed over time. Haas also notes that the UN's success has varied with the types of challenges that it has faced. Its greatest successes have come when global peace is threatened, and its greatest difficulties have come when it is dealing with

Table 6.6 UN PEACEKEEPING MISSIONS

Latin America

IAPF. Inter-American Peace Force, 1965–66: Moderate civil strife in the Dominican Republic (dispatched by the Organization of American States; UN representative and military observer present concurrently with IAPF).

Africa

ONUC. French initials for the UN Operation in the Congo, 1960–64: Keep peace and order, preserve unity.

UNAVEM. UN Angolan Verification Mission, 1988-present: Verify withdrawal of Cuban forces.

UNTAG. UN Transition Assistance Group, 1988-present: Supervise elections in Namibia

Europe

UNMOG. UN Military Observers in Greece, 1952–54: Investigate incidents along borders with Albania, Yugoslavia, and Bulgaria.

UNFICYP. UN Force in Cyprus, 1974-present: Keep law and order and peace between Greek and Turkish communities.

Middle East

UNTSO. UN Truce Supervision Organization in Palestine, 1948-present: Supervise armistice among Israel, Jordan, Lebanon, and Syria.

UNEF. UN Emergency Force, 1956–67, 1973–79: Prevent Israeli-Egyptian hostilities, keep peace and order in Sinai and Gaza Strip.

UNOGIL. UN Observer Group in Lebanon, June-December 1958: Police Lebanon-Syria border.

UNDOF. UN Disengagement Observer Force, 1974-present: Maintain cease-fire between Syria and Israel.

UNIFIL. UN Interim Force in Lebanon, 1978-present: Police Lebanon-Israel border.

UNYOM. UN Yemen Observation Mission, 1963–64: Report on withdrawal of Saudi Arabian and Egyptian forces.

UNGOMP. UN Good Offices Mission in Afghanistan and Pakistan, 1988-present: Monitor Soviet troop withdrawal

UNIMOG. UN Iran Iraq Oberserver Group, 1988-present: Observe cease fire that went into effect in August, 1988.

Asia/Pacific

UNMOGIP. UN Military Observer Group in India and Pakistan, 1948-present: Supervise cease-fire in Jammu-Kashmir.

UNCFI. UN Commission for Indonesia, 1949–51: Settle dispute with Netherlands.

United Nations Command in Korea, 1950-present: Established to repel armed attack by forces from North Korea and restore international peace in Korea.

UNSF. UN Security Force, 1962–63: Facilitate transfer of West Irian to Indonesia.

UNIPOM. UN India-Pakistan Observation Mission, 1965–66: Supervise cease-fire in Rann of Kutch.

Source: Harry Young, *Atlas of United States Foreign Relations* (Washington D.C.: U.S Department of State, 1985), p. 20.

scattered and low-level disputes. He suggests that this pattern may represent a "second best solution" to the problem of war. Wars will never be totally eliminated, but a mechanism seems to be in place for holding in check the most serious challenges to peace.

As the United States and the Soviet Union moved toward détente during the early 1970s, the logic behind preventive diplomacy lost much of its force and a fourth UN began to take shape. This one was also dominated by Third World states, but instead of being used as a protective shield, it was used as a sword. The target was what Third World states perceived to be the exploitative nature of the international economic system. The goal was to bring into existence a New International Economic Order (NIEO) that would be based on the principles of "equity, sovereign equality, interdependence, common interest, and cooperation among all states."[20] Among the long-term tasks that were deemed necessary were the elimination of Third World economic dependence on Western-based multinational corporations, the strengthening of economic ties among Third World states themselves, and the introduction of a global resource management system.

The specific goals of the NIEO are laid down in numerous UN documents. One of the most important of these is the United Nations General Assembly Resolution of 1975 on "Development and International Economic Co-Operation." It recommended that 69 specific measures be taken to bring about a NIEO. They were divided into seven categories: (1) international trade, (2) the transfer of resources for financing development, (3) science and technology, (4) industrialization, (5) food and agriculture, (6) co-operation among developing states, and (7) restructuring the economic and social sectors of the UN system. These goals were not entirely new. They were part of an agenda that Third World states had been advancing since the early 1960s. The vehicle for expressing their demands was the United Nations Conference on Trade and Development (UNCTAD), whose meetings they dominated through the formation of a bargaining coalition that came to be known as the "Group of 77." This name remains in use today, although the group's membership has grown to well over 100.

By and large, the fourth UN disappointed the Third World. The goal of an NIEO remains unrealized. The United States and the West have not moved beyond accepting the idea in principle. They have shown little interest in taking the necessary concrete steps to bring it into existence, preferring instead to seek ways of reforming the existing international economic order. In part, the failures of the fourth UN can be traced to events that took place outside the UN. Southern unity was severely shaken by the Iran-Iraq war; the economic slowdown in the global economy made Western states unwilling or unable, or both, to take part in international economic reforms; and the reintensification of the cold war sharply reduced the role that the UN could play in world politics. Problems also arose, however, from what Western states saw as the internal radicalization of the UN. Signs of this radicalization were everywhere. The UN agreed to allow the Palestine Liberation Organization (PLO) to address the General Assembly and gave it observer status. The South West African People's Organization (SWAPO) in Namibia was also given observer status. As a consequence of this designation and in spite of the fact that neither of these entities is a state, both are able to draw upon UN funds. In other moves, Israel was expelled from UNESCO and South Africa was barred from attending meetings of the assembly because of its racial policies. Calls were also heard in the General Assembly for Puerto Rican independence.

In time this radicalization produced a backlash of anti-UN sentiment in the United States. Congress voted to reduce the level of U.S. funding to the UN from 25 to 20 percent if steps were not taken to reform the UN's one-state-one-vote decision-making system. Repeatedly out-voted by Third World states unsympathetic to its interests, the United States wanted a weighted voting system to be used, similar to the one employed by the World Bank and IMF. Voting strength would be tied to the level of a state's financial contribution to the UN (the United States, Japan, West Germany, and France account for slightly more than 50 percent). While it did not change the voting system, the UN did put into place budgetary and staffing reforms that caused President Reagan to continue funding at the existing level. The United States also gave notice that it intended to withdraw from UNESCO in 1984 as a sign of its displeasure over UNESCO's treatment of Israel and the manner in which UNESCO's secretary-general was running the organization. The United States was troubled by what it saw as financial and managerial irregularities and the attempt by UNESCO's secretary-general to impose a New International Information Order, which would have allowed Third World governments to place restrictions on foreign (i.e., Western) media operating within their territories.

Today, signs point to a fifth UN coming into existence. The key transforming event leading to its birth would be Mikhail Gorbachev's ascent to power in the Soviet Union and the changes his government has brought to Soviet foreign policy. After being forced to sit on the sidelines and watch the superpowers or their proxies fight in Vietnam, Afghanistan, Nicaragua, Angola, and the Middle East, the fifth UN appears to be rediscovering the concept of preventive diplomacy. It is the United States and the Soviet Union, not the Third World states, who pursued this course of action during the third UN and are now using it to further their national interests. Both appear to be in agreement that they can no longer afford the high costs and limited benefits that have come from involvement in Third World wars. The search for a mechanism to control these costs has led them back to the UN. As a result, during the late 1980s the UN became active in peace mediation efforts in the Iran-Iraq war, the Soviet evacuation of troops from Afghanistan, and Angola. It is monitoring the independence of Namibia, and there were also talks of sending a UN Peacekeeping Force to the Nicaragua-Honduras border with the blessings of the United States. Further evidence of the dawning of a new UN was the setback dealt to the PLO's 1989 efforts to join the World Health Organization as a full member. The PLO lost when a resolution to defer the question for one year was introduced by 10 neutral states and was passed by a vote of 83–47. The Soviet Union backed the resolution, and the U.S. threatened to cut off funding to the WHO, a move that would have crippled the organization.

CONCLUSION: INTERNATIONAL COOPERATION

Three inescapable conclusions confront anyone studying international cooperation. First, cooperation is not a prerequisite for solving all foreign-policy problems. In some cases, a natural harmony of objectives exists; in others, a state may achieve its goals by imposing its will on other states. Cooperation is necessary when goals can be realized only when foreign policies are brought into conformity with one another through a process of mutual accommodation and compromise.

Second, when it is necessary, cooperation is not easily realized. States operate in an environment that places a premium on self-help, sovereignty, and the unrelenting pursuit of power. Domestic political considerations also complicate the pursuit of cooperative ventures. To be successful, cooperative arrangements must not only "solve" the problem but also enjoy domestic political support.

Third, when cooperation is supposed to take place, it often does not or does so only imperfectly. In part this is due to the complexity of the problems that confront states. Existing mechanisms that allow states to cooperate cannot be designed to deal with every contingency. A certain amount of slippage is thus inevitable. The frailty of cooperative arrangements can also be traced to the constraints under which they operate. "Sovereignty and autonomy mean that translation costs are never negligible since it is always difficult to communicate, monitor performance, and especially to enforce compliance with rules."[21]

Finally, international cooperation does take place with great regularity and probably does so more than most of us realize. World politics is not a zero-sum game in which the benefits gained by one state must by definition come at the expense of another state.

The two principal means for realizing international cooperation are international law and international organization. Each must overcome serious tests if they are to move international cooperation to a new plateau. International law must become truly global in nature. Global conferences, especially in the environmental area, appear to be the chosen avenue for bringing this about. As we judge the pace and result of these deliberations, it may not be much of an exaggeration to suggest that the universality of international law that many claim has been lost due to Third World communist challenges never really existed. It was always Western international law that had a global reach because of the economic and military power of Europe. If this is true, then international law today is in the same state of development that it was before the nineteenth century, when there also was no common culture or overarching political order.

International organizations face a different challenge. How long can their numbers continue to expand? Is there an upper limit to how many international organizations can effectively serve the international community? Nineteen states currently belong to at least 100 IGOs; Denmark leads the way, belonging to 164 IGOs. In 1970, only seven states belonged to more than 100 IGOs, and France belonged to the most, with 131 memberships. On a per capita basis, New Zealand belongs to 1 IGO for every 42,466 citizens; for Cape Verde Islands, the ratio is 1:11,571, while for the United States it is 1:1,850,500. Yet, while the creation of new international organizations has slowed down slightly, it continues at a rapid pace: In 1980, 42 new IGOs and 151 new INOs were created; in 1985, 9 new IGOs and 82 new INOs were created. If we are approaching a saturation point, what alternative forms of international organization should be pursued? Should international organizations be consolidated? Is world government the answer? Should the emphasis be switched from universal organization to regional organization?

NOTES

1. The material in this section is drawn from Craig Morton, "The Shooting of Korean Air Lines Flight 007," in W. Michael Reisman and Andrew Willard, eds., *International Incidents* (Princeton, N.J.: Princeton University Press, 1988), pp. 202–237; and G. F. Fitzgerald, "The Use of Force Against Civil Aircraft, *Canadian Yearbook of International Law* 22 (1984): 291–310.

2. Roger Masters, "World Politics as a Primitive Political System," *World Politics* 16 (1964): 595–619.

3. This section draws heavily upon the discussions found in Michael Akehurst, *A Modern*

Introduction to International Law, 3d ed. (London: Allen & Unwin, 1977), 30–47; and "Legal Argumentation in International Crises: The Downing of Korean Air Lines Flight 007," *Harvard Law Review* 97 (1984): 1198–1213.

4. Richard Sterling, *Macropolitics* (New York: Alfred Knopf, 1974), p. 272.

5. This section is based upon *A Study of Soviet Foreign Policy* (Moscow: Progress Publishers, 1975), pp. 27–31.

6. Quoted in K. J. Holsti, *International Politics: A Framework For Analysis* 5th ed. (Englewood Cliffs, N.J.: Prentice-Hall, 1988), p. 375.

7. K. J. Holsti, *International Politics*, pp. 370–371.

8. Steve Chan, *International Relations in Perspective* (New York: Macmillan, 1984), p. 311.

9. For a valuable collection of essays on international organizations, see Paul Diehl, ed., *The Politics of International Organizations* (Chicago: Dorsey Press, 1989).

10. Theodore Coulombis and James Wolfe, *Introduction to International Relations*, 3d ed. (Englewood Cliffs, N.J.: Prentice-Hall, 1986), p. 277.

11. Inis Claude, *Swords into Plowshares*, 4th ed. (New York: Random House, 1984).

12. Claude, *Swords into Plowshares*, p. 87.

13. Much of the discussion in this section builds upon the account of the UN that can be found in A. LeRoy Bennett, *International Organizations*, 4th ed. (Englewood Cliffs, N.J.: Prentice-Hall, 1988).

14. Claude, *Swords into Plowshares*, p. 45.

15. John Stoessinger, *The Might of Nations*, 3d ed. (New York: Random House, 1969), pp. 251–255.

16. This discussion is based upon and extends the discussion presented by John Spanier in *Games Nations Play*, 6th ed. (Washington, D.C.: Congressional Quarterly Press, 1987), pp. 576–599.

17. Claude, *Swords into Plowshares*, p. 313.

18. Ernst Haas, "Regime Decay: Conflict Management and International Organizations, 1945–1981," *International Organization* 32 (1983): 189–256.

19. Jonathan Wilkenfeld and Michael Brecher, "International Crises, 1945–1975: The UN Dimension," *International Studies Quarterly* 28 (1984): 45–62.

20. For documents and commentary on the idea of a NIEO, see Karl Sauvant and Hajo Hasenpflug, eds., *The New International Economic Order* (Boulder Colo.: Westview Press, 1977). The material cited in this paragraph can be found in that book.

21. Robert Keohane, "International Institutions: Two Approaches," *International Studies Quarterly* 32 (1988): 386–387.

PART TWO

The Military Dimension

Chapter

7

Historical Overview of the Post-World War II Era

While the phrase "cold war" is familiar and much has been written about it, its essential characteristics are not easily defined and continue to be debated. For many, the cold war continues to be "the most enigmatic and elusive international conflict of modern time." It symbolizes a period of competition, hostility, and tension between the United States and the Soviet Union, in which each perceives its national security to be threatened almost by the very existence of the other. Our purpose in this chapter is twofold. First, we will review the history of the cold war in order to provide a context for later chapters, which will discuss nuclear strategy, crisis management, terrorism, guerilla warfare, and the broader question of why nations go to war. Second, we will examine some of the key issues that have surrounded the history of the cold war. Before taking up these points, we will begin by examining the seminal cold war event: the Cuban missile crisis.

THE CUBAN MISSILE CRISIS

Perhaps at no time has the world come closer to a nuclear war than during the October 1962 Cuban missile crisis.[1] President Kennedy put the odds of avoiding war at between one out of three, and Soviet Premier Nikita Khrushchev observed that "the smell of burning hung in the air." Estimates projected the probable deaths resulting from such a conflict as 100 million in the United States, more than 100 million in the Soviet Union, and several million in Europe. At the heart of the crisis was the discovery that the Soviet Union had secretly placed 42 medium-range missiles in Cuba, each of which had an estimated range of 1,100 miles.

In October 1962, the United States enjoyed a substantial lead over the Soviet Union in intercontinental ballistic missiles (ICBMs): The U.S. had 226 ICBMs to the Soviet Union's estimated 75; it had a 144–0 advantage in submarine-launched ballistic missiles; and it had a 1,350–190 advantage in long-range bombers. These numbers translated into a U.S. capacity to attack the Soviet Union with nuclear weapons without a corresponding Soviet capability to attack the United States. Missiles in Cuba effectively negated this edge. All but a small portion of the United States could now be reached by Soviet missiles.

The Cuban missile crisis involved more than just nuclear saber rattling. Soviet weapons shipments to Cuba had been taking place at an uneven pace since the summer of 1960 and involved far more than just medium-range missiles. By the beginning of September 1960, the Soviet inventory in Cuba included 12 intermediate-range missiles; 144 surface-to-air missile launchers, with four missiles per launcher; 42 MIG-21 fighters; and cruise missiles, patrol boats, and large quantities of transportation, electrical, and construction equipment. Some 5,000 technicians and military personnel had also been sent to Cuba. This number grew to 22,000. In responding to the Soviet action, the United States drew upon virtually every part of its military establishment: Military forces around the world were put on alert, tactical fighters were moved to air bases within striking range of Cuba, 14,000 air force reservists were called up, over 180 ships patrolled the Caribbean and imposed a naval blockade on Cuba, and plans were drawn up for a surgical air strike of Cuba to be followed by a 100,000-man invasion force.

Cuba was important to the Soviet Union for several reasons. First, as we have already noted, it was an excellent base from which it could offset the U.S. edge in ICBMs. As a result of advances in reconnaissance technology, by 1961 the Kennedy administration had realized that the United States was ahead in the intercontinental ballistic missile race (the so-called missile gap). Soviet leaders feared that, armed with this knowledge, the United States would practice nuclear blackmail against them. A quick and economically inexpensive fix was necessary to counter the U.S. advantage and to buy time for the Soviet Union to build up its nuclear inventory. Second, as we shall discuss later, Khrushchev had just suffered a series of foreign-policy setbacks in trying to get the Western powers out of Berlin. A dramatic foreign-policy success in Cuba not only would do much to bolster Khrushchev's control over the Communist party but also might provide an additional bargaining chip to use against the United States somewhere in Europe. Finally, there was the problem of defending Cuba from the United States. On the one hand, the problem was symbolic (could the Soviet Union allow a Communist government to be overthrown?), but, on the other hand, it was also a very real problem.

Cuba had become an obsession with U.S. policymakers almost from the moment that Fidel Castro's guerrilla forces overthrew the corrupt Batista regime in January 1959. By the end of 1959, the Central Intelligence Agency (CIA) was advocating

Castro's "elimination." In March 1960, President Eisenhower approved a plan calling for the training of a small band of Cuban emigrés for guerrilla activities within
Cuba. By the time it was implemented by the Kennedy administration, the plan had
been altered to call for an invasion of Cuba by the emigrés. Little went according to
plan. On April 17, 1961, some 1,400 Cuban exiles landed at the Bay of Pigs. Within
two days they were surrounded by 20,000 well-equipped and loyal soldiers. On the
third day, the 1,200 survivors were marched off to prison camps.

Rumors had begun to build during the summer of 1962 that the Soviet Union
was placing missiles in Cuba, but the United States was slow to move on this information for several reasons. No single conclusive piece of evidence existed to support
the charge, and much of the evidence came from unreliable sources. For example,
Cuban refugees arriving in the United States had been reporting the arrival of Soviet
missiles in Cuba before any Soviet military equipment reached Cuba. Moreover, not
all of the evidence was available for analysis at the same time and place. On September 19, the U.S. Intelligence Board reached the conclusion that the Soviet Union
would not try to put offensive missiles in Cuba. A second factor inhibiting a response
to signs that the Soviet Union might be placing missiles in Cuba was the unwillingness or inability of key figures in the Kennedy administration to believe that this, in
fact, could be happening. Khrushchev had promised Kennedy that the Soviet Union
would do nothing "to complicate the international situation or aggravate the tension
in relations between our two countries" before the fall congressional elections.

John McCone, who was head of the CIA, believed that the Soviet Union was
putting missiles in Cuba. As the evidence mounted to support his view, a U-2 reconnaissance flight was ordered. Conclusive evidence of Soviet missiles in Cuba was not
obtained until October 14. On October 22, President Kennedy went on national
television to reveal the discovery, to announce the imposition of a naval blockade,
and to set a deadline for a Soviet response.

The naval blockade was only one of several options that were considered by
Kennedy and his advisors. Others were: Do nothing, put diplomatic pressure on the
Soviet Union, make a secret approach to Castro, launch an invasion, and conduct a
surgical air strike. None of these options were without drawbacks, and the naval
blockade was chosen as much for what it did not do as for what it accomplished. The
blockade, by itself, could not get the missiles out of Cuba (they were there already),
but it did signal U.S. resolve to end the situation without initiating armed conflict
with the Soviet Union. It also placed the responsibility for the next move and for a
possible escalation in the level of violence with the Soviet Union.

The crisis ended on October 28, when Khrushchev publicly agreed to remove
Soviet missiles from Cuba in return for a U.S. pledge not to intervene in Cuba. The
Soviet Union used the need to defend Cuba from U.S. aggression as its reason for
putting missiles in Cuba, and this formula allowed both sides to claim victory. This
compromise was not easily reached. Evidence suggested that Khrushchev was not
totally in control of the Communist party and the Soviet government during the
crisis and that at one point he had almost been removed from power. Only a creative
diplomatic response by the United States to contradictory signals from Moscow, regarding its willingness to end the crisis on terms acceptable to the United States,
may have kept Khrushchev in power and ended the crisis peacefully. Disagreement

on how to resolve the crisis also existed within the U.S. government. On October 27, one day before Khrushchev offered to remove the missiles, Kennedy gave his approval to an October 29 air strike against missile silos, air bases, and antiaircraft facilities. An air strike had originally been set for October 20 but was postponed in favor of the naval blockade, which was less dangerous. The blockade succeeded in stopping any additional material from reaching Cuba, but it did not get the missiles out. In fact, the construction of missile bases was accelerated, and 20 medium-range missiles had become operational. Because of this, on the same day that Kennedy approved the air strike, Secretary of Defense McNamara concluded that an "invasion had become almost inevitable" and that at least one missile would be successfully launched at the United States.

Members of Kennedy's inner decision-making circle also disagreed over the propriety of making a secret deal to end the crisis. While Kennedy had publicly rejected Khrushchev's call for removing U.S. missiles from Turkey in exchange for the removal of Soviet missiles from Cuba, he agreed to do so in a secret offer made on October 27. The Soviet Union was told that a response was needed the next day and that the offer was conditional on its keeping the agreement secret.

For some twenty-five years the foregoing account of the Cuban missile crisis was recited as the "standard" interpretation of what transpired in October 1962. On the basis of documents recently declassified and a joint U.S. and Soviet conference on the Cuban missile crisis held in 1987, this interpretation is now considered to be incorrect or incomplete in several respects. Not only are these revelations important for the new light they shed on the Cuban missile crisis, but they are a warning to us not to become too comfortable with our interpretation of events or to be too quick to draw conclusions about "crisis management techniques" or the "nature of the U.S.-Soviet rivalry," because the data we are basing our conclusions on may be incorrect.

We need to revise our thinking about the Cuban missile crisis in at least five respects. First, the decision to place missiles in Cuba appears to have been made by Khrushchev in April and was discussed in the following months by top Soviet leaders. He did so not to test Kennedy's resolve but to deter the U.S. from attacking Cuba and to correct the strategic imbalance. Khrushchev apparently believed that, confronted with a fait accompli, the United States would not take any military action but learn to live with the missiles just as the Soviet Union had learned to live with missiles on its borders. Second, it is now clear that the Soviet Union introduced 42,000 troops into Cuba and not 22,000 as assumed by U.S. policy-makers during the crisis. Third, President Kennedy was far more committed to a peaceful resolution of the crisis than was believed to be the case. A military strike against Cuba does not appear to have been in the offing in the last stages of the crisis. In fact, through an intermediary Kennedy had made a secret approach to the UN enlisting its help. Fourth, Khrushchev agreed to remove the missiles not because he feared a general war but because he was convinced that the United States was prepared to invade Cuba. Finally, the contradictory tone of Moscow's messages at the end of the crisis was not due to a power struggle but to the changing nature of the intelligence making its way to Soviet leaders. The conciliatory message came on the heels of information that the United States was about to invade Cuba. The more defiant message was written after it became clear to Moscow that there would be no invasion.

THE COLD WAR DEBATED

The Cuban missile crisis is only one episode in the cold war between the United States and the Soviet Union that has cast a shadow over virtually all major conflicts in the post-World War II era. The length and scope of this conflict are remarkable. First focused on Europe, it became global in nature. The cold war has lasted longer than such famous conflicts as the Thirty Years War between Catholics and Protestants in the seventeenth century, the Peloponnesian War between Athens and Sparta, the warfare in Europe that accompanied the French Revolution and Napoleon's reign, and the combined length of World War I, World War II, and the interwar period.[2] While frequently intense, this struggle has never risen to the point of direct military warfare. Instead, the war has remained "cold," with diplomacy, psychological warfare, economic coercion, foreign aid, ideological competition, covert action, arms races, and proxy wars being used alone and in combination to advance U.S. and Soviet interests.[3]

Numerous disputes have surrounded the way in which the cold war has been "played" by the United States and the Soviet Union. One disputed point is over the date of its inception. At least four different starting points have been given to the cold war. The immediate post-World War II period is the most frequently used starting point and the one that we will employ here. World War II is also used by many to mark its beginning. Less frequently employed are the period 1917–1920, the time of the Russian Revolution and civil war, and the interwar period. Evidence can be found to support all of these positions. In the final analysis, the choice of a starting point depends largely upon what we hold to be central to the cold war. For example, viewed as a conflict between rival ideologies, the 1917–1920 era may be the most appropriate starting point, for it was then that communism established itself in the Soviet Union and the Western powers intervened into Soviet affairs. If the cold war is seen as a struggle between the United States and the Soviet Union first for the control of Europe and then for global influence, the immediate post-World War II era is a logical starting point for the cold war, for it was only then that the United States began to act with an appreciation of the importance of Europe and international affairs in general for American national security interests.

A second point of dispute is whether or not the cold war has ended. Some see the Cuban missile crisis as signaling an end to the cold war. According to this view, there followed a period of relative calm in U.S.-Soviet relations when cooperative ventures, especially in the area of arms control, had as much of an impact on the temperament of world politics as did the ongoing competition between the two superpowers. The changed nature of the U.S.-Soviet relationship was formalized in the early 1970s by the term "détente." It, in turn, gave way to a second cold war. The continued Soviet military buildup and efforts to extend its influence in the Third World, plus the growing conservatism of the American public, combined to lay the foundations for a renewed wave of conflict and hostility between the United States and the Soviet Union.

As the 1990s began, there was renewed speculation that the cold war had come to an end. Signs of increased pragmatism in Soviet foreign policy abounded: Troops were withdrawn from Afghanistan, overtures were made to China, no attempt was made to block the democratization revolution in Eastern Europe, and arms control initiatives were put forward across virtually the entire spectrum of weapons systems. The United States also gave signs of pursuing a less confrontational foreign policy as it withdrew active support for the Contras in Nicaragua. Moreover, both sides began to talk of working through international organizations to solve regional and global problems. Many commentators, however, urged caution. Former President Nixon wrote that "those who parrot today a fashionable slogan—'the cold war is over'— trivialize the problems of Western security." He argued that Gorbachev brilliantly changed the rules of the cold-war game and that the situation the U.S. faces in the 1990s is infinitely more complex than that of 40 years ago.[4]

Controversy also surrounds the question of responsibility. Who caused the cold war? The orthodox interpretation of the cold war places the blame upon the Soviet Union.[5] The United States is portrayed as trying to hold in check the inherent expansionist tendencies of the Soviet Union. Revisionists assign responsibility to the United States for its constant exaggeration of Soviet power, misreading of Soviet goals, expansionist tendencies of its own, and obsession with communism.[6] In their view, U.S. foreign policy left the Soviet Union with no choice but to act forcefully to protect its legitimate security interests. A third point of view holds that neither superpower can be blamed. The cold war was inevitable and had its roots in the basic nature of world politics. In the eyes of some, it was the fourth great war fought to establish a balance of power in Europe.[7] (The other three were the Napoleonic wars, World War I, and World War II.) According to a fourth point of view, the United States and the Soviet Union are both victims, locked into a conflict spiral from which escape is very difficult.[8] The initial moves that were made by each side during the cold war were deliberately undertaken to cope with the actions of the other side. Over time the conflict began to feed upon itself, as fear and mutual suspicion began to distort each state's view of its own actions and those of its adversary. As the cycle of mistrust continued, states found it more and more difficult to control their actions. Economic or political exhaustion and war are the basic methods for breaking out of the conflict spiral, but none of them prevent the process from beginning anew.

THE COLD WAR: A HISTORICAL OVERVIEW [9]

1945–1949

The basic outlines of the cold war took shape in the short period between the concluding months of World War II and the outbreak of the Korean War in 1950. Numerous conferences had been held during World War II between the United States, Great Britain, and the Soviet Union in an effort to work out the details of the postwar international order. These attempts failed, and the diplomatic record of these conferences, particularly Yalta and Potsdam, contributed to the distrust and acrimony that came to divide the victors.

U.S. President Franklin D. Roosevelt, British Prime Minister Winston Churchill, and Soviet Marshal Joseph Stalin came to the Yalta Conference (February 1945) with different concerns. Churchill's principal interest was to secure a buffer zone in Germany to protect France from future attacks and to stop Soviet expansion into Poland. Stalin wanted reparations (compensation for war damages) so that he could rebuild the Soviet economy, domination over Poland, a weakened Germany, and possessions in Asia. The United States wanted to see the United Nations established, to have the Soviet Union enter the war against Japan and reduce its influence in Poland, and to have China given Great-Power status. The compromise reached at Yalta was heavily influenced by the military realities of the moment: The Soviet Red Army had already begun its liberating march through Eastern Europe, Western forces were stalled in Belgium at the Battle of the Bulge, and Japanese forces continued to put up stiff resistance, forcing U.S. military planners to contemplate the need for an invasion of the Japanese home islands. The United States and Great Britain agreed to Stalin's demand that Poland's borders be moved westward, giving Poland part of prewar Germany and the Soviet Union part of prewar Poland. It was also conceded that, while the Communist-led government operating in Poland would form the nucleus of the postwar government, a "more broadly based" government would be established and "free and unfettered elections" would be held. Germany was to be divided, and some form of German reparations were agreed to, but the actual amount was not decided. The Soviet Union promised to enter the war against Japan within two or three months. A compromise was reached on the membership of the UN and the voting procedures it was to use.

Events moved quickly after the Yalta Conference. Roosevelt died in April 1945 and Germany surrendered in May. In July, the United States, Great Britain, and the Soviet Union met as wartime allies for the last time in Potsdam. Germany and Poland dominated the agenda. The United States was now less interested in dismembering Germany than it was in economic reconstruction, but the Soviet Union continued to press hard for reparations. In a compromise decision, it was agreed that Germany would be divided into four military occupation zones but treated as a single economic unit and that each of the victors could take reparations from their own occupation zone. British complaints about the absence of free elections in Poland were met with Soviet complaints about British domination of Greece. Stalin again promised to enter the war against Japan; however, the United States was now less anxious for this to happen, because on the second day of the conference the first successful test of an atomic bomb had taken place in New Mexico. Several issues were not resolved at Potsdam, and soon they would be numbered among the first battlegrounds of the cold war.

One trouble spot was Iran. Iran had long existed under British domination, and Great Britain had major oil interests there in the Anglo-Iranian oil company. British and Soviet forces went into Iran in 1941 in an effort to prevent Hitler from gaining access to Iranian oil. American forces also had entered Iran to supervise the shipment of wartime lend-lease aid to the Soviet Union. By agreement, all foreign forces were to leave Iran within six months after the end of the war. By the withdrawal date of March 2, 1946, U.S. and British forces had already left. Soviet forces, however, remained firmly encamped in northern Iran, and the Soviet Union announced the creation of the "autonomous republic" of Azerbaijan there. The issue was brought to the UN, and President Truman issued an ultimatum to Stalin, demanding the withdrawal of Soviet forces. In the end, the Soviet Union agreed to withdraw its troops in return for the future establishment of a joint Soviet-Iranian oil company and the peaceful settlement of the Azerbaijanian situation. Neither took place. The Iranian parliament refused to create such a company, and the Iranian army marched into northern Iran, defeating the pro-Soviet forces.

Conflict also broke out over the Dardanelles Strait. Under a 1936 international agreement, Turkey had control over navigation of the Bosporous and Dardanelles Straits and the right to close them in times of war or if Turkish security were threatened. Not only did these straits regulate Soviet access to the Mediterranean Sea, but, during World War II, Turkey had permitted German warships to pass through into the Black Sea. In 1945, the Soviet Union demanded that unilateral Turkish control be replaced by a system of joint Soviet-Turkish governance. It also wanted naval and land bases in the straits. Turkey rebuffed these Soviet advances with the help of the United States. In 1946, Truman warned Stalin that the United States would provide Turkey with military support, and he sent the Sixth Fleet to the eastern Mediterranean as a sign of support. The crisis eased in late 1946 but would be resurrected in 1947 with the announcement of the Truman Doctrine.

On February 21, 1947, the British informed the United States that it could no longer afford to guarantee the defense of Turkey and Greece, as it had traditionally done in the past. Soviet pressure on Greece had been building up since 1944. During World War II, two rival resistance groups—one pro-Communist and one pro-British—operated there, fighting each other as much as they fought against the Germans. Backed by the liberating British Army and later by U.S. military and economic aid, the pro-British forces managed to gain a tenuous advantage in the civil war that followed the German defeat. Expectations were that, stripped of its British support, Greece would fall within a matter of weeks. On March 12, 1947, Truman addressed a joint session of Congress and requested $400 million in economic and military aid for Greece and Turkey. Just as important as this request for aid was the language that Truman used to justify U.S. support for these two governments. Known as the Truman Doctrine, he argued that the United States must "support free peoples who are resisting attempted subjugation by armed minorities or by outside pressure."

Three months later, the United States took another step in linking its defense with that of Europe when Secretary of State George Marshall announced that the United States was prepared to underwrite a plan for European economic recovery. All European states were invited to participate in the drafting of a collective plan. The Soviet Union chose not to participate and was able to prevent East European states from joining. It was unwilling to take part in a program dominated by the United States, in which its economic recovery decisions would be subject to any form of approval by other states. The Marshall Plan also presented a threat to Soviet control over Eastern Europe. The Soviet Union had not yet established complete control over this region, and the sudden influx of large amounts of recovery aid (aid that the Soviet Union could not supply, given its weak economic position) was not wanted. Evidence suggests that the United States anticipated a Soviet rejection and was never interested in securing its participation in the Marshall Plan but saw its invitation as a way of scoring a propaganda victory.

In 1949, the economic division of Europe was reinforced by its military partition. On April 4, 1949, the North Atlantic Treaty Organization (NATO) was signed by the

United States, Great Britain, France, Canada, Belgium, the Netherlands, Luxembourg, Denmark, Iceland, Norway, Italy, and Portugal. Greece and Turkey joined in 1952, followed by West Germany in 1955. This last act prompted the Soviet Union to organize its East European allies, or satellites, as they were then referred to, into the Warsaw Pact Treaty Organization. Its members were the Soviet Union, Bulgaria, Czechoslovakia, Hungary, Poland, Romania, and East Germany. Notably absent from this list was Yugoslavia. The Communist party under the leadership of Josip Tito had come to power in Yugoslavia largely through its own anti-Nazi resistance efforts, and it resisted Soviet demands that it subordinate Yugoslav foreign-policy goals to those of the Soviet Union. Because of this independent attitude, in 1948 Stalin expelled Yugoslavia from the international communist movement (the COMINFORM) and tried to bring Tito down with a program of economic warfare.

Pressure against Yugoslavia was only one facet of an evolving Soviet policy that was designed to tighten its control over Eastern Europe. Only a few months earlier, the democratically elected coalition government in Czechoslovakia had been replaced in a "peaceful coup" by a loyal Communist government, which moved the country away from neutrality and toward satellite status. The year before, in 1947, noncommunists had been removed from the governments in Hungary, Bulgaria, and Romania. Soviet domination over Poland had been realized even earlier. Much to the consternation of the West, the promised free elections never took place. When challenged on this point, Stalin pointed to U.S. policies in Italy and Japan, and those of Great Britain in Greece—countries occupied by their armies and in which communist parties were all but excluded from power.

Tito's expulsion from the COMINFORM also coincided with the first Berlin crisis. It had been agreed that Germany was to be divided into occupation zones. The same fate befell Berlin, its capital, which lay deep in the Soviet occupation zone. In the first years of the cold war, the "German problem" took many forms. In part it was a military question: Should Germany be rearmed, and, if so, should it be brought into an alliance? Let us recall that it was West Germany's entrance in NATO that prompted the Soviet Union to create the Warsaw Pact. It was a political question as well: Should Germany be united, and, if so, what would its foreign policy look like? It was also an economic question: Was German economic recovery necessary for the recovery of all of Europe? If the answer was yes, then what should be done about reparation payments to the Soviet Union? These last two questions formed the heart of the 1948 Berlin crisis. In December 1946, the British and American occupation zones were combined into Bizonia. The rationale given for this move was that consolidation would speed the economic recovery of Germany. The Soviet Union saw the move as the first step in an effort to create a pro-Western German state. On June 18, 1948, on the heels of the announcement of proposed currency reforms for Bizonia, the Soviet Union withdrew from the Allied Control Council that theoretically ruled over all of Germany. It also set up a blockade of Berlin and informed the West that it no longer had any right of access to the city. Three days later the United States and Great Britain launched a massive air supply operation to provide West Berlin with food, fuel, and other basic necessities. Three hundred and twenty-four days later, in May 1949, the blockade was lifted. That same month, the French occupation zone was joined with Bizonia to form the Federal Republic of Germany. In

October, the Soviet Union transformed its zone into the German Democratic Republic.

The final chapter of the cold war in the 1940s was played out in Asia. Initially, the United States and the Soviet Union expected Chiang Kai-shek to defeat Mao Zedong in the civil war that was being fought for control of China. Both powers seemed content to see a coalition government established, but neither of their Chinese allies were interested in such a solution. The Soviet Union's primary interest in China was for it to be a weak and compliant neighbor. In 1945 it signed a Treaty of Friendship with Chiang Kai-shek. The price for this treaty (which brought official Soviet recognition to Chiang's government) was to recognize many long-standing Russian claims on Chinese territory. United States aid to Chiang never approached the level of funding provided to Europe by the Marshall Plan, and much of the aid that was given quickly fell into Mao's hands. Unable to defeat Mao on the battlefield and unwilling to do anything about the widespread corruption within his government or the steadily worsening economic conditions in China, Chiang saw his power decline after mid-1947. In 1948 Mao's forces launched a major offensive that ultimately brought all of Manchuria and then northern China under communist control. In September 1949, Mao announced the formation of the People's Republic of China, and by the year's end Chiang Kai-shek and his followers had fled to the island of Taiwan located 100 miles off the Chinese coast. Mao promptly aligned China with the USSR, a move that the United States viewed as significantly increasing Soviet power.

1950–1959

As the 1950s began, attention remained focused on Asia. In June 1950, North Korean forces crossed the thirty-eighth parallel into South Korea. The invasion caught the United States by surprise. Statements by U.S. policymakers had given the impression that the Korean peninsula was not regarded as vital to U.S. national security interests, but, once the attack began, the United States reversed its position and sent in forces to fight under the UN flag. It took the UN forces three months to stop the North Korean advance and to reclaim South Korea. In October 1950, President Truman authorized these forces to cross into North Korea. Chinese warnings that such a move would cause it to intervene in the Korean War were discounted, and the United States was surprised a second time when in November Chinese troops crossed the Yalu River en masse. It was not until March 1951 that Chinese forces were pushed back behind the thirty-eighth parallel and a stalemate in the fighting was reached. Peace talks began that July, but a truce was not signed until July 1953.

The "fall of China" and the Korean War both had the effect of internationalizing the cold war and the U.S. policy of containment. The rationale behind containment was first put forward in 1947 by George Kennan in an article published in *Foreign Affairs*. In it he argued that "the main element of any United States policy toward the Soviet Union must be that of a long-term, patient but firm and vigilant containment of Russian expansionist tendencies." He urged the United States to adopt a policy centering on the "adroit and vigilant application of counterforce at a series of constantly shifting geographical and political points, corresponding to the shifts and manoeuvres of Soviet policy."[10] The Marshall Plan and the creation of NATO were logical applications of this containment policy and had the effect of placing a ring around the Soviet Union's European border. In the early 1950s, U.S. policymakers sought to extend this ring around the remainder of the Soviet Union. Bilateral defense agreements were signed with Japan, Taiwan, South Korea, and the Philippines. A mutual defense pact (the ANZUS Pact) was signed by Australia, New Zealand, and the United States in 1951. After French forces withdrew from Indochina in 1954, the United States joined with France, Britain, New Zealand, Australia, Pakistan, the Philippines, and Thailand in creating the Southeast Asia Treaty Organization (SEATO). In 1955 it led in the establishment of the Baghdad Pact, whose members included Great Britain, Turkey, Iraq, Iran, and Pakistan. The Korean War extended the containment policy to China. It also led to the militarization of containment, with a military buildup in Western Europe, including the movement of more U.S. forces there.

By the 1950s, Europe was firmly divided into East and West. In Western Europe, the 1950s were a decade of diplomatic initiatives designed to bring about a greater degree of cooperation that many hoped would make future wars impossible. Tangible gains were made in the economic arena, but efforts to extend West European military cooperation beyond the framework of NATO met with repeated failure. On hotly debated proposal was for a European defense community, which would create a European army. European states were reluctant to rearm Germany, but in the aftermath of the Korean War they agreed that Europe needed to be strengthened militarily. The answer ultimately chosen was to admit Germany to NATO. This was done in 1955.

Alliance politics in Eastern Europe were quite different. Stalin's death in March 1953 set in motion a prolonged power struggle within the Kremlin. While Nikita Khrushchev emerged as the eventual victor, it was Georgi Malenkov who held center stage initially. He sought to continue Stalinist political practices while at the same time reducing the harshness of his economic policies. In doing so, Malenkov "seemed to take the permanence of the Soviet bloc too much for granted."[11] Within months following Stalin's death, rioting broke out in East Germany, and it was put down only with the help of the Soviet army. Khrushchev would face even stiffer challenges. In 1956, he delivered a secret speech to the Twentieth Party Congress, denouncing Stalin's excesses. The reform movement, set in motion first by the economic "new course" of Malenkov and then accelerated by Khrushchev's de-Stalinization speech, severely challenged the legitimacy and methods of control that the orthodox Stalinist Communist parties in Eastern Europe exercised over their people. In Hungary and Poland rioting broke out in 1956, and the old Stalinist leaders were pushed aside. In Poland, Wladyslaw Gomulka, a dissident nationalist with few ties to the Soviet Union, took power, and under his leadership the Communist party was able to reestablish order. In Hungary the situation proved to be more serious. Nationalistic Communist party leaders were not able to regain control over events. In the face of declarations that Hungary was withdrawing from the Warsaw Pact and that the Communist party no longer held a monopoly on political power, Khrushchev ordered a military invasion in order to reestablish effective Communist rule.

The West, while condemning the Soviet invasion of Hungary, made no move to counter it. In fact, the Western allies had problems of their own, which limited their ability to speak with one voice in criticism of the Soviet action. Virtually at the same time that Soviet tanks were rolling into Budapest, the British, French, and Israelis were trying to take the Suez Canal away from Egypt. Gamal Nasser had come to power in Egypt in 1952 as the result of a military coup that ousted King Farouk. Nasser quickly established himself as a spokesperson for Arab nationalism and opposed efforts by the United States and Great Britain to retain their influence in the Middle East through the Baghdad Pact and the manipulation of foreign aid. In 1955, Nasser stunned the world by accepting the first large-scale shipments of Soviet weapons to any country not under its control. He also recognized the government of Communist China. U.S. policymakers retaliated in response to what they saw as the overly close relationship developing between the Communist world and Egypt by announcing that, contrary to what had been previously decided, the United States would not provide funds for the building of the Aswan Dam, a project that Nasser had placed at the center of Egyptian development plans. Nasser, in turn, retaliated by seizing the Suez Canal, stating that, in the absence of Western aid, he would be forced to use revenues from it to build the Aswan Dam.

Great Britain and France, who jointly owned the canal, persuaded Israel, which had territorial designs of its own on the Gaza Strip which was controlled by Egypt, to launch an invasion against Egypt on October 29, 1956. Great Britain and France then issued Egypt and Israel an ultimatum, calling for a cease-fire and a joint Anglo-French occupation of key positions. When Nasser rejected these terms, as it was certain he would, British and French forces began their attack on Egypt and occupied Cairo. Everything went according to plan, except that the United States reacted strongly. Great Britain and France had expected the United States to acquiesce, but instead the United States called a special meeting of the UN Security Council and called for Israel to withdraw its forces and for all other states to stay out of the conflict. France and Great Britain vetoed the resolution. At this point, Khrushchev announced that Soviet "volunteers" were ready to aid Egypt. Determined to keep the Soviet Union out of the Middle East, the United States pressured Great Britain into abandoning its military plans, thus ending the crisis.

The effects of the Suez crisis were many. Unable to act on their own, France and Great Britain could no longer argue that they were powers on the same level as the United States and the Soviet Union. Western prestige in the Middle East had also been badly damaged, while the stature of the Soviet Union had grown considerably. In an effort to regain the initiative in the region, the United States put forward the Eisenhower Doctrine in 1957. It stated that the United States would give aid to any Middle Eastern state that was threatened by aggression from "a country controlled by international communism." One year later, the Eisenhower Doctrine provided the rationale for sending 14,000 troops to Lebanon. The catalyst for this move was the overthrow of the pro-U.S. Iraqi monarchy by nationalist forces. Fearful that events in Iraq would embolden nationalist groups elsewhere in the Middle East, the United States dispatched soldiers to Lebanon and Great Britain sent paratroopers to Jordan.

The cold war returned to Europe with dramatic suddenness in 1958. Once again, the problem area was Berlin. To Khrushchev and his East German allies, the "Berlin problem" had to be solved soon. Not only had the West refused to recognize the existence of East Germany and continued to call for unification and free elections, but, since 1949, each year some 150,000 East Germans had used the divided city of Berlin as their point of departure to the West. Many of these were skilled workers and professional people whose skills were necessary if East Germany was to recover and develop economically. In November 1958, Khrushchev announced a six-month deadline for the commencement of talks on the future of Germany. In the absence of such talks, the Soviet Union would sign a separate peace treaty with East Germany and would turn over control of East Berlin to it. Ultimately, he argued that Berlin should be given the status of a free city, in which no foreign troops would be stationed. Berlin is a city of great political significance to Europeans, and the Western powers would not accept any plan that would force them out of Berlin. Further complicating the issue was the fact that U.S., British, and French forces were in Berlin as a result of agreements made among the occupying powers. By giving East Germany control over its sector of Berlin, the Soviet Union effectively would be terminating these agreements. The West refused to hold high-level talks on Germany under these conditions, but Khrushchev did not go through with his threat, accepting instead a foreign minister's meeting on the matter, which did little to clarify the issues at stake.

The timing of Khrushchev's ultimatum on Berlin was closely tied to the launching of *Sputnik*, the first man-made satellite, in October 1957 and the successful testing of the first intercontinental ballistic missile (ICBM) two months before that. The ability of the Soviet Union to send warheads great distances meant that the United States would no longer be able to commit itself to the defense of Europe without having to consider the possibility that it too might become a target in any war that might erupt. No longer was the threat of nuclear war a one-way street in which the Soviet Union would be under the gun of U.S. bomber forces stationed in Europe and the United States would be largely, although not entirely, beyond the reach of Soviet bombers. This was not the first time that a Soviet technological breakthrough created problems for U.S. national security planners. In 1949, much to the surprise of the United States, the Soviet Union broke the American monopoly on atomic weapons. Truman's response was to order the development of the more powerful hydrogen bomb. The United States exploded its first thermonuclear device in November 1952, with the Soviet Union following suit in August 1953.

1960–1969

Although temporarily defused, the Berlin problem did not go away, and the overall problems remained essentially unchanged. From the Soviet perspective, the mass exodus of East Germans had to be stopped, and from the West's perspective, nothing could be done to call into question its right to have forces stationed in Berlin. Berlin was to be one of the topics of a summit meeting between Eisenhower and Khrushchev in Paris in May 1960. This meeting never took place, because on the eve of the conference the Soviet Union announced that it had shot down a U-2 spy plane over its territory. At first the United States denied the Soviet allegation, but then it was forced to admit its truth when the Soviets were able to produce the plane's pilot, Gary Francis

Powers. U-2s had been flying over the Soviet Union since 1956, collecting data on Soviet missile systems and production facilities. It was largely as a result of this data along with information from spy satellites and Soviet defector Oleg Perkovsky that the United States was able to establish that the Soviet Union did not possess an advantage in missiles and that the "missile gap" favored the United States.

Berlin was also on the agenda when Kennedy and Khrushchev met for the first time in Vienna in June 1961. The meeting did not go well. Khrushchev again demanded that Berlin be given the status of a free city and threatened to negotiate a peace treaty with East Germany. Kennedy sought to demonstrate toughness and resolve, but accounts suggest that Khrushchev came away with the opposite impression. In a matter of months, Berlin became the testing ground in yet another battle of wills. The conflict escalated rapidly. In July, Kennedy went on television and, citing the need to reaffirm the American presence in Berlin, asked Congress for an additional $3.2 billion in defense spending and the authority to call up reservists. He also asked for funding for a fallout shelter program. Early August saw the Soviet Union erect barbed-wire barriers around East Berlin. It took four days for the West to issue a public protest, and when the United States did not make any significant military countermove, a wall was put up sealing off East Berlin from West Berlin.

The test of wills did not end with Berlin. Instead, it moved to Cuba. As we indicated in the beginning of this chapter, Kennedy, as did Eisenhower before him, had become convinced of the need to force Castro out of power. Khrushchev's interest in Cuba lay in his need to find a quick fix to offset the U.S. missile advantage. Berlin may have also entered into his calculations. In many ways, erecting the Berlin Wall had been a shallow victory. He had faced down the United States, and the population outflow from East Germany had been stopped, but Western forces were still in West Berlin, and the Berlin Wall was a propaganda nightmare. For the United States, "victory" in the Cuban missile crisis proved to be less than complete. Evidence suggests that the Soviet Union reached the conclusion that only by achieving nuclear parity could it prevent future defeats at the hands of the United States in conflicts in which nuclear weapons would be brought into play. Thus, in the mid-1960s, U.S.-Soviet relations in the area of nuclear weapons moved simultaneously in two quite different directions. On the one hand, a burst of creative arms control activity took place. In 1963, the "Hot Line" was set up, which established direct communications between Washington and Moscow, and a Test Ban Treaty was signed. In 1967, an Outer Space Treaty was agreed to, and a Non-Proliferation Treaty was approved the following year.[12] On the other hand, the Soviet Union undertook a massive buildup of its nuclear forces. It also bears noting that not all states shared the U.S. and Soviet interest in arms control. China conducted its first atomic-bomb test in 1964 and followed this by detonating a hydrogen bomb in 1967. In 1974, India became the sixth state to demonstrate a nuclear capability when it detonated a "peaceful nuclear explosion."

Progress in arms control was halted by the Soviet invasion of Czechoslovakia and changes in U.S. foreign-policy priorities that were brought on by its deepening involvement in the Vietnam War. In Czechoslovakia, Antonin Novotny, a loyal Soviet ally, was replaced by Alexander Dubcek as head of the Czech Communist party. Under his leadership, the party sought to shed its rigid Stalinist past. It began to experiment with economic reforms based on free-market principles; it instituted freedom of the press, religion, and assembly; it called for secret elections; and it acknowledged the right of citizens to travel abroad. The Czechs hoped that by staying in the Warsaw Pact and leaving the Communist party firmly in control they they would be free to establish "communism with a human face." Soviet leaders read events in Czechoslovakia differently. What they saw was a Communist state slipping back toward capitalism and the possibility that the "Prague Spring" might spill over and infect other East European states. Both eventualities were unacceptable. The ideological justification for the Soviet invasion, dubbed the "Brezhnev Doctrine" by the West, was that Communist states had the right and responsibility to intervene in the domestic affairs of a Communist ally whenever the danger existed that capitalism might reestablish itself. More important than either the legality or ideological justification for the Soviet invasion was the signal that it sent to other Communist states: It was the Soviet Union, not the Czechs or anyone else, who determined the outer boundaries of reform efforts and the standards for loyalty to Moscow.

Berlin and Czechoslovakia aside, the primary cold-war battleground of the 1960s was the Third World. By 1960, the process of decolonization was well underway. Thirty-seven African, Asian, and Middle Eastern colonies had become independent states between 1949 and 1960. Eighteen more colonies received their independence in 1960. In 1958 alone, 28 guerrilla wars took place.

The traditional American way of thinking about foreign policy created problems for the United States in its dealings with the newly independent states of the Third World. Because of its emphasis on legalistic and technical solutions to problems and its tendency to universalize American values, the United States had difficulty relating to Third World independence movements, which advocated violence as the means for achieving their goals and which questioned the worth of Western values.[13] Early U.S. dealings with the Third World were also complicated by more concrete factors. One was the way in which containment had been implemented. Kennan had argued for bringing to bear a broad array of foreign-policy instruments to contain Soviet expansionist tendencies. Instead, U.S. policymakers had come to rely almost exclusively on military power, and herein lay the crux of the problem for many Third World leaders. Alliances such as the Baghdad Pact and SEATO, which the United States said were designed to contain communism, looked to the Third World like efforts on the part of the United States to replace the British and French as neocolonial masters. Reinforcing this fear was the fact that, by its actions in Iran (1953), Guatemala (1954), and Cuba (1959), the United States had demonstrated a willingness to engage in covert action in order to overthrow Third World governments that it defined as Communist or hostile to U.S. interests.

Soviet involvement in the Third World had been limited under Stalin. While he acknowledged that decolonization had weakened the imperialist powers, Stalin apparently did not appreciate fully the revolutionary potential inherent in the drive for independence.[14] Soviet policy changed under Khrushchev. Whereas under Stalin the leaders of the Third World, such as Nasser, Nehru, and Sukarno, were viewed with suspicion, under Khrushchev they were embraced as allies. He endorsed the efforts of the 29 "nonaligned" states that met at the 1954 Bandung Conference to chart a neutral course in the cold war, and he was generally optimistic about the potential of radical and anti-Western politicians and rebel leaders to promote Soviet interests in the Third

World. By 1961, Khrushchev was pledging Soviet support "fully and without reservation" to wars of national liberation. The fruits of this policy proved to be disappointing. Few permanent successes were realized, since, in many cases, pro-Soviet leaders were either subsequently overthrown or changed their policies. Khrushchev was removed from power in 1964, and many believe that his failures in the Third World, along with the great expense of these undertakings, were factors that contributed to his ouster. Under Leonid Brezhnev, Khrushchev's successor, the Soviet Union adopted a much more pragmatic and strategic outlook toward the Third World for the remainder of the decade. Foreign aid and trade agreements were defined in terms of mutual benefit, and justifications were given for *nonintervention* on behalf of Soviet allies. In a significant move, the Soviet Union also began to establish a naval "presence" in the Indian Ocean and Mediterranean Sea.

A long-standing anchoring assumption behind U.S. foreign policy was the existence of a unified Sino-Soviet bloc. It was only very slowly that the United States came to recognize and then to accept that by the end of the 1960s the monolith no longer existed. The Sino-Soviet alliance formally began in 1949, when, after 10 weeks of negotiations, Mao Zedong and Stalin signed a series of treaties replacing the agreement that Stalin had signed with Chiang Kai-shek in 1945. Included among them was a 30-year alliance and friendship pact. Up until the late 1950s, the two states supported each other's diplomatic and military initiatives. For example, the Soviet Union backed Chinese active participation in the Bandung Conference, and China supported the Soviet Union in its invasion of Hungary. In the late 1950s, strains began to appear in the relationship. By 1964, the Communist bloc had split into two separate parts, and in 1980 the alliance formally ended when China chose not to renew the now expired treaty of friendship and alliance.

There are many reasons why the Sino-Soviet split took place. Three of them stand out as especially important.[15] First, the Chinese and Soviets disagreed over the utility of Soviet nuclear weapons as a means of furthering the interests of international communism. The Chinese were far more willing to take risks and to bring the specter of a nuclear war into its confrontations with the United States than was the Soviet Union. The 1958 Quemoy Islands crisis illustrated the differences in their thinking. Once before, in 1954, China had shelled the Nationalist-controlled islands of Quemoy and Matsu as part of its announced goal of incorporating Taiwan into the People's Republic. China targeted these islands, not only for their symbolic value, but also because Chiang Kai-shek had used them as a staging base for military raids into China. Each time, the United States came to the aid of the Nationalists. In 1954 it signed a treaty of mutual defense with Taiwan, and in 1958 it sent the Seventh Fleet to escort Nationalist ships to the islands and helped them break through the Chinese blockade. The Soviet Union did not support China as fully as Mao had wanted. While it gave diplomatic support, the Soviet Union did not provide military assistance. In fact, the Soviet Union was taking steps to cut back its military support for China by suspending the shipment of atomic materials to China. In 1959, it unilaterally terminated a 1957 agreement to provide China with atomic aid.

Ideological differences were a second contributing factor in the Sino-Soviet split. Each saw the other as having deviated from the true path of Marxism-Leninism.

Mao argued that the Soviet Union had fallen victim to "rightist" tendencies in both its foreign and domestic politics. Its foreign policy was too accommodating. China saw the United States as a "paper tiger" and argued that the Soviet Union was crediting the United States with having more power than it really did. The Chinese also viewed de-Stalinization with suspicion. For its part, the Soviet Union saw China as "leftist." Chinese foreign policy was pictured as adventurous and risky. It rejected claims that through such policies as the Great Leap Forward, with its emphasis on rural communes and small industrial plants, China could accelerate the pace of building communism or could provide a more relevant development model for Third World states.

A third contributing factor in the Sino-Soviet split was a series of conflicts of national interest that had built up over the years. Included among them was the termination of Soviet economic aid in 1969, when some 1,390 Soviet technicians were withdrawn, 343 technical aid contracts were cancelled, and 257 scientific and technical projects were stopped. There was also an ongoing competition for leadership of the international Communist movement. Most serious were competing territorial claims. In all, China claimed that nine unequal treaties had been imposed upon it by the Tsars and that some 580,000 square miles of Soviet territory in the Far East rightfully belonged to it. Border incidents began as early as 1960 and numbered in excess of 4,000. The most serious occurred in 1969. On March 2, 1969, Chinese forces attacked Soviet frontier guards on Damansky Island, which lies in the Ussuri River that marks part of the Sino-Soviet far eastern border. The Soviets retaliated on March 15 by launching a counterattack, in which missiles, heavy artillery, and tanks were used.

1970–1979

The U.S. involvement in the Vietnam War ended in 1975. In all, it spanned six administrations, beginning with Truman's underwriting of the French war effort and ending with Congress' rejection of President Ford's request for emergency military, economic, and humanitarian aid for the South Vietnamese government in the final days of its existence. The history of the war and the central place that it occupies in post-World War II U.S. foreign policy have already been discussed at some length in Chapter 3. Rather than repeating that account, our focus here will be on its long-term consequences for the cold-war struggle between the United States and the Soviet Union.

The Vietnam War led to three policy changes in U.S. thinking about how to contain the Soviet Union. They were predicated on the twin assumptions that (1) the American public was unlikely to support any major or prolonged military campaign designed to protect American allies, especially those in the Third World, from Communist led or inspired challenges to their security, and (2) that such challenges would continue. A first change was to augment U.S. power with that of other states, thereby making it more difficult for the Soviet Union to challenge the United States. The key state in this scenario, both because of its power potential and its geographic location, was Communist China. U.S. policymakers came to see China as a trump card that could be held in reserve and played at a crucial point in future U.S.-Soviet confrontations. Knowing that the United States possessed the "China card," the Soviet Union would think twice before challenging U.S. interests.[16]

The second policy change involved placing a greater emphasis on the ability of U.S. allies to defend themselves without involving U.S. troops and to use selected regional powers as surrogates in keeping the peace and containing the Soviet Union. Large-scale arms transfers became the primary method by which the Nixon administration sought to effect this policy change.

The third policy change sought to minimize future Soviet challenges by treating it less as a rival and more as a managing partner in the international system. The goal was to create a framework for limited cooperation between the two superpowers within the context of ongoing competition and conflict. "Détente" was the name given to this policy. Its central component was the strategy of linkage, which sought to substitute a network of linked rewards and punishments for the application of military power as the primary means of containing the expansion of Soviet power and influence. Détente's greatest successes were in the area of arms control, most notably with the signing of the SALT I and SALT II agreements. SALT I was a 1972 agreement that limited each side to two antiballistic missile (ABM) defense systems and that placed a five-year cap on the number of offensive missile launchers that each could possess. SALT II, signed in 1979 but never ratified by the United States, placed a series of numerical ceilings on each side's missile and bomber forces. Détente's major failing—and one that contributed greatly to the breakdown of superpower arms control talks in the early 1980s—was an inability to place effective limits on Soviet activity in the Third World. The remainder of our discussion of the 1970s is devoted to an overview of the major Third World trouble spots that came to be associated with Soviet adventurism.

For much of the 1970s, the Middle East was the foremost trouble spot in international politics. To understand these conflicts, we must first examine the legacy left by the 1967 Arab-Israeli War. The precipitating event leading up to that war was Egypt's announcement that it was closing off the Straits of Tiran at the mouth of the Gulf of Aqaba to Israeli shipping. The Israeli-initiated Six-Day War took Arab leaders by surprise, and Israel's victory was decisive. Arab losses were heavy and were measured in more than men and material. Much territory was also lost: Israel took Jerusalem and the West Bank from Jordan, the Golan Heights from Syria, and the Sinai Peninsula and Gaza Strip from Egypt.

The June 10 cease-fire, a result of U.S. and Soviet pressure, did not end the fighting in the Middle East. Egypt and Israel continued to trade military blows across the Suez Canal, and Palestinian guerrillas continued their raids into Israeli territory. International efforts to bring about an end to the violence focused on implementing UN Resolution 242. Passed after the war ended, it called for Israel to withdraw its troops from the "territories occupied in the recent conflict" in return for Arab "termination of all claims of belligerency and respect for acknowledgement of the sovereignty, territorial integrity, and political independence of every state in the area and their right to live in peace within secure and recognized boundaries." Not only did the ever-deepening Arab and Israeli distrust for one another work against UN Resolution 242, but also both sides had turned to the superpowers (Israel to the United

States, and Egypt and Syria to the Soviet Union) for weapons to replenish their depleted arsenals. The role of arms supplier was only one dimension of superpower involvement in the Middle East. For a time, the United States and the Soviet Union also sought unsuccessfully to incorporate a negotiated settlement to the Arab-Israeli conflict into the framework of détente.

The pace of events quickened in 1972. Anwar el-Sadat now headed the Egyptian government. He was not only convinced that the status quo in the Middle East was intolerable, but also he was willing to risk defeat in a new Arab-Israeli war in order to bring about political conditions that would be better suited to realizing Egypt's goals. After being rebuffed by the Soviets in his request for additional military aid, Sadat expelled thousands of Soviet military advisors and technicians in the summer of 1972. The level of surprise in reaction to this action was minor compared to that experienced on October 6, 1973 when Egyptian and Syrian forces attacked Israel. The first days of the war favored the Arabs. Their armies recaptured much of the territory lost in the 1967 war and inflicted heavy casualties on the Israeli army. As the fighting progressed, Israel reestablished its military dominance, encircling the Egyptian army and almost bringing about its complete destruction. A measure of how deeply the Middle East had become embroiled in the cold-war struggle between the United States and the Soviet Union was that, while neither superpower had felt compelled to involve itself in the 1967 war, in 1973 neither felt it could afford not to get involved. Both the United States and the Soviet Union airlifted military aid to their respective allies during the war. They also engineered a cease-fire. The war took on a truly global dimension when Israel ignored the cease-fire and continued its advance into Egyptian territory, leading Brezhnev to announce that the Soviet Union would not allow the destruction of Egypt. Later, President Nixon put U.S. forces on a global alert in order to deter a reported Soviet decision to send its own troops into the region in order to impose a truce. The United States also increased pressure on Israel to accept the cease-fire. Israel agreed to do so on October 25.

For the remainder of the decade, a great deal of the United States' diplomatic energies were focused on trying to devise a formula for bringing stability to Middle Eastern politics. Henry Kissinger was first to do so with his "shuttle diplomacy." Maneuvering in rapid fashion between Cairo and Tel Aviv, Kissinger succeeded in obtaining an agreement in January 1974 that called for Israel to reposition its forces in the Sinai so that Egypt would have full control over the Suez Canal. By employing the same methods, he was able to get an agreement between Syria and Israel in May 1974 regarding the disposition of forces on their frontier and a second Israeli withdrawal from the Sinai in 1975.

Conditions in the Middle East hardened along several fronts soon after Kissinger's last diplomatic breakthrough, and the Carter administration confronted a quite different alignment of forces. Whereas at the height of the 1973 war the Soviet Union had sought Kissinger's help in bringing about an end to the conflict, it now objected to his "shuttle diplomacy." One of the things that the Soviet Union expected from détente was the recognition from the United States that no problem in the world could be settled without its participation and "shuttle diplomacy" gave it no role in the Middle East. The Soviet Union argued that a Geneva conference, in which all interested parties would be present, was the proper forum for settling the Arab-Israeli conflict. Meanwhile, Menachem Begin, a hard-liner who was uninterested in making further compromises with the Arab world, became Prime Minister of Israel, while Egyptian president Sadat's position as a leader in the Arab world fell sharply. Radical Arab regimes and guerrilla groups now condemned him for his willingness to work with the United States and Israel. There were limits to the types of compromises that Begin was willing to accept and that Sadat could make.

Confronted by this reality, the Carter administration's initial impulse was to call a Geneva conference; however, its thinking switched to a narrowly focused U.S.-Egyptian-Israeli agreement when Sadat made a dramatic visit to Jerusalem in 1977. In September 1978, Carter invited Begin and Sadat to Camp David. Under Carter's prodding, an agreement was reached on a timetable for an Israeli withdrawal from the Sinai in return for an Egyptian pledge to establish full diplomatic relations with Israel. Not only was a peace treaty signed between these two states, but also it was expected that the Camp David formula would provide the basis for agreements on the West Bank and Gaza Strip. This hope was never fully realized. The normalization of relations did not transform Egypt and Israel into allies, and it did not become the first element in a comprehensive Middle East settlement.

While Carter was conducting his Camp David diplomacy, widespread anti-Shah rioting became commonplace in Iran. In January 1979, the Shah went into exile, opening the way for the Ayatollah Khomeini to return from exile and set up a theocracy in Iran. In November, angered by the fact that the Shah had been admitted to the United States for cancer treatment, militant Iranian students seized the U.S. embassy, taking 63 Americans hostage. In Chapter 2 we detailed the problems that the United States faced as it attempted to secure the release of the hostages. Here it is important to stress the link between events in Iran and the December 1979 Soviet invasion of Afghanistan. The outburst of Moslem fundamentalism and militancy in Iran undoubtedly fueled Soviet fears about the consequences of the growing turmoil in Afghanistan and the potential for spillover into Soviet Central Asia. The Soviet invasion of Afghanistan, about which we will have much more to say in a later chapter, is cited by many as being the final and decisive Soviet action that brought an end to détente and set the stage for a U.S. military buildup during Reagan's administration.

The Western debate over how to interpret the invasion of Afghanistan (Was it a self-contained defensive measure or was it intended to be the first step in a strategy designed to extend Soviet influence to the Persian Gulf?) was intensified because of the Soviet Union's ongoing involvement in two African trouble spots. In Angola, the Soviet Union's involvement was indirect. It was the presence of Cuban forces, presumed to be acting as proxies for the Soviet Union, that disturbed Western leaders. In January 1975, the Portuguese government and three rival independence groups reached agreement on a formula that resulted in Angolan independence in November. Almost immediately, the international community began to take sides. The United States, along with such states as China, France, North Korea, and India, gave its support to an alliance between the National Front for the Liberation of Angola (FLNA), led by Holden Roberto, and the national Union for the Total Independence of Angola (UNITA), led by Jonas Savimbi. The Soviet Union, Cuba, Yugoslavia, Sweden, Nigeria, and others gave their support to the Popular Movement for the Liberation of Angola (MPLA). The MPLA was losing the war in the early stages, but the balance shifted dramatically in its favor when 2,800 Cuban troops arrived in November 1975.

Angola was more than a foreign-policy problem for the United States. It became the symbol for a major test of wills between Congress and the president. Angola was the first significant post-Vietnam cold-war battleground. It also came on the heels of revelations that the CIA had orchestrated the overthrow of President Salvador Allende of Chile in 1973. The legacy of suspicion and distrust left by the Chilean undertaking was now reinforced by revelations that, contrary to official U.S. government statements, the CIA was sending funds directly to Angolan forces and that CIA personnel were in Angola helping to manage the war effort. In 1975, CIA covert operations in Angola cost $32 million. President Ford was planning to earmark another $25 million for weapons when Congress, concerned over the consequences of the deepening U.S. commitment, passed legislation restricting the extent to which the United States could get involved in the civil war. The most severe restriction was the Clark amendment, which forbade funds from any source from being spent for "any activities involving Angola directly or indirectly." The amendment stayed in effect from 1976 until 1985, when it was repealed.

The other major Soviet involvement on the continent was in the Horn of Africa. In 1974, Ethiopian Emperor Haile Selassie, a long-time U.S. ally, was overthrown in a military coup. A Provisional Military Administrative Council (the Dergue) took power and announced that Ethiopia was now a socialist state. Within the country, widespread resistance to its policies of nationalization and land reform developed, and human rights violations became commonplace. Resistance was particularly strong in the province of Eritrea, where a national liberation movement had long been in existence. In February 1977, the pro-Western elements of the Dergue leadership were eliminated and the pro-Soviet faction under the leadership of Haile Mariam-Mengistu assumed full control of the government. In April, Mengistu expelled U.S. military advisors and closed U.S. bases. The following month, he signed a major aid package with the Soviet Union and the first Cuban forces began to arrive.

Ethiopia's actions placed the Soviet Union in a complicated position. On the one hand, the Soviet Union welcomed this move. Ethiopia is a large and populous state, so an alliance with it offered the prospect of increased access to naval ports along the Horn of Africa. These ports were critical if the Soviet navy was to achieve a global presence. However, support for Ethiopia placed it on both sides of two ongoing regional conflicts. First, the Soviet Union had supported the Eritrean guerrillas in their bid for Eritrean independence when Haile Selassie was in power in Ethiopia. The new Marxist government was just as committed to preventing an Eritrean secession. Second, Somalia had been an ally since 1974, and Ethiopia and Somalia were long-standing enemies with conflicting claims to the Ogaden region. In July 1977, Somalia invaded the Ogaden (using Soviet-made weapons) in an effort to annex the region and its Somali-speaking majority. The Somali bid failed. Backed by Soviet advisors and some 16,000 Cuban combat troops, Ethiopia succeeded in evicting the

Somalis from the Ogaden in early 1978. Faced with the Soviet Union's decision to switch sides, on November 13, 1977 Somalia canceled its treaty of friendship with the Soviet Union and began pursuing closer ties with the United States. Soviet weapons and Cuban advisors were also used against the Eritrean rebels.

1980–1989

The cold war during the 1980s can be characterized as a decade of reversals. Most fundamentally, Soviet activism was replaced by U.S. activism. The Soviet Union found itself besieged with problems, not the least of which involved the death of three leaders of the Communist party in rapid succession: Leonid Brezhnev (1982), Yuri Andropov (1984), and Konstantin Chernenko (1985). Because of its economic weaknesses, the Soviet Union had become a "one-dimensional power."[17] It could neither offer economic aid to other states nor continue to support the level of military spending needed to operate its large military establishment. A less adventurist foreign policy and arms control agreements were logical prerequisites for the success of Mikhail Gorbachev's reform agenda. Foreign-policy disappointments were plentiful. The activism of the 1970s in the Third World had created problems for the United States, but it had produced few clear-cut permanent victories for the Soviet Union. Nowhere was this so evident as in Afghanistan. It was 1988 before the Soviet Union was able to negotiate the terms for a face-saving withdrawal.

In retrospect it is easy to see the first sign of a crack in the iron curtain that separated Eastern Europe from the rest of the continent. It appeared in 1981 with the birth of the Solidarity trade-union movement in Poland under the leadership of Lech Walesa. While Solidarity succeeded in disgracing the leadership of the Polish communist party and forcing it from power, it was not able to take over the reins of government. Power passed to others in the party under the leadership of General Wojciech Jaruzelski. Serious economic problems continued to plague Poland throughout the decade and though it remained officially outlawed, Solidarity remained a visible and popular critic of the communist party's rule. The year 1989 again brought the communist party and Solidarity into a contest of wills. This time a quite different outcome took place. After months of negotiation between the two groups, an agreement was reached in April to legalize Solidarity and permit it to run candidates for a limited number of seats in a June election. In a stunning rebuff of the communist party's leadership, Solidarity-endorsed candidates won 260 of the 261 seats that they were allowed to contest. In September history was made once again when a 24 member coalition cabinet containing only 4 communists was formed to govern the country.

Events in Poland proved to be a spark that engulfed the rest of Eastern Europe in a wave of prodemocracy movements that culminated in the opening of the Berlin Wall and proclamations that the cold war was over. In Hungary, as in Poland, old-line communist party leaders offered little resistance in stepping down. They were not so much forced out of office by mass public pressure as they were worn down and discouraged by the repeated—failed—efforts at economic reform. East Germany served as a bridge linking the peaceful, elite-driven revolutions of Poland and Hungary with the popular mass uprisings of Czechoslovakia, Bulgaria, and Romania. At first communist party leaders in East Germany took a hard-line stance against the demands for greater democracy and open borders. However, by the winter it was clear that this strategy was not working. Some 80,000 East Germans had fled to the West and about 100,000 citizens had taken part in an unauthorized prodemocracy protest rally in Leipzig. In November 1989 the Berlin Wall was officially opened, and in December the parliament amended the constitution eliminating the communist party's right to a monopoly of power.

The East German action came three days after the Czechoslovak parliament had taken a similar action. In Czechoslovakia, the prodemocracy movement encountered large-scale violence for the first time. In October the police used clubs to break up a prodemocracy protest and in November tear gas and clubs were used against students. In the weeks that followed protest meetings attended in some cases by more than 200,000 people were held and a two-hour general strike was called. The year ended with longtime dissident Vaclav Havel, himself only released from jail in May, being installed as the first noncommunist Czech president in over four decades. Large-scale protests were also held in Bulgaria but there was little violence as the Bulgarian communist party was forced to give up its monopoly on power. Romania was a different story. Here, long-time communist party leader Nicolae Ceausescu desperately sought to hold on to power. He unleashed his private security force, the *Securitate*, against the protestors and the military, which had gone over to their side. Before the fighting was over it was estimated that hundreds of Romanians were killed by Ceausescu's forces, and Ceausescu and his wife were captured and executed by the prodemocracy forces.

In the early 1980s, the Reagan administration sponsored a large-scale expansion and modernization of U.S. military capabilities in an effort to catch up with and neutralize what it perceived as the military advantage that the Soviet Union had gained over the United States during the 1970s. Among the weapons systems it advocated were the MX missile, the B-1 bomber, the Trident II submarine, a greatly expanded surface navy, and the Strategic Defense Initiative (popularly known as "star wars").

Many of the early foreign-policy initiatives of the Reagan administration were low-risk, high-profile, short-term undertakings designed to restore America's pride. Most prominent among these were the invasion of Grenada, the attacks on Libya for its support of international terrorism, and the sending of marines to Lebanon (this last action proved to be costly when in 1983 terrorists attacked marine barracks in Beirut, killing 241). Reagan's strategy only partially succeeded. Although he succeeded in rejuvenating America's self-confidence, he was unable to generate a societal consensus behind one of his principal sustained ventures into projecting U.S. military power abroad: stopping the spread of communism in Central America.

Forty years of arbitrary, oppressive, and corrupt family rule came to an end in Nicaragua on July 17, 1979 when President Anastasio Somoza Debayle went into exile. Within two days, the Sandinistas assumed power, setting the stage for confrontation with the United States over the legitimacy of its rule and the exporting of revolution to other states in the hemisphere. Somoza's deteriorating political position had created a dilemma for the Carter administration. Somoza was a staunch ally of the United States in its efforts to keep communism out of the hemisphere and to create a stable climate for U.S. businesses. Twice he had allowed Nicaragua to be used as a staging area for CIA paramilitary operations (against Guatemala in 1954 and against Cuba in 1961), and Nicaraguan troops had participated in the occupation of the Dominican Republic in 1965. At the same time, his continued rule was clearly incompatible with the Carter administration's stated intent to make the defense and extension of global human rights the "soul" of its foreign policy. Caught on the horns of this dilemma, the Carter administration vacillated. It tried to follow a middle-of-the-road approach, urging the Somoza government to improve its human rights record.

A massive uprising in August-September 1978 caused the Carter administration to become more actively involved in efforts designed to bring into existence a post-Somoza government. In January 1979, it was clear that these efforts had failed when Somoza rejected a proposal for a plebiscite supervised by the Organization of American States (OAS). The Sandinistas' seizure of power that followed six months later more nearly represented the culmination of a war of national liberation than it did the end of a civil war.[18] No major segment of society or region of the country came forward to defend the Somoza regime on its own accord.

The new Sandinista government pledged itself to political pluralism and a mixed economy, and it quickly received the support of other Latin American states. Faced with this hemispheric show of support, the Carter administration asked Congress for $75 million in economic assistance. Conservatives objected, and these funds were not approved until July 1980. As the Carter administration drew to a close, its stance toward the Sandinista government hardened. Carter canceled plans to negotiate a renewal of PL-480 international loans to finance the sale of wheat and cooking oil to Nicaragua; he delayed spending of the final $15 million of the $75 million in aid that had been approved by Congress; and in January 1981 the Carter administration failed to renew its certification that Nicaragua was not aiding, abetting, or supporting acts of violence or terrorism in other countries. Such certification was a necessity before any country could receive U.S. aid.

Tensions between Nicaragua and the United States escalated rapidly and along many fronts after the Reagan administration took office. At first, hostile U.S. rhetoric outpaced hostile actions, but by 1982 the Reagan administration had begun to agree on a military solution to the Sandinista problem. The chosen instrument was the CIA. Forces loyal to Somoza (the Somocistas) had begun using Honduras as a staging base for raids into Nicaragua shortly after the July 1979 revolution. In November 1981, Reagan signed a presidential finding, authorizing the spending of $19 million to transform this largely ineffective fighting force into one that would be capable of intercepting the flow of Sandinista arms into El Salvador. Especially important to the success of this effort was the creation of a perception that these opposition forces (the Contras) were not just remnants of the hated Somoza regime.

Both Congress and the Sandinistas reacted strongly to the Reagan administration's covert paramilitary initiative. Many in Congress doubted the stated goal of the CIA-led operation. Suspicions formed that the real purpose for organizing a 5,000-person Contra force was to overthrow the Sandinista regime. To prevent this from happening, in December 1982 Congress passed the Boland amendment to the Continuing Appropriations Resolution, which barred the use of funds by the CIA or

Department of Defense for the purposes of overthrowing the Nicaraguan government or provoking a military exchange between it and Honduras. Within Nicaragua, the Sandinistas used the Contra threat as a justification to tighten their control over Nicaraguan society.

In spite of increased U.S. support and growing popular dissatisfaction with the Sandinista regime, the fortunes of the Contras showed little improvement. The Reagan administration was unsure of how to proceed and of what it wanted to accomplish. Some called for isolating and containing the Sandinista government, while others saw the Sandinista regime as a major threat to U.S. national interests in the region because of its Marxist leanings. A third perspective was provided by the Kissinger Commission, which President Reagan appointed to review U.S. policy in Latin America. It concluded that Central America was a region of importance to the United States and that El Salvador and Nicaragua were particularly sensitive areas, with much of the unrest there due to domestic and historical factors. While the Soviet and Cuban involvement in the region required a strong U.S. response, the Kissinger Commission urged the Reagan administration to pursue a negotiated settlement along the lines of the 21-point plan put forward by the Contadora states (Mexico, Colombia, Venezuela, and Panama) in September 1983. The Reagan administration did formally endorse the plan but with very little enthusiasm, and little came of the peace initiative.

The year 1984 was notable because of revelations of highly questionable CIA activity in Nicaragua. First it was revealed that the United States had helped mine Nicaraguan harbors. Later it was discovered that the CIA had produced a psychological warfare manual *(TAYACAN)* for the Contras, which had sections that could be interpreted as calling for assassination. Beginning with President Ford's Executive Order 11905, the CIA had been officially barred from using assassination as a means of accomplishing its assigned objectives. During Reagan's second term, even greater attention was given to finding ways of covertly aiding the Contras. At the heart of the Reagan administration's plan was a scheme to divert to the Contras money generated by the sale of weapons to Iran as part of a plan to free American hostages. The possibility of using these funds in this manner surfaced in early 1986 at a time when the Contras were facing a gloomy future. In January 1986, President Reagan requested $100 million in military aid for the Contras. It was feared by some, including Lieutenant Colonel Oliver North, that Congress would not act quickly enough to approve this money, which could result in the Contras operating without any U.S. aid sometime in the spring. The size of the sum involved (an estimated $3.5 million out of a total profit of $30 million) and the existence of explicit presidential approval for the diversion could not be determined by the Tower Commission, which was set up by the president to investigate the arms sale.

During Reagan's second term, diplomatic initiatives to bring peace to the region centered on a plan put forward by Costa Rican President Oscar Arias, for which he was awarded the 1987 Nobel Peace Prize. The Arias plan was signed on August 7, 1987. It contained provisions for amnesty, a cease-fire, national reconciliation and dialogue, democratic reforms, prohibitions on the use of the territory as a staging ground by groups seeking to destabilize the region, an end to overt or covert support for irregular forces, and verification provisions. The peace process received a major blow when June 9 face-to-face talks between the two sides were broken off. The Reagan administration's efforts to regain the diplomatic initiative met with little success, and Reagan's presidency ended with the Democratic-controlled Senate and the White House still at odds over the makeup of a Contra aid plan. The Reagan administration pushed for acceptance of a plan that would allow the immediate shipment of military aid to the Contras, while the Senate endorsed a plan that only provided for humanitarian aid.

The first major post-Reagan Nicaraguan initiative came not from the United States, but from the presidents of Nicaragua, Costa Rica, Honduras, El Salvador, and Guatemala. At a February 14, 1989 meeting, they agreed to disarm the Contras, dismantle their bases in Honduras, and repatriate them voluntarily to Nicaragua. Linked to these actions was a pledge by Nicaraguan leaders to allow more democracy within the country and to hold an election in February 1990 (which to the surprise of all concerned, the Sandinistas lost). After the February meeting of the Central American heads of states, Secretary of State James Baker III began negotiations with Congress on constructing an aid package for the Contras. One day after having been elected president, George Bush indicated that military aid for the Contras would have a "high priority" in his administration. The package that emerged from these White House-Congress negotiations was quite different. Congress authorized President Bush to make available $66.6 million to keep the Contras in existence through the February 1990 elections. Of this, $49.8 million was to be allocated for direct humanitarian aid: food, clothing, shelter, medical assistance, nonmilitary training, and replacement batteries for communication equipment. The remainder of the funds would pay for such things as transporting the aid to the Contras and providing medical assistance for civilian war casualties. Perhaps even more controversial than its content was a provision that made the continuation of aid beyond November 30, 1989 contingent on the approval of Congress. Commentators from across the political spectrum said it represented an end to the "Contra era." In place of a military-oriented strategy designed to bring down the Sandinista government, the Bush administration had endorsed a strategy designed to bring about political liberalization within Nicaragua and noninterference into the affairs of neighboring states.

CONCLUSION: THE 1990s

For all of the proclamations that the cold war is over, it may be premature to write its obituary. Once before, during the period of détente, people spoke of an end to the cold war. The situation in the 1990s is quite different in a number of respects from that which existed in the 1970s. Most significantly, both U.S. and Soviet leaders seem to be in agreement that the primary danger to their respective national security interests stems not from the actions of the other but from a generalized condition of unpredictability and instability in Eastern Europe and the Third World. Still, the potential for conflict between the two continues to exist. As we shall see in the next chapter, war is a recurring feature on the landscape of world politics, and war between Great Powers is not uncommon. Furthermore, there are many causes of war, and some of those most frequently discussed causes lie beyond the control of national leaders.

NOTES

1. A large number of histories have been written about the Cuban missile crisis. This account draws most heavily upon Graham Allison, *The Essence of Decision: Explaining the Cuban Missile Crisis* (Boston: Little, Brown, 1971); Theodore Sorensen, *Kennedy* (New York: Harper & Row, 1965); and Richard Ned Lebow, *Between Peace and War: The Nature of International Crisis* (Baltimore: Johns Hopkins University Press, 1981).

2. Joseph Nogee and John Spanier, *Peace Impossible and War Unlikely* (Glenview, Ill.: Scott, Foresman, 1988), p. 2.

3. For a compilation of articles that deals with the cold war, see Part IV of Erik Hoffmann and Frederick Fleron, Jr., *The Conduct of Soviet Foreign Policy* (New York: Aldine, 1980), pp. 213–288.

4. Richard Nixon, "American Foreign Policy: The Bush Agenda," *Foreign Affairs* 68 (1989): 199–219.

5. For an orthodox perspective, see Herbert Feis, *Between War and Peace: The Potsdam Conference* (Princeton, N.J.: Princeton University Press, 1960).

6. For a revisionist perspective, see William A. Williams, *The Tragedy of American Diplomacy*, rev. ed. (New York: World, 1962).

7. Louis Halle, *The Cold War as History* (New York: Harper & Row, 1967).

8. For a discussison of the concept of a conflict spiral, see Robert Jervis, *Perception and Misperception in International Politics* (Princeton, N.J.: Princeton University Press, 1976).

9. This overview of the cold war was drawn principally from the following accounts: James Dougherty and Robert Pfaltzgraff, Jr., *American Foreign Policy: FDR to Reagan* (New York: Harper & Row, 1986); Peter Beckman, *World Politics in the Twentieth Century* (Englewood Cliffs, N.J.: Prentice-Hall, 1984); Thomas Paterson, J. Garry Clifford, and Kenneth Hagan, *American Foreign Policy: A History Since 1900*, 2d ed. (Lexington, Mass.: D.C. Heath, 1983); Nogee and Spanier, *Peace Impossible and War Unlikely*; and John Spanier, *American Foreign Policy Since WW II*, 10th ed. (New York: Holt, Rinehart & Winston, 1985).

10. George Kennan (X), "The Sources of Soviet Conduct," *Foreign Affairs* 25 (1947): 566–582.

11. Zbigniew Brzezinski, *The Soviet Bloc: Unity and Conflict*, rev. and enlgd. ed., (Cambridge, Mass.: Harvard University Press, 1971), p. 158.

12. These treaties are discussed in more detail in Chapter 11.

13. For a discussion of U.S. national style, see Spanier, *American Foreign Policy Since WW II*.

14. Nogee and Spanier, *Peace Impossible and War Unlikely*, p. 238.

15. For a discussion of the Sino-Soviet conflict, see Joseph Nogee and Robert Donaldson, *Soviet Foreign Policy Since WW II* (New York: Pergamon, 1981), pp. 208–218.

16. For a discussion of the "China card," see Banning Garrett, "China Policy and the Strategic Triangle," in Kenneth Oye, Donald Rothchild, and Robert Lieber, *Eagle Entangled* (New York: Longman, 1979), pp. 228–263.

17. Nogee and Spanier, *Peace Impossible and War Unlikely*, pp. 111–112.

18. The growing involvement of the United States in Nicaragua can be traced in the yearly articles on Central America in the annual edition of *America and the World*, put out by *Foreign Affairs*. See also Christopher Dickey, *With the Contras: A Reporter in the Wilds of Nicaragua* (New York: Simon & Schuster, 1985).

Chapter
8

Why States Go to War

In this chapter we will review some of the most important arguments concerning the causes, amount, and place of war in the international system. We will also introduce some ideas that have been put forward for ending wars. Probably no aspect of world politics has been more intensely studied than that of war. Yet, for all of the attention that it has received, no consensus exists on these questions or on what is perhaps the most fundamental question of all: Why do states go to war? In fact, we lack both a single agreed-upon framework for posing these questions and a standard for accepting an answer as true. By way of introduction, we begin with an overview of the recent war between Iran and Iraq. As you read, you should keep several questions in mind. Is the war unique, or does it share common characteristics with other past or present wars? What lessons does it hold for future wars? What could past wars have told us about this war?

THE IRAN-IRAQ WAR

Less than one year after the Soviet invasion of Afghanistan occurred, Iraqi forces invaded Iran in September 1980. While technically this made Iraq the aggressor, Iran had done much to provoke it. For nearly one year preceding the actual beginning of the war, Iran and Iraq had engaged in a series of border skirmishes and had repeatedly interfered in each other's domestic affairs. Particularly notable were efforts by Iranian fundamentalists to incite revolution throughout the region by urging Shi'ite Moslems in neighboring states to overthrow their Sunni Moslem rulers. Iraq was a principal target of these appeals. Not only is the Shi'ite population a majority in Iraq, but also it is heavily concentrated. Among the areas it dominates are the shrine cities of al-Najaf and Karbala, both of which are of great symbolic importance to the Iranian revolutionaries. The Sunnis and Shi'ites originally split over the question of Mohammed's successor, but there are doctrinal differences as well. Where the Sunni Moslems believe that each person has a private relationship with Allah, Shi'ite Moslems believe that each person communicates with Allah through his appointed intermediaries—the ayatollahs. The religious animosity between these two Moslem sects is so great that, shortly after fighting began, the leaders of both sides declared the conflict to be a *jihad*, or holy war.

A host of secular controversies reinforced and heightened the underlying religious hostility that separated these two states. Iraqi leader Saddam Hussein felt that the Iranian revolution provided his country with an opportunity to become the unchallenged leader of the Moslem world. For his part, Iranian leader Ayatollah Khomeini "had a personal score to settle" with Iraq. For nearly 15 years, he had lived in exile at al-Najaf in Iraq only to suffer the embarrassment of being expelled to France in 1978 at the Shah's request. Also abhorrent to Khomeini was the fact that in 1975 Iraq had struck a deal with the Shah. Under its terms, the international boundary of the Shatt-al-Arab estuary was moved from the Iranian side to the center point and in return the Shah agreed to stop supporting the Kurdish insurrection that was draining Iraqi reserves. (Kurds make up one-quarter of the Iraqi population and have long felt themselves to be an oppressed minority. In the hope of escaping this status, they have been fighting a lengthy guerrilla war and hope to establish their own state of Kurdistan.) Neither Khomeini nor Hussein was happy with this agreement. Khomeini objected in principle to any state entering into agreements with the Shah, while Hussein objected to the content of the agreement.

At first, the fighting favored Iraq. With the air support provided by Soviet-built MIGs, which bombed military targets and oil fields, the Iraq army pushed 500 miles into Iran. The ineffectiveness of the initial Iranian response can be traced to two main factors. First, Iran had not foreseen the possibility of an Iraqi attack and was therefore unprepared to deal with it. Second, the revolution that catapulted the Ayatollah Khomeini into power had left the Iranian military disorganized and demoralized. However, it was not long before Iraq's advance into Iranian territory encountered problems. Many of them were of Iraq's own making. Its military tactics were highly orthodox and unimaginative. Iranian resistance also stiffened as the regular military regrouped and irregular Pasadaran forces asserted themselves. By December, the war had settled into a series of "9-to-5 artillery exchanges, occasional air sorties, and rare naval action."[1] This situation represented a major setback for Iraq. Although its forces had succeeded in capturing some important Iranian territory, they had failed to achieve a breakthrough that was significant enough to induce Iran to accept a settlement that would bring Iraq uncontested rights to the Shatt-al-Arab waterway.

The military situation then deteriorated sharply for Iraq. Though hastily planned and poorly executed, an Iranian counteroffensive pushed Iraqi forces back into its own territory and raised the possibility that Iraq might soon be defeated. Under conditions described by many observers as "desperate," Iraqi forces successfully repelled three massive Iranian assaults. In one engagement, an estimated 250,000 Iranian soldiers were massed opposite the Iraqi city of Basra. The tactics employed by the two sides made the fighting particularly frightful. Iranian forces relied upon brute force and employed "human-wave" tactics reminiscent of those used in World War I in their efforts to smash through Iraqi lines. Newspaper accounts of these battles made frequent mention of teenage Iranian boys blowing themselves up in Iraqi mine fields in order to make way for Iranian tanks. To counter these attacks, Iraq began to use chemical weapons, a practice that Iran also came to employ.

From 1982 until early 1988, the ground war between Iran and Iraq remained at a stalemate. Iran and Iraq faced each other across a 730-mile front that stretched from Turkey to the Persian Gulf. The front can be divided into three sectors.[2] The central sector saw particularly bloody fighting but failed to produce a military breakthrough for Iran. Until 1988, the focus of Iranian operations was in the south. The objective was to break Iraqi morale by cutting off its access to the Persian Gulf and by bringing Iraq's second largest city of Basra within the range of Iranian artillery. Iran's single major success along the southern sector of the front came in 1986 when its forces captured the Fao peninsula and, with it, Iraq's major naval base. Iraqi forces managed to encircle the invading Iranian army, and in 1988 it retook the entire region. The year 1988 also saw the first major fighting along the northern sector of the Iraq-Iranian front. Iranian forces succeeded in capturing several Kurdish towns, as well as in bringing important oil fields and a dam used to generate much of Baghdad's electric power and water within the range of its artillery. Iraq was able to blunt this attack only by calling in air power, moving in large numbers of reinforcements, and using chemical weapons. Some 5,000 Kurdish civilians were also reported to have been killed in the fighting.

The key ingredients to the stalemate were Iran's continued ability and willingness to bear heavy casualities and Iraq's continued access to modern foreign weapons.[3] Iran possessed an overwhelming manpower advantage. Out of a population of 45.2 million, it had an estimated 6.2 million men available for military service. Iraq had a population of 15.5 million, but only an estimated 2.03 million men were fit for military duty. These base figures translated into a 1988 Iranian army composed of 2.55 million first-line ground troops, 500,000 second-line militia, and 1 million reservists. In comparison, Iraq's army consisted of 450,000 first-line troops (up from the 200,000 it began the war with), 450,000 second-line forces, and 75,000 trained reservists. This translated into a 4.8-1 Iranian advantage in mobilized ground forces and a 13-1 advantage in reserve forces. Iraq compensated for its disadvantage in manpower with an overwhelming superiority in weaponry. Its advantage in aircraft was estimated to be as great as 20-1. It also possessed more tanks (4,000–1,040) and armored fighting vehicles (3,000–750). Only the Iranian navy was superior to its Iraqi counterpart. Quantitative superiority was only part of the Iraqi advantage. It was also able to secure more sophisticated weapons from foreign suppliers than Iran. Most notably, France supplied it with a fleet of Super-Etendard fighter planes that

Table 8.1   SHIP ATTACKS IN THE GULF 1981–7

Year	1981	1982	1983	1984	1985	1986	1987
By Iraq	5	22	16	53	33	66	76
By Iran	—	—	—	18	14	41	87
Total	5	22	16	71	47	107	163

Source: Strategic Survey, 1987–1988 (London: The International Institute for Strategic Studies, 1988), p. 131.

were equipped with Exocet missiles, and the Soviet Union supplied a large consignment of tanks. In contrast, Iran was forced to buy second-rate weapons from states such as North Korea, Libya, Syria, and China.

The stalemate on the ground led each side to expand the war into the Persian Gulf. This aspect of the war began in earnest in 1984 when Iraqi forces began to bomb Iran's major oil terminal—Kharg Island—and to attack commercial oil shipping in the Persian Gulf. Economically, Iraq had very little to lose by forcing the war into the Persian Gulf. Its crude-oil exports had already been severely curtailed by Syria's decision to close the pipeline going through its territory, which was used by Iraq to handle much of its exported oil. Only its pipeline to Turkey remained operational. For its part, Iran was totally dependent on Persian Gulf shipping lanes for its oil revenue, as well as for food and war supplies. By raising the possibility of oil shortages and price hikes, Saddam Hussein hoped to destroy the Iranian economy and to bring international pressure to bear on Khomeini in order to force him to end the war. Iran retaliated with attacks of its own on oil tankers. Its objective was to intimidate Kuwait and others into abandoning the financial support for Iraq, which allowed it to purchase foreign weapons. Table 8.1 provides an overview of the shipping war in the Persian Gulf. It shows that both sides escalated their military activity in the last years of the war and that, during much of the war, Iraq was responsible for most of these attacks. The combined Iraqi and Iranian attacks on Persian Gulf oil tankers proved to be indecisive from a military point of view, and they left both states virtually bankrupt. In 1986, Iraq's foreign debt approached $50 billion and Iran's was not much less.

In 1986, confronted with Iranian-sponsored terrorism within its borders and attacks on its ships in the Persian Gulf, Kuwait sought out foreign protection for its oil exports. The Soviet Union was the first to respond favorably. Intent upon keeping the Soviet Union out of the region, the United States agreed to place 11 Kuwaiti tankers under the U.S. flag, a move that would entitle them to protection by the U.S. navy. This was not the first time that the United States had provided military services for Persian Gulf states to ward off Iranian attacks. In the early stages of the war, Saudi Arabian jet fighters repelled Iranian attacks with the help of U.S. AWACS (Airborne Warning and Control System) aircraft.

Both the Soviet Union and the United States found out firsthand the risks attendant to a Persian Gulf presence. In May 1987, a Soviet-chartered tanker hit a mine off the Kuwaiti coast. That same month, 37 U.S. sailors were killed when the *USS Stark* accidentally was struck by an Iraqi aircraft. In April 1988, the United States enlarged its naval presence by extending protection to non-U.S. neutral shipping following further military action against Iranian targets. On July 3, having just engaged in combat earlier that morning with several small Iranian boats, the *USS Vincennes* picked up a plane on its radar. Believing it to be an Iranian military aircraft, the *Vincennes* fired two missiles and destroyed the target. Tragically, it was not a military aircraft but a civilian airliner. Two hundred and ninety persons died as a result of the attack. They joined the more than 600,000 Iraqis and Iranians who are estimated to have died as a result of the war.

Efforts to end the Iran-Iraq War began soon after fighting broke out. In January 1981, an Islamic Conference called for a cease-fire and formed a mediation committee. Khomeini rejected their appeal and pledged that Iran would fight until it achieved victory. Faced with an Iranian counteroffensive, Iraq twice offered to end the war in 1982, the second time coupling the offer with a unilateral cease-fire. Both times, Iran rejected the proposal. The following years saw no real movement toward ending the war. Peace came unexpectedly in August 1988 after Iran startled the international community by announcing its willingness to accept a cease-fire under the terms of UN Security Resolution 598 (passed in August 1987). UN authorities had been trying to get Iran to accept these terms since December 1987. Foremost among the procedural points blocking an agreement was Iran's insistence that, before a cease-fire could begin, an international tribunal would have to determine which side was responsible for starting the war against Iraq's insistence that a cease-fire should be the first step in ending the war.

Iran's surprise decision of July 18 to accept the terms of Resolution 598 was due to its rapidly deteriorating military situation. In December 1987 and January 1988, Iran was unable to find enough volunteers to launch a planned major offensive against Basra. On February 27, Iran and Iraq renewed their "war of cities." From that date until March 10, Iraq staged 56 attacks on Iranian cities and Iran launched 25 attacks on Iraqi cities. An estimated 1,150 people died and 4,000 were wounded before both sides agreed to end the bombing on April 20. In battle after battle, Iran's swiftly weakening position was evident. At Shalamcheh, the majority of the Iranian prisoners taken by Iraq were 14–16-year-old boys. At Majnoun Island, some 2,000 Iraqi tanks stormed Iranian positions, defended by only 60 tanks. Within Iran, these defeats brought forward calls from two of Iran's leading ayatollahs for Khomeini to "end the conflict with honor." However, Iraq now balked at ending the war. Experiencing success on the battlefield, it put forward additional demands and launched a new offensive. A cease-fire was officially declared on August 20, and peace talks began on August 25. Not unexpectedly, the talks quickly became deadlocked, but, as 1989 came to an end, the cease-fire remained in place.

CLASSIFYING WARS: WAR IN THE INTERNATIONAL SYSTEM

A first step for us to take in order to understand the Iran-Iraq War is to compare it to other wars. This, in turn, requires that we possess a classification scheme based on clearly stated and easily measurable features so that we can group similar wars together. This is easier said than done. Significant definitional and methodological problems face any student who is interested in the study of war. Consider the following decisions that must be made in deciding what international conflict situations qualify as wars.

Must there exist an official announcement that a state of war exists? Quincy Wright, a pioneer in the study of war, argued that, properly understood, war involved a "state of law and a form of conflict."[4] In his survey of international conflict from 1480 to 1964, he restricted his data set to declared wars. A moment's reflection brings to mind numerous "wars" that would be omitted from such a listing. Among the most prominent are the Korean War, the Vietnam War, all of the Arab-Israeli wars, and the Falkland Islands/Malvinas War. Because of this, Wright's approach has not been followed by more recent research projects.

How long must the fighting last? Is there a minimum amount of time and space that a war must occupy? How connected must a series of separate battles be in order to qualify as a war when they are added together? Most studies of war imply the presence of "sustained conflict" as a definitional requirement. War involves something more than isolated or sporadic acts of violence. The problem is, as Wright correctly points out, that, while from a legal point of view wars have distinct beginning and end points, militarily they do not. Are the Arab-Israeli wars of 1948, 1956, 1967, and 1973 four distinct wars or only one long war punctuated by periodic truces? In a similar fashion, is World War II best studied in its own right or, as some suggest, should the logical conclusion of World War I with the interwar period be treated as a prolonged truce? Questions could also be raised as to whether the war in Vietnam began in the 1960s or whether it can be dated from Ho Chi Minh's pre-World War II efforts to end French colonial rule.

Is there a minimum threshold of violence that a conflict must cross before it is defined as a war? If so, what is that threshold? Wright focuses his attention on the number of troops involved. A problem with this approach is that we must decide what troops to count. Do we adopt a minimalist position and count only those troops that actively engage in battle, or do we expand it to include active duty forces that are not yet involved in combat? How do we count reserve forces and service forces? Disagreements on these points plagued conventional arms control efforts in the interwar period and have been a repeated point of contention in the ongoing efforts to negotiate a conventional arms control agreement in Europe. The alternative preferred by most researchers is to focus on the number of battle-connected casualities. Here too, however, we encounter disagreements. Lewis Fry Richardson, one of the first to attempt a scientific study of war, included all "deadly quarrels" that resulted in at least 317 deaths in his data set of wars that occurred between 1820–1949.[5] Jack Levy, in his study of war in the Great Power System from 1495–1975, used both the number of casualties (at least 100) and the number of active combat participants (at least 1,000).[6] Perhaps the most frequently employed floor is 1,000 battle-connected deaths. It forms the starting point for the highly influential Correlates of War project led by J. David Singer and Melvin Small, which has examined war in the international system between 1816 and 1980.[7] Focusing on casualties instead of troops does not eliminate the need to make decisions on what to count. For example, are civilian and military casualties counted toward the floor of 1,000 deaths, or are only military deaths counted? A narrowly cast definition of war would rely on the latter approach, but the nature of modern warfare points to use of the former. We can recall the problems that the United States encountered in Vietnam and the Soviet Union encountered in Afghanistan in distinguishing between civilians and enemy soldiers. Finally, no matter which approach is used, there is also the problem of making an accurate count. It is becoming ever more rare to find enemy armies opposing each other in periodic set-piece battles. Rival forces in a guerrilla war may not even be able to see each other. The accuracy of the weekly "body counts" that were reported by the U.S. military in Vietnam became a major source of controversy as the war dragged on.[8]

Must a war involve fighting between two armies, or can a war involve fighting between the army of a government and portions of its own population? Should the following be counted as wars: colonial wars of independence; wars of secession, such as the Ibo tribe's failed attempt to create the state of Biafra out of part of Nigeria or Bangladesh's pulling out of Pakistan; large-scale insurgencies, such as those of the Contras in Nicaragua or the rebels in El Salvador; bloody coup d'etats, such as in Haiti; situations characterized by prolonged terrorist violence, such as in the Middle East; or civil rioting, such as in South Korea in the late 1980s? Typically, studies of war do not include these types of conflicts in their data sets. Their focus is on war as "armed conflict involving the organized military forces of independent political units" or, at a minimum, "direct international violence."[9] When they are included, these types of conflict tend to be grouped under a separate heading, such as "civil war" or "internal war." We will follow this same practice in our discussion of war.

The choices made with regard to these types of questions matter because they determine which past wars are looked at for insight into the nature of contemporary or future wars. Depending upon how the categories are defined, the number of relevant wars may be quite small or quite large. When the number of cases are small, it can be difficult for researchers to reach meaningful conclusions, and the inclusion or exclusion of one or two wars can produce quite different results. For example, one subset of international wars that has received a great deal of attention of late is "hegemonic," or "global," war. While the definitions used vary from research project to research project, they are seen as highly destructive, if not unlimited, wars, involving nearly all of the Great Powers, and they are seen as wars in which control of the international system is at stake. Researchers agree that very few international wars qualify as hegemonic wars, but they disagree on which ones do qualify. Jack Levy has compiled a list of such wars, which was used by nine researchers. It is presented in Table 8.2. A total of 11 wars dating back to the Italian Wars of 1494–1525 qualified for inclusion as global wars, but no one war appeared in every listing of hegemonic wars.[10] Five researchers treat World War I and World War II as a single global war. If one purpose for studying war is to prevent a global World War III, then the question of which of the 11 wars to look to for guidance is more than just a sterile academic debate.

HOW MUCH WAR HAS THERE BEEN?

What percentage of all wars is accounted for by these 11 global wars? To repeat the central point of our discussion of war to this point, the answer depends upon which definitions are used. In order to structure the presentation of data, we will divide

Table 8.2   COMPARISON OF COMPILATIONS OF GENERAL WARS

War	Dates	Levy	Toynbee	Modelski/Thompson	Wallerstein	Gilpin	Doran	Farrar	Mowat
Italian Wars	(1494–1525)		X	X					X
War of Dutch Independence/ Spanish Armada	(1585–1609)	X	X	X			X	?	
Thirty Years' War	(1618–1648)	X			X	X	X		X
Dutch War of Louis XIV	(1672–1678)	X	X			X	X		X
War of the League of Augsburg	(1688–1697)	X	X	X		X	X	X	X
War of the Spanish Succession	(1701–1713)	X	X	X		X	X	X	X
War of Jenkins' Ear/Austrian Succession	(1739–1748)	X							X
Seven Years' War	(1755–1763)	X							X
French Revolutionary and Napoleonic Wars	(1792–1815)	X	X	X	X	X	X	X	X
World War I	(1914–1918)	X	X	X	X	X	X	X	X
World War II	(1939–1945)	X		X	X	X	X	X	—

Source: Jack Levy, "Theories of General War," *World Politics* vol. 37, no. 3 (April, 1985) p. 373. Copyright © 1985 Princeton University Press. Table 2, "Comparison of Compilation of General Wars" reprinted with permission of Princeton University Press.

wars into four categories: (1) civil wars, (2) international wars, (3) Great Power wars, and (4) global wars. The last two are subsets within the category of international war. Given the nonsuperpower status of Iran and Iraq, the limited involvement of the United States and the Soviet Union, and the large number of deaths involved, most Western analysts would classify the Iran-Iraq War as an international war.

Civil War

The popular perception is that the number of civil wars in the international system has increased dramatically in the post-World War II era, and, to some extent, the data support this conclusion. Small and Singer identified 106 civil wars during the period 1816–1980.[11] Far more civil wars (41) began in the post-World War II era than at any other time. While only an average of 0.5 civil wars per year was taking place between 1816–1947, there was an average of 1.5 civil wars per year after that.[12] The length of time they lasted (a total of 1,191.4 months) increased dramatically over early periods.

Their data also reveal that civil wars are not a totally unique phenomenon. Points of similarity exist between contemporary civil wars and earlier ones. The percentage of civil wars that became "internationalized" through large-scale outside military intervention during the period 1948–1980 (25%) was not out of line with earlier periods, and, while the number of battle deaths (3,022,300) had never been higher, it had been approached before, most notably during the periods 1849–1881 (2,891,600 battle deaths) and 1915–1947 (2,622,300 battle deaths). Civil wars have been a frequently recurring phenomenon on the world scene. Small and Singer calculate that civil wars were underway in 134 of the 165 years, or 80 percent of the time, during the period 1816–1980. One obvious reason for the increased frequency of civil wars is the rise in the number of states. If the number of states is controlled for (i.e., if, rather than look at the total number of civil wars taking place, we divide that number by the number of states), the frequency of civil war in the international system during the period 1948–1980 was actually slightly less than for the 1816–1948 period.

International War

Small and Singer identified 118 international wars in the 1816–1980 time period. An estimated 31 million combat fatalities resulted from these wars. Their study showed that international wars were a constant feature of international politics. Each of the five time periods covered included the onset of at least 20 international wars, with the most (28) occurring during the period 1849–1881. The 1945–1980 period had the second largest number of wars (26). When our attention shifts from when wars began to how many wars were underway at any one time, we find that only 20 out of the 165 years in the period 1816–1980 (12.1 percent) were truly peaceful in the sense that no war was taking place. Although the data suggest that the number of wars has increased, as with civil wars, if the number of states is controlled for, a different picture emerges. Small and Singer conclude that "whether we look at the number of wars, their severity, or their magnitude, there is no significant trend upward or downward over the past 165 years."[13]

Using a different definition of war, as well as different starting and ending points, Wright reached somewhat different conclusions. He identified at least 308 wars between 1450–1964.[14] From Wright's perspective, several distinct trends in the nature of warfare were evident. We will highlight two of his conclusions.

First, the average length of war is declining. From the sixteenth through the eighteenth centuries, major wars often lasted for more than 10 years and averaged about 5 years. During the nineteenth century, they averaged 3 years in length, and during the twentieth century they have been averaging 4 years. Second, wars involved more and more states. An average of 2.4 states participated in any given war from the late fifteenth century through the end of the sixteenth century. During the eighteenth century, that number jumped to 3.7 states, and, after a slight decline in the nineteenth century, it had grown to an average of 5 states per war in the twentieth century.

Regardless of which data set is used, two facets of modern warfare produce general agreement. The first concerns the geographic location of wars. Increasingly, wars are a Third World phenomenon. One researcher has compiled lists of wars (civil and international) during the nineteenth and twentieth centuries that have resulted in over 100,000 deaths.[15] During the nineteenth century, there were 14 such wars. Six of them took place in Europe or the United States, while the remainder occurred in the Far East and Latin America. Through 1986, there were 43 wars of this magnitude during the twentieth century. Including World War I and World War II, only

8 of these wars were fought on European soil. All the rest took place in the Third World.

The second point of general agreement concerns the cost of modern warfare. The costs in terms of casualties and military spending are readily computed. The total number of deaths resulting from the 14 wars during the nineteenth century was 5,817,000. The 43 wars during this century killed 83,642,000 people. Worldwide, military spending was estimated to have approached the $900 billion figure in 1985, compared to just over $300 billion in 1974, and appeared to be little affected by global economic problems.[16] When this is adjusted for inflation, real increases in military spending of 5.9 percent and 7.2 percent were registered for 1984 and 1985, respectively, using 1974 as a base. Third World states accounted for 20 percent of the world total in 1984, compared to only 8 percent in 1960. Table 8.3 presents the relative burden that military expenditures placed on societies in 1984. At one extreme were Kampuchea (Cambodia) and Laos, each of which had per capita GNPs of under $200 and devoted over 10 percent of their total GNP to military expenditures. At the other extreme were Japan, Luxembourg, and Iceland, which had a per capita GNP of over $10,000 and allocated less than 1 percent of their total GNP for military purposes.

More difficult to measure are the "opportunity costs" or trade-offs that accompany war. Simply put, the money that governments spend preparing for, fighting, or recovering from war cannot be spent on improving the quality of life enjoyed by their citizens. Ruth Sivard makes the following paired comparisons in addressing this issue:

> Three governments in five spend more to guard their citizens against military attack than against all the enemies of good health.

> Between 1975 and 1985, arms imports of developing countries amounted to 40 percent of the increase in their foreign debt in that period.

> In the USSR, more than twice as much money goes to military defense as to education and health expenditures combined.

> The United States now devotes over $200 billion per year to military defense against foreign enemies, but 45 percent of Americans are afraid to go out alone at night within one mile of their homes.

> The cost of a single new nuclear submarine equals the annual education budget of 23 developing countries with 160 million school-age children.

> At a cost of less than half an hour's world military outlay, the UN's Food and Agricultural Organization destroyed a plague of locusts in Africa, saving enough grain to feed 1.2 million people for one year.[17]

Great-Power Wars

An important subset of international wars is Great-Power wars—those wars involving at least one Great Power on each side. Many studies of war do not include the iden-

Table 8.3   RELATIVE BURDEN OF MILITARY EXPENDITURES, 1984

ME/GNP* (%)	GNP per capita (1983 dollars)					
	Under $200	$200–499	$500–999	$1,000–2,999	$3,000–9,999	$10,000 and over
10% and over	Cambodia† Laos		Yemen (Aden) Egypt Yemen (Sanaa)	Iraq Korea, North Syria Jordan Nicaragua Mongolia†	Oman Israel Saudia Arabia Libya Soviet Union	Qatar
5–9.99%	Ethiopia	Cape Verde† China Vietnam† Zambia Somalia	Angola Lesotho Zimbabwe El Salvador	Lebanon† Peru Taiwan	Bulgaria Greece Iran Germany, East	United Arab Emirates United States
2–4.99%	Burma Burkina Faso Equatorial Guinea† Guinea-Bissau† Mali	Pakistan Afghanistan† Mauritania† Mozambique† India Burundi Kenya Tanzania Guinea†	Morocco Guyana Honduras Thailand Botswana† Bolivia	Cuba Korea, South Turkey Albania† South Africa Chile Malaysia Argentina Yugoslavia	Czechoslovakia Poland Singapore United Kingdom Romania France Hungary Bahrain Netherlands	Kuwait Germany, West Sweden Norway Denmark Canada Switzerland

ME/GNP*								
1–1.99%	Bangladesh, Malawi, Chad, Nepal	Central African Republic†, Haiti, Sri Lanka, Sao Tome & Principe†, Zaire, Uganda	Cameroon, Papua New Guinea, Nigeria, Swaziland, Ivory Coast, Philippines	Senegal, Madagascar, Indonesia, Benin, Togo, Liberia, Rwanda†	Guatemala, Paraguay, Ecuador, Colombia, Fiji, Dominican Republic, Costa Rica	Portugal, Tunisia, Uruguay, Algeria, Congo, Suriname, Panama	New Zealand, Ireland, Venezuela, Cyprus, Austria	Belgium, Australia, Italy, Trinidad and Tobago, Spain, Gabon
								Finland
Under 1%		Niger, Sierra Leone, The Gambia†				Brazil, Jamaica, Mexico, Mauritius		Barbados, Malta, Ghana
								Japan, Luxembourg, Iceland

Source: World Military Expenditures and Arms Transfers, 1986 (Washington, D.C.: U.S. Arms Control and Disarmament Agency, 1986), p. 5.

*Countries are listed within blocks in descending order of ME/GNP.

†Ranking is based on a rough approximation of one or more variables for which 1984 data or reliable estimates are not available.

tity of the belligerent as a defining characteristic in their classification schemes. Jack Levy holds that this is a mistake.[18] He argues that, just as the study of world politics gives special status to the role and actions of the Great Powers, so too should the study of war. Only by separating these wars from those fought by lesser powers can we hope to come to a real understanding of the causes of war that pose the greatest threat to international peace and stability. His data show that Great Powers—those that are both relatively self-sufficient with regard to their own security and are able to project military power abroad—have participated in an unusually high proportion of all wars. Reworking Wright's figures, Levy concludes that over 70 percent of his 308 wars involved at least one Great Power. According to his own calculations, 119 wars involving the Great Powers occurred between 1495 and 1975, and 64 of them were Great-Power wars.

Levy found that Great Powers were at war for 75 percent of the 480 years covered in his study. Sixty percent of the time they were engaged in a Great-Power war. On average, a Great-Power war broke out every seven or eight years, and in a typical year two and one-half Great Powers were at war and there was slightly less than one Great-Power war underway. The typical Great-Power war lasted four years, involved more than two Great Powers, and resulted in 34,000 battle deaths. Although Great-Power wars are decreasing in frequency, the more recent ones were much more serious than earlier ones in virtually every respect except for duration. Table 8.4 lists the 20 most recent Great-Power wars.

General or Hegemonic War

An even smaller subset of international wars is general or hegemonic wars. The most powerful states always attempt to structure and organize the international system in such a way that their goals and interests are best served. This does not mean that other states do not benefit by the way in which the international system is structured, but it does not guarantee that they will either. Furthermore, when the goals and aspirations of the lesser states conflict with those of the dominant states, it is the dominant states that will win. Only by assuming the role of a dominant state can a frustrated lesser state bring into existence a system that favors its foreign-policy agenda. Since few dominant, or hegemonic, states are likely to give up their dominance over the international system voluntarily, a war most likely would be required to bring such a change about. For most researchers, it is this quality that separates a hegemonic or general war from all others.[19] Robert Gilpin has identified three defining characteristics of a hegemonic war: (1) It involves a direct contest between the dominant power(s) and the rising challenger(s), (2) the fundamental issue at stake is the nature and governance of the system, and (3) it is an unlimited war with respect to both geography and means.[20]

Gilpin has also identified three preconditions for such a war.[21] First, a "closing in" of time and space must take place. As territory, markets, and resources become more and more scarce, conflicts between states become more frequent. Moreover, international politics starts to take on the quality of a "zero-sum game" in which gains made by one state can only come at the expense of losses incurred by another. Second, a perception arises in one of the Great Powers that a major historical change is

Table 8.4 THE TWENTY MOST RECENT
GREAT-POWER WARS

Korean War	1950–1953
World War II	1939–1945
Russian Civil War	1918–1921
World War I	1914–1918
Russo-Japanese War	1904–1905
Franco-Prussian War	1870–1871
Austro-Prussian War	1866
War of Italian Unification	1859
Crimean War	1853–1856
Napoleonic Wars	1803–1815
French Revolutionary Wars	1792–1802
War of the American Revolution	1776–1783
War of the Bavarian Succession	1778–1789
Seven Years' War	1755–1763
War of Austrian Succession	1739–1748
British-Spanish War	1726–1729
War of the Quadruple Alliance	1718–1720
War of the Spanish Succession	1701–1713
Second Northern War	1700–1721
War of the League of Augsburg	1688–1697

Source: Jack Levy, *War in the Modern Great Power System* (Lexington, Ky.: University of Kentucky Press, 1983), pp. 72–73.

taking place and that time is working against them. As a result, policymakers may come to view their choice as one of making war now while they still possess an advantage rather than one of waiting and fighting later under less favorable conditions. Third, events begin to escape human control.

Given the defining characteristics of a hegemonic war, it is clear that, should there ever be another, it would have to be an unlimited nuclear war fought on a global scale. Are the preconditions in place for such a war? Gilpin argues that they are not.[22] More troubling is the question of whether such a war (or any other type of war) *must* take place? In order to answer this question, we need to come to an understanding of the role of war in world politics and why states go to war.

WHY STATES GO TO WAR

There is no shortage of reasons for why states go to war. Many of these reasons strike observers as plausible or interesting, but little empirical evidence exists to support their claims. For other explanations, the evidence is inconclusive. No single explanation has yet emerged that can provide the basis for a general theory of war. In all likelihood, none ever will. Explaining, predicting, or preventing war will require moving beyond single-factor arguments. Combining variables into a theoretically sound and empirically verifiable framework, however, cannot be easily done for something as recurrent, varied, and complex as war. At the risk of some oversimplification, the many different explanations given for why states go to war can be divided into two categories. In the first category are those explanations that see war as a disease.[23] Its root causes are found in the environment in which policymakers operate. War is something that happens to them. The second category is comprised of explanations that start from the assumption that war is the product of deliberate choice. Policymakers go to war because they believe that they will win and because of the benefits that they expect to realize from victory.

War as a Disease

The Security Dilemma   The origins of the security dilemma lie in the anarchic structure of world politics, which makes the pursuit of power both necessary and self-defeating. In the absence of agreed-upon laws, norms, or rules that regulate international competition, a state must build up its own power relative to that of other states in order to protect its national interests. The problem is that by increasing its power—and thereby feeling less threatened—a state simultaneously lessens the ability of other states to protect their own national interests. The logic of world politics demands that they, too, must try to increase their power. If successful, these states will now be in a less threatening situation, but the state that originally felt threatened now finds itself back in a vulnerable position. The cycle then repeats itself, moving to ever higher levels of potential violence. With the completion of each cycle, actions tend to become less and less controllable and the likelihood of war becomes greater. War is not, however, inevitable. Economic exhaustion may also bring an end to the conflict spiral, since neither side is able to continue acquiring additional increments of power.

Many see the arms race as the most dangerous manifestation of the security dilemma in the contemporary international system: State A acquires a new weapons system to improve its security, but in doing so it increases the vulnerability of state B to attack or threats. This forces state B to develop a new weapons system of its own, which has the effect of negating the benefits that state A expected from its development of new weapons. State A must now develop still another weapons system, which will prompt yet another response in kind by state B. The fear that the U.S.-Soviet arms race will go out of control and explode into war is a major force behind calls for arms control and disarmament. While not disputing the existence of the security dilemma itself, some observers have challenged the notion that the weapons acquisition process involving the United States and Soviets is a result of this kind of competition. They argue that domestic, technological, and bureaucratic factors are better explanatory variables. In a particularly influential series of articles, Albert Wohlstetter argued that, in fact, the opposite of an arms race took place during the period 1962–1971. The United States underreacted to the Soviet military buildup, reducing by two-thirds the amount of funds (measured in constant dollars) that it spent on strategic weapons.[24]

Structure of the System   The structure of the international system is a second environmental feature cited by many as a cause of war. The crux of the argument centers on the relative merits of bipolarity versus multipolarity. One school of thought holds that bipolar systems are war-prone because of their rigidity. By definition, a bipolar system is one in which there are two competing powers locked into what each perceives as a struggle for survival. Each power is at the core of an alliance system over which it has virtually complete control. Neutrality is impossible in this system, and each conflict is treated as significant because of the fear that it may represent the first in a series of "falling dominoes." Far preferable is a multipolar system with its flexibility and deemphasis on ideology. A multipolar system is one in which there are at least five major actors, all of whom are relatively equal in power. Because ideological differences are not held to be significant, states are free to ally with any other state and to change alliance partners as the situation requires. There are no permanent friends or enemies. Such a system encourages the development of multiple and cross-cutting ties between states, which makes it difficult for wars to break out.

Working from the same definitions, a second school of thought holds that multipolar systems are the most susceptible to war. Instead of being condemned for its rigidity, bipolarity is championed because of the amount of control that the two powers possess over all others in the system. This control is seen as capable of preventing the occurrence of small or accidental wars that could escalate into major confrontations. Such wars, as well as their potential for escalation, are seen as critical problems in multipolar systems because of the large number of potential enemies. With attention spread over at least four states, the very possibility arises that threatening actions or potentially explosive situations will not be recognized in time for corrective actions to be taken. This is not likely to be the case in a bipolar system, in which there is only one enemy who receives the full and undivided attention of the other major power.

The historical record as interpreted in various research projects does not offer conclusive support for either argument.[25] One study found that bipolarity was not associated with the outbreak of war in the eighteenth century but that it has been associated with it in the twentieth century. Another study found that bipolar systems tended to have fewer wars than did multipolar systems, that wars in bipolar systems tended to last longer, and that wars in multipolar systems tended to produce more casualties.[26] Still another study concluded that a curvilinear relationship existed, with the probability of war being at the apex, when there were either very few poles or large numbers of power centers in the international system.[27]

The Distribution of Power in the International System   Regardless of how the international system is structured (bipolar, multipolar, etc.), the distribution of power in that system affects the ability of policymakers to gauge accurately the prospects for victory. When there are clearly visible gaps in the power potential of states, leaders will have a relatively easy time anticipating the probable outcome of the war. War is unlikely in such a situation, because the inferior state knows that it cannot win and will not fight, and, for the same reason, the dominant state knows that it does not need to go to war in order to realize its objectives. The situation is quite different when a balance of power exists among states. Under these conditions, it is difficult for policymakers to determine which state is more powerful because of how closely grouped the power potentials of the states are. Thus, leaders are apt to miscalculate the odds of victory and go to war when they should not. For this reason, rather than being a stabilizing factor in world politics, as is generally maintained, a balance of power may actually contribute to the onset of war.

The Power Transition   For other analysts, it is not the distribution of power in world politics that causes war but the rate at which the distribution of power is changing. In this view, even if a balance of power exists among states, the probability of war breaking out will not increase as long as the distribution of power remains constant. Long-term stability in the power ranking and spacing among states allows leaders to estimate correctly the consequences of their actions and the responses of other states. The primary threat to peace lies with rapid changes in the distribution of power. The more rapid the rate of change, the more difficult it is to predict the outcomes of conflicts or to accommodate demands for greater prestige and power within the international system. Knowing that the power gap is shrinking, dissatisfied states may become sufficiently emboldened to challenge the dominant state. At the same time, the dominant state may be less sure of its ability to withstand this challenge without resorting to war. Furthermore, the dominant state must consider the possibility that, if it does not fight a war now, it may have to fight one in the future under even less favorable conditions.

War Cycles   A fifth explanation for why states go to war focuses on the existence of long-term cycles. Different reasons are given for why such cycles exist. In our discussions of international systems change and hegemonic war, we introduced one version of the argument: Wars occur with great regularity because over time a contradiction develops between the distribution of rewards and benefits conveyed by a given international system and the actual distribution of power in it. The roots of this contradiction lie, on the one hand, in the increasing costs and declining benefits of world leadership and, on the other hand, in the diffusion of military and economic technology in the international system, which strengthens the relative power position of challenging states. An alternative version of this argument emphasizes human nature instead of the inherent dynamics of world politics. In the immediate aftermath of a war, people experience a sense of "war weariness."[28] Tired and disillusioned by what war has brought into their lives, citizens in neither the victorious state nor the defeated one are anxious to fight again. Over time these memories fade, and a new generation of leaders assumes power. Recollections of the horrors of war are replaced by concerns about the need to stand firm in the face of enemy challenges, the need to regain lost prestige, the desire to realize once again some long-standing goal, and a general nostalgia for the past.

Here again, empirical testing of the war cycle hypothesis has produced mixed results.[29] Those researchers that have found that there are cycles in war have been unable to agree on their duration. For example, Wright argued that periods of war were separated by 50-year intervals of peace, while Richardson maintained that a 200-year cycle separated the peak years of war. When the focus shifts from the outbreak of wars to the amount of war underway, a clearer pattern is evident. Singer and Small found that the amount of war in the international system peaked at 15–20-year intervals. The variation in the frequency and amount of war in the international system is important, because it casts doubt on the likelihood that war can be explained solely on the basis of the structure of the system or of some underlying characteristic. If this were the case, then war should be a constant phenomenon. Periods of peace, however short and irregular they may be, suggest that the disease-like qualities of war that reside in the international system can be moderated or muted by other factors.

Type of Government   One of the most popular explanations for why states go to war has to do with the type of government that exists in the state that started the war. Democratic governments are seen as inherently peaceful, slow to go to war, and, most frequently, the victim of aggression rather than the instigator of it. Authoritarian governments are held to possess the opposite characteristics: They are aggressive and quick to go to war. Furthermore, democracies almost never seem to go to war against other democracies. The historical record, however, suggests that there is at least as much myth as substance to this view of the pacific nature of democracies. A listing of the 10 most war-prone countries shows that democracies are as likely to go to war as authoritarian states. During the 165 years covered by the Singer and Small study, 2 democratic states—France (50 years and 4 months) and Great Britain (34 years and 2 months)—were at war most often. Germany, an authoritarian state for much of this time period, came in tenth. The Soviet Union and the United States were both found to have been at war about the same amount of time, 23 years and 10 months, and 21 years and 10 months, respectively. In a variation on this argument, some analysts have argued that, regardless of their form of government, newer states are more apt to go to war than older ones.

Nationalism   The terms "nation" and "state" are often used interchangeably or even together in hyphenated fashion, as "nation-state." In reality, these terms refer to two quite different concepts, and the lack of congruence between "nation" and "state" is frequently cited as reason for war. The concept of nation refers to a "we" feeling; that is, it is a shared sense of group identity that builds upon the perception of a common past and a shared vision of the future. Language, culture, and religion are the most common bonds that forge a people into a nation. The state is an abstract legal entity, whose prominence in world politics can be traced back to the Treaty of Westphalia in 1648.

Nations and states share an uneasy coexistence in contemporary world politics. The geographic boundaries of nations and states are anything but identical. Nowhere is this more true than in Africa, where the Europeans carved out colonial boundaries without regard for existing national ties. As a result, not only were segments of the same nation placed in different colonies, but also historically hostile nations were placed in the same colony. This problem is not unique to either Africa or other states in the Third World. Virtually no continent is free from this type of war disease. Neither are the major powers. Great Britain faces ongoing violence in Northern Ireland, with the Catholic minority there demanding that it be allowed to become part of predominantly Catholic Ireland. The United States has periodically had to deal with demands, often accompanied by terrorist-type actions, for Puerto Rican independence. In 1988, the Communist party leadership in the Soviet Union faced multiple challenges. Estonia attempted to declare its sovereignty, ethnically based rioting occurred in the Transcaucasian republics of Armenia and Azerbaijan, and there were continued disagreements with China over territory in Siberia. In 1990 Lithuania declared its independence.

As even these few examples suggest, not all nationalistic wars are alike. They can be divided into two categories: *separatist* wars, in which one nation seeks to leave a state, and *irredentist* wars, in which part of the territory of one state (or, in the extreme, an entire state's territory) is claimed by another state on nationalistic grounds. Prominent separatist wars in the past include those preceding the establishment of Israel, the U.S. Civil War, the secession of East Pakistan from Pakistan to form Bangladesh, and the failed attempt by the Ibo tribe to establish the independent state of Biafra out of Nigeria. Irredentist claims are evident in the dispute between Greece and Turkey over Cyprus, in the hard-line Arab claims that Israel has no right to exist, and in Hitler's annexation of Austria and his claims on the Sudetenland in Czechoslovakia. Particularly problematic and prone to war are those situations in which a nation-state cannot be created simply by one separatist or irredentist act. Such a situation exists in the Persian Gulf, where, as we have already noted, the Kurds wish to establish the nation-state of Kurdistan but in order to do so must incorporate territory presently held by Iran, Iraq, Turkey, and the Soviet Union.

There is yet one more way in which nationalism can become a cause of war. Throughout history, many people have felt that their nation was superior to others and that this superiority gave their nation a right to dominate others. Since such beliefs, and the demands that grew out of them, were not likely to go unchallenged, wars were common where such ideas were in vogue. War also tends to be glorified in nations where such beliefs are held, with the game of world politics being equated to a Darwinian struggle of survival of the fittest. In these nations, war is seen as the primary mechanism for settling disputes over which culture is superior and for passing power from old, decaying states to young, vibrant ones. Feelings of nationalist superiority played prominent roles in the Fascist and Nazi ideologies. Benito Mussolini, leader of Fascist Italy, stated that the tendency for states to expand was a sign of their vitality. Adolph Hitler asserted that the German people needed living space (*Lebensraum*) and that they had a right to take what they needed from their old and decaying neighbors.

Relative Deprivation   Of greater importance for some than the type of government or the lack of fit between the boundaries of nations and states, are socioeconomic factors. Given the high incidence of war in the Third World, a great deal of speculation has centered on the question of whether states are more prone to go to war at certain levels of economic development. According to this theory, war is seen as a product of poverty. It is something that happens when socioeconomic conditions deteriorate beyond a certain point. The available evidence suggests that this hypothesis is incorrect. There does not seem to exist a poverty line below which states are more warlike.[30] A more promising line of inquiry focuses not on absolute levels of poverty, but on relative deprivation. War is most likely to come about when segments of society feel deprived relative to some other groups. In place of the status quo, a "fair share" of society's wealth is demanded. The problem for policymakers is that the definition of "fair share" is as much psychological in nature as it is economic. Simply improving the standard of living of those who are demanding change is no guarantee of success. If other societal groups continue to advance at an even faster rate, if the gap between the dissatisfied group and the other groups remains the same, or if gains are threatened by reversals, societal discontent will continue to grow.

Relative deprivation appears to be an especially important concept for understanding civil wars in the Third World because of the side effects of certain economic development strategies. Rising inequality often accompanies economic development. The initial growth in GNP tends to benefit the wealthier elements of the population, often at the expense of those at the lower end of the social ladder, particularly those living in rural areas. Expectations rise faster than opportunities. Where expectations cannot be met, people are susceptible to revolutionary rhetoric. Even where inequality is not a factor, relative deprivation can occur if the government causes people to believe that they will receive greater benefits than the society is able to provide. Here the gap is between where people are and where they were led to expect they would be, rather than where they are relative to some other group. Events in China, with the Beijing student demonstrations, suggest what can happen when the government raises expectations through limited reform and then fails to carry through with that reform.

The more developed countries are not immune to the effects of denying rising expectations. To some extent, the urban riots that the United States experienced during the late 1960s were a result of failed expectations. Studies of those who were involved in the riots found that participants tended to come from the better educated, slightly better off segments of the ghetto communities. They were people who had been led to expect that conditions would get better but who had become impatient and alienated in the face of restricted opportunities.

Contagion   If some diseases are contagious, might not war be contagious too? This question forms the starting point for yet another set of inquiries into why states go to war. Disagreement exists over where to look for the source of the infection. Most frequently mentioned are internal violence, past wars, and wars taking place elsewhere in the international system. While this theory is intuitively persuasive (it always seems that wars, coups, terrorist attacks, etc., come in waves), researchers have not yet been able to establish that wars are contagious. The presence of high levels of domestic violence within a state has not been found to be related in a consistent manner to high levels of external aggression. Civil wars and other forms of internal violence may provide an opportunity for foreign states to involve themselves in a war, but they do not automatically spill over into the global arena. International wars also do not appear to beget more international wars. In studying wars over the past five centuries, Levy found that "there may be a slight tendency for the occurrence of a war to increase the likelihood of the outbreak of a second war, but only while the first is underway and independent of its characteristics. Once a war (or a series of wars) is over, neither its incidence nor seriousness has any impact on the likelihood of war in the period immediately following. . . ."[31]

War as Conscious Choice

An Expected Utility Theory of War   Where some see war as a disease that infects world politics, others see it as a conscious policy choice in which policymakers weigh the costs and benefits of going to war versus those of remaining at peace. This position has been argued most forcefully by Bruce Bueno de Mesquita.[32] In his formulation of the problem, the decision to go to war is made by a single dominant leader on the basis of his or her estimate of the costs and benefits of doing so and on the basis of the leader's comprehension of right and wrong. In making this decision, the leader behaves as if he or she has made calculations regarding (1) the expected utility of a two-country war, (2) the expected utility of a war in which other states come in on the side of the attacking state, and (3) the expected utility of a war in which other states come in on the side of the attacked state. Only when all three sets of calculations favor the attacking state will the decision to go to war be made. Bueno de Mesquita stresses that leaders are concerned with more than the probability of victory and the size of the payoff. They also take into account possible future changes in the policies of the target state: Are they likely to be more to the liking of his or her state in the absence of war or only as a result of war?

An important contribution made by the "expected utility" theory of war is its ability to explain why there have been four times as many wars between states that had defensive pacts with one another as between states that were enemies. Bueno de Mesquita argues that alliance ties not only bind states together but also serve as a source of intelligence about policies and future plans. In the absence of this intelligence, it is difficult to predict with any accuracy what future policy changes may take place, and therefore such considerations will not heavily influence the decision about whether or not to go to war. However, the knowledge that an already friendly state is considering a course of action that will make it less friendly on occasion provides leaders with a rational incentive to go to war with an ally.

Bueno de Mesquita is not the first or only researcher to see war as the product of deliberate choice. With varying degrees of explicitness, at least three other important explanations of war also start from this assumption. All three emphasize factors that make it difficult for policymakers to calculate the odds of victory.

Individuals   For some, war is inherent in human nature. A central principle of realism holds that human nature is neither good nor perfectible. People are seen as power-seeking and as inherently flawed, with a capacity for evil.[33] A wide variety of theoretical explanations have been put forward in support of this view. They draw upon such diverse fields of study as biology, anthropology, psychology, animal behavior studies, and religion. As is the case for explanations that find the root cause of war as residing in the fundamental nature of world politics, human-nature-oriented explanations are unable to account for the variability of war. If human nature is the cause of war, then war should be present all of the time. Because it is not, the influence of human nature must be less than absolute. As Ted Robert Gurr puts it, "human nature allows war to occur but does not make it occur."[34]

Personality is an alternative focus to human nature in a consideration of the individual as a cause of war. Conceptualized this way, not all leaders are equally prone to lead his or her state to war. Some policymakers are more predisposed to go to war than others. The assumption seems plausible and is implicit in the many "great men" histories that have been written about past wars. The problem is one of moving from a plausible explanation of why states go to war to a verified explanation. How do we establish the link between actions or statements and personality? While political scientists tend to treat personality as a single variable, psychologists note that, in fact, the concept of personality actually encompasses a large number of variables. Finally, questions must be asked regarding the types of generalizations that can be drawn about the impact of personality on war when these studies tend to adopt widely differing theoretical starting points of what many might consider to be aberrant personalities (Stalin, Hitler, Gandhi, Nixon, Wilson, etc.).

Misperceptions   Finally, another school of thought holds that the major impediment to making rational calculations regarding the outcome of a hypothetical war or the consequences of any foreign-policy action lies in our inability to perceive correctly the world around us. Proponents of this view hold that, while in one sense it may be true that we live in a world defined by our imagination, it is also quite possible for us to distinguish between our individual images of a situation and the situation as it actually exists.[35] Both are important for an understanding of world politics. A focus on images helps us to understand why leaders acted as they did. The gap between images and reality helps us to understand why some courses of action succeed while others fail.

Four misperceptions have been found to be especially prevalent in decisions on whether or not to go to war. They are (1) the leader's self-image, (2) the leader's view of the adversary's character, (3) the leader's view of the adversary's intentions, and (4) the leader's view of the adversary's power and capabilities.[36] Routinely, leaders on the brink of war expected to realize a quick and relatively painless victory. Compared to individual-focused explanations of why states go to war, which focus on human nature and personality, the focus on perceptions is relatively optimistic regarding our long-term ability to prevent wars. While there is little that can be done to prevent war if human nature and personality are responsible, perceptions are learned. Logically, therefore, if policymakers have learned to view adversaries in a certain light, they can be taught to view them more accurately. Much of the literature on misperceptions and surprise in world politics is directed at this very purpose.

ENDING WARS

Why Wars Are Difficult to End

While the causes of war are widely disputed, few challenge the assertion that ending wars is easier said than done. Regardless of whether we are looking at World War I, World War II, the Korean War, the Vietnam War, the Iran-Iraq War, or the

Soviet invasion of Afghanistan, a frequently voiced opinion is that these wars lasted too long. A number of factors came together to produce situations such as these. First, one side cannot end a war unilaterally. Both sides must agree that the war is over. So long as either side believes that by continuing the war it may achieve victory or lessen the political costs of defeat, fighting will continue.

The need for both sides to agree that the war is over points to a second factor that makes ending wars difficult: As the war continues, the goals being pursued may change. New goals may arise in the course of fighting a war, secondary goals may increase in prominence, or leaders may simply come to feel that they have already paid too high a political price to admit defeat. The Defense Department's study of the Vietnam War, commonly known as *The Pentagon Papers*, provides an example of the first possibility. In it, an official defined U.S. war aims in the following terms: 70 percent to prevent a humiliating defeat for the U.S.; 20 percent to prevent South Vietnam from falling into the hands of China; and 10 percent to allow the people of South Vietnam to enjoy a freer way of life. It is not hard to imagine that an internal Soviet military study of the war in Afghanistan would produce a parallel set of conclusions. Clearly, these were not the war aims at the outset for either the United States or the Soviet Union.

A third factor that can complicate efforts to end wars is the lack of clarity over how wars end. Tradition has it that wars end with a peace treaty, and, until World War I, most did.[37] Of the 311 wars that occurred between 1480 and 1970, 179 ended with a peace treaty or peace treaties (World War I ended with the signing of five peace treaties to resolve the 79 different declarations of war). In fact, the use of peace treaties became the norm. Where in the sixteenth century only one-third of all wars ended with a peace treaty, one-half of all wars ended this way in the eighteenth century, and two-thirds did so in the nineteenth century. However, since World War I, no war has ended in a peace treaty. In some cases, one side emerged as the victor and imposed a peace upon the loser; in other cases, the fighting simply ended, or a temporary truce became permanent, while, in still others, formal negotiations took place that produced something other than a peace treaty. In this light, the ending of the Iran-Iraq War was quite normal. As the 1990s began, no peace treaty was signed. The war ended with a cease-fire that led to inconclusive peace talks. The Korean War, the Vietnam War, the invasion of Afghanistan, the various Arab-Israeli wars, the Falkland Island War, and the fighting in Nicaragua all ended on terms short of a traditional international peace treaty.

Possible Tactics

Designing a line of action to bring about an end to war requires an understanding of why the war began. If the war is seen as a disease, then a judgment must be made as to whether a cure exists. Perhaps there is little that can be done except to let the war run its course while an attempt is made to lessen the pain and suffering that accompanies it and to take steps to speed up the process of recovery. The most effective line of action might be to approach a potential war situation in terms of preventive medicine that can be applied before the war disease breaks out. Working from a game theory perspective, Kenneth Oye has suggested three ways in which the likelihood that cooperation rather than conflict will mark the relations between states can be increased, given the anarchic nature of the international system.[38] As we have already noted, one of the most frequently identified sources of the war disease relates to some aspect of the international system. Therefore, Oye's argument can serve as an illustration of the type of corrective action that might be prescribed to prevent war as a disease from occurring.

First, the structure of the payoff can be altered to increase the benefits of cooperative behavior. Second, policymakers can be taught to extend the time frame of their thinking beyond the immediate conflict at hand and further into the future. Important here is the realization that world politics is made up of an ongoing series of periodic conflicts and that what matters is not winning the conflict at hand but the fitness of the state in the long run. Third, the number of players in the game can be reduced through the formation of alliances or the creation of international organizations, so that it is easier for policymakers to identify and realize common interests.

If war is seen as a product of conscious choice instead of a disease, tactics can focus on ending a current war rather than on preventing the next war from starting. The challenge is for states to devise tactics that will allow their opponent to say that the war is over. One way in which this might be done is for the conflict to escalate. Implicit in this strategy is the notion that societies possess a certain pain level and that, once pain is inflicted beyond that level, they will stop fighting. This was the logic behind the U.S. bombing of North Vietnam, the dropping of the atomic bomb on Hiroshima, and Hitler's bombing of Great Britain. After reviewing several attempts at what he labels "bombing for peace," Ernest May concludes that a strategy of escalation is capable of producing a "yes" answer only under special circumstances.[39] It is particularly important that the leaders who began the war be replaced by others who are less wedded to the reasons for going to war. He also concludes that the notion of a societal pain level is misleading. The threat of inflicting greater pain appears to be far more effective in influencing an enemy's decision-making process than actually doing so. This is because societies find out that they can endure far more than they thought possible. Unless it reaches unprecedented proportions, escalating the level of violence thus may simply raise the stakes without bringing about an end to the conflict.

A second strategy takes the opposite approach. Rather than escalating the conflict it suggests fractionating it.[40] It is hoped that, by dividing the conflict into smaller pieces, common interests and points of agreement can be found. This is the logic behind Kissinger's shuttle diplomacy and Carter's Camp David peace plan. Rather than trying to end the series of Arab-Israeli wars with one comprehensive formula, they broke down the problem into smaller pieces: the states involved, the issues addressed, the principles on which long-term solutions would be based, and so on. They believed that, over time, all the small agreements would be brought together to create the conditions for a viable Middle East peace.

These efforts also illustrate three interrelated problems with this approach toward ending wars. First, great care needs to be taken when a large problem is broken down into smaller ones. The complexity of war means that there are multiple ways to proceed, but not all are equally well suited to serve as the foundation of a lasting peace. Second, there is nothing inevitable in the process of moving from agreement in one area to agreement in another. Domestic political pressures are likely to make policymakers pay close attention to the costs and benefits of each agreement. In fact, as the process of building agreements and binding them together progresses and as the pluses and minuses become clearer and clearer, policymakers may feel that they have less and less room to make concessions. Third, this is a time-consuming process. The ultimate danger is that, by the time it nears completion, the situation may have changed so much that the agreement is no longer relevant to the problem.

A third strategy treats war as if it were a rung on a ladder of violence, with the goal being to move down the ladder to a more peaceful condition. Developed by Charles E. Osgood, the GRIT strategy (Graduated and Reciprocated Initiatives in Tension Reduction) asks that one side unilaterally move a rung or two down the ladder of violence and invite an equivalent response from the opponent.[41] The exact nature of the response is not specified, but it is made clear that any attempt to exploit this effort at tension reduction will produce a forceful counterreaction. If a positive response is forthcoming, the initiating state is expected to repeat the process by taking another step down.

While experimental evidence exists that indicates that GRIT has the potential for reducing international tensions, policymakers have yet to apply it systematically to any real-world problem.[42] One major impediment to its use is the difficulty encountered by states who try to convince their opponent that the first unilateral step down is not an act of appeasement. If this step is taken by the losing state, the winning state may read it as affirmation that its policies are succeeding and may press on with the war effort, even if it means renewed or more intense fighting. If this step is taken by the winning state, the losing state may read it as a sign of war weariness and may conclude that additional fighting may bring even better terms of surrender. Problems also exist when judgments are made about the comparative worth of tension-reducing measures. Can policymakers in one state accurately measure and appreciate the military or political value of concessions made by "the enemy"? A related issue involves the scope of the permissible trade-offs. In an Arab-Israeli or India-Pakistan dispute, the reciprocal initiatives would take place in a narrowly defined area, but what of the U.S.-Soviet rivalry? Can a U.S. unilateral initiative in Angola or Nicaragua be matched by a Soviet response in Afghanistan or Europe?

CONCLUSION: THE ROLE OF WAR IN WORLD POLITICS

One final question needs to be asked: Must there be more wars? At the heart of the answer to this question lies a judgment as to whether war is an inherent feature of world politics or an aberration. Three different answers can be given as to whether there must be more wars. Realists respond in the affirmative. Not only is war rooted in the anarchic nature of world politics, but also it is an important policy instrument that states rely upon to realize foreign-policy objectives. The observation made in the eighteenth century by Karl von Clausewitz is still held to be valid: War is merely an extension of diplomacy by other means. War is also held to play an important role in the operation of the international system. It is held as the primary mechanism by which fundamental shifts in system change take place. This is especially true for hegemonic war.

Globalists take exception with realists' starting assumptions. They see the advent of an interdependent international system as tempering much of the anarchy that is seen by the realists, making war a dysfunctional tool of diplomacy and system change. They are divided, however, on the implications that interdependence holds for the likelihood of future wars. Optimistic globalists see interdependence as an ushering in of a new era in world politics—one in which growing sense of world community and mutually beneficial interactions will make wars between major states all but disappear. Pessimistic globalists fear that interdependence between states may instead lead to attempts by some to exploit the growing vulnerability and sensitivity that societies now have to events taking place elsewhere in the international system. Whether the resulting conflicts will escalate to the level of war is an open question and one that cannot a priori be dismissed as impossible.[43]

Still a different answer is given by Soviet Marxist scholars. Traditionally, they have argued that wars between capitalist states are held to be an inherent feature in the development of capitalism and that only with the defeat of capitalism will it be possible to create a truly peaceful international system. Looking beyond these ideological assertions, we find that Soviet scholars have often characterized wars along two dimensions. First, they identify what kind of war it is. Here they are concerned with the political content of the war: Does it have a progressive or a reactionary influence on the development of society? In the former case, it is a just war, while, in the latter case, it is an unjust war. Second, wars are classified according to their type, with the type of wars in existence being dependent upon the main social contradictions of each historical epoch. In the present historical epoch, the fundamental social struggle is between socialism and imperialism. This gives rise to five pure types of war, which, in practice, often intermix with one another or change back and forth from one type to another: (1) wars between opposing social systems, (2) civil wars that find the proletariat and bourgeoisie locked in a violent struggle for control of state power, (3) wars of national liberation, in which the oppressed people in colonial and dependent states are fighting for their independence, (4) wars between capitalist states, and (5) wars in defense of the socialist motherland.

NOTES

1. J. C. Hurewitz, "The Middle East: A Year of Turmoil," *Foreign Affairs*, 59 (1981): 564.
2. David Segal, "The Iran-Iraq War: A Military Analysis," *Foreign Affairs* 66 (1988): 946–953.
3. Dankwart Rustow, "Realignments in the Middle East," *Foreign Affairs* 63 (1985): 586–587.
4. Quincy Wright, *A Study of War*, abr. ed. (Chicago: University of Chicago Press, 1964), p. 7.
5. Lewis Fry Richardson, *Statistics of Deadly Quarrels* (Pittsburgh: Quadrangle Books, 1960).

6. Jack Levy, *War in the Modern Great Power System, 1495–1975* (Lexington, Ky.: University of Kentucky Press, 1983).

7. J. David Singer and Melvin Small, *The Wages of War, 1816–1965: A Statistical Handbook* (New York: John Wiley & Sons, 1972); and Melvin Small and J. David Singer, *Resort to Arms: International and Civil Wars, 1816–1980* (Beverly Hills, Calif.: Sage, 1982).

8. David Farnsworth makes this point in his discussion of war in *International Politics: An Introduction* (Chicago: Nelson-Hall, 1988), p. 208.

9. Jack Levy, *War in the Modern Great Power System, 1495–1975* (Lexington, Ky.: University of Kentucky Press, 1983), p. 51; and Francis Beer, *Peace Against War* (San Francisco, W. H. Freeman, 1981), p. 6

10. Jack Levy, "Theories of General War," *World Politics* 37 (1985): 344–371.

11. Singer and Small, *Resort to Arms*, 1982.

12. Farnsworth, *International Politics*, p. 207.

13. Singer and Small, *Resort to Arms*, p. 141.

14. Wright, *A Study of War*, p. 11.

15. Ruth Leger Sivard, *World Military and Social Expenditures, 1986* (Washington, D.C.: World Priorities, 1986), p. 26.

16. *World Military Expenditures and Arms Transfers, 1986* (Washington, D.C.: Arms Control and Disarmament Agency, 1987).

17. These comparisons as well as others can be found in the introductory comments made in Ruth Sivard's series, *World Military and Social Expenditures*. These statements are from the 1986 and 1983 editions.

18. Levy, *War in the Modern Great Power System*.

19. See Levy, "Theories of General War."

20. Robert Gilpin, *War and Change in World Politics* (Cambridge, Mass.: Cambridge University Press, 1981), pp. 199–200.

21. Gilpin, *War and Change in World Politics*, pp. 200–202.

22. Gilpin, *War and Change in World Politics*, p. 234.

23. This is the formulation used by Francis Beer in his *Peace Against War* (San Francisco: Freeman, 1981).

24. Albert Wohlstetter, "Is There a Strategic Arms Race?" *Foreign Policy* 15 (1974): 3–20; and "Rivals but No 'Race'," *Foreign Policy* 16 (1974): 48–81.

25. See J. David Singer and Melvin Small, "Foreign Policy Indicators: Predictors of War in History and in the State of the World Message," *Policy Sciences* 5 (1974): 291.

26. Michael Hags, "International Subsystems: Stability and Polarity," *American Political Science Review* 64 (1970): 98–113.

27. Michael Wallace, "Alliance Polarization, Cross-Cutting, and International War, 1815–1964," *Journal of Conflict Resolution* 17 (1973): 575–604.

28. Geoffrey Blainey, *The Causes of War* (New York: Free Press, 1973).

29. For a lengthier review of these findings, see Charles Kegley Jr., and Eugene Wittkopf, *World Politics*, 2d ed. (New York: St. Martin's, 1985), pp. 429–431.

30. Charles Kegley Jr. and Eugene Wittkopf, *World Politics*, p. 424.

31. Levy, *War in the Modern Great Power System*, p. 166.

32. Bruce Bueno de Mesquita, *The War Trap* (New Haven: Yale University Press, 1981). For a sympathetic discussion of his argument and a review of criticisms of it, see James Ray, *Global Politics*, 3d ed. (Boston: Houghton Mifflin, 1987), pp. 438–454.

33. For a review of the literature on human nature and other individual traits as a cause of war, see James Dougherty and Robert Pfaltzgraff, Jr., *Contending Theories of International Relations*, 2d ed. (New York: Harper & Row, 1981); and Michael Sullivan, *International Relations: Theory and Evidence* (Englewood Cliffs, N.J.: Prentice-Hall, 1976).

34. Ted Robert Gurr, *Why Men Rebel* (Princeton, N.J.: Princeton University Press, 1970).

35. Harold Sprout and Margaret Sprout, *Toward a Politics of Planet Earth* (New York: Van Nostrand, 1971), chap. 9 and 11.

36. John Stoessinger, *Why Nations Go to War,* 4th ed. (New York: St. Martin's, 1985), pp. 202–219. For another formulation, see Jack Levy, "Misperception and the Causes of War," *World Politics* 36 (1983): 76–99.

37. Quincy Wright, "How Hostilities Have Ended," in William Fox, ed., *The Problems of War Termination* Vol. 392 (New York: American Academy of Political and Social Science, 1970), pp. 51–61.

38. Kenneth Oye, "Explaining Cooperation Under Anarchy," *World Politics* 38 (1985): 1–24.

39. Ernest May, *"Lessons" of the Past* (New York: Oxford University Press, 1978), pp. 125–142.

40. Roger Fisher, *International Conflict for Beginners* (New York: Harper & Row, 1969).

41. Charles E. Osgood, *An Alternative to War or Surrender* (Urbana, Ill.: University of Illinois Press, 1962).

42. Robert Axelrod, "More Effective Choice in the Prisoner's Dilemma," *Journal of Conflict Resolution* 24 (1980): 3–25.

43. For a discussion that distinguishes between optimistic and pessimistic globalists, see Ray Maghroori, "Introduction: Major Debates in International Relations," in Ray Maghroori and Bennett Ramberg, eds., *Globalism Versus Realism* (Boulder, Colo.: Westview, 1982).

Chapter 9

International Crises and Low-Intensity Conflict

CRISES AND CRISIS MANAGEMENT

Conflict and competition between states are widely considered to be routine features of world politics. A state need not be at war in order to use, or threaten to use, military force. A wide range of circumstances short of war often present themselves, in which military force is a potential option. These circumstances vary in terms of characteristics such as the amount of underlying hostility between those involved, the extent to which fundamental values are at stake, the degree to which policymakers are surprised, and the likelihood that war will break out. In this chapter, we will look at four of these situations: international crisis management, covert action, terrorism, and guerrilla warfare. The last three we will group under the heading "low-intensity conflict." This term, although commonly used, is misleading. Many events that are termed "low intensity," particularly guerrilla warfare, in fact, produce many deaths and great suffering among the people who are directly affected. Low-intensity conflict generally refers to protracted political-military struggles that involve challenges to the existing social order. The term is usually applied to Third World conflict situations.[1]

One of the most studied forms of international conflict and competition is international crises. They represent an acute departure from the norm and stand as a type of no-man's-land between the normal give-and-take of world politics and the existence of a state of war. The point at which a crisis actually begins is not easily established. Newspaper and television commentaries tend to attach the label "crisis" to a much wider range of events than most analysts of world politics feel is appropriate. They tend to define a crisis by one of two sets of criteria.

First, from a decision-making perspective, a crisis occurs when policymakers feel that there exists a major threat to the core national interests of their state and that they have little time within which to formulate an effective response.[2] Viewed this way, international crises are a type of competitive bargaining or negotiating situation in which the objective is to influence the perception of the other state through a demonstration of will and resolve so that the crisis is resolved on acceptable terms. "Crisis management" is the phrase that is often used to describe this bargaining process.

Alternatively, an international crisis can be defined as "a sequence of interactions between the governments of two or more sovereign states in severe conflict, short of actual war, but involving the perception of a dangerously high probability of war."[3] Some analysts argue that in the contemporary international system crises have become a substitute for war. Traditionally, wars were the primary means for passing power and influence from one state to another, and a normal way by which foreign-policy objectives were realized. With the arrival of nuclear weapons, war can no longer play this role, at least not for the superpowers or anywhere that the possibility of superpower involvement exists. Still, in the absence of well-established and effective, peaceful ways for resolving disputes, some mechanism must exist for resolving conflicts that involve the use or threatened use of military force. International crises fulfill just such a role. Nuclear weapons have also transformed the basic nature of international crises. Today, policymakers must balance two potentially contradictory motives in resolving a crisis: They must attempt to win and to avoid war. This was not as true for prenuclear crises, in which the costs of having a crisis evolve into war were far less severe.

The ever-present risk that a crisis might escalate into a war can be traced to the inherent uncertainty of crisis situations and the nature of crisis decision making. Crises are confusing, volatile, and explosive situations. Because they represent a sudden departure from the norm, no one can be certain of where events will move next. Attaching the correct interpretation to individual acts, such as the movement of troops or the burning of diplomatic codes, is not easily done. Too much happens too quickly, and very often the more information collected, the more confusing the picture becomes. Particularly dangerous are accidents that happen in the course of a crisis that either one or both sides interprets as part of the other's strategy. There is also the danger that policymakers will get so caught up in the game of move and countermove that they will lose control of events. Finally, communicating resolve, signaling intentions, and arranging a settlement of the dispute under these conditions is a tricky matter.

For their part, policymakers tend to be confident about their ability to manage crises. One observer goes so far as to suggest that crises hold a type of "macabre fascination for policymakers" because, in the absence of war, a crisis "is the ultimate moment of truth, the time when his will, ability, wisdom, and leadership qualities are all stretched to the utmost."[4] In his study of "nuclear-tinged" crises, those in which either the United States or the Soviet Union threatened to use nuclear weapons, Richard Betts found that this self-image was not entirely accurate. He notes that presidents and their key advisors rarely were able to face up to the potential consequences of what they were doing or to think through carefully whether or not they would be willing to carry out their nuclear threats. "In a sense, people at the top sometimes appeared to grit their teeth, close their eyes, and forge ahead."[5]

Different Types of International Crises

Successful crisis management begins with a clear understanding of the nature of the crisis that one is facing. However, just as there are different forms of international conflict, there are also different types of crises. Richard Lebow has identified three different types of international crises: the *justification-of-hostilities crisis*, the *spin-off crisis*, and the *brinksmanship crisis*.[6] This further complicates the task of crisis management, because not every response is equally appropriate for all crises. For example, rather than bringing a crisis to a successful and peaceful conclusion, under certain circumstances injecting military force into a crisis might almost guarantee the coming of war.

In the *justification-of-hostilities crisis*, the initiating side has made the decision to go to war before the crisis has even begun and is using the crisis as a pretext to justify its actions. Policymakers have no interest in reaching a peaceful accommodation of the dispute; rather, they are trying to place responsibility for the upcoming war on the shoulders of the adversary and to mobilize support for themselves, both among their own people and within the international community. The actual event that triggers the crisis may take several forms. Often it is an unanticipated event or accident that policymakers in the initiating state seize upon. In other cases, policymakers purposefully create or invent an incident, or take actions that all but invite the adversary to take aggressive actions that then can be exploited. Most justification-of-hostilities crises follow a five-step formula.

1. Exploit a provocation to arouse public opinion.
2. Make unacceptable demands upon the adversary in response to this provocation.
3. Legitimize these demands with reference to generally accepted international principles.
4. Publicly deny or understate your real objectives in the confrontation.
5. Employ the rejection of your demands as a *casus belli* (cause for war).

The *spin-off crisis* may be the most unmanageable of the three types of crises. None of the parties involved really desire war or even the crisis confrontation itself. Their primary attentions are elsewhere—with another adversary or another problem. This type of crisis quite literally "spins off" from an ongoing conflict in one of two ways and then takes on a life of its own. The first path to a spin-off crisis occurs when one of the parties to an ongoing conflict makes unacceptable demands upon a third party. The second path to a spin-off crisis comes when a third party, which is being adversely affected by the primary conflict, issues an ultimatum to one of the states involved in it. In either case, rejection of the ultimatum sets the crisis in motion. Not every war or conflict produces a spin-off crisis. Four factors appear to increase the likelihood that such a crisis will occur. They are (1) geographic proximity, (2) the length and intensity of the primary conflict, (3) a shift in the internal balance of power in favor of the military in one of the belligerent states involved in the primary conflict, and (4) public attitudes, which compel policymakers to adopt a course of action that will lead to the issuing of an ultimatum or the adoption of a provocative policy line.

The *brinksmanship crisis* is the most common type of crisis. It comes about when one state deliberately employs threats of force against another in hopes of getting the adversary to back down, thus allowing it to achieve its political goals without having to go to war. Several factors tempt policymakers to instigate a brinksmanship crisis. Most important is the expectation that the international balance of power will soon shift in favor of the adversary. Under these circumstances, a brinksmanship crisis represents one way of realizing important national-security goals while there is still time to act. Typically, policymakers seek to force an adversary to abandon an important commitment, to force an adversary to make a concession elsewhere in return for ending the crisis, or to humiliate the adversary by demonstrating his weakness.

Also important to the decision over whether or not to provoke a brinksmanship crisis is the policymakers' reading of the political situation within their country. Lebow found that brinksmanship crises frequently occurred when either the leader of the initiating state was politically vulnerable, when the entire government was weak, or when there was a struggle for power among elites over who would rule. A brinksmanship crisis can help a policymaker's domestic political standing by directing the public's attention away from internal problems and toward what hopefully will be foreign-policy successes. Domestic political problems may also make a brinksmanship crisis more likely, because a weak policymaker may be unable to dampen pressures for an aggressive foreign-policy line. Taken together, these factors led Lebow to conclude that "aggression is less a function of opportunity than it is of need."[7] Policymakers do not so much actively seek to take advantage of opportunities presented to them as they feel compelled to act for reasons of domestic politics or because of the direction of international trends.

July 1914: Three Types of Crises in One

No one wanted war in 1914, or, at least, no one wanted the war they got. Even Germany's Kaiser Wilhelm, who was willing to fight *a* war, was unprepared for what followed. Moreover, European leaders seemed incapable of avoiding what was to be the first truly continental war since the Napoleonic wars. It is this combination of characteristics—accidental, yet inevitable—that makes World War I fascinating and frightening to modern analysts of world politics. Many see it as an omen of how a nuclear World War III might begin—not as the result of conscious deliberation and planning, but as a result of actions of world leaders who were stumbling forward with no sense of how to prevent its happening.[8] Our brief overview of the events leading up to World War I will emphasize the way in which all three different types of crises became interwoven with one another to produce a "compound crisis." Austria's ultimatum against Serbia is an example of a justification-of-hostilities crisis. Its effort to keep Russia out of the war is an example of a brinksmanship crisis. Finally, Germany's actions against Belgium and Great Britain provide an example of a spin-off crisis.

The triggering incident that set in motion the events that culminated in the outbreak of World War I was the June 28, 1914 assassination of Austrian Crown Prince Franz Ferdinand by a Serbian radical. Even before the Archduke was assassinated, many Austrian leaders had reached the conclusion that the maintenance of the Austro-Hungarian Empire demanded military action against Serbia. The Austro-Hungarian Empire was a multiethnic state dominated by Germans and Magyars (Hungarians). Over time, the other ethnic groups—the Czechs, Poles, Romanians, Croats, Italians, Slavs, Slovaks, and Slovenes—came to demand greater representation in the army, civil service, and legislative assemblies of the empire and equal cultural standing with the Germans and Magyars. Serbia was an independent Balkan state that bordered the Austro-Hungarian Empire. It had long been viewed as the potential centerpiece for a Slavic state by many of the southern Slavic peoples, who longed for independence from the Austro-Hungarian Empire. For their part, Serbian leaders had been conducting a propaganda campaign directed at Slavs within the empire in hopes of speeding up its disintegration. Defeating Serbia and annexing it into the empire would accomplish two objectives. It would be a severe blow to the strength of the pan-Slav movement and would serve as a signal to other states that, in spite of a series of foreign-policy setbacks that dated back to the turn of the century, Austria-Hungary remained a force to be reckoned with in European politics.

The chief of the general staff seized upon the assassination as a pretext to realize these goals, and he urged quick military action against Serbia. He argued that in this way Austria would be able to capitalize on international sympathy for the royal family, as well as catch the other major military powers off guard. Others within Austria opposed military action. Most notably, the emperor was uncertain of Germany's willingness to support Austria in a war, and the president argued that military action would only arouse sympathy for Serbia and paint Austria as the unjustified aggressor. Steps were taken to overcome both sets of objections. An anti-Serbian propaganda campaign weakened the force of the president's protests, while a clarification of Germany's views was obtained by the Austrian foreign minister, who also favored war but felt Germany's support was crucial.

German leaders were in agreement with the prowar forces within Austria that a war with Serbia was in Austria's interests. They also believed that the war could be localized and that the German army would keep Russia from intervening on the side of Serbia as it had done in an earlier Balkan crisis in 1909. Consequently, on July 5, Germany gave the Austrian foreign minister what amounted to a blank-check endorsement for any action that Austria might undertake against Serbia. On July 14, after further political maneuvering within Austrian political circles, it was agreed that an ultimatum would be issued to Serbia. The ultimatum was issued with the expectation that Serbia would not agree to all of its terms, and, without full capitulation, Austria was determined to go to war. Two days after its receipt, Serbia responded by accepting most, but not all, of the conditions laid down by Austria. Within days, on July 28, the Austro-Hungarian Empire declared war on Serbia.

Following its declaration of war against Serbia, Austria mobilized 8 of its 16 army corps. It did so in the hopes of realizing a quick victory over Serbia but also to frighten the tsar into staying out of the conflict. Russia countered this move by ordering a partial mobilization of its own, hoping that, if frightened by the prospect of a Balkan war, Austria would not invade Serbia. At this point, Germany, with British encouragement, sought to pull Austria and Russia back from the brink of war. The kaiser sent a telegram to Tsar Nicholas II, his cousin, urging restraint. As events unfolded over the next several days, the kaiser came to feel that Russia was intent upon war and was using the time provided by his mediation efforts to strengthen its military position. Accordingly, on July 31, he issued a 12-hour ultimatum to the tsar, in which he demanded that Russia demobilize its forces. Russia refused, and the kaiser ordered that Germany's forces be mobilized for war.

German leaders had been sure that Russia would not go to war to protect Serbia. In part, their confidence was based on the events of 1909 when, with German backing, Austria had successfully issued an ultimatum to Serbia. The year 1914, however, was not to be 1909 revisited. In 1909, Austria had provoked a crisis with Serbia and Russia by unilaterally announcing that it was going to annex Bosnia-Herzogovina, a province of the old Ottoman Empire. They did so in an effort to dampen the growing sentiment within the region for a Slavic state. Annexing Bosnia-Herzogovina would make impossible a union between it and Serbia. At first Serbia and Russia resisted this move. Both demanded financial compensation from Austria for taking this territory, and Serbia mobilized its army as an added show of displeasure. However, in the end both states accepted Austria's action. Diplomatically isolated because the French were not interested in fighting a war over the Balkans and having just been beaten by Japan in the 1905 Russo-Japanese War, Russian leaders felt that they had little choice but to give in. Austria's demands in 1914, however, were of a far greater magnitude. The very independence of Serbia was now at stake. Traditionally, Serbia enjoyed Russian protection in times of crisis. Russia saw itself as the protector of all Slavic peoples, and to acquiesce to Austria's demands would have called into question its ability to fulfill this role as well as its role as a Great Power. Also, unlike 1909, the French were willing to support Russia in a war against Austria.

Upon becoming convinced that Russia was preparing to go to war to protect Serbia, Germany issued an ultimatum to Belgium in which it demanded that its armed forces be granted free passage through the country. They did so because German thinking assumed that, should it ever go to war with Russia, it would also find itself at war with France. Moreover, the German general staff had long ago concluded that Germany could not fight a two-front war and that either France or Russia would have to be dealt with first. As the stronger of the two states, France, they decided, would have to be attacked first. Accordingly, the German war plan, the Schlieffen Plan, called for massing German military units for an attack on France while leaving only a reserve force to fight a delaying and holding action against the Russian army. Having defeated France, German armies would be raced across the continent by train to defeat Russia before Great Britain could mobilize its naval power in defense of its continental allies. Speed was of the essence in this plan, and, because the Franco-German border was not well suited for the rapid movement of military forces, the Schlieffen Plan called for an invasion of France through Belgium.

Belgium rejected the demand and was promptly invaded. The kaiser had also demanded that France adopt a position of neutrality in the conflict over Serbia and that it turn over its border fortifications to Germany. France rejected these demands. Germany's August 3 declaration of war against France and its invasion of Belgium brought it into direct conflict with Great Britain, which, along with Germany, had promised to guarantee Belgium's neutrality. Prior to the invasion, sentiment within Great Britain was mixed on the question of whether or not the country should involve itself in a war over Serbia. After the invasion, little question remained that Great Britain would have to go to war to protect its interests. Not only did Belgian ports provide the best embarkation points for an invasion of Great Britain, but, more fundamentally, British security was seen as resting upon the existence of a balance of power on the continent. Should Germany succeed in defeating both France and Russia, there would exist no effective check on its power in Europe. Yet, in spite of the logic that pointed to an inevitable British involvement in a continental war should Germany invade Belgium in order to attack France, German leaders were convinced that Great Britain would remain neutral. Britain went to war on August 4.

LOW-INTENSITY CONFLICT

"Low-intensity conflict" is a term that came into popular usage during the Reagan administration but that lacks an agreed-upon definition. Daniel Papp defines it as including small skirmishes along borders or at sea, acts of individual or small-group violence, and sporadic conflict. Former Secretary of State George Shultz includes worldwide terrorism, fighting between the Sandinistas and Contras in Nicaragua, Soviet-sponsored interventions in Angola and Ethiopia, the invasion of Grenada, and Cambodian resistance against Vietnam as examples of low-intensity conflict.[9] We will use the term to cover three types of conflict situations that fall short of international war: covert action, terrorism, and guerrilla warfare.

Covert Action

Covert action seeks results by means of secretly altering the internal balance of power within a state. It can be practiced in a number of ways. The most common form of covert action is clandestine support for individuals and organizations. This support takes such forms as personnel training, giving technical advice, and providing support services and financial aid. Journalists, reporters, unions, political parties, church groups, and professional associations are among the most prominent covers used. Clandestine support was a major form of CIA covert action in postwar Europe. In West Germany, both major political parties and most of their leadership received CIA subsidies. Between 1948 and 1968 the CIA spent over $65 million on these types of programs. The Soviet Union has made heavy use of front organizations on a number of occasions to further its foreign-policy goals. The CIA estimates that, at a minimum, the Soviet Union spends $63 million per year on organizing and operating front organizations.[10] In 1977, the Soviet Union mobilized groups in Istanbul, Accra, Stuttgart, Frankfort, Düsseldorf, Bonn, and Lima to protest U.S. production of the neutron bomb, to demonstrate in front of U.S. embassies, and to engage in letter-writing campaigns.

A second category of covert action is *black propaganda*. Unlike the *white propaganda* of the United States Information Service, in which the identity of the sender is known, in *black propaganda* the sender is either not known or is falsely identified. At its peak, CIA propaganda assets numbered over 800 news and public information organizations and individuals. Clandestine radio stations played a prominent part in CIA propaganda efforts. The best known covertly founded radio broadcasting systems were Radio Free Europe, which was directed at Eastern Europe, and Radio Liberty, which was directed at the Soviet Union. Other notable CIA radio systems included Radio Free Asia, which broadcast into China from 1951 to 1955, and a network of radio stations that were targeted at Castro's Cuba.

The CIA has also relied heavily upon the print media for spreading propaganda. As a matter of normal practice, the CIA has sent out facts, themes, editorial outlines, and model essays to its Third World stations, which were to be reworked for local consumption. It has also been actively involved in the publication of books and journals. More than 200 English-language books have been financed or produced by the CIA since the early 1950s. The CIA has also subsidized a number of social democratic magazines in countries such as West Germany, France, India, and Argentina in an effort to project the existence of a viable center-left alternative to communism.

The Soviet Union has also made heavy use of covert propaganda. David Jameson, a former CIA covert-action specialist, divides Soviet propaganda operations into two groups.[11] The first of these are thematic campaigns. They usually begin with a public announcement of the official Soviet position on an issue, which is then followed by the reworking of that theme by the various Soviet front groups, agents-of-influence, and disinformation specialists. Recent thematic campaigns have targeted the neutron bomb, NATO's modernization of its theater nuclear weapons, sowing discontent among NATO members, and creating tension in the U.S.-Egyptian relationship. The second category of Soviet covert-action propaganda operations is directed at enduring targets. Among the principal Soviet concerns in this area have been attacks on the United States and China, distancing West Germany from other NATO members, and destabilizing the situation in South Africa.

Like the United States, the Soviet Union has made use of covert radio stations and the print media. In the early 1970s, 11 clandestine radio stations were located either in the Soviet Union or Eastern Europe. Secret broadcasts into Iran by "The National Voice of Iran" first began in 1959 and allowed the Soviet Union to pursue a two-track policy against the shah. Although official Soviet policies were proper and cordial, the Soviet Union sought to weaken the shah's rule through its clandestine broadcasts. By using the print media, the Soviet Union has placed special emphasis on exploiting individual writers and not the newspaper or magazine per se. One of the most famous "agents-of-influence" was French writer Charles Pathe, who was arrested in 1979 and confessed to having been a Soviet agent for 19 years. During that time, he wrote pieces championing Soviet disarmament proposals, extolling the virtues of Soviet science, attacking the United States, and defending French nationalism from corrupting U.S. influences.

A third category of covert action involves economic operations. Comparatively few economic operations have been undertaken by the CIA, and they have not been very successful. Their general purpose has been to deny the enemy access to a particular commodity or technology, or to sabotage one of its economic operations. The Soviet Union has also engaged in this type of economic covert action. Additionally, it has sought to manipulate economic transactions in order to realize political gain. For example, the Soviet Union once offered to sell coal to several West European states at a reduced price. According to the CIA, the purpose was to gain added political influence in those states. In another case, Soviet representatives in a joint trading company tried to replace a number of local representatives with ones more agreeable to the Soviet Union.

The fourth form of covert action involves the assassination of foreign leaders. The Church Committee investigated five cases of alleged U.S. involvement in the assassination of foreign leaders:

Cuba: Fidel Castro

Congo (Zaire): Patrice Lumumba

Dominican Republic: Rafael Trujillo

Chile: Rene Schneider

South Vietnam: Ngo Dinh Diem

The committee concluded that the cases of Cuba and the Congo involved plots conceived by the United States to kill their foreign leaders. The plots directed against Castro will be outlined later in this chapter as part of the case study on CIA covert action against Cuba. In the Congo, events overtook U.S. policy, and Lumumba was killed by political rivals. U.S. authorities had authorized Lumumba's assassination in the fall of 1960, and CIA plans had gone so far as to send vials of poison to the Congo for use against him. It was only following the assassination of Chilean General Rene Schneider that a CIA directive was issued banning assassinations. Since then, this prohibition has been part of every presidential executive order. Actions taken by the Reagan administration in support of the Contras have raised doubts about the current status of the ban on assassinations. In 1984, the CIA was linked to the production of a psychological warfare manual, sections of which could be interpreted as calling for assassination.

The Soviet Union, through the KGB and its predecessors, was involved in killing foreigners as early as 1926.[12] In 1936, the Administration of Special Tasks, or "wet affairs," was created to carry out assassinations. Its original targets tended to be dissident foreign communists, such as Leon Trotsky. During Khrushchev's tenure, evidence suggests that top party leaders collectively approved major projects carried out by the now renamed Department 13. In late 1962 or early 1963, Soviet leaders made the decision that assassinations were only to be carried out under special circumstances, and, by the mid-1960s, Department 13's primary concern was with sabotage.

The fifth category of covert action involves paramilitary operations. Ted Shackely, a former practitioner of covert operations, defines paramilitary operations as those programs furnishing covert military assistance and guidance to unconventional and conventional foreign forces and organizations. He argues that it represents a highly valuable "third option" between sending in the marines and doing nothing. CIA paramilitary operations were initially targeted against the Soviet Union and its East European allies. Aid was given to Ukrainian resistance fighters, and attempts were made to create Polish and Albanian underground organizations. In the early 1950s, the CIA also undertook paramilitary operations in China. None of these operations were very successful, and some were outright failures.

As the 1950s progressed, the most significant CIA paramilitary operations took place in the Third World. In 1953, the United States and Great Britain undertook a joint venture, Operation *AJAX*, to bring down the Iranian government of Prime Minister Mossadegh, who had nationalized the Iranian oil industry and pursued anti-Western policies. In 1954, the CIA helped bring down the government of Jacobo Arbenz in Guatemala. His program of social reform and modernization was considered to be "distinctly unfriendly to U.S. business interests."

These paramilitary operations were quite modest in scale. In Iran, the CIA exploited and encouraged local opposition groups, while in Guatemala it organized a small invasion force. In the latter part of the decade and into the early 1960s, CIA paramilitary operations proved to be less successful yet grew considerably in scale. In 1958, the agency supported the abortive coup against President Sukarno of Indonesia. A still greater embarrassment came in 1961 with the failure of the Bay of Pigs invasion of Cuba. The Bay of Pigs put a temporary dent into Washington's fascination with covert action, but it did not bring an end to it. By the end of the 1960s, the CIA was involved in two major paramilitary operations in Southeast Asia—one in Vietnam and the other in Laos.

A former chief of the CIA's covert action staff, who is an advocate of its continued use, lamented that during the 1970s covert action was rapidly becoming a "dying art form." All of this changed during the 1980s. In the Reagan administration's first term, the number of paramilitary operations jumped to seven or eight per year. In 1985, the CIA was supporting the Afghan rebels, the Contras in Nicaragua, anti-Qaddafi forces, pro-Western forces in El Salvador, anti-Khomeini Iranian exiles in Turkey and France; training the Thai military for raids against heroin production and processing centers; conducting a joint operation with China to supply arms to the forces of former Kampuchean (Cambodian) ruler Pol Pot in his struggle with the Vietnamese-supported Kampuchean government; and training, arming, and financing military forces in Ethiopia, Angola, and the Sudan.

Either directly or through surrogates such as the Cubans and East Germans, the Soviet Union frequently has provided clandestine military assistance to participants in "national wars of liberation" in the Third World. In its report to the House Intelligence Committee, the CIA presented several examples of Soviet paramilitary operations. In late 1979, the Soviet Union approached the Zimbabwe African People's Union (ZAPU), noting that it was "fully prepared to provide whatever amount of military aid was necessary to achieve a military victory." This offer came after the Patriotic Front temporarily withdrew from negotiations with Great Britain over the future of Rhodesia (Zimbabwe). The CIA report noted that later that year officers from the main political directorate of the Soviet armed forces conducted a training course in covert action for senior ZAPU leaders. A second example given of a Soviet covert paramilitary operation was the presence of 25,000 Soviet "advisors" in Afghanistan prior to the invasion there. Many times these advisors have been directly engaged in military combat operations. Operating more secretly, the Soviet Union has also air dropped supplies to Kurdish guerrillas operating along the Iranian border.

Covert Action Case Studies

U.S. Covert Action Against Castro   The U.S. covert-action program that was directed against Fidel Castro in Cuba made use of virtually all of the techniques that we have identified. The best known of these programs was the effort to remove Castro from power in the Bay of Pigs invasion. Originally conceived during the Eisenhower administration, the plan was approved by President Kennedy in April 1961. Later that month a brigade of some 1,400 Cuban exiles was put ashore in Cuba, where it was expected that they would link up with Cuban opposition forces and topple the Castro regime. Everything went wrong. On the first day of the invasion, two of the four supply and ammunition ships were sunk and the other two fled. On the second day, the brigade was surrounded by 20,000 well-armed and loyal Cuban soldiers. On the third day, the 1,200 surviving members of the invasion force surrendered. Almost two years later, they were released in exchange for $53 million in food and drugs. Critics argue that the Bay of Pigs was doomed for at least two reasons. First, it was poorly conceived. Said to be modeled after the successful operations in Guatemala and Iran, the Bay of Pigs invasion lost sight of the fact that in both cases the paramilitary operation was of secondary importance to the central role played by propaganda and psychological warfare. Furthermore, in both cases the paramilitary force built directly upon rebels who had easy access to a target that faced real domestic opposition and lacked a skilled army at its disposal. Second, the action cannot be properly classified as a covert paramilitary operation because it was too large and reports about preparations for the invasion were reported in major newspapers. Similar complaints have been made about more recent CIA covert-action programs in Nicaragua and Angola.

The Church Committee found concrete evidence of at least eight plots to assassinate Castro between 1960 and 1965. Proposed assassination devices included arranging "an accident," poison cigars, poison pills, poison pens, placing deadly bacterial powder in Castro's skin-diving suit, and rigging a seashell to explode while Castro was skin diving. While most of these plans never went beyond the discussion stage, on one occasion weapons and other assassination devices were provided to a Cuban dissident. Among the most controversial aspects of these plans was the reliance on underworld crime figures. Twice individuals with close ties to organized crime syndicates were part of attempts to assassinate Castro by using poison pills.

The principal economic covert operation directed against Castro was Operation Mongoose, which was authorized by President Kennedy in November 1961. It was designed to "use our available assets . . . to help Cuba overthrow the communist regime." The first act of this operation, which had been planned to look like an inside job, was to have been the demolition of a railroad yard and bridge. It was called off when the saboteurs were spotted approaching Cuba by boat. The CIA did have its successes. European shippers turned down Cuban delivery orders, a German firm sent off-center ball bearings to Cuba, British buses destined for Cuba were sabotaged on the docks, and a shipment of Cuban sugar headed for the Soviet Union was contaminated while the ship was being repaired in Puerto Rico. Operation Mongoose was canceled in June 1963, but covert economic operations continued into the 1970s.

Finally, covert propaganda was also employed against Castro. The CIA subsidized several U.S.-based anti-Castro publications such as *Advance* and *El Mundo*, and it set up Radio Free Cuba, which was not a radio station but consisted of broadcast time bought on Florida and Louisiana radio stations that could be picked up in Cuba.

U.S. Covert Action Against Allende   The United States repeatedly sought to block the election of Salvador Allende as president of Chile through the use of covert action. It successfully worked to block his election in 1958 and in 1964 but failed to do so in 1970. Between 1964 and 1969, the CIA spent almost $2 million on training anti-Communist organizers among Chilean peasants and slum dwellers. It spent $3 million on the 1964 elections and almost $1 million on the 1970 elections. In addition, the CIA provided International Telephone & Telegraph (ITT) with the names of two "secure" funding channels that could be used to get money to anti-Allende candidates. In 1970, Allende won a plurality of the vote and, according to Chilean custom, he would be picked by the Chilean Congress as the next president. In an effort to stop this from happening, President Nixon adopted a two-track strategy. Track I was approved by the 40 Committee, the National Security Council committee that was charged with overseeing CIA covert operations. Track II was kept secret from it. In Track I the CIA was ordered to engage in political, economic, and propaganda tactics designed to influence political events. As part of this strategy, $25,000 was authorized, but never spent, to bribe members of the Chilean Congress, whose votes would elect the next president. The economy was also a major target of Track I activity. The general goal given to the CIA's economic covert-action program was "to make the economy scream." U.S. multinational corporations were asked to cut off credits and the shipment of spare parts to Chile. This campaign continued even after Allende was elected president. Over $6 million were channeled into efforts to bring down his regime. An additional $1.5 million went to *El Mercurio*, an influential Chilean newspaper. Agents and contacts with *El Mercurio* allowed the CIA to generate one or two editorials per week in their efforts to unseat him. Other funds were spent on subsidizing right-wing think tanks and on training white-collar trade union leaders. Evidence also points to continued CIA support for labor unions and trade associations for the purpose of engineering social chaos and, while it has not been firmly established, the CIA has been linked to the economically crippling truckers' strikes of 1972–1973.

Track II involved efforts to organize a military coup. Over a two-week period, the CIA made over 21 contacts with Chilean military leaders to assure them of U.S. support for a coup d'état. Chief of Staff General Rene Schneider was a strong supporter of the military's noninvolvement in politics and emerged as the main obstacle to a coup. In an effort to remove Schneider from the political scene, the CIA supplied weapons to Chilean leaders who were planning to kidnap him. The first two attempts failed, but General Schneider was killed in the third attempt. Evidence indicates that CIA weapons were not involved in the fatal kidnapping, and at no point does it appear to have been the intent of the kidnappers of the CIA to assassinate General Schneider.

Soviet Forgeries   One of the mainstays of Soviet covert-action black propaganda or disinformation campaigns are forgeries. They take one of two forms: (1) altered or distorted versions of actual U.S. documents obtained secretly and (2) documents that are entirely fabricated.[13] During the early 1960s, many Soviet forgeries were aimed at disrupting U.S.-NATO member relations. Beginning in 1976, a new series of NATO-oriented forgeries began. The first falsification to appear was a State Department airgram that was altered to make it appear as if U.S. embassies in Western Europe were being asked to obtain information that could be used to bribe local officials and develop economic covert-action plans. The actual document requested publicly available economic, commercial, and financial data. Three forgeries in the series sought to exploit tensions between Greece and Turkey. A totally fabricated speech by President Carter contained unflattering references to the role of Greece within NATO, a bogus Defense Department intelligence directive instructed U.S. personnel to spy on Greek political parties, and a U.S. government document was altered to make it appear as if the United States favored Greece over Turkey. In 1978, a counterfeit letter from NATO Secretary-General Joseph Luns was made public. It contained references to the existence of a Belgian Defense Ministry list of journalists opposed to the neutron bomb. The implication was that action was contemplated against these journalists. Finally, in 1979 a letter written on U.S. embassy stationery confirmed the existence of chemical and biological warfare stockpiles near Naples. This letter confirmed a rumor that Soviet propagandists were circulating in Italy.

One particularly successful disinformation campaign centered on a forged U.S. Army *Field Manual* (FM 30-31B), which contained instructions on interference in the affairs of the host state, the subversion of foreign political and military officials, and the use of extremist organizations to protect Americans in friendly states whenever it appeared that communists might enter the government. The existence of this manual (FM 30-31B really does exist) was first reported in a Turkish newspaper in 1975, and it was printed in two Spanish publications in 1978. Since then, it has been the subject of news stories in over 20 states. Soviet propagandists have cited it as supporting evidence that it was the United States and not Red Brigade terrorists who were responsible for kidnapping and killing former Italian Premier Aldo Moro. The forgery was skillfully carried out. There are a minimum number of errors in style, phraseology, and format, and a suitable typewriter and paper were used.

Forgeries have also played a key part in Soviet Third World covert operations. During the late 1970s, at about the same time that the NATO series of forgeries appeared, a succession of forgeries aimed at undermining U.S.-Egyptian relations surfaced. One of these reported on an interview supposedly given by Vice President Mondale in which he made derogatory remarks about Egyptian President Sadat. Another was a letter to Director of Central Intelligence Stansfield Turner from U.S. Ambassador Herman Eilts. In it Eilts said that, if Sadat refused to go along with the

U.S. peace initiative, the United States "must repudiate him and get rid of him without hesitation." It went on to discuss U.S. efforts to bring about a shift in the PLO's policy toward Israel and continued with, "I know you possess the necessary capability and resources in this regard."

Terrorism

We will define *terrorism* as violence for purposes of political intimidation. The study of terrorism is marked by a troubling duality: It is intensely commented upon but seldom objectively analyzed. Disagreement exists regarding virtually every facet of the term: Who is a terrorist? What is terrorism? How much terrorism exists? How do we deal with it? Regardless of how it is defined—and ours is only one of over 100 different definitions—terrorism carries a larger meaning in the minds of most people. It has become a code word that evokes a set of images which complicates the task of analysis. Terrorists are the enemy. They are fanatics who stand for things we disagree with. Those whose goals we support are called "freedom fighters," not terrorists. Terrorists also tend to be identified with lost causes, utopian quests, or unsuccessful struggles. Spokespeople for crusades that triumph are instantly transformed into national leaders or are treated as visionaries.

This larger symbolism also affects efforts to organize the international community against terrorism. While few states hesitate to condemn terrorism in the abstract, many Third World states are reluctant to condemn specific acts of terrorism or terrorist groups, citing as justification, "the inalienable right to self-determination and independence of all peoples under colonial and racist regimes and other forms of alien domination and the legitimacy of their struggle, in particular the struggle of national liberation movements, in accordance with the principles of the [UN] Charter and the relevant resolutions of the organs of the United Nations." The remainder of this section examines each of the questions about terrorism that we raised in the previous paragraph.

Who is a Terrorist?   In 1989, at a cost of $71,000 and countless hours for compiling and printing, the U.S. Defense Department gave its answer to this question when it released a list of 52 of the world's key international terrorist groups.[14] This inventory is presented in Table 9.1. The study finds that terrorist groups are present on every continent and are headquartered in at least 28 states. Not all specialists in terrorism would agree that this list is either accurate or complete. It is heavily biased in the direction of left-wing terrorism. No mention is made of the Salvadoran Death Squads, which engage in right-wing terrorism. Also absent are references to terrorism conducted by governments. Finally, while the Contras and Afghan rebels are omitted, presumably because they are considered to be guerrilla groups, the Farabundo Marti National Liberation Front (FMLN) in El Salvador, which many consider to be a guerrilla group, is included in the list.

A different picture of who a terrorist is emerges if we sort terrorists into groups on the basis of the political agenda that they seek to promote. Approached from this perspective, there are four types of terrorists. First, there are what can be described as "states-in-waiting" terrorist organizations. These are groups whose goal is the creation of a homeland where none currently exists. The Irish Republican Army (IRA), the Pal-

Table 9.1   TERRORIST GROUPS IDENTIFIED BY THE DEFENSE DEPARTMENT

Middle Eastern terrorism

Abu Nidal Organization
Arab Organization of 15 May
Democratic Front for the Liberation of Palestine
Fatah
Hizballah
Lebanese Armed Revolutionary Faction
Organization of the Armed Arab Struggle
Palestine Liberation Front
Popular Front for the Liberation of Palestine
Popular Front for the Liberation of Palestine—General Command
Popular Struggle Front
Sa'iqa

West European terrorism

Armenian Secret Army for the Liberation of Armenia
Basque Fatherland and Liberty
Combatant Communist Cells
Direct Action
First of October Anti-Fascist Resistance Group
Iraultza
Irish National Liberation Army
Justice Commandos of the Armenian Genocide
Popular Forces 25 April
Provisional Irish Republican Army
Red Army Faction
Red Brigades
Revolutionary Cells
Revolutionary Organization 17 November
Revolutionary Popular Struggle

Latin American terrorism

Alfaro Lives, Damn It!
Bandera Roja (Red Flag)
Cinchoneros Popular Liberation Movement
Clara Elizabeth Ramirez Front
Farabundo Marti National Liberation Front
Guatemalan National Revolutionary Unity
Lorenzo Zelaya Popular Revolutionary Forces
19th of April Movement
Macheteros
Manuel Rodriguez Patriotic Front
Movement of the Revolutionary Left
National Liberation Army
Popular Liberation Army
Revolutionary Armed Forces of Colombia
Ricardo Franco Front
Shining Path
Tupac Amaru Revolutionary Movement

Asian terrorism

Chukaku-Ha
Japanese Red Army
Liberation Tigers of Tamil Eelam
New People's Army
Sikh Terrorism
Dal Khalsa
Dashmesh Regiment

African Terrorism

African National Congress

Source: Terrorist Group Profiles (Washington, D.C.: U.S. Department of Defense, 1989).

estine Liberation Organization (PLO), the Armenian Secret Army for the Liberation of Armenia (ASALA), and Basque Homeland and Freedom (ETA) are prominent contemporary examples of states-in-waiting terrorist organizations. Second, terrorism is carried out by radical political groups. Their goal is not to carve out a new state or to realign international boundaries, but to bring about a radical transformation of the values that guide political life within a country. Examples of terrorist groups espousing a left-wing, anticapitalist ideology include the Red Army Brigades in Italy, the Weathermen in the United States, the Baader-Meinhof Gang in West Germany, and the Japanese Red Army. A listing of right-wing radical terrorist groups would include the Esquadro del Muerte (Death Squad) in Guatemala, the National Democratic Organization in El Salvador (ORDEN), and the Ku Klux Klan (KKK) in the United States.

State terrorism is the third type of terrorism. This is terrorism practiced by a government against its own people. Hitler's use of the police and security forces against communists and the Jewish community in Nazi Germany; Stalin's purges of the ruling elite and his intimidation of the general population; the more recent Soviet practice of sentencing political dissidents to mental hospitals and psychiatric wards; Argentina's "dirty war" of 1976–1983, when more than 340 clandestine jails and torture centers were set up and almost 9,000 prisoners still remain unaccounted for; and the genocide of Pol Pot in Kampuchea (2 million dead) and Idi Amin in Uganda (100,000–500,000 dead) are all examples of this type of terrorism. As with the two previously mentioned forms of terrorism, the purpose of state terrorism is to create a climate of fear among the people that can be exploited for political gain. The objective is to make it easier for the government to rule.

The fourth label that can be attached to acts of terrorism is "state-sponsored terrorism." This is terrorism used as an instrument of foreign policy by a state. It is often linked with the actions of the other types of terrorism, because these groups are the primary beneficiaries of its aid. The United States has officially identified five states as practitioners or supporters of international terrorism, which it defines as terrorism involving citizens or territory of more than one country. These states are Libya, South Yemen, Syria, Iran, and Cuba. Of the four categories of terrorism, it is this one that provokes the most intense political debate. Just what is meant by "state-sponsored terrorism"? Is it giving money; donating supplies; providing moral support; allowing one's territory to be used as a sanctuary; training terrorists; or must state officials actually plan and provide leadership for a terrorist attack? At issue here is how much control a foreign state exercises over terrorists, and, therefore, to what extent it should be held accountable for their actions. Do we blame the Irish Republican Army for attacks on British police forces or Libya for providing it with weapons and training? Critics of U.S. foreign policy argue that, unless the United States adopts a narrow interpretation of "state-sponsored terrorism," it could be accused of sponsoring terrorism itself. Presently, the United States provides weapons and related internal security technologies and training in interrogation techniques to Third World police and militia forces. If these are known to be involved in acts of state terrorism, then U.S. support amounts to "state-sponsored terrorism."[15]

What Is a Terrorist Act? Inseparably linked with the question of what is a terrorist is the issue of what constitutes an act of terrorism. U.S. government statistics identify six varieties of terrorism. Figure 9.1 presents a graphic depiction of how frequently these six types of terrorism occurred in 1987. Bombings were the most common (56.7 percent), followed by arson (18 percent), armed attacks (15.9 percent), kidnapping (6.4 percent), sabotage (0.7 percent), and skyjackings (0.1 percent). Left out of this accounting are acts of terrorism conducted by governments against their own people. Measuring state terrorism is difficult, because no one in a position of authority is keeping count. It has traditionally fallen to groups such as Amnesty International to make "guesstimates" about what type and how much government terror has occurred in various countries. It reports that in 1985 there were over 4,500 known political prisoners. Prisoners had been tortured or cruelly treated in more than 60 countries. The organization investigated 74 reported cases of extrajudicial

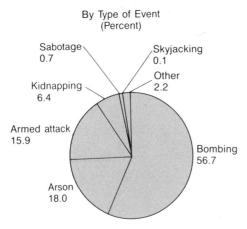

Figure 9.1 International Terrorist incidents, 1987 by type of Event. (*Source: Patterns of Global Terrorism, 1987* Washington, D.C.: U.S. State Department, 1988, p. vii.)

killings or disappearances. Those who oppose labeling these actions as terrorism argue that "an act of unjustifiable government violence should be called an atrocity, a massacre, barbarism, or even genocide, but not terrorism."[16]

According to U.S. government figures, in 1987 there were 832 international terrorist incidents, which resulted in 633 deaths and 2,272 persons being wounded. These figures include casualties suffered by the terrorists themselves. In 1987, 24 percent of all terrorist attacks were directed at business facilities. The next most common targets were government and military facilities. The most common victims of terrorist attacks in 1987 were military personnel (11.9 percent), followed by government personnel, diplomats, and businesspeople. Terrorists do not restrict themselves to these victims and targets. As Figures 9.2 and 9.3 document, the largest category is "other." How do these figures compare with previous years? Is the amount of terrorism on the rise? Is the problem about the same as in the past, or is it declining?

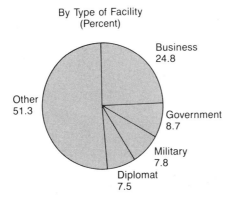

Figure 9.2 International Terrorist Incidents, 1987 by Facility. (*Source: Patterns of Global Terrorism, 1987* Washington, D.C.: U.S. State Department, 1988, p. vii.)

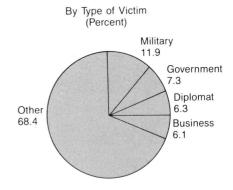

Figure 9.3 International Terrorist Incidents, 1987 by Victim. (*Source: Patterns of Global Terrorism, 1987* Washington, D.C.: U.S. State Department, 1988, p. vii.)

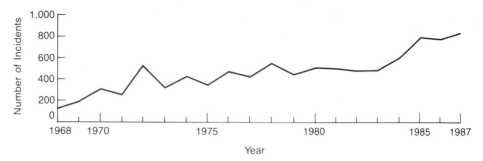

Figure 9.4 International Terrorist Incidents Over Time. (*Source: Patterns of Global Terrorism: 1987* Washington D.C.: U.S. Department of State, 1988, p. 2.)

How Much Terrorism Exists?   Comparing the amount of terrorism today with that in previous years is not an easy task because of the different definitions that people employ in measuring terrorism. Figure 9.4 presents U.S. government figures. It shows that since 1968 there has been a steady increase in the number of incidents of international terrorism. During the early 1980s terrorism leveled off but then increased sharply in 1985. The 1987 figure of 832 incidents represents a 7 percent increase over the 1986 total of 774. What this graph does not tell us is why the trend looks the way it does. The State Department, for example, notes that 1987 was marked by an absence of "terrorist spectaculars" in the Middle East. It also notes that much of the increase in 1987 was due to "a wave of high-casualty bombings in Pakistan carried out by agents of the Soviet-trained and -organized Afghan intelligence service." Newspaper accounts also attribute much of the surge in international terrorism to drug-related activities.

There is also a question of what to measure in creating such a graph. Different measures of terrorism do not necessarily produce the same answers. For example, Ted Gurr looked at the amount of terrorism between 1961 and 1970 in terms of the number of incidents and number of deaths. His findings are presented in Figures 9.5 and 9.6.[17] Two quite different pictures emerge. Viewed in terms of the number of deaths, the amount of terrorism during the 1960s peaked in 1967 and then fell to levels below those in the early part of the decade. Approached from the perspective of the number of terrorist incidents, 1967 was the second most terrorist-free year, and terrorism at the end of the decade was far greater than it was in the early part of the decade.

While the victims of terrorist attacks are often important people in their own right, of central importance to terrorists is their symbolic values. The specific identity of the person, building, or plane is often not as important as the fact that the victim is an American, a member of the armed forces, a leader in the business community, or that the building is a police headquarters. Targets are chosen in this way because, by definition, terrorists succeed to the extent to which their acts of violence intimidate onlookers. Others must identify with the victim or target and in the process change their way of thinking or acting, such as when Americans see the results of a terrorist attack on a Greek or Italian airport and cancel plans to vacation in Europe.

The terrorists' need to reach a wide audience places the media, especially televi-

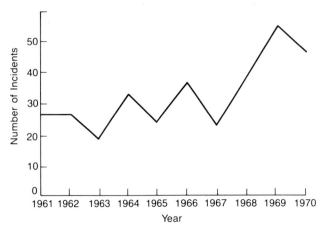

Figure 9.5 Terrorism as Measured by Number of Incidents. (*Source:* Ted Robert Gurr, "Some Characteristics of Political Terrorism in the 1960s," in Michael Stohl (ed.), *The Politics of Terrorism* New York: Marcel Dekker, 1979, p. 32.)

sion, in a very difficult and highly controversial position as it reports a terrorist attack that has been directed at a government. Silence may buy time for government officials to formulate and implement a strategy to negotiate with or punish the terrorists. Yet, many would argue that silence is a disservice to the public and that the media has a responsibility to inform the public about acts of terrorism. On the other hand, by presenting accounts of terrorist incidents, by reading terrorist demands, or by showing films of hostages made by terrorists, the media is helping terrorists publicize their cause. Excessive news coverage can also generate tremendous pressure on public officials to do something about the problem of terrorism or at least look as if they

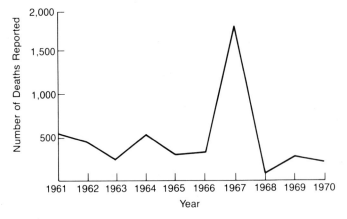

Figure 9.6 Terrorism as Measured by Number of Deaths. (*Source:* Ted Robert Gurr, "Some Characteristics of Political Terrorism in the 1960s," in Michael Stohl (ed.), *The Politics of Terrorism* New York: Marcel Dekker, 1979, p. 31.)

are in control of the situation. Finally, it needs to be noted that a different type of problem confronts the media when the issue is state terrorism. Here, the government often does not wish its terrorist acts to be well known beyond the immediate circle of individuals at whom the terrorism is targeted.

How Should We Deal with Terrorism   How should one respond to the problem of terrorism? Broadly speaking, three options exist, each of which approaches terrorism from a different perspective. The first line of action addresses the underlying causes of terrorism. The roots of terrorism lie in perceived social, political, and economic injustices. Terrorist acts are designed to draw attention to these conditions (as well as to bring notoriety to the terrorists themselves). One strategy for dealing with terrorists is to deal with the sources of their grievance. If the poverty, discrimination, or inequities that the terrorists hope to highlight and use to bring more people to their side can be ameliorated, then the terrorists will be less able to present themselves as freedom fighters and it will be easier for governments to treat them as criminals. Applied to the Middle East, this strategy would give priority to creating some type of Palestinian homeland. In Northern Ireland, it would emphasize bringing about some form of reconciliation between Protestants and Catholics.

Designing strategies that address the underlying causes of terrorism is not an easy task. Not only are the problems complex, but also the political resolve to make the necessary changes is often lacking. Even if it is successful, such a strategy will not bring about a complete end to terrorism. There will always be individuals dissatisfied with the existing order who are willing to resort to violence to press their case. Contemporary world conditions reinforce the continued reliance on terrorism as a tactic.[18] Among the most significant are the following: the trend toward smaller weapons, the high level of integration among the social, economic, political, and communications systems of modern industrial societies and their vulnerability to disruption, and the difficulty that democratic societies have in responding to terrorism. Finally, it must also be remembered that terrorism is not a new phenomenon. Studies have detailed its existence as far back as the campaign of Jewish zealots against the Romans in Palestine during the period 6–135 A.D. One of the earliest cases of state terrorism involved the "reign of terror" that followed the French Revolution.[19]

The second option open to states that are confronted with a terrorist problem is retaliation. The reprisals need not take the form of military action, such as the 1986 U.S. bombing of Libya in retaliation for the bombing of a nightclub in West Berlin or repeated Israeli air and ground attacks on PLO positions. Diplomatic retaliation could take the form of recalling or expelling diplomats, closing an embassy, or withdrawing recognition of a government. Economic sanctions could take the form of bilateral restrictions on trade, technology transfers, foreign assistance, credits, or access to international funds, such as those dispersed by the IMF or World Bank. Covert action represents yet another retaliatory option that falls short of involving the open and direct use of military force.

Retaliating against an act of terrorism with military force presents many problems. First, a series of tactical obstacles must be overcome. The state must be sure of who the terrorists are and where they are hiding. Determining the identity of those responsible for a terrorist act has proven to be very difficult. Controversy still surrounds the 1986 U.S. retaliation against Libya. One school of thought maintains that Syria, not Libya, was behind the attack and that the United States took military action against Libya because (1) it was a more vulnerable target, (2) Syria was more closely associated with the Soviet Union, and (3) Syrian cooperation was vital in solving the problem in Lebanon. Second, the morality of such an action must be addressed. How is the military act of retaliation different from the original terrorist act? Both could be interpreted as acts of violence for purposes of political intimidation. Third, the long-term strategic consequences of military retaliations must be considered. Did the U.S. bombing of Libya in 1986 put a damper on Qaddafi's support of international terrorism? The wave of terrorism with which many predicted Libya would respond never materialized. Was this due to the bombing? Perhaps, but as a Congressional Research Service Report notes, it may also have been due to sanctions imposed by the European Community after the raids.[20] The question may also be raised as to whether a connection existed between the retaliatory raids on Libya and its subsequent heightened interest in chemical warfare.

The third option for dealing with terrorists emphasizes security enhancement efforts. These may take a variety of forms, depending upon whether the purpose is to make it more difficult for the terrorists to strike or to deter terrorism through anticipation. Included in the first category are the development of contingency plans for dealing with a terrorist attack, training law enforcement officials in antiterrorism techniques (something done by the Department of State's Anti-Terrorism Training Assistance Program), international exchanges of information on terrorist organizations, and the signing of international agreements on the prosecution of terrorists. The International Convention Against the Taking of Hostages and the Convention on the Physical Protection of Nuclear Materials are examples of such international agreements. The former requires that signatory states either extradite or prosecute alleged hostage-takers found within their jurisdiction, regardless of where the act occurred. The latter agreement requires that anyone who commits a serious offense involving nuclear material be punished.

Can terrorist acts be anticipated and prevented? The public and many policymakers routinely assume that they can. Acts of terrorism bring forward charges of an intelligence failure and investigations into what went wrong. Such was the case with the 1983 terrorist attack on the U.S. Marines in Beirut.

The Terrorist Attack on U.S. Marines in Beirut   At 6:22 A.M., on October 23, 1983, a single terrorist, driving a yellow Mercedes Benz truck drove through the public parking lot south of the Battalion Landing Team Headquarters in the marine compound at the Beirut International Airport and crashed into the lobby of the building. In doing so, the truck went through a barbed wire and concertina fence, passed between two marine guard posts without drawing fire, entered an open gate, passed around one sewer pipe barrier and between two others, and flattened a guard's sandbag booth. The explosion produced by the over 12,000 pounds of TNT that the truck was carrying occurred while most in the building were asleep. It had sufficient force to rip the building from its foundation and to cause it to implode. From that attack, 241 marines died and over 100 were injured. Not quite four months later, President Reagan announced the withdrawal of the remaining 1,600 marines from Lebanon.

The presence of the U.S. Marines in Beirut had its roots in the June 6, 1982 Israeli invasion of Lebanon, whose military objective was to secure southern Lebanon and destroy the PLO. The invasion's political objective was twofold. The first political objective was to alter the political climate within Lebanon in order to lay the foundation for a Christian-dominated Lebanon. The second political objective was to give Israel a freer hand in dealing with the West Bank and Gaza Strip—Arab-populated territories that it had occupied since the 1967 war. The initial stages of the military campaign were highly successful. Within three days, Israeli forces reached the outskirts of Beirut, and by June 14, they had linked up with the Christian Lebanese militia in East Beirut. On July 2, Israeli forces set up a military blockade around Beirut, and in August PLO and Syrian forces within the city were surrounded. At this point, the Lebanese government called for an international presence in Beirut to oversee the safe evacuation of these forces. A United Nations force was not acceptable to Israel, and in its place a Multilateral Force, consisting of French, Italian, and U.S. troops, was dispatched to Lebanon. The marine unit involved in the Multilateral Force was no stranger to Lebanon. It had recently carried out the successful evacuation of U.S. citizens from the port city of Juniyah. The withdrawal of the 15,000 PLO and Syrian forces took place between August 25 and September 9. On September 10, the Multilateral Force was withdrawn from Lebanon.

The situation in Lebanon took a decisive turn for the worse in mid-September. On September 14, President-elect Bashir Gemayel was assassinated, and from September 16 to September 18 Phalangist forces massacred Palestinian and Lebanese civilians in the Sabra and Shatila refugee camps, both of which were technically under the control of Israeli forces. In the wake of these events, the Lebanese government requested the return of the Multilateral Force. On September 26, the French and Italian contingents returned. They were joined by the U.S. Marines on September 29. The 1,200 U.S. Marine force took up positions near the Beirut International Airport, thus separating the Israeli forces from the populated areas of Beirut. U.S. Ambassador Philip Habib stated that the basic objectives of the marines were (1) to bring about the withdrawal of all foreign forces from Lebanon, (2) following that, to restore the full sovereignty of the Lebanese government over its territory, and (3) to see to it that Lebanon would not be used as a source of hostile actions against Israel.

While the stated objectives of the U.S. presence in Beirut did not change, the conditions under which the marines operated changed dramatically. At first, the marines encountered a generally "passive attitude." General James Mead characterized Beirut as "minimally threatening," in large part, because the marines were seen as impartial peacekeepers. Gradually, however, this view of the marines became transformed, and a consensus emerged that the U.S. forces were really biased in favor of the Christians, who were allied with the Israelis. Support for this view came from the U.S. training of the Lebanese Armed Forces and the continuing failure to do anything about the political imbalance in the Lebanese government, in which there were few Moslem officeholders.

As views of the marine presence changed, the level of violence increased. Beginning in January 1983, Israeli defense forces came into repeated contact and conflict with marine positions. In March, five marines were slightly wounded by a terrorist hand grenade in a southern Beirut suburb. On April 18, a pick-up truck, loaded with explosives, destroyed the U.S. embassy in Beirut, killing 57 people, including 17 U.S. citizens. In an attempt to curb the heightened fighting between the Christian and Druze forces, the Lebanese government and Israel signed an agreement that provided for the departure of Israeli troops and the establishment of a security zone in southern Lebanon. Israeli troops never left Lebanon. As a condition for its withdrawal, Israel insisted upon the simultaneous withdrawal of Syrian and PLO forces from Lebanon. The problem was that neither of these two forces had been a party to the agreement, so they refused to leave. The collapse of the accord further angered the Moslem population and produced a backlash of anger against the government.

Fighting continued to escalate throughout the summer. In the course of this fighting, mortar and rocket fire landed on the marine positions. The situation became even more complex after the Israeli forces pulled out of the Alayh and Shaf districts of Beirut. This set off another wave of massacres and additional shelling of the U.S. positions. On September 19, U.S. Navy destroyers provided gunfire support for the Lebanese army in its efforts to defend Suq-al-Gharb, the high ground overlooking the U.S. Marine position. While successfully accomplishing its military objective, the shelling reinforced the Moslem community's belief that the United States supported the Christians and that it was not a neutral peacekeeper. On October 23, slightly more than one week after the leaders of Lebanon's warring factions agreed to reconciliation talks in Geneva, 241 marines died in the bombing of the compound.

What Went Wrong?   The practical problems involved in anticipating a terrorist attack are illustrated by this incident. Three major investigations were conducted to determine what went wrong in Beirut. All three agreed that there was a virtual flood of information on terrorism. Between July 1 and October 23, the marines received descriptions of over 100 potential car bombs. Between September 15 and October 23, one section of the intelligence network provided the marines with over 170 pieces of information. General Mead recalls that he received so many warnings about a white Mercedes Benz that he would tell his driver to count the number of white Mercedes that they passed. All three reports also stressed the existence of a processing failure. Although abundant information was available, no parallel capacity existed to analyze it. Among the specific failings cited were a 30–40-hour backlog in processing information between the task force in Beirut and the one offshore, and the absence of analysts who specialized in terrorism. The picture, however, was not totally negative. The Defense Department report acknowledged that intelligence provided a good picture of the broad threat that was facing the marines. Intelligence officials also pointed out that,

> Along with the normal flow of information to the Marines, the National Intelligence Digest, a daily summary of significant intelligence information, contained several reports on threats in Beirut during the summer and fall, including one published on October 20 that specified that American forces in Beirut might soon be the target of a major terrorist attack.

Could the attack have been foreseen at the time? In answering this question, it must be kept in mind that, even if the specifics of a terrorist attack had been obtained, the terrorists would always have had the option of not striking if the defender looked too prepared. Moreover, it would have been very difficult for the terrorists' target to maintain a high state of vigil over a long period of time, regardless of how specific the threat was. Alert fatigue would have set in. As General Mead noted: "Initially after the American Embassy went, we went into a condition one-type situation. But then I began thinking . . . I'm wearing my men down. . . ."

Furthermore, policymakers cannot be forced to listen or to act upon the intelligence that they are given. Frequently, they feel that they cannot act on it because doing so will either undermine their overall policy or make the situation even worse. This was the case in Beirut. Committed to opposing terrorism and having a highly visible diplomatic presence in Beirut left the Reagan administration with little leeway in responding to warnings about an impending attack. Pulling the marines out of Lebanon was not considered to be an option; it would have been seen as capitulation in the face of terrorism—something that would have encouraged other terrorist groups. Dispersing the marines into smaller units or closing off access to the airport would have made the marines more "invisible" and harder to attack, but this too was not considered to be an option. The marines were in Beirut on what was essentially a political mission. Success required a visible but noncombat presence. Finally, even moving the marines away from the Beirut airport to another location was not possible, given the nature of the mission. The airport was being run by the Lebanese government as a symbol of the continued authority and viability of the central government. If the marines left and the airport were closed or overrun, the legitimacy of the government would be called into doubt.

Guerrilla Warfare

Guerrilla warfare and terrorism are often viewed as two different forms of the same phenomenon. This is not the case. While both rely upon terror as a tactic in advancing their cause, guerrilla warfare and terrorism are two distinct forms of conflict. A first difference lies in the area of military strategy. For guerrillas, terror is a tactic to be relied upon most heavily at a specific stage in the struggle against the governing authorities. For terrorists, terrorism is the only weapon. A second difference is that guerrilla warfare contains both a military and a social-political dimension. Moreover, it is generally held that victory is possible only by triumphing in the social-political sphere. Terrorism is unidimensional. Its concern is solely with undermining the legitimacy of the government. No effort is directed at establishing the terrorists as credible alternative rulers.

The specific number of stages to the military dimension of a guerrilla war varies from theorist to theorist, but the logic linking them together is essentially the same. Our discussion is based upon the formula suggested by Mao Zedong, one of the most successful practitioners of guerrilla warfare. The first stage, often referred to as the "strategic defensive," is concerned with establishing a safe zone from which to build up one's own organization and carry out operations against the government. Given the limited resources of guerrilla groups at this stage, both in terms of materiel and members, their major problem is not so much defeating the enemy as it is ensuring their own continued survival. The principal tactics employed by guerrilla groups in this first stage are terrorism, covert political activity, and propaganda. At this point, the guerrillas are fighting a "war without frontiers." Attacks are possible anywhere and everywhere as the guerrillas try to maximize the chaos produced by small numbers of dedicated individuals.

The second stage, the "strategic stalemate," is characterized by the emergence of clearly identifiable areas, which are either under the control of the guerrillas or progovernment forces. In this stage, guerrilla units begin to supplement their reliance upon terrorism with hit-and-run attacks and small-scale military operations against government targets. Direct confrontations are avoided. Typical of this stage is the scenario in which the guerrillas overrun a government outpost during daylight hours and retreat at night before government reinforcements arrive to retake the position. As Mao Zedong put it, "when guerrillas engage a stronger enemy, they withdraw when he advances; harass him when he stops; strike him when he is weary; pursue him when he withdraws."[21]

The third and final stage, the "strategic counteroffensive," resembles conventional warfare, with large-scale battles taking place between the military forces of both sides. According to Mao, the guerrillas should not move to this stage until victory is all but certain. If it is handled properly, it is not a long stage. Demoralized and themselves questioning the legitimacy of the ruling elite, government forces will not put up an effective resistance but will instead melt away under the pressure of the guerrilla offensive.

Guerrilla wars are protracted wars. They do not easily move through these three stages. Regardless of what stage the guerrilla war is in, Mao counsels that victory cannot be achieved on the battlefield alone. It will only come from separating the people from the government. Military encounters must be designed with this purpose in mind. Acts of terrorism, for example, cannot be seen by the population at large as random acts of violence that are ultimately directed at them. Instead, terrorist acts must be seen as "an extragovernmental effort to dispense justice long overdue and it must have the effect of freeing the local communities from the felt constraints of coercive authority."[22] The same principle holds for ambushes and large battles. The goal is not to take a piece of territory away from the government or to destroy its army but to demonstrate to the people that, due to its military incompetence and general pattern of behavior, the government no longer deserves their continued support. In the early post-World War II period, most guerrilla wars were directed at speeding up the process of decolonization. More recently, they have sought to bring down what the guerrillas believe to be oppressive and illegitimate governments. Guerrilla-war theorists are in disagreement over whether or not guerrillas must wait for popular grievances to harden to the point where revolutionary struggle is possible or if they themselves can create the required climate of exploitation and oppression.

The process of separating the people from the government also takes place away from the battlefield. In fact, guerrilla-war theorists argue that at all times primacy must be given to the social-political dimension of a guerrilla war over the military dimension. The key to success is the ability of the guerrillas to present themselves as champions of the people. This is rarely accomplished by simply reciting ideological principles or by proclaiming their virtues over those espoused by the existing political order. Far more successful is a strategy where the guerrillas as a group promote those concrete issues on which popular opposition to the government is based (i.e., land reform, an end to corruption, self-rule) and in which they as individuals act as model soldiers and citizens. Once in control of territory, guerrillas set up political institutions and social programs, which often correct these injustices and are based upon proper codes of behavior. Mao argued that these activities serve a dual purpose. Not only do they demonstrate that life under the guerrilla organization is superior to that under the government in power, but also they keep the guerrillas occupied during the long periods when there is little military activity. This prevents boredom and improves morale.

Just as guerrillas cannot triumph solely by achieving victories on the battlefield, they cannot be defeated by military means alone. Established authorities must also wage a two-front struggle against the guerrillas. Through military successes and social-political reforms, they must win back and keep the loyalty of the people, thereby isolating them from the guerrillas. Major obstacles stand in the way of government success in both of these areas of required action. In the military dimension, the problem is structural and grows out of the fundamental asymmetry in strength between the guerrillas and the government forces and the differing military requirements facing each side. It has been argued that government forces must outnumber guerrilla forces by at least 5 to 1 in order to defeat them. According to Henry Kissinger, "the guerrilla wins if he does not lose. The conventional army loses if it does not win." Stalemate thus works to the advantage of the guerrillas, and stalemate is likely, because the population recognizes that the guerrillas are weak and therefore it is difficult for the government (or its outside protector) to justify mobilizing the resources necessary to defeat them. The government thus finds itself fighting a limited war, while the guerrillas are using all of their available energies to defeat it. The longer the war drags on, the more disadvantaged the government's position becomes. "A war with no visible payoff against an opponent who poses no direct threat will come under increasing criticism as battle casualties rise and economic costs escalate."[23]

Social-political reforms are not easily undertaken. The government must overcome the opposition of well-entrenched political and economic groups that benefit by a continuance of the status quo, whether it is corruption, an uneven distribution of land, an unfair tax code, or ethnic discrimination. Often these groups make up the very core of the ruling elite. In other cases, such as in El Salvador, these groups may launch a countercampaign of violence and terrorism. For example, when the government of El Salvador, under pressure from the United States, instituted a land reform program, right-wing elements used the program to identify and eliminate potential "troublemakers." Some who applied for land under the program were kidnapped and murdered, as well as a U.S. advisor who was sent to help carry out the program.[24] An additional problem facing governments is that reform can actually worsen political instability by raising the expectations of the people beyond what the government intends. Once the government begins to institute change, it is very dangerous for it to stop or to attempt to turn back.

While governments face real obstacles in meeting the challenges posed by a guerrilla war, victory for the guerrillas is far from automatic. The 1988 *Social Science Index* referenced articles on guerrilla wars taking place in 19 separate states in Latin America and the Middle East. Of these, only the Afghan guerrilla war could be labeled a success at that time. Many times guerrilla wars are conducted under circumstances in which the necessary prerequisites for success are absent. Among the most commonly cited preconditions are (1) an extensive territory within which to maneuver, (2) a relatively high percentage and density of rural population, (3) a common frontier with a sympathetic state so that sanctuaries may be created, (4) the inability of the government to launch counterattacks by air, and (5) a government army that is not large enough to protect its lines of communication. Based on a consideration of these factors, Regis Debray concluded in 1967 that Latin America was not well suited for guerrilla warfare.[25] Che Guevara, one of Fidel Castro's lieutenants in the Cuban revolution, had reached the opposite conclusion. He felt that, because of its large number of rural areas and underdeveloped lines of communication, Latin America was a highly promising candidate for revolution. Guevara died in an unsuccessful attempt to bring down the Bolivian government through a guerrilla war in 1967.

The Soviet Invasion of Afghanistan The roots of the Soviet invasion of Afghanistan and the ensuing guerrilla war can be traced back to the 1973 coup d'etat, in which King Zahir Shah was overthrown. While the Soviet Union did not engineer the coup, it did give it its tacit support. Within a short period of time, the new regime came under internal attack from two different factions of the Marxist People's Democratic Party of Afghanistan (PDPA). One faction, the Khalq (masses), is Maoist in outlook, and the other, known as the Parcham (flag), is pro-Moscow in orientation. In April 1978, the Khalq led a bloody coup. The Soviet Union appears not to have planned the coup, but its penetration of the Afghan military was so thorough that most believe Moscow had foreknowledge of it. In December 1978, a 20-year friendship and cooperation pact was signed with the Soviet Union.

One year later, in 1979, Soviet forces invaded Afghanistan. The intervening year had seen widespread rioting against the radical social, economic, and education policies that the new regime attempted to impose on Afghanistan's largely tribal society. The government faced armed opposition in a majority of Afghanistan's 28 provinces and was cautioned by the Soviet Union to slow down the pace of its reform agenda. The Soviet Union also found it necessary both to step up its shipments of military equipment and to send combat personnel to help the government in the rapidly escalating civil war. In September, a rival Khalq faction seized control of the government. It too refused to follow Moscow's instructions and followed an even more radical reform program. As a result, rioting and opposition to communist rule in Afghanistan became even more widespread. Once again the Soviet Union increased the size of its military presence, this time tripling its garrison inside Afghanistan so that, by the time the invasion took place, 4,500 Soviet military advisors were present. Then, on December 27, determined to bring order to this increasingly chaotic situation and to prevent what appeared to be the otherwise inevitable triumph of the Islamic rebel forces, more than 50,000 Soviet forces invaded Afghanistan and installed Babrak Karmal, who headed the rival Parcham faction and had been out of the country in exile, as the new president.

A decade after the invasion, Western observers continued to disagree among themselves as to the reasons for the Soviet invasion. Whereas some stressed the defensive nature of the Soviet invasion of Afghanistan (a concern for instability on its southern border and a fear of the spread of Islamic fundamentalism into the Soviet Asiatic republics), others saw the Soviet move as fundamentally aggressive (Afghanistan was to be the first step in a long-range plan to extend Soviet influence throughout the Persian Gulf region). Whatever the motivation, disagreement also appeared to have existed within the Politburo over the wisdom of sending Soviet forces into Afghanistan. Brezhnev and Mikhail Suslov, the Communist party leader in charge of ideology, reportedly supported the invasion and gained a narrow Politburo majority for the invasion over the objections of then KGB Chief Andropov.

The original Soviet military plan called for the Afghan army to bear the bulk of the responsibility for pacifying the Afghan population. Wholesale defections quickly negated this strategy. Before the 1978 coup, the strength of the Afghan army was placed at 100,000 men. By the end of 1980, this figure had fallen to 30,000, and only 10,000–15,000 of these were valued as an effective fighting force. As a result, within one year of the Soviet occupation, the Soviet army grew to 110,000, with several thousand more service troops stationed just north of the Soviet-Afghan border. An estimated 15,000–20,000 of these Soviet troops have been actively engaged in fighting. The collapse of the Afghan army also meant that Soviet forces had to bear the primary responsibility for fighting the guerrillas, or Mujahadin.

Initially, Soviet forces attempted to conduct conventional-style military operations against the Mujahadin. Armed with missiles, heavy armor, and antiaircraft weapons, they sought to achieve victory on the battlefield through the application of superior firepower. After initially sustaining heavy losses, the Mujahadin countered by retreating into the mountains out of the reach of Soviet forces. So ineffective was the Soviet Union's strategy, that the Afghan government exercised effective 24-hour per day control of over no more than 10 percent of the country. Faced with this situation, the Soviet Union adjusted its tactics. Heavy reliance came to be placed on the use of helicopter gun ships and the type of search-and-destroy missions that had been common in the Vietnam War. The Soviet Union also employed chemical warfare and destroyed entire villages in retaliation for Mujahadin attacks on Soviet forces. In 1986, 500,000 were estimated to have died from the combination of civil war and the Soviet invasion.

The Soviet Union's inability to defeat the Mujahadin on the battlefield was paralleled by its inability to stabilize the political order in Afghanistan. Karmal was neither able to unite the two factions of the PDPA nor generate popular support for his government. In 1986, in yet another effort to end the factional infighting within the PDPA, the Soviets removed Karmal from power and replaced him with the KGB-trained, former head of the secret police, Najibullah. At first, Najibullah and the Soviet Union attempted to broaden support for the PDPA regime by pursuing a policy of national reconciliation. One year later, in 1987, in a virtual admission that the policy of national reconciliation had been a failure, the emphasis shifted to building up the core of the PDPA and concentrating power within Najibullah's hands.

During the early 1980s, Soviet leaders became increasingly disillusioned with the political, economic, and social costs of a continued military stalemate and began to explore the possibility of a negotiated settlement to the war, but it was not until

1988 that such an agreement was reached. In the interim, the scale of the fighting escalated. "Bleeders" in both Pakistan and the United States sought to keep the pressure on the Soviet Union rather than allow it to withdraw.[26] American military aid to the Mujahadin rose from $120 million in 1984 to $630 million in 1987, bringing the accumulated value of U.S. military aid to $2.1 billion. Not counted in this figure was U.S.-orchestrated aid from China, Egypt, Saudi Arabia, and Western Europe. Pakistan had become an important player in ending the war for two reasons. First, much Western aid intended for the Mujahadin was channeled through it. Second, by 1988, the number of Afghan refugees in Pakistan had grown to 3.5 million and refugee camps on the Afghan border were fertile recruiting grounds for the Mujahadin. The Soviet Union also escalated the level of its involvement in the war. Gorbachev tried to achieve a military victory by raising the number of Soviet forces in Afghanistan to 115,000.

The diplomatic deadlock over ending the Soviet involvement in Afghanistan broke in February 1988, when Gorbachev announced that he was prepared to remove Soviet troops within 10 months and that this withdrawal would begin on May 15. Shortly thereafter, on April 14, Afghanistan and Pakistan signed three bilateral agreements, spelling out the ground rules for their relations in the postinvasion era. The Soviet Union and the United States also signed a "Declaration on International Guarantees." Collectively, these documents are referred to as the Geneva Accords. They specify that (1) neither state would interfere in the other's internal affairs, (2) refugees would be returned, and (3) there would be a phased withdrawal of Soviet forces but this would be settled by the Soviet Union and Afghanistan.

The Soviet withdrawal was not without its problems, but it did take place on schedule. Approximately 50,000 Soviet soldiers left in August 1988, and the remainder left in February 1989. The war in Afghanistan entered a new phase at that point, because, for all practical purposes, conventional warfare replaced guerrilla warfare as the dominant form of military interaction between the opposing sides. Many expected President Najibullah's government to collapse almost instantly, but it did not. Instead, the Mujahadin experienced a great deal of difficulty in making the change-over from guerrilla to conventional warfare, and in maintaining their unity in the absence of Soviet forces.

The progress of the guerrilla war in Afghanistan shows the importance of those factors cited by Mao and theorists as necessary for success. Militarily, the Mujahadin avoided large-scale direct military engagements with the Afghan army as long as Soviet forces were in the country. Instead, it focused its efforts on demoralizing the Soviet forces and separating the Afghan people from the Soviet-backed government. The Mujahadin owed much of its success to the availability of large rural areas within which it operated, U.S.-supplied weapons, and sanctuary in Pakistan. Just as the United States had tried and failed to substitute technology and firepower for meaningful social-political reforms in Vietnam, so the Soviet Union tried and failed in Afghanistan. The Mujahadin also showed signs of lacking a key ingredient: leadership. Because the resistance was heavily localized and tribally based, the unity that came from fighting Soviet forces was often more than offset by differences based upon such factors as whether individuals were locally based Mujahadin or members of a resistance group in Pakistan; a tribesman or an Islamic fundamentalist; a monarchist or antimonarchist; or members of the Pushtan ethnic group. So deep were these divisions that, even before the Soviet exodus was completed, some observers speculated that, if the alliance of resistance forces was not able to establish a provisional government before the Soviet Union withdrew from Afghanistan, it would disintegrate.[27]

CONCLUSION

Our discussion of crises and low-intensity conflict only begins to suggest the many different forms that international conflict can take, short of international war. For example, excluded from our accounting are cases of economic warfare and the "political use of force" such as sending a naval squadron to foreign waters as a show of force. Our discussion also points to the impact that technology has had on the nature of warfare in the twentieth century. As we have seen, low-intensity conflict and crises do not directly translate into few deaths or minimal destruction; nor are these types of conflict situations necessarily more easily resolved than international wars. If anything, they may be even more intractable—appearing to policymakers as a safe way of pursuing national interests in a world haunted by the specter of nuclear war.

NOTES

1. Michael T. Klare and Peter Kornbluh, eds., *Low Intensity Warfare* (New York: Pantheon Press, 1988).
2. See Charles Hermann, "International Crisis as a Situational Variable," in James Rosenau, ed., *International Politics and Foreign Policy* (New York: Free Press, 1969) for a decision-making approach to defining international crises. In this article, he included surprise as one of the key features of a crisis. In a later work he drops it. See his *International Relations: Insights from Behavioral Research* (New York: Free Press, 1972).
3. Glenn Snyder and Paul Diesing, *Conflict Among Nations* (Princeton, N.J.: Princeton University Press, 1977), p. 6.
4. Phil Williams, "Crisis Management," in John Baylis, et al., eds., *Contemporary Strategy* (New York: Holmes & Meier, 1975), p. 152.
5. Richard Betts, *Nuclear Blackmail and the Nuclear Balance* (Washington, D.C.: Brookings Institute, 1987), p. 9.
6. Richard Lebow, *Between Peace and War* (Baltimore: The Johns Hopkins University Press, 1981).
7. Lebow, *Between Peace and War*, p. 276.
8. For a discussion of the similarities and differences between World War I and a possible future world war in the nuclear age, see the symposium, "The Great War and the Nuclear Age," *International Security* 9 (1984): 3–186.
9. Daniel Papp, *Contemporary International Relations* (New York: Macmillan, 1984), p. 449; and George Shultz, *Low Intensity Conflict* (Washington, D.C.: U.S. State Department, Current Policy #783, 1986). See also Klare and Kornbluh, *Low Intensity Warfare*.
10. "CIA Study: Soviet Covert Action and Propaganda," printed as part of testimony before the House Intelligence Committee, *Hearings*, Subcommittee on Oversight of the Perma-

nent Select Committee on Intelligence, House of Representatives, February 6, 1980 and February 19, 1980.

11. Donald Jameson, "Trends in Soviet Covert Action," in Roy Godson, ed., *Intelligence Requirements for the 1980's: Covert Action* (New York: National Strategy Information Center, 1981), pp. 169–184.

12. John Barron, *KGB* (New York: Bantam, 1974), pp. 413–448.

13. Richard Shultz and Roy Godson, *Dezinformatsia* (Washington, D.C.: Pergamon-Brassey's, 1984).

14. U.S. Department of Defense, *Terrorist Group Profiles* (Washington, D.C.: Government Printing Office, 1989).

15. Michael Klare, *American Arms Supermarket* (Austin, Tex.: University of Texas Press, 1984), chap. 9.

16. James Ray, *Global Politics*, 3d ed. (Boston: Houghton Mifflin, 1987), p. 385. Ray also presents an excellent discussion of the problems involved in defining *terrorism*.

17. Ted Gurr, "Some Characteristics of Political Terrorism in the 1960s," in Michael Stohl, ed., *The Politics of Terrorism* (New York: Marcel Dekker, 1979), pp. 23–50.

18. John Spanier, *Games Nations Play*, 6th ed. (Washington, D.C.: Congressional Quarterly Press, 1987), pp. 375–376.

19. Donna M. Schlagheck, *International Terrorism* (Lexington, Mass.: Lexington Books, 1988), pp. 15–18; and Charles Learche, Jr., and Abdul Said, *Concepts of International Politics*, 3d ed. (Englewood Cliffs, N.J.: Prentice-Hall, 1979), pp. 294–295.

20. James Wootten, *Terrorism: U.S. Policy Options* (Washington, D.C.: Congressional Research Service, November 3, 1987).

21. Quoted by Leon Baradat, *Political Ideologies*, 3d ed. (Englewood Cliffs, N.J.: Prentice-Hall, 1988), p. 212.

22. Peter Paret and John Shy, *Guerrillas in the 1960s* (New York: Praeger, 1962), p. 32.

23. This argument is taken from Andrew Mack, "Why Big Nations Lose Small Wars: The Politics of Asymmetric Conflicts," *World Politics* 27 (1975): 175–200.

24. Lawrence Simon, "Social Ethics and Land Reform: The Case of El Salvador," *Agriculture and Human Values*, 1, no. 3, (Summer 1984): 31–35.

25. Regis Debray, *Revolution in the Revolution* (New York: Harmondsworth, 1967).

26. Selig Harrison, "Inside the Afghan Talks," *Foreign Policy* 72 (1988): 32.

27. *Strategic Survey, 1987–1988* (London: International Institute for Strategic Studies, 1988), p. 135.

Chapter
10

National Security and Military Power in the Nuclear Age

Military power can advance a state's national security interests in many ways. A state can use it to defend itself from an attack or to attack another state. It can be used to compel, or force, another state to do something that it would otherwise not do or to stop it from doing something. It can also be used to deter an opponent, to prevent or discourage that opponent from doing something by arousing fear or uncertainty. In this chapter, we will examine the ability of nuclear weapons to fulfill these three roles. Our emphasis will be on nuclear deterrence, because, up until recently, it was widely held that this was the only task for which nuclear weapons were suited. We will also examine nuclear compellence and nuclear-war scenarios. During the 1980s, these topics received a level of attention by policymakers and scholars that had not been present for many years. Before turning to these issues, we will first introduce the world's nuclear arsenals.

NUCLEAR ARSENALS

Nuclear weapons are not interchangeable. Differences in such areas as accuracy, payload, speed, vulnerability, and control make them suitable for some military purposes and disqualify them for others. Traditionally, nuclear weapons have been grouped into three categories: strategic, theater, and battlefield. We will discuss strategic weapons because they play the most prominent role in thinking about nuclear deterrence.

Strategic Weapons

Strategic weapons are most readily distinguishable from one another in terms of their delivery systems. Manned bombers are the original delivery system of the nuclear age. They have been joined by land-based intercontinental ballistic missiles (ICBMs) and submarine-launched ballistic missiles, so that now both of the superpowers have a triad of delivery systems.[1] The backbone of the U.S. strategic bomber force is the B-52 Stratofortress. The B-52 first flew in 1952. Today it is capable of carrying up to 20 nuclear short-range attack missiles and 4 nuclear gravity bombs. A second strategic bomber in the U.S. inventory is the B-1. It is capable of flying 6,400 miles without refueling, attaining a speed of Mach 1.25 and carrying 32 nuclear missiles or cruise missiles, or 115,000 pounds of conventional bombs. Bombers play a less significant role in the Soviet nuclear arsenal. The primary heavy bomber in the Soviet inventory is the Tu20 Bear. The Bear was first introduced into service in 1956, and the most recent version is capable of carrying from 4 to 12 cruise missiles. Currently, the Soviet Union is working on adding the Blackjack to its bomber force. It will be the world's largest and heaviest bomber and will have an unrefueled combat radius of some 4,533 miles and a speed of Mach 2.0. Foremost among the advantages that the manned bomber possesses over the other two legs of the triad are its ability to carry high payloads and deliver them with great accuracy, and that it can be recalled after it has been dispatched against a target. On the negative side, bombers have a long flight time, which gives the enemy ample warning time that an attack has been launched. Bombers are also readily detected by radar and vulnerable to enemy air defense systems and prelaunch attacks while they are still on the ground. Several steps can be taken to increase the survivability of bomber forces. First, the United States has equipped many of its bombers with air-launched cruise missiles, which allow them to release their weapons before encountering Soviet air defense systems. Second, it always keeps a portion of its manned bomber force on airborne alert. Third, in an on-again-off-again fashion, it has entertained plans to deploy a new generation of manned bombers, the B-2, which would possess "stealth" technology, making it virtually invisible to most Soviet radar systems.

Land-based intercontinental ballistic missiles (ICBMs) have the virtue of being a highly accurate delivery system and the fastest reacting one. The Soviet Union tested the first ICBM in 1957. Early generations of ICBMs were powered by liquid fuel that was stored separately from the missile, stationed above ground, and possessed one warhead. Today, ICBMs are propelled by solid or storable liquid fuels, and launch times of 1–2 minutes are considered normal. It would take an ICBM warhead approximately 30 minutes to fly 7,000 miles. ICBMs have also been fitted with multiple independently targeted warheads (MIRVs), so that today one missile can launch warheads at several different targets. The U.S. MX and the Soviet SS-18 are capable of carrying 10 warheads. Historically, Soviet warheads have also been larger than their American counterparts. For example, the warhead carried by the Minuteman III has a yield of 170 kilotons (170,000 tons of TNT), while an older version of the Soviet SS-9 was capable of carrying either a huge, single 25-megaton (25 million tons of TNT) warhead or three 4–5-megaton warheads. The MX is an exception to this rule. It is a 100-ton missile that was designed explicitly to approach the size of Soviet land-based ICBM counterparts. In large part, the reason for this disparity in size lay in the Soviet Union's inability to master the art of miniaturizing weapons systems technology. Until recently, the large size of Soviet missiles was seen as a weakness. Advances in ICBM accuracy have transformed it into a source of potential strength, because it raises the possibility of being able to destroy hardened targets.

Circular Error Probability (CEP) is the measure used to gauge a missile's accuracy. It is defined as the radius of a circle in which 50 percent of the warheads fired by a missile on a given target will fall. In 1963, the U.S. Titan II had a CEP of 4,250 feet. Today, the MX has a CEP of 300–400 feet. Soviet missiles have undergone a parallel increase in accuracy. Where in 1962 the SS-7 had a CEP of 9,000 feet, today the SS-18 has a CEP of 800 feet. ICBM accuracy is so great, that no amount of "hardening" can make a missile site completely invulnerable to a surprise enemy attack, and this vulnerability is the primary liability of the ICBM. Recognizing this, both the United States (the MX) and Soviet Union (SS-24 and SS-25) have begun to deploy mobile ICBMs.

Submarine-launched ballistic missiles (SLBMs) have been in service since 1958. Early SLBMs were greatly limited in their range (so they had to be deployed near their targets), and they were also fairly inaccurate (because it was difficult to pinpoint exactly where they were). The newest generation of SLBMs possess both great range and are highly accurate. For example, the Polaris A3, which became operational in 1964, had a range of only 2,880 miles and a CEP of 2,600 feet. The Trident II, the sixth and newest U.S. SLBM, has a range of 4,000–6,000 miles and a CEP of 400 feet. The United States, and to a lesser extent the Soviet Union, have also MIRVed their SLBMs. The U.S. Poseidon submarine carries 16 missiles that are equipped with 10–14 warheads. Trident submarines carry 24 missiles, each equipped with 8-10 warheads of 100 kilotons each. When coupled with the continuing problems of vulnerability of ICBMs and manned bombers, these advances in SLBM technology have led nuclear strategists to place increasing emphasis on the deterrence role of SLBMs. SLBMs are also valued for their invulnerability. Notwithstanding recent advances in the technology used to detect submarines, submerged ballistic missile submarines are widely considered to be the most invulnerable leg of the strategic triad.

The very invulnerability of SLBMs to detection also creates command, control, communication, and intelligence problems (C^3I, pronounced "see-cubed-eye"), problems that are greater than those facing the other legs of the triad. Launching a U.S. ICBM requires the receipt of a validated order and the coordinated action of four individuals. Located in two separate command capsules (two per capsule), both members of each crew must turn a key at virtually the same time to affect a launch. Similar safeguards have been incorporated into the launching of nuclear weapons from U.S. bombers. According to the Strategic Air Command (SAC), unless "di-

Table 10.1   THE STRATEGIC NUCLEAR BALANCE

A. Current US strategic forces under SALT and START counting rules

Counting rules	SALT/ START	SALT		START	
	Launchers deployed	Warheads/ launcher	Total warheads	Warheads/ launcher	Total warheads
ICBM					
Minuteman II	450	1	450	1	450
Minuteman III	511	3	1,533	3	1,533
MX	39	10	390	10	390
Subtotal (ICBM)	1,000		2,373		2,373
SLBM					
Poseidon C-3	256	14	3,584	10	2,560
Trident C-4	384	8	3,072	8	3,072
Subtotal (SLBM)	640		6,656		5,632
Subtotal (ICMB + SLBM)	1,640		9,029		8,005
Bombers					
B-1B	99	12	1,188	1	99
B-52G/H (non-ALCM)	105	12	1,260	1	105
B-52G (ALCM)	98	20	1,960	10	980
B-52H (ALCM)	60	20	1,200	10	600
Subtotal (bombers)	362		5,608		1,784
Total	2,002		14,617		9,789

rected otherwise by the President of the United States," the bombers will return to their bases. A "go code" would have to be authenticated at several command levels, including two crew members. The weapons on board are not armed until the "go code" is received. This type of tight control is not possible over SLBMs because of the difficulty that radio waves have in penetrating the ocean. As a result, submarine commanders possess the technical authority to use their weapons without having first to receive a positive "go code." They cannot, however, sanction the use of nuclear weapons without the concurrence of several crew members.

Table 10.1 presents an inventory of the major weapons in the U.S. and Soviet strategic nuclear arsenals. Two points about this table merit special attention and must be kept in mind when we are discussing arms control and nuclear strategy. First, the current size of the U.S. and Soviet strategic arsenals is consistent with the limits allowed by the unratified SALT II agreement. Second, the overall balance in numbers found in these two nuclear inventories has not always been present. Only since 1970 has nuclear parity existed between the United States and the Soviet Union. In 1949, the year in which the Soviet Union exploded its first atomic bomb, the United States inventory stood at 100–200 weapons. By 1957, the year in which the Soviet Union sent Sputnik into earth orbit and successfully tested the first ICBM,

Table 10.1   Continued

B. Current Soviet strategic forces under SALT and START counting rules.

Counting rules	SALT/ START	SALT		START	
	Launchers deployed	Warheads/ launcher	Total warheads	Warheads/ launcher	Total warheads
ICBM					
SS-11	420	1	420	1	420
SS-13	60	1	60	1	60
SS-17	138	4	552	4	552
SS-18	308	10	3,080	10	3,080
SS-19	350	6	2,100	6	2,100
SS-24	10	10	100	10	100
SS-25	100	1	100	1	100
Subtotal (ICBM)	1,386		6,412		6,412
SLBM					
SS-N-6	256	1	256	1	256
SS-N-8	286	1	286	1	286
SS-N-17	12	1	12	1	12
SS-N-18	224	7	1,568	7	1,568
SS-N-20	100	9	900	10	1,000
SS-N-23	64	10	640	4	256
Subtotal (SLBM)	942		3,662		3,378
Subtotal (ICBM + SLBM)	2,328		10,074		9,790
Bombers					
Bear (ALCM)	70	20	1,400	10	700
Bear (non-ALCM)	100	2	200	1	100
Bison	5	4	20	1	5
Subtotal (bombers)	175		1,620		805
Total	2,503		11,694		10,595

Source: The Military Balance, 1988–1989 (London: The International Institute for Strategic Studies, 1989), p. 230.

it is estimated that the United States possessed approximately 2,000 nuclear bombs, compared to a few hundred in the Soviet arsenal. Spurred on by fears that the Soviet accomplishments had produced a "missile gap," the United States began a large-scale buildup that did not begin leveling off until 1967, at which time the United States had a 2,280-755 advantage in warheads over the Soviet Union. The Soviet Union began to build strategic nuclear weapons in earnest following the Cuban missile crisis. By September 1968, the U.S. lead had been reduced to 2,275-1,135. At the time the SALT agreement was signed in 1972, virtual equality existed. The United States had 2,140 warheads, compared to 2,142 for the Soviet Union.

Second, although the Soviet and United States strategic arsenals are roughly comparable in size, they are not symmetrical. U.S. forces are distributed relatively

Table 10.2   DEPLOYED INF MISSILES, DECEMBER 31, 1986

	System	Approximate range (miles)	Launchers (missiles)	Warheads
LRINF[a]				
USSR	SS-20	311	441 (441)	1,323
	SS-4	1242	112 (112)	112
U.S.	Pershing II	1118	108 (108)	108
	GLCM	1553	52 (208)	208
SRINF[a]				
USSR	SS-12	559	100+	100+
	SS-23	311	Being deployed	
U.S.	None			

[a]Long-Range Intermediate Nuclear Forces

[b]Short-Range Intermediate Nuclear Forces

Source: Negotiations on Intermediate-Range Nuclear Forces Special Report no. 167 (U.S. Department of State, July 1987), p. 3.

evenly (in terms of their survivability in case of an attack) among all three legs of the triad: SLBMs make up 50 percent of the total of warheads, ICBMs account for 19 percent, and warheads carried by bombers make up the remaining 31 percent. Sixty-eight percent of the Soviet strategic warheads are in their ICBM force. SLBMs account for an additional 24 percent, with warheads on bombers comprising only 8 percent. Not only does this lack of symmetry make it difficult to construct arms control reduction formulas, but it presents each superpower with different types of strategic problems. For example, fixed land-based ICBMs are the most vulnerable of the three legs of the triad to attack. This creates a type of "use-them-or-lose them" pressure on policymakers. Because the Soviet Union has such a preponderance of its forces in this category, it has a far greater problem than does the United States, and this accounts, in part, for the long-standing Soviet emphasis on the preemptive use of its strategic nuclear forces.

Theater and Battlefield Nuclear Weapons

A second category of nuclear weapons is composed of theater nuclear weapons, which are often subdivided into intermediate-range missiles (those with a range of 621–3,416 miles) and short-range missiles (those with a range of 311–621 miles). Table 10.2 presents the U.S. and Soviet theater nuclear arsenals as they existed in 1986. By the end of 1991, this table will be empty, as a result of the signing of the Intermediate Nuclear Forces (INF) Treaty. According to its terms, the United States will dismantle and destroy a total of 283 deployed and nondeployed launchers and 867 missiles. The Soviet Union will destroy a total of 851 launchers and 1,836 missiles.

One final category of nuclear weapons exists: battlefield nuclear weapons.[2] Figuring most prominently in this category are aerial bombs, short-range artillery rounds, lance missiles, atomic land mines, and air defense missiles in and at sea around Europe. First put in Western Europe in 1954, by the end of the 1970s approximately 7,000 battlefield nuclear weapons were located there. U.S. nuclear artillery shells and atomic land mines are also stored in South Korea and Guam. At that time, a decision was made to begin reducing the size of this arsenal. The 1979 decision to withdraw 1,000 battlefield nuclear warheads was followed by a 1983 decision to take out another 1,400. Because many are located near the front lines, there was a strong feeling that battlefield nuclear weapons carry too high a political price tag and have limited military significance because of the speed with which they must be used in order to stop a Warsaw Pact advance. In 1989, plans for the modernization of battlefield nuclear weapons were a major point of controversy between the United States and West Germany. The United States wanted NATO to back its decision to proceed with a new generation of Lance missiles. West Germany urged that the United States postpone such an action and advocated that it negotiate the complete elimination of these weapons in Europe. Table 10.3 presents an inventory of U.S. and Soviet weapons in this category.

Other Nuclear Arsenals

The United States and the Soviet Union are not the only states in the world that possess nuclear power. Three other states publicly acknowledge that they possess nuclear forces (Great Britain, France, and China), and one has acknowledged testing a nuclear device (India). Of these, Great Britain and France possess a complement of strategic, theater, and tactical nuclear weapons. Their nuclear inventories are presented in Figure 10.1. It is also widely believed that Israel possesses a stockpile of nuclear warheads, that South Africa may have tested a nuclear device, and that Pakistan is actively attempting to join the nuclear club. Recently, new light was shed on the development of the French nuclear force.[3] Contrary to public perceptions that the French nuclear force had been developed independently from the United States, it appears that the United States engaged in a sustained and substantial covert operation, dating back to the Nixon administration, to provide France with aid in the areas of miniaturization, shielding warheads from the debilitating effects of electromagnetic radiation generated by nearby explosions, and delivery system technology. Unlike U.S. cooperation with the British, actual weapons designs were not exchanged. The net result of these revelations is that they point to the existence of a much closer (and perhaps illegal) relationship between the Western nuclear powers. For example, it now appears that both the French and British nuclear forces operate with two alternative target lists: One list would be used independently as an instrument of last resort and national survival, and a second list would be used in conjunction with NATO forces.

Table 10.3   BATTLEFIELD NUCLEAR WEAPONS IN EUROPE

United States

Weapon	First Deployed	Range	Warhead	Launchers	Missiles
Lance	1976	4-71 miles	1-100 kt	88	700

Soviet Union

Weapon	First Deployed	Range	Warhead	Launchers	Missiles
SCUD	1965	170 miles	1-10 kt.	661	1,200
SS-21	1976	9-75 miles	10,100 kt.	289	400
Frog-7B	1965	7-44 miles	1, 10 or 25 kt.	658	1,500

Other Nuclear Forces

The North Atlantic Treaty Organization also maintains 1,364 nuclear-capable aircraft, and has 400 U.S. sea-based nuclear weapons under its control. The British separately control 64 nuclear missile warheads deployed at sea. The French separately control 256 long-range, nuclear missile warheads, 48 short-range missiles, and 18 nuclear-capable aircraft. These British and French forces are expected to more than double by the mid-1990s. The United States wants to deploy a new, nuclear-tipped air-to-surface missile in Europe, and a new short-range missile.

The Warsaw Pact has roughly 2,349 nuclear-capable aircraft in Europe. Soviet long-range nuclear missiles are also capable of striking targets in Europe.

Note: These tallies do not include U.S. and Soviet missiles with a range between 300 and 3,000 miles, which are to be eliminated by June 1, 1991. Numbers of Soviet missiles are best rough estimates. U.S. officials believe the total number of Soviet short-range missiles is between 3,000 and 6,000, and that more than half have nuclear warheads.

Source: The Washington Post, May 31, 1989.

A NUCLEAR TUTORIAL[4]

The destructive potential of the nuclear arsenals possessed by the two superpowers is not easily grasped. Some turn to the World War II bombing of Hiroshima and Nagasaki for insight. Approximately 64,000 civilians died as a result of the Hiroshima bomb.[5] While they should never be forgotten, the bombings of Hiroshima and Nagasaki are probably not valid examples for us to use in anticipating the death and destruction that would accompany a possible future nuclear war.[6] Not only were the Hiroshima and Nagasaki bombs the only two in existence at the time, but also their destructive potential pales in significance when they are compared to those that exist today. The uranium bomb dropped on Hiroshima was 12.5 kilotons, and the plutonium bomb dropped on Nagasaki was equivalent to 22 kilotons. It is estimated that the combined strategic arsenals of the United States and the Soviet Union contain the destructive potential of approximately 1 million Hiroshimas. To capture more

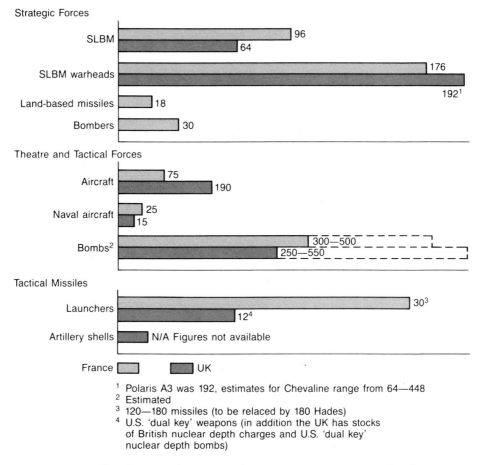

Figure 10.1 French and UK Nuclear Forces. (*Source:* Martin, Laurence, *The Changing Face of Nuclear Warfare* New York: Harper & Row, 1987).

clearly the nature of a nuclear attack, we will examine a hypothetical scenario involving an attack on one U.S. city by the Soviet Union. The scenario, casualty figures, and amount of physical destruction have been taken from a study done by the U.S. Office of Technology Assessment. The 1-megaton bomb that we will use as an example to illustrate the theoretical effects of a nuclear explosion is equivalent to 75 Hiroshima bombs.

The Effects of a 1-Megaton Explosion[7]

It is 11:08 P.M. on a Thursday evening in early January. The weather over Detroit is clear, with a visibility of 10 miles and winds from the southwest at 15 miles per hour. The lead story on the evening news deals with the fate of a tax reform bill in the Michigan legislature. The only international news item presented so far in the broadcast examines an ongoing disaster relief effort in Mexico, which suffered a major earthquake three days earlier.

Without warning, a 1-megaton nuclear warhead, launched from a Soviet submarine, detonates at ground level at the intersection of I-75 and I-94, virtually on top of the Detroit Civic Center and some 3 miles from the entrance to the Detroit-Windsor tunnel. This is the only bomb that explodes on Detroit. No other part of the United States is attacked.

The death and destruction brought on by the detonation of a nuclear warhead is a result of the way in which energy is released in a nuclear explosion. It needs to be stressed that these effects can only be calculated by making a series of arbitrary assumptions concerning such factors as the altitude at which the bomb was detonated, weather conditions, wind velocity, the geography, and the identity of the target. Before we look at the specifics involved in our scenario, we will present a theoretical overview of the type of damage that can be done by a 1-megaton explosion.

Fifty percent of the energy released by a nuclear blast is emitted as thermal radiation (heat) within 10 milliseconds of the explosion. On a clear day, a 1-megaton bomb could produce second- and third-degree burns over an area 7–8 miles from the blast site, ignite clothing up to 13 miles away, and produce retinal burns at distances of up to 53 miles. Second-degree burns over 25 percent of the body and third-degree burns over 30 percent of the body are generally considered to be fatal.

A shock wave traveling outward from the blast site at supersonic speeds is the second major component of a nuclear explosion. It is the overpressure (measured in pounds per square inch, or *psi*), produced by the instantaneous compression of air from the blast, that military strategists rely upon to destroy targets. A frame house will collapse at 5 psi, and a reinforced-concrete building will collapse at 100 psi. The hardness of a military target (its ability to withstand overpressure) determines the altitude at which a warhead must be detonated. Destroying a hard target (such as a Minuteman missile site) requires a near-to-earth explosion. Soft targets (such as government buildings, communications centers, and military bases) can be readily destroyed by detonating warheads high in the atmosphere. Ten seconds after detonation, the shock wave from a 1-megaton bomb has traveled 3 miles; 50 seconds after detonation, it has traveled about 12 miles from the blast site and is moving slightly faster than the speed of sound.

A 1-megaton bomb detonated at 6,000 feet would destroy every structure within a 2.7-mile radius; from 2.7 to 4 miles from the blast site, individual residences would be destroyed; from 4 to 7 miles from the blast site, there would be widespread damage; and finally, from 7 to 10 miles from the blast site, there would be only light damage to commercial structures. Almost no one in the inner 2.7-mile circle who was not in a blast shelter could survive such a blast. About one-half of the population located from 2.7 to 4 miles from the blast would be killed, largely as a result of falling buildings and flying debris. The greatest danger for people from 4 to 7 miles from the blast site would be from the fires that would probably burn for 24 hours and would consume one-half of all buildings. Moderate fatalities because of secondary effects of a nuclear explosion would occur in the 7–10-mile zone. Figure 10.2 shows

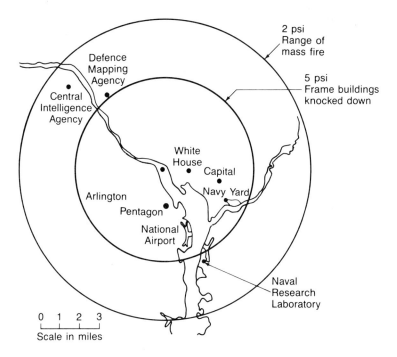

2 psi
Range of
mass fire

5 psi
Frame buildings
knocked down

Defence
Mapping
Agency

Central
Intelligence
Agency

White
House
Capital

Navy Yard

Arlington

Pentagon

National
Airport

Naval
Research
Laboratory

0 1 2 3
Scale in miles

Figure 10.2 Effects of a Single One-Megaton Airburst on the Washington, D.C., Area. (*Source:* Theodore Postol, "Targeting," in Ashton Carter, John Steinbruner, and Charles Zraket (eds.), *Managing Nuclear Options* Washington, D.C.: Brookings, 1987, p. 393.)

the area of destruction that would accompany the dropping of a single 1-megaton bomb at ground zero near the White House.

The damaging effect that large dosages of nuclear radiation have on living cells is the third major component of nuclear explosion. Severe illness sets in at about 200 rems, and a dose of 300 rems can be expected to kill about 10 percent of its victims. Exposure in the range of 600 rems over a 6- to 7-day period will be fatal to 90 percent of those who have been exposed. As we think about nuclear radiation, we need to make a distinction between prompt and residual radiation. Prompt radiation is given off in the first minute. Even exposures to smaller dosages of radiation have significant long-term health consequences. For example, a dose of 50 rems generally has no short-term effects, but over the long run, 0.4 to 2.5 percent of those who have been exposed to this level of radiation will die of cancer. A 1-megaton surface blast, with a constant 15-mile-per-hour wind and no precipitation, would expose 1,000 square miles to a total dosage of 900 rems and approximately 4,000 square miles to over 100 rems. The amount of residual radiation produced would depend upon the nature of the explosion. The greatest quantities of radiation are generated when the explosion is close to the surface of the earth (something necessary to destroy hard targets) because of the amount of debris sucked up by the explosion, which returns to earth as fallout. A 1-megaton surface blast will excavate a crater hundreds of meters in diameter and discharge between 100,000 and 600,00 tons of soil into the atmosphere. A 15-megaton explosion over Bikini Atoll in 1954 spread fallout with a substantial amount of contamination over more than 7,000 square miles.

The fourth component of a nuclear blast poses no direct threat to human survival, but it is capable of destroying virtually everything that relies upon solid-state electronics, including the control systems on airplanes and the guidance systems of missiles. An electromagnetic pulse (EMP) is a pulse of energy that produces an electric field of up to 50,000 volts per meter. In 1954, a 1.4-megaton bomb that detonated over Johnson Island set off burglar alarms and street lights on Oahu, some 800 miles away. It is estimated that a 1-megaton explosion 311 miles over Nebraska would create an EMP that would be powerful enough to shut down the electrical grid for the continental United States.

What It Means for Detroit

The hypothetical 1-megaton blast in downtown Detroit would excavate a crater about 1,000 feet in diameter and 200 feet in depth. Around its rim there would be an area of about 2,000 feet that would be covered with highly radioactive soil that would have been thrown out of the crater. Moving outward from ground zero, we could identify four rings: (1) 0–1.7 miles, (2) 1.7–2.7 miles, (3) 2.7–4.7 miles, and (4) 4.7–7.4 miles. These rings are superimposed over a map of Detroit in Figure 10.3.

Virtually none of the 70,000 people whose homes would be within the first ring would survive. Of the 250,000 people who would have homes 1.7–2.7 miles from ground zero, 130,000 could be expected to die and 100,000, injured. Most deaths would be due to collapsing buildings. The ratio of deaths to injuries would change dramatically in the third ring. Out of a population of 400,000, only 20,000 would die and 180,000 would suffer injuries. The greatest immediate danger to people at this distance would be fire, which would spread much more rapidly if the buildings were partially damaged rather than if they were completely flattened. Fires could be expected to continue for at least 24 hours and to consume about 50 percent of all buildings. An additional 150,000 injuries could be expected at a distance of 4.7–7.4 miles. Total estimated casualties in these four rings would number 220,000 dead and 430,000 injured. If the attack had occurred on a weekday during normal business hours, 130,000 deaths and 45,000 injuries would have to be added to these figures due to the larger downtown population at such times.

If we turn our attention from people to buildings, virtually nothing recognizable would be found within a radius of 0.6 miles. It would only be at the outer limits of the first ring that buildings, bridges, or other structures would remain standing. The overpressure in this first ring would be 12 psi. At a distance of 1.7–2.7 miles from the blast, the overpressure would be 5 psi. Commercial and multistory residential buildings would have their walls completely blown out. Individual residences would be totally destroyed. In the third ring, low residential buildings would be destroyed. Depending upon their construction, large buildings would lose windows, interior partitions, and possibly upper floors would be blown off. Damage to heavy industrial plants, such as the Cadillac plant, would be severe, and most planes and hangars at

Figure 10.3 One Megaton Surface Burst in Detroit, Michigan. (Source: Office of Technology Assessment, *The Effects of Nuclear War* Washington, D.C.: Office of Technology Assessment, 1980, p. 29)

the Detroit City Airport would be destroyed. Overpressure in the third ring would be 2 psi. In the outermost ring, commercial buildings would suffer only light damage and residential buildings would suffer moderate damage, as the force of the overpressure would be only 1 psi.

The capacity of buildings to withstand a nuclear explosion would be of vital significance if medical aid were to be given to the survivors. Thermal burns would now pose a life-threatening danger for those who had survived the nuclear attack: Of the 120,000 in the second ring who would be alive, 1,200 would eventually die from burns, given a 10-mile visibility at the time of the attack; of the 380,000 survivors in the third ring, 3,800 would eventually die; and of the 600,000 survivors in the fourth ring, 2,600 would eventually die and 3,000 would suffer burn injuries. Had the attack occurred on a weekend afternoon during the summer, the figures would be far worse due to the large number of people who would have been outdoors and unshielded from the effects of the blast. For example, in the second ring, instead of 1,200 eventual deaths due to burns, the number would be closer to 30,000, and, in the third ring, the number would jump from 3,800 to 95,000.

Providing medical aid to these people would be no easy task. In 1980, the area in and surrounding Detroit had 63 hospitals containing approximately 18,000 beds. Fifty-five percent of those beds were within the first two rings and now would be completely destroyed. Only 5,000 beds lay outside the region where major damage would have taken place, and they would be enough to treat only 1 percent of the injured. In 1977, the entire United States had only 85 specialized burn centers, and they had a capacity to service only 1,000–2,000 cases. Transportation of the sick and wounded out of Detroit would be difficult because of the debris clogging the streets and the damaged motor vehicles. The blast would have destroyed all automobiles parked anywhere in the second ring and would have made most heavier commercial vehicles, such as fire trucks and tow trucks, useless. Initial recovery operations would also have to take place in the absence of electricity, water, and gas. Service from these utilities could be restored with surprising speed, because most of the key plants would be relatively far removed from ground zero and because in this scenario only Detroit would have been attacked. Help could therefore be expected from other municipalities, states, and Canada. Because winds had been from the southwest, clean-up efforts at the Detroit airport would not be able to begin for approximately two weeks because of the fallout.

The outward movement of radioactive fallout away from the blast could vary greatly. The idealized pattern is that of an elongated feather, with its base located at ground zero. Within it, we could identify four zones, based upon how much radiation would have accumulated over a seven-day period: 3,000 rems, 900 rems, 300 rems, and 90 rems. As we can see from Figure 10.4, in our scenario, it would spread over sparsely populated farmlands in Canada. If the winds were from the northwest, then fallout would be distributed over Cleveland, Youngstown, and Pittsburgh. People in the first contour in the map in Figure 10.4 (3,000 rems) who had stayed and had not found shelter would receive a fatal dose of radiation within one week. People in the second contour (900 rems) would become very sick from radiation if they had stayed indoors and would probably receive a fatal exposure if they had spent much time outdoors. In the third contour (300 rems), people would become sick and run a high

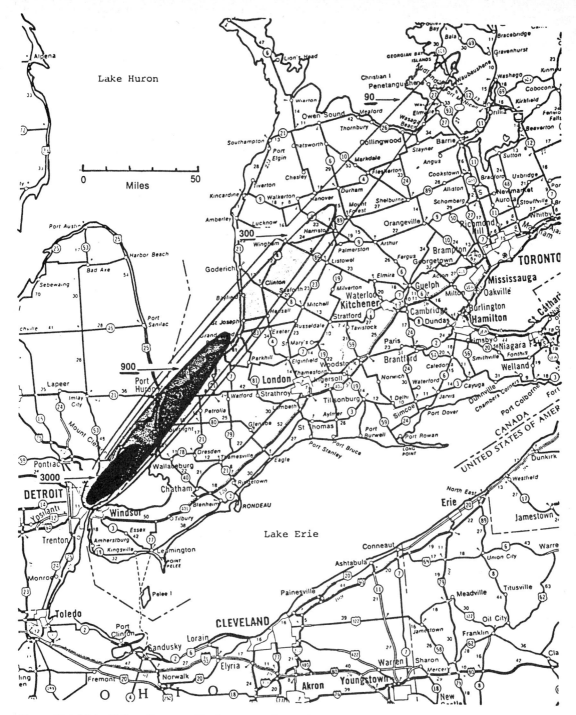

Figure 10.4 Main Fallout Pattern—Uniform 15 mph Southwest Wind (1-Megaton Surface Burst in Detroit). (Contours for 7-Day Accumulated Dose (Without Shielding) of 3,000, 900, 300, and 90 Rem.) (*Source:* Office of Technology Assessment, *The Effects of Nuclear War* Washington, D.C.: Office of Technology Assessment, 1980, p. 24.)

risk of succumbing to other deadly diseases. In the fourth contour (90 rems), people would suffer few immediate visible effects, but they would have a shortened life expectancy because of an increased risk of cancer.

The consequences of a nuclear war, even one involving only a single 1-megaton bomb, would not necessarily end here. Many fear that the sunlight-blocking action of the dust particles raised into the atmosphere by a nuclear explosion, along with the smoke from the fires that would break out, would have a major impact on the earth's climatic patterns. The resulting "nuclear winter" would threaten all survivors with cold, starvation, and shortages of fresh water.[8] One recent study speculated that a nuclear war, in which only one-half of the world's nuclear arsenal was used, would result in an 18–55-degree Fahrenheit temperature drop in most of North America and Eurasia. If the war occurred just before or during the growing season, virtually all plants in the Northern Hemisphere would be killed or damaged. Continued cold temperatures and the loss of sunlight could hold dire consequences for the size of future harvests. Figure 10.5 presents one expert's view of the long-term effects of a nuclear war on such crucial issues as medical supplies, contagious diseases, food shortages, and psychiatric disorders.

DETERRENCE: HOW DOES IT WORK?

Above all else, deterrence is designed to prevent a nuclear war that would transform this hypothetical scenario into a real case study. However, deterrence cannot be willed into existence or simply assumed to exist. Instead, it rests on the successful integration of three elements: capability, credibility, and communication. A state's deterrence capability has two parts. First, it must possess the means of inflicting an unacceptable level of damage on a potential attacker. Second, it must possess a strategy for using its weapons that makes sense, given its deterrence goals and weapons. Credibility can be translated as "believability." A potential attacker must come to believe that a state has the will to carry out its deterrence strategy, regardless of the consequences for itself or the global community. Finally, both a state's capabilities and its resolve to carry out its deterrence strategy must be communicated to a potential attacker. If a state assumes that the opponent thinks as it does or that the opponent understands what it is saying, this can be an invitation to disaster. The United States took it for granted that the presence of the heart of its Pacific fleet in Pearl Harbor was a deterrent—that a Japanese attack would occur in the Philippines or somewhere else. From the Japanese perspective, because U.S forces were concentrated there, Pearl Harbor was the only logical point of attack. Attacking anywhere else would have left intact the U.S. retaliatory capability.

Deterrence Strategies

In selecting a deterrence strategy, a state must make a number of fundamental choices. A traditional starting point used in distinguishing between deterrence strategies is the possession of a first- or second-strike posture. In a *first-strike* strategy, a state seeks to deter a potential attacker because a state threatens to attack first in a

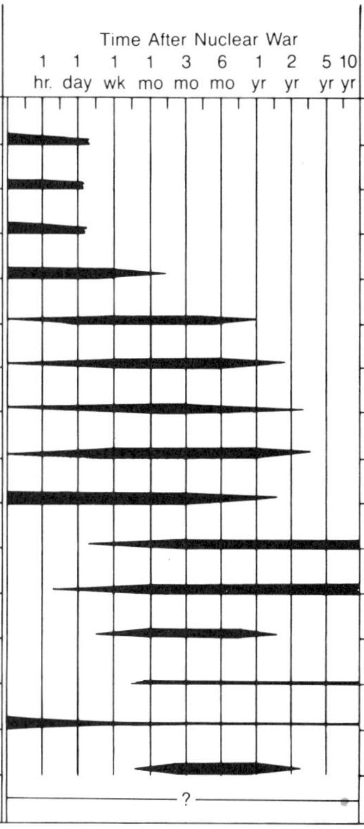

Effect	Time After Nuclear War 1 hr.	1 day	1 wk	1 mo	3 mo	6 mo	1 yr	2 yr	5 yr	10 yr	U.S./S.U. Population at Risk	N.H. Population at Risk	S.H. Population at Risk	Casualty Rate Those at Risk	Potential Global Deaths
Blast											H	M	L	H	M–H
Thermal radiation											H	M	L	M	M–H
Prompt ionizing radiation											L	L	L	H	L–M
Fires											M	M	L	M	M
Toxic gases											M	M	L	L	L
Dark											H	H	M	L	L
Cold											H	H	H	H	M–H
Frozen water supplies											H	H	M	M	M
Fallout ionizing radiation											H	H	L–M	M	M–H
Food shortages											H	H	H	H	H
Medical system collapse											H	H	M	H	M
Contagious diseases											M	M	L	H	M
Epidemics and pandemics											H	H	M	M	M
Psychiatric disorders											H	H	L	L	L–M
Increased surface ultraviolet light											H	H	M	?	?
Synergisms					?						?	?	?	?	?

H—Heavy
L —Light
M—Moderate
? —Something else

Figure 10.5 Possible Long Term Effects of a Nuclear War. (*Source:* Carl Sagan, "Nuclear Winter and Climatic Collapse," *Foreign Affairs* 62 1983/84, p. 262.)

conflict situation. It envisions a massive use of force that makes it impossible for the potential attacker to retaliate with a nuclear strike of its own. In a *second-strike* strategy, a state seeks to prevent war through the possession of a nuclear force that is capable of absorbing an enemy's nuclear attack and of retaliating with so much force that an unacceptable level of damage could be inflicted upon the attacking state. How much retaliatory damage must a state be able to inflict in order to deter an enemy from attacking first? No one knows for sure. Historically, the United States has stressed the need to inflict an overwhelming amount of damage in a retaliatory attack. Robert McNamara, who was the secretary of defense under Presidents Kennedy and Johnson initially put the figure at 25 percent of the Soviet population and 50 percent of Soviet industry. President Carter's Secretary of Defense Harold Brown defined it in terms of the ability to destroy the 200 largest Soviet cities. This would kill 34 percent of the Soviet population and lay waste to 62 percent of the Soviet industrial base.

Where U.S. strategists have stressed the need for a large second-strike force,

French strategy has held that all that is required to deter an attack is the possession of a small nuclear force capable of destroying a carefully selected target list within the attacking state. Not only would the threat of less than a near total amount of damage deter the Soviet Union from attacking France, but also, French strategists have argued, a minimum size French nuclear force would be a more credible nuclear deterrent for this purpose than would a large U.S. force. They have argued that only the leadership of a country faced with the prospect of a nuclear war could credibly threaten nuclear retaliation. Charles de Gaulle, longtime president of France and one of the key figures in the development of the French nuclear force, defended its credibility this way:

> Once reaching a certain nuclear capability . . . the proportion of respective means has no absolute value. In fact, since a man and country can die only once, deterrence exists as soon as one man can mortally wound the potential aggressor and is fully resolved to do so, and he is well convinced of it.[9]

Some strategists argue for the adoption of nuclear strategies that move away from the shared presumption of first- and second-strike strategies that deterrence is best achieved by threatening to inflict an unacceptable level of damage on the potential attacker. They believe that such threats are simply not credible to deter anything but a large-scale enemy attack. What is needed are strategies that are flexible enough so that a state can respond effectively to any level of threat. The umbrella term currently used for these strategies is *limited strategic options.* Included among them are strategies calling for the limited first use of nuclear weapons. According to this line of thought, a nuclear war will not be a short-lived affair, nor will each side simply launch all of its missiles at the other side in one gigantic, almost spasmotic, exchange. It may last weeks or months. Thus, the threatened opening salvo in such a war could take many forms, ranging from a demonstration strike on one city (as in our Detroit example) or military installation, to a significant but still less-than-total attack on the enemy's military forces and command centers.

A second basic choice is the selection of a target list. In theory, two broad options exist. First, a state can adopt a *counterforce* posture, in which it targets the potential attacker's offensive weapons systems that are capable of striking its homeland and its command and control support systems. Second, a state can adopt a *countervalue* posture. In this posture, the potential attacker's population and economic infrastructure are targeted and held "hostage." The rational, potential attacker is assumed to be deterred by the knowledge that, no matter how successful its initial use of nuclear weapons may be, large portions of the potential attacker's urban areas would be destroyed in any nuclear exchange. Targets cannot be selected independent from the basic posture being followed (i.e., first strike, second strike, limited nuclear options). The primary targets for a first-strike attack must be segments of the enemy's offensive nuclear forces and its command and control systems. To allocate too many weapons for any other purpose increases the possibility that enough of the opponent's weapons will survive to inflict serious damage on its own society. On the other hand, if a state has adopted a second-strike deterrence posture, focusing too heavily on counterforce targeting is dangerous. The state runs the risk of blowing up empty holes in the ground, because the missile sites that it has targeted no longer contain missiles. They have been used to attack it. Accordingly, countervalue targets receive primary emphasis in second-strike strategies.

Limited strategic-options strategies tend to have a more varied target list. They are neither purely counterforce nor countervalue in nature but lean heavily toward the former. (As can be readily appreciated, in practice, the theoretical distinction between counterforce and countervalue targets is difficult to maintain, because key economic, administrative, and political targets are frequently located in and around cities). The almost infinitely large number of potential military targets allows for far greater fine-tuning of nuclear options than do attacks on cities of different sizes or locations. Moreover, nuclear explosions of any magnitude on population centers are unlikely to bring forward a measured response from the attacked state. The targets most frequently added to a pure counterforce target relate to key Soviet economic and administrative assets. At the same time, logic dictates that countervalue attacks cannot be completely ruled out because it would free a state's population from being held hostage while leaving its own still subject to "the hostage effect." Were this the case, the enemy might still feel it had an incentive to strike first, no matter how flexible its counterforce-oriented targeting policy might be.

A third choice centers on whether or not it makes sense for a state to add a defensive component to its deterrence strategy. Should it try and protect its society or its retaliatory weapons systems from an enemy attack? For two reasons, the traditional answer given to civilian defense is no. First, a system of civilian defense (fallout shelters, evacuation plans, etc.) is seen as being so impractical or so costly that it is not worth the money. Second, it is seen as destabilizing. When both sides are able to hold the other's population hostage in a retaliatory second-strike attack, *mutual assured destruction* (MAD) is said to exist. Advocates of MAD see it as a stabilizing factor in world politics, because it denies both sides an incentive for going first. By definition, anything that makes a population less vulnerable or threatens the survivability of a state's retaliatory forces is destabilizing. Proponents of MAD thus objected to President Reagan's original vision of his "Star Wars" program as a population shield because they felt that it violated the requirement that populations must always be vulnerable to a retaliatory nuclear attack. In the abstract, a state that possesses such a shield might be tempted to use its nuclear weapons, feeling that the attacked state could not mount a retaliatory strike against its homeland. In contrast, they endorsed scaled-down versions of the plan that were designed to protect ICBM sites from attack because they added to the requirement of invulnerable retaliatory forces. On the other hand, defensive measures are central to the success of a first-strike or limited strategic-options strategy. Without some ability to restrict the damage that can be inflicted upon its own society or military forces, it makes little sense for a state to get into situations that call for protracted wars or limited nuclear exchanges.

Credibility

While the fundamental credibility problem is the same for any deterrence strategy (i.e., it is believable), credibility takes different forms, depending on the goal being pursued. We can distinguish two types of deterrence situations: One in which an attack is a distinct possibility (immediate deterrence) and one in which there is a more imprecise and widespread fear that the opponent might use force to gain an advantage should the opportunity for success present itself (general deterrence).[10] The essence of the credibility problem of immediate deterrence is, given a situation in which the danger of war is imminent, how does one state convince another state that it cannot and will not back down, even if it means mutual suicide? The problem of establishing this type of credibility increases as the coverage of deterrence is extended further and further away from the state's own territory. Few would doubt the credibility of American threats intended to deter an attack on the United States, but what of attacks on Western Europe, Japan, Israel, Korea, or Saudi Arabia? A public opinion poll in 1986 revealed that the American public was not nearly as interested in protecting these areas as were American leaders.[11]

Often, such pledges of support are written into a treaty (as is the case with NATO) or take the form of highly visible public statements of the United States (as with Israel). Most observers feel that this is not enough to guarantee the credibility of extended deterrence, because the history of world politics is littered with broken treaties and promises. More effective would be setting up a "trip wire," an imaginary line that, once broken, automatically brings about an American military response. The United States currently has trip wires in place in Western Europe and South Korea. They take the form of U.S. troops that are stationed in the path of a possible Soviet or North Korean invasion. Their numbers are too small to repel the attack itself, but the death of these troops would leave an American president with virtually no choice but to join the fighting. To do otherwise would be political suicide. Clear communications are a crucial part of setting up a trip wire, because not every placement of U.S. troops overseas serves this purpose. For example, troops are often dispatched to defend an ally, to make a symbolic statement, or to engage in a training exercise.

The core of the credibility problem of general deterrence lies in the lack of trust between states and has its roots in the necessity of making decisions about weapons systems and strategies under conditions of uncertainty. To protect themselves from the worst possible outcome, policymakers feel that they have no choice but constantly to seek more military power. The problem is that, while every added increment of military power makes policymakers in state A feel more secure, it also has the effect of undermining the ability of state B's military forces to deter an attack. Operating under the same conditions of uncertainty and mistrust, policymakers in state B feel that they have no choice but to upgrade their military capability. The net result is an arms race in which forces that originally were intended to deter a potential threat have the paradoxical outcome of increasing the level of military preparedness in the enemy state, thus calling into question the credibility of a state's own deterrence strategy.

Communication

As we have discussed at several points throughout this text, communicating with leaders in other states is often a highly problematic undertaking. Cultural and bureaucratic factors, as well as time constraints, often produce perceptual distortions that result in unintended surprises. Inherent uncertainty over the correct interpretation of data also plays an important part in this problem. Major events simply do not come in nice neat packages, nor do they automatically become more understandable as information accumulates. In fact, it is often only through hindsight that we can distinguish between the important bits of information from the natural clutter of useless information that surrounds all events.[12]

To better ensure that clear communication occurs during deterrence situations, the United States and the Soviet Union have entered into a number of cooperative ventures, beginning with the 1963 agreement to establish the "Hot Line" (a direct communications link between Moscow and Washington). More recently, considerable interest has been expressed in the establishment of crisis management or risk reduction centers. Such centers could be used to provide virtually instantaneous communications between military, diplomatic, and political leaders in times of high tension and would be intended to reduce the risk of nuclear war due to accident, miscalculation, or misunderstanding.[13] In 1987, a treaty establishing Nuclear Risk Reduction Centers in Washington and Moscow was signed by the United States and the Soviet Union. Unlike some other schemes, they are not intended to serve as crisis management centers. Their purpose is to serve as a point of information exchange and government-to-government notifications that are specified in existing arms control agreements.

A new twist has been added to the communications problem with the interest in limited strategic options. Communication with the enemy must be maintained throughout the fighting, *and* communication must also be maintained with a state's own forces so that they can be used in a purposeful fashion. In the past, the focus was on ensuring the clarity of U.S.-Soviet communications before war broke out. A concern for the ability to communicate with the opponent under wartime conditions has led many to advocate rejecting targeting policies that call for "decapitating" the enemy's leadership structure. Rather than crippling the military effectiveness of the enemy's response, critics maintain that it would only exacerbate the problem of control by forcing local military authorities to make uniform decisions about whether or not to use the nuclear weapons under their control. Virtually all observers agree that, in its present form, the U.S. command, control, communications, intelligence system C^3I cannot accomplish this second task under wartime conditions. In simplified form, what is needed is a "shoot-look-shoot" capability. The United States must be able to fire nuclear weapons at Soviet targets in a controlled fashion, evaluate the amount of damage inflicted, assess the consequences of a Soviet counterattack, and use this information to retarget surviving U.S. forces against a revised list of Soviet targets. The cycle then would repeat itself.

U.S. DETERRENCE STRATEGY

It is an often noted phenomenon in world politics that great differences can exist between what states say their foreign policy is and what they actually do. Nuclear deterrence strategies are no exception to this rule. In the following two sections, we will provide an overview of U.S. and Soviet strategic thought. In each case, our concern will be with the fit between what each state says it will do (its declaratory strategy) and what it is actually planning or prepared to do (its deployment strategy).

U.S. Declaratory Deterrence Strategy

U.S. strategists have shown little interest in pursuing a first-strike strategy. The controlling debate has been between advocates of second-strike and the limited strategic-options strategies. Recognition that nuclear weapons were unique came very slowly. It was only in the mid-1950s that nuclear strategy per se came into its own as a field of study. Up until then, U.S. planning for World War III was based on the assumption that it would be a compressed replay of World War II: Long-range bombers would deliver their payloads on the enemy's industrial and population centers; atomic weapons would be used first, and, when they were exhausted, conventional bombs would be used.

The Eisenhower administration put forward the first fully articulated strategy for the use of nuclear weapons that acknowledged their unique nature. It emphasized their deterrent function. The doctrine of *massive retaliation* pledged the United States to respond with nuclear weapons, if need be, to communist aggression around the world "at times and in places of our choosing." The United States had the capability to execute such a threat. It possessed a significant advantage in nuclear weaponry, and while the Soviet threat to the United States was not negligible, it did not match the potential U.S. threat to the Soviet Union. ICBMs did not yet exist. It would be easier for the United States to attack the Soviet Union with manned bombers, because U.S. bombers could attack Soviet targets from bases in Europe. The principal weakness of massive retaliation is its lack of credibility. Critics argued that it simply was not believable that the United States would launch a massive attack against the Soviet Union because an ally had been attacked with conventional weapons. Many also questioned the wisdom of being so vague over what constituted a trip wire or of implying that the trip wire was everywhere.

The dual Soviet successes in 1957 of launching Sputnik and an intercontinental ballistic missile added a new dimension to the ongoing debate on the merits of massive retaliation. It was now only a matter of time until the United States would itself be very vulnerable to a Soviet nuclear attack. The Kennedy administration replaced the doctrine of massive retaliation with that of *flexible response*. It was now held that the Soviet Union would be deterred, not through the threat of a large-scale attack, but by the knowledge that the United States possessed a wide range of nuclear and nonnuclear options from which it could choose to respond to an act of aggression. Nuclear options were envisioned as growing out of a strategy of controlled response, wherein the selection of nuclear weapons and targets would be tailored to the importance of the political objectives at stake in the conflict. In terms of our earlier discussion, flexible response seeks to deter war by giving the United States limited nuclear options and a war-fighting capacity.

The Johnson administration jettisoned flexible response and replaced it with *assured destruction*. Once again, the United States sought to deter the Soviet Union by threatening to destroy its population and industrial centers. The Cuban missile crisis was largely responsible for this change in outlook. The way in which the crisis was played out strongly suggested that a type of nuclear "firebreak" existed. All of the fine gradations in level and type of nuclear options paled in significance to the absolute nature of nuclear deterrence and the prospect of nuclear war. U.S. policy-makers were no longer convinced that nuclear war could be controlled. The purpose of assured destruction was to raise the nuclear firebreak as high as possible. Assured destruction was not, however, a return to massive retaliation. It neither tried to extend the U.S. deterrent shield to cover all types of Soviet aggression nor to be vague on what the United States was prepared to do. Assured destruction promised that, in the event of a Soviet attack on the United States, U.S. nuclear forces would retaliate against Soviet population centers in a large-scale countervalue attack.

The late 1950s and early 1960s were the golden age of U.S. strategic thought. The one major change in U.S. deterrent strategy since then came when the Nixon administration replaced the second-strike doctrine of assured destruction (which it relabeled *strategic sufficiency*, in recognition of the fact that nuclear parity now existed) with the strategy of *flexible targeting*. As its name implies, thisstrategy represented a return to an emphasis on counterforce targeting and controlled nuclear responses, characteristic of a limited strategic-options deterrent posture. Developments since then have largely been variations on a theme. Successive administrations have changed the label attached to U.S. deterrent strategy largely for political and symbolic purposes. For example, Carter's countervailing strategy essentially replicated Nixon's doctrine of flexible response. Both are limited strategic-options defensive postures, designed to deter the Soviet Union through the possession of a warfighting capability. Carter's doctrine, formally contained in Presidential Directive 59, merely brought to the public's attention and made official the change in thought that had begun under Nixon. Reagan only modified Carter's strategic doctrine at the margins. His administration placed added emphasis on damage limitation measures, stressed the need to be prepared to "endure" a long nuclear confrontation, and formally stated that the goal of the United States in a nuclear confrontation with the Soviet Union was to "prevail."

U.S. Deployment Policy

The changes in U.S. declaratory deterrence policy first outlined implies that repeated and simultaneous changes took place in U.S. targeting policy. A review of U.S. deployment policy suggests that this has not been the case. The classification of targets has remained constant, as has the inclination to plan for the use of all available weapons. What has changed is the number of preplanned attack options from which policymakers can choose.

During the 1950s, each military command developed plans for using those weapons under its control. Three types of targets were identified: nuclear capable, other military, and urban-industrial. In 1956, the Strategic Air Command had selected 2,997 targets. In 1960, the Eisenhower administration approved the creation of a National Strategy Target List (NSTL) and a Single Integrated Operations Plan (SIOP) after war games indicated that over 300 duplicate targets existed. The first NSTL

Table 10.4   THE U.S. SHIP

1. *Nongenerated Options Plan:* 3,840 weapons would be expected to arrive on Soviet targets.

Nuclear targets	1,761
Other military targets	935
Leadership targets	423
Economic and industrial targets	2,300 (1,793 aim points)
Total targets	5,419

2. *Generated Options Plan:* 7,160 weapons would be expected to arrive on Soviet targets.

Nuclear targets	2,018
Other military targets	1,603
Leadership targets	736
Economic and industrial targets	4,400 (3,572 aim points)
Total targets	8,757

Source: U.S. Arms Control and Disarmament Agency, *Effectiveness of Soviet Civil Defense in Limiting Damage to Population,* ACDA Civil Defense Study Report No. 1 (Washington D.C.: November 1977), pp. 18–20.

identified 2,600 separate targets and 1,050 ground zeros from an overall list of 4,100 targets. Only 151 of these targets were urban-industrial in nature. Plans called for launching all 3,500 nuclear warheads if time permitted. If sufficient warning was not available to do this, then an alert force of 800 bombers and missiles would attack approximately 650 designated ground zeros. Chief of Naval Operations Admiral Arleigh Burke noted how ill-suited the emerging SIOP was for U.S. deterrence purposes: "Counterforces receives higher precedence than is warranted for a retaliatory plan, and less precedence than is warranted for an initiative plan."[14]

In putting together SIOP-63, President Kennedy's Secretary of Defense Robert McNamara combined the three target categories into five basic attack options, each of which could be further modified: Soviet nuclear delivery forces; Soviet military forces and resources located away from cities; command and control centers; Soviet military forces and resources near cities; and an all-out attack. In spite of the identification of flexible response as a second-strike posture, the SIOP included provisions for executing a preemptive strike. It also appears that it was put together in such a way that all U.S. weapons would be used rather than one that was tailored to meet the needs of the policy laid down by the Kennedy administration. When McNamara abandoned flexible response for assured destruction, there was no indication that this SIOP would ever be reworked.

Put forward by the Reagan administration in 1983, SIOP-6 currently is still in force. It contains some 50,000 potential targets (up from the 25,000 in SIOP-5). The targets are divided into four principal groups and organized around four scenarios. The number of targets far outstrips the capacity of the U.S. nuclear arsenal. At best, only about 20 percent could be hit. One official study has estimated that, if U.S. forces were to be on a generated alert status, more than 8,500 targets would be destroyed. Approximately 5,400 would be destroyed in a nongenerated alert situation. Table 10.4 presents the projected breakdown of targets for each scenario. Press reports during the summer of 1989 indicated that the Bush administration was following through with the development of SIOP-7, which was begun in the last year of the Reagan administration.[15] Central to it is an unprecedented emphasis on decapitation attacks on Soviet leadership targets in the early phases of a war.

SOVIET DETERRENCE STRATEGY

Soviet Declaratory Strategy

U.S. and Soviet deterrence strategies are neither identical nor easily compared. In large measure this is because, unlike Western writings on deterrence, which tend to use the terms "doctrine" and "strategy" interchangeably, Soviet commentators assign these terms very precise and distinct meanings. Military doctrine is the official view of the type of warfare that the Soviet military must be prepared to fight and the political purposes of that war. Its content is set by the Communist party leadership and tends to be quite stable. When change has occurred, it has been a result of major political or military developments, such as the death of a leader or a shift in nuclear balance. Military strategy is part of military science and is concerned with the theory and practice of preparing for and waging war. The purpose of Soviet military strategy is to ensure that the Soviet military is prepared to fight the type of war anticipated by its military doctrine. Strategy is thus subordinate to doctrine (in the sense that doctrine determines the problem that strategy must solve), but, at the same time, along with political and economic factors, it is an important influence in the formation of that doctrine.

Early Soviet writings on nuclear strategy were greatly concerned with the possibility of a surprise nuclear attack on the Soviet Union and with the nature of a future war in Europe. The surprise-nuclear-attack scenario dominated Soviet writings throughout the 1950s and for much of the 1960s. In 1955, a Soviet military journal contained an article that stated that "surprise attack with the massive employment of new weapons can cause the rapid collapse of a government whose capacity to resist is low as a consequence of radical faults in its social and economic structure. . . . the duty of the Soviet Armed Forces is not to permit an enemy a surprise attack on our country. . . ."[16] While it is still frequently written about, a surprise attack is no longer held by the Soviet Union to be the most probable path to nuclear war. An important reason for this change in outlook is its nuclear parity with the U.S.[17] As the Soviets see it, parity has made war less likely because it raises the cost to the United States of either threatening the Soviet Union with nuclear weapons or of using those weapons to further U.S. foreign-policy objectives. Soviet writings about the next war in Europe argued that escalation from conventional to nuclear war was inevitable. Over time, a softening in the language has occurred: nuclear war went from being "inevitable," to "most likely," and then to "probable." By the mid-1970s, Soviet writings voiced the possibility that a conventional war in Europe might remain just that—a possibility.[18] Warsaw Pact military exercises, however, continue to be structured around scenarios in which the threat of a NATO nuclear strike is present, and many scenarios simulate escalation to actual nuclear exchange. The most frequently discussed scenario pictures conventional war escalating directly into a full-scale nuclear conflict. This is expected to happen anywhere from 10 to 15 days after the beginning of hostilities and to be brought on by a significant loss of territory or forces by NATO.

Contemporary Soviet strategic thinking contains several important themes. Among them are:[19]

1. *The best deterrent is an effective war-fighting capability.* Soviet writers assume that the rationality of the enemy cannot be counted upon to prevent a war. Because of this, the Soviet Union has given considerable attention to questions of civil defense and damage limitation. Experts disagree on the effectiveness of these systems and the extent to which the Soviet leadership has faith in them.

2. *Theoretically, victory is possible.* This point almost logically follows from the first. It does not follow, however, that the Soviet Union wants war or prefers war over peace. Even with their civil defense programs and damage limitation measures, the Soviets do not believe that victory would be easily achieved or that the Soviet Union would escape tremendous destruction.

3. *It pays to strike first.* The importance of surprise, initiative, and momentum are prominent themes in Soviet writings. Soviet writings, however, do not speak in terms of a first-strike attack. As in a first-strike attack, a Soviet preemptive strike would be targeted on military objectives. There is, however, no expectation that this would be a disarming strike that would leave the United States crippled and unable to respond with a nuclear attack of its own. The stated purpose of a preemptive strike is to cut Soviet losses— to limit the damage that the soon-to-be-launched American nuclear attack could inflict on it. The importance of preemption in Soviet writings recently appears to have declined.

4. *Restraint is foolhardy.* Once deterrence fails, the purpose of strategy is to defeat the enemy as quickly as possible. Soviet writings give little attention to such Western concepts as crisis management, limited war, or escalation control.

5. *Numbers matter.* Soviet writings specify neither a minimal nor an ideal number of weapons that must be possessed for deterrence to work. What Soviet military planners do appear to want is to have as many weapons at their disposal as possible. The emphasis on large inventories exists across the entire spectrum of nuclear and conventional forces. It is especially notable in the Soviet tendency not to "retire" an old weapons system when it has been overtaken by a more modern one (as is done by the United States) but to keep both the new and the old weapon in their inventory.

Many observers feel that the preconditions necessary for a shift in Soviet doctrine are now in place. In particular, they point to domestic difficulties, the reform agenda of Mikhail Gorbachev, and the call for "new political thinking" on security matters. The long-term impact of many of the ideas that are now being debated is difficult to determine because they are so closely associated with Gorbachev's bid to consolidate his power base. Should that bid fail or his stay as General Secretary be short-lived, then the new political thinking may amount to nothing more than a brief footnote in the development of Soviet doctrine. By mid-1987, six basic threads in

Gorbachev's new political thinking had emerged.[20] Three of them can be said to represent potentially significant departures from previous doctrinal pronouncements. The remaining ones accentuate existing trends, build upon current concepts, or are still too vague in their presentation to allow for even a preliminary judgment about their importance.

One potentially significant change is the added emphasis that is being given to the possibility of accidental war. All but ignored in Soviet writings for a long time, it is now held to be a likely path to nuclear war. In a second departure from tradition, Soviet security is no longer viewed in a zero-sum context. Instead of being brought about by increasing the insecurity of the United States, Soviet security is now being talked about as inevitably linked with U.S. and global security. Also potentially significant is the concept of "defensive defense." It calls for creating a Soviet military force structure that, while it would be capable of conducting a strategy of offensive denial, would be incapable of threatening the enemy's territory. Historically, Soviet forces have been prepared to go deep into enemy territory as part of its "defensive" strategy.

Soviet Deployment Policy

As can well be imagined, far less is known about Soviet deployment decisions than about U.S. deployment decisions. One researcher has put together a set of likely Soviet target sets and has combined them into a plausible "Russian Integrated Strategic Operational Plan (RISOP).[21] Based on Soviet military doctrine, Desmond Ball expects Soviet nuclear forces to be used massively and against a wide array of targets. Urban areas would not be attacked simply to produce some minimum number of casualties, but they would not be avoided either if they contained or were near important targets. He identifies five target categories: (1) enemy military forces, particularly strategic nuclear forces; (2) theater nuclear weapons and associated systems; (3) other military targets, such as large ground troop-and-tank concentrations; (4) political-administrative targets; and (5) economic-industrial facilities. Table 10.5 indicates how the RISOP might have looked in 1982 under two alternative scenarios: when Soviet forces are intact and on high alert (generated) and when they have suffered a U.S. counterforce attack (nongenerated). After examining Soviet military planning literature, military histories, and force structure and deployment data, another researcher concludes that there is no single Soviet strategy for waging nuclear war and that, just as in the United States, the Soviet RISOP would offer policymakers a series of graduated options from which to choose, depending upon the circumstances. These options appear to include: preemption, launch on tactical warning, launch under attack, and second strike.[22]

There are also indications that a less-than-perfect fit between declaratory and deployment strategy also exists in the Soviet Union. For example, policymakers in the United States have worried a great deal about either a surprise Soviet nuclear attack or a Soviet preemptive attack. However, even though the percentage of Soviet ICBM forces on day-to-day alert status has increased over time, Soviet strategic forces are operationally incapable of instigating these types of attack. No Soviet strategic bombers are kept on alert status, only a small fraction of Soviet SLBMs would

Table 10.5 ALLOCATION OF SOVIET RISOP WARHEADS TO TARGET CATEGORIES IN GENERATED AND NONGENERATED SITUATIONS, JULY 1982

	Generated	Nongenerated
Baseline force	7,420	7,420
Weapons deliverable to target	4,840	3,352
Target category		
Strategic C^{3}I targets	400	400
U.S. SIOP forces	2,302	2,302
French and British strategic nuclear forces	80	80
Theater nuclear forces capable of hitting the Soviet Union	250	250
U.S.-NATO conventional power projection forces	200	50
U.S.-NATO administrative-governmental targets	150	50
U.S.-NATO economic-industrial, war supporting, and economic recovery targets	1,250	200
Reserve warheads, including warheads allocated to targets in China	208	20

Source: Reprinted by permission of the publisher. From *The Soviet Calculus of Nuclear War,* edited by Roman Kolkowicz and Ellen Propper Michkiewicz (Lexington, Mass: Lexington Books, D.C. Heath and Company). Copyright 1986, D.C. Heath and Company.

be available for use because of the low on-station rates of Soviet submarines, and the Soviet civil defense system requires at least one week start-up time if it is to protect Soviet industrial targets from retaliation.[23] U.S. intelligence collection and early warning systems would be able to detect changes in the readiness levels of all of these areas.

NUCLEAR COMPELLENCE

In a strategy of compellence, a state uses nuclear weapons to realize political objectives by getting the enemy to stop what it is doing or to force it to do something that it otherwise would not do. William Kincade argues that nuclear compellence has been a recurring tactic in U.S.-Soviet relations. In the 1950s, both the United States and the Soviet Union unsuccessfully engaged in nuclear compellence. He notes that, when paired with such other elements of Eisenhower's foreign policy toward the Soviet bloc as "rolling back the iron curtain," massive retaliation contains a veiled compellent threat: Stop engaging in aggression and supporting subversion, or else we will attack with our nuclear forces. As support for this hidden agenda, he cites Secretary of State John Foster Dulles' comment after *Sputnik* and the Soviet Union's testing of an ICBM occurred: "all we really have that is meaningful is a deterrent."[24] Kincade argues that Khrushchev brandished the Soviet Union's supposed superiority in nuclear weapons in order to compel the United States to enter into a series of arms control agreements that would have been favorable to the Soviet Union.

Two recent changes in U.S. strategic policy also contain a strong dose of compel-

Table 10.6 NUCLEAR THREATS AND EAST-WEST CRISES

Low-Risk Crises	High-Risk Crises
1. The Berlin blockade, 1948 (the United States issues the threat)	1. The Berlin crisis, 1958–1959 (the United States)
2. The Korean War, 1950–1953 (the United States)	2. The Berlin crisis, 1961 (the United States)
3. Indochina and the Taiwan Straits, 1954–1955 (the United States)	3. The Cuban missile crisis, 1962 (the United States)
4. Suez, 1956 (the Soviet Union)	4. The Yom Kippur War, 1973 (the United States)
5. Lebanon, 1958 (the United States)	5. The Carter Doctrine and the Persian Gulf, 1980 (the United States)
6. Taiwan Straits, 1958 (the United States)	
7. Soviet-Chinese border clashes, 1969 (the Soviet Union)	

Source: Richard Betts, *Nuclear Blackmail and Nuclear Balance* (Washington, D.C.: Brookings Institute, 1987).

lence. In 1974, Secretary of Defense James Schlesinger announced with great fanfare that U.S. nuclear policy now embraced the idea of limited strategic options. Kincade argues that, because such options had been present ever since SIOP-63, the real reason for revealing it in this fashion was to try to compel the Soviet Union not to exploit its advantage in missile throw weight (the amount a missile can lift). The larger size of Soviet missiles would (and has) allowed them to place more warheads on each missile than the United States is capable of with MIRV technology. Finally, he argues that President Reagan's Strategic Defense Initiative has a compellent role. In part, its purpose is to neutralize what many American conservatives see as the potential for blackmail inherent in the Soviet Union's large missiles when combined with a strategy of first-strike.

Kincade's work speaks to one type of compellence, in which the threat is general in nature, as is the case with general deterrence. Compellence can also be practiced in quite specific situations, in which the type of action that a state wants stopped or begun is immediate and precise. Richard Betts has found at least 12 crises in which either the United States or the Soviet Union suggested that nuclear weapons might be used if a dispute were not settled on acceptable terms.[25] He groups these crises into two categories: low risk and high risk. They are listed in Table 10.6. As we can see from an examination of this table, these threats were made far more frequently by U.S. policymakers and tended to be in areas at the margins of superpower interest.

Betts found that U.S. and Soviet behavior in these situations cannot be explained by the same factors. The willingness of U.S. policymakers to threaten nuclear coercion was not strongly influenced by assessments about the nuclear balance of power. The favorable nuclear balance during the 1950s and 1960s did not lead them to believe that the United States could escape an unacceptable level of damage if nuclear war were actually to come about as a result of their actions. By the same token, nuclear parity has not made them any less willing to practice nuclear coercion. Betts terms the primary motivating factor behind U.S. actions as an overly casual reliance on the "balance-of-interests" argument. U.S. policymakers believe that they have more at stake than does the Soviet Union and therefore are in a position to risk more in order to resolve the crisis. He found Soviet actions to be much more consistent with a "balance-of-power" argument: The Soviet Union backed down in each case because the United States was seen as more powerful, regardless of whose interests were more threatened.

The differences in motivation are important. If in the past Soviet policymakers backed down because they felt that the Soviet Union had less power than the United States, what will they do now that nuclear parity exists? In neither of the last two crises examined by Betts (Nixon's raising of the alert level of U.S. strategic forces during the 1973 Yom Kippur War to prevent the Soviet Union from unilaterally sending in Soviet peacekeeping forces, and the Carter administration's announcement following the invasion of Afghanistan that it was now considering the use of tactical nuclear weapons in areas outside of Europe) did the United States really compel the Soviet Union to accept an unfavorable outcome. Just as troubling is the fact that, although the Soviet Union has backed down in the past, there is no precedent for the United States to back down from going to the brink of nuclear war.

NUCLEAR-WAR FIGHTING

A nuclear-war fighting posture seeks to accomplish political goals through the skillful use of military power on the battlefield. Deterrence theorists have tended to avoid this question, and the absence of explicit attention to the question of how a nuclear war would be fought should deterrence fail is one of the most telling criticisms made of second-strike strategies. In this section, we will deal with two closely related questions: (1) How might deterrence fail and (2) how might a nuclear war be fought?

How Might Deterrence Fail?

Detterence can fail. Although strategists differ on the number of paths that might lead to a nuclear war, the specifics of the scenarios that make up each path, and the likelihood that a nuclear confrontation lies at the end of each, we can identify five possible "nuclear nightmares."[26]

The first path to nuclear war proceeds via the escalation of a conventional war. In one sense, this is the path by which we arrived at Hiroshima. For many, the possibility that nuclear war might emerge out of a conventional conflict remains highly plausible, especially in Europe, where both U.S. and Soviet military plans have long incorporated the possibility of escalating from a conventional to a nuclear war. Complicating matters further is the large concentration of troops there. Within the territories of the two Germanies, the Benelux countries, Poland and Czechoslovakia alone (roughly one and one-fourth times the size of Texas), NATO deploys 796,000 active ground forces and the Warsaw Pact deploys 995,000. If reserves are added, the numbers jump to 922,000 and 1,030,000, respectively.

The second path to nuclear war involves a surprise attack, in which the calm of peacetime is suddenly shattered by the unleashing of a nuclear attack. This is not a nuclear Pearl Harbor scenario. While the Japanese attack caught the United States by surprise, it did not come out of the blue. U.S.-Japanese relations had been deteriorating for several years, and expectations were high that an official state of war would soon exist between them. A more accurate, but still incomplete, historical analogy is Hitler's surprise 1941 attack on the Soviet Union. Stalin recognized that war with Germany was all but inevitable; however, he was convinced that the Soviet Union could remain at peace with it until 1942 or that he would at least be served with a German ultimatum of some kind before the war would begin. Most commentators believe that fears about the surprise-attack scenario are exaggerated and that this is a very unlikely path by which deterrence might fail.

The third and fourth paths to nuclear war center on the existence of a major international crisis. They may be termed *crisis preemption* and *crisis escalation*.[27] Crisis preemption involves the use of nuclear weapons before a crisis situation has erupted into open military conflict. It involves striking first in self-defense just before it is believed the fighting will begin. It is a very real option for a state (Israel or the Soviet Union) or an alliance (NATO) that is convinced that war is inevitable and is unsure of its ability to triumph in either a conventional conflict or one in which it must absorb the first nuclear blow. A crisis escalation involves the use of nuclear weapons after a crisis has precipitated fighting. Both the winning and the losing sides may avail themselves of this option. The winning state may see it as a way of bringing the conflict to a quick end through the delivery of a knockout blow. The losing side may see it as the only way of avoiding an even greater defeat and of compelling the winning side to stop its war effort because the price of victory has gotten too high.

The fifth, and final, path to nuclear war that we will examine is one in which nuclear war comes about accidentally. The most popular version of the accidental nuclear-war scenario involves an unauthorized nuclear attack.[28] Far more problematic to deal with, as well as more likely to come about than unauthorized use of nuclear weapons, is a scenario built around human responses in the early warning systems of the United States and Soviet Union to technical accidents.

Accidental nuclear war is possible because the early warning systems are not foolproof. Experts distinguish between a Type I error (in which the system fails to indicate that the United States is under attack) and a Type II error (in which the system incorrectly concludes that an attack has been launched). There have been Type II errors. During the 1950s, a flock of migrating Canadian geese were read by the Distant Early Warning (DEW) line of radars as a Soviet missile attack. In 1960, meteor showers and lunar radar reflections caused the Ballistic Missile Early Warning System to conclude that an attack had been launched. In 1979, without informing those who were monitoring the system, a technician at NORAD headquarters loaded a test tape into the computer that showed a Soviet attack was underway. Before it was discovered to be a mistake, 10 fighters from three different bases were airborne, and U.S. missiles and submarine bases had gone on a heightened alert status. In 1980, a 46-cent computer chip malfunctioned, causing about 100 B-52 bombers and the president's emergency aircraft to be readied for takeoff. The airborne command post of the U.S. commander in the Pacific actually did take off. Because these accidents occurred in times of peace, the system was quickly able to correct itself. Critics fear that, if such an accident or a series of accidents happens in a time of crisis, this would not be the case. Under time pressures to act and already on the alert for signs of an escalation of fighting in Europe or the Middle East, military officers and policymakers might not be capable of responding to warning signals with restraint or skepticism.

How Might a Nuclear War Be Fought?

Earlier in this chapter, we examined the consequences that would follow from a surprise nuclear attack on Detroit. Many consider this scenario to be among the least likely paths to nuclear war. In this section, we will examine more plausible scenarios that might come about in the event of a nuclear war, given current U.S. and Soviet strategic war-fighting doctrines. A Soviet attack on the United States might take any one of a number of forms. One possibility is an attack on key military-industrial targets, such as those used to produce missile systems, command and control systems, and antitank missiles. A second possibility is an attack limited to key U.S. strategic and nuclear targets. A third possibility involves a full-scale attack on U.S. strategic targets.[29] In the first two scenarios, it is assumed that the Soviet attack will employ 100 1-megaton bombs against 100 U.S. targets. In the last scenario, 2,839 warheads, equivalent to 1,342 megatons would be used against 1,215 targets. The target list and allocation of weapons for the Soviet attack is presented in Table 10.7. It is expected that an attack on military-industrial targets would result in 11–29 million deaths and 23–35 million casualties. The attack on key strategic targets would kill 3–11 million Americans and injure 10–16 million others. Finally, a full-scale Soviet attack would result in 13–34 million dead and 25–64 million injured. The wide disparity in figures is due to different ways of calculating the effects of a nuclear explosion. In each case, the lower figures are based on the overpressure model used to calculate the effects of the attack on Hiroshima. The higher figures are the product of a conflagration model, which adds to the deaths produced by overpressure the effects of large "superfires" with asphyxiating gases and gale-force winds that would be produced by megaton-sized explosions over urban areas.

The same methodologies were used to estimate the consequences of U.S. limited nuclear attacks on the Soviet Union.[30] A full-scale attack on Soviet strategic and nuclear forces was estimated to involve 1,740 targets and to require the use of 4,108 warheads with a total yield of 844 megatons. The target list is found in Table 10.8. It is estimated that such an attack would result in 12–27 million fatalities, would kill or injure 25–54 million people in the short run, and cause 2–14 million to suffer radiation-induced cancer in the long run.

CONCLUSION: PROBLEMS WITH DETERRENCE THEORY

Regardless of the specific strategy selected, many feel that deterrence theory is built upon a number of highly questionable assumptions. The extent to which they are unsound makes suspect the ability of deterrence to prevent war or to provide for

Table 10.7　HYPOTHETICAL MAJOR ATTACK ON U.S. STRATEGIC-NUCLEAR FORCES

Target type	Number	Mode of attack		
		Number of warheads on each	Yields (megatons)	Height of burst
Missile silos	1016	1	0.5	Low Airburst
		+1	0.5	Groundburst
Strategic bomber and tanker bases	34	1	1.0	Groundburst
		+14	0.2	Airbursts (pattern)
Nuclear-navy bases	16	1	1.0	Airburst
		+1	1.0	Groundburst
Nuclear weapon storage facilities	9	1	1.0	Airburst
		+1	1.0	Groundburst
Missile launch-control facilities	100	1	0.5	Airburst
		+1	0.5	Groundburst
National command posts and alternate headquarters	7	1	1.0	Airburst
		+1 (5 sites)	1.0	Groundburst
Early warning radars	5	1	1.0	Airburst
Navy radio transmitters	10	1	1.0	Airburst
Strategic Air Command radio transmitters	9	1	1.0	Airburst
		+1 (2 sites)	1.0	Groundburst
Satellite command transmitters	9	1	1.0	Airburst
Totals	1215 targets	2839 warheads	1342 megatons	

Source: William Daugherty, Barbara Levi, and Frank von Hippel, "The Consequences of 'Limited' Nuclear Attacks on the United States," *International Security* 10 (1986): 30.

U.S. national security. We will briefly identify four of these assumptions. First, deterrence theory assumes that governments are unitary and rational actors. States are "black-boxed:" No effort is made to analyze decision-making procedures, personality factors, or the domestic pressures on policymakers, because states are seen as responding with one voice to the challenges confronting them. In doing so, they are assumed to be acting on the basis of a cost-benefit type of calculation, in which all available options and consequences have been considered and a value-maximizing choice has been made. Critics argue that both parts of this assumption are flawed. Governments are not monolithic. Different parts of governments frequently disagree with each other over what to do, and policymaking is often a response to internal stress rather than to external pressures. Experimental research and case studies of crisis decision making also call into question the ability of policymakers to make rational decisions under conditions of great stress.

Second, traditional deterrence theory assumes the existence of a world in which there are only two nuclear powers. However, in actuality, there are more than two nuclear powers. Can a deterrence scenario be played out in the Middle East without taking into consideration the existence of an independent Israeli nuclear force? If

Table 10.8 HYPOTHETICAL COUNTERFORCE ATTACK ON SOVIET STRATEGIC FORCES

Target type	Number of targets	Attack assumptions	
		Groundbursts	Airbursts
Missile silos			
SS-4	112	0.1-megaton	0.1-megaton
SS-11	448	0.1-megaton	0.1-megaton
SS-13	60	0.1-megaton	0.1-megaton
SS-17	150	0.35-megaton	0.17-megaton
SS-18	308	0.35-megaton	0.17-megaton
SS-19	360	0.35-megaton	0.1-megaton
Missile launch-control centers			
SS-4, -11, -13	66	1.2-megaton	0.17-megaton
SS-17, -18	48	0.35-megaton	0.17-megaton
SS-19	36	0.35-megaton	0.1-megaton
ICBM test silos	27	0.1-megaton	0.1-megaton
Bases for Mobile Missiles			
SS-25 bases	3	1.2-megaton	16 0.1-megaton (barrage attack)
SS-20 bases	16	1.2-megaton	16 0.1-megaton
Antiballistic-missile launcher sites			
Exo-atmosphere interceptors	2	0.1-megaton	0.1-megaton
Endo-atmospheric interceptors	7	0.1-megaton	0.1-megaton
Nuclear navy bases			
Ballistic missile submarines	8	1.2-megaton	1.2-megaton
Other nuclear-capable ships	8	1.2-megaton	1.2-megaton
Naval yards	5	1.2-megaton	1.2-megaton
Bomber bases			
Long-range (Bison & Bear)	3	1.2-megaton	16 0.1-megaton (barrage attack)
Arctic staging	5	1.2-megaton	16 0.1-megaton
Intermediate-range (Backfire)	10	1.2-megaton	16 0.1 megaton
Medium-range (Badger, Blinder, Fencer)	6	1.2-megaton	16 0.1-megaton
National and strategic rocket forces HQs			
Underground	19	0.1-megaton	0.1-megaton
Base for airborne command posts	1	1.2-megaton	16 0.1-megaton
Communication facilities			
Early warning and ABM radars	13		0.1-megaton
Radio transmitters	19		0.1-megaton
Totals	1740 Targets	4108 attacking warheads, 844 megaton Total Yield	

Source: Barbara Levi, Frank von Hippel, and William Daugherty, "Civilian Casualties from 'Limited' Nuclear Attacks on the USSR," *International Security* 12 (1988): 174.

not, can the presence of an Israeli nuclear capability be factored into the picture? One way of doing so is by relying upon insights from game theory—a mathematical form of decision-making theory that includes a focus on decision-making situations in which more than two actors are present. The problem is that these computations become exceedingly complex. For example, in a world in which there are four nuclear powers—a point that we have already passed—the enemy is not one individual state but every one of the nine possible coalitions of the remaining three states. Serious questions can be raised about the real-world ability of policymakers to comprehend and to act upon such complex alternative scenarios.

Third, there is the problem of cause and effect. How do we know that deterrence is responsible for preventing something from happening? War might have been prevented from occurring for reasons that are totally unrelated to deterrence. War might also never have been contemplated. One way to measure the success of deterrence would be to remove it (i.e., troops in Europe, ICBMs, etc.) and see what happens. If no war takes place, then deterrence can be judged to be superfluous to the problem of protecting a state's national security interests. For obvious reasons, policymakers are reluctant to conduct such an experiment. The cost of being proven "right" is too high. The point remains, however, that we cannot be sure that deterrence means the difference between peace and war. It may be, as some have recently argued, that nuclear weapons are irrelevant to the stability of the post-World War II international system, that this long period of peace is, instead, the logical conclusion of the process of historical evolution in relations between economically developed states.[31]

We conclude with a discussion of what many experts and concerned citizens consider to be the most troubling aspects of deterrence theory: its morality. Questions about "nuclear ethics" can be raised at many levels.[32] Many find the prospect of nuclear war to be so appalling that the only morally correct position would be to do away with nuclear weapons. For some, this means a strategy of disarmament. Others embrace the vision put forward by President Reagan when he introduced the strategic defense initiative (SDI, or "Star Wars") and stated that its purpose was to make nuclear weapons obsolete. We will examine both of these positions in a later chapter. Here we will briefly review the debate between those who accept the fundamental morality of using nuclear weapons to protect national security and those who reject the use of nuclear weapons as an instrument of foreign policy.

At the center of this controversy is the morality of holding millions of citizens in the United States and the Soviet Union hostage as part of a second-strike strategy. The hostage effect has been defended on the grounds that, while we may wish it to be otherwise, there is nothing that can be done to escape from this situation. MAD is not so much the product of policy choices as it is a basic condition of the nuclear age.[33] In 1983, the National Conference of Catholic Bishops spoke out strongly against countervalue targeting:[34] "Under no circumstances may nuclear weapons . . . be used for purposes of destroying population centers or other predominantly civilian targets." In the end, however, their pastoral letter states that deterrence "may still be judged morally acceptable but that it is not an adequate strategy as a long-term basis for peace."

Advocates of limited strategic options also question the morality of the hostage effect, but even more so do they question its efficacy. Albert Wohlstetter puts the case this way: Because the Soviet Union values its military power more than the lives of its citizens, attacks directed only at its population centers are unlikely to deter them, and it is dangerous and absurd to leave our civilian population vulnerable to their missiles, thereby forcing us into a position of either carrying out such an attack or capitulating in the face of a Soviet threat. Wohlstetter also criticizes the Catholic bishops for condemning the use of nuclear weapons while at the same time appearing to endorse threats of using them.[35]

An important point that has become attached to the question of morality is the ability of the United States to conduct a limited nuclear war. Advocates of this doctrine argue that, unlike the 1950s and 1960s, advances in missile technology now make counterforce targeting a credible strategy. The Catholic bishops take exception to this conclusion, stating that there are no moral grounds whatsoever for using nuclear weapons in a first-strike and that the case for limited nuclear war has yet to be proven. Advocates of the continued adherence to a second-strike strategy base their case on Clausewitz's concept of "friction":

> Everything in war is very simple, but the simplest thing is difficult. The difficulties accumulate and end by producing a kind of friction that is inconceivable. . . .[36]

In particular, they argue either that (1) by its very nature nuclear war cannot be kept limited and (2) if it were possible, the technology for doing so does not now exist.[37] Others point to an additional complicating factor. Even if the United States could conduct a limited nuclear attack, it is quite possible that the Soviet Union would not be able to recognize it as such. Given the way in which Soviet targets are concentrated in the same area, the limitations in Soviet technology, and the pressures of time, prudence might force Soviet leaders to treat any nuclear attack as a full-scale attack.

NOTES

1. The data presented in this section are taken primarily from Laurence Martin, *The Changing Face of Nuclear War* (New York: Harper & Row, 1987).
2. Battlefield nuclear weapons are discussed by the authors in Andrew Pierre, ed., *Nuclear Weapons in Europe* (New York: Council on Foreign Relations, 1984).
3. Richard Ullman, "The Covert French Connection," *Foreign Policy* 75 (1989): 3–33.
4. Office of Technology Assessment, *The Effects of Nuclear War* (Montclair, N.J.: Allanheld & Osmun, 1980).
5. The data for this paragraph are taken from Eric Chivan, et al., eds., *Last Aid: The Medical Dimensions of Nuclear War* (San Francisco: Freeman, 1982).
6. The subsection heading is taken from Robert Jay Lifton, "Is Hiroshima Our Text," in Robert Jay Lifton and Richard Falk, *Indefensible Weapons* (New York: Basic, 1982).
7. The figures associated with a nuclear blast can vary considerably, depending upon how the blast is defined, the time frame used, and a number of other factors. Data in this section were drawn from a number of sources, not all of which presented identical figures. See Office of Technology Assessment, *The Effects of Nuclear War*; William Daugherty, Barbara Levi, and Frank von Hippel, "The Consequences of 'Limited' Nuclear Attacks

on the United States," *International Security* 10 (1986): 3–45; Leo Sartori, "Effects of Nuclear Weapons," *Physics Today* 36 (1983): 32–58; and Dietrich Schroeer, *Science, Technology, and the Nuclear Arms Race* (New York: John Wiley, 1981).

8. For discussions of the concept of nuclear winter, see Paul Ehrlich, et al., *The Cold and the Dark: The World After Nuclear War* (New York: Norton, 1984); Richard Turco, et al., "The Climatic Effects of Nuclear War," *Scientific American* 251 (1984): 33–43; The Committee on the Atmospheric Effects of Nuclear Explosions, et al., *The Effects on the Atmosphere of a Major Nuclear Exchange* (Washington, D.C.: National Academy Press, 1985); and Carl Sagan, "Nuclear Winters and Climatic Catastrophe: Some Policy Implications," *Foreign Affairs* 62 (1983–1984): 257–292.

9. Quoted in David Yost, "French Nuclear Targeting," in Desmond Ball and Jeffrey Richelson, eds., *Strategic Nuclear Targeting* (Ithaca, N.Y.: Cornell University Press, 1986), p. 129.

10. Patrick Morgan, *Deterrence: A Conceptual Analysis*, vol. 40 (Beverly Hills, Calif.: Sage Library Social Research, 1977), pp. 35–47.

11. John Rielly, "America's State of Mind," *Foreign Policy* 66 (1987): 39–56.

12. The distinction between *noise* and *signals* is made in Roberta Wohlstetter, *Pearl Harbor* (Stanford, Calif.: Stanford University Press, 1962).

13. See Barry Blechman and Michael Krepon, *Nuclear Risk Reduction Centers* (Washington, D.C.: Center for Strategic and International Studies, 1986).

14. Quoted in Desmond Ball, "U.S. Nuclear War Planning, 1945–1960," in Ball and Richelson, *Strategic Nuclear Targeting*, p. 55.

15. Robert Toth, "U.S. Shifts Nuclear Response Strategy," *Los Angeles Times*, July 23, 1989.

16. Quoted in David Holloway, *The Soviet Union and the Arms Race* (New Haven, Conn.: Yale University Press, 1983), p. 37.

17. See Holloway, *The Soviet Union and the Arms Race*, pp. 43–58; and Stephen Meyer, "Soviet Perceptions on the Paths to Nuclear War," in Graham Allison, Albert Carnesale, and Joseph Nye Jr., (eds.), *Hawks, Doves, and Owls: An Agenda for Avoiding Nuclear War* (New York: Norton, 1985), pp. 167–205.

18. See Meyer, "Soviet Perceptions on the Paths to Nuclear War," and his "Soviet Nuclear Operations," in Ashton Carter, John Steinbruner, and Charles Zraket (eds.), *Managing Nuclear Operations* (Washington, D.C.: Brookings, 1987).

19. This list is taken from Benjamin Lambeth, "How to Think About Soviet Military Doctrine," in Douglas Murray and Paul Viotti, *The Defense Policies of Nations* (Baltimore: Johns Hopkins University Press, 1982), pp. 148–151.

20. These points are discussed in Stephen Meyer, "The Sources and Prospects of Gorbachev's New Political Thinking on Security," *International Security* 13 (1988): 124–163.

21. Desmond Ball, "Soviet Strategic Planning and the Control of Nuclear War," in Roman Kolkowicz and Ellen Mickiewicz, eds., *The Soviet Calculus of Nuclear War* (Lexington, Mass.: Lexington Books, 1986), 49–67.

22. Meyer, "Soviet Perspectives on the Paths to Nuclear War," p. 195.

23. Meyer, "Soviet Perspectives on the Paths to Nuclear War," p. 177.

24. William Kincade, "Arms Control or Arms Coercion," *Foreign Policy* 62 (1986): 24–46. Dulles' quote is on pg. 29.

25. Richard Betts, *Nuclear Blackmail and Nuclear Balance* (Washington, D.C.: Brookings Institute, 1987).

26. For general discussions of alternative scenarios, see Nigel Calder, *Nuclear Nightmares: An Investigation into Possible Wars* (New York: Penguin, 1979); Albert Carnesale, et al., *Living with Nuclear Weapons* (New York: Bantam 1983); Allison, Carnesale, and Nye, *Hawks, Doves, and Owls*; Kurt Gottfried and Bruce Blair, eds., *Crisis Stability and Nu-*

clear War (New York: Oxford University Press, 1988); and Miroslav Nincic, *United States Foreign Policy: Choices and Trade-offs* (Washington, D.C.: Congressional Quarterly Press, 1988).

27. For a possible scenario involving a preemptive crisis in Europe, see Gottfried and Blair, *Crisis Stability and Nuclear War*, p. 227. For a discussion of a scenario involving a crisis escalation in the Middle East, see Louis Renes Beres, *Apocalypse: Nuclear Catastrophes in World Politics* (Chicago: University of Chicago Press, 1980), pp. 52–68.

28. For an extensive discussion of this possibility, see Beres, *Apocalypse*, pp. 52–68.

29. These scenarios, plus ones centered on population attacks, are presented in Daugherty, Levi, and von Hippel, "The Consequences of 'Limited' Nuclear Attacks on the United States," 3–45.

30. Barbara Levi, Frank von Hippel, and William Daugherty, "Civilian Casualties from 'Limited' Nuclear Attacks on the USSR," *International Security* 12 (1987/1988: 168–189.

31. See the exchange between John Mueller, "The Essential Irrelevance of Nuclear Weapons: Stability in the Postwar World," and Robert Jervis, "The Political Effects of Nuclear Weapons: A Comment," *International Security* 13 (1988): 55–90.

32. See Joseph Nye, *Nuclear Ethics* (New York: Free Press, 1987); and Douglas Lakey, *The Ethics of War and Peace* (Englewood Cliffs, N.J.: Prentice-Hall, 1989), chap. 5.

33. Spurgeon Keeny, Jr., and Wolfgang Panofsky, "MAD Versus NUTS: Can Doctrine or Weaponry Remedy the Mutual Hostage Relationship of the Superpowers," *Foreign Affairs* 60 (1981/1982): 287–304.

34. *The Challenge of Peace: God's Promise and Our Response* (Washington, D.C.: United States Catholic Conference, 1983).

35. Albert Wohlstetter, "Bishops, Statesmen, and Other Strategists on the Bombing of Innocents," *Commentary* 1983: 15–35.

36. Quoted in Harry Summers, Jr., *On Strategy* (Novato, Calif.: Presidio Press, 1982), p. 33.

37. Desmond Ball, *Can Nuclear War Be Controlled* (London: International Institute for Strategic Studies, Adelphi Papers #161, 1981); and Ashton Carter, "The Command and Control of Nuclear War," *Scientific American* 252 (1985): 32–39.

Chapter
11

Arms Control and Disarmament

In their book, *Thinking in Time: The Uses of History for Decision Makers*, Richard Neustadt and Ernest May argue that policymakers must resist the temptation to treat each problem that comes before them as if it were "new," then making a decision about what to do and moving on to the next one.[1] They must recognize that contemporary policy problems do not exist in total isolation from past events. One of the keys to successful policymaking is to recognize that the problems that are being dealt with are but the latest in a stream of connected events. Neustadt and May urge that policymakers create time-lines within which they can place policy decisions and against which they can judge the merits of proposed policy options.

Our concern in this chapter is with arms control and disarmament. We will survey attempts to eliminate or, at least to curb, the spread and use of a variety of weapons systems, ranging from chemical and biological weapons to nuclear weapons. No single arms control and disarmament time-line exists. Understanding current efforts to eliminate chemical weapons requires that we tell a different story than is the case when the issue before us is nuclear proliferation. Not only must we create different time-lines, but choices must be made regarding how the story is to be told and what the time-line should look like. Telling the wrong story can be a major factor contributing to the failure of a policy. According to Neustadt and May, this is just what happened during the Carter administration. The staff prepared a history of the Strategic Arms Limitation Talks (SALT), yet what Carter really needed was an understanding of how the U.S. and Soviet nuclear arsenals came to be what they are today.

To illustrate the process of creating a time-line, we will examine the efforts to negotiate a conventional arms control agreement in Europe. Success or failure in these efforts will be realized in two sets of autonomous negotiations, which began in Vienna on March 9, 1989: the negotiations on Conventional Armed Forces in Europe (CFE), which is being carried out between representatives from NATO and the Warsaw Pact states and deals with weapons and forces stationed from the Atlantic Ocean to the Ural Mountains; and the negotiations on Confidence and Security-Building Measures (CSBMs). Both the CFE and CSBM negotiations are being carried out within the framework of the Conference on Stability and Cooperation in Europe (CSCE). The most ambitious agenda lies before the CFE negotiators. In May 1989 the United States, with NATO's support, proposed that common ceilings be established on the number of combat forces, tanks, armored troop carriers, and artillery pieces that each alliance may possess. According to the U.S. plan, 30,000 American combat troops would be withdrawn from Europe and brought back to the United States, where they would be demobilized. This is the first time that the United States has expressed a willingness to negotiate troop reductions. In addition, the United States has endorsed the principle long argued for by the Soviet Union that common ceilings also be set on the number of land-based combat aircraft and helicopters that can be stationed in Europe. While the opening proposals put forward by the Soviet Union did not differ greatly from those advanced by the West, its negotiators asserted that Bush's goals and timetable for arriving at an agreement within one year were "unreachable" because of the number of troops and weapons that would have to be cut

Remarkable as this proposal was, by the year's end it looked timid. Events in Eastern Europe—the demise of communist governments, opening the Berlin Wall, talk of East German reunification with West Germany, and the Soviet Union's expressed willingness to remove its troops from Eastern Europe—pointed to the possibility of making even deeper cuts in Europe's conventional military balance. Accordingly, it came as no surprise that in early 1990 at a meeting in Ottawa, the United States and Soviet Union agreed to a revised conventional arms control framework. Under this plan, each side would be permitted to station 195,000 troops within a central region made up of five West European states and four Eastern European states. The United States would also be restricted to placing 30,000 U.S. troops on the periphery of Western Europe, while the Soviet Union would not be permitted to station any of its forces just outside the central region in Romania or Bulgaria.

Neither the CFE or CSBM talks are without precedent, as conventional arms control negotiations have become a familiar feature on the European political landscape. Our time-line will have three parts: past diplomatic initiatives, the shifting military rationale for having conventional forces in Europe, and the domestic politics of conventional arms control talks.

CONVENTIONAL ARMS CONTROL TALKS IN EUROPE

Past Diplomatic Initiatives

The time-line for understanding European conventional arms control and disarmament begins with the First Hague Conference of 1899, which discussed the use of dum-dum bullets, asphyxiating gases, and weapons launched from balloons, but failed to reach an agreement. Likewise, little headway was made at the Second Hague Conference (1907), in which discussions on arms limitations consumed all of 20 minutes. Plans for a Third Hague Conference were undermined by the outbreak of World War I. The next major international conference that dealt with conventional arms control and disarmament issues was the Washington Naval Conference. In 1922 negotiators reached agreement on a pact that provided for limitations on battleships and aircraft carriers; a 10-year ban on the construction of new capital ships; and limitations on replacement ratios for future capital-ship construction. Less well remembered than the agreements that came out of these negotiations is the fact that their acceptance was made possible by the simultaneous conclusion of a political agreement organized on the basis of the existing status quo in the Pacific. U.S. policy-makers had become increasingly uncomfortable, because its Pacific possessions and commercial interests were far removed from the United States and also vulnerable to Japanese pressure. By 1934, relations between the United States and Japan had deteriorated to the point where the existing restrictions on naval armaments lost their restraining ability and Japan formally gave notice of its intention to withdraw from them.

At this point, a break occurred in the conventional arms control and disarmament time-line. Calls for conventional force reductions in postwar Europe began again in 1954, when the Soviet Union proposed a conference to settle the still unresolved issues growing out of World War II. The initial Soviet proposal called for a withdrawal of all occupation forces from Germany and a 50-year European collective security pact. A primary stimulus behind the Soviet proposal was the fact that the integration of West Germany into NATO was nearing completion. America's West European allies rejected the proposal, because it did not provide for any U.S. participation. The Soviet Union repeated its call for some form of European security treaty three more times during the 1950s (1955, 1957, and 1958). Each appeal was rejected by the West.

It was only during the late 1960s that real movement began toward an agreement on conventional forces in Europe. Conventional arms control was seen by some as a way of countering the political appeal of renewed Soviet calls for a European security conference. West Germany, which was embarking upon its policy of Ostpolitik (a set of foreign policy initiatives that was intended to reestablish normal diplomatic relations between West Germany and the Communist bloc states of Europe, including the Soviet Union), was among those in the lead. The 1968 Soviet invasion of Czechoslovakia put a temporary hold on the growing interest in arms control. Movement began again in 1969 when the Warsaw Pact formally proposed a European Security Conference to "strengthen political, economic, and cultural links." Finland offered

Helsinki as the conference site. In December 1969, NATO indicated that it was willing to attend such a conference, but only if progress was first made in normalizing German relations with the East (Ostpolitik) and in settling Berlin-related issues. Progress came quickly. In relatively short order, West Germany and the Soviet Union signed a treaty recognizing "the frontiers of all states in Europe as inviolable"; West Germany and Poland established normal diplomatic relations; a four-power agreement was signed on the status of Berlin; and a pact was signed by East and West Germany.

A major remaining obstacle to European conventional arms control talks fell by the wayside in 1971 when Brezhnev dropped the Soviet Union's long-standing insistence that troop reduction talks be conducted under the auspices of a European security conference. He agreed that there could be separate talks on European security issues and troop reduction schemes. The signing of a nuclear arms control agreement, SALT I, in May 1972 and the accompanying spirit of détente provided the final ingredient necessary for the beginning of these talks. On consecutive days in November, SALT II and the Soviet Union's long sought-after Conference on Security and Cooperation in Europe (CSCE) talks began.

The CSCE talks, which ran from July 1973 to July 1975, produced a four-part agreement, commonly known as the Helsinki Accords. The first part, or "Basket I," deals with security and confidence-building measures that outline such principles as sovereign equality, the inviolability of frontiers, and restraints on the use of force. "Basket II" deals with measures to increase trade and economic, scientific, and environmental cooperation in Europe. "Basket III" addresses humanitarian issues, such as family reunification and the free flow of people, ideas, and information. "Basket IV" provides for follow-up conferences to continue to evaluate the CSCE process. The second follow-up conference was held in Madrid (1980–1983). It was the Madrid Conference that mandated the establishment of the Conference on Confidence and Security-Building Measures (CDE) talks.

Begun in January 1984 in Stockholm, the CDE talks were attended by 35 states (members of NATO, the Warsaw Pact, and European neutral and nonaligned states). These talks operated with an expansive "Atlantic-to-the-Urals" geographic focus, and they produced the first post-World War I agreement on the use of conventional forces in Europe. Much of the time, the United States lacked a high degree of interest in the conference. U.S. allies pushed hard in the final months for the United States to pay attention and to adopt a flexible approach. The CDE talks did not focus on questions of human labor, equipment, or force levels, but, rather, on how to make the existing military situation less dangerous. Attention was directed at minimizing the ability of either side to launch a surprise attack and at reducing the likelihood of accidental military confrontations due to miscalculation, misperception, or the general sense of uncertainty and threat that accompanies a crisis. Among the most significant provisions of the agreement are the following:

1. Each state must give all other signatory states two years' advance notice of any military exercise that would involve more than 75,000 troops, and one year's advance notice of exercises that would involve between 40,000 and 70,000 troops.

2. Each state must provide a yearly calendar of all out-of-garrison military formations of more than 13,000 troops or 300 tanks. When that number exceeds 17,000 troops, all signatories must be invited to send observers.

3. Each state must accept three verification challenges per year, by which another state can come into an operational area within 36 hours. No state can issue more than one challenge per year to another state.

Two months after the CSCE talks began, the Mutual and Balanced Force Reduction (MBFR) talks got underway. Attended by the 12 members of NATO and the 7 Warsaw Pact states, the focus of the MBFR was on enhancing the stability in Central Europe by establishing parity at lower troop levels. No international agreement was ever reached in these negotiations, and, with the convening of the CFE talks, the MBFR talks were terminated and allowed to fade into history. One of the major difficulties in negotiating an MBFR treaty was the differing arms control objectives of the two sides. The Soviet Union's primary objective was to ratify the conventional military balance (or imbalance) in Central Europe. Therefore, it was unwilling to discuss specific numbers, so it concentrated on establishing ceilings for individual national forces. The United States' principle objective was to reduce the Warsaw Pact advantage in force levels and thereby create what it saw as a more stable equilibrium in Central Europe.

The Shifting Military Rationale for Conventional Forces in Europe

As we enter the 1990s, NATO is making the uncertain transition from a military alliance into a political one, and the Warsaw Pact is simply trying to survive. To place these changes in perspective and understand the type of impact these changes will have on conventional arms control talks it is necessary to go back to the original purposes of these two organizations.

From the outset, NATO conventional forces have had two primary military functions: to deter a Soviet attack on Western Europe and to defend Western Europe should deterrence fail. They have also served a political purpose: to demonstrate the United States' commitment to Europe. Originally, neither the United States nor the other members of NATO were quick to contribute troops, largely because it was assumed that U.S. nuclear weapons provided an adequate protective shield. The Korean War cast doubt upon this assumption, so in 1951 four U.S. divisions were sent to Europe in order to clarify and reaffirm the U.S. commitment to NATO. The emphasis, however, continued to be on the military protection afforded by U.S. nuclear weapons. During the late 1950s and early 1960s, the presence of conventional forces in Europe took on a new strategic significance. The growing number and reach of Soviet nuclear weapons called into question the ability of the United States to use its nuclear weapons to defend Europe without running the risk of Soviet retaliation toward the United States. Recognizing this, NATO's strategy became one of flexible response, in which conventional forces would bear the brunt of an initial Warsaw Pact attack and nuclear weapons would be used only if necessary.

While the potential effectiveness of flexible response has long been suspect because of the imbalance between NATO and Warsaw Pact forces, little has been done to correct this situation, due to the domestic political and economic costs of staffing a larger standing army. Furthermore, so long as a nuclear option existed, NATO did not have to face up to the strategic dilemma posed by an inadequate conventional capability. All of this changed with the signing of the 1987 Intermediate Nuclear Forces (INF) Treaty, which largely stripped NATO conventional forces of its nuclear shield. A properly constructed arms control agreement now came to be seen by many as both a way of achieving a military balance in Europe and of avoiding an expensive arms buildup.

Soviet conventional forces in Europe also serve military and political purposes. By virtue of their numbers and strategic doctrine, Soviet-led Warsaw Pact forces pose at least a theoretical threat to Western Europe. As we noted in Chapter 10 in the section on deterrence, the Soviet Union traditionally has placed a great deal of emphasis on preemption and has rejected the concept of limited nuclear war. While the military potential of the Warsaw Pact forces cannot be discounted, continuing questions about the political reliability of its East European allies and the need to allocate forces to ensure their loyalty does call into question the military utility of its troops and equipment advantage. From a political standpoint, the Warsaw Pact has served as a two-pronged instrument of political domination. First, the network of military-administrative organizations, joint military maneuvers, shared military doctrines, and integrated officer education systems has allowed the Soviet Union to establish a vantage point for controlling the internal affairs of its East European allies. Second, in times of crisis, Warsaw Pact forces have been actively used by the Soviet Union to put down challenges to its domination. This happened in East Germany (1953), Hungary (1956), and Czechoslovakia (1968). Twice (1956 and 1980–1981) Warsaw Pact forces were used to threaten Polish leaders.

The Domestic Politics of Conventional Arms Control Talks

Negotiating international agreements is a two-faceted project. Not only must policymakers reach an understanding with other states on what is to be done or not done, but they must forge a consensus within their own government on what can be agreed to. This latter task can be every bit as difficult as reaching an agreement with other states. Conventional arms control proposals, for example, raise dissimilar issues and problems for different parts of a government. For the military, the primary issue is the effect the proposals would have on the ability of the armed forces to accomplish its assigned objectives. For diplomats, the key issues center around the consequences that an agreement would have on relations with other states. Treasury officials are likely to evaluate the merits of a proposed conventional arms control agreement either in terms of its impact on a state's balance of payments situation or of the relative costs of keeping forces stationed abroad versus the expected costs of monitoring the agreement. Finally, elected officials and their advisors place greatest emphasis on the domestic political consequences of signing a proposed agreement. In fact, the initial U.S. interest in European conventional arms control agreement grew directly out of these kinds of domestic political considerations.

During the mid-1960s, there was both a growing disillusionment with the war in Vietnam and a perception that U.S. European allies were not carrying their fair share of the defense burden. This latter concern intensified as the value of the dollar fell and the cost of stationing U.S. troops abroad rose. In 1966, Senator Mike Mansfield turned these concerns into a concrete policy proposal when he introduced a Sense of the Senate Resolution to reduce the number of U.S. forces stationed in Europe. Agreeing to conventional arms control talks was one way in which U.S. administrations have tried to deflect congressional pressures for unilateral reductions. No action was taken on Mansfield's resolution, but he offered it annually. In 1971, Mansfield changed tactics. Instead of introducing a resolution, he attached a force reduction measure as an amendment to a defense appropriations bill. His proposal called for a 50-percent reduction in the number of troops that could be stationed in Europe. Before debate on his measure ended, five alternative troop reduction plans had been introduced, and, while all failed, 60 senators had voted yes on at least one proposal. Senator Sam Nunn has taken up where Mansfield left off. During the early 1980s, he introduced an amendment that called for a 33-percent reduction in U.S. forces in Europe if NATO allies did not bolster their military contributions to the defense of Europe.

Nunn also wasted little time in attacking the Ottawa agreement. Barely one month after it was announced he criticized the troop ceiling of 30,000 on the periphery of the central region as insufficient to meet U.S. defense needs in Europe should all U.S. troops be forced out of the central region. Moreover, opponents of the agreement criticized the Bush administration for not consulting with Congress or top civilian and military leaders in the Pentagon before agreeing to the deal.

Soviet leaders have also had to look inward in formulating their conventional arms control positions. In his December 1988 speech to the United Nations, Gorbachev announced a unilateral Soviet conventional arms control measure: 50,000 troops and 5,000 tanks would be withdrawn from Europe. Western commentators were quick to label the announcement a "striking defeat" for the Soviet military, which had "waged an extended [and] unusually public campaign of opposition."[2] Speculation also began concerning "the price" that the military may have extracted from Gorbachev for its support. One Moscow publication suggested that the military may have been promised that some of the savings expected to be realized from the troop reductions would be earmarked for better military training and equipment.

Table 11.1 puts the various strands of our time-line together and shows how the legacy left by previous efforts to negotiate an agreement and domestic political considerations interact to limit the options open to U.S. policymakers as they wrestle with the problem of conventional arms control in Europe during the 1990s.

FRAMING THE PROBLEM: ARMS CONTROL AND DISARMAMENT

While constructing a time-line allows us to understand better the dynamics behind attempts to reach disarmament and arms control agreements in a given area, a different approach is necessary if our goal is to compare efforts and agreements in one area with those in another. These comparisons are potentially valuable, because the

Table 11.1 CONVENTIONAL ARMS CONTROL TIME-LINE

1899	First Hague Conference
1907	Second Hague Conference
1922	Washington Naval Conference
1934	Japan gives notice that it will withdraw from existing disarmament agreements
1949	NATO established
1951	Korean War
1953	Soviet Union uses force to put down riots in East Germany
1954	Soviet Union calls for conference to settle unresolved issues relating to World War II
1955	West Germany joins NATO, and the Warsaw Pact established
1956	Soviet Union sends troops into Hungary
1966	Senator Mike Mansfield proposes Sense of Senate Resolution calling for reducing number of U.S. troops in Europe; the proposal would be regularly reintroduced in following years
1968	Soviet Union invades Czechoslovakia
1969	Warsaw Pact calls for a European security conference
1971	Senator Mansfield attaches amendment to a defense appropriations bill, calling for 50-percent reduction in number of troops stationed in Europe
1972	SALT I signed
1973	Helsinki CSCE talks begin; produce agreement on the need for security and confidence-building measures
1979	SALT II signed
1980	Follow-up CSCE conference in Madrid begins; mandates the establishment of a Conference on Confidence and Security-Building Measures (CDE talks)
1982	Congress passes provision limiting number of active-duty personnel in Europe to 315,600; president is allowed to waive limitation if he declares there to be an "overriding national security requirement" for more troops
1984	CDE talks begin in Stockholm
	Mutual and Balanced Force Reduction (MBFR) talks begin
1987	Intermediate Nuclear Forces Treaty signed
1988	Gorbachev announces unilateral Soviet conventional arms control measures in Europe
1989	Negotiations on Conventional Armed Forces in Europe begin
	NATO takes up issue of modernizing battlefield nuclear weapons
	Berlin Wall is opened
1990	Ottawa agreement reached limiting each side to 195,000 troops in a central region and limiting the U.S. to 30,000 troops on the periphery

history and practice of disarmament and arms control in the area of nuclear proliferation may hold important lessons for policymakers who are concerned with halting the spread of chemical and biological weapons or with keeping weapons off the seabed. In order to do this, we need standards for comparison and a common vocabulary. To practitioners and advocates of disarmament and arms control, these terms hold very different meanings. Traditionally, the two have been seen as incompatible. Either they have pursued a policy of arms control (defined as restraint in the use of force) or have sought disarmament (defined as a reduction in arms). Efforts to realizing one were often seen as threats to the integrity of the other. For example, it is possible for arms control to be realized through an increase in the number of weapons, if the possession of those additional weapons makes policymakers feel more secure in their ability to deal with whatever developments might arise out of a crisis. It is also possible that by reducing the number of weapons in existence disarmament might actually increase the likelihood that war would break out. This would be the case if a state possessed such few weapons that in the midst of a crisis policymakers would come to believe that they were in a "use it or lose it" situation.

In contemporary usage, the distinction between "arms control" and "disarmament" is fading. These terms now compete for attention with such newly minted phrases as "arms limitation" and "arms reduction." The net result of this proliferation of terms is that "arms control" has taken on an almost generic meaning to cover attempts to place limits of any type on weapons and weapons systems. While we recognize that this has happened, it is still important that we understand the differences between the two terms. Consequently, in this section, we will present an introductory overview of the language and logic of each term. In the following section, we will review arms control and disarmament efforts in areas other than conventional weapons in Europe.

Disarmament

All disarmament proposals are based on a single premise: Weapons are the primary cause of war. Thus they share a single concern: Remove these weapons. Historically, disarmament has been practiced in two very different ways.[3] First, after a war, disarmament has been imposed on the defeated state by the victor. The Treaty of Versailles limited the post-World War I German army to 100,000 troops, thereby effectively eliminating an army that could be capable of offensive activity, and the same restriction was placed on it after World War II. Historically, the victors have been unable to remain united and unwilling to act together to enforce these prohibitions. Nazi Germany established training areas and munitions factories in the Soviet Union after World War I without suffering any penalties, and as the cold war intensified after World War II, a primary concern of U.S. foreign policy became rebuilding the military might of Japan and West Germany.

The other type of disarmament is voluntary disarmament, in which states seek to negotiate a mutually acceptable framework within which all parties will reduce the size of their military establishments. The Hague Conferences and the Washington Naval Conference and its follow-up meetings in London and Geneva are examples of efforts to institute voluntary disarmament. As we have already seen, the successes of these conferences were limited both in their scope and duration.

While the ultimate logic of disarmament points to the total elimination of all weapons, our examples show that concrete disarmament proposals often have had a more limited focus. Three different types of disarmament plans can be identified. The first is typified by attempts to reduce the size of the German armed forces to the bare minimum. The principle of disarmament down to the point at which a state's military establishment is capable of acting like little more than a national police force was part of Woodrow Wilson's Fourteen Points. The underlying assumption was that the public did not want war and that, if leaders tried to use some of their now greatly reduced military force to attack another state, they would be vulnerable to an uprising at home. The second type of disarmament is general and complete disarmament

(GCD). Disarmament plans falling under this heading seek the total elimination of all weapons. If this ever happened, the fundamental nature of world politics as envisioned by realists would be radically transformed. GCD proposals draw their inspiration from a variety of sources. Most important are the deeply felt moral and ethical objections to war as an instrument of foreign policy, continuing fears about the growing influence of the military over society, and concerns over the economic costs of war. The utopian nature of this quest has not limited its appeal. In fact, it makes GCD proposals attractive to states that are engaged in a struggle for power. Public opinion both at home and abroad is almost sure to react favorably to a GCD proposal. It is left to the state that declines to agree to the plan to explain why it is opposed to peace and remains in favor of continuing an arms race or international hostilities. Unfortunately, these same utopian qualities lead most analysts to conclude that, even if a GCD proposal were accepted, it would be impossible to realize.

A case in point was the 1986 Reykjavik Summit, in which General Secretary Mikhail Gorbachev proposed—and President Reagan accepted—a plan for the elimination of all nuclear armed ballistic missiles by 1996. The proposal added to Gorbachev's image in Europe and throughout the world. The proposal also put the United States on the defensive and raised questions about Reagan's leadership and grasp of nuclear matters. Strategists, such as former Secretary of Defense James Schlesinger, complained that, in accepting Gorbachev's proposal for total strategic nuclear disarmament, Reagan had "jettisoned twenty-five years of deterrence doctrine" and "two of the three traditional legs of the triad," leaving the United States with little in the way of weaponry or strategy to protect U.S. national security. Schlesinger argues that European "confidence in American leadership has been significantly weakened [and] in the immediate aftermath of the summit some began to cast around for alternative methods, other than American protection, to provide for their security."[4]

A third form of disarmament is regional disarmament. It seeks to reduce or to eliminate weapons from a particular geographic area. During the post-World War II era, regional disarmament plans have frequently taken the form of proposals for nuclear-free zones. A major roadblock to the successful negotiation of such agreements is that, once a state in a region has acquired nuclear weapons, it is almost impossible to prevent others from doing likewise. To a large extent, it is this imbalance that stands in the way of implementing the often proposed South Asian Nuclear-Free Zone. India has already exploded a (peaceful) nuclear device, and Pakistan is unlikely to accept an agreement that prohibits it from at least duplicating the Indian feat.

A similar situation holds when one state has an incentive to acquire nuclear weapons. During the 1950s, the Soviet Union and Warsaw Pact states put forward the Rapacki Plan in an effort to block the placement of nuclear weapons on West German soil. It would have created a nuclear-free zone in Central Europe. The United States and NATO rejected the Rapacki Plan because it would have added a nuclear imbalance to the already existing imbalance in conventional forces.

The history of regional disarmament is not all negative. Four major regional disarmament agreements are in effect. In 1967, the Treaty for the Prohibition of Nuclear Weapons in Latin America, also known as the Treaty of Tlatelolco, was signed. As of 1986, it has been signed by 24 states, and it prohibits the testing, possession, and deployment of nuclear weapons within the region. The United

States, Great Britain, and the Soviet Union cannot sign the agreement, but all have endorsed it. Thirty states have signed the Antarctic Treaty of 1959, which bans the use of Antarctica for military purposes, including nuclear testing. Seventy-four states have signed a 1971 treaty, which prohibits states from placing nuclear weapons on the seabed. A fourth "regional" disarmament agreement is the 1967 Outer-Space Treaty. Signed by 83 states, it bans the placing of nuclear weapons in earth orbit or stationing them in outer space. In addition to these agreements, a South Pacific Nuclear-Free Zone Treaty was signed by 9 states in 1985 but has yet to be ratified.

Today, several of these regional disarmament pacts are under stress.[5] Nowhere is this more apparent than in outer space. While the 1967 Outer-Space Treaty has prevented the placement of nuclear weapons in outer space, space is anything but demilitarized. Since ICBM technology was perfected in the late 1950s, both the United States and the Soviet Union have treated space as a legitimate area of military activity. Both rely heavily on satellites to communicate with their own forces and to monitor and provide warning of military action taken by the other. It has been estimated that since 1960 they have sent more than 2,000 military payloads into orbit. The U.S. Defense Department has spent over $70 billion on military activities in space. Concern today centers on the possible placement of defensive weapons, such as laser beams, in outer space. Such weapons are central to most "Star Wars" scenarios, and while technically they are not "weapons of mass destruction" and therefore not prohibited by the Outer-Space Treaty, introducing them would violate the spirit of the pact and represent a further militarization of space.

Arms Control

Varieties and Forms of Arms Control   Arms control approaches the problem of curbing international violence from a different perspective than does disarmament. It seeks not to reduce the number of weapons in existence per se but to place restraints on the use of force. The guiding assumption behind arms control is that the root causes of international conflict lie in the political realm. They can be found in such areas as disagreements over territory, ideology, security needs, access to resources and markets, and prestige. Weapons aggravate tensions between states but do not cause them. Therefore, getting rid of weapons does not address the root cause of the problem. Proponents of arms control further assume that, in spite of their differences, potential enemies have an interest in cooperating so that the most damaging and disruptive features of a conflict will not come to pass.

When we think of arms control, we think of formal international agreements such as SALT I and SALT II. This need not be the case. In their pioneering account of arms control, Thomas Schelling and Morton Halperin define its essence as including "all forms of military cooperation between potential enemies in the interest of reducing the likelihood of war, its scope, and violence if it occurs, and the political and economic costs of being prepared for it."[6] Nothing in this definition equates arms control with formal, internationally negotiated agreements. In fact, Schelling and Halperin warn against equating the two. They stress that it is not the formal agreement itself that constitutes arms control, but the spirit of self-restraint that lies behind it. In addition to formally negotiated agreements, arms control can take the form of informally agreed-upon "traffic rules" and unilateral restraints. The former include such things as the tacit understanding that has developed between the United States and the Soviet Union to limit their assistance to Third World allies so that it stops short of creating combat situations in which U.S. and Soviet military personnel must face each other. Examples of the latter would include Gorbachev's announcement that the Soviet Union was suspending its nuclear-testing program and the Christmas bombing moratoriums that the U.S. instituted in Vietnam.

Keeping the qualification in mind that not all arms control efforts involve formally negotiated international agreements, two main categories of arms control can be identified. The first involves agreements that are intended to avoid or to control crisis situations. The second category of formal arms control agreements deals with questions related to the size and structure of a state's military forces. Approached in these terms, the MBFR talks on conventional weapons in Europe fall into the second category, while the CSCE talks are an example of the first type of arms control.

Other types of arms control agreements that can be included in the first grouping are:

> *The Hot Line and Modernization Agreements, 1963.* Established direct radio, wire-telegraph, and satellite communication links between Moscow and Washington to ensure that the leaders of the United States and the Soviet Union can communicate to one another in times of crisis.

> *The Accidents Measures Agreement, 1971.* Pledges that the United States and the Soviet Union will upgrade their system of safeguards against the accidental or unauthorized use of nuclear weapons.

> *The Prevention of Nuclear War Agreement, 1973.* Requires that the United States and the Soviet Union enter into consultations if there is a danger of nuclear war.

> *The Incidents at Sea Agreement, 1972.* Regulates and restricts dangerous surface and aerial actions and also establishes provisions for increased communication at sea and for regular naval consultations and exchanges of information.

Included in the second category of arms control undertakings are the following agreements:

> *The Limited Test Ban Treaty, 1963.* Bans the testing of nuclear weapons in the atmosphere, outer space, and underwater, and prohibits underground explosions that send radioactive material across international borders.

> *The Non-Proliferation Treaty, 1968.* Provides that states possessing nuclear weapons will not transfer these weapons to nonnuclear states; that nonnuclear states will not try to acquire nuclear weapons; established the International Atomic Energy Agency, whose job it is to prevent the diversion of nuclear material from peaceful to military purposes.

The Threshold Test Ban Treaty, 1974. Signed but not ratified, forbids the underground testing of nuclear devices that have a yield above 150 kilotons.

The Peaceful Nuclear Explosions Treaty, 1974. Signed but not ratified, bans "group" explosions that have a yield greater than 1,500 kilotons and requires on-site inspection for explosions with a yield of over 150 kilotons.

The SALT I Agreements, 1972. Consist of two parts. The first part takes the form of a treaty that is of unlimited duration and limits each state to two antiballistic missile (ABM) complexes. The second part is in the form of an executive agreement of five years' duration. (Unlike treaties, executive agreements do not have to be voted on and approved by the Senate.) It places limits on the size of each state's strategic weapons forces. For all practical purposes, these limits reflect the number of missiles and launchers that were in existence or under construction in 1972. The SALT I agreement limits the United States to 1,054 ICBMs and 656 SLBMs or 1,000 ICBMs and 710 SLBMs. It limits the Soviet Union to either 1,618 ICBMs and 740 SLBMs or 1,408 ICBMs and 950 SLBMs.

The SALT II Agreements, 1979. Can be divided into three parts. The first part consists of a treaty that was never ratified by the United States and has since expired. It limits the United States and the Soviet Union to a total of 2,250 launchers with sublimits set for heavy ICBMs and MIRVed missiles. Unlike the SALT I agreement, this limit included bombers thereby setting a cap on the number of strategic nuclear weapons possessed by each side. The second part is a protocol to the treaty which sets qualitative restrictions on improvements in weapons research and development. The third part of the agreement is a statement of principles. It identifies areas in which no agreement has been reached and topics that are to serve as the agenda for SALT III negotiations.

The Intermediate Nuclear Forces (INF) Treaty, 1987. Provides that the Soviet Union will destroy missiles capable of delivering over 1,600 nuclear warheads and the U.S. will give up its Pershing II and Ground-Launched Cruise Missile forces. The INF Treaty also contains unprecedented provisions for an ongoing system of on-site inspections.

The Geneva Protocol of 1925. Outlaws the use of asphyxiating, poisonous or other gases, and bans bacteriological warfare.

The Biological Weapons Convention, 1972. Forbids the development, production, and stockpiling of biological and toxic weapons, and requires states to take steps to destroy their existing inventory of such weapons.

The Problem of Verification   One of the most difficult problems in negotiating an agreement centers on verification of the terms of the agreement. At the outset, a distinction must be made between *monitoring* and *verification*. The former refers to the task of collecting and analyzing information regarding the treaty-related actions of other parties to the agreement. The latter involves a political judgment about whether or not the monitored behavior constitutes a violation of the treaty. In order to understand the current controversy surrounding verification, we need to break the problem into three interrelated parts: techniques, points of emphasis, and standards of judgment.

Verification techniques can be subdivided into three categories: on-site inspection, national technical means, and cooperative measures. Throughout the 1950s, the United States argued for—and the Soviet Union opposed—provisions for on-site inspection. Advances in remote collection technologies provided a way of breaking the impasse, and, in 1963, the United States accepted national technical means for verification (NTM) as a passable substitute for on-site inspection.

Today, national technical means have become the primary technique by which the United States and the Soviet Union verify arms control agreements. They were specified by SALT I and SALT II as the means for verification. In the SALT I treaty, each side pledged not to take steps to interfere with the other's ability to conduct NTM verification. SALT II extended this pledge by prohibiting either state from deliberately denying the other *telemetry* necessary for verification. Telemetry refers to the electronic signals given off by a missile during testing. Scientists use telemetry to evaluate a missile's performance. A wide variety of technologies are covered by the phrase "national technical means." Perhaps the most important of these are reconnaissance satellites (others of note are the seismic detection of underground tests, high-flying planes, radars, and land-based listening posts). Reconnaissance satellites perform four tasks: photoreconnaissance, early warning of missile launchings and nuclear tests through the use of infrared detecting devices, radar reconnaissance, and electronic surveillance.[7]

The capabilities of these systems highlight the central problem that exists with any verification system. According to a former director of the Central Intelligence Agency, a skilled photo interpreter working with pictures taken from space can tell the difference between Guernsey and Hereford cows grazing in open fields. The SR-71 spy plane is capable of filming 60,000 square miles in one hour, and, by using its product, a pilot can pick out a mailbox on a country road. Reportedly, U.S. signals intelligence stations in Japan "can pick up a Russian television broadcast in Sakhalin or an exchange of insults between Chinese and Soviet soldiers on the Sino-Soviet border."[8] The point of these examples is that, inevitably, more information than is necessary is collected, and, at some point, verification and espionage become virtually indistinguishable. At the same time, it must be recognized that, even if no arms control agreement existed, there would still be a need for monitoring the behavior of other states.

While the capabilities of NTM verification systems are impressive, they are not without limits. For example, at distances of greater than 625 miles, seismic detectors have great difficulty distinguishing between a nuclear explosion of a few kilotons and an earthquake. A particularly vexing problem centers on the fact that, while counting the number of missiles can be done with some confidence, counting the number of warheads on a missile is another matter. To deal with this problem, the United States and the Soviet Union have agreed upon a set of artificial counting rules: Once a missile is tested in a given MIRV configuration (i.e., with 3, 5, or 10 warheads), all deployed missiles of that type will be assumed to carry the same number of warheads. The counting rules were changed during the START talks (discussed next). Under START counting rules, the number of warheads assumed to be on each ICBM remains the same, but arbitrary and lower number of warheads have been assigned to SLBMs.[9] Counting rules have also been a major negotiating point with regard to the capabilities of manned bombers.

These inherent limitations, plus a steady stream of allegations of Soviet noncompliance by the Reagan administration, produced a renewed U.S. interest in on-site inspection during the 1980s. In a remarkable turnabout, the Soviet Union agreed to include provisions for on-site inspection in the 1987 INF treaty. The terms of the treaty provided for a system of inspections that would establish the number of missiles to be destroyed, would observe the actual destruction of those missiles, would allow for the inspection of installations that no longer contained missiles or serviced them, would permit inspections on short notice at agreed-upon facilities, and would provide for continuous monitoring at agreed-upon missile factories.

Michael Krepon, an expert on verification matters and a former official in the Carter administration, cautions against treating on-site inspection as a panacea for verification problems. As he puts it, "if all goes well, inspections can only provide intelligence analysts with high confidence of compliance at individual sites just prior to, during, and immediately after the visit."[10] Krepon urges that greater attention be paid to cooperative measures, such as agreed-upon counting rules for determining the number of warheads on a launcher and data exchanges covering the production and transportation schedules of missiles to facilitate inspection by NTM technologies.

In constructing an arms control agreement, choices must be made regarding which types of activities are permissible, which are required, and which are prohibited. Verification technologies are an important factor in determining how the agreement will be worded. The traditional point of emphasis in arms control agreements has been on deployed missiles. The choice was a logical one, since by means of NTM verification systems, inspectors could count deployed missiles but could not look inside buildings. Alternatively, we can identify research and development or production as the chief concern. Of the two, research and development presents the greatest difficulties. How does a state know how much research is being conducted or where? Furthermore, how does a state distinguish between "peaceful" or "basic" research and "weapons" research? National technical means of verification systems cannot do so and, as Krepon notes, it is unlikely that on-site inspection can do so with complete confidence. The problem posed by verifying restrictions on research and development recently came into sharp focus when President Reagan proposed his Strategic Defense Initiative (SDI). In addition to limiting the number of ABM sites that each country would be allowed to have, the ABM Treaty, which was part of the SALT I accords, permitted continued research and development so long as it stopped short of system and component testing. This prohibition represents an almost insurmountable barrier to the development of an SDI system on the magnitude envisioned by Reagan. To get around this barrier, the Reagan administration advocated a "broad" interpretation of the ABM treaty. Opponents of an SDI system countered that only one interpretation of the ABM treaty existed at the time it was negotiated and ratified and that the Reagan administration was not free to reinterpret the treaty without the consent of the Senate.

It is impossible to verify compliance with absolute confidence. There also does not exist a single standard or set of criteria to apply to an arms control treaty. For example, in sharp contrast to the detailed on-site inspection provisions of the INF Treaty or the reliance upon NTM verification systems in the SALT agreements, the 1972 biological weapons treaty contained no verification provisions and only required signatories to consult and cooperate with one another through the appropriate United Nations bodies when problems arose. This arrangement was settled upon because what was most important to the United States was getting the Soviet Union to agree in principle to ban such weapons—a position that the United States had taken unilaterally. The question that lies at the heart of compliance debates is how great a risk a state is willing to run that one of two things will *not* occur: that the enemy will cheat and will get away with it or that permissible behavior will be misinterpreted and viewed as an incidence of noncompliance. Risk assessment is a political question and cannot be solved simply by examining the available evidence. Instead, the standard selected will reflect the overall state of relations between the parties to the treaty and the domestic political balance of power among those who supported and opposed the treaty.

The United States has employed two different verification standards. Between 1963 and 1979 the United States standard was one of adequate verification, which President Nixon defined as "whether we can identify attempted evasion if it occurs on a large enough scale to pose a significant risk, and whether we can do so in time to mount a sufficient response."[11] The Reagan administration set a different standard: effective verification. Although the difference between adequate verification and effective verification has never been spelled out, the implication of the charges that were leveled by the Reagan administration of Soviet arms control violations is that effective verification is a more demanding standard. This interpretation is reinforced by the fact that many of the practices classified by the Reagan administration as arms control violations were held to be acceptable or unverifiable by earlier administrations. Among the Soviet actions that have been singled out as violations of existing arms control agreements are the construction of the Krasnoyarsk radar system, Soviet missile testing and development programs, the encryption of telemetry, and the use of chemical and biological weapons. The Soviet Union has its own list of charges of U.S. violations. Included in it are the construction of SLBM early warning radar systems, the installation of new radars in Greenland and Great Britain, the placement of shelters on minuteman silos, and the Strategic Defense Initiative.[12] In late 1989, in a virtually unprecedented move, the Soviet Union admitted that the Krasnoyarsk radar station was in violation of the ABM agreement. U.S. satellites had spotted the construction of the radar station in mid-1983. For several years, an intense debate raged between the two states over the purposes of the Krasnoyarsk system: The Reagan administration charged that it was designed for detecting and tracking ballistic missiles, and the Soviet Union maintained that its purpose was to track objects in space, which was permitted under the ABM treaty.

Allegations of arms control violations such as those surrounding the Krasnoyarsk radar station lie at the heart of compliance diplomacy. Krepon argues that we should not be surprised by such allegations but should treat them as a natural extension of the negotiating process. They are inevitable, not because states will cheat—something they often do—but because of the ambiguity of wording and unforeseen contingencies. The mechanism that currently is in place for dealing with compliance issues is the Standing Consultative Commission (SCC). Created by SALT I, the SCC is a small body whose purpose is to arbitrate misunderstandings in a quiet and confidential atmosphere. Presidents Nixon, Carter, and Ford used the SCC as the primary vehicle for dealing with possible violations. The Reagan administration adopted a more public and accusative approach. It viewed the SCC as simply having papered over Soviet arms control violations by redefining them as acceptable practices.

The on-site inspection provisions of the INF Treaty have added another dimension to compliance diplomacy. An On-Site Inspection Agency (OSIA) has been created to implement its inspection provisions. The first Soviet inspection of a U.S. military facility on short notice took place in February 1989. At issue was a U.S. decision to convert a plant that produced unassembled ground-launched cruise missile parts into one that would produce sea-based weapons not covered by the INF Treaty. The Soviet Union maintained that media accounts suggested that missiles had been assembled at the plant and that these missiles were not included in the official INF tally submitted by the United States. A U.S. official described the inspection as "uneventful." Prior to the Soviet inspection, the United States had conducted six inspections in the Soviet Union and the Soviet Union had conducted three inspections in Western Europe.

CONTEMPORARY ARMS CONTROL PROBLEM AREAS

U.S.-Soviet Nuclear Weapons Inventories

In the previous chapter, we presented a detailed breakdown of the number of weapons in the U.S. and Soviet nuclear arsenals. Table 11.2 shows how these two nuclear arsenals took their present shape. The process of growth documented in Table 11.2 is referred to as "vertical proliferation" and is distinguished from "horizontal proliferation," which deals with the spread of nuclear weapons from one state to another. Efforts to end or place a ceiling on the vertical proliferation of nuclear weapons date back to the very earliest years of the nuclear age, but they have not been pursued with equal seriousness. These efforts can be divided into three periods.

The first period is 1946–1957. Little of significance was achieved in this period because the primary focus on each superpower was on building up their nuclear capabilities and on developing strategies for their use. Classical disarmament proposals dominated the agenda but tended to be put forward more with an eye to their propaganda and image-creating potential than to their substantive merits. The first disarmament proposal to command global attention was the Baruch Plan. Put forward by the United States at the 1946 meeting of the United Nations, it called for placing all aspects of nuclear-energy production and use under international control. It proposed that an international organization should be created, the International Atomic Development Authority (IADA), which would be able to hand out "immediate, swift, and sure punishment" to states that sought to acquire atomic bombs. Once the IADA was in place, the United States promised to destroy its atomic arsenal and

Table 11.2   GROWTH OF THE U.S. AND SOVIET NUCLEAR ARSENALS, 1964–1981

	U.S.		USSR
1964: January—Johnson Freeze Proposal; balance on July 1.	834	ICBMs	190
	416	SLBMs	107
	630	Bombers	175
	1,880	Total	472
1967: January—first SALT proposal by U.S.	1,054	ICBMs	500
	576	SLBMs	100
	650	Bombers	155
	2,280	Total	755
1968: September—SALT due to begin.	1,054	ICBMs	875
	656	SLBMs	110
	565	Bombers	150
	2,275	Total	1,135
1969: November—SALT begins.	1,054	ICBMs	1,140
	656	SLBMs	185
	525	Bombers	145
	2,235	Total	1,470
1972: May—SALT Accords signed; balance on June 30	1,054	ICBMs	1,527
	656	SLBMs	459
	430	Bombers	156
	2,140	Total	2,142
	3,858	Missile IRVs	1,986
	5,700	Missile + bomber warheads	2,500
1974: November—Vladivostok Accord; balance on June 30.	1,054	ICBMs	1,567
	656	SLBMs	655
	390	Bombers	156
	2,100	Total	2,378
	5,678	Missile IRVs	2,222
	7,650	Missile + bomber warheads	2,500

Table 11.2   Continued

	U.S.		USSR
1979: June —SALT II Treaty signed; balance on September 30.	1,054	ICBMs	1,400
	656	SLBMs	923
	348	Bombers	156
	2,058	Total	2,493
	7,274	Missile IRVs	5,375
	9,200	Missile + bomber warheads	6,000
1981: January 1	1,052	ICBMs	1,398
	576	SLBMs	950
	316	Bombers	150
	1,944	Total	2,498
	7,065	Missile IRVs	6,375
	9,000	Missile + bomber warheads	7,000

Source: David Holloway, *The Soviet Union and the Arms Race* (New Haven Conn.: Yale University Press 1983), pp. 58–59.

make its expertise on atomic bombs available to all states that pledged not to acquire atomic bombs. The Soviet Union rejected the Baruch Plan. It called upon the United States to destroy its atomic arsenal first and then to work to establish an international control organization. The Soviet Union also insisted that this organization operate under a system of vetoes and not majority rule as the United States was proposing.

Two other arms control proposals of note took place during this period. In 1953, the Eisenhower administration introduced the Atoms for Peace Plan, and in 1957 it presented the Open Skies Proposal. The United States had hoped to use the Open Skies plan as a way of getting around the problem of on-site inspection. The Soviet Union, however, saw it as an attempt by the United States to legitimize spying and rejected it. The Atoms for Peace Plan did not produce significant movement in the direction of curbing vertical proliferation, but it did lead to the establishment of the International Atomic Energy Agency (IAEA).

The second period took place between the years 1958 and 1972 and was dominated by arms control proposals rather than plans for nuclear disarmament. The Cuban missile crisis added an element of urgency and importance that had not been present before to efforts to curb the superpower arms race. This was a period of great activity, and many of the agreements whose contents we have already specified were negotiated and signed in this era: the Limited Test Ban Treaty; the Non-Proliferation Treaty; and the ABM Treaty and SALT I Accords. Schelling argues that the closing of this period also marks the end point of successful arms control efforts. Since then, he maintains, the United States has lacked "any coherent theory of what arms control is supposed to accomplish." He finds that the current period, 1973 to the present, is dominated by public accusations of wrongdoing and by the transformation of arms control from an instrument of restraint to a mechanism for continuing and justifying the arms race.

Schelling's comments pertain most directly to strategic arms control talks. First, weapons such as the Trident missiles and MX missile, which were built as "bargaining chips," are never cashed in because, since their very existence produced a countermove by the other side, they are now considered to be too valuable to give up. Second, weapons ceilings are set so high that no real reductions of forces—planned or operational—are required by either side.

The Reagan administration's position on strategic arms control talks took shape slowly. During his campaign against Carter, Reagan argued that SALT II was flawed and should not be ratified because it left the Soviet Union in a position of military superiority. Accordingly, the first priority of his administration was arms modernization and expansion, not arms control. In 1981, the Reagan administration announced its readiness to enter into strategic arms control talks with the Soviet Union but not within the framework of SALT. Its preferred acronym was START (Strategic Arms Reduction Talks).

Real movement toward a START agreement did not come until Reagan's second term. In 1985, there occurred the first Reagan-Gorbachev Summit, and this was followed in 1986 by the highly controversial Reykjavik Summit, in which Reagan apparently agreed to eliminate all strategic nuclear weapons but refused to make a deal on SDI. Not only was the substance of these negotiations controversial but so too was the Reagan administration's lack of preparation for them and its failure to consult with either Congress or U.S. allies. The closing months of the Reagan administration saw one last push for a START pact. Although at times an agreement seemed possible, no treaty was signed. At the core of the agreement is a limit of 1,600 launchers; a limit of 6,000 warheads of certain types and sublimits on the number of permissible warheads on ballistic missiles and heavy missiles; and a reduction of about 50 percent in Soviet aggregate ballistic missile throw-weight. The emerging START agreement differs markedly from the SALT framework in its focus on limiting warheads and in the way numbers of SLBM and bomber warheads are calculated. Under the SALT framework, all deployed missiles of a certain type were assumed to carry the maximum number of warheads with which any missile of that type had been tested. Under START, agreed upon numbers of warheads were assigned to certain missiles. For example, the number of warheads on the Soviet SS-N-20 increases from 9 to 10 while the number on the U.S. Poseidon C-3 drops from 10 to 4. Similarly, U.S. B-52 bombers are now counted as having 20 air-launched cruise missiles rather than 12. The numbers for Soviet *Bear* and *Bison* go up to 20 from 2 and 4 bombs per bomber respectively.

Schelling's pessimistic assessment of the arms control record during the current period is less true for intermediate-range nuclear weapons. As we have already noted, in this category, the United States and the Soviet Union negotiated a pathbreaking agreement that not only did away with an entire class of operational and militarily valuable nuclear weapons systems but also allowed a system of on-site inspections. One consequence of the INF Treaty has been to focus attention and controversy on short-range nuclear missiles. Upon coming into office, the Bush administration followed the lead of its predecessor in pushing for a modernization of the short-range Lance missile. West Germany, however, took the position that no decision on modernizing these missiles should take place until 1991 or 1992. West German Chancellor Helmut Kohl also spoke of a willingness to examine the "third zero option" under which all of NATO's and the Warsaw Pact's short-range nuclear missiles would also be scrapped.

Nuclear Proliferation

By commonly accepted counting methods, there currently exist six nuclear states. These are the United States, the Soviet Union, Great Britain, France, China, and India. Officially, no other state has "gone nuclear" since then. The purpose of the 1968 Non-Proliferation Treaty (NPT) is to prevent this number from getting any larger. In the immediate period after the signing of the NPT, a feeling existed that, to a large extent, the problem of proliferation had been solved. The initial concern of arms controllers had been to keep other advanced industrial states, particularly the two Germanies, from acquiring nuclear weapons, and this had been accomplished. While France had not signed the NPT, it did agree not to undermine its operation. Today, concern for the problem of nuclear proliferation has increased, and the focus has shifted from horizontal proliferation to other advanced industrial states to vertical proliferation to the Third World. In order to understand the dimensions of the nuclear proliferation problem, we need to break it down into smaller parts.

The initial point that must be addressed is definitional in nature: When is a state a nuclear military power? Without a clear distinction between nuclear and nonnuclear status, there is no way of judging whether or not proliferation is taking place. A number of possibilities exist. A state could be treated as a nuclear power when it has stockpiled enough nuclear-grade material that it could assemble a nuclear weapon on short notice; when it has a stockpile of nuclear weapons; when it has detonated a nuclear device; or when it possesses both an inventory of tested weapons and a full-fledged ability to deliver warheads against enemy targets.[13] The traditional rule of thumb is that a state is considered to be a nuclear power only after it has detonated a nuclear device. The primary difficulty that many people have with this definition is that it excludes states such as Israel, considered by many to possess a stockpile of nuclear weapons but never to have tested them, and South Africa, which is widely believed to have exploded a nuclear device but for which conclusive proof does not yet exist. The question becomes, if the standard is to be changed, what should it be changed to?

Creating a consensus around a new standard, or even maintaining the consensus around the traditional one, will be difficult for several reasons. First, there has never existed a global consensus that nuclear proliferation is undesirable and must be halted. Many Third World states accuse the United States and the Soviet Union of having a double standard. While they have repeatedly attempted to stop other coun-

Table 11.3   NUCLEAR WEAPONS CAPABILITY WITHIN THIS CENTURY

Possession	Little motivation	Some motivation	High motivation
United States	Australia	Argentina	Iraq
Soviet Union	Austria	Brazil	Libya
Great Britain	Belgium	Chile	Pakistan
France	Canada	South Korea	South Africa
China	Czechoslovakia	Taiwan	
India	Denmark		
Israel (?)	East Germany		
	Egypt		
	Finland		
	Iran		
	Italy		
	Japan		
	Mexico		
	Netherlands		
	Norway		
	Poland		
	Romania		
	Saudi Arabia		
	Spain		
	Sweden		
	Switzerland		
	West Germany		
	Yugoslavia		

Source: The Harvard Study Group, *Living with Nuclear Weapons* (New York: Bantam, 1983), p. 222.

tries from acquiring nuclear weapons, they have done little to reduce the size or sophistication of the weapons in their own nuclear inventories. Many Third World states also tend to view the attitude of the United States, the Soviet Union, and the other advanced industrial states that possess nuclear-energy capabilities as patronizing. A reason frequently given by these states for stopping nuclear proliferation is that the potential (Third World) recipients are not mature or stable enough to manage this material. The implication is that the advanced industrial states *are* mature enough to do so—a point challenged by the events at Chernobyl and Three Mile Island. A related problem that has received less attention is not the absence of political maturity in the Third World but the absence of the technological infrastructure needed to control the production and storage of nuclear-weapons grade material.

An additional factor that any proliferation standard must take into account is a state's motives for developing nuclear weapons. The technological ability to do so is a poor predictor of a state's potential for joining the nuclear "club." Table 11.3 presents a listing of states that might belong to this club before the end of this century. All states commonly labeled as "advanced industrial societies" are found in the "little motivation" category. The greatest challenge will come from keeping three types of states from acquiring nuclear weapons: pariahs, pygmies, and paranoid states. These categories which deal with the motivation for going nuclear are not mutually exclusive, and a state may fit into more than one. Pariah states are international outcasts. They have few allies and feel themselves to be surrounded by hostile states. Israel (classified by the table as a possible nuclear state), South Africa, and Taiwan are pariah states. A pygmy state is a small state existing next to a large neighbor, which feels that its security can only be realized through the possession of nuclear weapons. Pakistan (next to India) and Taiwan (next to China) are two such states. South Korea, with its fear of North Korea and its potential ally China, can also be defined as a pygmy state. Paranoid states tend to view world politics in terms of conspiracy theories. Israel also qualifies as a paranoid state, as do Libya and Iraq, which combine their paranoia with a sense of revolutionary fervor. An additional proliferation problem is nuclear terrorism. Acquiring the necessary component parts to make a deliverable nuclear weapon is not impossible. For example, Pakistan has reached the nuclear threshold by importing allegedly commercial nuclear fuel-reprocessing plants from Europe, building its own uranium enrichment plant, and acquiring a tested design for a nuclear weapon from China. If states such as Pakistan can obtain nuclear weapon-related material illicitly, there is every reason to assume that a determined terrorist organization could do likewise. Writing in 1978, one author estimated that there have been at least 175 incidents of violence or threats of violence against U.S. nuclear facilities since 1969.[14]

Clarity is also needed in order to realize a nonproliferation policy. For example, while the first nuclear explosion that a state conducts is politically important, it is unlikely to be militarily significant. Military significance comes after an inventory of weapons has been created and is coupled with effective delivery systems and command and control technologies. The question thus becomes whether the focus of a nonproliferation agreement should be on preventing the first nuclear explosion by a state or on preventing the prolonged testing of nuclear warheads, the transfer of delivery systems, or the acquisition of command and control technologies. Joseph Nye, Deputy Undersecretary of State for Security Assistance during the Carter administration, argues that the goal must be to maintain an international presumption against proliferation.[15] He notes that the prospects for preventing another explosion are gloomy and that efforts might better be directed at slowing down the rate and degree of proliferation. Such efforts might take the form of negotiated "halts" or "plateaus" among regional nuclear rivals.[16]

The final dimension to the nuclear proliferation question centers on what strategies can be employed to bring it under control. The available strategies can be grouped in any number of ways. One frequently employed approach distinguishes among technological, legal, and political strategies.[17] A second approach classifies strategies into one of two categories, depending upon whether the focus is on altering the incentives to acquire nuclear weapons (demand-side approaches) or on making it more difficult for a state to obtain nuclear weapons (supply-side approaches).[18] Demand-side approaches include providing would-be nuclear states with additional amounts of conventional weapons with the hope that this would satisfy their desire for added security or prestige; extending strengthened security guarantees to would-be nuclear states; providing would-be nuclear states with an alternative fuel supply to nuclear power; and toughening the economic and political penalties applied to states that do achieve nuclear capabilities. Supply-side measures include export controls on sensitive technologies and increasing the inspection capabilities and powers of the IAEA to ensure that nuclear material intended for peaceful uses is not diverted either intentionally or secretly for military purposes.

None of these approaches is without its drawbacks, and this is one of the reasons why halting the spread of nuclear weapons is so difficult. Does the United States want to give South Korea or Israel an ironclad defense guarantee in return for a pledge not to develop nuclear weapons? What type of leverage will it have on human rights issues if it does? How closely should the United States be identified with South Africa or Pakistan? Should it ignore their (often illegal) efforts to acquire nuclear weapons in the interests of larger defense concerns or break off relations with these governments? Will providing a state with added quantities of conventional weapons really curb its nuclear appetite? From the perspective of a state that is seeking to possess nuclear weapons, are conventional weapons—no matter how sophisticated they may be—a substitute for status as a nuclear power? Do not the same types of trade-offs (human rights versus security interests) that are encountered in dealing with nuclear proliferation come into play in the transfer of conventional weapons? Finally, is conventional arms proliferation really safer or any more desirable than nuclear proliferation?[19]

Chemical and Biological Warfare

International controls regulating chemical and biological warfare have been in place since 1925, when the Geneva Protocol banned the use of asphyxiating and poisonous gases, as well as bacteriological methods of warfare. Additional controls were added in 1972 when a Biological Weapons Convention was signed, which banned the development, production, and stockpiling of biological and toxic weapons. These prohibitions against the use of chemical and biological weapons have never been totally effective. One problem is that the Geneva Protocol did not prohibit all activity related to chemical and biological warfare. Signatory states were legally entitled to develop, produce, possess, and transfer such weapons. Additionally, in signing the protocol, many states reserved the right to retaliate in kind if chemical weapons were used against them. One source estimates that up to 34 states and two nonstate actors—the Palestine Liberation Organization and SWAPO (a Namibian independence organization)—may currently possess such weapons.[20]

For much of the post-World War II era, violations of the Geneva Protocol were rare. Documented cases of the use of chemical and biological weapons include the Yemen civil war (1963–1967), during which Egyptian aircraft dropped poison gas on pro-Royalist forces, and the Vietnam War, during which poison gases were used for riot control, to flush Vietcong out of bunkers or other confined spaces, and in conjunction with air attacks or other military actions in large areas in order to drive the enemy into the open. There have also been a number of allegations concerning the use of chemical weapons.

During the late 1970s and 1980s, there was a pronounced weakening of the ban against the use of chemical and biological weapons. Three developments refocused international attention on the problem. First, there was the use of chemical and biological warfare in the Iran-Iraq War. It is estimated that over 50,000 people may have been killed as a result of its use. (In World War I, an estimated 90,000 soldiers were killed and an additional 1.2 million injured due to the use of chemical weapons.) Second, the United States alleged that Libya was constructing a huge chemical weapons factory, and news stories indicated that the Reagan administration had discussed the possibility of taking military action against the suspected factory. Third, the United States announced that it was resuming the production of chemical weapons, thereby ending a nearly 20-year, self-imposed moratorium. U.S. officials maintained that renewed production was necessary because, while the U.S. stockpile had deteriorated and was now of questionable military value, the Soviet Union had for a period of time continued its testing program and possessed more sophisticated chemical weapons.

It was in this context of growing international concern that President Reagan addressed the United Nations in September 1988 and proposed an international conference that would consider ways of strengthening the 1925 Geneva Protocol and of reversing its progressive erosion. The conference called for by Reagan took place in France in January 1989 and was attended by over 140 states. The five-day conference ended with a pledge by those who attended to refrain from using chemical weapons and with an expression of concern that such weapons "remain and are spread." This wording was a compromise. Nonaligned states and others objected to using the term "proliferation" in the final communiqué. The U.S. proposal for international sanctions against new poison gas use was also omitted. Third World states objected to the U.S. condemnation of Libya at the same time that it was going ahead with a modernization of its chemical weapons inventory. Consistent with this position, in late 1989, the Bush administration indicated that the United States intended to continue producing chemical weapons, even if a new global treaty authorizing their destruction took effect. This conference also revealed a growing feeling among Arab states that chemical weapons were a legitimate counter to the suspected Israeli nuclear capability—something which in the past they did not possess. Also disturbing was the fact that, in early March, no more than two months after the meeting adjourned, there were press reports concerning Egypt's acquisition of components for a poison gas plant.

This 1989 international conference on chemical weapons was not the only forum that dealt with the problem. For over 20 years, there have also been ongoing talks in the Conference on Disarmament over additional prohibitions on the use of chemical and biological weapons. Forty states attend these talks. The main problem has been agreeing on the selection of a verification system. National technical means of verification are not effective in monitoring chemical weapons production. On-site inspection is needed. Furthermore, to be truly effective, such inspections must be conducted on civilian production centers, not just military ones. In 1986, the Soviet Union agreed to almost all of the U.S. verification demands. Many analysts believe that the Soviet Union changed its position because it felt that a new treaty was the only way to stop the United States from producing "binary" chemical weapons. Unlike older "unitary" chemical weapons that are filled at the factory, "binary" chemical weapons are made up of two otherwise harmless chemicals that only become deadly when they mix in flight. The Soviet Union does not possess any binary weapons, and U.S. research and development in this field places it at the forefront of chemical warfare technology. Still unresolved at the Conference on Disarmament talks was the proposal put forward by France in 1987 that smaller states be allowed to retain and possibly even to acquire a "minimum security stockpile" of chemical weapons during the projected 10 years that it would take for the United States and the Soviet Union to eliminate their inventories.[21]

Conventional Arms Proliferation We began this chapter with a case study on conventional arms control. We will end our survey of arms control problems with a discussion of conventional arms proliferation. Although the problem of controlling the spread of conventional arms has received far less attention than its nuclear counterpart, it is seen as increasingly important. There are significant differences between nuclear arms control and conventional arms control. Even the language is different. In addressing the pace and consequences of the spread of conventional weapons, policymakers and commentators speak of "arms transfers," not "proliferation." In many ways, the problem of controlling the spread of conventional weapons is far more difficult than that of controlling nuclear weapons proliferation, because arms transfers have become an almost commonplace occurrence in world politics and an accepted instrument of foreign policy. In the Iran-Iraq War, for example, at least 41 states were involved in supplying the two combatants with weapons: 4 states supplied weapons to Iraq but not to Iran (Egypt, Jordan, Ethiopia, and the Philippines), 12 states supplied weapons to Iran but not to Iraq (numbered among them were, Canada, Israel, Libya, Mexico, Taiwan, and Vietnam), and 25 states supplied weapons to both sides (they included the United States, Great Britain, China, the Soviet Union, and South Africa). Eleven other states sold support equipment or supplied advisors during the war.

Arms transfers during the Iran-Iraq War represent only the tip of the iceberg when it comes to the proliferation of conventional arms. Each year the United States receives approximately 10,000 requests from foreign governments for equipment or services that are classified as arms and 20,000 applications from firms for licenses to export equipment or services.[22] In 1985, at roughly the midpoint of the Iran-Iraq War, the worldwide trade in arms was valued at approximately $43 billion. U.S. arms exports in 1985 accounted for 20 percent of all arms that were exported, and they were valued at $12.3 billion. The Soviet Union accounted for 35 percent ($15.3 billion) of all arms transfers in 1985. The cumulative value of world arms transfers for the period 1982–1986 is estimated at nearly $224.5 billion.

The dollar value of the international trade in arms tells only part of the story. A number of other trends must be kept in mind in developing strategies for curbing the flow of weapons across international borders. First, the quality of the weapons crossing borders has increased dramatically. Prior to the 1970s, most arms transfers involved World War II vintage equipment or weapons systems that supplier states were phasing out. Today, many of the weapons systems being made available on the international arms market are among the most sophisticated that are possessed by the supplier state.

A second important trend involves the emergence of Third World states as the primary recipients of arms transfers. Up until the mid-1960s, most arms transfers went to the European allies of the Soviet Union and the United States. This changed with the U.S. involvement in the Vietnam War, when Southeast Asia became the primary end point for arms transfers. Since the 1970s, the Persian Gulf and the Middle East have been the principal recipients of arms transfers.

A third important trend is that arms transfers today tend to involve the sale of weapons rather than the use of military assistance programs or grants. In large measure, this is a result of the emergence of the Middle East states as major recipients of arms transfers. With their treasuries enriched as a result of the oil price hikes of the early 1970s, these Middle Eastern states were in a position to pay for top-of-the-line weapons systems.

A fourth trend that holds serious consequences for any attempt to address the problem of conventional arms proliferation is the increased prominence of Third World states as arms exporters. Third World arms sales accounted for almost 15 percent of total world sales in 1984 and about 18 percent of all sales to Third World markets. Table 11.4 presents a list of the world's major arms exporters in 1985.

No international agreement exists governing the transfer of conventional weapons. The one major effort to construct such an agreement came during the Carter administration. Alone among recent U.S. administrations, Carter's administration sought to stem the tide of arms sales. Among the policy guidelines that it established were a ceiling on the total dollar value of arms sales and, in a unilateral act of arms control, a pledge not to introduce new and sophisticated weapons into the Third World and not to produce weapons solely for export. Gradually, however, the Carter administration found it difficult to work within its own guidelines. The dollar ceiling became a numbers game that was maintained only through creative accounting procedures, and, by 1980, U.S. arms sales had risen from $12.8 billion in 1977 to $17.1 billion. As part of its efforts to curb the international arms trade, the Carter administration initiated talks with the Soviet Union on establishing a system of bilateral restraints.

The Conventional Arms Transfer (CAT) talks began in 1977, and four negotiating rounds were held before these talks collapsed in 1979.[23] Many factors contributed to the failure of the CAT talks. Three stand out as particularly important. First, the United States and the Soviet Union entered the CAT talks with conflicting agendas. The Carter administration was concerned with the influx of Soviet weapons into the Middle East and hoped to establish a "code of conduct" governing superpower arms transfers to that region. The Soviet Union saw the CAT talks as an opportunity to legitimize its Third World activities and to place restraints on Western arms shipments to states along its border, most notably Iran and China. Second, the conventional arms limitations focus of the CAT talks became obscured when U.S. negotiators chose to place the political nature of arms transfers rather than weapons characteristics at the center of the talks. Conflicts quickly arose over what regions were to be discussed. The United States proposed starting with Latin America and sub-Saharan Africa. The Soviet Union agreed, provided China would also be taken up, to which the United States replied that China was not a region. Third, the level of political cooperation between the United States and the Soviet Union that had made the SALT agreements possible was quickly evaporating.

Table 11.4 ARMS SUPPLIERS IN 1981–1985, BY GROUP AND SCALE OF EXPORTS

Millions of current dollars (cumulative)	Warsaw Pact	Other Communist	NATO	Other non-Communist	
				Developed market	Third World
	• Soviet Union				
50,000					
			• United States		
20,000					
			• France		
10,000					
			• United Kingdom		
			• West Germany		
		• China			
5,000					
			• Italy		
	• Poland				
	• Czechoslovakia				
3,000					
	• Romania	• North Korea	• Spain		• South Korea
2,000					
	• Bulgaria	• Yugoslavia		• Switzerland	• Israel
	• East Germany		• Belgium	• Japan	• Brazil
1,000					
	• Hungary		• Canada	Austria	Pakistani
			• Netherlands	• Sweden	• Egypt
				• Finland	• Saudi Arabia
500					
			Portugal		• Libya
			• Turkey		
200					
			• Greece	• Australia	
					• Syria
					• Argentina
100					
		• Cuba	• Norway		• Singapore
					Peru
60					
				• South Africa	• Taiwan
					India
			• Denmark		• China
36					

Source: Joseph Clare, Jr., "Whither the Third World Arms Procedures?" (Washington, D.C.: U.S. Arms Control and Disarmament Agency, 1987), p. 23

CONCLUSION

Advocates of arms control face three major problems in their attempt to create an awareness that possibilities exist for cooperation and mutual restraint. First, if it is to succeed, arms control must be viewed as something that contributes to a state's national security. To the extent that it is equated with appeasement of the enemy or treated merely as a symbolic statement about the evils of war, arms control will fail. A key factor influencing receptivity to arms control is the nature of a state's strategic posture. Advocates of mutual assured destruction (MAD) are more likely to view arms control efforts in a positive light than are those who advocate a policy of limited strategic options (LSO). This is because, while MAD strategists are concerned with stabilizing the nuclear balance, LSO strategists are concerned with preparations for fighting a nuclear war and are likely to see proposals that reduce or constrain the use of nuclear weapons as unwarranted restrictions on their ability to "service" their targets.[24]

Second, arms control cannot be oversold in terms of what it can produce. Richard Burt, a former U.S. ambassador to West Germany and director of the Bureau of Political-Military Affairs of the State Department, argues that "a central fallacy of the existing approach to arms control is the belief that the primary function of negotiations is to alleviate sources of military instability."[25] Furthermore, he says that what arms control can do is catalog and legitimize an existing balance of forces and ratify (as opposed to transform) the status quo. Burt goes on to note that arms control often becomes controversial because, in the process of freezing an existing military balance, it places a spotlight on a state's military deficiencies.

Finally, arms control negotiations must regain a measure of the credibility that they have lost over the years. To many, arms control has been transformed from a means of introducing restraint into an adversarial relationship and a cover for perpetuating the arms race. At issue is the slow pace and lengthy time required to negotiate an agreement. U.S.-Soviet bargaining over SALT I was conducted over a two-and-one-half-year period, during which there occurred seven negotiating rounds and almost 100 meetings. It took five years and almost 100 joint sessions to negotiate the SALT II treaty. Critics contend that, by having transformed the talks into endurance contests, there exists a built-in incentive for stalling and using weapons systems as bargaining chips.

NOTES

1. Richard Neustadt and Ernest May, *Thinking in Time: The Uses of History for Decision Makers* (New York: Free Press, 1986).
2. *The Washington Post*, December 9, 1988, p. 16.
3. Frederick Hartmann, *The Relations of Nations*, 6th ed. (New York: Macmillan, 1983), pp. 268–269.
4. James Schlesinger, "Reykjavik and Revelations," *Foreign Affairs* 1987 (65): 426–446.
5. For a discussion of the negotiating history and operation of various arms control and disarmament regimes, see Alexander George, Philip Farley, and Alexander Dallin, eds., *U.S.-Soviet Security Cooperation* (New York: Oxford University Press, 1988).

6. Thomas Schelling and Morton Halperin, *Strategy and Arms Control* (New York: Twentieth Century Fund, 1961), p. 2.

7. John Gaddis, "The Evolution of a Reconnaissance Satellite Regime," in George, Farley, and Dallin, *U.S.-Soviet Cooperation*, pp. 353–372.

8. Quoted in Jeffrey Richelson, *American Espionage and the Soviet Target* (New York: Quill, 1987), p. 95; also see Jeffrey Richelson, *The U.S. Intelligence Community* (Cambridge, Mass.: Ballinger, 1985); and James Bamford, *The Puzzle Palace* (New York: Penguin, 1982).

9. See the discussion in *The Military Balance, 1988–89* (London: International Institute for Strategic Studies, 1988), pp. 231–232. The one exception on lowering the number of SLBM warheads is the Soviet SS-N-20, which goes from 9 to 10.

10. Michael Krepon, *Arms Control, Verification and Compliance*, Headline Series #270 (New York: Foreign Policy Association, 1984), p. 25.

11. Quoted in Krepon, *Arms Control*, p. 17.

12. Thomas Longstreth, John Pike, and John Rhinelander, *The Impact of U.S. and Soviet Ballistic Missile Programs and the ABM Treaty* (Washington, D.C.: National Campaign to Save the ABM Treaty, 1985); and *Soviet Noncompliance with Arms Control Agreements*, Special Report #136 (Washington D.C.: Bureau of Public Affairs, U.S. State Department, 1985).

13. Michael Nacht, "Controlling Nuclear Proliferation," in Kenneth Oye, Donald Rothchild, and Robert Lieber, eds., *Eagle Entangled* (New York: Longman, 1977), p. 147.

14. Louis Renes Beres, "The Nuclear Threat of Terrorism," *International Studies Notes* 5 (1978): 14–17.

15. Joseph Nye, "Sustaining the Non-Proliferation Regime," in Charles Kegley, Jr., and Eugene Wittkopf, eds., *The Nuclear Reader* (New York: St. Martin's, 1985), p. 187.

16. Harvard Study Group, *Living With Nuclear Weapons* (New York: Bantam, 1983), p. 224.

17. John Spanier, *Games Nations Play*, 6th ed. (Washington, D.C.: Congressional Quarterly Press, 1987), pp. 354–357.

18. William Potter, "Strategies for Control," in Burns Weston, ed., *Toward Nuclear Disarmament and Global Security* (Boulder, Colo.: Westview, 1984), pp. 429–462.

19. These issues are raised in Richard Burt, "Nuclear Proliferation and the Spread of New Conventional Weapons Technology," in Stephanie Neuman and Robert Harkavy, eds., *Arms Transfers in the Modern World* (New York: Praeger, 1980), pp. 89–108.

20. Frederic Pearson and Martin Rochester, *International Relations*, 2d ed. (New York: Random House, 1988), p. 366.

21. *Strategic Survey, 1987–1988* (London: International Institute for Strategic Studies, 1988), pp. 55–62.

22. Richard Wilcox, "Twixt Cup and Lip: Some Problems in Applying Arms Control," in Neuman and Harkavy, *Arms Transfers*, pp. 27–36.

23. Janne Nolan, "The U.S.-Soviet Conventional Arms Transfer Negotiations," in Alexander George, Philip Farley, and Alexander Dallin, eds., *U.S.-Soviet Security Cooperation* (New York: Oxford University Press, 1988), pp. 510–523.

24. Donald Snow, *National Security* (New York: St. Martin's, 1987), pp. 225–250.

25. Richard Burt, "Defense Policy and Arms Control: Defining the Problem," in Richard Burt, ed., *Arms Control and Defense Postures in the 1980s* (Boulder, Colo.: Westview, 1982), p. 5.

THREE

The Economic Dimension

Chapter
12

The Politics of International Economics: The View from the North

Unlike postwar military interactions, the international economy does not provide us with a single dominating struggle such as the cold war around which we can organize our discussion. Instead, we will explore the politics of international economics from three vantage points. In this chapter we will focus on the developed market economies. In Chapter 13, we will look at the poorer and newly industrialized states of the Third World. These two sets of states are often referred to geographically. The developed market economies (with the exception of Australia) are located in the Northern Hemisphere and are referred to as the North; the less developed states are concentrated south of the equator and are referred to as the South. In Chapter 14, we will adopt a global perspective and take up issues that, while they have an economic dimension, also raise important questions concerning social welfare and the ability of the global community to meet the needs of the earth's ever-growing population.

A PRIMER ON THE INTERNATIONAL MONETARY SYSTEM AND TRADE

We will explore two issues in depth in order to give a sense of how Northern states have dominated and organized the international political arena during the post-World War II era. These issues are the international monetary system and trade. In

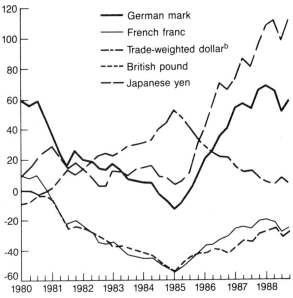

a Change relative to selected foreign currencies, compared with
March 1973.
b Relative to 16 major currencies, weighted by 1979—1980 trade
in manufactures.

Figure 12.1 Selected Developed Countries: Percent Change
in Value of Currencies Relative to the US Dollar,[a] 1980–88.
(*Source:* Central Intelligence Agency, *Handbook of Economic Statistics, 1989* Washington, D.C.: Government Printing Office, 1989.)

discussing trade, we will include a focus on European integration and the use of
trade as a weapon against the Communist states of the East. It is impossible to carry
out such a discussion without using the language of international economics. Therefore, before we begin our overview of the politics of international trade and monetary
policy, we need to introduce certain key economic terms.

International Monetary Terminology

International economic transactions involve the buying and selling of goods, valued
in different currencies. Consequently, some mechanism has to be established for
converting one state's currency into another's. The standard that is used is the *international exchange rate*. The exchange rate can be set by international agreement or
by market forces. For each country, it consists of the rate at which the state's central
bank will exchange local currency for foreign currency. Figure 12.1 illustrates the
value of the dollar against several national currencies between 1980 and 1988. When
currency is determined by market forces, it is said to *float*. Market forces affect the

exchange rate primarily through trade. When one country over time imports more from a particular country than it exports to that country, then a *trade deficit* develops. If the United States is buying more Japanese goods and Japan is buying fewer American goods, then more dollars must be exchanged for yen than vice versa. Since there is a greater demand for yen, its value goes up relative to that of the dollar. The exchange rate can also be affected by speculation. Investors buy currency when it is relatively cheap and then sell it when its value goes up. This affects the market for the currency.

Debate has been persistent over the question of fixed versus floating rates. In a system of *fixed* rates, each country's currency is valued against some standard. Rates may be permanently fixed, periodically adjusted, or adjusted around some point. Fixed rates require an international agreement and apply only to those countries that join in the agreement. *Floating* rates may float freely with no intervention, may float with intervention designed to smooth out "abnormal" fluctuations, or may float with a limitation on the amount of fluctuation allowed within one year's time.[1] Fixed rates are convenient for planning purposes. Although they change, there is considerable intervention to keep them stable. Floating rates, however, probably give a more accurate picture of the relative worth of each country's currency.

Obviously, the prices of goods and services flowing across international borders are affected by the current exchange rate. When one state's currency is valued highly vis à vis another state's currency, that state's purchasing power expands. Imports rise, but since that state's own products are more expensive to purchasers in the other state, exports fall. In theory, when exchange rates are allowed to fluctuate freely, a self-correcting mechanism is built into the system. As the value of a state's currency goes down relative to that of a trading partner, its goods become cheaper and exports increase, thus restoring a balance to trade.

A state's *balance of payments* includes all currency exchanged with other states, including trade and other areas such as tourism and foreign aid. States attempt to build up *reserves* of commonly exchanged currencies, such as the dollar, the pound, the mark, and the yen, in order to meet balance-of-payments deficits at times when the balance of trade is not bringing in a surplus of these or other currencies. Additionally, states can draw on reserves maintained by the International Monetary Fund (discussed next).

International Trade Terminology

International trade is rooted in the unequal distribution of natural resources, technology, people, and capital among states. If a product or a resource is needed and cannot be produced in sufficient quantity within a state's own borders, the state must either go without it, find a domestic alternative, or trade for it. Going without the product or resource may mean that certain economic or political goals must be abandoned. Substitutes are not always available, and, even if they are available, they may carry a high price tag. International trade thus becomes the most appealing of the three options. The question then becomes one of what to trade. One answer is provided by the principle of *absolute advantage*, which says that a country should only *export* goods and resources that it produces in abundance and cheaply and should only *import* goods and resources that it lacks completely or cannot produce more efficiently than others.

However, economic theory argues that a state should actually follow the principle of *comparative advantage* in deciding what to trade. This principle holds that, in making trade decisions, the key point of comparison is not with the efficiency of the same industry in other states (the automobile industry in the United States versus the automobile industry in Japan), but the relative efficiencies of one's own industries (the U.S. automobile industry versus U.S. shoe manufacturing). Even if a state can produce everything more efficiently than other states, trade still makes sense if that state concentrates its resources on producing those goods or resources that it does best. A state has a comparative advantage over another state if, in producing some commodity, it can do so at a relatively lower opportunity cost in terms of the alternative commodities that it must forego.

In a world that contains over 100 states and that has countless products moving across international boundaries, we are far removed from the British-cloth-for-Portuguese-wine example that David Ricardo used in 1817 to illustrate the principle of comparative advantage. Today we need to think in terms of states as having lists of goods that are potentially exportable and importable.[2] At the top of the list are goods for which their comparative advantage is so great that they are sure to be exported. At the bottom of the list are goods for which the state is at such a great comparative disadvantage that they are certain to be imported. In between is a grey area where the costs of producing goods in two states are so similar that the decision to export or import will be based on factors such as transportation costs.

Advocates of comparative advantage argue that where *free trade* prevails, that is, where there are no barriers to the movement of goods, services, or resources across state boundaries, everyone benefits from international trade. Trade between states does more than serve as a mechanism for optimizing the use of global resources and producing wealth. It also provides policymakers with an array of tools that can be used to further domestic and foreign-policy goals. Free trade, itself, can serve and has served as an instrument of foreign policy. From 1944 to 1962, the United States used free trade in the guise of access to U.S. markets as the principal inducement to get other states to adopt policies it favored, such as strengthening military alliances, promoting the economic recovery of Japan and Europe, and creating markets for U.S. exports.

Although many countries support the notion of free trade in principle, they restrict trade in practice. Restrictions on trade can also be used as instruments of foreign policy. *Tariffs*, or taxes on foreign-made goods entering a country, typically are applied in order to protect domestic industries against foreign competition or to raise revenue, but they can also be manipulated to serve foreign-policy goals, such as defeating communism or punishing states for adopting discriminatory economic policies. Closely related to tariffs are *nontariff barriers* (NTBs), among which are quantitative restrictions or quotas on goods coming from one state into another, and qualitative restrictions such as health and safety requirements. NTBs are often instituted for domestic reasons, but these too can be used for foreign-policy purposes. An *embargo* is a refusal to sell a commodity or a good to another state. Embargoes are generally put into place to deny a state access to goods or services that are either in short supply or that could be used against a state in a future conflict situation. Finally, a *boycott* is a refusal to buy products from a certain state, and it is generally applied in an effort to place pressure on a state to change an objectionable policy. This was the case in the late 1960s, when the UN sponsored a boycott of Rhodesian products in an attempt to get that government to accept the principle of majority rule.

INTERNATIONAL MONETARY POLITICS

In July 1944, representatives from 44 countries met in Bretton Woods, New Hampshire, in order to establish international institutions for regulating the international economic system in the post-World War II era. From 1875 to 1914, the world economy operated on the basis of the gold standard. This period of relative stability revolved around a core mechanism—fixed values of national currencies were set in relation to the price of gold. This system ended with World War I and was never effectively reestablished. During the depression of the 1930s, international economic collaboration among states reached a low point and the international monetary and trade systems deteriorated. Many blamed the nationalist economic policies practiced during this period for the outbreak of World War II. Although they differed in the specifics of implementation, the states meeting at Bretton Woods were united in their belief that an open system would enhance the welfare of all; that nationalist economic policies lead to instability, chaos, and war; and that world communism threatened their survival.

Together they created the Bretton Woods system that lasted for nearly two decades. Its viability depended on two major factors—the absence of a group of states that was both able and willing to challenge the system and the existence of a dominant power to ensure that the system worked (hegemony). The Articles of Agreement of the International Monetary Fund attempted to establish a stable economic system to be implemented following the war. The agreement established the International Bank for Reconstruction and Development (World Bank) and the International Monetary Fund (IMF). Exchange rates were to be fixed without being rigid. Countries would declare a value (referred to as the *par value*) for their currencies and would maintain exchange rates within 1 percent of this amount. However, in the event of a "fundamental disequilibrium" in their balance of payments, a state could alter its par value. Since states were not to devalue their currency at will, the IMF was established to provide reserves that each state could draw on if needed. Member nations were assigned quotas and were to pay a specified amount into the IMF. Few countries were in a position, however, to make their payments to the IMF during the years following the war.

In addition to providing reserves, the IMF would administer the rules regulating currency exchange and would provide an institution for managing monetary relations among states. Voting power within the IMF was related to the quotas. Under the Articles of Agreement, each state would receive 250 votes, plus one vote for each $100,000 of its quota. Quotas were established on the basis of the perceived economic importance of the country. During the late 1980s, the United States, West Germany, the United Kingdom, Japan, and France together controlled 40.9 percent of the votes. In 1990, Japan moved into second place behind the United States.

The World Bank was established to aid in reconstruction after the war. It would make loans from its own funds and would underwrite loans from private sources. Additionally, it could raise new funds by issuing securities. It soon became clear that the World Bank could not handle the needs for postwar reconstruction and that the IMF could not deal with Europe's huge deficits. In 1947, the United States assumed responsibility for managing the international monetary system. During the period from 1947 to 1960, the United States was both willing and able to manage the system.

The Europeans and the recently defeated Japanese were in no position to challenge U.S. hegemony. Because of its geographic isolation, the United States had escaped the physical and economic destruction suffered by the other combatants. In fact, most states were quite willing and anxious to allow the United States to dominate the international monetary system. A measure of the importance of the United States to global economic recovery can be seen in the fact that in 1946 Europe had a balance-of-payments deficit of $5.8 billion, while the United States had a balance-of-payments surplus of $6.7 billion, and that in 1948 it had reserves of over $26 billion. Clearly, the United States was in a position to provide capital and goods to other states. In the course of doing so, the dollar became an international currency. It was valued at $35 per ounce of gold, and the United States committed itself to maintaining this exchange rate. Other countries soon began to value their currency vis à vis the dollar.

The U.S. government met any domestic objections to its international economic policy by citing the importance of economic stability in Japan and Europe to U.S. national security interests. It argued that the cold war required that some domestic economic interests be subordinated in the interests of survival. As long as the cold war persisted, the United States tolerated a number of actions undertaken by the other market economies, which were actually at odds with the principles of a liberal system, and during the 1940s and 1950s, it encouraged a huge outflow of dollars in the form of aid programs and loans. Since much of this money was spent on American goods and services, the U.S. economy flourished as the European and Japanese economies recovered. This period of hegemony was marked by frequent intervention by the United States in the world economy. By 1960, however, the outflow of dollars had reached the point at which the United States was facing an undesirable deficit and was reluctant to continue managing the monetary and trade systems. Between 1957 and 1963, U.S. gold holdings fell from $22.8 billion to $15.5 billion. The stability of the world's economy was threatened by American deficits, and a number of economic crises occurred. In 1971, the United States ran a disastrous balance-of-payments deficit—$10.6 billion—and imports exceeded exports for the first time in the twentieth century.

As the cold war eased and their economies recovered from the war, the European nations were less and less willing to accept U.S. dominance. Disagreement existed on how to reform the system. The United States and Great Britain favored reform that would preserve the dollar as the preeminent currency. France desired a return to the gold standard. The French position represented a challenge to U.S.

power. A return to the gold standard would have seriously weakened U.S. economic strength by requiring it to pay, in gold, for dollars that other states held. As these states demanded payment, the United States would have to resolve its balance-of-payments deficit. This could only be accomplished by seriously reducing U.S. military presence worldwide. West Germany supported a middle position and negotiated a compromise, whereby Special Drawing Rights (SDRs) would be used to relieve pressure on the dollar and the European states would receive greater voting rights in the IMF. SDRs are sometimes referred to as *paper gold*. They are a fictional international currency whose value is based on a weighted mix of the world's most important currencies—dollar, yen, mark, franc, and pound. This agreement marked the end of U.S. control over the monetary system and the beginning of multilateral management.

During the period of multilateral management, which prevailed in the 1960s, there were three important elite groups involved in the management of the international monetary system. The Group of 10 was composed of finance ministers from 10 industrial market economies—Belgium, Canada, France, Germany, Italy, Japan, the Netherlands, Sweden, the United Kingdom, and the United States. In 1961, it created a fund independent of the IMF. The purpose of this fund was to supplement the reserves of the IMF, which were not thought to be great enough to handle a major crisis. The Group of 10, in addition to managing this fund, served as a forum for negotiation and was responsible for the creation of SDRs, which are allocated by the IMF. A second elite group was composed of bankers. Known as the Basel Group, they agreed in 1961 to establish a "gold pool" to control speculation. They controlled the gold market until 1968 by buying gold when the price fell and holding it until the price rose. The third group was a committee of finance ministers in the Organization for Economic Cooperation and Development (OECD). The OECD is composed of the developed capitalist economies, including the West European states, the United States, Canada, Australia, and Japan, and was formed to provide technological assistance and to work toward cooperation in the international economy. Although the United States continued to occupy a central position in world economic affairs, for the first time in its history it was not able to make domestic fiscal policy without constraints from abroad. The Smithsonian Agreement of 1971 devalued the dollar relative to the mark, the yen, and gold, and the United States rescinded its guarantee to convert dollars to gold on demand. This decision marked the end of the Bretton Woods system.

In the post-Bretton Woods era, the international monetary system has been marked by flexible exchange rates, with the value of the dollar reflecting fluctuations in perceptions of U.S. economic strength. Gold has been less important and has been traded at market prices. In 1981, the Reagan administration announced that it would no longer intervene in foreign-exchange markets. During the 1980s, monetary power was more widely dispersed. Table 12.1 indicates holdings of gross international reserves for the developed countries. Although the United States remains the most powerful state, it is no longer able or willing to manage the system. Although economic summits during the 1980s did establish a desire for cooperation, real reform was not accomplished. Without reform, crisis management rather than preventive maintenance is likely to be the norm. One suggestion for reform consists of gradually replacing the dollar as the medium for exchange with SDRs. Holders of

Table 12.1 GROSS INTERNATIONAL
RESERVES FOR
SELECTED DEVELOPED
COUNTRIES, 1988

Total (market economies)	610,996
Canada	10,961
France	63,450
Germany (Federal Republic)	88,941
Italy	46,049
Japan	51,727
Switzerland	54,339
United Kingdom	25,853
United States	139,884

Source: World Bank, *World Development Report, 1988,* from Table 15. (New York: Oxford University Press, 1988).

SDRs can exchange them directly for foreign currency. Because the value of SDRs fluctuates less than any single currency, it is a more stable medium of exchange. Extensive international cooperation will be required before SDRs become the standard unit.

TRADE

In 1947, the Western powers created a mechanism—the General Agreement on Tariffs and Trade (GATT)—to organize and encourage world trade. GATT was originally seen as a temporary measure, but it became permanent because of the failure to reach an agreement on a more ambitious system that was to be organized around the Havana Charter and the International Trade Organization (ITO). As envisioned by the United States, the Havana Charter would have established rules for tariffs and nontariff barriers, including detailed provisions on commodity agreements, employment, and restrictive business practices. These would have been enforced by the ITO, which was to have the authority to ensure compliance with trade rules.

After lengthy negotiations in which each country pushed for protections and special exemptions, a compromise was reached. It fell far short of the original proposal. Faced with considerable domestic opposition to the Havana Charter, President Truman declined to submit this compromise to Congress. GATT, which had already been established as an agency of the ITO, became the mechanism for managing trade. GATT has a small, permanent staff based in Geneva, Switzerland, and regularly schedules conferences to negotiate tariff reductions. Members of GATT agree to abide by three principles (as well as a number of other conditions): nondiscrimination, transparency, and reciprocity. A nondiscriminatory policy is one in which all of the trading partners of a given country are treated equally. Transparency requires that, if barriers to trade exist, these should be primarily tariffs rather than nontariff barriers. Those nontariff barriers (such as health and safety regulations) that exist should be established and applied in such a way that they do not act merely as a tool for protecting domestic interests in the face of foreign competition. Finally, reciprocity provides that, if one country lowers its tariffs on another's products, the other country should reciprocate. GATT consists of a set of rules that are designed to promote free trade and are legally binding for member states. Under GATT, the international system has approximated the ideal of open trade in industry only. Agricultural products remain protected, and, additionally, under GATT there is an escape clause that allows a country temporarily to protect other products endangered by competition and in case of balance-of-payments difficulties. The membership has grown from 23 to 93 members, and, in all, about 122 countries follow its rules. In theory, each member adheres to the most-favored-nation principle (nondiscrimination), but exceptions are granted for customs unions, free-trade associations, and developing nations. GATT has no authority to apply sanctions or force against members who fail to comply with its policies.

International mechanisms for regulating trade have proven to be more problematical than those concerning monetary policy. Historically, monetary policy has been left up to economic and political elites. In the United States, it has provoked little domestic interest, and the executive branch has been relatively free to pursue its policies without Congressional interference. In contrast to monetary policy, trade policy has a clear impact on particular industries and localities. When an industry is threatened by foreign competition, management and workers turn to government for protection. When a particular industry fails, other industries that provide inputs into the state's production process also suffer, as well as any businesses that depend on the market provided by the now unemployed workers. For example, in 1980, U.S. automobile manufacturers lost $6 billion and laid off more than 200,000 employees. The public, particularly in the geographic areas most affected, perceived a direct relationship between unemployment and lower wages in the automobile industry (and other resulting economic woes) and the importation of Japanese cars. Management and unions demanded trade policies that would raise the prices of Japanese cars to make them less desirable to the American consumer. Consequently, the U.S. government negotiated voluntary quotas on Japanese automobile imports. This scenario has been played out many times in many countries, particularly in the areas of agricultural imports and textiles.

Like unemployment, inflation is also affected by trade policy. By easing restrictions on imports, competition for higher-priced items can be obtained, which causes prices to fall. Similarly, export restrictions can cause more of a domestically produced good to remain in the domestic market, thereby reducing its price. Since trade policy has an immediate impact on the crucial domestic issues of unemployment and inflation, few governments are able to pursue a policy based on ideology alone. For this reason, it was inevitable that the system of open trade, although agreed upon in principle by the market economies, would soon break down. In fact, some would argue that the system fell victim to political forces before its existence was fully established, since the International Trade Organization that would have been created by the Havana Charter never came into existence. Nevertheless, under GATT, tariffs have been substantially reduced, particularly in the immediate postwar period.

The United States, anxious to accelerate economic recovery in Europe and Japan after World War II, initiated six trade negotiations between 1947 and 1967. During this time, the system worked well and world trade grew rapidly. Trade among the industrialized market economies more than quadrupled between 1963 and 1973. The World Bank reports that average tariffs on manufactures fell from about 40 percent during the 1950s to less than 10 percent by 1974.

Given the close relationship between international monetary policies and world trade, it was likely that the forces responsible for change in the monetary system would also affect trade. In fact, changes in monetary policy and trade have tended to occur at roughly the same time. During the period when the monetary system was relatively stable and the United States dominated the international economy, the other market economies remained supportive of open trade. Given the primacy of the U.S. market, other nations could not afford to impose trade restrictions without U.S. approval. Tariffs dropped, and world trade grew rapidly. Until about 1960, trade issues among the market economies were depoliticized. Disputes were settled by negotiation.

In this period, the United States was willing to maintain open trade while allowing Europe and Japan to follow more protectionist policies. The United States enjoyed a trade surplus and was anxious to rebuild the European and Japanese economies. During the 1960s, Japan and Europe began to challenge the United States economically and domestic interests in the United States demanded protection. Additionally, six European states came together to form the European Economic Community (EEC), now called the EC. Although none of these states alone could have challenged U.S. hegemony, together they constitute a powerful bloc. The member nations of the EC—there were 10—enjoyed free internal trade, including the movement of labor and capital and a common agricultural policy (CAP). The CAP blocks agricultural imports through high tariffs and maintains domestic price supports, which make local goods competitive with the more cheaply produced U.S. products. U.S. exports of protected products to EC countries have been seriously affected by the CAP. In addition to the preferential trade agreements among its members, the EC has established preferential treatment for former colonies and has established trade agreements with nonmember states in the Mediterranean region. Many of the EC's policies are inconsistent with the principles of GATT, although customs unions are permitted under the agreement.

By 1971, the United States was no longer willing to support an open economic system at the expense of its own interests. The Nixon administration developed a "New Economic Policy," which, among other things, imposed a 10-percent surcharge on all imports that were eligible for duties. Negotiations with Europe and the Japanese led to a multinational trade meeting in September 1973 in Tokyo. The Tokyo Round, as it came to be known, produced a declaration of continued commitment to open trade. The Tokyo Round reduced tariffs in a number of areas. Table 12.2 presents figures for tariffs on finished and semifinished manufactured goods. In spite of these reductions, the Tokyo Round negotiations actually opened a new era of protectionism. Currency crises, resource scarcity (the oil crisis), high unemployment, and recession and inflation fueled domestic pressure for government intervention and protection in many states. At the same time, competition from Japanese

Table 12.2   PRE- AND POST-TOKYO ROUND TARIFFS FOR TWELVE PROCESSING CHAINS

Stage of processing	Product description	Tariff rate	
		Pre-Tokyo	Post-Tokyo
1	Fish, crustaceans, and mollusks	4.3	3.5
2	Fish, crustaceans, and mollusks, prepared	6.1	5.5
1	Vegetables, fresh or dried	13.3	8.9
2	Vegetables, prepared	18.8	12.4
1	Fruit, fresh or dried	6.0	4.8
2	Fruit, provisionally preserved	14.5	12.2
3	Fruit, prepared	19.5	16.6
1	Coffee	10.0	6.8
2	Processed coffee	13.3	9.4
1	Cocoa beans	4.2	2.6
2	Processed cocoa	6.7	4.3
3	Chocolate products	15.0	11.8
1	Oilseeds and flour	2.7	2.7
2	Fixed vegetable oils	8.5	8.1
1	Unmanufactured tobacco	56.1	55.8
2	Manufactured tobacco	82.2	81.8
1	Natural rubber	2.8	2.3
2	Semimanufactured rubber (unvulcanized)	4.6	2.9
3	Rubber articles	7.9	6.7
1	Rawhides and skins	1.4	0.0
2	Semimanufactured leather	4.2	4.2
3	Travel goods, handbags, and so on	8.5	8.5
4	Manufactured articles of leather	9.3	8.2
1	Vegetable textiles and yarns (excluding hemp)	4.0	2.9
2	Twine, rope, and articles; sacks and bags	5.6	4.7
3	Jute fabrics	9.1	8.3
1	Silk yarn, but not for retail sale	2.6	2.6
2	Silk fabric	5.6	5.3
1	Semimanufactured wood	2.6	1.8
2	Wood panels	10.8	9.2
3	Wood articles	6.9	4.1
4	Furniture	8.1	6.6

Note: Rates are the unweighted average of the tariffs actually facing developing country exports (under the Generalized System of Preferences, the most-favored-nation rule, other special preferential arrangements, and so forth) in the EC; Austria, Finland, Norway, Sweden, Switzerland; Australia, New Zealand, and Japan; and Canada and the United States.

Source: World Bank, *World Development Report, 1987* (New York: Oxford University Press, 1987), p. 138.

imports and manufactured goods from newly industrialized countries (NICs) threatened local industry. Prior to 1970, growth in trade occurred among the industrialized market economies and was largely intraindustry. A rise in imports resulted in a rise in exports. In contrast, the growth from the NICs tended to be concentrated in a few products, which threatened labor-intensive domestic industry in the importing country. Since labor costs were lower in the NICs, goods could be produced more cheaply there, and since the same industries were labor-intensive in the industrialized country, their potential failure threatened many jobs. Meanwhile, exports to the NICs tended to come from industries employing fewer workers. Growth in these industries could not be enough to absorb workers displaced by imports. At the same time, the markets in the NICs were intensely competitive, making it difficult for the industrialized countries to compete. These factors influenced calls for protectionism.

The Kennedy Round of GATT negotiations in 1968 was the last truly successful conference. Although the Tokyo Round (1974–1979) cut tariffs further, a number of other barriers to liberalization of trade have remained unchanged or in some cases have increased. The liberal trade system has been undermined since the mid-1970s by the implementation of nontariff barriers (NTBs). These include quotas on particular foreign products, subsidies on domestic products (particularly agricultural products), product specifications (particularly health regulations), government buying policies that favor domestic producers, and administrative regulations. By using NTBs, governments can restrict imports while technically adhering to GATT regulations. For example, a government might argue that, in order to protect the health of its citizens, it will not import beef containing antibiotics. In reality, such a restriction may have more to do with protecting the domestic beef industry than with protecting health and safety. Major trade areas affected by NTBs are textiles and agricultural products.

There are numerous indications of the breakdown of open trade. Agricultural trade has become more protected as the industrial nations have increased subsidies and barriers to imports. Regional trade organizations have eliminated barriers among their members but have created new barriers with nonmember countries. Existing protections on textiles have been strengthened. The 1962 agreement on textiles, which protects cotton, evolved into the Multifibre Arrangement (MFA), which extended protection to synthetics in 1974. In 1977 and 1982, more restrictive agreements were adopted. In 1986, silk, linen, ramie, and jute were added to the fibers previously covered. Between 1981 and 1986, nontariff barriers increased significantly in Canada, the United States, and the EC.

Although it has the world's third largest gross national product and consistently carries a favorable balance of trade, Japan continues to pursue protectionist policies. In 1984, the United States ran a trade deficit with Japan of $37 billion, and the EC had a deficit with Japan of $13 billion. Japan is accused of nurturing its industries behind highly protectionist trade barriers, including quotas, and by maintaining an undervalued yen. Protectionism continued to be a major concern in the 1990s.

The World Bank attributes increased demands for protectionism worldwide to three factors: structural changes in trade, reduced flexibility, and recession and instability in the international economy. Structural changes refer to the rise in Japanese and NIC exports as a percent of world trade. The second factor, reduced flexibility in labor markets, particularly in Europe, makes it difficult for those economies to reduce unemployment. Labor laid off in one area is not readily employable in another. Where jobs are threatened, workers demand protection. Finally, recession and instability have slowed the growth of the industrialized economies. Unemployed workers become harder to absorb. Meanwhile, unstable exchange rates have resulted in appreciated currency, which affects the competitiveness of exports.

The agenda of the current Uruguay Round of GATT negotiations includes tariffs, nontariff barriers to trade, agricultural and tropical products, safeguards, and textiles. The Uruguay Round marks the first of the GATT negotiations in which the less-developed nations are full participants. An issue that is important to the United States and to the Third World is the regulation of trade in services, such as transportation, banking, insurance, and tourism. These account for at least one-fifth of all global trade. Presently, there are few rules governing trade in services, and the Uruguay Round is the first of the GATT negotiations to include this topic. Presently, states are free to establish whatever restrictions they desire. These include technical standards, licensing requirements, monopolies, and procurement policies. Often, in an effort to protect domestic firms, states apply these rules differently to foreign and domestic companies. The United States desires to liberalize trade in services. Major U.S. interests that would benefit from fewer restrictions are the insurance industry, financial institutions, data processing and telecommunications firms, and the motion picture industry.

Third World nations have voiced serious reservations concerning the liberalization of trade in services. India and Brazil have emerged as representatives for these states. They argue that liberalizing trade in services threatens their sovereignty. Negotiating access to transportation, communications, and financial networks will restrict their ability to manage development strategy and may threaten their national security. They also contend that they need to protect their own infant industries. Trade in services is expected to be a tough issue on which agreement can be reached.

REGIONAL INTEGRATION

One of the most significant developments for the politics and economics of international trade has been the emergence of an increasingly unified Europe as a powerful force on the world scene. By 1982, the members of the European Community represented a market of approximately 270 million consumers, compared with approximately 225 million consumers in the United States. They accounted for one-quarter of the world's imports and one-fifth of its exports—figures that are roughly equivalent to those of Japan and the United States. Since its founding in 1957, private spending by its citizens has increased seven times, compared with a fourfold increase in spending by Americans. At first, the United States encouraged this process, because it saw a strong and healthy Europe as a valuable ally against the Soviet Union. More recently, however, the United States has come to see the EC as a competitor. In this section, we will examine the growth and development of European economic cooperation. We will also take a look forward to 1992, when European economic cooperation (and competition with the United States) may reach unprecedented heights. As will soon become evident, economics and politics are all but inseparable in the recounting of efforts to bring about greater economic cooperation in Europe.

Integration Theory

The body of ideas and concepts that underlies what European leaders are trying to achieve is *integration theory.* The close, but uncertain, connection between politics and economics is evident in theories about how greater integration (the coming together of separate states or other political units under a common authority) can be brought about in Europe.[3] One school of thought focuses exclusively on political integration, which entails the development of a shared sense of identity, community, and obligation by people who once thought of themselves as belonging to separate and often competing political systems. It seeks to transpose onto the international scene national political institutions. This approach believes that the only way a larger unit can be created is by means of a frontal attack on state sovereignty through the creation of new institutions (legislatures, bureaucracies, and judiciaries) that centralize important political powers in the hands of international authorities. Once these institutions are in place, advocates of this approach are confident that policy and attitudinal integration will follow. Piecemeal approaches, in which national power is slowly whittled away and is taken over by regional authorities, are seen as bound to fail because they cannot generate sufficient momentum to overcome the inevitable resistance of national policymakers to efforts to strip them of power. The most popular approach to integration based on this logic is *federalism.* Working largely on the basis of the U.S. historical experience, federalists incorporate democratic safeguards, the concept of separation of powers, and "states rights" provisions into their plans for regionally integrated governments.

Functionalism is a second possible path to integration. It seeks to realize political integration through economic integration. Economic integration involves the merging of economic activities that once took place almost exclusively within the borders of separate states. Trade in goods and services, investment and planning decisions, monetary policy, and labor policy stand out as the leading economic sectors in which integration has been attempted. Believing that there is not likely to exist enough political will for a frontal attack on state sovereignty, functionalists propose an indirect and minimal attack. Emphasis is placed on developing narrowly focused regional bodies that would deal with specific policy problems in the above-mentioned policy areas rather than on creating supranational political institutions.

Central to functionalist logic are three interconnected propositions. First, politics and economics can be treated as two separate areas. Decisions in the political arena are made through bargaining and negotiation; decisions in the economic arena are made according to technical and objective criteria. Second, the types of economic problems facing the modern state cannot be resolved at the state level. Thus, while policymakers will resist challenges to their political authority from a regional power structure, they will respond differently to plans for economic integration that appear to be nonpolitical in nature and therefore do not threaten state sovereignty. Third, the ultimate result of economic integration is political integration. Political integration occurs because the benefits of regional problem-solving organizations are so great that not only do states find it very difficult to withdraw from them but also pressure builds to create additional organizations to deal with other problems. For the functionalist, the end result of the integrative process will not be the creation of a larger sovereign state, as is envisioned by the federalists. Functionalists seek only to establish the minimum amount of integration necessary to solve common problems. Their ultimate goal is to make sovereignty irrelevant by enmeshing the state in a series of overlapping technical and administrative regional organizations.

A third approach to integration is *neofunctionalism.* Neofunctionalists have been termed "federalists in functionalist clothing." Like the functionalists, their approach encompasses a minimal assault on state sovereignty that emphasizes economic integration over political institution building. Neofunctionalists differ from functionalists in that, rather than relying upon the nature of the problems facing society to dictate where integration will take place, they consciously select areas that are politically important but in which a technically oriented problem-solving approach will work. The ultimate goal of neofunctionalism is federalist in nature: the creation of a larger political unit. To that end, the neofunctionalist strategy emphasizes setting up political institutions that will speed up the integrative process by producing "spillover" from one area of international cooperation to another. Early neofunctionalists were confident that spillover would occur for two reasons. First, policymakers who experienced success in integrating one area would naturally be inclined to try to duplicate that success elsewhere. Second, integration in certain areas almost demands integration in related policy areas if it is to succeed. By carefully selecting the areas in which integration would occur, neofunctionalists felt they could engineer the assault on state sovereignty.

As our discussion of European integration and Third World integration (to be discussed in Chapter 13) will show, efforts to put integration theory into practice have had mixed results. This has led observers to reexamine the logic behind their integration formulas. This has been particularly true for neofunctionalism, which has proven to be the most influential theory of integration and on which efforts at European integration are based. Neofunctionalists have lost some of their optimism over the efficacy of their spillover strategy. Phillipe Schmitter, for example, notes that most political activity occurs within a zone of indifference, in which existing grants of authority are simply taken as a given. When policymaking breaks out of this zone, spillover is only one possible path that might be followed. Others include retrenchment, "spill back," muddling about, and "spill around." His argument is presented in Figure 12.2. Added attention has also been given to specifying the environmental conditions that are conducive to integration. Foremost among these are (1) the economic compatibility or "fit" of the states being integrated, (2) the existence of interest groups that are capable of lobbying for additional integration and energizing the spillover process, (3) the presence of strong leaders who share the same values and are supportive of integration, (4) domestic political stability that allows states to adapt and respond to pressures for integration, and (5) "catalytic" factors, such as a common enemy, a natural disaster, or economic distress, which lead to demands for integration.

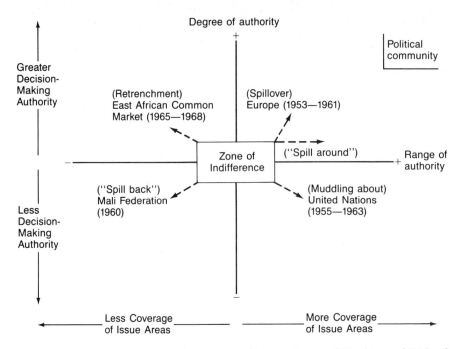

Figure 12.2 Possible Directions of Integration. (*Source:* Raymond Hopkins and Richard Mansbach. *Structure and Process in International Politics* New York: Harper & Row. 1973, p. 280.)

The European Community

Growth and Development   The foundation for the European Community (EC) was created in 1957 when Belgium, France, Italy, Luxembourg, the Netherlands, and West Germany signed the Treaty of Rome, which set up the European Economic Community (EEC) and the European Atomic Energy Commission (EURATOM). It has been more successful than any other regional economic organization, and today the EC has 12 members and stands on the verge of moving integration to a level not thought possible a decade ago. While carving out a new and unique place for itself on the political landscape of Europe, the EC had long intellectual and institutional roots to draw upon. The notion of a unique entity called "Europe" dates back about 15 centuries to the latter days of the Roman Empire, and, though politically divided, Europe remained an informal community throughout the Medieval and early modern eras. Formal international cooperation among European states can be dated back as far as 1815, when the Central Commission for the Navigation of the Rhine was established to allow states to take commercial advantage of the development of the steamship. Other international organizations were then created to deal with telegraphic communications, mail delivery, and standardizing weights and measures.

The post-World War II period also provided institutional predecessors for the EC. The oldest European postwar organization is the Council of Europe. Founded in

1949, its purpose was, and still is, to bring about greater European unity and cooperation and to stimulate democracy and human rights. A second step toward European unity was taken in 1950, when French Foreign Minister Robert Schumann proposed the creation of the European Coal and Steel Community (ECSC). The purpose behind the ECSC was to make another war in Europe impossible. Steel is a primary component in any state's war-making potential, and iron and coal are required to make steel. Before World War II, Europe's richest iron deposits were located on the French side of the Franco-German border in Lorraine, while its greatest coal deposits were found on the German side in the Ruhr and the Saar. Not surprisingly, France and Germany had repeatedly come into political and military conflict over control of these resources. Under Schumann's plan, the ECSC would place these resources under a common high authority, which would have the power to set production quotas in the member states, fix rail charges and other transportation costs, provide retraining and housing for workers displaced in these industries, and prevent unfair competition. On April 18, 1951, the same six states that would later unite to form the EC signed a treaty creating the ECSC.

Not all pre-EC attempts at European unification succeeded, nor did they all contribute to the creation of the EC. One notable failure was the attempt to establish a European Defense Community. As with the ECSC, the proposal for a European Defense Community came from France, but, unlike the ECSC, the impetus behind the proposal was provided by events outside of Europe. War in Korea had made the United States fearful of a Soviet attack on Western Europe. To counter such a threat, it was felt that West Germany should make a military contribution to NATO. In an effort to curb European fears regarding German rearmament, France proposed creating a European army under the authority of a European Defense Community that would be modeled on the ECSC. Before it could come into existence, the parliaments of all six member states were required to give their approval. Heated debates took place in each country over both the question of German rearmament and the desirability of placing national military forces under European control. After four years, only two states had voted their approval. The death blow was delivered in August 1954, when the French National Assembly rejected the plan by a vote of 319–264, with 43 abstentions.

With the failure of the European Defense Community, attention shifted back to economic integration. The culmination of efforts to advance economic integration and negotiations over how to prevent another negative vote by France was the formation of the EEC and EURATOM. Particularly important to France was protection for its industries, many of which were likely to find themselves at a competitive disadvantage in a larger and open common market, and the adoption of a common agricultural policy by the EEC. In the end, West Germany agreed to the French demands in order to obtain a greatly expanded tariff-free market for its industrial goods. At the outset, the EEC was basically an economic union, although it was clear to its founders that some form of political union would ultimately be necessary. The short-term objectives of the EEC were to remove obstacles to trade within its boundaries. This required that there be:

1. No customs duties or quotas on goods moving within the EEC

2. Uniform customs duties on goods entering any member country from outside the EEC

3. The right of any citizen of any member state to live and work in any member state with equal benefits and pay

4. Provisions for any company in any member state to operate in any other member state subject to the same laws and taxation as companies originally registered in that state

5. Rules against governments unfairly helping citizens and their businesses in competition with citizens in other member states

6. No restrictions on the free transfer of capital from member state to another

The early years of the EEC brought remarkable economic success to its members. The first serious political crisis faced by the EEC came in 1962 when Great Britain applied for membership. Although it was Winston Churchill who in 1946 first suggested the idea of creating a "United States of Europe," Great Britain repeatedly had declined to participate in the creation of new international institutions in Western Europe. In fact, just after its founding, Great Britain had sought to envelop the EEC in a larger economic organization by creating a free-trade area that would include both EEC members and nonmembers. In the end, French opposition to the plan brought about its undoing, and, in 1960, Great Britain, Denmark, Norway, Sweden, Switzerland, Ireland, and Portugal—all non-EEC members—set up a European Free Trade Association. Only trade in manufactured goods was covered by the new organization, and there was no hint of creation of supranational political institutions.

It was French opposition in 1962 that stood in the way of Great Britain's entry into the EEC. All other EEC members supported the British application. President Charles de Gaulle vetoed the request for admission, primarily because he feared that British membership would serve as an entry point for greater U.S. influence in EC decision making. De Gaulle was also fearful that British membership would transform the EEC into a federal superstate, in which French influence would be diminished through the presence of another large state. De Gaulle's decision angered other EEC members and left a legacy of distrust that paralyzed EEC decision making for some time. In a very real sense, the deadlock was broken only with his resignation from the French presidency in 1969.

Along the way, however, a compromise was reached that allowed the EEC to limp along. It recognized the right of the EEC, as opposed to only the member states, to initiate policy with France maintaining that on matters of "vital" national interest it reserved the right to exercise a veto. The net result of this compromise was to shelve any plans for European unification and the development of supranational institutions. For the time being, the EEC would remain a customs union. The next major step toward 1992 came in 1965, when the original six members signed a treaty merging the ECSC, EEC, and EURATOM into the European Community (EC), which would become effective in 1969. This was done by combining the governing bodies of each into one Council of Ministers and by having the EEC Commission, its bureaucratic administrative body, also take over the responsibility for managing the day-to-day affairs of the ECSC and EURATOM.

Great Britain continued to seek membership in the EEC. A 1967 application was never officially acted upon, and it was only in 1970 that negotiations were formally opened with Great Britain. Ireland, Denmark, and Norway also applied for membership at this time. France placed fewer obstacles in Great Britain's path this time. In part, this was because de Gaulle was no longer in power, but it was also due to French unease over West Germany's growing economic power. It now saw Great Britain as a potential counterweight to growing German influence within the EC. Still, the negotiations over the terms of British membership were complex, far more so than with the other three states, whose small size meant that they would only have a marginal effect on the economy of the EC as a whole. Particularly troublesome was Great Britain's insistence on special terms for imports from the commonwealth countries. A precedent for this already existed. The former French and Belgian colonies were linked to the EC and given special trading status by the Yaounde Conventions. Due to expire in 1975, these agreements were rewritten to allow the participation of nearly all the commonwealth countries and territories in Africa, the Caribbean, and the Pacific. In the end, all four applications were accepted, but Norway declined to join following a national referendum that rejected EC membership. The other three states formally became members of the EC in 1973.

The EC expanded once again in 1981, when Greece became a member, and in 1986, when Portugal and Spain joined. Currently, Austria and Turkey are seeking to become the EC's next members. A step backwards of sorts was taken in 1985, when Greenland, which had come into the EC as part of Denmark, elected to withdraw. None of these expansions was without its difficulties or controversies, and, to some extent, expansion brought with it renewed paralysis. Agriculture and budget policy debates found the EC deeply divided, with Great Britain often alone in its opposition to the rest of the Community. The OPEC oil shocks of the 1970s and the economic recessions that followed them produced further decay, as members erected trade barriers in an effort to protect their own economies. The environment for integration improved significantly during the mid-1980s, as the world economy rebounded and protectionist sentiment receded. Just as important, in 1984, Great Britain finally reached an agreement with other EC members on how to divide up Community bills, and in January 1985, Jacques Delors of France became President of the EC Commission. A strong advocate of European unity, Delors actively began to seek out ways of moving a united Europe forward. He considered the idea of pushing defense or monetary integration but rejected doing so because of the political opposition these would arouse. Instead, he settled on the idea of creating a single internal market within Europe. Structured as it was, many felt that European national markets were too small to compete with Japan and the United States and that a single, unified market would be needed to ensure the economic vitality of Europe in the next century. EC leaders approved the plan in principle at a summit in June 1985, and they identified December 1992 as the target date for creating a true common market.

1992 and Beyond   Conceptually, the 1992 blueprint represents a grand compromise between the rich states of northern Europe, who wanted to take advantage of the markets in southern Europe, and the poorer states of the EC, who saw the plan as a way to spur economic growth. As part of the compromise, the richer EC states also agreed to provide the four poorest states (Spain, Portugal, Greece, and Ireland) with considerable amounts of aid to allow them to improve their infrastructure. The actual negotiations to remove the fiscal, technical, and physical barriers that still separate the members of the EC have been long and difficult. Very often the discussions have found Prime Minister Margaret Thatcher on one side and the rest of the EC on the other. The British see 1992 as providing them with a major economic opportunity but are reluctant to abandon any national policymaking powers that would accompany a unified single market. Problems also arise from the fact that the British, the French, and the Germans do not subscribe to the same economic philosophy. Prime Minister Thatcher is strongly monetarist in orientation, while French President François Mitterand and German Chancellor Helmut Kohl are more Keynesian in their thinking. This means that Mitterand and Kohl are likely to attempt to manipulate supply and demand to influence economic performance, while Thatcher is more likely to try to manipulate the money supply.

As the 1980s ended, 107 of the 279 implementing directives issued by the European Commission, whose job it is to see to it that all barriers are removed that stand in the way of creating a true common market—one in which there are no obstacles whatsoever to the free movement of people, products, and money across borders—had been adopted and tentative agreements had been reached on two dozen others. Many of the areas in which no agreement had been reached are highly political. Included among them are the abolition of customs and immigration checks at internal EC borders and the narrowing of tax policy differences among the 12 EC states. The Commission's job has been made somewhat easier by a 1987 decision, known as the Single European Act, to amend the Treaty of Rome and replace the unanimity rule with a complicated majority rule formula.

While within Europe many view 1992 with a sense of enthusiasm that has been absent since the 1960s, many outside Europe have mixed feelings. The EC is already the United States' single largest export market, with U.S.-EC trade valued at nearly $133 billion per year. On the positive side, 1992 will make Europe an even more attractive market as barriers to trade disappear. If all goes according to schedule, the EC will become the world's third largest trading bloc, controlling almost 18 percent of the world's output. On the negative side, U.S., Japanese, and Canadian firms are alarmed over the prospects of a "Fortress Europe," in which non-European firms will be excluded from competing in this new and enlarged market. For example, Europe is the destination of nearly one-half of all U.S. computer and computer part exports. Prior to 1992, for a computer chip to be considered European it simply had to be assembled and tested in Europe. After 1992, companies must complete the expensive and highly technical fabrication process in Europe. This will require them to build plants costing between $200 and $400 million. So that it can compete after 1992, Texas Instruments is building a major plant in Italy. While this will create jobs in Italy, it will mean fewer jobs at Texas Instrument operations elsewhere.

Finally, there is the question of what comes after 1992. Is a true common market the end of the road for European integration, or is more to follow? Jacques Delors, President of the EC Commission has spoken of creating an embryonic European government, capable of taking over 80 percent of the economic and social decision

Table 12.3 CATEGORIES OF ECONOMIC INTEGRATION

	No tariff or quotas	Common external tariffs	Free flow of factors	Harmonization of economic policies	Unification of policies, political institutions
1. Free-Trade Area	X				
2. Customs Union	X	X			
3. Common Market	X	X	X		
4. Economic Union	X	X	X	X	
5. Total Economic Integration	X	X	X	X	X

Source: Bela Balassa, The Theory of Economic Integration (Homewood, Ill.: Dorsey Press, 1961).

making in Europe within 10 years. Prime Minister Thatcher's response to this was that the idea was "quite absurd" and would never happen in her lifetime. One unfinished piece of business is the creation of a single European currency. Monetary reform is not part of the 1992 agenda, but many feel that it is the logical next step and one that must be undertaken if all of the economic benefits of a single, unified market are to be realized. Only limited progress has been made on this front. European leaders have been talking about creating a single monetary unit since the mid-1970s. To date, the major accomplishment has been the creation of the European Monetary System, which stabilizes European currencies relative to one another. At present, 8 of the 12 EC states (all but Great Britain, Portugal, Spain, and Greece) participate in this program. In 1989, EC leaders considered a three-stage plan to integrate further European currencies. Stage 1 specified that all currencies would be part of the European Monetary System by July 1990. Stages 2 and 3 would see the creation of an EC central banking system, an irrevocable system of interlocking exchange rates, and the possibility of a single European currency. Success in this endeavor is made doubtful by the British refusal to go beyond stage 1.

One way of assessing just how far the EC has moved toward the creation of an integrated Europe and just how much remains to be done is to examine the range of possible outcomes discussed in the literature on integration theory. For some there exists only one possible end point, which represents the culmination of the integrative process. This is the establishment of a supranational political unit, one that possesses the authority to make binding decisions in the integrated areas. Anything that falls short of this condition is not properly referred to as "integration." For others, integration is a process that can have many end points.

The range of institutional possibilities in the economic area and how they relate to one another is presented in Table 12.3.[4] The least integrated region is a Free Trade Area, where the sole unifying feature is the absence of tariffs or quotas for trade among member states. A Customs Union adds to this common external tariffs on goods or services entering the region. The most thorough form of economic integration adds to these two properties three others: the free flow of factors of produc-

Table 12.4   LEVELS OF POLITICAL INTEGRATION
_____

Low Integration

1. All policy decisions are made by individual governments by means of purely internal processes or are made in other nonnational settings.
2. Only the beginnings of regional-level decision-making authority have appeared.
3. Substantial regular policymaking goes on at a regional level, but most matters are still decided by purely domestic political processes.
4. Most decisions are taken jointly, but substantial decisions are still taken autonomously at the nation-state level.
5. All choices are subject to joint decision in a regional decision-making system.

High Integration
_____

Source: Adapted from Leon Lindberg and Stuart Sheingold, *Europe's Would-Be Polity* (Englewood Cliffs, N.J.: Prentice-Hall, 1970), pp. 68–69.

tion such as labor, material, and capital; the harmonization of economic policies; and institutional and policy unification.

Political integration can be seen as varying along an analogous scale.[5] As depicted in Table 12.4, the least amount of political integration occurs when only the most rudimentary forms of regional decision-making authority are present and all important decisions are made in the national capitals of member states, with little regard for how these decisions will affect the region as a whole. One step above this is a situation in which regional policymaking regularly takes place but final decisions are still made in the national capitals. A still higher form of political integration exists when most decisions are taken jointly, although national leaders still retain some autonomous decision-making power. The highest form of political integration exists when all policy choices are made jointly and at the regional level.

INTERACTION BETWEEN THE NORTHERN MARKET ECONOMIES (THE WEST) AND THE EASTERN BLOC COMMAND ECONOMIES[6]

During the period immediately following World War II, the United States considered Soviet participation in the international economy to be important to world peace and prosperity. The Soviet Union and the East European countries were invited to participate in Bretton Woods. Although under Stalin the Soviet Union participated in the conference, it refused to join the institutions created by the agreements. It created a new and separate economic system with the states of Eastern Europe by establishing satellite regimes in these states and by restructuring their economies around state ownership and central planning. In this way, the Soviet Union hoped to deny the West access to East European markets, while making available to itself raw materials and other resources.

As an alternative to membership in the IMF, World Bank, and GATT and in response to the Marshall Plan, the Eastern bloc established its own economic institution, the Council for Mutual Economic Assistance (CMEA or COMECON) in 1949. Among the East European states, only Yugoslavia failed to join. Presently, it is composed of 10 members: Bulgaria, Cuba, Czechoslovakia, the German Democratic Republic, Hungary, Mongolia, Poland, Romania, USSR, and Vietnam. Yugoslavia is an associate member. Additionally, there are three countries that have cooperative agreements (Finland, Iraq, and Mexico) and seven observers (Afghanistan, Angola, Ethiopia, Laos, Mozambique, Nicaragua, and Yemen). Its purpose was to promote technical cooperation, planning, and trade among its members for the purpose of rebuilding their war-torn economies. By 1953, a majority of the trade among the East European states was within the Eastern bloc.

Trade relations among the CMEA nations tended to benefit the Soviet Union during the years following the war. Under the guise of war reparations, Soviets dismantled factories in Germany, Hungary, Bulgaria, and Romania and claimed goods amounting to approximately $20 billion. The Soviets negotiated favorable trade deals with the CMEA nations, including the transfer of large amounts of Polish coal to the Soviet Union at a low price. Disagreement exists over whether trade patterns since the 1960s have worked to the advantage of the Soviets or of the Eastern Europeans. While the Soviet Union has been able to impose quantities of imports and exports different from what its trading partners would have freely chosen, it has traded on terms less favorable than what it would have received from other markets. Additionally, East European states have been able to purchase Soviet products at a lower cost than from a non-CMEA source. At the same time, restricted trade with the West has slowed technological development.[7]

In the West, economics came to be seen as a weapon for use in the cold war. The United States set up an embargo to deny the Soviet Union critical resources, established credit restrictions, and denied access to U.S. markets.[8] A persistent debate has centered over whether a strategic embargo, or more serious restrictions, was an appropriate policy. A strategic embargo allows most exports but prohibits those exports that make a direct and significant contribution to military capability. A more extensive set of limitations, referred to by some as "economic warfare," limits strategic exports but also limits those exports that are thought to make a significant contribution to the economic growth and development of the country in question. Under this theory, anything that benefits economic growth in general will also contribute to military power. Thus, technology and other resources are denied to the target country, even when they are not directly designed for military use. Many U.S. planners were convinced that the Soviet economy was a "war economy," thus industrial and military potential were synonymous.[9] The U.S. Export Control Act of 1949 gave the president the authority to prohibit or to curtail commercial exports to the Communist states and to other destinations from which they might be passed on to prohibited areas. On the domestic scene, there was little effective opposition during the early 1950s. Anti-Communist sentiment was strong enough to dissuade corporations from espousing Soviet trade, and a broad majority in Congress supported trade restrictions. There was also consensus at the bureaucratic level among officials at the State, Defense, and Commerce Departments. By 1950, the list of items of primary and secondary strategic significance contained nearly 500 categories. In consultation with other Western states, the United States set up a committee to draw up an international list of restricted items. In 1949, CoCom was formed to coordinate U.S. and West European trade with the Communists. Although the Europeans agreed to most of the United States' items that had a direct military application, they were reluctant to include other items. Unlike the United States, Western Europe traditionally had strong trade ties with Eastern Europe and was dependent on its raw materials. Although the State Department argued against coercion, Congress, as an incentive to the European states to comply with U.S. policy, passed an act that would authorize the president to deny assistance to any country that permitted the shipment of strategic goods to a Communist country. In spite of the European allies being in almost continual violation of the act, the president never cut off aid. Although Europe accepted U.S. restrictions from 1950 to 1951, by 1954 it had substantially reduced the number of restricted items on the CoCom list. If the United States retained its own much longer list, domestic firms would have been at a decided disadvantage. Additionally, in order to avoid having items that were shipped to Western Europe find their way to the Soviet Union, the United States might find it necessary to modify trade with Europe. In order to avoid these problems, the United States revised its own list to match more closely the CoCom list. Although nonmilitary items were removed from the list, a strategic embargo remained in force and the United States continued to practice a more restrictive trade policy than did Western Europe.

Additionally, the United States used a law that was already in existence—the Johnson Debt Default Act of 1934—to deny credit assistance to the Eastern bloc. The law prohibited private persons or institutions from granting credit to any foreign government in default on past debts to the United States. After World War II, it was amended to exclude any state that was a member of the IMF or World Bank. Of the Eastern states, only Yugoslavia was a member, and, among the nonmember countries, only Albania, Bulgaria, and East Germany had no outstanding debts. Consequently, the major impact of the act fell on the Eastern bloc. The United States was unsuccessful in its attempts to get the West European states to restrict credit.

The United States also sought to close its market to the Eastern bloc countries, with the exception of Yugoslavia. It denied trade concessions to these countries, with the result that they were subject to significantly higher tariffs than were other states. Several European states also established barriers to trade with the Communist countries. As a result, during the early 1950s, East-West trade was lower than before World War II. With Stalin's death in 1953, restrictions were eased somewhat. Between 1953 and 1963, trade increased substantially. Nevertheless, significant restrictions on trade remained.[10]

Although trade between the East and the West began to improve during the era of détente, trade between the superpowers remained relatively unimportant. A trade agreement reached in 1972 would have improved relations by granting the Soviet Union most-favored-nation status if the Soviet Union agreed to make payments on their World War II debt. However, the agreement was canceled as a result of congressional opposition. Congress added the Jackson-Vanik amendment, which linked most-favored-nation status and bank loans to free policies of emigration. Although the Soviets at one point agreed to changes in emigration policies, Congress imposed restrictions on bank credits, and the agreement was nullified in 1975. Trade relations were also complicated by the sale of grain to the Soviet Union at low prices. A subsequent rise in the price of grain angered American farmers, who had not shared in the profits realized by the grain traders, and consumers, who were paying higher food prices. In 1975, the United States negotiated a grain agreement whereby the Soviets could buy up to 8 million tons of grain per year, unless the total grain crop fell to below 225 million tons.[11]

In response to the Soviet invasion of Afghanistan, President Carter called an embargo on all sales of wheat and other grains to the USSR above 8 million tons, an embargo on sales of certain types of technological goods, including oil exploration and production equipment, and restricted access to U.S. ports by Soviet vessels. Trade in these areas was picked up by other countries, particularly Canada, Australia, and Argentina. Although the Reagan administration lifted the grain embargo, it continued to use trade embargoes and restrictions on currency transfers to punish Soviet actions. U.S. allies remained reluctant to follow its lead in trade relations with the Soviets. Over the United States' objections, West European governments cooperated in building a natural gas pipeline between the USSR and Europe. When Poland, under pressure from the Soviets, instituted martial law and arrested Solidarity members, the United States acted to deny U.S. designs and technology to the construction of the pipeline. These restrictions caused considerable friction between the European governments of Great Britain, West Germany, France, and Italy and the United States. When the United States extended the restrictions to include sanctions against any foreign firm that exported U.S. technology to the Soviet Union, the European states ordered companies to ignore the restrictions.

In 1983, the relations between the Soviet Union and the United States began to improve, and the two countries signed a new five-year grain agreement, in which the Soviet Union would buy a minimum of 9 million and a maximum of 12 million metric tons of wheat and corn per year. However, when the Soviets shot down a Korean airliner that had strayed over Soviet territory, relations deteriorated. In 1983, Soviet imports from the United States fell by 25 percent and had not risen by 1987.[12]

Gorbachev's domestic political and economic reforms within the Soviet Union and the pro-democracy wave that swept through Eastern Europe in 1989 caused many in the West to rethink the East-West economic relationship. Rather than using its economic power as a weapon to punish these states, thought is now being given to ways in which to use economic power to continue the liberalization process and permanently integrate these economies into the (capitalist) international economic order. Movement in this direction is clearly visible as Poland and Hungary have received increased amounts of Western foreign and financial aid. Even more significant is the fact that Romania and Hungary are now members of IMF, and Romania, Hungary, and Poland are members of the World Bank. Several CMEA members have also joined GATT.

Success in this endeavor will not be easily realized. Five problem areas can already be identified. First, there is a lack of funding for East European and Soviet development projects. The United States has made it quite clear that it does not possess the financial resources to carry out a "Marshall Plan" for Eastern Europe. A large scale international effort will be needed, and this points to the second problem. To be successful, a high degree of international cooperation will be needed, not only between states but between states and private businesses seeking to gain entry into the East European market. The dangers here are many. Eastern Europe could become the next trade battleground between U.S., Japanese, and European investors. One of the reasons that U.S. business leaders lobbied for eased trade restrictions in the early 1970s was that they saw Japanese and West European firms closing them out of the Soviet market. The rush to get international aid to Eastern Europe could also have the effect of denying much needed aid to Africa and other impoverished regions.

A third question to be answered is that of the relationship between the opening up of Eastern Europe and a reunified Germany, and progress in unifying West European economics. Will German energies and attention be directed toward their traditional markets in Eastern Europe and cause them to become less interested in "1992," or will the interest of these states in joining Europe cause the integration process to accelerate? Fourth, it needs to be stressed that not everyone is convinced that increased trade with the Soviet Union and Eastern Europe is in the long-term interests of the United States. Opponents note that not only is the ultimate purpose of Gorbachev's reforms to make the Soviet Union a strong and powerful state (and, therefore, a strong and powerful competitor of the United States), but there is no guarantee that this reform agenda will not be reversed and communism reimposed. Both the Reagan and Bush administrations have been divided over the merits of increased high technology trade with the East and it was only in December 1989 that Bush approved the sale of personal computers to Eastern Europe. Finally, as we have just suggested, questions exist surrounding the political and economic stability of the Soviet Union and Eastern Europe. Potentially disruptive social and economic reforms will be needed in order to create a business environment that attracts Western firms and aid. Foremost among these will be monetary reforms. Traditionally Soviet and East European currencies were inconvertible; that is they could not be freely bought and sold on international money markets. Instead, each currency's value was artificially fixed by its own government and this was done with little reference to its actual value or to world trading conditions. In making currencies convertible, these governments run the risk of injecting unprecedented rates of inflation, unemployment, and government spending cuts into their societies. Coming at the same time as the first experiments with democracy, the results are anything but certain.

CONCLUSION

For many years, the international economic system was dominated by two major powers—Great Britain in the nineteenth century and the United States in the twentieth century. This was followed by a period of multilateral management, in which the industrialized market economies cooperated in setting monetary policy. Although disagreements occurred among the major actors in the system, there was agreement on fundamental ideology and there was congruence among the participants' domestic economies. Although the industrialized market economies remain dominant in today's international economy, their position is being seriously challenged by the emergence of newly developed economies and by the entry into the international system of the centrally planned economies of the East.

Multilateral cooperation in trade and monetary policy remains problematical today. The breakdown of existing institutions has not been met with the construction of new international regimes for managing the economy. The international economic order is characterized by crisis management. Successive crises have been met and dealt with through negotiation, but no reforms of the kind that might prevent future crises have been agreed upon. Joan Spero attributes the breakdown of multilateral cooperation to changes in the structure of the economic system, primarily increasing interdependence and pluralism. Monetary interdependence was created in part by the growth of international financial institutions, as banks began to open branches abroad. By 1974, there were 125 U.S. banks that had foreign branches with assets in excess of $125 billion. At that same time, foreign banks held assets in the United States of $56 billion. Interdependence was also furthered by the growth of multinational corporations. The importance of these businesses will be discussed more fully in Chapter 14.

In April 1989, 100 nations that were participating in the GATT negotiations in Geneva (called the Uruguay Round because the talks began there in 1986) announced a compromise settlement on four key issues. The talks had become deadlocked over farm subsidies, trade sanctions against the piracy of patented products, GATT rules allowing countries to impose temporary measures to curb imports when domestic industries are seriously injured by a surge of foreign goods, and a move by textile exporters to win an end to import curbs on their products. The United States had opposed farm subsidies, arguing that they distorted trade by encouraging overproduction and by reducing market prices. The European community refused to agree to eliminate protectionist supports. The United States retreated from its position in the interests of reaching an agreement, noting that Europe had agreed to concessions. The negotiators also agreed to set and to enforce standards designed to eliminate the theft of intellectual property, such as patents and trademarks, to move ahead on clarifying rules for temporary import curbs, and to find ways to end curbs by the more industrialized countries on textile imports from less-developed counries. Additionally, the talks moved forward on 11 other trade agreements, including the establishment of rules for free trade and in-service industries, such as banking and engineering. The United States hailed the agreements as a breakthrough in the protection of free trade.

NOTES

1. Jan S. Hogendorn and Wilson B. Brown, *The New International Economics* (Reading, Mass.: Addison-Wesley, 1979). p. 35.
2. Hogendorn and Brown, *New International Economics*, p. 223.
3. This discussion is based upon Joseph Nye, *Peace in Parts*, (Boston: Little Brown, 1971)

pp. 48–54. A fourth approach to integration that has not been discussed here is based upon communications theory. For a discussion, see Raymond Hopkins and Richard Mansbach, *Structure and Process in International Politics* (New York: Harper & Row, 1973), pp. 282–283.

4. Bela Baalassa, *The Theory of Economic Integration* (Homewood, Ill.: Richard Irwin, 1961).

5. This discussion is based upon and modifies that presented by Leon Lindberg and Stuart Sheingold, *Europe's Would-Be Polity* (Englewood Cliffs, N.J.: Prentice-Hall, 1970). pp. 68–69.

6. The material in this section is based largely on Joan E. Spero's discussion in *The Politics of International Economic Relations*, (New York: St. Martin's, 1985), pp. 343–385.

7. Philip Hanson, "Soviet Trade with Eastern Europe," in Karen Dawisha and Philip Hanson, eds., *Soviet-East European Dilemmas*, (London: Heinemann, 1981), pp. 91 ff.

8. Henry Bretton argues that, although the stated purpose of the economic isolation of Eastern Europe was to hasten the downfall of capitalism, more than likely it was dictated by Moscow's desire to benefit economically from Eastern European resources and markets. See his *International Relations in the Nuclear Age* (Albany, N.Y.: SUNY Press, 1986), p. 243.

9. Michael Mastanduno, "Trade as a Strategic Weapon: American and Alliance Export Control Policy in the Early Postwar Period," *International Organization*, 42, no. 1 (Winter 1989): 126.

10. Spero, *Politics of International Economic Relations*, p. 351.

11. Spero, *Politics of International Economic Relations*, pp. 373–374.

12. Karl Ryavec, *United States-Soviet Relations* (New York: Longman, 1989), p. 214.

Chapter
13

The Third World and the International Economy

The Bretton Woods agreement was essentially an American-British plan in which the interests of the other developed economies were barely considered. Many of the Third World states had not yet achieved independence, and many states that were technically independent were, in fact, dominated by a major power. As a result, the conference at Bretton Woods, New Hampshire, paid little attention to the special needs of developing countries. Over time, Third World states have come to see themselves as being systematically discriminated against by the rich states of the North and by the institutions that these rich states created to organize the post-World War II international economic system in such areas as finance, trade, aid, and debt. To rectify this situation, Third World states have proposed the creation of a New International Economic Order. They have also sought to acquire more political clout in international economic decision making through the formation of common markets and resource cartels, and through the adoption of aggressive economic development policies. In the first part of this chapter, we will examine the reasons why the Third World is dissatisfied with the international economic order set up by the North and we will introduce the concept of a New International Economic Order. In the last part of the chapter, we will look at some of the efforts by Third World states to improve their individual and collective standing in the international economic system.

THE INTERNATIONAL MONETARY FUND AND THIRD WORLD FINANCE

As we discussed in the previous chapter, the IMF was designed to provide short-term loans to states that ran into balance-of-payments problems. States could draw from the fund while taking steps to correct the disequilibrium. Each state was given a quota, which was divided into slices or *tranches*. The state's first tranche was in gold and could be drawn from without restrictions. The state could draw from the second tranche with the consent of the fund's managers. Beyond this level, a state had to enter into consultation with the fund and agree to take those measures that the fund considered necessary to solve the problems that led to the imbalance. No provision was made for the long-term problems associated with economic development. At the conference, India proposed amendments that would have called upon the IMF to assist in development with special attention to the needs of the less-developed states. However, the Articles of Agreement did not distinguish between more and less developed states. As many critics have pointed out, equal treatment of unequal partners is bound to produce unequal results.

Most Third World states have chronic balance-of-payments problems, and few choose to avoid membership in the IMF. Although the amount borrowed directly from the fund is less than that borrowed from private sources, commercial lenders often use IMF guidelines to determine whether or not to make loans. States that cannot get IMF approval generally find their credit opportunities severely restricted; thus, IMF policies have a serious impact on Third World economies. For example, although Julius Nyerere of Tanzania at one point broke off negotiations with the IMF, arguing that Tanzania would not have its economic policy dictated by the Fund, he subsequently returned to the IMF and submitted to its requirements.

The IMF is committed to a liberal economic order. It operates on the assumption that the growth of international trade benefits all members of the system, and, consequently, its policies are aimed at preserving that system. Policies reflect the belief that a restrictive monetary policy and adherence to financial orthodoxy and the free-market mechanism for regulating prices will work toward reestablishing equilibrium. The balance-of-payments deficit is thought to be caused by excessive demand. Cuts in government spending, restrictions on credit, and lower wages reduce demand. Additionally, removing food subsidies reduces the real income of the people. As a larger portion of income is spent on food, less is available for imports. Devaluation of the state's currency also helps by raising the price of imports and making exports cheaper for other currencies. IMF lending policies have come under considerable criticism from Third World authorities. Generally, IMF-imposed cuts on government spending, particularly regarding food subsidies, place serious burdens on an already poor population. Spending cuts, combined with controls on wages, are politically unpopular, and there have been numerous instances of riots and instability following the institution of policies prescribed by the IMF. The Venezuelan riots during the spring of 1989, in which 300 people were killed and 1,500 were wounded, were a response to austerity measures (specifically an 89-percent rise in gas prices and an increase in bus fares) imposed after the government had reached an agreement with the IMF.

Additionally, IMF policies are criticized for their failure to address underlying structural problems. It is argued that, even if IMF policies restore equilibrium in the short run, problems will recur without structural changes, such as the expansion of the industrial sector, more equitable income distribution, and land reform.

Third World leaders charge that the IMF exists to protect the international economic order as it is and that this perpetuation of the status quo is not in the interest of less developed states. Voting in the IMF is based on a system of quotas, which determines not only how much money a state must pay into the fund but also how many votes it receives. As we noted earlier, five industrialized countries hold 40.9 percent of the votes. Third World states argue that their interests cannot be adequately represented under this arrangement. In an April 1989 statement calling for a comprehensive debt-reduction plan, the Group of 24 (an organization made up of the poorer members of the IMF), asked for an adjustment in the allocation of votes that would allow them more voting power than that to which their quotas entitled them. Adjustments concerning quotas and voting were scheduled for consideration at the fall 1989 meeting.

The IMF has responded to some requests for change. Until 1972, the IMF was run by the Group of 10, all of whom represented industrialized states. This was expanded to 20, including some less-developed states. The Compensatory Finance Facility provides funds to meet balance-of-payments difficulties that result from factors beyond the control of the borrower, and the Oil Facility of 1974 makes loans to states to help them with rising energy costs. These loans are made under less stringent conditions than usual. Furthermore, the fund has extended the grace period within which states must show stabilization and has coordinated activities with the World Bank to link stabilization policies with structural reform.

Other reforms have been rejected, particularly those that would fundamentally alter the balance of power in the IMF. When SDRs were created in 1967, the Third World responded with interest and attempted to use this device to redistribute income. They proposed that, whenever SDRs were issued, more should be given to poorer states and less to wealthy states. This idea was rejected by the developed market economies. The distribution of SDRs heavily favors the wealthier states—75 percent is distributed to the 25 wealthiest states. However, even without redistribution, SDRs could be of value to the less developed states. They could provide a base in which the exchange rates of Third World currencies with all Western currencies could be established and the value of their reserves could be stabilized. Second, the allocation of SDRs made on a system of quotas could provide a more rational distribution of reserves than would be provided by the distribution of gold that now exists for historic reasons.[1] By 1980, the total value of allocated SDRs was in excess of $18 billion. To this amount, $3.6 billion was reserved for the non-oil-exporting less developed states.[2] Presently, SDRs remain a small fraction of the IMF's stock of reserves, but, ultimately, the IMF hopes to see SDRs replace currency and gold reserves.

The future of relations between the less developed states and the IMF is unknown, but most analysts expect some degree of reform in the system. Some have observed that the IMF may be forced by the debt crisis (which will be discussed in more detail in a later section) to pay more attention to Third World needs. The debt crisis has emphasized the interdependence of North and South economies. The less developed states cannot default on their debts without doing considerable harm to the banking industries of the Western economies. It is noted that Third World states will have no incentive to play by the rules in a system that remains stacked against them and could, if they chose to, use the threat of default to change the system.[3] Others have argued that as the developed economies move toward economic nationalism, they will become less and less likely to reform the system.

TRADE AND INDUSTRIALIZATION

Following World War II, the less developed states specialized in the production of primary commodities, which were exported in exchange for manufactured products from the industrialized states. Classical economic theory encouraged these states to focus on those exports that were generally labor- and land-intensive and/or for which there were abundant resources. It was argued that, under a system of free trade, every state is better off concentrating on whatever it can produce most efficiently (the theory of comparative advantage). It was also believed that gradually wages would rise and the price of capital would fall in these states, and economic development would occur. Liberals continue to argue that both rich and poor states need to adhere to an open-trade policy. The more-developed states must accept the comparative advantage that newly industrialized countries have in such areas as leather goods and textiles. Meanwhile, the less developed states should allow competition from abroad for their own industries, since competition results in improved efficiency and quality. Although free trade may, in fact, produce the benefits ascribed to it in theory, this system has not truly existed, and inequality between states has increased.

Many Third World states have become poorer in relative terms during the last few decades. After 1980, the yearly growth rates of the less developed states dropped from an average of 5.4 percent, which occurred between 1973 and 1980, to 3.9 percent per year between 1980 and 1987.[4] The less developed states have come to see themselves as disadvantaged by the international economic system, particularly in the area of trade. Most developing states have small domestic markets and so are very dependent on trade. A major concern of these states has to do with the production for export of primary products, such as raw materials, minerals, and food. Conventional wisdom holds that the price of primary products, in the long run, declines relative to that of manufactured goods. There are several reasons why this is thought to be true: the inelasticity of demand, the substitution of synthetics for natural products, and improved technologies that require lower inputs of raw materials. Inelasticity of demand refers to the phenomenon that, as incomes rise, the proportion of wealth spent on primary goods falls. As a simple illustration, consider this phenomenon in terms of the family. A family with a very low income will spend a large proportion of that income on food. However, at some point, as income rises, the proportion (although not the actual amount) spent on food declines—people can only eat so much. This situation also applies to trade among states. As income rises, proportionally more of the state's wealth will be spent on manufactured goods, so the prices of

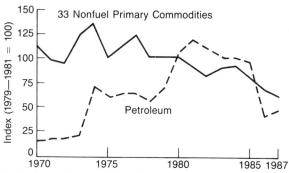

Note: Real prices are annual average nominal prices in dollars, deflated by the annual change in the manufacturing unit value index (MUV), a measure of the price of industrial country exports to developing countries.

Figure 13.1 Real commodity prices, 1970 to 1987. (*Source:* World Bank, *World Development Report, 1988* New York: Oxford University Press, 1988.)

primary commodities tend to fall relative to that of manufactured goods. In addition, the prices of primary commodities are thought to fall as the use of synthetics increases in areas as diverse as rope manufacturing (in which plastics have been substituted for sisal), tire production (with the introduction of synthetic rubber), and textiles (where acrylic is substituted for wool). Further, with improved technologies, the manufacturing process often involves a lower level of raw materials to produce a finished product.[5] Figure 13.1 illustrates the decline in real commodity prices between 1970 and 1987.

Third World states continue to specialize in the export of primary products. Over three-fourths of the total commodities that are exported by the poorer states are primary products. Although there has been some progress in expanding exports of manufactured goods, much of this has taken place in very few states. South Korea, Taiwan, Hong Kong, and Singapore alone account for over 60 percent of manufactured exports from less developed states. In some areas, particularly sub-Saharan Africa, exports are concentrated in a relatively few products, such as cocoa and coffee. Three-fourths of the Third World nations receive 60 percent or more of their export receipts from as few as three products.[6]

Although some states have achieved a high standard of living, primarily from the production and export of food and raw materials, most of the less developed states believe that industrialization is the road to improved conditions and have sought development strategies that would increase their rate of industrialization. The World Bank identifies two broad strategies concerning trade and industrialization that are followed by these countries. Inward-oriented strategies, generally referred to as *import substitution*, promote industrialization for the domestic market at the expense of the export sector. Countries pursuing a policy of import substitution establish tariffs, quotas, and strict licensing requirements, which are designed to discourage imports and protect infant industries. Although sometimes there are also policies to encourage exports, controls on imports generally create a disadvantage for exports by overvaluing the exchange rate and by raising the costs of domestic and imported inputs into the production of exports. These factors result in export prices that are not competitive with those of other countries.

Outward-oriented strategies are characterized by the absence of restrictions on trade or by the slow removal of import barriers at the same time that exports are encouraged. In these states, policies do not discriminate between production for the domestic market and production for export or between the purchase of domestic and foreign goods. Proponents of a liberal trade policy argue that outward-oriented strategies perform better in terms of economic development, and, in fact, a number of indicators support this argument. From 1973 to 1985, the growth rates for gross domestic product for outward-oriented states averaged 7.7 percent, in comparison with 2.5 percent for states pursuing import substitution. Per capita income grew 5.9 percent in those states with outward-oriented strategies and declined by 0.1 percent in those states with inward-oriented strategies. However, the direction of the relationship is uncertain; that is, it is unclear whether outward-oriented strategies produce higher standards of living or whether higher standards of living make it possible for countries to pursue successfully outward-oriented strategies. The World Bank, which espouses a liberal trade policy, concludes that an outward-oriented strategy promotes development by encouraging an efficient use of resources, since states are forced to compete internationally. Some economists note, however, that the basic assumptions of free-trade theory do not hold for Third World states. They argue that the beneficial aspects of trade have accrued disproportionately to wealthy states and to the wealthier individuals within the poor states and that Third World states would be wise to pursue policies of collective "self-reliance" by entering into economic agreements with other developing states.[7]

Presently, many less developed states continue to pursue protectionist strategies. Even if the evidence supporting an open-trade policy as a tool for development were conclusive, political factors within these countries would continue to influence trade decisions. These factors are no less important in determining trade policy in the less developed states than in the industrialized states. First, protected industries develop a vested interest in continuing that protection. Their owners and managers are often among those who possess political clout, and they resist any effort to remove tariffs or other protective devices. Second, fear that unemployment will occur if local industries are driven out by competition by foreigners is a major consideration of policymakers. Most Third World states have significant problems with unemployment and underemployment, as well as with considerable political unrest. Their leaders are particularly sensitive to unemployment as an issue. In several countries (for example Brazil, Sri Lanka, and Indonesia, among others), there is no evidence that increased unemployment occurred with liberalization. However, as Chile opened to trade, a number of jobs were lost in the manufacturing sector. It is estimated that more than 11 percent of the 1974 labor force in manufacturing had lost jobs by 1979. These losses were only partially offset by a gain in jobs in the agricultural sector. Third, additional political problems revolve around questions of nationalism and fear of foreign penetration. Fourth, tariffs are the major source of revenue for many less developed states. Fifth, tariffs discourage imports and thus help with balance-of-payments difficulties. Finally, there is considerable evidence showing that, for a liberal trade policy to work, there must be decisive leadership and political stability. Many Third World governments are characterized as weak states. Their policymakers are faced with major constraints on their decision-making autonomy. These governments may lack the authority necessary to pursue open trade.

The less developed states have also been influenced by their weak positions in the world economy. The Havana Charter would have given developing states access to decision making and would have exempted them from a full commitment to free trade. GATT, however, made no such concessions. It contained no provisions for aiding development in the Third World. GATT provisions did allow each state to use discriminatory import restrictions, with the prior approval of GATT members, to aid development, but these provisions have been useless in reality. The institutional character of GATT puts the less developed states at a disadvantage for a number of reasons, but principally because of the most-favored-nation principle and reciprocity. The most-favored-nation principle eliminates preferential trading for development. An industrialized state cannot aid a less developed state by lowering tariffs or other barriers without opening itself up to competition from other industrialized states. This restriction is particularly important when it influences trade relations with former colonies that generally maintain strong economic ties with the former mother country. The poorer states are also disadvantaged by their weak bargaining position. This weakness can be attributed to several factors. First, these states import relatively few goods for consumption; their imports have consisted heavily of necessary inputs for production. They are unable to threaten retaliation when a richer state establishes a tariff because, by putting tariffs on products that they use in manufacturing, they would raise the price of their own manufactured goods. Second, their markets are small and they cannot offer much in exchange for concessions. Third, as they are rarely among the principal suppliers of an item, they are left out of negotiations when those topics are considered, and they are not powerful enough to get the items that most concern them on the agenda. Finally, the less developed states have lacked the sophistication and full-time technical support needed to be influential. Many of the poorer states have refrained from joining GATT, arguing that a system of equal treatment is inherently unfair when all parties are not equal in strength.

Largely as a result of their inferior status concerning the GATT negotiations, the poorer states have gained less than the industrialized states from the GATT reductions that have taken place. After the Tokyo Round, the average tariffs on those goods in which less developed states specialized in producing remained higher than for those products produced by the industrialized states. While tariffs on many manufactured goods were reduced to less than 5 percent, tariffs on textiles, processed metals, and wood were not lowered and in some instances were actually raised. Additionally, agricultural products continue to face a variety of NTBs, which are designed to protect agriculture in industrialized states.[8]

The less developed states are also at a disadvantage because tariffs are higher on processed goods, so if they try to expand their manufacturing sector by first processing the raw materials they export, they are faced with higher tariffs, which in some cases may actually lower their profits. For example, the tariff rate on coffee beans is 6.8 percent, but on processed coffee it is 9.4 percent, and, while the tariff on rawhides and skins is 0 percent, on leather it is 4.2 percent and on goods manufactured from leather it is 8.2 percent. Overall, during the period of GATT negotiations, the less developed nations' share of world trade declined from 31 percent in 1950 to 26 percent in 1982.[9]

Consequently, the tendency in the less developed states has been to reject the arguments concerning liberal trade and to increase restrictions on trade. Their representatives have argued that, although liberalization of trade by developed states might help the plight of the Third World somewhat, it would not address the roots of the problem, which lie in the unequal structure of the world economic system. Rich states must extend preferential treatment to overcome problems. In 1964, the less developed states formed the United Nations Conference on Trade and Development (UNCTAD) to challenge GATT as the forum for decisions regarding world trade. Subsequently, there have been a number of UNCTAD meetings. At approximately the same time as UNCTAD, the Group of 77 was formed by 77 less developed states, which sponsored the Joint Declaration of the Developing Countries. It established goals for UNCTAD. The Group of 77 has become a permanent political group, representing 120 less developed states in 1985. The existence of UNCTAD has institutionalized Third World trade interests. It established a conference that meets every three years, four committees that meet yearly, and a trade and development board that meets twice yearly. It is viewed by the less developed states as the proper forum for negotiation on all matters concerning the world economy. UNCTAD has faced strong difficulties since its inception. The richer states have refused to recognize it as the proper forum for negotiation and have not considered themselves bound by its proposals. Additionally, UNCTAD and the Group of 77 have been plagued by the enormous diversity found among their members. First, member states differ in their level of wealth and development. They range from wealthy oil-exporting states like Saudi Arabia, to middle-income states like Brazil, to newly industrialized states like South Korea, to the states of the Fourth World like Bangladesh. Second, they range in ideology from market economies to centrally planned Communist economies. Third, they differ in their economic ties to other states. Some are tied to the European Economic Community; some, to the United States or Japan; and some, to the Communist bloc. Each of these differences affects their orientation toward trade issues. Nevertheless, UNCTAD has had some success in placing its concerns on the world agenda.

Presently, world trade continues to work to the disadvantage of many less developed states. Those producing primary commodities are subject to wide fluctuations in the prices of their commodities and to declining demand. Those producing manufactured goods for export face increasing trade barriers from the developed states. GATT permits trade preferences for the less developed states, but only a small percentage of Third World exports are affected.

UNDERDEVELOPMENT AND FOREIGN AID

If we use a broad definition, all resource transfers from one country to another can be defined as *foreign aid*. However, economists generally use a more specific definition in order to distinguish aid from commercial transactions and to differentiate

Table 13.1   MAJOR SOURCES OF DEVELOPMENT AID (IN MILLIONS OF US DOLLARS)

Country	Amount 1975	Percent GNP	Amount 1980	Percent GNP	Amount 1985	Percent GNP
Canada	$ 950	0.44	$1,042	0.41	$1,634	0.46
France	2,100	0.66	4,082	0.64	3,807	0.71
Germany	1,706	0.41	3,543	0.43	2,827	0.42
Italy	202	0.09	683	0.16	1,126	0.26
Japan	1,205	0.23	3,529	0.31	3,939	0.29
Netherlands	686	0.84	1,688	0.99	1,150	0.85
United Kingdom	916	0.42	1,745	0.39	1,456	0.31
United States	4,139	0.26	7,179	0.26	9,294	0.23

Source: World Bank, *World Development Report, 1988,* from Table 21 (New York: Oxford University Press, 1988).

developmental and humanitarian assistance from military aid. The concept as it is commonly used today is defined as all official grants and concessional loans broadly aimed at transferring resources from developed to less developed states for the purposes of development or income distribution.[10] Concessional loans are those for which the interest rate and repayment period are less stringent than for commercial loans. Given this definition, foreign aid excludes transfers that are purely for national security purposes, but, in reality, it is often impossible to distinguish aid given for humanitarian and development purposes from aid designed to promote the security of the donor state. The amount of foreign aid given by the developed states has grown substantially over the years, quadrupling between 1970 and 1983.[11] The total value of development assistance that was given in 1986 was $37 billion. Although the absolute amount of foreign aid has risen steadily for the last few decades, aid as a percentage of the donor state's GNP has fallen. Presently, the United States gives less than 0.3 percent of its GNP in aid. Although in absolute amount the United States gives more in assistance than any other state, it ranks seventeenth among developed states in terms of aid as a percent of GNP. Also ahead of the United States are several OPEC members, which give an average of 1.05 percent of their GNPs in development assistance. Table 13.1 summarizes the major sources of development aid.

Motives for Giving Aid

States have diverse motives for granting foreign aid. Political interests have usually been the most important of these motives. Aid can be used to strengthen an ally or to keep an ally from switching sides in the East-West struggle (either through keeping political elites favorably disposed or by maintaining friendly regimes in power). The first major post-World War II aid package, the Marshall Plan, involved the transfer of resources from the United States to Europe to rebuild the war-torn economies there. A major purpose of the Marshall Plan was to fight the spread of communism by providing economic security. Other early U.S. aid payments were for military assistance and were granted to states bordering the USSR and China. During the mid-1950s, when the Soviets began aiding a number of Third World countries, U.S. interest in that region increased. Believing that economic development would raise incomes, lead to stability, and thus weaken the appeal of Marxism there, the United States extended development assistance to a number of states in the Third World. The success of Castro in Cuba in 1959 and the subsequent establishment of a Communist government there, aided by the Soviet Union, raised the possibility of a Communist threat from the south. In its wake, the United States stepped up economic aid to Latin America (through the Alliance for Progress), with the intent of preserving friendly regimes. National security concerns also prompted the United States to extend its aid to countries in the Middle East and Asia during the 1960s and 1970s. During the Reagan administration, U.S. security assistance to the developing states amounted to $78.1 billion, compared to $51.4 billion in development aid.[12] In addition to those directly involving national security, political concerns can also include the spread of a particular ideology (demonstrating the advantages of capitalism over socialism) or religion (Islam). The United States is not alone in its ability to be influenced by political interests. Great Britain, France, and the Soviet Union, among others, have also tied aid to their national-security interests.

Humanitarian motives also influence the granting of aid. Aid that is designed to raise incomes or food consumption is an example of humanitarian aid. Famine relief and direct food aid programs are geared not toward development but rather toward the short-term alleviation of problems. Other food aid programs are designed to increase agricultural productivity to alleviate long-term food shortages. Even here, political and economic motivations can play a role. The bulk of U.S. food aid often is not given to those countries with the hungriest people, nor does it always reach the most needy in those states that do receive it. The top recipients of food under the Food for Peace Program in 1986 were Egypt, India, El Salvador, and the Sudan. These states were chosen for strategic, rather than for humanitarian, reasons.

Economic interests constitute another set of reasons for the granting of foreign aid. Economic growth in Third World states is beneficial to commercial interests in the developed countries for the simple reason that rising incomes help to create new and expanded markets for their products. Aid can also ensure that the developed states can maintain access to natural resources produced by less developed states. In the aftermath of the Arab oil embargo in 1973, Japan granted large amounts of aid to Indonesia and other oil-producing states.[13] In addition, the developed states have an economic interest in maintaining a stable political climate in areas where their business interests have investments. Often aid carries requirements that the aid must be spent on goods produced by the donor state and shipped by firms headquartered there; consequently, aid provides a subsidy to domestic businesses, thus providing benefits to the donor state's economy. Finally, aid given as commodities can help to dispose of surpluses that would drive prices down if they were sold on the domestic market.

Bilateral Versus Multilateral Aid

Aid given directly from one state to another is called *bilateral aid*, while aid funneled through international organizations is termed *multilateral aid*. Bilateral aid accounts for the largest portion of foreign aid. In 1980, approximately 28 percent of aid from developed states was channeled through multilateral agencies; the remainder was in the form of direct transfers from one state to another. In 1988, the breakdown for U.S. aid was 88.9 percent in bilateral aid and 11.1 percent in multilateral aid. A good bit of bilateral aid is based on past associations; thus, much of the aid given by the colonial powers is to their former colonies. There are a number of multilateral-aid agencies that disperse assistance contributed by a number of states. The most visible are the agencies of the United Nations, such as UNICEF and the World Health Organization. These agencies grant aid on humanitarian terms. They can nevertheless be affected by political pressure. In 1989, the World Health Organization declined to admit the Palestine Liberation Organization as a member after the United States threatened to withdraw its funding for the agency.

The World Bank has become an important source of funds for Third World states. Created as part of the Bretton Woods system, it was originally designed to aid in the development and reconstruction of Europe. Because it was not supposed to compete with private capital, its loans were given only for specific projects and then on hard terms—interest rates were based on the market rate and had to be repaid in hard currencies. It was not until the 1950s that growing Third World membership in the United Nations and U.S. concern with Soviet influence in the less developed states combined to create a new interest among developed states in aid for development. In 1956, the members of the World Bank created the International Finance Corporation (IFC) to finance loans for private investment in less developed states. In 1958, the lending capacity of the World Bank was increased from $10 billion to $20 billion, and the flow of funds shifted from developed to less developed states. In 1983, over $10 billion in aid was disbursed under the auspices of the World Bank.[14] The International Development Association (IDA), an affiliate of the World Bank, grants loans under concessional terms. Credit is usually extended for 50 years, with no interest, a nominal service charge, and a 10-year grace period.[15] Other major multilateral agencies include those of the United Nations, the European Economic Community, and various consortia designed to coordinate aid programs.

One disadvantage for the donor state that grants aid through multilateral agencies is that often control over how the money is spent is lost. For the recipients, this constitutes an advantage. There are usually fewer strings attached to multilateral aid, and thus there may also be fewer political consequences from accepting the aid. Unlike bilateral aid, multilateral aid is not usually tied to trade with the donor state. Donor states can use multilateral aid to demonstrate their commitment to humanitarian principles.

Some aid is also funneled through voluntary agencies such as CARE, World Vision, and Catholic Relief Services. Under the Reagan administration, the proportion of U.S. aid that was given through these organizations increased from 16.2 percent to 24 percent. Aid distributed by these private groups is thought to reach the most needy more directly than official aid; however, even here there can be a political component. By channeling aid through private organizations, a state can send humanitarian aid to states where direct aid is thought to be inappropriate. For example, the U.S. government was able to get aid sent to Haiti under Duvalier and the Philippines under Marcos by granting it to private organizations.[16]

Consequences of Aid

Analysts are divided over the consequences of aid programs. Many view the continuance of aid programs as essential for Third World development and argue that aid has helped to promote growth and stability. Hollis Chenery and Nicholas Carter examined the effect of foreign assistance on development performance in the decade of the 1960s and concluded that many aid recipients achieved significant growth, which reduced their future aid requirements.[17] Others argue that aid programs have not significantly helped development. The gap between rich and poor states has grown during the era of development aid. Aid has not brought about development or stability. Although many observers point to the failure of aid programs, they are divided as to the wisdom of continuing assistance. Some critics argue that properly funded and administered programs could be helpful. Their criticisms are aimed not at the concept of aid but rather at the amount of aid that has been granted and at the way in which its administration has diminished its usefulness. Granting more aid and ending practices such as tying aid to the purchase of goods and services in the donor state would improve the efficiency of aid programs. Critics also argue that, since most aid is granted as loans with concessional terms, it adds to the enormous debt burden that less developed states face. Giving more outright grants-in-aid rather than loans would solve this problem. Both donors and recipients are reluctant to switch to outright grants-in-aid, however. Recipients feel less dependent when they accept loans, and donors can argue that they are getting something back. Thus, both are more comfortable with loans than with grants.

Other critics argue that aid actually hinders development, and therefore granting more aid would not solve the problems associated with it. Aid has been criticized for reinforcing existing inequalities, particularly between the urban and rural sectors; for retarding reform by making it easier for governments to preserve the status quo; for increasing dependency; for emphasizing industry at the expense of agriculture; and for reinforcing inefficiency. Aid also has been criticized for reducing the autonomy of Third World governments, which must be careful to avoid decisions that could lead to a reduction in aid. Aid, it is argued, does not address fundamental political, cultural, and structural problems and therefore cannot bring about development.

Future of Aid

During the decade of the 1980s, the commitment of the more developed countries to providing aid has weakened. Joan Spero suggests that three crises—in food, energy, and anti-inflationary policies and recession in the developed countries—had profound impacts on the flow of aid.[18] She argues that at the same time that these crises created a greater need for economic aid, they undermined political support for aid in the North. In particular, economic recession undermined the richer states' commitment to aid, but political factors also played a role. Conservative governments in the United States and the United Kingdom argued that private investment rather than aid should play a greater role in development. Additionally, the Reagan administration's focus on East-West tensions led to an interest in offering unilateral military aid rather than multilateral development assistance. The United States reduced its annual contribution to the International Development Association and cut back on its commitment to IFAD. At the same time, the debt crisis has led to a focus on the more heavily indebted nations of South America and the question of restructuring the debt rather than on providing development assistance to the poorer states in Africa and Asia. Those who believe that aid is important for the alleviation of poverty and for improving the living standards of people in less developed states argue that aid must be geared to the real development needs of recipients, should take the form of outright grants untied to donor exports, and should be distributed by multilateral assistance agencies whose political motivations are less narrowly defined.[19] Many observers are pessimistic about the future of aid. They see no evidence that patterns in the granting of aid will change sufficiently to enhance development.

DEBT

The World Bank has identified 17 states as being highly indebted.[20] All but one of these are Third World states, and 11 are found in Latin America. These states do not have the world's largest debts, in terms of amount owed. They are judged as being at risk because large portions of their debt are owed to commercial lenders at variable rates. Debt in and of itself does not create a problem. Many states have large external debts, and commercial banks are not interested in seeing this debt paid off as long as interest payments are met. This type of debt should not be confused with consumer debt, which is nonproductive. The deeply indebted consumer is simply living beyond his or her means and must eventually either seriously restrict spending or declare bankruptcy. In contrast, commercial debt, when it has been properly invested, can produce substantial revenue, which can then be used in part to pay the interest and principal on the debt. Thus debt can finance growth. Problems from these loans arise when the debt cannot be serviced. *Debt service* refers to the annual interest and principal payments that are due.

Between 1970 and 1980, the external debt of oil-importing less developed states had increased from $48.0 billion in 1970 to $301.3 billion in 1980. In constant 1978 dollars, this is an increase of about two and one-half times. By 1989, the external debt of developing states had increased to $1,283 billion.[21] Important characteristics of this debt are: (1) It has outstripped the capacity of the borrowers to generate foreign exchange sufficient to make interest and principal payments; (2) it is held largely by the newly industrialized and middle-income developing states; (3) it was made at floating, rather than fixed, rates, and (4) it comes largely from a relatively few commercial sources, primarily the nine major U.S. banks and two British banks. Each of these points is discussed in more detail in the next section.

Origins of the Debt Crisis

Michael Todaro argues that the origins of the debt crisis of the 1980s lie in the period between 1974 and 1979. In 1974, developing states were becoming increasingly important to the world economy. The average growth rate for these states from 1967 to 1973 was 6.6 percent. To meet their growth needs, many of these states had begun heavily importing capital goods, oil, and food. With the first major OPEC oil price increase, these states sought to preserve their high growth rates by borrowing. Increasingly, they turned to commercial sources for credit. In part this was a response to the insufficiency of official funds, and in part it was an attempt to avoid meeting IMF policies (usually in force for official loans) requiring greater austerity. Commercial banks were ready and willing to lend the surplus OPEC dollars that they were holding, particularly in view of the declining demand for capital from the developed states, which were experiencing recession and thus slower growth rates. Bankers were anxious to lend to those middle-income and newly industrialized states that had been showing such high growth rates. Little thought was given to the possibility of default. One bank president went so far as to note that the loans could not go bad because "countries do not fail to exist."[22]

Unlike the earlier loans given by the IMF and the World Bank, which were concessional loans (i.e., they were given at lower-than-market interest rates and for longer periods), loans from commercial banks were general-purpose loans made on nonconcessional terms and often at variable rates. When a loan has a floating interest rate, the nominal rate is the amount of interest on paper. The real interest rate is the difference between the rate of inflation and the nominal interest rate. If the nominal rate is 10 percent and the rate of inflation is 8 percent, then the real interest rate is only 2 percent. During the decade of the 1970s, the average real rate paid on these loans was −0.8 percent. Under these conditions, it made sense to borrow. During the 1980s, nominal interest rates did not fall as much as inflation, so real rates rose. Figure 13.2 demonstrates this phenomenon. At the sums borrowed, a 1 percent rise in rates could mean billions of dollars more owed.

The second round of increases in the price of oil in 1979 created a situation in which the export earnings of many Third World states were not sufficient to meet loan-servicing requirements. Developed states sought to stabilize their own economies through sharp increases in interest rates. At the same time, slowed growth and protectionism in the developed economies meant less demand for Third World exports. Thus, these states were faced simultaneously with lower earnings and increased debt service demands. It also needs to be noted that sometimes the money from loans was not used in ways that would have produced the income necessary to service the loans. In Venezuela, the water company billed customers for only 35 percent of the water delivered and ran up a $775 million deficit, then used borrowed funds to meet that deficit. In other cases, loans were used for imported consumer goods and thus generated no revenue at all.

Further complicating the situation was the problem of capital flight. Enormous deposits in foreign banks have been made by Third World nationals. Between 1983 and 1985, Mexico borrowed $9 billion. At the same time it is estimated that $16 billion left the country.[23] Sixty-two percent of Argentina's and 71 percent of Mexico's growing debt is thought to be a result of capital flight.[24] Finally, falling oil prices seriously hurt oil-exporting countries like Algeria and Nigeria, which had borrowed heavily to finance development on the expectation that oil revenues would provide them with adequate earnings to service their debt.

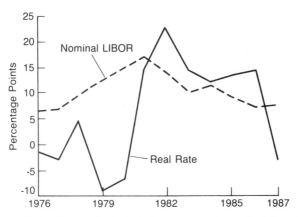

Note: The nominal rate is the average six-month dollar LIBOR during each year; the real rate is the nominal LIBOR deflated by the change in the export price index for developing countries.

Figure 13.2 Interest rates on external borrowings of developing countries, 1976 to 1987. (*Source:* World Bank, *World Development Report, 1988* New York: Oxford University Press, 1988.)

Although the developing states can be held partially responsible for the accumulation of debt, the responsibility is not theirs alone. One economist estimates that almost 85 percent of the total increase in the external debt of the non-oil-producing Third World countries can be attributed to factors outside their control, notably the OPEC oil price increases, the rise in interest rates during the early 1980s, the decline in their export volume as a result of worldwide recession, and a fall in commodity prices.[25]

Consequences of the Debt Crisis

In August of 1982, the finance minister of Mexico announced that his country did not have the resources necessary to make its annual payment on its debt. Financial institutions were thrown into a state of near panic. The nine leading U.S. banks had up to two and one-half times their total capital and assets in loans to Third World countries.[26] Just three countries (Argentina, Brazil, and Mexico) owed approximately 40 percent of the Latin American debt held by U.S. banks.[27] The extent to which the debt is concentrated makes the problem of default more critical. If these Latin American debtors defaulted, the banks would collapse and the entire international financial system would be threatened. There would be serious political consequences of default as well. A state that defaulted on a loan would be highly unlikely to receive future loans. Unless it could find a state willing to grant it aid for political reasons, it would have to fund every development project with cash. Furthermore, its creditors would move to seize all assets held abroad. Thus, there is agreement on virtually all fronts that default is an option to be avoided.[28] Nevertheless, these states continue

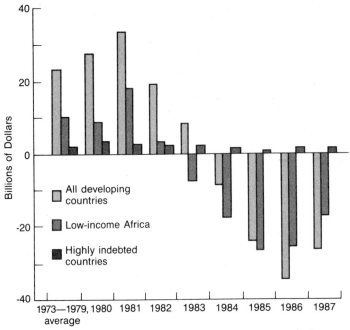

Note: Net resource transfers are defined as disbursements of medium-and long-term external loans minus interest and amortization payments on medium-and long-term external debt.

Figure 13.3 Net resource transfers to developing countries, 1973 to 1987. (*Source:* World Bank, *World Development Report, 1988* (New York: Oxford University Press, 1988).)

to face difficulties in debt service. In September 1989, Brazil failed to make $1.6 billion in interest payments to creditor banks. Peru and Ecuador have also suspended payments.

Economically and politically, the consequences of the debt crisis have been profound. Twenty-eight Latin American and Caribbean nations that have undergone economic stabilization programs as a consequence of debt were able to finance $145 billion in debt payments between 1982 and 1988 but faced economic stagnation, rising unemployment, and a 7-percent decline in per capita income.[29] Real wages declined in Mexico by 50 percent during this period. The increase in debt service and the deterioration in lending to less developed countries has led to net resource transfers from the poorer to the richer states. A net resource transfer is the amount of external loans made minus the amount of interest and amortization payments being made on external debt. It amounts to a transfer of wealth. Between 1977 and 1982, the developing states received a positive resource transfer of $147 billion. Since then there have been negative transfers of $85 billion. (See Figure 13.3) Currently, about $30 billion per year is flowing north from Latin American countries.

Payments on existing loans and limits on future lending seriously affect development in the Third World. As interest rates rose and exports fell or stagnated, the cost of servicing debt increased from 27.1 percent of export earnings to 38.8 percent from 1980 to 1982. Thus, a greater portion of export earnings must go to interest payments rather than to financing development at the same time that less credit is available to finance these projects. Complicating matters further, the less developed states' share of international trade has dropped during the period of the debt crisis. To increase their foreign-exchange earnings, debtor states must curtail imports. This affects the industries of the developed states, which rely on these markets. The U.S. balance of trade with Latin America changed from a surplus of $2 billion in 1980 to a deficit of $13 billion by 1986.

Economic problems have created significant political problems for the fragile democracies that exist in many Latin American countries. Reaction to economic stagnation, high rates of inflation, and the implementation of austerity measures has ranged from rioting to the defeat of incumbent parties, sometimes replacing moderate with more extremist parties. The riots in Venezuela, the election of the Peronist party in Argentina, and the election of a right-wing government in El Salvador have all raised concerns about the future of democracy in this region. In a number of states, nationalist movements on both the left and the right have seen increases in their strength as a result of the debt crisis. In response to instability, foreign investment has declined, thus worsening the economic situation further.

Managing the Debt Crisis

The International Monetary Fund (IMF) has taken on a major role in the debt crisis. The highly indebted states have had to turn to the IMF to finance foreign exchange. The IMF first assesses the economic situation, works out a standby loan, and monitors the state's economic policies to ensure that it adheres to the conditions of the loan. Private lenders generally view IMF certification as an indication that the debtor state is attempting to solve its economic problems and is therefore worthy of additional credit. Thus, in order to renegotiate loans with a private lender, the debtor state must agree to IMF stabilization policies. The stabilization program, which typically calls for devaluation of currency and austerity measures to control inflation, is politically unpopular and puts a significant burden on the poorer population in the debtor states. Recently the IMF has shown greater flexibility in the economic programs that it has negotiated with Third World governments. IMF policies were discussed in more detail in Chapter 12.

Recently, a number of proposals have been advanced for managing the debt crisis. The Baker Plan, proposed in 1985, was designed to encourage renewed lending to support economic growth in the debtor states. It proposed a three-way agreement among debtors, creditor states, and private creditors. The debtors would open their economies to trade and multinational investment, privatize aspects of their economies, and adopt market-oriented policies. The creditor states would stimulate their own economies and open them to debtor exports and expand the role of the World Bank in lending. The commercial lenders would loan an additional $20 billion to the debtors to facilitate policy changes and to increase economic development. This plan was seen as significant because it marked a recognition on the part of the

United States that the debt crisis was long-term and because it did not rely entirely on Third World efforts to improve their own situation.[30] The Baker Plan failed, largely because the banks were reluctant to make new loans. Critics charged that, even if it had succeeded, it would only create more debt, not less.

The Brady Plan, proposed in 1989, represented a shift toward debt reduction by recognizing that some debtor states could not pay back their loans in full, even if the payment period were extended.[31] Banks were asked to reduce voluntarily principal or interest charges on loans to less developed states. Debt would be reduced through buy backs, conversion of debt into bonds at lower principal or interest, or debt-equity swaps. In return for an agreement on the part of creditors to reduce principal or interest, the IMF and the World Bank would guarantee part of the remaining principal or interest. In July 1989, Mexico, which owed $35 billion, became the first state to reach an agreement with its creditors along the lines suggested by the Brady Plan. The Philippines reached an agreement shortly thereafter.

Problems are to be addressed on a case-by-case basis. To qualify for relief under the plan, a state must agree to adopt economic policies to encourage domestic savings, foreign investment, and the return of flight capital. The plan has been praised for addressing the need to reduce the debt burden of less developed states. It has been criticized for providing too little relief. Loans would be reduced by about $70 billion over three years. Additionally, critics have argued that, if economic conditions worsen and states are unable to make their payments, the banks will turn to the IMF and the World Bank, which then must make good on their promise to guarantee the payments. Since the IMF and the World Bank are supported by the member states, this amounts to a bailout of the banks on the part of the taxpayers of these states. The plan is also criticized because it applies only to those states that are willing to adopt politically unpopular austerity measures. Some fear that those states not affected by the plan will be more likely to radicalize and repudiate their debts.

THIRD WORLD RESPONSES

The New International Economic Order

As we noted earlier, Third World states created UNCTAD as a forum for advancing their demands for reworking the basic nature of the international trading system. UNCTAD doctrine is based on dependency theory, as originally developed by the Argentinian economist Raul Prebisch.[32] Under this theory, the developed states of the Northern Hemisphere constitute the center of the world's economic system, and the less developed states of the Southern Hemisphere constitute the periphery. Decisions are made primarily to advance the interests of center states. Production in the periphery states is geared toward the needs of those in the center. The international market works against the interests of periphery states through the decline in terms of trade for primary products and the protectionist policies of the industrialized states that discriminate most heavily against periphery exports. The international system must be restructured to redistribute resources.

A complete assessment of dependency theory is beyond the scope of this chapter, but it should be noted that a number of studies have called into question many of its basic assumptions.[33] Nevertheless, in terms of the issues discussed in this chapter, there is considerable evidence that the less developed countries are at a disadvantage because of the international economic system as it presently exists. Michael Todaro identifies five major ways in which the poorer states are affected.[34] First, there is an imbalance in the distribution of international monetary reserves. The Third World, which accounted for 70 percent of the world's population in the 1970s, controls only 4 percent of the international reserves. The structure of the international monetary system is controlled by the more developed states, which can create and manipulate reserves for their own benefit. Second, poor states get back only a small fraction of the final price from international purchases of their products, since they often do not control processing, shipping, and marketing. Third, the richer states give only lip service to liberal principles. These states use tariffs and NTBs to protect inefficient domestic industry, particularly the labor-intensive industries that constitute much of Third World manufactured goods, and they restrict immigration to protect jobs. One of the best examples of the richer states' abandonment of liberal principles is the Multifiber Arrangement (MFA), which restricts trade in textiles, an area of manufacturing in which Third World states have a comparative advantage. Fourth, multinationals have in many instances negotiated contracts, leases, and concessions that have benefited themselves at the expense of the host states. Finally, the less developed states traditionally have been left out of critical decisions concerning the world economy. Principally for these reasons, UNCTAD has challenged the existing economic order by calling for a New International Economic Order (NIEO). The NIEO touched on a number of issues, including:

Renegotiating Third World debt

Reforming the IMF, particularly in its decision-making process

Stabilizing the value of primary product exports by tying commodity prices to those of manufactured goods

Creating a common fund to be used to establish buffer stockpiles

Lowering tariffs on Third World exports

Increasing technical assistance in agriculture

Increasing development assistance from the developed states to a minimum of 0.7 percent of their respective GNPs

The greatest area of progress has been in trade, but even here reforms have been limited. In 1965, UNCTAD asked states to give priority to avoiding increases and reducing barriers on products that comprise the principal exports of the less developed states and to grant exceptions to free-trade rules for less developed states. In 1968, UNCTAD II developed the Generalized System of Preferences (GSP), which was passed by the UN in 1976 and extended in 1980. The original idea behind the GSP was to exempt the exports of developing states from trade barriers. Eventually, 19 developed states agreed to the GSP, but different states passed different versions, none of which were as pervasive as that envisioned by the UNCTAD pro-

Table 13.2 IMPORT COVERAGE OF THE GENERALIZED SYSTEM OF
TARIFF PREFERENCES, 1976 (MILLIONS OF DOLLARS)

	Nonfuel merchandise imports from developing countries		
	Total value	Under GSP	
Country or trading group		Value	Percentage of total
Austria	$ 647	126	19
Australia	1,268	179	14
Canada	2,031	303	15
EEC	15,155	4,446	29
Finland	415	21	5
Japan	12,314	1,789	14
Norway	556	22	4
Sweden	1,247	145	12
Switzerland	1,042	257	25
United States	24,499	3,154	13
Total	$59,174	10,442	18

Source: World Bank, *World Development Report, 1981* (New York: Oxford University Press, 1981).

posal. The U.S. version put a ceiling on the quantity and value that an import could reach to receive special treatment. Once the quota was reached, normal tariff rates would apply. It also excluded textiles, watches, shoes, and a number of other products particularly important to Third World states. The United States also reserved the right to deny preference to states under certain circumstances, such as their membership in cartels like OPEC. The GSP has had a limited impact on U.S. trade with Third World states. Table 13.2 shows the percentage of nonfuel merchandise covered by the GSP that was imported by developed states in 1976. In 1983, the United States imported $10.8 billion under the GSP, but this accounted for only 14 percent of its imports. Further, only 5 states accounted for nearly two-thirds of the imports under GSP.[35] The EC adopted a GSP that accepts certain products from 51 African, Caribbean, and Pacific states without tariffs. These account for 29 percent of its nonfuel imports from less developed states.[36] Overall however, the less developed states have been hurt by the increase in trade barriers established by much of the developed world in the 1980s.

A second area in which there has been progress is commodity trade arrangements. The less developed states have had success in placing commodity issues on the world agenda but little concrete success in achieving stability for commodity prices. UNCTAD proposed in 1976 an Integrated Program for Commodities (IPC), which would have imposed export quotas, international buffer stocks, a common fund, and compensatory financing for 10 core commodities (cocoa, coffee, tea, sugar, cotton, jute, sisal, rubber, copper, and tin). Some commodity producers have provided funds for establishing buffer stockpiles. Commodities are bought and stored when prices are low and then sold when prices rise, thus stabilizing prices. The less developed states have asked for a common fund to finance these buffer stock agreements. Although an agreement has been reached on the establishment of a common fund, it has not yet been put into effect. In spite of a shared interest in the area of commodity production, agreements exist on only 6 commodities.

Resource Cartels

The Rise and Fall of OPEC[37]

The First Oil Shock: 1973–1974   The morning of October 6, 1973 saw the beginning of a fourth Arab-Israeli War as Egyptian troops crossed the Suez Canal and Syrian forces attacked along the Golan Heights. Initially, the Arab armies proved superior. By the end of the first week, however, Israeli forces stopped the Arab advance, and, during the second week, Israel gained the upper hand in the fighting. On October 17, as a show of support for Egypt and Syria, the Arab members of the Organization of Petroleum Exporting Countries (OPEC) announced an oil embargo against those states supporting Israel. The United States and the Netherlands were singled out for a total embargo, while Japan and some European states were to be subjected to progressive reductions of 5 percent per month. Saudi Arabia took the lead in this collective action by cutting its oil production by 25 percent and halting all oil sales to the United States.

The oil embargo did not in itself greatly disrupt Western economies. What did create economic havoc were a series of price increases that followed the embargo. Two days before the war began, the price of a barrel of crude oil was $2.70. The Arab members of OPEC, acting through the Organization of Arab Exporting Countries (OAPEC), were first to act. They raised the price of their oil to $5.12 per barrel. Just before Christmas, OPEC followed suit and unilaterally raised the January 1, 1974 selling price of oil to $11.65 per barrel.

OPEC was able to raise the price of oil in large measure because of the way in which the international oil system had developed. The international oil industry was an oligopoly. Virtually from the beginning, it was dominated by a small number of oil companies, commonly known as "the Seven Sisters." They were Standard Oil of New Jersey (today known as Exxon), Standard Oil of California, Texaco, Mobil, Gulf, British Petroleum, and Royal-Dutch Shell.[38] The first five of these oil companies are American firms, and the last is a joint British-Dutch venture. Early on, each of these firms had managed to establish vertically integrated operations; that is, each firm controlled all aspects of the oil industry from exploration, production, and refining through transportation and marketing. To reinforce their position of dominance, the Seven Sisters not only engaged in joint exploration and production ventures but also fixed prices and divided world oil markets and sources up among themselves. These characteristics are important, because they provided OPEC with a ready-made mechanism by which it could control both the flow of oil and its price.

Just as important as the nature of the system set up by the Seven Sisters was the gradual erosion of their ability to dominate it. New competitors—"independents"—entered the international oil system, setting up operations in states such as Algeria,

Libya, and Nigeria. These companies were not vertically integrated, and their presence in the oil fields greatly reduced the control that the Seven Sisters exercised over the international oil market. In 1952, the Seven Sisters produced 90 percent of all crude oil outside of North America and the Communist states. In 1968, they produced only 75 percent. Additionally, because these new independents did not recognize agreements to divide up the world's oil regions into exclusive exploration zones, they also provided oil-producing states with the opportunity to realize more profit from their oil reserves. No longer confronted with either a single buyer or group of buyers working within a fixed price structure, oil-producing states were able to renegotiate the price at which they allowed companies to extract oil from their territory. As a result, the bank accounts of oil-producing states grew rapidly. Whereas in 1964 the level of official reserves of the major oil-producing states was valued at $2.87 billion, in 1970 it had jumped to $5.17 billion and in 1971 it stood at $8.18 billion. This increase was important, because it put the oil-producing states in a financial position in which they could afford a short-term loss of revenue that would follow from a production cutback and embargo.

Developments within the Seven Sisters' home states also weakened their dominance of the international oil system. On the economic front, the advanced industrial economies of North America, Europe, and Japan had become increasingly dependent on inexpensive imported oil. In 1972, 30 percent of all the oil consumed in the United States was imported, with approximately 15 percent being imported from North Africa and the Middle East. By 1972, Europe relied upon oil for 60 percent of its energy needs, with 80 percent being imported from North Africa and the Middle East. That same year, imported oil accounted for some 73 percent of Japan's oil needs, with 79 percent coming from North Africa and the Middle East.

Politically, Western governments were no longer willing or able to protect "their" oil companies from the aggressive policies of Third World leaders, as they had done in the past. Whereas, in 1951, Great Britain and the United States took covert action that was designed to remove Iranian Premier Muhammad Mossadegh from power when he nationalized the Anglo-Iranian Oil Company, no such help was forthcoming in 1970 when Colonel Muammar al-Qaddafi's government demanded that, if they wished to avoid nationalization, oil companies operating in Libya would renegotiate the price at which they sold Libyan oil on the world market.

Finally, the dominance of the Seven Sisters was weakened by the growing strength and unity of the oil-producing states. OPEC was formed in 1960 by Iran, Iraq, Saudi Arabia, Kuwait, and Venezuela. By the end of the decade, its membership had grown to 15 states, which collectively accounted for 85 percent of the world's oil exports. Nevertheless, it was not much of a match for the Seven Sisters. OPEC's founding members had come together in an attempt to find ways of halting the decline in world oil prices that had followed the U.S. oil embargo. Little progress was made in raising oil revenues until 1970, when the international oil market began to tighten and Qaddafi demonstrated that the oil companies were no longer invincible. In rapid succession, OPEC states succeeded first in raising the price of oil and then in gaining a larger voice in decision making. In spite of these gains, OPEC states continued to feel exploited, as events in the international economy outpaced their efforts to reap the benefits of higher oil prices. Oil companies, not OPEC members, were profiting by the continuing surge in oil prices. Meanwhile, the downward drift of the dollar lessened the purchasing power of OPEC's oil revenue. Consequently, in September 1973, OPEC summoned the oil companies to Caracas for yet another round of negotiations. After two weeks, the oil companies requested an adjournment so that they could consult with their home governments on OPEC's demand for a substantial price hike. As Joan Spero notes, "the adjournment, it turned out, was not for two weeks but forever."[39]

The Second Oil Shock: 1978–1979   A crisis atmosphere returned to the international oil marketplace in 1978 and 1979. In late 1978, political unrest became widespread in Iran, as public opposition to the shah's rule mounted. Domestic violence took a heavy toll on Iran's capacity to produce oil. This was soon followed by the Soviet invasion of Afghanistan. There resulted a bidding war for oil on the "spot market," that is, for oil that is not sold on a long-term contractual basis but that is available to meet short-term needs. At one point, for example, the spot price for oil was $8 per barrel over the established OPEC price for oil sold under long-term contracts. By October 1979, the OPEC price for oil had skyrocketed to $34 per barrel. Because OPEC was unable to manage the price of oil at this time, the international oil system was largely out of control.

By mid-1980, the worst seemed over. However, just as Saudi Arabia and other OPEC moderates appeared to be on the verge of bringing order back to the international oil system, war broke out between Iraq and Iran. This had the effect of reducing the world's oil supplies by an estimated 3.5 million-barrels-per-day (mbd), or 10 percent of all world oil exports. Largely because of increases in the level of oil production by other OPEC members and a reduced demand for oil brought on by a recession in the West, the Iran-Iraq War did not paralyze the international oil system. Still, it did result in yet another price increase, because, in December 1980, OPEC raised the ceiling price for oil to $41 per barrel.

Oil Glut: 1981-   The price of oil had climbed to such heights and had remained there for so long that it simultaneously reduced the demand for oil and brought in new oil producers. The demand for imported oil by Western industrialized economies fell 40 percent under the combined weight of economic recession, conservation, the development of alternative energy sources, and increased domestic oil production. Whereas in 1979 these states had received two-thirds of their oil from foreign sources, in 1983 they imported less than one-half of their oil needs. Among the new non-OPEC oil exporters who arrived on the scene in the 1980s were Mexico, China, Egypt, Malaysia, Norway, Great Britain, and the Soviet Union. Their production was so great that, by 1983, OPEC members accounted for only 33 percent of world oil exports. This was down from its 63 percent share of the world market in 1973 and its 48 percent share in 1979. OPEC's management task was made even more difficult by the increased prominence of the spot market. In 1973, less than 5 percent of the world's oil was sold on the spot market. The remaining 95 percent was sold on the basis of long-term contracts. In 1983, at least 20 percent of the world's oil was sold on the spot market.

The full extent to which OPEC's position of dominance had been eroded became clear in the first months of 1983. Shortly after an emergency OPEC meeting in Geneva, which failed to produce agreement on production quotas, it was announced that the price of (non-OPEC) North Sea oil would soon be reduced. Fearing that this would set off a new round of OPEC price cheating, OPEC was forced to seek the help of non-OPEC oil producers in stabilizing the international oil system. Stability was achieved, but the price of oil continued to drop. In 1981, it stood at $34 per barrel, and, by mid-1986, it had fallen to as low as $10 per barrel before rebounding to approximately $18 per barrel in 1988. Adjusted for inflation, this put the price of oil near where it had been in 1973.

Why Success; Why Failure   The history of OPEC's rise and fall as a dominant force on the international economic scene is instructive for what it tells us about the political and economic conditions necessary for the successful operation of a natural resource cartel. More agreement exists on the economic requirements of a successful cartel than on the political ones. A first economic requirement is that the cartel possess export control of the commodity. It need not control all of the global reserves for that resource—just that portion of it that is traded on the world market. Second, all major exporters must belong to the cartel. It is far less likely that the cartel's policies will be frustrated if only small exporters are nonmembers. Third, demand for the resource should be *inelastic*. Demand is said to be inelastic when changes in price do not affect how much of a product or a resource people want or need. Fourth, there should be no readily available and affordable substitutes for the resource. Together, these last two points insure that prices can be raised without fear that consumers will either simply stop buying the product because it has become too expensive or turn to alternative products.

For OPEC, all four of these requirements were present in 1973, but they had largely vanished during the 1980s. As we have seen, its control over the world oil market fell from 63 percent to 33 percent in the span of one decade. Important oil exporters such as Mexico, Norway, and Great Britain also came on the scene and remained outside of OPEC's management structure. Just as damaging to OPEC's position was the fact that some of its members (Algeria, Ecuador, and Gabon) were running out of exportable oil, while others (Indonesia, Venezuela, Nigeria, and Libya) will probably have to cut back on their oil exports in the 1990s. While trapped into a short-term dependence upon oil from which they could not escape, gradually consumers turned to substitutes and began to put into practice energy conservation measures. Demand for OPEC oil fell from a high of 31 mbd in 1977 to 14 mbd in February 1983.

The central political requirement for a successful cartel is unity of purpose—something that is not easily achieved or sustained over time. The key event that galvanized OPEC was the 1973 Arab-Israeli War. Sympathy for the Arab cause served as a unifying factor within OAPEC, which outweighed all of its splintering tendencies. OAPEC's success, in turn, caused the remaining OPEC members to follow suit, giving the appearance of a united front. In the long run, unity of purpose requires that cartel members share three properties. The first requirement is ideological homogeneity. Political cooperation between governments of vastly differing ideologies is difficult to achieve. In 1973, all three major OPEC producers (Saudi

Arabia, Kuwait, and Iran) were politically conservative states. By the 1980s, the shah had been replaced by the fundamentalist regime of the Ayatollah Khomeini. Additionally, two OPEC members (Iran and Iraq) were at war with one another.

The second requirement is partially economic: economic policies of cartel member states should be both complementary and capable of withstanding retaliatory action by the consumer states or any short-term economic hardship that would come with an an embargo. OPEC unity was always somewhat weak on this point. Conflicting economic goals caused some OPEC members to emphasize short-term profits and other OPEC members to stress the long-term consequences of their actions for the health of the Western economies and demand for oil.

The third political requirement is the presence of a state capable of placing the cartel's long-term interests above its own or, alternatively, a state that sees the cartel's interests and its own national interests as being identical. In the case of OPEC, the role of balancer had been played effectively for a long time by Saudi Arabia. With its abundance of oil and limited development goals, Saudi Arabia adjusted its prices and production levels as necessary to maintain the health of the international oil system. Today, Saudi Arabia is unable to do so. As we have already noted, in part, the reasons are economic, but they are also political. As cheating became more common and as its own economic reserves began to shrink due to falling oil prices, Saudi Arabia experienced many of the same self-doubts about the cost of leadership that the United States has entertained about the cost of its role as protector of the international free-trade system.

Other OPECs   In the immediate aftermath of the 1973 oil crisis, a great deal of attention was given to the question of whether OPEC was an aberration or would serve as a model for other resource-rich Third World states.[40] The answer to both parts of the question has proven to be yes: OPEC has served as a stimulus for the creation of other resource cartels, but its success has not been duplicated. Prior to 1960, the year in which OPEC was established, there existed only one cartel. It regulated the international tea market. During the late 1980s, there were 19 cartels. Numbered among the cartels in existence today are the International Council of Copper Exporting Countries (CICPEC), the International Bauxite Association (IBA), and the International Coffee Organization (ICO). OPEC had a multiplying effect, not only because of its success in raising oil profits, but also because many Third World states share its members' fate as producers of a limited number of commodities. Table 13.3 shows just how pervasive this problem is for Third World states.

The problems that producers of resources face in meeting the requirements for the successful formation and operation of a cartel can be seen by examining the bauxite industry. IBA was established in 1974. The driving force behind its creation was Jamaica, whose economy was sputtering under the pressure of rising prices for imported oil and food. Other charter members were Surinam, Guyana, the Dominican Republic, Haiti, Ghana, Guinea, Sierra Leone, Yugoslavia, Australia, and Indonesia. Together these 11 states controlled 85 percent of the world non-Communist production of bauxite. Optimism ran high at first. Consumer states were heavily dependent upon imported bauxite (the United States, for example, imported 89 percent of its bauxite, and 86 percent of that came from Jamaica). Demand was relatively inelastic,

Table 13.3 PERCENTAGE OF
MERCHANDISE EXPORTS
DERIVED FROM PRIMARY
COMMODITIES, 1986*

State	Percentage
Argentina	73
Burkina Faso	87
Burundi	88
Central African Republic	67
Colombia	70
Cote d' Ivoire	85
Dominican Republic	56
El Salvador	75
Ethiopia	97
Ghana	68
Guatemala	66
Honduras	82
Kenya	70
Madagascar	81
Mauritania	65
Nicaragua	88
Panama	77
Paraguay	81
Rwanda	94
Somalia	98
Tanzania	79
Thailand	54
Uganda	98

*Excluding fuels, minerals and metals.
Source: World Bank, *World Development Report, 1988* (New York: Oxford University Press, 1988).

and the structure of the bauxite industry resembled that of oil in that it was dominated by a few large, vertically integrated, multinational corporations such as Alcoa, Alcan, Reynolds, and Anaconda. Not only the economic prerequisites of success but also the political ones were present. Jamaica, Surinam, and Guyana were linked by geography and ethnic ties, and Jamaica's domination of bauxite production put it in a position of playing the role of leader.

It did not take long, however, for internal dissension to surface. With the global economy in a recession due to OPEC's price hikes, IBA members were quick to adopt "me-first" policies. Australia and Guinea, whose taxes on bauxite exports were lower than those of other IBA members, quickly moved to increase their levels of bauxite production as the multinational corporations began to search for alternative sources of supply. The major losers were the Caribbean producers. Whereas the percentage of bauxite mined in Australia and Guinea rose from 30 to 45 percent between 1973 and 1979, Caribbean production dropped from 34 percent to 23 percent. Political and economic unity were lessened further in 1979 when Australia announced that it would not respect a common IBA base price for bauxite. With its treasury weakened by reduced bauxite sales, Jamaica was unable to play the role of balancer, and it retaliated by reducing its export tax in return for a commitment by the aluminum companies to purchase more of its bauxite. Making matters worse was the fact that Brazil, an exporter of potential importance with one-fifth of the world's bauxite reserves, was a nonmember. Finally, consuming states took steps to lessen their long-term dependence on bauxite when in 1979 the U.S. Bureau of Mines and four American aluminum companies began a search for commercially feasible substitutes. Similar histories of less-than-successful attempts to form resource cartels have been written for bananas and copper.[41]

Third World Common Markets

Third World states have also attempted to build regional economic organizations to further their growth and development. From an economic point of view, regional economic integration is appealing to the Third World because of the opportunity that it provides for existing industries to take advantage of the economies associated with large-scale production and because of the stimulus that it provides for the creation of new industries. Long-term economic benefits can also be realized from the possibility of engaging in coordinated industrial planning.[42] The 1960s and early 1970s saw the creation of the Andean Group (1969), the Association of South East Asian Nations (1967), the Caribbean Community and Common Market (1973), the Central American Common Market (1960), the Central African Customs and Economic Union (1964), the West African Economic Community (1973), the Latin American Free Trade Association (1961), and the Economic Community of West African States (1975).

An example of a subregional group that focuses on coordinating development activities rather than on trade among members is the Southern African Development Coordination Conference (SADCC).[43] Established in 1979, the SADCC is composed of nine states: Angola, Botswana, Lesotho, Malawi, Mozambique, Swaziland, Tanzania, Zambia, and Zimbabwe. During the colonial era, countries in this region were able to ship goods from ports on coasts of both the Atlantic and Indian Oceans. However, transportation and communication across the area has been disrupted in recent years by war. Consequently, much of the shipping has been done through the Republic of South Africa. This route is less economical, and one of the purposes of the SADCC was to lessen dependence on trade through South Africa. The member states have agreed to cooperate in the areas of transportation and communications, agriculture, industry and trade, energy, labor development, mining, tourism, and finance with individual states coordinating specific functional activities. There are no provisions for establishing a free-trade area, because the member states believe that the establishing of customs unions leads to the uneven development of members. A number of projects have been drawn up, but these require external financing, and only 16 percent of them have been funded, mostly by Belgium, the Netherlands, and the Scandinavian countries. At its 1987 annual conference, SADCC adopted the theme "Investment in Production," which focused on the development of intra-regional investment and trade.

Agreements reached among members are flexible enough to allow states to continue to pursue their own interests. This flexibility creates problems, however. For the organization to realize its goal of increasing development and lessening dependence, it is important to coordinate efforts, yet individual countries are reluctant to cooperate when their security is at stake. Thus, Zimbabwe decided to meet its additional electricity requirements by expanding its own coal-powered facility rather than by buying electricity from Zambia or Mozambique. Unless leaders perceive that it is in their own self-interest to do so, they are not likely to cooperate, even though such cooperation would enhance development in the region as a whole. Although a stated aim of the organization is to lessen members' economic dependence on the Republic of South Africa, exports from that country to the area have actually increased.

Attempts at Third World economic integration have not matched the level of success attained by the European Community. Some of these organizations have passed out of existence. For example, the Caribbean Community and Common Market replaced the Caribbean Free Trade Association, which was founded in 1968, and in 1980 the Latin American Integration Association was established to replace the Latin American Free Trade Association. The difficulties of integrating Third World economies can be attributed to several of the factors that we have already identified as affecting the integrative potential of any region. Some of the reasons are political in nature: the natural tendency for elites to favor the status quo over change; the dominance of nationalism over regionalism as the primary goal among the elite; the absence of interest groups to push for greater integration; and a lack of the bureaucratic resources necessary to forge progressively more binding linkages among economic areas. Others are economic. Because they are less developed, it is more difficult to establish linkages among Third World economic sectors. Low levels of income and low levels of industrialization are also seen as making societies more sensitive to inequalities in the distribution of the economic benefits that come with integration. In essence, in many Third World states, "a greater number of economic issue areas tend to become highly politicized than is the case in more developed settings."[44] Despite this lack of success, Third World leaders continue to look to regional economic organizations as a means of fostering political stability and economic growth. Thus, in February 1989, Algeria, Morocco, Tunisia, Mauritania, and Libya announced the formation of the Arab Maghreb Union.

Newly Industrialized Countries

As we have seen, during the 1970s, OPEC was seen by many in the North as the primary troublemaker of the 1970s in the international economy and by many in the South as a model to be followed. With OPEC's success in raising oil prices becoming a thing of the past, many observers have turned their attention to a new kind of

Table 13.4   U.S. MERCHANDISE
             TRADE DEFICIT, 1988

State	Millions of dollars
Japan	$ 52,070.0
Taiwan	12,679.9
Canada	10,059.4
EC	9,065.0
OPEC	9,041.9
South Korea	8,899.6
Brazil	5,034.6
Hong Kong	4,552.0
Mexico	2,633.5
Singapore	2,225.7
Others	2,461.2
Total	$118,715.8

Source: The Washington Post, May 26, 1989.

Third World troublemaker or model, depending upon one's perspective. The objects of their concern are not resource exporters organized into producer cartels, but a small group of states that do not belong to a common organization yet are collectively known as "newly industrialized countries" (NICs, often pronounced as *nickels*): South Korea, Taiwan, Singapore, Hong Kong (the Gang of Four), Brazil, and Mexico. The source of their strength lies in their ability to produce large quantities of low-cost manufactured goods for export. Originally, NICs concentrated in such industries as textiles, clothing, shoes, and simple electronic devices. They now have expanded into the production of automobiles, videocassette recorders, and computers. In 1978, these six states, plus India, accounted for 70 percent of the Third World's manufacturing exports, and, as can be seen in Table 13.4, these states dominated the list of states running merchandise trade imbalances with the United States in 1988.

On the whole, NICs have adopted one of two industrialization models. The Asian Gang of Four has pursued an export-led growth strategy. Its basic features can be illustrated by looking at Taiwan.[45] In order to attract foreign investors who would use their country as an export platform, Taiwanese leaders offered a number of incentives designed to reduce production costs and increase profitability. Among them were tax holidays, accelerated depreciation programs, and tax exemptions for exports. Taiwan also set up an Investment Commission within the Ministry of Economic Affairs to approve business ventures, monitor their activities, sanction any changes in plans from those agreed upon when the firm entered Taiwan, and see to it that, where appropriate, these firms purchase locally made products for use in their business operations. A Foreign Exchange Bureau also approved the inflow and outflow of all foreign exchange.

We need only to look at the success that the Gang of Four has experienced in gaining a share of the world's export market to appreciate the extent to which these Third World states are challenging the long-standing global division of labor between the manufacturing North and the agricultural and natural resource-rich South.[46] In 1979, the combined exports of these four Asian states were valued at $60.5 billion. In 1985, they stood at $113.9 billion—an 88 percent increase. Growth was equally spectacular in individual sectors and for individual countries. Textile and clothing exports grew 60 percent, from $14.6 billion to $23.4 billion. South Korean automobile exports grew from $300 million to almost $1 billion. Hong Kong's exports of footwear doubled in value from $125 million to $250 million. Making these figures even more remarkable (i.e., threatening from the North's point of view and heartening from the South's point of view) is the fact that it took place against a background of slowed economic growth in the advanced industrial economies and falling commodity prices. The real GNP of Northern states only grew an average of 4 percent per year between 1976 and 1979 before it slowed even further to an annual rate of 1.25 percent in 1980 and 1981. The picture in the South was just as bleak. World food commodity prices fell an average annual rate of 15 percent between 1981 and 1985; the price for agricultural raw materials fell at an average annual rate of 7 percent; and the price for minerals and metals fell 6 percent.

Brazil and Mexico have adopted policies of "assertive industrialization." This process can be illustrated by looking at the development of the Brazilian computer industry.[47] During the early 1970s, many Brazilian leaders came to the conclusion that a prime source of Brazil's underdevelopment lay in its dependence on foreign technology. Creating a domestic computer industry was seen as an avenue for escaping this dependence and realizing real growth. At that time, even though it was quite large, growing rapidly, and ranked as the twelfth largest computer market in the world, Brazil's computer industry was what one would have expected of a Third World economy. It was dominated by foreign multinational corporations; no local capital was involved in the production of data processing equipment; and the government had no special policy with regard to foreign investment in the area.

In 1977, foreign computer firms lost the right to manufacture minicomputers and microcomputers in Brazil. The first Brazilian computers appeared on the market in 1978 and accounted for only 2 percent of the total value of all computers installed that year. This figure rose to 19 percent in 1982. By 1983, there were approximately 100 Brazilian computer companies employing 18,000 workers and gross sales of $687 million or 46 percent of total gross computer sales in Brazil. U.S. companies dominated the global computer market at the time these actions were being taken. Collectively, they controlled 80 percent of the market, with IBM, alone, controlling 60 percent. U.S. firms applied pressure on both Brazil and the U.S. government to get restrictions on foreign production lifted or eased. They argued that, if Brazil was not stopped, other Third World states would follow its lead and exclude foreign investors from key market sectors. These efforts also failed. Rather than intimidate Brazilian leaders, this pressure produced a wave of nationalist sentiment that strengthened the government's hand. In the end, U.S. multinationals did succeed in getting around some restrictions on their business activities, but they were forced to accept the principle that microcomputers and minicomputers were to be the special preserve of domestic Brazilian firms.

CONCLUSION: THE FUTURE OF THE THIRD WORLD IN THE INTERNATIONAL ECONOMIC ORDER

The emergence of NICs as important economic actors raises two important questions about the future. The first deals with the difficulty that the United States has had in responding to their success. The second revolves around whether they can serve as a role model for other Third World states.

Peter Evans see the United States as a "declining hegemon."[48] A hegemonic state is one that has access to raw materials, controls major sources of capital, maintains a large market for imports, and holds a comparative advantage in the production of highly valued goods. Hegemonic states are valuable economically because they are seen as capable of organizing the international economic system in a stable and productive manner.[49] For most of the post-World War II era, the United States was a hegemonic state. Now that it is in a state of decline, Evans sees the United States as striking out aggressively in an effort to defend specific economic interests under the pretense of attempting to preserve a free-trade system. Not only has this strategy not been very successful, but also it contains two inherent dangers. First, if Brazil, Taiwan, and other NICs reject U.S. efforts to portray its actions as in the global interest—as simply opposed to benefiting the U.S. computer, automobile, or textile industry—the post-Bretton Woods international economic order may unravel even faster than it is unraveling at the present time. Second, U.S. relations with important Third World allies may be seriously damaged as the diplomatic fallout from these disputes spreads into other issue areas. NATO allies, such as Portugal and Turkey, have already begun to demand increased economic aid and trade concessions as part of the price tag for renewing leases on important U.S. military bases located there. It is not unreasonable to expect NICs to practice their own version of linkage politics. Finally, U.S. policymakers are confronted with a dilemma, because, in spite of the dangers intrinsic to this strategy and its lack of success, they have little choice but to follow it. They lack the political and economic resources to pursue either the option of increasing domestic competitiveness or of reestablishing a Bretton Woods free-trade system.

Some 30 states (see Table 13.5) are seen as potentially able to join the ranks of NICs. Should they? Should NICs serve as the development model for other Third World states? The answer given by the World Bank and the International Monetary Fund (IMF) to these questions is yes. Of the 9 Third World states to receive structural adjustment loans worth more than $50 million from the World Bank in the late 1970s and early 1980s, 7 were would-be NICs and 1 was an NIC. A similar pattern holds for IMF loans. Of the 20 Third World states to receive loans of this magnitude, 12 were would-be NICs and 2 were NICs. The appeal of NICs as

Table 13.5   POTENTIAL NICs

Argentina	Morocco
Chile	Pakistan
Colombia	Paraguay
Costa Rica	Peru
Cyprus	Philippines
Dominican Republic	Rawanda
Ecuador	Senegal
Egypt	Sri Lanka
Guatemala	Syria
Honduras	Thailand
Indonesia	Tunisia
Ivory Coast	Turkey
Jordan	Uruguay
Kenya	Venezuela
Malaysia	Zambia

Source: Robin Broad and John Cavanagh, "No More NICs," *Foreign Policy* 72 (1988): 83.

a development model lies in their apparent success in breaking the bonds of dependency.

Recently, voices have been raised challenging the wisdom of this advice.[50] It is pointed out that no new NICs have joined the original 6 and that only 2 of the 30 would-be NICs (Malaysia and Thailand) appear to have any hope of doing so. Critics note that, to be successful, the NIC development strategy requires a supportive international environment. Continuous access to foreign technology must be maintained (recall that Brazil did not try to exclude all foreign computer firms from operating there, but only those in the minicomputer and microcomputer fields), markets must exist, and funds must be available to finance these projects. Third World indebtedness, slowed global economic growth, and the changing nature of technology transfers (from entire industrial production processes in the 1960s to only segments of scattered assembly lines in the 1980s) constitute a far less hospitable setting. Additionally, Third World populations may well be the big losers in the race to become full-fledged NICs. Competition between these states has already led government officials to offer potential investors investment incentives, as well as promise them a docile and cheap labor force if they will locate in their state as opposed to a rival would-be NIC. The alternative suggested by Robin Broad and John Cavanagh is that these Third World states should follow a strategy of growth based on maximizing industrial linkages with agriculture.[51] In particular, they stress the benefits that would come from focusing on industrial-agricultural linkages in the production of agricultural inputs, the processing of farm products, and the production of consumer goods, the demand for which will increase as the purchasing power of those residing in the countryside grows.

NOTES

1. Joan Robinson, *Aspects of Development and Underdevelopment* (Cambridge Mass.: Cambridge University Press, 1981), p. 99

2. Michael Todaro, *Economic Development in the Third World*, 4th ed. (New York: Longman, 1989), p. 404.

3. Caroline Thomas, *In Search of Security: The Third World in International Relations* (Boulder, Colo.: Lynne Riemer Publishers, 1987), p. 60.

4. World Bank, *World Development Report 1988* (New York: Oxford University Press, 1987), p. 23.

5. Some analysts have questioned the decline of commodity prices for a number of reasons, including questions of supply due to limits in natural resources and the existence of resource-poor industrializing states. However, available data do suggest a long-term decline according to economists at the World Bank.

6. Todaro, *Economic Development in the Third World*, p. 370.

7. Todaro, *Economic Development in the Third World*, pp. 396–397.

8. "Hard-core" NTBs are those most likely to have significant restrictive effects. They include import prohibitions, quotas, and voluntary export restraints, among others.

9. David H. Blake and Robert S. Walters, *The Politics of Global Economic Relations* (New York: Prentice-Hall, 1987), p. 37.

10. Todaro, *Economic Development in the Third World*, p. 482.

11. Organization for Economic Cooperation and Development, *Development Cooperation, 1984 Review* (Paris: OECD, 1984), p. 64.

12. Larry Minear, "The Forgotten Human Agenda," *Foreign Policy*, 73 (Winter 1988–89): p. 82.

13. David Blake and Robert Walters, *The Politics of Global Economic Relations* (Englewood Cliffs, N.J.: Prentice-Hall, 1987), p. 144.

14. Blake and Walters, *Politics of Global Economic Relations*, p. 147.

15. E. Wayne Nafziger, *The Economics of Developing Countries*, (Belmont, Calif.: Wadsworth, 1984), p. 435.

16. Minear, "The Forgotten Agenda," pp. 85–86.

17. Hollis Chenery and Nicholas Carter, "Foreign Assistance and Development Performance, 1960-1970," *American Economic Review*, 63, no. 2: 459–468.

18. Joan Spero, *The Politics of International Economic Relations* (New York: St. Martin's, 1985), pp. 197–215.

19. Todaro, *Economic Development in the Third World*, p. 496.

20. These are Argentina, Bolivia, Brazil, Chile, Colombia, Costa Rica, Cote d'Ivoire, Ecuador, Jamaica, Mexico, Morocco, Nigeria, Peru, Philippines, Uruguay, Venezuela, and Yugoslavia. For more information, see Todaro, *Economic Development in the Third World.*

21. Todaro has an excellent discussion on the debt crisis. See Todaro, *Economic Development in the Third World*, pp. 415–425. This section draws heavily from that work, particularly regarding the explanation for the origins of the crisis.

22. Quoted in Susan George, *A Fate Worse Than Debt: The World Financial Crisis and the Poor* (New York: Grove Press, 1988), p. 13.

23. "Economic and Financial Indicators," *The Economist* (March 14, 1986).

24. Todaro, *Economic Development in the Third World*, p. 418.

25. This analysis, attributed to William Cline, is discussed in Todaro, *Economic Development in the Third World*, p. 423.

26. At the end of 1982, the nine major U.S. banks had 287.7 percent of their capital in loans to Third World states. By the end of 1988, this had been reduced to 108.0 percent, according to the Federal Financial Institutions Examination Council.

27. Robert Gilpin, *The Political Economy of International Relations* (Princeton, N.J.: Princeton University Press, 1987), p. 321.

28. Fidel Castro is a notable exception. He called upon the Latin countries to band together and to refuse to pay the debt owed.

29. Todaro, *Economic Development in the Third World*, p. 421.

30. Gilpin, *The Political Economy of International Relations*, p. 326.

31. For a lucid discussion of the Brady Plan, see Jeffrey Sach, "Making the Brady Plan Work," *Foreign Affairs*, 68, no. 3 (Summer 1989): 87–104.

32. Raul Prebisch, *The Economic Development of Latin America and Its Principal Problems*, Economic Commission for Latin America (Lake Success, N.Y.: United Nations, Department of Economic Affairs, 1950).

33. See Gabriel A. Almond's review of criticisms of dependency theory in "The Development of Political Development," in Myron Weiner and Samuel Huntington, eds., *Understanding Political Development* (Boston: Little, Brown, 1987), pp. 450–468.

34. Todaro, *Economic Development in the Third World*, pp. 598–599.

35. Blake and Walters, *Politics of Global Economic Relations*, p. 42.

36. Nafziger, *The Economics of Developing Countries*, p. 400.

37. The account presented here draws upon Joan Spero, *The Politics of International Economics*, 3d ed. (New York: St. Martin's, 1985); Robert Lieber, *No Common Power* (Glenview, Il.: Scott Foresman, 1988), pp. 201–224; Dennis Pirages, *The New Context for International Relations: Global Ecopolitics* (North Scituate, Mass.: Duxbury, 1978), pp. 120-145; and Dennis Pirages, *Global Technopolitics* (Pacific Grove, Calif.: Brooks/Cole, 1989), pp. 75–81.

38. For a history of the international oil companies, see Anthony Sampson, *The Seven Sisters* (New York: Viking, 1975).

39. Spero, *The Politics of International Economic Relations*, p. 304.

40. For an exchange of views, see Fred Bergsten, "The Threat from the Third World," *Foreign Policy* 11 (1973): 102-124; and Stephen Krasner, "Oil is the Exception," *Foreign Policy* 14 (1974): 68–84.

41. See Spero, *The Politics of International Economic Relations*, pp. 331–338.

42. Todaro, *Economic Development in the Third World*, p. 455.

43. See Paul Cammack, David Pool, and William Tordoff, *Third World Politics* (Baltimore, Md.: Johns Hopkins University Press, 1988), pp. 223–227, from which this discussion was taken, for more information on this organization, particularly concerning its relation to trade with the Republic of South Africa.

44. Joseph Nye. "Comparing Common Markets," in Leon Lindberg and Stuart Sheingold, eds., *Regional Integration* (Cambridge, Mass.: Harvard University Press, 1971), p. 228.

45. This account is based upon Steve Chan, "The Mouse That Roared," *Comparative Political Studies* 20 (1987): 251–292; and Chi Huang, "The State and Foreign Investment," *Comparative Political Studies* 22 (1989): 93–121. Not all Asian NICs have followed the same development strategy. Huang's article presents a comparison of the different paths that Taiwan and Singapore have followed in becoming NICs.

46. Robin Broad and John Cavanagh, "No More NICs," *Foreign Policy* 72 (1988): 81–103.

47. The following account of Brazil draws upon Peter Evans, "Declining Hegemony and Assertive Industrialization," *International Organization* 43 (1989): 207–238; Peter Evans, "State, Capital, and the Transformation of Dependence," *World Development* 14 (1986):

791–808; and Emanuel Adler, "Ideological 'Guerrillas' and the Quest for Technological Autonomy: Brazil's Domestic Computer Industry," *International Organization* 40 (1986): 673–706.

48. Peter Evans, "Declining Hegemony and Assertive Industrialization," *International Organization* 43 (1989): 207–238.

49. For a discussion of hegemonic states, see Robert Keohane, *After Hegemony* (Princeton, N.J.: Princeton University Press. 1984).

50. See Broad and Cavanagh, "No more NICs," pp. 81–103.

51. Broad and Cavanagh, "No more NICs," pp. 81–103.

Chapter
14

Global Issues

Today as in the past, the dominant unit of analysis in international relations is the sovereign state. As a result, problems of world politics tend to be conceptualized in terms of an individual state's foreign-policy responses. During the last few decades, a number of issues in world politics that transcend national boundaries and whose effective resolution lies beyond the reach of any single state have risen to prominence. Solutions to these problems will require either regional or global cooperation. Attacking these issues not only involves directing our attention away from the state but also raises a series of fundamental political questions concerning what we wish to achieve and what we wish to avoid, what types of trade-offs we are willing to accept, how benefits will be distributed, and who pays the costs.

This chapter will address three sets of global issues: (1) global environmental issues, such as depletion of our resources and pollution; (2) the global human issues of human rights violations and refugee politics; and (3) the global economic and political issues involved in controlling multinational corporations. In our conclusion, we will return to the three perspectives on world politics that we introduced in Chapter 1 and will use these issues to illustrate how each of these perspectives views the world political environment differently.

THE TRAGEDY OF THE COMMONS AND WORLD POLITICS

Finding solutions to the problems discussed in this chapter is complicated by the nature of the issues themselves. While each of them requires marshalling a great variety of highly sophisticated technological skills, expertise alone will not bring about a solution. These are also not problems that can be addressed through the use of military power; nor are they problems that can be clearly labeled in terms of national security. A state's immediate short-term interests may conflict with the long-term global interest of preserving humanity while maintaining a certain quality of life.

The Tragedy of the Commons is a concept that many have found to be quite helpful as they tried to understand the political issues involved in resolving these types of issues. This metaphor was developed by Garrett Hardin.[1] He asks us to imagine an old English village with a common pasture area on which all residents are free to graze their livestock. This arrangement works well for all concerned as long as the pasture is large enough to accommodate the demand for it. However, if more and more animals graze on the common pasture, then eventually the pasture will be destroyed as a common resource. Although it is in each villager's individual interest to continue to add to his or her herd, such behavior endangers the community as a whole.

Tragedy is almost certain to occur because of two factors. First, the impact of individual action on depleting the resource is delayed. If a villager adds a single additional cow or sheep, it does not cause the ruin of the commons. Thus, there is not an observable cause-and-effect relationship for each villager's action. This makes it psychologically easier for each villager to act on the basis of self-interest, and it makes it more likely that the problem will not be addressed until crisis threatens. Second—and more importantly—there is the "free-rider" problem. If some villagers restrain themselves but others do not, then the conscientious villagers are unfairly bearing the costs of conservation, and the end result of overgrazing eventually will take place anyway. Thus, it is more rational in terms of individual behavior for each villager to continue to add animals. Only cooperation and foresight among the villagers can avert catastrophe.

ENVIRONMENTAL ISSUES

A concern with the environment as a major global issue surfaced during the 1970s.[2] In 1972, a group of computer scientists at the Massachusetts Institute of Technology published a study called *The Limits to Growth*, which was commissioned by a group of businessmen and academicians.[3] They created a computer model of the world that involved five major issues: (1) population growth, (2) the depletion of nonrenewable resources, (3) pollution, (4) levels of industrialization, and (5) capital accumulation. It pessimistically predicted that growth could not be sustained and that within the next 100 years there would be an uncontrollable decline in population and industrial capacity. The report received a lot of attention in the media throughout the world.

A second study, commissioned by the Club of Rome, but less well known, was *Mankind at the Turning Point.*[4] It predicted that catastrophes would occur on a regional level long before the middle of the next century. The *Global 2000 Report to the President,* published in 1980, used data from a number of federal agencies in the United States.[5] It predicted water shortages, more pollution, resource depletion, the deterioration of cropland, population problems, and the increasing extinction of species. These studies assume that rates of technological development will continue, that existing environmental policies will remain stable, and that there will be no major or economic crises.

Critics of these "doomsday" studies argue that assumptions concerning available resources are incorrect and that forecasting based on current trends ignores important changes that occur. In particular, *The Limits to Growth* was criticized for using models that exaggerated consumption and population growth. The population growth rate has actually declined in recent years, forcing the United Nations to alter its earlier projections on the size that the world population would reach by the end of this century. The more optimistic studies are criticized for using data selectively and for making unrealistic assumptions concerning technological development and the avoidance of international catastrophes such as war.

International concern with these problems was evidenced by the convening of the United Nations Conference on the Human Environment that was held in Stockholm, Sweden, in 1972. It was preceded by a number of joint ventures that studied the earth's environment and addressed specific problems. The Stockholm Conference brought together the developed market economies, the command economies, and the developing states in order to consider the environment, broadly defined as: "Land, water, and climate, the polar icecaps and remote ocean deeps, . . . space, . . . the human situation, . . . and the relationship between man-made and natural environments."[6] The conference created the United Nations Environment Program (UNEP) as a forum for raising environmental issues. A number of international conferences have followed the Stockholm Conference, addressing a wide range of environmental issues, from acid rain to ocean pollution. Recently, the 1989 Economic Summit in Paris devoted the largest share of its time to environmental issues.

Resource Scarcity[7]

Food   Presently, there is an adequate amount of food produced globally to meet the nutritional needs of the world's population. Current food shortages are a result of distribution problems. Some regions of the world produce an excess of food, whereas in others food production has not kept up with population growth. Production of an agricultural surplus in one region does not ensure that all people will have access to food supplies. Even within states that are food exporters, such as Brazil, relatively large numbers of people are malnourished because of income inequality. Food production may also be inefficient, as when grain is produced to feed cattle. When converted into meat, grain loses from 65 to 90 percent of its protein value.[8] A simple measure of nutrition is the number of calories consumed per day. The average daily caloric intake required to meet basic nutritional needs is between 2,300

Table 14.1 AVERAGE
NUMBER OF CALORIES
CONSUMED PER CAPITA
PER DAY, 1985

Country	Calories
Bangladesh	1,804
Brazil	2,657
China	2,620
El Salvador	2,155
Haiti	1,784
Japan	2,695
Thailand	2,399
United States	3,682
Zimbabwe	2,144

Source: World Bank, *World Development Report, 1988,* from Table 1 (New York: Oxford University Press, 1988).

and 2,500 calories. Table 14.1 shows the average number of calories consumed per day in selected developed and less developed states. Although Table 14.1 gives us some idea of how access to food is distributed in the world, it fails to provide a complete picture, since food is also poorly distributed within states.

The food crisis that exists in some Third World states was created by development strategies that emphasized industry and urban development at the expense of agriculture, by high population growth rates, and by natural disasters. This crisis is worst in Sub-Saharan Africa. Per capita food production in Africa declined about 1.1 percent per year from the early 1970s through the early 1980s. Presently, 24 Sub-Saharan African states are suffering from food shortages. Persistent drought has brought famine to areas of Africa, particularly in the Sahel region. Although considerable attention was given to food aid during the 1970s (assistance grew by 18 percent in constant prices from 1973 to 1978), attention began to fade by 1978, and food aid increased by only 2.6 percent between 1978 and 1981.[9] Aid has often been given for major projects that ignore the small farmer, yet increasing agricultural productivity in these states requires that small-scale agriculture be given attention.

Food production can be raised by increasing the amount of land in production or by increasing the yield per acre. Although there is now new land that can be brought into production, the amount available is finite. Existing and potential cropland is lost to cities, homes, highways, and parking lots and through desertification and erosion. In many areas, remaining land that can be brought into production is marginal, requiring extensive fertilization or irrigation. During the 1950s and 1960s, increases in food production came about largely through increasing yields. The Green Revolution has applied technology in order to develop new high-yield varieties of staple crops. Although yields have increased significantly, there have been problems. The varieties developed require large inputs of fertilizers, pesticides, irrigation, and the use of certain types of agricultural tools, Generally, these are not available to the subsistence-level farmers who most need to improve their yields. It is also argued that these varieties are often more prone to disease and more sensitive to climatic fluctuations than the traditional varieties that were already in existence. These varieties are dying out in some areas as farmers switch to the higher-yield seeds. Monoculture (the use by farmers of a single species of plant) is potentially dangerous, since a disease or weather condition that attacks the species could wipe out an entire region's crop. Nevertheless, many observers believe that crop yields will continue to improve as a result of technological advances, particularly those in genetic engineering. Others are less optimistic.

Although food production could now adequately feed the world's people if the food were evenly distributed, many observers believe that food production will not be able to keep up with demand in the future. Lester Brown argues that, since 1973, the race between food production and population growth has been a standoff.[10] Solving the world's food problem will require extensive cooperation among governments and aid-granting agencies and worldwide changes in distribution and consumption patterns.

Nonrenewable Resources Fossil fuels have provided the energy for most of the world's industrialization. However, the supply of these fuels is finite and nonrenewable. Within the foreseeable future, petroleum supplies will be depleted. The Complex Systems Research Center at the University of New Hampshire prepared a model of the energy future of the United States in 1982. It predicted the following: The United States will import over two-thirds of its oil within 10 years; the United States' oil will be virtually depleted by 2020, and the world's oil will be depleted by 2040; and, since agricultural production in the United States depends heavily on oil, we may be unable to export food by the year 2000.[11] (Coal is in greater supply, and its production is not expected to peak for more than 100 years. However, coal burning poses environmental hazards.) The authors of *The Limits to Growth* predicted that, if the then current patterns of usage continued, we could exhaust reserves of petroleum within 20 years along with other important minerals such as copper, tin, silver, lead, mercury, and zinc. These predictions have not been borne out, but there is no argument that these are finite resources that eventually will be exhausted.[12] Table 14.2 presents figures on reserves of essential mineral resources.

As the less developed states industrialize, demands on the world's resources will increase. Presently, the developed states account for the bulk of energy use. The United States consumes about 30 percent of the energy used globally each year, yet it contains less than 7 percent of the world's population. Table 14.3 illustrates per capita energy consumption for developed and developing countries. It is estimated that the world energy demand will increase 125 percent by the year 2025.[13] In addition to exhausting energy supplies, this increase will lead to additional pollution.

Solutions to the depletion of nonrenewable resources call for the adoption of conservation policies and the search for alternatives to those resources now used. Using presently existing technology, conservation could cut the projected growth in

Table 14.2 LIFE EXPECTANCIES OF 1976 WORLD RESERVES OF SELECTED MINERAL COMMODITIES AT TWO DIFFERENT RATES OF DEMAND

	1976 Reserves	1976 Primary demand	Projected demand growth rate	Life expectancy in years[a]	
				Static at 1976 level	Growing at projected rates
			percent		
Fluorine *(million short tons)*	37	2.1	4.58	18	13
Silver *(million troy ounces)*	6,100	305	2.33	20	17
Zinc *(million short tons)*	166	6.4	3.05	26	19
Mercury *(thousand flasks)*	5,210	239	0.50	22	21
Sulfur *(million long tons)*	1,700	50	3.16	34	23
Lead *(million short tons)*	136	3.7	3.14	37	25
Tungsten *(million pounds)*	4,200	81	3.26	52	31
Tin *(thousand metric tons)*	10,000	241	2.05	41	31
Copper *(million short tons)*	503	8.0	2.94	63	36
Nickel *(million short tons)*	60	0.7	2.94	86	43
Platinum *(million troy ounces)*	297	2.7	3.75	110	44
Phosphate rock *(million metric tons)*	25,732	107	5.17	240	51
Manganese *(million short tons)*	1,800	11.0	3.36	164	56
Iron in ore *(billion short tons)*	103	0.6	2.95	172	62
Aluminum in bauxite *(million short tons)*	5,610	18	4.29	312	63
Chromium *(million short tons)*	829	2.2	3.27	377	80
Potash *(million short tons)*	12,230	26	3.27	470	86

Note: Corresponding data for helium and industrial diamonds not available.

[a]Assumes no increase to 1976 reserves.

Source: The Global 2000 Report to the President (Washington, D.C.: U.S. Government Printing Office 1980)

demand for energy in half. Because a relatively few states now consume so much of the world's energy, conservation in those states alone would have profound effects. For example, raising automobile fuel efficiency to 40 miles per gallon in the United States would save as much energy as Brazil now consumes.[14] Alternative sources of energy include nonrenewable and renewable substitutes for petroleum. Nuclear power and coal can be substituted for oil in a variety of usages. Both of these power sources create problems concerning pollution. Solar energy, hydropower, wind power, and alcohol fuels appear to be the most promising sources of renewable energy. However, even these sources of energy have problems attached to their use: Harnessing hydropower often involves environmental damage; raising crops to cre-

Table 14.3 PER CAPITA ENERGY CONSUMPTION (KILOGRAMS OF OIL EQUIVALENT), 1986

Bangladesh	46
Brazil	830
Canada	8,945
Ethiopia	21
Germany (East)	5,915
Germany (West)	4,464
Haiti	50
India	208
Japan	3,186
Mexico	1,235
Morocco	246
Thailand	325
United Kingdom	3,802
United States	7,193
Zimbabwe	517

Source: World Bank, *World Development Report, 1988,* from Table 10 (New York: Oxford University Press, 1988).

ate alcohol fuels takes land out of food production; and, so far, the technology for producing solar energy and wind power is expensive and unlikely to be developed without tax credits.

Nonfuel minerals are thought to exist in greater supply than fossil fuels, but these too are finite. As with fuels, conservation and the development of alternatives provide possible solutions to a depletion of major minerals. Recycling could also significantly extend our supply of minerals. Additionally, some have looked to the exploration of space and mining on other planets.

The ocean depths are another potential source of resources. Many Third World states view the wealth of the seas as a common heritage. In a first-come-first-served policy, the Third World states would be the losers, since they lack the capacity to exploit seabed minerals. In 1973, the third UN Conference on the Law of the Sea (UNCLOS III) met to address the issue. Coastal states were staking claims to larger and larger offshore areas. By the end of the 1970s, states had reached an agreement to establish a 12-mile territorial sea with a 200-mile economic zone. An International Seabed Authority was established to regulate deep-sea mining. An agreement was readied for consideration by 1980. The Law of the Sea Treaty has been signed by 150 countries. However, the Reagan administration opposed the treaty, and the United States is the only major power that has not signed it.

Under the UNCLOS III treaty, states share in the proceeds of deep-sea mining, even if they are not involved in the process. Any firm applying for a mining permit would have to submit two sites to the International Seabed Authority. The Authority would decide which of the sites to award to the firm. It would retain the other for its own exploitation, which would be shared by the international community. Although the United States has stated its intention to abide by the other provisions of the treaty, it continues to oppose the Authority and the provisions on deep-sea mining.

Pollution

The Greenhouse Effect and Ozone-Layer Depletion There are no national boundaries and no rights to sovereignty as far as the earth's atmosphere is concerned. Air moves freely around the world, and activities in one state can have a profound impact on the lives of people everywhere. The largest source of air pollution is the burning of fossil fuels, and by far the greatest use of fossil fuels is in the richer states of the North.

The use of coal, oil, and natural gas releases large amounts of carbon dioxide into the atmosphere. Since the middle of the nineteenth century, there has been an increase of 25 percent in the level of CO_2 in the air. The increased concentrations of carbon dioxide along with other gases, notably methane and chlorofluorocarbons (CFCs), are held responsible for what has been labeled "the greenhouse effect."[15] Although the entire globe is affected, the problem has been created largely by the industrialized states. In 1985, 62 percent of the CO_2 released into the atmosphere came from the developed states, even though these states contain less than one-third of the world's population. The industrialized states are also a major source of chlorofluorocarbons. Chlorofluorocarbons are thought to be responsible for 15–20 percent of the global warming trend. The entire developing world has contributed only a little more than 2 percent of the chlorofluorocarbons emitted. Although the less developed states have contributed relatively little to the greenhouse effect in the past, as they industrialize they will significantly worsen the problem. They are now thought to contribute about 25 percent of all greenhouse gas emissions. Deforestation, which presently claims more than 1 acre per second in the equatorial region, is thought to be the source of at least 20 percent of the global release of CO_2 and much of the methane. Tropical forests are being cleared at a rate of 50 to 100 acres per minute. Methane is also produced by rice cultivation and cattle raising in wetlands.

Although an international scientific consensus supports the existence of this problem, scientists are divided over the anticipated consequences. One of the expected effects for which there is considerable evidence and agreement is a global rise in sea level of up to 1–7 feet by the year 2075. Large numbers of people living in coastal regions around the world would be displaced. For example, a rise of only 3 feet would flood part of the Nile delta in Egypt, which constitutes between 12 and 15 percent of the country's arable land. In Bangladesh, 11.5 percent of the country's land area would be flooded and 9 percent of the population would be displaced.

Other greenhouse effects are less certain. A rise in temperatures in the middle latitudes could seriously affect agricultural production in some of the world's most productive areas, notably the American Midwest. It is expected that tropical areas would experience the most severe changes. Arid areas might become even drier, and humid areas could become hotter and wetter, with more tropical storms and other natural disasters.

A related problem to the greenhouse effect is ozone-layer depletion. In the lower atmosphere, ozone contributes to pollution. It is a major component of smog. However, in the upper atmosphere, ozone is beneficial, blocking out harmful ultraviolet rays from the sun. A major source of ozone-layer depletion is the use of chlorofluorocarbons as refrigerants, computer solvents, and propellants. CFCs do not break down until they reach the upper atmosphere, where they release chlorine, destroying ozone. Other sources of chlorine in the stratosphere are methyl chloride and carbon tetrachloride, which are solvents used to clean machinery. In 1988, scientists reported that ozone loss over North America and Europe has nearly doubled since 1969. It has been estimated that reduced ozone in the upper atmosphere will cause a significant increase in skin cancer each year. Additional health problems will include an increase in cataracts and damage to the human immune system. Ozone-layer depletion also contributes to the greenhouse effect by allowing more of the sun's rays to reach the earth.

Solutions to these problems will require considerable cooperation among the world's states. Stabilizing concentrations of CO_2 will require cutting global emissions by one-half. By using present technologies to produce more energy-efficient appliances and automobiles, we could reduce CO_2 emissions in the United States by 14–18 percent.[16] This could be achieved without sacrificing our present standard of living. The United States accounts for 24 percent of the emissions that produce global warming. Major reductions in CO_2 emissions from industrialized states would also require energy conservation and the use of renewable energy sources. Renewing the world's forests and slowing deforestation would also help.

Significant steps have already been taken to reduce the introduction of CFCs into the atmosphere. The United States was the first state to take seriously the threat of ozone-layer depletion. It banned the use of CFCs in nonessential aerosols in 1978. In 1987, the Montreal Protocol on Substances That Deplete the Ozone Layer vowed to halve the production and consumption of CFCs by 1999. By March 1989, it had been ratified by 31 states, and another 19 were giving it serious consideration. In an attempt to influence those states that have not agreed to the accord, it includes a ban on the imports of controlled substances from states that are not parties to the agreement. In 1989, the members of the European Community agreed to attempt to ban the use of CFCs by the year 2000.

Recently, there have been a number of international conferences on these issues. In March 1989, an international conference on the ozone layer involving 123 countries took place in London, followed quickly by a 24-nation meeting in the Netherlands. The latter conference, which excluded the United States, the Soviet Union, China, and Great Britain, called for increased authority in the UN to police the global atmosphere, including a search for appropriate enforcement measures. It also recommended, as did the conference in London, that poorer states receive financial aid to help ease the burden of meeting antipollution standards. In the late spring of 1989, representatives from 30 states met at a UN-sponsored conference in Geneva. In November 1989, a conference sponsored by the Dutch government, the UN Environment Program, and the World Meteorological Organization was held in the Netherlands. Several European states sought to establish a ceiling on carbon dioxide emissions by industrialized states to reduce global warming. Arguing that the magnitude and impact of global warming remains uncertain and that reductions in carbon dioxide emissions would hurt the economy, the Bush administration opposed the ceiling. Joining the United States in its opposition were Japan, the Soviet Union, and Great Britain.

Acid Rain, Contamination of the Oceans, and Species Loss   The ozone-layer depletion and the greenhouse effect are not the only issues in the area of atmospheric pollution. High levels of sulphur dioxide and nitrogen oxides in the atmosphere produce rain with a high acidic content. Coal burning is a major source of sulphur pollution. The use of petroleum releases nitrogen oxide. Normal rainfall has a level of acidity near 5.6. Presently, the average rain in the eastern part of North America has a pH of 4.6. This is 10 times as acidic as normal rain. Acid rain retards the growth of forests and may be responsible for killing trees. It reduces the number of fish in lakes, first by retarding reproduction, and then at higher levels by suffocating them because of the concentrations of minerals that clog their gills. In Ontario, Canada, 400 lakes have become biologically dead and life is threatened in an additional 48,000. In Sweden, 4,000 lakes are biologically dead.[17] Acid rain has significant economic effects, as well as contributing to the corrosion of stone and metal. In one area of Poland, the speed of trains is limited to 40 kilometers per hour because rails are so badly corroded from acid rain. Additionally, the acid rain is thought to dissolve heavy metals in the soil, increasing the risks of metal pollution to rivers and streams.[18] Acid rain falls far from the source of pollution, often across international borders, largely because of the use of high smokestacks. These were constructed to disperse the pollutants over a larger area, thus, in theory, diluting their harmful effects. Consequently, industry in the United States releases sulphur and nitrogen, which react with sunlight and water vapor to form acid rain that falls in Canada. Industry in England has polluted lakes in Sweden. The original purpose of the Stockholm Conference of 1972, called by Sweden, was to address the issue of acid rain. The declaration adopted at this conference says that states have a responsibility to ensure that activities within their boundaries do not damage the environment of other states. The 1979 Treaty on Long-Range Transboundary Air Pollution was signed by the United States and most of the other developed countries, including the Soviet Union and most of Eastern Europe. It requires states to limit and gradually to reduce air pollution, particularly sulphur dioxide. States also agreed to cooperate on research on the problem.

Land-based pollutants dumped into lakes, rivers, and streams eventually find their way into the world's oceans. Fertilizers and pesticides used on land also pollute the sea through runoff. Consequently, even when rivers do not cross international boundaries, water pollution becomes an international issue. Ocean pollution is derived from sewage, agriculture, industry, mining, and oil transport. No one is sure of the extent to which the oceans are polluted, nor are the consequences of low levels of pollutants clear. It is known that mercury and other heavy metals can concentrate in fish and shellfish. These can then poison people who eat them. Water pollutants are also known to affect phytoplankton—an essential part of the food chain. Additionally, coastal areas are often fragile ecosystems that are easily disrupted by pollution. A number of species are already threatened by overdevelopment of coastal areas. Pollution makes their existence even more precarious.

Oil spills have received more media attention than has low-level pollution. Their consequences are direct and dramatic. Even a relatively small spill will kill birds, fish, and marine mammals and pollute beaches. The 1989 Exxon *Valdez* accident once again reminded the world's people of the potential for disaster. On March 24, 1989, it spilled 10 million gallons of crude oil into Prince William Sound off the coast of Valdez, Alaska. Although in terms of volume, the accident was not a major spill, it was particularly damaging because the characteristics of the sound prevented the oil from dispersing. By April 24, clean-up crews had counted 3,000 dead animals. Six months later, workers had recovered the carcasses of 33,126 sea birds, 138 bald eagles, and 980 sea otters. These make up only a fraction of the number that died. The oil spill threatened the $750 million per year fishing industry, particularly salmon and herring fishing. Although they figure prominently in the headlines, oil spills account for only a small fraction of the ocean's oil pollution. When oil is removed from tankers, some of the empty tanks are filled with water to keep the ship stable. Before reloading, this water, now mixed with the oily residue from the tanks, is discharged into the ocean. Ships also commonly wash sludge out of tanks directly into the ocean. It is estimated that from 150,000 to 450,000 birds are killed yearly by chronic oil pollution.[19]

The oceans have long been recognized as a public or common good that belongs to all peoples. Although states have long had rights over territorial waters (historically, for 3 nautical miles from the coast but now extended to 12), no one may exercise sovereignty over the high seas. Because there was already a body of international law pertaining to the seas, a consensus on the rights of all states to use them, and the existence of monitoring institutions, it has been easier to formulate international policy concerning ocean pollution. The International Maritime Organization (IMO) was established in 1958. It is an agency of the UN and has over 100 members. After a disaster in 1967, involving a British ship that spilled 29 million gallons of oil off the coast of Cornwall, pollution from vessels became one of its major concerns. This disaster resulted in a treaty that makes the owner of the ship responsible for pollution damage and cleanup. The International Convention for the Prevention of Pollution from Ships, formulated in 1973, contains regulations on procedures to reduce oil pollution and imposes special requirements on shipping in highly vulnerable areas such as the Mediterranean Sea. A number of other treaties have addressed the issue of preventing oil spills. Enforcement is a serious problem. It is up to the state under which a ship is registered to enforce regulations. These regulations apply only to those states that are signatories to the treaties. States like Panama and Liberia have set themselves up as havens from regulations, and they register most of the tankers now operating on the open seas. These registrations are known as "flags of convenience," since nearly all of the ships are owned by foreign businesses. A UN treaty that was adopted in 1982 gives port states the authority to prosecute the captains of vessels who are in violation of policies, regardless of where the ship is registered or where the violations actually occurred.

The question of pollution from land is not within the province of the IMO. UNEP has aided states in drawing up regional agreements on this subject, most notably the Barcelona Conventions, which were aimed at preventing pollution of the Mediterranean Sea.

Acid rain and pollution of the oceans have contributed to the actual and threatened extinction of species by destroying habitats. Clearing of land for agriculture or development also destroys habitats and leads to species extinction. It is estimated that, of the 3 million species of plants and 10 million species of animals that exist, 10 percent of flowering plants and over 1,000 vertebrates are threatened.[20] Even more of the smaller species, particularly insects, are thought to be affected. *The Global 2000 Report to the President* estimated that 15–20 percent of living species could be extinct by the year 2000.

The tropical forests cover only about 7 percent of the world's surface, but they are home to more than one-half of the world's plant and animal species. Many plant species have medical and industrial uses, and it is almost certain that species not yet studied have potential benefits for humanity. For example, the rosy periwinkle of Madagascar, used in the treatment of childhood leukemia, was discovered relatively recently. Dozens of potentially beneficial plants may be lost forever through deforestation. Most deforestation is a result of the expansion of farming and raising of livestock. However, the land converted to agricultural uses is often poor for this purpose. The nutrient content of the soil diminishes rapidly, and, in just a few years, farmers are forced to move on, clearing more land. Thus, species are irrevocably lost, with no real gain for humanity.

Trade in wildlife products also threatens some species—often those that are already threatened by land development. Elephants are endangered by a combination of habitat loss and the international ivory trade. Six of seven species of sea turtles are threatened by the demand for their hides, shells, and meat. Rhinos are hunted for their horns, and exotic birds are smuggled from tropical forests. Although the animal trade does not pose the same threat as habitat loss, it has been directly responsible for the extinction of some species.

HUMAN ISSUES

Human Rights

Although the idea that people have basic rights to which all are entitled can be traced back for centuries, the issue of international human rights seized the attention of the world following World War II. The Nuremberg trials formally charged the leaders of Nazi Germany with committing crimes against humanity. These trials established that individuals have rights under international law, regardless of where they reside, and that these rights cannot be abridged through domestic law.

In 1948, the General Assembly of the United Nations passed the Universal Declaration of Human Rights. It urges governments to work toward the fulfillment of political, economic, and social rights. Political and civil rights covered by the document include such things as the right to freedom of movement, freedom of conscience and expression, participation in government, and freedom from arbitrary imprisonment and torture. Social and economic rights include the right to work in just conditions, with equal pay for equal work, to form trade unions, to a decent standard of living sufficient to provide for food, clothing, shelter, and medical care, and the right to free fundamental education. These are considered entitlement rights; that is, people are entitled to these rights by virtue of their humanity. Thus, these rights belong to all people, regardless of whether or not their government is a signatory to the declaration. Although the declaration itself has no enforcement mechanisms, it has been followed by over 100 other resolutions, covenants, conventions, and protocols on political rights, genocide, racial discrimination, and economic rights, which are legally binding on the signatories. Three important agreements—the Genocide Convention, International Covenant on Civil and Political Rights, and the International Covenant on Economic, Social, and Cultural Rights—would give the force of law to the principles recognized in the Universal Declaration of Human Rights, but these agreements have only been signed by about one-half of the world's states. The United States has signed the Genocide Convention but has not ratified the others.

Although most of the world's states have signed the Universal Declaration of Human Rights, violations of basic rights are common. Even among those states that seek to abide by the document, there is considerable room for interpretation. For example, the United States has argued that the assertion of a right to a decent standard of living for all citizens obligates a state to work toward that goal but does not require immediate implementation. Other states have argued that participation in government does not have to mean participation through competitive parties and elections, as these are divisive and may actually exacerbate tensions leading to human rights abuses. Other forms of participation, they assert, can be meaningful. The declaration lists the right to life as the most fundamental of rights, and most of the developed states have abolished capital punishment as a violation of human rights. However, the United States and many developing states argue that, if it is imposed as a result of a fair trial, the death sentence is not a violation of basic human rights. Some analysts have argued that, although the concept of basic human rights is a sound one, the present interpretation of those rights reflects the Western bias toward the individual, ignoring the rights of the community as a whole.

While many states disagree over interpretations of human rights, other states give lip service to the concept while violating rights that they have officially recognized. Other states refuse to recognize that individual rights exist at all. Massive violations of human rights have occurred in all parts of the globe. In 1965, following an attempt to overthrow the government, the Indonesian army and supporters of the fundamentalist Islamic party killed over 500,000 people. During the rule of Pol Pot in Kampuchea (Cambodia), the government killed between 1 and 3 million people. Idi Amin's government in Uganda killed 500,000 people, mostly members of particular ethnic groups; the government of his successor, Milton Obote, continued the slaughter, merely changing the groups targeted for murder. In El Salvador, over 10,000 civilians were killed in 1981 alone. In South Africa, the black majority have been denied the most basic human rights through a system of institutionalized racism—apartheid. Throughout the world, people are tortured, imprisoned without trial, denied free speech, and forbidden to organize unions and political parties.

When they attempt to justify their actions, governments often claim that these measures are necessary in the face of political and social unrest. They assert that allowing dissent will result ultimately in greater violations of human rights and that they must protect the majority of law-abiding citizens from the disruptive efforts of the few. In Argentina between 1976 and 1979, leftist guerrillas killed about 700 people. In response, the military eliminated thousands of citizens, arguing that this "dirty war" was necessary to fight communism. Those dead included 1,000 pregnant women and 100 children under the age of 7. In the spring of 1989, students in China staged a peaceful demonstration in Tiananmen Square. The triggering event was the death of Hu Yaobang, an official who was fired for being "soft" on student demonstrators in 1986. Hu Yaobang had become a hero to the students. The underlying cause was student dissatisfaction with the progress of reforms. The Chinese government had instituted a variety of economic reforms. These had created new opportunities for favoritism and corruption. The reforms were also creating a wealthier class. Meanwhile, the students saw their professors teaching in miserable conditions with inadequate supplies, often unable to buy needed textbooks. The students were concerned about their own future prospects, and, among other things, wanted more respect and a better standard of living for the intellectual class.

The goals of the students were not particularly radical. They did not require sweeping changes in the Chinese government. Although they called for democracy, they were not really asking for democracy as we know it. They wanted greater freedom of the press but were very supportive of the Communist party and the principles of socialism and did not call for competitive parties or elections. Their own movement was organized along authoritarian lines. Their placards contained slogans such as "Support the Correct Policies of the Communist Party." In spite of their vast numbers (it was estimated that there were more than 1 million demonstrators in Tiananmen Square), the students were remarkably well behaved. They were courteous to police, and they directed snarled traffic and helped emergency vehicles pass.

Nevertheless, in June, troops moved into Tiananmen Square and opened fire. Estimates on the number of students killed vary widely, ranging from 500 to 3,000. In the aftermath of the massacre, the government arrested more than 1,650 people, often using videotapes made by Western media sources during the demonstration to identify participants. Some of those arrested were quickly tried for treason. By July 24, 27 students had been executed. By the fall of 1989, the Chinese government had begun implementation of a number of measures to control the population, including indoctrination sessions at universities and a requirement that high school and university students work in factories on a regular basis.

The world's response to the Tiananmen Square massacre illustrates the problems with protecting human rights. These abuses occur within sovereign states, and no state is willing to set a precedent for direct intervention by either other states or international agencies. Prior to the massacre, various governments urged the Chinese to proceed cautiously, but in the end China chose to ignore that advice even at the risk of incurring economic sanctions against it. Although the U.S. government immediately issued a statement deploring the killings, the Bush administration was reluctant to impose harsh sanctions, since it views friendly relations with China as important to U.S. national interests. It did suspend foreign military sales and loans and, at Congressional insistence, imposed relatively minor economic sanctions. Even in the face of minor sanctions, China's economy will suffer. Billions of dollars of low-interest loans from the World Bank and other international institutions have been placed on hold. It has been estimated that China will lose almost $1 billion in lost tourist revenues.

International rights groups such as Amnesty International instituted campaigns to stop the executions, but the only apparent effect was that China attempted to block press coverage of the executions. A major weapon against human rights abuses is publicity. The United Nations Human Rights Commission, regional human rights commissions, and voluntary groups such as Amnesty International, Freedom House, and Americas Watch collect instances of abuses and publicize them. Few states are absolutely immune to adverse world opinion. Amnesty International has documented many cases in which prisoners received better treatment once officials learned that people outside the country were aware of the prisoners' existence and were monitoring their treatment. The South African government spends large sums of money every year in an attempt to counter world opinion. Although progress on human rights has been very slow, it has been affected by publicity. Many of those gains that have been made would not have occurred without world pressure.

Economic sanctions can have an effect on human rights abuses under the right circumstances. Obviously, the extent of the sanctions and the degree to which the target state's economy is likely to be affected are key variables, as well as the resolve of government officials. In China, officials were apparently so concerned with consolidating power that they were willing to risk the economic consequences of cracking down on the students. Sanctions against South Africa have not wrecked that state's economy, nor have they achieved the goal of ending white minority rule. Certainly they have had an effect on opinion among some business leaders within South Africa who have increasingly supported reform, and they have no doubt contributed to the morale of activists fighting to change the system. It is impossible to measure these kinds of effects. In El Salvador, the human rights picture did improve considerably after President Carter instituted his policy of denying aid to states that were in violation of human rights. El Salvador's government is dependent on U.S. aid for its continued survival in the face of insurgency. Although human rights violations continue, there is no doubt that numerous lives have been saved as a result of U.S. pressure.

Refugees

The right to leave a state is recognized by the UN Declaration of Human Rights. There is, however, no accompanying right to be permitted entry into a state. The right to decide whom to admit and under what conditions is one of the most fundamental principles of sovereignty. According to international legal conventions, a refugee is any person who has left his or her state because of a well-founded fear of persecution due to race, religion, nationality, or membership in a social group or political organization. Individuals classified as refugees are entitled to certain protection and services that are unavailable to those who seek entry to states for other reasons. The most significant of these protections is *nonrefoulement*, the prohibition on sending a refugee back to a state where he or she will risk persecution.

The key international document defining the conditions for granting refugee status is the 1951 UN Covenant Relating to the Status of Refugees. This document was drafted after World War II in an attempt to solve the European refugee problem brought on by war and the division of Europe. Its terms were set by statute to be applicable only to the victims of events occurring before January 1, 1951. Once these refugees were resettled, it was anticipated that the refugee problem would pass. Events have not supported this expectation. Even within the confines of European politics, refugee problems have continued to surface, and, by the 1960s, the flow of refugees had become an increasingly prominent feature of Third World politics.[21]

At the end of 1987, there were an estimated 13 million refugees in the world. The worst hit areas were the Middle East, including South Asia and Africa. There are presently more than 3.5 million refugees in Pakistan, most of whom are Afghans who have fled the war in their home country. Another 2 million Afghan refugees are in Iran. In all of the Middle East and South Asia, there are approximately 8.8 million refugees. War has also created refugees in Africa. Overall, there are more than 3.5 million refugees there. Since gaining independence in 1975, Mozambique has been plagued by civil war. The rebels were initially mobilized by the white minority in Rhodesia and have continued to receive support from the white government of South Africa. By the end of 1987, more than 2 million people had been displaced within the country and another 800,000 had sought refuge in surrounding countries. In Angola, civil war has caused 400,000 refugees. To the north, conflict in Ethiopia and the Sudan continues to produce refugees.[22]

States have jealously guarded their right to protect their borders and typically try to make the decision of whether to grant refugee status on a case-by-case basis. States also try whenever possible to screen refugee applicants before they arrive at the border. Sometimes, however, circumstances make this impossible. The United States has long had such a policy and sought to implement it to deal with the 1980 exodus from Cuba. Early indications were that the Cuban refugees would first be flown to Costa Rica and then sent on to other states for the purposes of receiving asylum. The United States announced that it would accept 10,000 refugees who met U.S. immigration standards. The strategy was frustrated when large numbers of Cubans began arriving in the United States directly as part of the Mariel boat lift.

In theory, refugee politics should be fairly straightforward. Any person who leaves his or her country because of a well-founded fear of persecution would be granted refugee status and would therefore be entitled to the protection of the UN. However, the issue of who is or is not entitled to refugee status is not at all clear. The legal definition of a refugee stresses the loss of political, civic, and legal rights. It is largely insensitive to the plight of individuals victimized by systemic economic deprivation or generalized conditions of insecurity and oppression.[23] Such individuals are typically classified as labor migrants or economic refugees who are responding to market forces rather than to political oppression. As such, their admission to a state, as well as any benefits to be extended to them, are entirely up to the host state.

Contemporary observers assert that this distinction between refugees and migrants is artificial and often misleading.[24] While few refugees may be able to document direct persecution, most are able to cite the existence of an exploitative political and economic environment that made life insecure and flight a necessity. Since many refugees are leaving states with economic problems, host states can nearly always label them economic migrants if they so desire. Political, economic, and social calculations enter into a state's decision.

In granting refugee status the host state is documenting persecution in the refugee's state. States are reluctant to accuse allies of persecution. Conversely, they may be anxious to accuse enemies of persecution. Thus, the United States generally labels Cuban immigrants refugees, even when they arrive during times of economic distress but at the same time resists granting refugee status to immigrants from El Salvador. Since Congress has tied aid to El Salvador to improvement of human rights there, recognition of persecution would threaten the continuance of aid. Pakistan has exhibited a similar double standard in dealing with refugees. Afghan refugees are openly welcomed and aided, while Iranian refugees are denied recognition. States whose political orientation is perceived as threatening will also be reluctant to accept refugees, particularly where there is already some agitation and unrest within the state.

Economic and social calculations are also important. Surveys have shown that Americans are quite open to receiving refugees in good economic times, but resist in times of high unemployment. States are disinclined to accept refugees who will add to the numbers of already existing minority groups.

The refugee problem is further complicated when states create refugees for political purposes. China has accused Vietnam of exporting refugees in order to extort money from them, to create social and economic problems throughout Southeast Asia, and to infiltrate agents into Association of Southeast Asia Nations (ASEAN) states. Some have argued that the Mariel boat lift, in which thousands of Cubans arrived in the United States, also may have been motivated by a desire on the part of Castro to create problems for the United States.

The use of refugee camps by rebels is a significant problem in many areas. Rebels fleeing government troops will cross a border and hide among refugees. It is often impossible to tell combatants from peasants. Honduras has referred to Salvadoran refugees within its borders as guerrillas without weapons and has been accused of allowing Salvadoran troops to cross the border and seize refugees. Refugee camps are also used to mask incursions across borders to attack villages in the host state. In Zambia, a number of Angolan refugees were tortured by Zambian security forces after repeated incursions by Angolan insurgent forces. An attack on a village in Zimbabwe by Mozambican rebels resulted in the beatings and deaths of Mozambican refugees. The army then forced 15,000 refugees back into Mozambique.[25]

A major international actor in refugee situations is the United Nations High Commissioner for Refugees (UNHCR). Its role is to coordinate relief efforts and to provide UN protection for refugees until they can be resettled. The UNHCR must be invited into a state before it can work with the refugees there. It is sensitive to the concerns of the host state and has been criticized for allowing political considerations to interfere with its primary mission of protecting refugees. Various voluntary organizations, including a number of religious groups, are also active in efforts to provide relief to refugees. Most of the money from states that is devoted to relief efforts for refugees is channeled through international refugee aid agencies. The largest donor is the United States, which gave $226.3 million in 1987.

Refugee problems are difficult to solve. Long-term solutions to refugee problems lie in addressing the underlying causes of the flow of refugees. As long as there are wars, economic deprivation, and human rights violations, there will be substantial flows of refugees. The causes of flows of refugees are internal to a state, but the consequences are international. For international organizations to have the power to address these issues, the sovereignty of states would have to be abridged considerably. Few states are willing to grant this kind of power to an outside agency. In the meantime, it has been suggested that the UNHCR be given increased power to protect refugees and that states adopt a humanitarian, rather than political, orientation when they are faced with a refugee situation.

MULTINATIONAL CORPORATIONS

Multinational corporations (MNCs), which are businesses that control assets (manufacturing plants, mines, sales offices, etc.) in two or more states, are not a new phenomenon. Their roots can be traced back to the British East India Company, the Hudson's Bay Company, the Portuguese Mozambique Company, and the Dutch East India Company. The 1602 charter of the Dutch East India Company permitted it to make war and peace, to seize foreign ships, to establish colonies, and to coin money. Moreover, among these corporations involved in international economic transactions today, there are several that have existed as MNCs for many years: Ford Motors had a plant in Europe in 1911, and Singer Sewing Machines had a Scottish assembly line operating in 1878. Still, it is only in the post-World War II international economic system that MNCs have emerged in large numbers from the shadows of state power to become important and independent economic actors. Between 1950 and 1963, the number of U.S.-based MNC affiliates increased from 7,000 to 23,000. They have also increased in size. A 1973 UN study concluded that so great was the size of MNCs, that firms with sales of less than $100 million per year could "for most practical purposes . . . be safely ignored."[26]

The UN study found both a great deal of concentration and variety in the pattern of MNC activity. Most MNCs were headquartered in the developed capitalist economies of the North. A full one-third of all foreign affiliates of MNCs were linked to U.S.-based parent firms. When these affiliates were combined with those linked to firms headquartered in Great Britain, France, and Germany, over three-quarters of all MNC affiliates had been accounted for. Manufacturing is the primary economic activity of MNCs, although its significance varies depending upon whether the host state is a developed or developing economy. In developed economies, 50 percent of foreign investment is in the manufacturing sector and 30 percent is in extractive industries. In developing economies, the situation is almost reversed, with 50 percent of foreign investment in extractive industries and 25 percent in the manufacturing sector. Geographically, MNCs show a preference for certain states over others.

This is particularly noticeable in the Third World. Argentina, Brazil, India, Mexico, Nigeria, Venezuela, and several Caribbean Islands have been found to account for 43 percent of the total stock of investment in Third World states. Another 30 percent of all Third World foreign investment was concentrated in 13 other states.

The size of MNCs can be measured in several ways. A sampling of figures concerning the overseas operations of several MNCs provides a sense of the scale of their activities. During the 1970s, Exxon had a tanker fleet larger than that of the Soviet Union and had three times as many employees posted abroad than did the U.S. State Department. Also at this time, IBM had operations in 126 states, plants in 13 states, research and development facilities in 8 states, and did business in 30 languages and more than 100 currencies. During the 1980s, U.S. MNCs formed over 2,000 alliances with European firms. Corning Glass, alone, has entered into 15 working agreements with firms based in Great Britain, Switzerland, West Germany, Italy, Belgium, Japan, South Korea, and Australia. Nestlé, a Swiss firm and the world's leading food company, has plants in more than 60 states and produces 200 different types of instant coffee. Finally, Japanese automobile makers have established plants in 6 U.S. states, and they have been followed by over 300 Japanese automobile parts companies. An appreciation of the size of MNCs can also be gained by comparing them with states. Table 14.4 ranks states by GNP and MNCs by gross annual sales. Of the top 50 entities, 42 are states and 8 are MNCs. Of the second 50 entities, 17 are states and 33 are MNCs. The highest-ranking MNCs are General Motors (23), Ford (29), Exxon (35), and Royal Dutch Shell (36). The latter is the highest-ranking non-U.S. MNC. Well over one-half of the MNCs are non-U.S. firms. The rankings of both states and MNCs have changed over time. For MNCs, movement up or down the power hierarchy is often a result of the overall health of the economic sector to which they belong.[27] In 1955, 9 of the top 50 MNCs were in the consumer industry, but in 1975 only 4 remained. An even harsher fate befell aerospace firms. In 1955, 5 of them were numbered among the top 50 MNCs, yet none remained on the list in 1975. Automobile and tire MNCs remained prominent, but their share of top 50 MNC sales fell from 30 to 21 percent. Not surprisingly, the biggest gains among the top 50 MNCs were posted by oil firms. They grew in number from 11 to 17, and their share of top 50 sales jumped from 27 to 46 percent. Accompanying these changes in the ranking of the largest MNCs has come a change in the identity of the home state. Whereas in 1960 127 of the top 200 MNCs were headquartered in the United States, only 91 were based there in 1980. On the other hand, the number of Japanese-based firms rose from 5 to 20.[28]

Raymond Vernon summarizes the dilemma that host states face in dealing with MNCs this way: "With different degrees of intensity, practically all countries feel that something has been lost if their national industries are not nationally owned; but most countries are also aware that at times more is lost by excluding the foreigner than by admitting him."[29] Given these conflicting forces, it is not surprising that a great deal of attention has been given to the matter of controlling MNCs. The problem is how to do so. Answers have been put forward at the international, regional, and national levels. Before we answer these questions, we need to look at the debate over why MNCs invest in foreign states.

Table 14.4   THE TOP 100 MNCS AND STATES RANKED BY WEALTH IN 1989 (IN BILLIONS OF DOLLARS)

MNCs and states	1989	MNCs and states	1989
1. United States	$4,862.0	51. Hong Kong	46.2*
2. USSR	2,500.0	52. *British Petroleum*	46.2
3. Japan	1,843.0	53. *IRI*	45.5
4. West Germany	1,120.0	54. *Daimler-Benz*	41.8
5. France	939.2	55. *Hitachi*	41.3
6. Italy	814.0*	56. Pakistan	39.4
7. United Kingdom	758.4	57. Israel	36.0
8. Canada	471.5	58. *Chrysler*	35.5
9. China	350.0	59. Malaysia	34.3*
10. Brazil	313.0	60. *Siemens*	34.1
11. Spain	288.3	61. *Fiat*	34.1
12. Poland	276.3	62. Iraq	34.0
13. India	231.0	63. *Matushita Electric Industrial*	33.9
14. Netherlands	223.3	64. *Volkswagen*	33.7
15. East Germany	207.2	65. Philippines	33.6
16. Australia	202.2	66. Portugal	33.5*
17. South Korea	171.0	67. *Texaco*	33.5
18. Czechoslovakia	158.2	68. Columbia	33.0*
19. Belgium	155.0	69. *E.I. DuPont*	32.5
20. Yugoslavia	154.1	70. Ireland	30.6
21. Romania	151.3	71. *Unilever*	30.5
22. Mexico	135.9*	72. *Nissan*	29.1
23. *General Motors*	121.1	73. *Philips*	28.4
24. Austria	118.1*	74. New Zealand	27.9*
25. Sweden	116.5	75. *Nestlé*	27.8
26. Switzerland	111.3	76. *Samsung*	27.4
27. Denmark	101.3*	77. *Renault*	27.1
28. Iran	93.5	78. *Philip Morris*	25.9
29. *Ford*	92.4	79. Egypt	25.6
30. Hungary	91.8	80. *Toshiba*	25.4
31. Taiwan	91.7	81. *ENI*	25.2
32. Finland	87.7	82. *Chevron*	25.2
33. Norway	82.6*	83. *BASF*	25.0
34. South Africa	81.0*	84. Singapore	23.7*
35. *Exxon*	79.6	85. *Hoechst*	23.3
36. *Royal Dutch Shell*	78.4	86. *Peugeot*	23.2
37. Nigeria	78.0	87. *Bayer*	23.0
38. Argentina	74.3	88. *Honda*	22.2
39. Saudi Arabia	74.0	89. United Arab Emirates	22.0
40. *IBM*	69.7	90. *CGE*	21.5
41. Indonesia	69.0	91. *Elf Aguitaine*	21.2
42. Bulgaria	67.6	92. *Amoco*	21.2
43. Turkey	62.6*	93. *Imperial Chemical Industries*	20.8
44. Algeria	59.0	94. Syria	20.3*
45. Thailand	52.2	95. Libya	20.0
46. *Toyota*	50.8	96. Peru	19.6*
47. *General Electric*	49.4	97. *NEC*	19.6
48. *Mobil*	48.2	98. Chile	19.4
49. Venezuela	47.3*	99. *Occidental Petroleum*	19.4
50. Greece	46.6	100. *Procter & Gamble*	19.3

Note: Wealth is measured in billions of dollars. It is calculated in terms of gross annual sales for MNCs and gross national product for states; *indicates that the state's wealth is valued in terms of gross domestic product.

Sources: The World Fact Book, 1989 (Washington D.C.: The Central Intelligence Agency, 1989); and *Fortune* (July 31, 1989), p. 282.

Why Multinational Corporations Invest in Foreign States

The World Manager's Vision[30]   If asked why their company has set up operations in Italy, Peru, or Thailand, managers of MNCs are likely to respond with one word: profit. Just as power is the driving force behind foreign policymaking for states, profit is the primary force shaping the foreign-policy decisions of MNCs. From the perspective of world managers, what is truly unique about MNCs is not their size but their world view. Of all the major international economic powers, only MNCs plan and act in global terms. For world managers, the state is an outmoded and obsolete institution. Jacques Maisonrouge, writing as chairman and chief executive officer of the IBM World Trade Corporation, stated that "the boundaries that separate one nation from another are no more real than the equator." He continues that in today's world "the seminal problem appears to be the lopsided distribution of the world's resources, both material and human. What is needed are mechanisms whereby those resources can be identified, managed, and more equitably distributed. One such mechanism—the international company—already exists. . . ." In his view, "purely political" solutions to these problems do not exist, and the record of generations of politicians attempting to deal with them must be judged as "sorry."

This self-image of the MNC as a citizen of the world stands in sharp contrast to the view held by many looking at MNCs from the outside. Quite apart from questioning the economic consequences of its presence within their borders, those in the host states often see MNCs as instruments of home state foreign policy and as threats to their sovereignty. In earlier chapters, we chronicled the events surrounding two of the best documented cases involving home state-MNC interference in politics: ITT involvement in discussions to remove Salvador Allende from power in Chile and CIA-orchestrated efforts to remove Jacobo Arbenz from power in Guatemala after he challenged the United Fruit Company. While they are extreme examples of home state-MNC interference in host country politics, they are not isolated ones. According to one otherwise sympathetic observer, the United States "has landed marines in half a dozen Caribbean countries, threatened to cut off aid to several dozen others from Peru to Sri Lanka, and at some point put other forms of pressure on almost every other government."[31]

Skepticism and hostility toward MNCs is not restricted to the Third World. In the late 1960s, J. J. Servan-Schreiber wrote of the "American challenge" to Europe.[32] He argued that modern technology requires large corporations and that states without their own MNCs are doomed to become colonies of those that do have them. Furthermore, this colonial status will extend beyond the economy of the state. It will also envelop its political, social, and cultural life. Echoes of European and Third World fears of the power and influence of MNCs were heard in the United States during the 1970s when there was a large and sudden influx of foreign investment into the United States.[33] Senate hearings brought forward expressions of concern over foreign domination of key industrial sectors, foreign penetration of defense industries, domestic scarcity and high prices in food and natural resource products, and technological dependence.

It should also be noted that where host state leaders tend to see MNCs as acting as extensions of a home state's foreign policy, home state policymakers tend to re-

member those cases in which its MNCs did not behave as desired. U.S. firms in
Libya did not send their American workers home in 1987 as requested by the Reagan
administration at a time when doing so would have made it easier for the United
States to carry out additional air strikes against Libya. Earlier in the decade, over
U.S. objections, Gulf Oil, which had large holdings in Angola, decided to continue
payments to that state's Marxist government at the same time that the CIA was
trying to engineer its downfall.

Oligopoly Competition[34]   The oligopoly competition model accepts the profit motive as the guiding force behind MNC behavior but comes to very different conclusions regarding its motives and the consequences of its actions. According to this
view, the MNC is not a force for peace or global prosperity. Rather, it is a predator,
taking advantage of market imperfections and exploiting the societies within which
it operates. Advocates of this interpretation build their case around three assertions.

First, they note that most direct foreign investment is carried out by a small
number of extremely large firms. This means that, instead of basing explanations of
MNC behavior on models built around the assumptions of free trade and perfect
competition, foreign investment decisions must be approached from the perspective
of oligopoly competition. An oligopoly can be likened to a small exclusive club, all
of whose members produce essentially the same product. The Seven Sisters in the
oil industry are such a club. Similar clubs can be found in the automobile, airline,
banking, newspaper, copper, and food industries. The cardinal rule governing the
behavior of club members is that "price competition, except on very limited occa-
sions, is an antisocial practice to be strictly avoided."[35]

Second, this position maintains that foreign investment occurs because of market
imperfections that produce a situation where not all firms are equally able to compete
in the marketplace. They can be grouped under four headings: (1) not all products
are perceived to be equally desirable by consumers due to marketing and advertising
skills, and price policies; (2) not all firms possess the same technology, resources, or
managerial skills to produce the product; (3) some firms are able to operate more
efficiently, given how they are organized and the scale of their operations; and (4)
government policies such as quotas and "buy American" legislation give certain firms
an unfair competitive advantage. In this view, multinational corporations are far better positioned to take advantage of these market imperfections than are most domestic firms.[36]

Third, once in control of an economic sector, the oligopoly competition model
sees MNCs as exploiting their advantage to the detriment of local interests. This
exploitation takes several forms.[37] Local firms soon are either forced out of the marketplace or become dependent upon MNCs through licensing agreements and other
arrangements for the technology that they need to stay in business. For example, at
one point, 46 percent of all U.S.-based MNC manufacturing activities in Latin
America initially came about as a result of purchases of existing firms. All told, in
1971, U.S. firms transferred $4.8 billion abroad for direct investment and took back
$9 billion from their subsidiaries. According to the oligopoly competition model, one
reason for this disparity is that so much MNC trade involves transactions between
different parts of the same company (i.e., General Motors of Brazil selling parts to

General Motors of Mexico). Under such circumstances, MNCs are in a position to set arbitrary prices (known as "transfer pricing") for the products being traded, thereby allowing them to take advantage of tax laws, export-import regulations, and labor laws. A study of MNC activity in Peru, Colombia, Mexico, and the Philippines concluded that one firm sold machinery to its subsidiaries at a price that was 30 percent higher than that being charged by an independent Colombian manufacturer for the same product.

Product Life-Cycle Theory[38]   A third interpretation, the product life-cycle theory, holds that MNCs have little choice but to go abroad if they wish to survive. Theirs is a defensively motivated expansion that is rooted in the nature of the industry's production technology. According to this view, the life history of a product can be broken down into three phases (the introductory phase, the maturing phase, and the standardized product phase), each of which places different survival requirements on the firm. The dominant characteristics of the introductory phase are the high costs and risk involved, and the lack of price sensitivity. Developing new products is an expensive process in which there are more failures than successes. The logical strategy for a firm to follow is to locate its production facilities in its target market, because this will allow the firm to make speedy and timely adjustments in its sales, marketing, or production strategies. For most major technological innovations during the post-World War II era, the target market has been the United States.

In the second phase, the maturing phase, the product has proven to be successful and competitors enter the picture. Because it is always cheaper for another firm to imitate or copy a product than to invent one, the competitor is in a position to sell its version of the product at a cheaper cost than can the inventing firm, which is still trying to recoup the cost of its research and development expenses. Now able to choose from multiple versions of the same product, consumers become price conscious. Faced with a shrinking share of the market and high costs, the innovating firm turns to export markets, where it believes that a demand for its product exists (such as Western Europe or Canada) and where it will once again possess a monopoly of the product. This new advantage is short-lived as local competitors imitate and copy the product. Faced with this pressure, the innovating firm now sets up foreign subsidiaries in an effort to cut its costs and compete with domestic firms.

The innovating firm is faced with still different pressures in the third, standardized product, phase. The production process has now become so routine that virtually any firm that desires to can manufacture a "generic" version of the product. This is now the case for many products in electronics, textiles, and footwear. Holding down production costs and conducting advertising campaigns that stress the virtues of the firm's name and products are now the central elements of the firm's survival strategy. In order to stay competitive, the firm now sets up "export platforms" in Third World states, where it will take advantage of their low-skilled, low-wage, and labor-intensive economies. As opposed to the second phase, in which the firm set up operations in Europe when it desired to sell its product in Europe, the firm is now not primarily concerned with setting up operations in Taiwan, South Korea, the Philippines, or Mexico in order to sell its product there. The intended market for these goods continues to be the advanced industrialized economies of the North.

Advocates of the product life-cycle model tend to acknowledge that the MNC can cause major problems for host states and that its behavior has not always been exemplary. Still, they view MNCs in a positive light because of the role that they play in transferring technical and managerial knowledge.[39] Along with foreign aid, trade, and economic assistance, MNC investment in Third World states is one of the four primary ways in which the conventional theory of development believes that the South can acquire enough capital and technology to produce sustained growth and overcome the development problems rooted in such domestic conditions as overpopulation, excessive military expenditures, and corruption.[40]

Controlling the Multinational Corporation

National Controls   Host states have borne the brunt of the burden in trying to control the actions of the MNC. They have relied upon a wide series of measures, many of which we have already come across in our overview of MNC operations.[41] The most publicized control-oriented action has been the nationalization of an MNC's assets. Chile and Zambia nationalized copper industries; Peru nationalized various banks, the fishmeal and fish oil industry, as well as the International Petroleum Corporation; and Mexico nationalized banks. Less visible but potentially more significant control efforts have centered on regulating the type of foreign investment allowed, limiting the sectors in which this investment may take place, limiting the amount of foreign ownership, regulating foreign acquisitions of existing firms, requiring joint ventures with local or state-owned firms, and limiting the amount of profits that can be taken out of the country.

The relationship between a host state and an MNC is not static. It changes over time. Theodore Moran emphasizes the roles that uncertainty and learning play in establishing the rules by which MNCs operate within a country.[42] His account is framed in terms of the interaction between a host state and a natural-resource-producing MNC. With allowances for some greater mobility on the part of manufacturing MNCs, it may also be applied to their relations with host states. At the outset, a great deal of uncertainty exists over the profitability of a possible investment opportunity, and virtually all of the bargaining advantages lie with the MNC. The host state desires to capitalize on its natural resource base, but, without the MNC, it has no way of doing so. It may even need the MNC to judge the risk involved in the venture or the possible revenue and jobs that might be realized from it. The MNC, with its greater expertise and experience, is thus likely to find itself balancing the merits of competing offers from similarly positioned states. As a result, the original contract will be weighted heavily in favor of the MNC. Moran notes that this will be the case no matter how "nice" the MNC is. The profit motive and the weakness of the host state guarantees it.

At some point after the investment has proven to be a success, the relationship between the MNC and the host state begins to change. The sense of uncertainty that led the state to grant the MNC highly favorable terms of entry is now replaced by the perception that it is being exploited and cheated. The position of the MNC has also changed. It now has an ongoing profitable enterprise in the host state. As such, it now also has something to lose in the bargaining process. The first indication that the host state is now in a position to drive a tougher bargain may surface in the terms of entry given to the next wave of MNCs that wish to invest in that industry.

As host state officials work their way up the learning curve, becoming more capable of monitoring MNC behavior and more familiar with such aspects of its operations as its accounting practices, corporate structure, and the nature of the international market for the natural resources, there is a cumulative shift of bargaining power away from the MNC to the host state. New surtaxes, contract renegotiations, forced adjustments in business practices, and recomputations of the way in which earnings are calculated are all signs that the pendulum is swinging in favor of the host state. Ultimately, a point is reached at which host state officials believe that elements within the country are capable of replicating the activities of the MNC. When this happens, the MNC has become as powerless as the host state was at the outset of the bargaining process.

Regional Controls   In the final analysis, the effectiveness of national level controls is limited by the fact that MNCs operate in more than one country. Single-state actions thus may not be sufficient to control an international manufacturing or refining process. There is also nothing inevitable about host state officials moving up the learning curve and positioning themselves to control MNCs. Because their focus extends beyond the boundaries of a single state but does not require global cooperation to succeed, regional efforts to control the actions of MNCs are particularly attractive to many observers as an improvement on host state control. OPEC's rise to preeminence in the 1970s can be interpreted as a successful regional effort to control MNCs. On balance, however, the success of Third World regional control efforts has been limited.

One of the most ambitious regional efforts by Third World states to control MNCs took place in 1970. The year before, Colombia, Ecuador, Bolivia, Peru, and Chile formed the Andean Pact of Regional Integration. The goal was to create an Andean Common Market. A potential threat to realizing the full economic benefits that might follow from the creation of an enlarged and unified market lay in the ability of MNCs to "jump over" the newly created protective tariff wall, buy out local firms, and dominate the economies of the region for their own gain. To prevent this from happening, the Andean group adopted Decision 24, which established a Standard Regime for the Treatment of Foreign Capital. Public utilities, the mass media, advertising, and banking were declared off limits to new foreign investments. MNCs already operating in these sectors were required to sell off 80 percent of their stock to local nationals within three years. Other MNCs desiring to take advantage of the new common-market tariff system were required to sell off 51 percent of their stock to local investors or states over a 15–20 year period. Finally, only 14 percent of the profits made by foreign firms could be repatriated.

Because of the divergent interests and development strategies held by these states, the full potential of these "fade out" provisions has never been realized. From the outset, problems have been encountered in seeing to it that the members of the Andean Common Market uniformly enforce the provisions of Decision 24. Venezuela applied the restrictions most vigorously, while Ecuador applied few of them. Most damaging from the perspective of regional control was the case of Chile. In 1974, following the ouster of Salvador Allende, the new Chilean military junta under the leadership of General Augusto Pinochet announced its intention to grant liberal tax, repatriation, tariff, and depreciation incentives to selected foreign investors. A short-lived compromise on rules governing foreign investment was reached in 1974, but, in late 1976, Chile withdrew from the Andean Pact.

International Controls Meaningful international controls remain more in the realm of future possibility than current reality. One potential approach that might be followed has been put forward by the 1980 Brandt Commission Report.[43] Its recommendations can be divided into three parts.

First, the Brandt Commission Report calls for the creation of an international investment regime that would establish codes of conduct for all MNCs, home states, and host states. Its principal features would include the following provisions:

1. Reciprocal obligations on the part of host and home states covering foreign investment, transfer of technology, and repatriation of profit, royalties, and dividends.
2. Legislation, coordinated in home and host states, to regulate transnational corporation activities in matters such as ethical behavior, disclosure of information, restrictive business practices, and labor standards.
3. Intergovernmental cooperation with regard to tax policies and the monitoring of transfer pricing.
4. Harmonization of fiscal and other incentives among host developing states.

Second, in the area of natural resource industries, the Brandt Commission Report stated that permanent sovereignty over natural resources is the right of all countries. It went on to note that nationalization should be accompanied by appropriate and effective compensation and urged that greater use should be made of international mechanisms for settling disputes when they arise.

Third, the Brandt Commission Report argued that a special effort must be undertaken to ensure that MNCs transfer appropriate technologies from the North to the South. The Brandt Commission wanted the selection of what technology to use in setting up operation in the Third World to be a conscious decision rather than one based on convenience or standard MNC operating procedures. It noted that appropriate technologies might include those using cheaper sources of energy; simpler techniques in the agricultural, natural resource, and manufacturing sectors that would save money; and smaller plants and scales of operation that would allow economic activity to be spread over a wider area. Among the corrective measures called for by the Brandt Commission Report in this area were (1) that more research and development take place in the South, (2) that there be a greater and more open flow of information about technology in the international system, and (3) that international aid agencies should not interfere with a recipient state's right to choose the type of technology it wishes to purchase or employ.

CONCLUSION

Analysts recognize that these global issues are increasingly important and will continue to occupy a prominent place on the international agenda. They raise important questions concerning the structure of the international system, the pursuit of national interest, and questions of sovereignty. Not only do these issues illustrate the interdependence of the world's states, but also they are interrelated with each other. First, there is a clear relationship between environmental and economic issues. At the economic summit meeting that occurred in Paris in the summer of 1989, environmental issues were the major topic under consideration. The environment has a profound impact on the international economy. The debt crisis is partly attributable to energy prices. The increased need for foreign aid is related to resource depletion and energy prices. If the environment is to be protected, the less developed states will need additional aid for programs to curb population growth and to install cleaner technologies. MNCs are important actors in international environmental politics, since Third World states neither possess the infrastructure necessary to enforce their compliance with environmental standards nor in some cases the inclination to do so. Second, economic issues are tied into questions of human rights and the flow of refugees, for economic and social rights cannot be guaranteed where there are no opportunities for employment, decent housing, adequate nutrition, or proper medical care. Where there is great inequality and economic hardship, there is insurgency, which can lead to the loss of political freedoms. Governments may respond to instability by curbing basic civil and political rights. The violation of human rights by governments, as well as the existence of insurgency, contribute to the flow of refugees. Finally, human rights issues can be related to environmental issues. Resource scarcity can contribute to political instability and human rights violations through its economic effects. Environmental disasters cause the displacement of persons, and, while these are not political refugees as defined by the UN, they contribute to the overall refugee problem. More directly, many would argue that a clean and livable environment is a fundamental human right.

In Chapter 1, we identified three major theoretical perspectives on world politics: realism, globalism, and dependency theory. Realism holds that the state is the only truly important international actor. States, as sovereign actors in an anarchic environment, must pursue their own narrowly defined national interests above all else because all other states can be expected to do the same. Because each state is acting in its own self-interest, it is unreasonable to believe that utopian solutions to world problems will ever be realized. Globalists argue that, although states are still the major actors, the world political scene increasingly involves important nonstate actors. Changing world issues have resulted in numerous situations in which cooperation, rather than competition for power, is the norm. The growing interdependence of states is leading to a world in which rules and institutions can be created to solve international problems. Dependency theorists argue that the dominant actors in the world arena are unequal classes. The richer states of the North dominate and exploit the poorer states of the South. The system is structured so that the capitalist elements in the Northern states benefit from virtually all international decision making. Reform of such a system is insufficient to address the fundamental issue of inequality. The system must be transformed.

These three perspectives view the global issues in this chapter differently. Realism stresses the continuity of world politics. The challenges facing policymakers during the last decade of the twentieth century are fundamentally the same as those that confronted earlier generations of leaders. As such, for some realists these issues are of secondary importance to the more significant and pressing military threats to state security. Policies designed to address questions of human rights, environmental pollution, and controlling MNCs must be formulated within the context of how they affect national power. The history of human rights and refugee policies is consistent with a realist perspective on how the international system works. Although there are international conventions for addressing both of these issues, in practice, national interest plays a key role. States are quick to condemn human rights violations in hostile states but are silent when they occur in friendly states. Governments accept refugees, ostensibly on humanitarian grounds, when it is in their political interests to do so, but label them economic migrants when it is not.

Solutions are most likely to be found under one of two conditions. The first is when a single hegemonic state exists, which is capable of imposing its will upon all others. As we have seen, this was the case in the first part of the post-World War II era when the U.S. dominated the world economy. The second possibility for cooperation grows out of a competitive bargaining process between states locked into a condition of interdependence. Realists are far less optimistic than their globalist counterparts over the peace-creating potential of interdependence. They see interdependence as translating into a potentially dangerous loss of state power and feel that increased interdependence and government intervention in national economies simply create more opportunities for conflict among states. The "solution" emerging from these negotiations will reflect the relative power positions of the states present, the bargaining skills of their diplomats, and the relative importance that states attach to resolving the problem. This problem-solving outlook helps explain why international conferences, such as the Law of the Sea negotiations, take so long and accomplish so little. At the start of the 1989 conference on ozone-depleting CFCs, in which 124 states took part, China and India indicated that they would not participate in a global ban on CFC pollution until the industrialized states committed themselves to financial and technological aid to the Third World. When asked to comment on its willingness to finance a possible global technology, a U.S. spokesperson noted that the Bush administration was working under "budgetary constraints" but hoped that international bodies such as the World Bank might help in its creation.

Many of the issues discussed in this chapter aptly illustrate the globalist contention that power, particularly military power, is becoming increasingly ineffective as a tool for wielding influence. Although in the short run military power could provide a state with access to dwindling resources, it can do nothing to stop their depletion. Nor has it always been a viable option for dealing with MNCs. As we have seen, not only have MNCs shown themselves willing to ignore powerful states, but also military power was of little help in dealing with OPEC and its challenge to the power of the Seven Sisters. Power has also proven ineffective in solving refugee crises. This has been clearly illustrated by the arrival of boat loads of Cuban and Haitian refugees in the United States. Additionally, some states, particularly in Africa, have acted in a humanitarian fashion. Refugees in Africa have been viewed as a problem that the African community must solve through cooperation. In spite of the costs to its own struggling economy, Tanzania, for example, has freely accepted refugees and has attempted to incorporate them into its own society.

The growing interdependence of states observed by the globalists is also evident.

Environmental decisions in one state can have long-term effects on the ecology of another. Deforestation in the tropics affects climate worldwide. Land-based pollution crosses international borders when it is carried by rivers and streams to the world's oceans. Human rights violations cross international borders in the form of flows of refugees. Interdependence can also be seen in the destruction of local customs, traditions, and values that often follows in the wake of MNC investment. The goal of the MNC is to produce a standard product for a global marketplace. This can only occur if tastes are standardized. Thus, the MNC enters a host state, not with the idea of altering its product to meet local conditions, but with a view toward altering local conditions to meet its product and profit needs. Perhaps the most infamous case of this involved Nestlé's marketing of infant baby formula in Africa. Nestlé argued that its product was as good as or better than breast feeding. The problems were that (1) unable to afford baby formula, mothers did not mix enough infant formula with water and (2) the water itself was often undrinkable. As a result, babies fed instant formula were often malnourished and unnecessarily exposed to numerous life-threatening diseases.

While globalists see the realists' emphasis on state power and national interest as explaining much of state behavior concerning these global issues, they argue that realism understates the amount of cooperation that exists among states and cannot provide adequate solutions to such problems. Without necessarily endorsing the globalist perspective, not all realists would take exception to this observation. Stanley Michalak argues that the scope of realist theory is largely confined to the implication of territorial issues for the distribution of state power and that realism is an inappropriate perspective for analyzing foreign-policy problems rooted in interdependence.[44]

For globalists, global, long-range interests, even if they conflict with national short-term interests, must be recognized. There is evidence that some progress has been attained on this front. Increasingly, multilateral organizations are playing a greater role in addressing international issues as states come to realize that it is in their enlightened best self-interest to adopt a global perspective. Third World states are important sources of markets and resources; thus development aid that helps these states prosper will in the long run benefit the entire world economy. In recent years, more assistance has been channeled through multilateral institutions. Progress is seen in other areas as well. Although pollution has not yet created intolerable living conditions and although energy resources are not yet depleted, states have come together to confront these problems, and some international agreements have been reached. States continue to work toward more respect for human rights, even when it is not in their own national interest to do so. Most of the world's states have signed the Universal Declaration of Human Rights, and there is considerable evidence that international pressure does affect state behavior on this issue.

Dependency theory looks at these issues differently. Underdevelopment in the South (periphery) is a function of the policies of the North (center) states, including the legacy of colonialism. MNC investment in Third World states from the oligopoly competition perspective is a good illustration of dependency. For many in the Third World, MNC investment is a continuation of colonialism in a slightly different form. Through MNCs, production is geared toward the needs of the center (North) states, rather than toward the requirements of the domestic economy. Thus, land is taken out of production of basic foodstuffs and turned over to beef production for the U.S. fast-food market. As a result, people are malnourished in areas that could produce adequate amounts of staple crops for domestic consumption. Meanwhile, MNCs engaged in manufacturing and services create an indigenous elite class whose tastes and interests are tied to those of their counterparts in the center states. Their decisions favor the interests of MNCs at the expense of domestic (periphery) interests. Goods are not produced that would meet the needs of local consumers, but, rather, production is geared toward consumer goods for the center state's markets.

Dependency theorists might find their views vindicated by the reactions of North states now that they are increasingly penetrated by foreign investment. In 1976, foreign firms controlled 57 percent of Canada's manufacturing industries, 73 percent of its petroleum and natural gas industries, and 57 percent of its mining and smelting industries. In an attempt to arrest this trend, the Canadian government established an agency with the power to review and block all proposed foreign takeovers valued at more than $5 million. Still, the pressures for increased foreign investment have been strong, and in 1988 the government of Prime Minister Brian Mulroney signed a free-trade agreement with the United States that over a 10-year period will remove all tariffs and most import-export restrictions between the two states and permit investment capital to move across the two borders more freely. In 1992, Canada will also stop reviewing indirect takeovers (those in which an American parent of a Canadian firm is taken over by another American firm). Among the advantages that the Mulroney government argues will accrue to Canada are a more flexible and innovative Canadian economy, a boost in Canadian real income, exploitation of economies of scale, lower consumer prices, and a net increase of 120,000 jobs for Canadians by 1993. At the same time, the Free-Trade agreement rekindled fears held by many Canadians that too much foreign investment would "recolonialize" the Canadian national identity. Even before the free-trade agreement went into effect, direct U.S. investments in Canada were valued at $66 billion, or about 20 percent of all overseas U.S. investments.

Dependency theory also addresses the environment. Once again, the interests of the center states take precedence over the needs of the periphery states. The focus is on equity. The North has created most of the pollution that now exists. Although it contains a minority of the world's peoples, it has used the lion's share of the world's resources that have been consumed. Now that the North perceives a problem, it wants the South to help bear the costs of finding solutions. While the developed world was industrializing, it had access to abundant and cheap energy and it operated in an environment free of expensive pollution controls. During this time, it made no attempt to conserve resources or to spare the environment. Now that these states are wealthy, they can afford the luxury of environmental protection. The less developed states are struggling to feed their people and to provide a better standard of living for them. Substituting more expensive resources for those nearing depletion and imposing pollution controls will add considerably to their burden. The Third World resents being told that it cannot clear its forests to provide more living area for its people by states who already have thriving cities and towns. Third World states accept the idea that the environment must be protected, but they argue that it is the North that should bear the costs of that protection. This includes the granting of aid to install cleaner, more energy efficient technologies and to find alternatives to deforestation.

As we have attempted to show throughout this text, the field of world politics is complex. For example, many of the issues that we examined in earlier chapters, such as nuclear weapons, arms control, debt, and foreign aid might quite justifiably be included in this chapter and approached as global issues. Our purpose in presenting material has not been to argue for one solution over others or for the use of one theoretical perspective to the exclusion of others. Rather, it has been to heighten awareness of how world politics affects our daily lives and to stimulate student interest in the problems of world politics. If we are to solve these problems, we need to become critical thinkers about the nature of the world around us, recognize where problems exist, and possess the ability to judge the merits of policy options put forward to deal with them. It is our hope that this text contributes to developing these skills and enhances the reader's understanding of current and future problems of world politics.

NOTES

1. Garrett Hardin, "The Tragedy of the Commons." *Science* 162: 1243–1248. This discussion of the tragedy of the commons is taken from Marvin S. Soroos, "The Tragedy of the Commons in Global Perspective," in Charles W. Kegley and Eugene R. Wittkopf, *The Global Agenda: Issues and Perspectives* (New York: Random House, 1988), pp. 345–357.
2. For a more comprehensive summary of some of the major environmental studies, see Kenneth A. Dahlberg, Marvin S. Soroos, Anne Thompson Feraru, James E. Harf, and B. Thomas Trout, *Environment and the Global Arena* (Durham, N.C.: Duke University Press, 1985), pp. 120–126.
3. Donella H. Meadows, Dennis L. Meadows, Jorgen Randers, and William H. Behrens, *The Limits to Growth* (New York: Signet, 1972).
4. Mihajlo Mesarovic and Edward Pestel, *Mankind at the Turning Point* (New York: E. P. Dutton, 1974).
5. Council on Environmental Quality and the Department of State, *The Global 2000 Report to the President, Volume I* (Washington, D.C.: U.S. Government Printing Office, 1980).
6. Quoted in Dahlberg, et al., *Environment and the Global Arena*, p. xiv.
7. Although the information in this and the following section on pollution is gleaned from a variety of sources, we have drawn most heavily on James E. Harf and B. Thomas Trout, *The Politics of Global Resources* (Durham, N.C.: Duke University Press 1986) and Dahlberg, et al., *Environment and the Global Arena*.
8. Hart and Trout, *The Politics of Global Resources*, p. 47.
9. Joan Spero, *The Politics of International Economic Relations* (New York: St. Martin's, 1985), p. 200.
10. Lester Brown, et al., *State of the World, 1985* (New York: W. W. Norton), p. 27.
11. John Gever, Robert Kaufmann, David Skole, and Charles Vorosmarty, *Beyond Oil: The Threat to Food and Fuel in the Coming Decades* (Cambridge, Mass.: Ballinger Publishing Company, 1987), p. xxix.
12. Estimating reserves of resources is a complex task, and it is impossible to know what new

sources will be discovered. It is almost certain, however, that new deposits of minerals and oil will be more costly to extract than those now being exploited.

13. Cited by William Chandler in "Increasing Energy Efficiency" in Brown, et al., *State of the World, 1985*, p. 148.

14. Brown, et al., *State of the World, 1985*, p. 149.

15. Projections concerning the greenhouse effect are imprecise, and different sources often give very different estimates. This discussion of the greenhouse effect is taken from David Wirth's excellent summary of the scientific literature in "Climate Chaos," *Foreign Policy*, 74 (Spring 1989): 3–22.

16. Wirth, "Climate Chaos," p. 15.

17. Kenneth Dahlberg, et al., *Environment and the Global Arena*, pp. 109–110.

18. Harf and Trout, *The Politics of Global Resources*, p. 125.

19. Dahlberg, et al., *Environment and the Global Arena*, p. 105.

20. Harf and Trout, *The Politics of Global Resources*, p. 134.

21. K. Newland, "Refugees: The New International Politics of Displacement," *Worldwatch Paper Number 43* (Washington D.C.: Worldwatch Institute, 1981).

22. Current figures given in this section for refugees are from *World Refugee Survey: 1987 in Review* (Washington, D.C.: U.S. Committee for Refugees, 1987).

23. A. Surhke, "Global Refugee Movements and Strategies of Response," in M. Kritz, ed., *United States Immigration and Refugee Policy* (Lexington, Mass. Lexington Books, 1983).

24. Aristide Zolberg, "Contemporary Transnational Migrations in Historical Perspective," in M. Kritz, ed., *United States Immigration and Refugee Policy* (Lexington, Mass.: Lexington Books, 1983).

25. U.S. Committee for Refugees, *World Refugee Survey*, p. 9.

26. United Nations Department of Economic and Social Affairs, *Multinational Corporations in World Development* (New York: United Nations, 1973. A significant portion of this study is reprinted in George Modelski, *Transnational Corporations and World Order* (San Francisco, W. H. Freeman, 1979), pp. 14–33.

27. George Modelski," International Content and Performance Among the World's Largest Corporations," in Modelski, *Transnational Corporations and World Order*, pp. 45–65.

28. Frederick Clairmore and John Cavanagh, "Transnational Corporations and Global Markets," *Trade and Development* 4 (1982): 155.

29. Raymond Vernon, "Future of Multinational Enterprise," in Charles Kindleberger, ed., *The International Corporation* (Cambridge, Mass.: MIT Press, 1970), p. 393.

30. See Jacques Maisonrouge, "How a Multinational Corporation Appears to Its Managers," in George Ball, ed., *Global Companies* (Englewood Cliffs, N.J.: Prentice-Hall, 1975), pp. 11–20; George Ball, "The Promise of the Multinational Corporation," *Fortune* 75 (June 1967): 80; and the account of the world manager's vision given in Richard Barnett and Ronald Muller, *Global Reach* (New York: Touchstone, 1974).

31. Quoted in Frederick Pearson and Martin Rochester, *International Relations* (Reading, Mass.: Addison-Wesley, 1984), p. 389. The original quote can be found in Raymond Vernon, "The Multinationals: No Strings Attached," *Foreign Policy* 33 (1978/1979): 121.

32. J. J. Servan-Schreiber, *The American Challenge* (New York: Avon, 1969).

33. Glenn Hastedt, "The United States Response to Direct Foreign Investment, 1973–1974," *Southeastern Political Review* 13 (1985): 39–64.

34. For elaborations on the oligopoly competition model, see Stephen Hymer, *The International Operations of National Firms* (Cambridge, Mass.: MIT Press, 1976); Barnett and Muller, *Global Reach;* and Charles Kindleberger, *American Business Abroad* (New Haven, Conn.: Yale University Press, 1969). Kindleberger does not share the negative evaluation of MNC activity described in this section.

35. Barnett and Muller, *Global Reach,* p. 32.

36. Kindleberger, *American Business Abroad,* pp. 14–27.

37. The data in this paragraph are reported in Steve Chan, *International Relations in Perspective* (New York: Macmillan, 1984), p. 283.

38. The product life-cycle theory is most closely associated with the work of Raymond Vernon. See his *Sovereignty at Bay* (New York: Basic Books, 1971).

39. Robert Gilpin, *U.S. Power and the Multinational Corporation* (New York: Basic Books, 1975), pp. 117–122.

40. This argument is outlined in Walter Jones, *The Logic of International Relations,* 6th ed. (Glenview, Il.: Scott Foresman, 1988), pp. 189–213.

41. For a discussion of control options at the state level, see Spero, *The Politics of International Economic Relations,* pp. 282–287.

42. Theodore Moran, *Multinational Corporations and the Politics of Dependence* (Princeton, N.J.: Princeton University Press, 1974).

43. *North-South: A Program for Survival,* The Report of the Independent Commission on International Development Issues under the Chairmanship of Willy Brandt (Cambridge, Mass.: MIT Press, 1980), pp. 187–200.

44. Stanley Michalak, Jr., "Theoretical Perspectives for Understanding International Interdependence," *World Politics* 32 (1979): 136–150.

Index